NORTH AMERICAN WOMEN POETS
IN THE 21ST CENTURY

The American Poets in the Twenty-First Century Series

EDITOR CLAUDIA RANKINE

2002
American Women Poets in the 21st Century:
Where Lyric Meets Language
    Edited by Claudia Rankine and Juliana Spahr

2007
American Poets in the 21st Century:
The New Poetics
    Edited by Claudia Rankine and Lisa Sewell

2012
Eleven More American Women Poets in the 21st Century:
Poetics across North America
    Edited by Claudia Rankine and Lisa Sewell

2018
American Poets in the 21st Century:
Poetics of Social Engagement
    Edited by Claudia Rankine and Michael Dowdy

North American Women Poets in the 21st Century

Beyond Lyric and Language

Edited by

Lisa Sewell

and

Kazim Ali

Wesleyan University Press · Middletown, Connecticut

Wesleyan University Press
Middletown CT 06459
www.wesleyan.edu/wespress
© 2020 Wesleyan University Press
All rights reserved

Manufactured in the United States of America
Designed by Dennis Anderson and Scott Cahoon
Typeset in Sabon and The Sans by Passumpsic Publishing

Library of Congress Cataloging-in-Publication Data
available upon request

Hardcover ISBN: 978-0-8195-7941-6
Paperback ISBN: 978-0-8195-7942-3
Ebook ISBN: 978-0-8195-7943-0

5 4 3 2 1

CONTENTS

ACKNOWLEDGMENTS

The editors would like to thank Suzanna Tamminen for her support of this project and to express gratitude to Claudia Rankine for her collaboration and advice. Many thanks as well to Katie Van Heest and Michelle Niemann for editorial assistance and to Christine Kelley, Christian Leithart, and Jesse Schwartz for invaluable administrative support. Permission to reprint copyrighted material has been obtained whenever possible. The editors gratefully acknowledge permission to reprint from the following sources.

Marilyn Chin. "So, You Fucked John Donne," "Blues on Yellow," and "Rhapsody in Plain Yellow" from *Rhapsody in Plain Yellow* © 2002 by Marilyn Chin; and "Black President," "Brown Girl Manifesto (Too)," "Twenty Five Haiku," "Beautiful Boyfriend," "Formosan Elegy," and "Quiet the Dog, Tether the Pony," from *Hard Love Province* © 2014 by Marilyn Chin; and "Brown Girl Manifesto, One Amongst Many," from Marilyn Chin, *A Portrait of the Self as Nation: New and Selected Poems* © 2018 by Marilyn Chin, are all used by permission of W. W. Norton & Company, Inc. Excerpts from "Exile's Letter: (Or An Essay on Assimilation)," from *Dwarf Bamboo* © 1987 by Marilyn Chin, which appear in Catherine Cucinella's essay, "Marilyn Chin's Hard Love Province: The Erotics of Grief," are used by permission of Greenfield Press; excerpts from "Cougar Synonymous," "Formosan Elegy," "Alba: Moon Camilla Lover," "Beautiful Boyfriend," and "Quiet the Dog, Tether the Pony," from *Hard Love Province* © 2014 by Marilyn Chin which appear in Cucinella's essay are used by permission of W. W. Norton & Company, Inc.

Fanny Howe. Excerpt from "Forty Days," from *The Lyrics* © 2007 by Fanny Howe; "A Hymn," from *Come and See* © 2011 by Fanny Howe; and "For The Book," "The Garden," "Parkside," "Evening," and "The Ninth Hour," from *Second Childhood* copyright © 2014 by Fanny Howe, are reprinted with the permission of The Permissions Company, Inc. on behalf of Graywolf Press, Minneapolis, Minnesota, www.graywolfpress.org. Excerpt from John Wieners, "Acts of Youth" from *Selected Poems, 1958–1984*, published by Black Sparrow Books, copyright © 1986 by John Wieners, reprinted by permission of the John Wieners Literary Trust, Raymond Foye Executor. Excerpts from "The Source," from *Gone* © 2003 by Fanny Howe, and from *Selected Poems* © 2000 by Fanny Howe which appear in Meg Tyler's essay, "A Place Apart: Sound, Silence, and Play in the Poetry of Fanny Howe," are reprinted by permission of University of California Press; excerpts from *For the Book* © 2014 by Fanny Howe and from *Winter Sun: Notes on a Vocation* © 2009 by Fanny Howe, which also appear in Tyler's essay, are reprinted with the permission of The Permissions Company, Inc. on behalf of Graywolf Press, Minneapolis, Minnesota, www.graywolfpress.org.

Alice Notley. "Dear Dark Continent" and "I the People" from *Grave of Light* © 2006 by Alice Notley, and "City of Ghostly Festivals" from *Songs and Stories of the Ghouls* © 2011 by Alice Notley, are reprinted by permission of Wesleyan University Press; excerpt from *The Descent of Alette* by Alice Notley © 1996 is reprinted by permission of Penguin Books; "Flowers" from *Mysteries of Small Houses* © 1998 by Alice Notley and "Carp Shoals and Tules" from *Culture of One* © 2011 by Alice Notley are reprinted by permission of Penguin Random House; "Growth of the Light Flat upon Her" from *Reason and Other Women* © 2010 by Alice Notley is reprinted by permission of Chax Press. Excerpts from *Culture of One* © 2011 by Alice Notley which appear in Elline Lipkin's essay, "Resist, Reframe, Insist: Alice Notley's Poetics of Inclusion," are reprinted with the permission of Penguin Random House; excerpts from *Grave of Light* © 2006 by Alice Notley which appear in Lipkin's essay are reprinted with the permission of Wesleyan University Press; excerpts from "Three Strolls" © 2007 by Alice Notley, from *Not For Mothers Only: Contemporary Poems on Child-Getting and Child-Rearing*, which appear in Lipkin's essay are used with the permission of Fence Books; excerpts from *Coming After: Essays on Poetry* © 2005 by Alice Notley which appear in Lipkin's essay are reprinted with the permission of The University of Michigan Press.

Claudia Rankine. Excerpts from *Citizen* © 2014 by Claudia Rankine are reprinted with the permission of The Permissions Company, Inc. on behalf of Graywolf Press, Minneapolis, Minnesota, www.graywolfpress.org. Excerpts from *Citizen* © 2014 by Claudia Rankine and *Don't Let Me Be Lonely* © 2004 by Claudia Rankine which appear in Kamran Javadizadeh's essay, "The Atlantic Ocean Breaking on Our Heads: Claudia Rankine and the Whiteness of the Lyric Subject," are reprinted with the permission of The Permissions Company, Inc. on behalf of Graywolf Press, Minneapolis, Minnesota, www.graywolfpress.org.

Martha Ronk. "I cannot remember anything about this journey other than this," "It is only a question of discovering how we can get ourselves attached to it again," and "The shadows of clouds scudded across the steep slopes and through the ravines," from *Vertigo* © 2007 by Martha Ronk, are reprinted with the permission of Coffee House Press; "The," and "Remembrance" from *Partially Kept* © 2012 by Martha Ronk are reprinted with the permission of Nightboat Books. "In a Landscape of Having to Repeat," "Trying," and "A Photograph of a Plate Glass Window" from *In a Landscape of Having to Repeat* © 2004 by Martha Ronk; "a glass bowl," "corroded metal," "the window," and "the book" from *Transfer of Qualities* © 2013 by Martha Ronk; and "A blurry photograph," "No Sky," "As I understand my job, it is, while suggesting order, to make things appear as much as possible to be the way they are in normal vision," and "Elegy (and a photograph by Robert Adams)" from *Ocular Proof* © 2016 by Martha Ronk are reprinted with the permission of Omnidawn Publishing. Excerpts from *Ocular Proof* © 2016 by Martha Ronk and excerpts from *In a Landscape of Having to Repeat* © 2004 by Martha Ronk which appear in Brian Teare's essay, "Martha Ronk's Distressed Lyrics," are reprinted with the permission of Omnidawn Publishing; excerpts from *Vertigo* © 2007 by Martha Ronk which appear in Teare's essay are reprinted with the permission of Coffee House Press; excerpts from *Why/Why Not* © 2003 by Martha Ronk which appear in Teare's essay are reprinted with the permission of University of California Press; excerpts from *Desire in L.A.* © 1990 by Martha Ronk and from *Eyetrouble* © 1998 by Martha Ronk which appear in Teare's essay are reprinted with the permission of the University of Georgia Press; excerpts from *Glass Grapes and Other Stories* © 2008 by Martha Ronk which appear in Teare's essay are reprinted with the permission of BOA Editions; excerpts from *Partially Kept* © 2012 by Martha Ronk which appear in Teare's essay are reprinted with the permission of Nightboat Books.

Leslie Scalapino. "Floating Series 1" from *Way* © 1988 by Leslie Scalapino, "Notes to Waking Life" from *Defoe* © 1994 by Leslie Scalapino, "Delay Rose" from *Day Ocean States of Stars' Night* © 2007 by Leslie Scalapino, and "Dead Souls" from *The Front Matter, Dead Souls* © 1996 by Leslie Scalapino are reprinted with the permission of the estate of Leslie Scalapino. Excerpts from *Zither And Autobiography* © 2003 by Leslie Scalapino which appear in Michael Cross's essay, "Leslie Scalapino's Anarchic Moment," are reprinted with the permission of Wesleyan University Press; excerpts from *The Return of Painting, The Pearl, and Orion: A Trilogy* © 1997 by Leslie Scalapino, from *Green and Black: Selected Writings* © 1996 by Leslie Scalapino, from *Defoe* © 1994 by Leslie Scalapino, from *Objects in the Terrifying Tense Longing from Taking Place* © 1993 by Leslie Scalapino, from *Considering how exaggerated music is* © 1982 by Leslie Scalapino, and from *that they were at the beach* © 1985 by Leslie Scalapino which appear in Cross's essay are all reprinted with the permission of the estate of Leslie Scalapino.

Cole Swensen. "May 21, 1420: The Signing of the Treaty of Troyes" and "December 25, 1456: Je Françoys Villon escollier" from *Such Rich Hour* © 2001 by Cole Swensen and "Shadow Puppets" from *The Book of a Hundred Hands* © 2005 by Cole Swensen are reprinted with the permission of University of Iowa Press; excerpts from *The Glass Age* © 2007 by Cole Swensen are reprinted with the permission of Alice James Books; "A Garden Is a Start" from *Ours* © 2008 by Cole Swensen and "A Ghost," "Kent," "One No," "Gravesend," and "Who Walked" from *Gravesend* © 2012 by Cole Swensen are reprinted with the permission of University of California Press; excerpts from *Landscapes on a Train* © 2015 by Cole Swensen and "Wordsworth," "George Sand: Promenades autour d'un village," "Debord" from *On Walking On* © 2017 by Cole Swensen are reprinted with the permission of Nightboat Books. Excerpts from *Noon* © 1997 by Cole Swensen which appear in

Lynn Keller's essay, "Truths Surpassing Fact: Cole Swensen's Research-Based Poetics," are reprinted with the permission of Sun and Moon Press; excerpts from *Such Rich Hour* © 2001 by Cole Swensen and *Try* © 1999 by Cole Swensen which appear in Keller's essay are reprinted with the permission of University of Iowa Press; excerpts from *Greensward* © 2010 by Cole Swensen which appear in Keller's essay are reprinted with the permission of Ugly Duckling Presse; excerpts from *Gravesend* © 2012 by Cole Swensen which appear in Keller's essay are reprinted with the permission of University of California Press; excerpts from *The Glass Age* © 2007 by Cole Swensen which appear in Keller's essay are reprinted with the permission of Alice James Books.

Natasha Trethewey. "Bellocq" from *Bellocq's Ophelia* © 2002 by Natasha Trethewey is reprinted with the permission of The Permissions Company, Inc. on behalf of Graywolf Press, Minneapolis, Minnesota, www.graywolfpress.org; "Theories of Time and Space," "Myth," "Elegy for the Native Guard," and "Incident" from *Native Guard* © 2006 by Natasha Trethewey and "Elegy," "Miracle of the Black Leg," "Calling," and "Enlightenment" from *Thrall* © 2012 by Natasha Trethewey are reprinted with the permission of Houghton Mifflin Harcourt Publishing Company; "Before Katrina" from *Beyond Katrina* © 2010 by Natasha Trethewey reprinted with the permission of University of Georgia Press. Excerpts from "'Why I Write': Poetry, History, and Social Justice," by Natasha Trethewey are reprinted with the permission of the author. Excerpts from "What the Body Can Say" from *Native Guard* © 2006 by Natasha Trethewey and excerpts from *Thrall* © 2012 by Natasha Trethewey which appear in Khadijah Queen's essay, "Natasha Trethewey's Palimpsestic Poetics," are reprinted with the permission of Houghton Mifflin Harcourt Publishing Company; excerpts from *Bellocq's Ophelia* © 2002 by Natasha Trethewey which appear in Queen's essay are reprinted with the permission of The Permissions Company, Inc. on behalf of Graywolf Press, Minneapolis, Minnesota, www.graywolfpress.org; excerpts from *Beyond Katrina* © 2010 by Natasha Trethewey which appear in Queen's essay are reprinted with the permission of University of Georgia Press.

Jean Valentine. "First Love" from *Dream Barker* © 1965 by Jean Valentine is reprinted with the permission of Yale University Press; "The Child and the Terrorist, The Terrorist and the Child," and "Pilgrims" from *Pilgrims* © 1969 by Jean Valentine are reprinted with the permission of Farrar, Straus and Giroux; "Trust Me," "The First Station," "The River at Wolf," "World-light," "Home," "Little Map," and "The Blue Dory, The Soul" from *Home. Deep. Blue* © 1989 by Jean Valentine are reprinted with the permission of Alice James Books; "In prison" from *Break the Glass* © 2010 by Jean Valentine and "A Child's Drawing, 1941," "[The ship] is slowly giving up her sentient life. I cannot write about it," "Song," and "Icebergs, Ilulissat" from *Shirt in Heaven* © 2016 by Jean Valentine are reprinted with the permission of Copper Canyon Press. Excerpts from *Shirt in Heaven* © 2016 by

Jean Valentine which appear in Lisa Russ Spaar's essay, "Skirting Heaven: Jean Valentine's Late Dream-Work in *Shirt in Heaven*," are reprinted with the permission of Copper Canyon Press; excerpts from *Door in Mountain: New and Collected Poems, 1965–2003* © 2004 by Jean Valentine which appear in Spaar's essay are reprinted with the permission of Wesleyan University Press.

Cecilia Vicuña. "Solitude," "Mastaba," "Mawida," "Teresa the Idiot," and "Librarian Expedition" from *Sabor A Mí* © 1973 by Cecilia Vicuña are reprinted with the permission of Cecilia Vicuna; "fables of the beginning and remains of the origin" from *Instan* © 2002 by Cecilia Vicuña and "Clepsydra" from *New and Selected Poems of Cecilia Vicuña* © 2018 by Cecilia Vicuña are reprinted with the permission of Kelsey Street Press; "The Quasar," and "The Undoer Doing (Muhammad Ali)" from *Spit Temple* © 2012 by Cecilia Vicuña are reprinted with the permission of Ugly Duckling Presse. Excerpts from *Sabor A Mí* © 1973 by Cecilia Vicuña which appear in Julie Phillips Brown's essay, "Return of the Disappeared: Cecilia Vicuña's *Saboramis*," are reprinted with the permission of Cecilia Vicuña; excerpts from *QUIPOem* © 1997 by Cecilia Vicuña which appear in Brown's essay are reprinted with the permission of Wesleyan University Press; excerpts from *Precario/ Precarious* © 1983 by Cecilia Vicuña which appear in Brown's essay are reprinted with the permission of Cecilia Vicuña; excerpts from *Unraveling Words & the Weaving of Water* © 1992 by Cecilia Vicuña which appear in Brown's essay are reprinted with the permission of Graywolf Press; excerpts from *Illuminations* by Walter Benjamin, translated by Harry Zohn © 1955 by Suhrkamp Verlag, English translation © 1968 and renewed 1996 by Houghton Mifflin Harcourt Publishing Company, which appear in Brown's essay are reprinted by permission of Houghton Mifflin Harcourt Publishing Company. All images that appear in Brown's essay are used by permission of Cecilia Vicuña.

Rosmarie Waldrop. "Evening Sun" from *Blindsight* © 2003 by Rosmarie Waldrop, "Feverish Propositions" from *The Reproduction of Profiles* © 1987 by Rosmarie Waldrop, and "Time Ravel" from *Driven to Abstraction* © 2010 by Rosmarie Waldrop are all reprinted with the permission of New Directions Publishing Corporation; "Initial Conditions" and "Intentionalities" from *Love Like Pronouns* © 2003 by Rosmarie Waldrop are reprinted with the permission of Omnidawn Publishing. Excerpts from *Driven to Abstraction* © 2010 by Rosmarie Waldrop which appear in Richard Greenfield's essay "Rosmarie Waldrop: Attending to Absence" are reprinted with the permission of New Directions Publishing Corporation; excerpts from *Dissonance (if you are interested)* © 2005 by Rosmarie Waldrop which appear in Greenfield's essay are reprinted with the permission of University of Alabama Press; excerpts from *Curves to the Apple* © 2006 by Rosmarie Waldrop which appear in Greenfield's essay are reprinted with the permission of New Directions Publishing Corporation.

NORTH AMERICAN WOMEN POETS
IN THE 21ST CENTURY

INTRODUCTION

Kazim Ali and Lisa Sewell

THE 1999 CONFERENCE, "Where Lyric Tradition Meets Language Poetry: Innovation in Contemporary American Poetry by Women," has had a long reach and multidirectional echoes. Featuring readings, panels, and roundtables that highlighted the work of nationally recognized women poets like Rae Armantrout, Lucie Brock-Broido, Jorie Graham, Barbara Guest, Lyn Hejinian, Brenda Hillman, Ann Lauterbach, Harryette Mullen, Alice Notley, Leslie Scalapino, Susan Howe, and Mei-Mei Berssenbrugge, the conference was the jumping-off point for this series that focuses on twenty-first-century women poets. The conference was, at least in part, a response to the so-called "poetry wars" of the 1990s; the organizers hoped to create a neutral zone that could foster a conversation across the dividing lines between the mainstream post-confessional "lyric tradition" that had dominated the field since mid-century, and the Modernist legacy of materialist experimentalism and Language-oriented writing—the two apparently opposing poles of contemporary American poetry at the end of the twentieth century.[1] Whether or not the conference succeeded in facilitating that conversation, it led to broader publication and exposure for many of the featured writers, and to this series, which continues to bring scholarly and critical attention to contemporary North American women's poetry.

The conference and the series were also conceived in response to the sense that while well-established poets like Armantrout, Hillman, Lauterbach, Scalapino, and Notley were clearly at the vanguard of contemporary American poetry, their work lacked the kind of critical and scholarly attention it deserved. The first anthology, *American Women Poets in the 21st Century: Where Lyric Meets Language* (Wesleyan University Press 2002), edited by Claudia Rankine and Juliana Spahr, featured many of the poets that participated in the conference, including Rae Armantrout and Lyn Hejinian, who fall on the experimental Language-oriented end of the continuum, and Jorie Graham and Lucie Brock-Broido, whose work is generally considered to be at the more expressive, lyric end. The next, which appeared in 2012 and was edited by Rankine and Lisa Sewell, included some of the poets who had not made it into the first collection, and also had a broader geographical scope, featuring poets from all of North America. At the time that follow-up was first proposed, it was so difficult to narrow down the list of poets to be included that a third volume was immediately planned. This is that volume.

This book, and the ones that preceded it in the series, also grew out of a desire to create a different kind of anthology, one that would place a generous selection of work alongside an author's statement of poetics as well as a critical essay. In the current collection, which features work by Marilyn Chin, Fanny Howe, Alice Notley, Claudia Rankine, Martha Ronk, Leslie Scalapino, Cole Swensen, Natasha Trethewey, Jean Valentine, Cecilia Vicuña, and Rosmarie Waldrop, we have continued to showcase women poets writing at various disciplinary intersections as well as at the intersections and interstices of different schools of poetics. The aesthetic range of the writers included here is also somewhat broader than in the previous anthologies, which were weighted more toward post-Language writing and innovative and experimental traditions. In fact, their relationship to traditional schools of poetics at times feels slippery and hard to categorize. Each has aesthetic commitments of her own that feel incompatible even with the notion of "hybridity," which in recent years has become a way of siting writers who work outside recognized poetic lineages.

In the years since the publication of the first collections in this series, the nature of the lyric has continued to be a source of contention and a focus of debate, for poets as well as critics, which is clear from the renewed scrutiny of the category of "lyric" by critics like Virginia Jackson, Yopie Prins, and Rei Terada.[2] In *Lyric Shame: The "Lyric" Subject in Contemporary American Poetry*, Gillian White observes that "lyric" remains "a charged word and concept: in poetry circles, it is a word and concept disparaged, defended, repurposed and much discussed . . . abjected by avant-garde antilyricism" and ambivalently defended by those still engaged in the "epiphanic, meditative mode."[3] The place of research, the documentary, and the political in poetry, as well as the virtues and hazards of conceptual poetry, have also been at the forefront of literary critical conversations.[4] Nevertheless, critics seem to have largely concluded that the "poetry wars" are over. The strict divide between experimentation and expression in American poetry has "fractured" into what Vernon Shetley describes as "microclimates," "niches structured by different, often radically different, ideas about poetry: about what constitutes a poem, about what ends poetry should serve, about the social role poetry performs, about the politics of the poet and the reader."[5]

This volume reflects this changed and changing landscape—though many of the writers would say such fragmenting and fracturing is nothing new, as they have been writing at the borders between genres and outside the purview of any defined tradition or ideology since the late 1970s. If any conclusion can be drawn about contemporary women's poetry based on this collection, it is that rubrics, schools, and movements always fail to fully account for the important work being produced in any period—especially work by writers outside the mainstream in terms of class, race, gender, sex, or institution.

Given that there is very little that unites the writers in this collection, it remains quite striking that many of them also cannot be aligned with a specific school, aesthetic, or political ideology. As far back as 2002, Lynn Keller suggested that two of the writers included here—Fanny Howe and Rosmarie Waldrop—were part of what she termed "an in-between generation."[6] Keller means this literally in that Howe and Waldrop were too young to be part of the generation included in Donald Allen's *The New American Poetry*, but born too early to be part of the Language poetry school. She also suggests that Waldrop and Howe were "in between" aesthetics:

> Being pulled between social conformity and deviance, straddling aesthetic camps, or finding a home in no language or nation were experiences that generated increasingly fractured senses of subjectivity and of reality. It would seem that such internal divisions and unstable positions ultimately pushed . . . Howe, and Waldrop to invent the forms that could do justice to the disjunctions they had been living.[7]

The difficulty of situating Waldrop and Howe—along with many of the other writers collected here—under a particular rubric has persisted. Leslie Scalapino, for example, is a writer who takes language as her subject but cannot be neatly aligned with the Language poetry movement, though for different reasons than Waldrop. Claudia Rankine's work explicitly engages with the discussion around lyric, presenting an "American Lyric" that largely takes shape as prose and intentionally troubles generic distinctions; her poetry has been described as post-confessional, experimental, documentary, and post-modern.[8] Where on the poetic spectrum do we position Jean Valentine, whose lyric poems "skirt" the boundary between self and other, inside and outside, body and spirit, and destabilize the singularity of the lyric "I?" Martha Ronk is also difficult to situate within any single school or movement, as are Alice Notley (can we really consider her as part of the New York School?), Cole Swensen, and Cecilia Vicuña.

The result is a chorus of voices that sometimes resonate, sometimes clash, and sometimes miss each other entirely. In one sense, placing a writer like Marilyn Chin alongside Cole Swensen or Cecilia Vicuña might even return us to the preoccupations of the original anthology and conference —not so much to stake out separate territories, nor even to explore a strong current of hybridity in contemporary American poetry, but rather to demonstrate how contemporary poetry by women draws from multiple streams and perhaps even complicates the old canon-centric notions of "lineage" and affiliation. It would be an interesting exercise, after the fact, to look at all the writers included since the beginning of the series and explore how different configurations and arrangements resonate. What narratives are created, however unintentionally, by the writers who are grouped together?

A narrative of some sort is unavoidable. Simply by the act of ordering writers within book covers (in this series, the poets have appeared alphabetically), questions of canonicity and omission are bound to arise. But rather than delimit or define, it is our hope that the chorus of writers collected here resounds in unexpected ways, ultimately rejecting overarching rubrics in favor of a healthy and contradictory eclecticism that acknowledges the varied terrain of contemporary poetry and provides new understandings that may have previously gone unnoticed. Having Rankine's version of the lyric come just before Brian Teare's discussion of Ronk's use of rhetoric and syntax to systematically disrupt lyric subjectivity is one of the serendipities of our alphabetical organization. But the possibilities for discourse multiply as these very diverse writers are brought into conversation. How does reading the sparse lyrics of Fanny Howe or Martha Ronk prepare you for Jean Valentine? What about the other way around? What are the resonances between the different transnationalisms of Alice Notley, Cecilia Vicuña, and Rosmarie Waldrop? How do Natasha Trethewey and Claudia Rankine's aesthetically contrasting ways of engaging with and unearthing American history and culture—especially as they relate to race—expand, contradict, or enrich one another?

Before providing an overview of the collection, it seems useful to point to a few areas of overlap and conflict that weave through these pages beyond the serendipitous juxtapositions that occur through alphabetical organization. Key areas of conflict and concern include genre and the nature of the lyric, connections between gender and aesthetics, and—echoing Shetley—the lack of consensus about what poetry is, what it should do, and what the responsibilities of the poet are. Marilyn Chin and Fanny Howe—two writers whose aesthetic choices and affiliations are quite disparate—both write about the continuity between their politics and their poetics. Chin insists that by asserting her "poetic 'I,'" she takes a stand against oppression:

> Through the spoken word, the "I" critiques, questions, corrects, annotates, examines, mocks, derides, offends, and talks back at the prevailing culture.
>
> When I perform my poetry, the "I" speaks not only as the "poet" but also through enacted "difference"—through a body inscribed by historical determinations: brown (dirty), immigrant (illegal alien), girl (unwanted, illegitimate).

Chin's sense that she has no choice but to push back against the dominant culture is clear throughout her poetics statement, and in her poetry as well. Howe also asserts that there is continuity between human circumstances and poetic production, tracing her knowledge and beginnings as a writer to a specific time and place, Boston in 1968, and to the politics of that moment: "imminent violence," she writes, "defines my life and poetry." But the ways in which politics inflects her work is vastly different from Chin and from other explicitly political poets like Trethewey, Notley, or Vicuña.

The nature of poetic language is another site of contention. Like Chin, Natasha Trethewey believes language can foster identity and make amends: "I write to claim my native land even as it has forsaken me, rendered me an outsider. . . . I write to tell a fuller version of American history, to recover the stories and voices of people whose lives have been marginalized, forgotten, erased, overlooked." This sense of purpose feels urgent, feels like the poet is taking on a *mission*, as it were. It also suggests a reliance on the referential powers of language, on the ability of language to represent those stories and lives. Other writers not only mistrust the intention of a writer seeking to take on a public role, they also mistrust language's or poetry's ability to fulfill that ambition. For Leslie Scalapino, "Writing simply has no connection to reality. The actual event is entirely absent. . . . Language is separate from one's sensational phenomenal action (such as walking)." Scalapino is not making the claim that writing has no impact in the world—rather she sees language as alive in the present tense and always "in process": "My poems are not 'autobiography' (implying one's completed view about one's formed life) in the sense that the category, as now conceived, separates from phenomenal relation in the way the word 'personal' means separation from 'the world.'"

In contrast to Scalapino, Alice Notley believes that poetry "is the closest to reality if not coincident with it," but she also denies that poetry has any "responsibility" to anything or anyone. She questions the purpose of poetry itself and the product-focused language that informs the "business" of poetry: "I don't see any bigger artistic risk . . . poetry achieves nothing and probably doesn't help. Is there something to be achieved?" Notley's stance is always resistant, a counterstream, but in the current political moment of global turmoil and domestic uncertainty, the question about what poetry does or does not achieve is especially relevant. While they may approach this new reality in different manners and from a range of philosophical positions, many of the poets here believe that poetry is precisely what we need in this moment. In her statement, Martha Ronk writes in defense of poetry as a way of thinking through confusion, difficulty, the loss of our ideals and hope for the future. She sees it as part of the strategy by which we may live through these difficult times. She goes on to suggest that poetry can compensate for loss:

> by means of a language outside the normative; it can make the familiar unfamiliar, edgier, more vivid, in a shifted frame. Or it can offer a way of finding

words for the unfamiliar, inexplicable. One is drawn to poetry, in part I believe, as it articulates the uncanny nature of both language and representation, a kind of thinking that allows for the silences and confusions, both private and public, in which we live.

For Valentine, poetry is also a strategy. She writes that "poetry is prayer" that approaches the inexplicable. Citing Deleuze and Guattari on "minor literature," Cole Swensen suggests that poetry exists as "disturbances, both on the surface of language and within its deeper structures" and connects this to its ability to "agitate":

> There's always a crisis in poetry because poetry simply is language in crisis —it doesn't exist any other way, and it's this aspect of it that allows it to do what it, socially and culturally, needs to do, which is to be agitated, and then, in turn, to agitate. For a crisis in poetry doesn't mean that something is happening to poetry, but that poetry is itself happening something to language —i.e., it makes to happen into a transitive verb.

For Swensen this understanding of poetry—as something that happens to language—helps explain the multiplying splinterings and iterations in aesthetic approaches in poetry. Waldrop also treats language as haunted and multiple: "The blank page is not blank. We always write on top of a palimpsest. This is not a question of 'influence,' but of writing as dialog with a web of previous and concurrent texts, with tradition, with the culture and language we breathe and move in." While it might seem counterintuitive to make an aesthetic connection between Waldrop and Trethewey, for example, Khadijah Queen's essay examines precisely this notion of "blankness" and palimpsest in Trethewey's poetry. Instead of treating language as multiple, in her poetics statement, Rankine focuses on the disruption of generic distinctions, and is interested in "extending the document beyond the limits of its genre" in order to create "contaminated fields of possibility."

Ronk's idea that, by definition, poetry is "outside the normative" is important to most of the poets in this collection, though they approach this outsideness in different ways. Notley, though she has taught off and on— like several other writers here, including Scalapino, Vicuña, Waldrop and Valentine—has functioned outside tenured academic life, as if in some way actualizing for herself a certain kind of fruitful "outsiderness." Even though Waldrop has been an important publisher of other writers (and situated at Brown University where her spouse taught), she still has mostly functioned outside those systems. Ditto for Valentine, who taught at Sarah Lawrence and New York University for many years, but never as a tenured professor.

Because all of these writers are women, questions of lineage, influence, and inheritance are also part of the context within which we have to think about their work. Rankine and Waldrop, like many of the writers here, emphasize the material aspects of language or blur the dividing lines between genres, but also seek to construct the poem beyond and despite the limits of gender. In her discussion of how poetry can function in these difficult times, it's telling that Ronk invokes private and public "silences and confusions," for the overlap between these two spheres—perhaps the fact that they are thought of as distinct spheres at all—is one of the defining characteristics of what has been thought of as "women's writing," though the valences and definitions of that term have shifted widely and deeply throughout the twentieth century and into the present moment. The separation then—between the public and the private, between a woman's unique experience of the world as opposed to everyone else's—plays itself out in these pages as well. Marilyn Chin posits that claiming a lineage at all is revolutionary for women of color, who have traditionally been excluded from both mainstream conventions and those at the forefront of experimentation: "Aren't Chinese girls allowed to have a surreal imagination?" she asks.

As was also true of the previous collections in this series, there is no clear consensus on feminism or other forms of identity politics, though the effects of gender and the construction of the feminine are very much in play in the work. More than a shared ideology, what unites the varied approaches of these writers is a commitment to creating new fields, new idioms, new vernaculars, new forms. To make the *new* is of primary importance to these writers and, for women poets, that often entails a negotiation of gender, whether it is Chin's explicitly feminist stance, Notley's "inclusive" and boundary-crossing poetics, or Howe's embrace of a philosophical and spiritual lyric space that feels nearly "old-fashioned" in the manner of Hopkins, Herbert, or Donne. It is remarkable, paging through the manuscript, to see how *visually* different all the poems are; this visual difference is a manifestation of both sonic difference and a difference in poetic approach to the treatment of subject and speaker.

Part of the work of this anthology is to explore and bring attention to these differences and, as we have already noted, part is compensatory: over half of the poets collected here have been writing and publishing for at least forty years and are widely considered to be major figures across the spectrum of contemporary poetry, and yet there are only a handful of significant scholarly considerations of their work. Despite a shifting cultural landscape, women's writing now, as in 1999, is still underrepresented, and more importantly, for our purposes, there is a noticeable dearth of serious critical assessment of women's poetry.[9] Our hope is that the essays, poems, and aesthetic statements collected here will help fill the considerable gap in serious criticism on contemporary women poets, while calling attention to the sheer variety of voices and forms, sparking conversation across lingering divides.

. . .

The collection opens with Marilyn Chin, whose poems underscore the notion that what gives this assembly coherence is each writer's singularity. Though she must be included under (and has made a significant contribution to) the broad and diverse umbrella of twentieth- and twenty-first-century Asian American literature, her work—like that of many of the poets here—cannot readily be aligned with any one aesthetic or ideological school or movement. Even the Asian American-ness in her writing is heterogeneous and multiple, as she draws on different sources in her work, from ancient Chinese practices to more recent Japanese and Vietnamese forms. Chin also invokes western traditions, from the compression of epigraphs and couplets, to the formal strictures of quatrains, sonnets, and blues stanzas. Chin's work is polyvocal and full of contradictions, enacting and describing hybrid subjectivity and experience on multiple levels—from the invention of hybrid forms to wild shifts in diction. Critic Dorothy Wang notes that Chin frequently draws on the trope of irony in her work, suggesting that it "allows her to mimic and dissect conflicting states of self-hatred, self-colonization, and erotic desire . . . [in] a formal manifestation —whose very structure captures the rivenness of subjectivity wrought by immigration, diaspora, and the violence of assimilation."[10]

In her poetics statement, "Brown Girl Manifesto, One Amongst Many," Chin's double-edged use of irony is in full view, as she deploys and questions the lyric "I" while making an argument for the ways poetry can help shape and express cultural identity. Perhaps more than any poet in this collection, Chin rejects the idea that poetry makes nothing happen; she offers no apology for the political nature of her work—or for her belief that part of her duty as a poet is to speak of and for those whose voices are silenced within our culture. Putting pressure on the very notion of polyvocality and multiculturalism, Chin asks why shouldn't she speak for "the veiled 'subaltern' from the (un)'Holy Lands'? the girl who is burned for a better dowry? the 24-year-old undocumented worker whom you both need and despise who died in the desert south of Dateland, Arizona traveling across the border?"

Chin's sense of obligation to be part of the resistance and her identification with the marginalized is clear in all of her books, and it is not surprising that scholarship on her work tends to emphasize the ways her poems challenge stereotypes and explicitly examine and enact the heterogeneous nature of Asian American identity.[11] While never losing sight of the importance of the political in Chin's work, Catherine Cucinella shifts the focus somewhat in her essay, "Marilyn Chin's *Hard Love Province*: An Erotics of Grief," calling attention to Chin's distinctive and innovative use of the elegy to express erotic desire, power, and rage, in addition to grief. As Cucinella shows, Chin transforms the elegy into a love poem and vice versa, developing a powerful "erotics of grief" that conflates absence and presence, reconfiguring our understanding of time while also foregrounding the power of feminine sexuality and desire. But while her losses are specific, Chin's mourning is broad and inclusive: "Her elegies," Cucinella explains, "make clear that she grieves from the margins and mourns the lives of those on the margins."

As we suggest above, Chin and Fanny Howe can be linked by a shared sense of community and political obligation, but aesthetically it would be difficult to find two more different writers. Where Chin shifts between compression and excess, Howe is consistently spare, reticent, and oblique, though as Meg Tyler suggests in her essay, "A Place Apart: Sound, Silence and Play in the Poetry of Fanny Howe," the poems are "oblique but not confounding, mystical but not mystifying." Just as crucially, Chin's sense of political exigency demands a kind of faith in language that cannot be found in Howe's work. In "A Hymn," Howe begins by suggesting that language, not experience, comes first:

> I traveled to the page where scripture meets fiction.
> The paper slept but the night in me woke up.
>
> Black letters were now alive
> and collectible in a material crawl.
>
> I could not decipher their intentions anymore.
> To what end did their shapes come forth?

But Howe's work is not purely self-reflexive or disjunctive. As she notes in her poetics statement, she has been interested from the beginning in "the inclusion of the unknown with the need to know," but she also, "like most poets," believes in "the healing power of beauty." Her work is often unpredictable and can be difficult to categorize because it engages strategies of disjunction, "creating phonetic and syntactical ambiguity" but retains an "unembarrassed confidence in her lyric self," as Geoffrey Treacle suggests in a review of her chapbook, *Forged* (2000).[12] Like several of the poets in this anthology, Howe both conforms to and radically challenges the conventions of the lyric, giving interiority a new, self-reflexive form.

In her essay, Tyler explores Howe's commitment to the difficult—"the unspoken, or the broken"—detailing the ways silence informs her work on multiple levels, from the structural—through fragments, broken lines, lack of punctuation—to the ethical, by syntactically drawing attention *away* from the self and the speaking subject. As Tyler observes, in place of lyric self-regard, "Howe offers . . . a kind of relentless questioning of . . . interiority (and our surroundings), things both seen and unseen," but also sees her actions and her writing "in concert with others, as part of a community." Her lyric poems are uncharacteristically full of silence "about the self."

Tyler also notes that despite the ways Howe's work resists lyric expressiveness and calls attention to the unreliability of language, she is in many ways distinct from the avant-garde and Language poetry movement, though she has spent most of her career associated with them. Of the poets in this collection, she seems to have more in common with Jean Valentine than Leslie Scalapino or Rosmarie Waldrop, and yet she clearly shares their interests in language as material and the provisionality of the lyric subject.

Alice Notley, whose work follows Howe's in this anthology, also gets associated with the avant-garde, and she too has created a body of work that is hard to categorize—despite her general association with the second generation of New York School poets like Anne Waldman, Ron Padgett, Joe Brainard, and her husband, Ted Berrigan. It is also hard to imagine two writers more different than Howe and Notley: compare Howe's "Hymn," with its koan-like self-reflexive lines and stanzas, to Notley's "Flowers" or "Growth of the Light Flat upon Her." Both writers work associatively, letting language lead and negotiating what Ira Sadoff has observed as the divide between "mimetic writing and writing where experience does not precede language."[13] But the effect in Notley's poems is of fullness and excess rather than sparseness. For Notley, poetry is "measured, layered and vibrates across itself," and exposes "the metaphysics of the universe." Even when she is working in short lines, as in "City of Ghostly Festivals," the lines, phrases, and sentences rush forward, constantly shifting time, point of view, and pronoun, making room for every turn and return of thought, as well as for the reader—a habit that makes Notley's own sense of responsibility to community and inclusiveness palpable. Like Howe, Notley is committed to resisting traditional understandings of lyric selfhood and the singularity of the lyric voice, and to exposing and exploring the fragmented nature of identity and the self.

In her essay, "Resist, Reframe, Insist: Alice Notley's Poetics of Inclusion," Elline Lipkin focuses on that particular aspect of Notley's work. Early in her career, Notley resisted the singularity of identity in a very literal way, including her children's actual speech and perspectives in her poems, emphasizing the fluid boundary between self and other, child and (m)other, in a way that echoes critical theory's problematizing of identity. Notley's specific project of resisting the singular, lyric "I" is explicitly feminist, though also pluralistic and polysemic. Lipkin shows that, through her poetics of "inclusivity," Notley calls attention to a multifaceted feminism that raises up everyone, not just people who identify as women. Lipkin demonstrates that this feminist inclusiveness is part of Notley's poetic praxis. Like Howe, "Notley is interested in offering to others the experience of joining into the intention of her poem, and (as an extension of her paradigm shift while writing and mothering) in also co-creating meaning as a way to free the lyric from the restrictive expectation of serving a singular consciousness." Looking first at early work, then turning to her epic poem, *The Descent of Alette*, Lipkin traces the different strategies Notley engages to forge "a poetics of inclusivity that is born out of the necessity to resist and react against the constrictions she felt as a female writer."

Claudia Rankine's mixed genre, polyvocal, post-confessional experimental work brings us with equal urgency to the problems of mimetic language, the need to resist the false singularity of lyric subjectivity and the cultural construction of the raced and gendered self. Whereas Howe traffics in broken lines and Notley in broken syntax, Rankine makes it clear in her poetics statement that she is specifically interested in crossing borders and disrupting boundaries in order to "extend the document," as Muriel Rukeyser put it. For Rankine, it is moving beyond genre's limits that produces the possibility of the communal voice which Chin, Howe, and Notley also aspire to. Such breaking is productive because it "contains . . . contaminated fields of possibility (contaminated because the habits of that genre are disrupted and generative because the perceived sense of unity contained in the habits of that genre are disrupted)." In her "American Lyric" series—*Don't Let Me Be Lonely* (2005) and *Citizen* (2015)—Rankine constructs a lyric speaker that is dispersed across shared experience, challenging the broad assumption that lyric is personal, singular, and introspective:

> You sit next to the man on the train, bus, in the plane, waiting room, anywhere he could be forsaken. You put your body there in proximity to, adjacent to, alongside, within.
>
> You don't speak unless you are spoken to and your body speaks to the space you fill and you keep trying to fill it except the space belongs to the body of the man next to you, not to you.

Both *Citizen* and *Don't Let Me Be Lonely* juxtapose lyric prose with a range of images, from newspaper photographs and fine art to prescription labels and medical diagrams, as well as other "evidence" drawn from the internet, television and other media.

In "The Atlantic Ocean Breaking on Our Heads: Claudia Rankine and the Whiteness of the Lyric Subject," Kamran Javadizadeh considers the connections between race and lyric at our contemporary moment, focusing on *Citizen* and the ways Rankine grapples with the problematic legacy of expressive lyric subjectivity. He asks, "What should the distribution of a lyric subject among a range of forms (here: poems, prose, portraits) have to do with the construction of that lyric subject's race, of his or her whiteness?" In order to answer his own question, Javadizadeh traces the connections between Rankine's *Citizen* and Robert Lowell's ur-text of confessional poetry, *Life Studies*, and between the twentieth- (and perhaps) twenty-first-century lyric and the construction of whiteness—a construction that assumes its own centrality and obliterates any signs of dissent or difference that threaten its inviolability. Focusing on the most pressing problems that *Citizen* brings to our attention—the cultural permeation of institutionalized racism, the construction of raced identity, and the reconciliation between a post-confessional lyric mode and a constructionist awareness of language and its effects—the essay also reconfigures our understanding of the confessional mode, suggesting that Rankine ultimately departs from that tradition "by making visible the privilege upon which its self-disclosures depended for their power."

Like Howe and Rankine, Martha Ronk is explicitly, even obsessively in conversation with the lyric and with the painfully mediated nature of language. In her poetics statement Ronk connects the lyric impulse in her work to memory and her "repeated effort to write about memory and the failures necessarily bound up with memory." As Brian Teare notes in his essay, "Martha Ronk's Distressed Lyrics," this focus has remained consistent. Over the course of a thirty-year career, she has developed "a virtuoso set of formally deconstructed variations on classic lyric themes like love, perception, grief, and the passage of time." Moreover, she is equally committed to finding ways "of acknowledging the imbedded nature of all verbal expression, [and] the fluid nature of a first-person pronoun." Like Howe and Notley, Ronk's aesthetic sensibility does not neatly align with any particular group or ideology—though she is often associated with the avant-garde and experimental writing. Though of the same generation as Leslie Scalapino and Lyn Hejinian, she was not part of the West Coast Language poetry scene, despite her interests, nor is her work purely invested in the anti-capitalistic disruptive, disjunctive practices associated with Language poetry.

In his essay on her work, Brian Teare puts questions about the place of the lyric in contemporary poetry front and center. Outlining the evolution of the so-called poetry wars and the hybrid poetics posited by anthologies like Cole Swensen's and David St. John's *American Hybrid* and Reginald Shepherd's *Postmodern Lyricisms*,[14] Teare positions Ronk's "postmodern lyrics" "on the major fault line of late twentieth-century poetic practice and literary critical discourse about poetics," the contested space between lyric self-expression and postmodern self-reflexiveness, between "the New Lyric Studies" and "post-language." Through incisive readings across several books, Teare outlines the ways Ronk's poetry presents "a serious revision of lyric tradition," emphasizing the ways she calls attention to the self-reflexive operations of language. Even as she seems to present what we think of as private utterance, "feeling recollected in tranquility," Ronk demonstrates that all expression is always already utterly and absolutely mediated.

While Ronk's work finds fruitful ground in the contested space between "new lyric" and "post-language," Leslie Scalapino seems squarely committed to some of the hallmark aspects of 1980s-era experimental writing, such as extreme fragmentation, decentering of the lyric "I," commitment to theory and theoretical underpinnings and, most importantly, a seriality of the work that dedicates itself to an identity as "writing," not as "poetry," and definitely not as "poems." On the other hand, Scalapino herself draws on interior experience in her work, and cites such personal references and influences as the ancient sage Nagarjuna, the Zen teacher Dogen, and the contemporary poet Philip Whalen (also a Zen abbot), whose work trafficked in the autobiographical and conversational terrain of poets like Notley, Joanne Kyger, and Frank O'Hara.

In both her poetry and her prose, Scalapino's aim is precisely to unbuckle time and space and identity, to explore the ways language can construct or deconstruct a world without such borders and demarcations. Her forms—detective novel, science fiction, pastoral poem, political screed, letter to the editor—are actually quite conventional. Inside each, however, furious storms brew. It's not that language lies or is ineffective, it's precisely the opposite. Scalapino is able to uncover fresh and new potential in the most hackneyed of genres with her wild approach.

Writing about her novel *Defoe*, which was, among other things, about the first aerial bombardments of Iraq in 1991, Scalapino says:

> I was writing a way of having motions be *before* they're conceived in/be *before* their entirety. Motions without/before becoming entity, the writing is a spatial conceiving of motions not determining these no thing already settled but forming. One is to be seeing ahead of there being event (an "event" as such would already be concluded), is to let go description that creates detachment of the individual from outside (let go the misconception that the outside is pre-formed).

One thinks here of Jean Baudrillard's argument that the 1991 Gulf War marked an end to "war" as the west knew it, that (in his words) the war "did not take place." What he meant was that the intention of the vocabulary had failed: that the new wars of the future would be fought at distance, by remote control, on a screen (he would turn out to be correct), more game than actual physical struggle for the "first world" invading forces. Scalapino's writing seems aimed at trying to create new configurations for understanding cause and effect, new contours of thinking for the information age.

At first Scalapino's attraction to Zen thinkers and Zen practice feels odd, further complicated by her stated aversion to *zazen* meditation, which she discusses in *The Public World/Syntactically Impermanence*.[15] But what she does in her work is slow down the mind, turn over and observe each single moment. In his essay, "Leslie Scalapino's Anarchic Moment," Michael Cross writes, "Scalapino's testing-space is precarious as both interior(s) and exterior(s) conform to structures of legibility (often through the habit of 'making sense'), and the mind struggles against the gravitational pull toward recognition, fighting to free itself from 'mind formation' while acknowledging that mind formation itself is the very apparatus by which we come to know anything at all." Cross goes on to explore the techniques and modes used by Scalapino in her decentering but ultimately "reterritorializing" work. "Even the Deleuzian model of the rhizome is not flexible enough for this work," he remarks, "as it still implies a fixed dimension," while Scalapino's mind travels in every direction at once and in four dimensions, maybe more.

Cole Swensen is similarly a poet of "experience." Her work investigates and challenges one's knowledge of a subject. Whether she is examining public gardens, the act of walking, traveling by train, cemeteries, or shared arts like painting, illuminated prayer books, or performance art, Swensen is exploring the notion of the "commons" or "public space." Though her approach and her structures may be thought of as avant-garde or experimental, her actual vocabulary and poetic structures (line and stanza) are fairly simple and accessible. Swensen accepts that poetry is an art with a greater potential for forcing change than prose. She invokes Deleuze and Guattari's notion of "crisis" and cites poetry as "a literature that coexists within another, dominant, one that it constantly disturbs, continually forcing the major literature to rethink itself, regroup itself, and reassert itself."

When she cites the ability of poetry to reveal the world in its "post-truth" state (now post-"alternative facts," post-"fake news") she actually sounds more like Natasha Trethewey than Leslie Scalapino, a poet with whom she is probably more frequently aesthetically aligned. On the other hand, Swensen's (and Scalapino's) deep commitment is to disrupt binary oppositions and open up a field of possibility, including new approaches to hybridity. It was this urge that led her to co-edit the anthology *American Hybrid* with David St. John. In her essay, "Truths Surpassing Facts: Cole Swensen's Research Based Poetics," Lynn Keller quotes Ron Silliman saying that rather than draw from the competing and separate influences of 'Language' and 'Lyric,' in *American Hybrid*, Swensen sought to "ameliorate the borders betwixt the two, to operate perhaps as if no chasm in aesthetic & cultural values gave rise to these traditions." This is a very different approach than many of the writers in this volume, who draw from one or the other lineage or seek to fuse them into new approaches. In Swensen, we instead find *both* the lyric and the language jostling alongside the "post-lyric" and "post-language."

Swensen, like Trethewey, Rankine and, to a lesser extent, Waldrop, engages in a "research-based poetics," and Keller explores how her commitment to "betweenness" influences and is influenced by the projects she undertakes. Keller finds a fascinating push and pull between the ludic and theoretical impulses in Swensen's work, a trait that characterized much of post-1990s critical theory and poetry alike. Her essay both explores and explicates the visual and the verbal, along with the ghosts of various kinds that haunt Swensen's books.

In one sense, Scalapino's unearthing of "phenomena," or the daily moments upon which history turns, is similar to the historical project of Natasha Trethewey, though Trethewey's writing is more recognizably lyric and narrative. As much as Scalapino had a politics and "poethics" (Joan Retallack's term) that called for eschewing the singular lyric voice, Trethewey is equally politically and "poethically" committed to her own approach.[16] In her poetics statement (excerpted from a longer piece titled "Why I Write"), she states,

> I write to claim my native land even as it has forsaken me, rendered me an outsider. . . . I write to tell a fuller version of American history, to recover the stories and voices of people whose lives have been marginalized, forgotten, erased, overlooked. I write in order to redress the omissions and errors in history, to confront the willed forgetting that haunts our interactions with each other and to create a vision of a more just society based on reckoning with our troubled past rather than forgetting it.

Like Howe, Trethewey finds herself witness to, and implicated in, historic moments. Unlike Scalapino, she does not at all feel the impetus to critique her positionality vis-à-vis the narrativizing of history, nor the luxury (one might say) of withdrawing from her own subjectivity. She does not take the problem lightly:

> Certainly there are many poets and critics out there who believe that all personal experience is passé—my famous poet professor said as much on many occasions—though I have never heard anyone simplistically admonish white poets by saying they'll write better poems when they stop writing from personal experience. Often, when poets who are from groups deemed "other" write about personal experience, some readers assume that the poems can't speak to universal human experience, thus imparting the work with a "message" some readers would rather not encounter.

Here Trethewey writes somewhat defensively as she champions the choice of personal experience and transparent language, though perhaps it is an earned defensiveness.

In "Natasha Trethewey's Palimpsestic Poetics," Khadijah Queen explores Trethewey's engagement with visual images and the historical events those images depict. As Queen suggests, Trethewey attempts to uncover those voices she earlier said were "marginalized, forgotten, erased" through the triple layering of verbal text, visual text, and historical event, creating anew the histories previously forgotten or effaced. For Queen, Trethewey's invocation of the photographs of Bellocq, the ordinary objects of quotidian African-American life, and the archives and oral histories surrounding Hurricane Katrina, points to a practical and intentional use of poetry as a form of recovery. Of the writers included here, Trethewey has had perhaps the most widely recognized success (in addition to winning a Pulitzer Prize, she served a term as U.S. Poet Laureate); it is possible that these laurels have inspired a greater obligation toward the so-called "role of the poet" in public life.

Jean Valentine is equally engaged with American culture and history as Trethewey, but while Trethewey writes narrative and lyric poems that engage with events directly, Valentine's mostly brief and hermetic lyrics remain oriented toward her internal life, often even a dream life. Through a long engagement with hospice caregiving and psychotherapy, Valentine has developed a poetic idiom that feels very personal yet honors mystery and unfixity. As we have already suggested, most of the writers cite multiple sources and influences, often ones who might not be ordinarily thought of as working in concert. Valentine—mostly thought of as a lyric poet in a lineage that includes Adrienne Rich, W.S. Merwin, and James Wright, for example—also discusses her affection, admiration, and passion for Language poetry.[17]

These qualities of hermeticism and deep internal focus, what Lisa Russ Spaar calls their "irresistible attraction and their perceived inaccessibility," have earned Valentine both praise and critique from various quarters. In spare and sometimes disjunctive language she nonetheless treats very ordinary occurrences. As in Swensen's work, both vocabulary and subject often involve simple daily moments, though in Valentine's case much is left unsaid, resulting in an associative and highly compressed lyric. The poems frequently lean on what is sometimes called "dream logic," meaning that though the reader may be confused there is the trust—for both poet and reader—that such "confusion" can lead to deeper understanding. Valentine has not written much critical prose, nor engaged in the kind of professional positioning more commonly seen in many of her (predominantly male) peers. In place of critical prose we have numerous interviews from throughout her career and, rather than provide a poetics statement for this volume, Valentine has allowed her previous discourses to serve. In an interview with Michael Klein, she addresses the issue of "clarity" in her work:

> I think I do everything I can to be understood but after a point there's nothing more I can do. When I say to my students, "be clear, be clear, be clear,"

they say to me "you're asking something of us that you don't give to your own work." Well, that's one thing I can do as a reader, is say when I'm with you and when I'm not. But there's a point where you can't change a poem any more, or the poem becomes not itself anymore. There's nothing left, there's no poetry left. It just becomes an explanation or something . . . It's a very thin line for me because I don't have any liking at all for obscurity, but I do love mystery.

The core energy of Valentine's work stems from this commitment, not to mystery for its own sake but, as in the lyrics of Fanny Howe, a recognition that the deeply spiritual and philosophical manifests concretely in one's daily life. Lisa Russ Spaar tracks these efforts in her essay, "Skirting Heaven: Jean Valentine's Late Dream-Work in *Shirt in Heaven*." Spaar notes that the poems in *Shirt in Heaven*, Valentine's most recent book, "are suffused with a new equipoise and tensility, hard-won by her ongoing, daring, open-minded working through the neural mesh, the ligatures, tendons, and sinews of oneiric liminality—where image and thought, dark and light, dream and waking permit one another to deepen and speak." In tracing Valentine's progression from a more or less straightforward lyric to these more recent poems, Spaar offers the reader numerous frameworks and contexts for all stages of Valentine's body of work.

Cecilia Vicuña's poems move not between dream and waking life but between contexts, between continents, between languages. As Julie Brown discusses in her essay, "Return of the Disappeared: Cecilia Vicuña's *Saboramis*," the 1973 coup in Chile strongly affected the young Vicuña's poetics as well as her political and linguistic development. Like Rankine, Vicuña draws on visual text and contemporary life to fashion a performative approach to the lyric that often includes ephemeral and improvisational practices that mirror her approaches to visual art, film, and sculpture—all of which she is also engaged with. According to Brown:

> [Vicuña] lays claim to simultaneously individual and communal identities. Her "shaman heart" locates her as a specific and individuated speaker, and yet she bears "the soul of all the Indians [she has] been" within her. In a more figurative sense, of course, this image invokes the speaker's indigenous roots, but if taken at face value, it also bears important implications for Vicuña's relationship to time: she is at once present and past, an ever-increasing fold of identities and times stretching into eras unknown.

Vicuña sees the making of the poem as an act itself; as in Scalapino's work, there is a present-tense moment that defies writing as a moment of inscribing reality and privileges "writing" (in some cases literally handwriting) or performance of a piece as a way of opening up possibilities, of dissolving borders. She says in her poetics statement, "I search for a *com*munal syntax arising from the space between *com* (together) and *un* (one): / the seed of language in dissonance, a clash, or double sound. / Not a denial of the individual, but its double realization, in solitude and togetherness. // I return to poems centered on dissolution, a way of being in language, listening to the tongues within tongues."

There is, in some way, a kind of bilinguality or polylinguality at work in much of the work in this volume. These poets contend with multiplicity of form, aesthetic positioning, subject, and sometimes—like Vicuña—even in the language of the poem itself. For Rosmarie Waldrop the border-crossing and exchange of language is not a weakness or a condition that must be dealt with; rather, it provides the entry into poetry: "In crossing the Atlantic my phonemes settled somewhere between German and English. I speak either language with an accent. This has saved me the illusion of being the master of language. I enter it at a skewed angle, through the fissures, the slight difference." Waldrop uses the structures of prose and paragraph but also the rhythms of poetry and the line to create poems that are simultaneously interrogative and phenomenological yet (in her term) also "driven by abstraction."

Waldrop's questions are like the questions asked of Joan of Arc during her trial (as pointed out by Anne Carson in an essay in her book, *Nay Rather*), meant not to solicit real answers from Joan, but rather to corral her, force her to implicate herself. If so often the question is used as an interrogation, for political purposes and with the "questioner" in the position of political power, in Waldrop's writing the questions serve to widen the field of understanding, creating new dissonances and consonances, previously unmapped. Waldrop sees this resistance to fixity as a feminist practice. She writes, "It was only gradually that I realized this challenge to a fixed subject-object relation has feminist implication. In many cultures, woman has been treated as object par excellence. These poems propose a grammar in which subject and object functions are reversible roles, where there is no hierarchy, but fluid and constant alternation."

In his essay on Waldrop's work, "Rosmarie Waldrop: Attending to Absence," Richard Greenfield examines her move to prose and the techniques she uses within that genre to open up the poetics of grammar and syntax. Like one of her invoked predecessors, Gertrude Stein, Waldrop is looking into the structure of language itself to find new meanings. Greenfield shows how Waldrop's singular use of the fragment is key to her explorations of history, historiography, metaphysics, and poetics through such interweavings as personal experience, scripture, and concepts from quantum physics.

The multiple approaches and grounding assumptions of the poets collected in this volume serve to enrich and extend the possibilities of poetry in the contemporary moment. Martha Ronk, in her poetics statement, invokes Barbara Guest as one writer who confronted these same issues in a time when there were very few women writers who were publishing in mainstream venues and were accepted by the literary establishment. Ronk writes, "Extending the work of her chosen predecessors, Guest radically changes the ways in which images are used, not as ways to complement an idea or scene, but as foreign substances that run counter to or athwart much that they seem to be connected to. . . . Images work as the energy that propels or attracts, that initiates thinking and creates movement."[18] Many of the writers throughout this series of anthologies have invoked one another as poetic or aesthetic influences, and that tendency continues in the statements collected in this most recent edition. That force of Guest's to "initiate" may be seen in all the writers here. They widen the lens of possibilities for poetry even if in their own work they focus deeply on one area or another. By finding their own unique voices amidst complex and sometimes vexed contexts, they have created a new American poetry.

NOTES

1. For an account of the "Poetry Wars" of the 1990s and earlier, see Hank Lazar, *Opposing Poetries: Part One: Issues and Institutions* (Chicago: Northwestern University Press, 1996) and Jed Rasula, *The American Poetry Wax Museum: Reality Effects, 1940–1990* (Urbana, IL: National Council of Teachers of English, 1996), which explores the divergences in the field by examining the processes and effects of the anthologization of poetry. Christopher Beach's essay, "Poetic Positionings: Stephen Dobyns and Lyn Hejinian," in *Contemporary Literature* 38.1 (Spring 1997) 44–77, usefully summarizes the differences between conventional mainstream poetry and Language-oriented writing.

2. In *Dickinson's Misery*, Jackson uses the nineteenth- and twentieth-century reception of Dickinson's work to argue that a particular understanding of lyric was invented and created by critics and editors who ignored other contiguous writing activities Dickinson was involved in. "Through the development of various reading practices," Jackson writes, "poetic subgenres collapsed into the expressive romantic lyric of the nineteenth century," which continues to be the model of what we consider to be lyric expression. For an introduction to the terms of the contemporary debate around "the new lyric studies," see the special section on lyric poetry in the January 2008 issue of *PMLA* (123.1), which includes essays by Jackson, Terada, Jonathan Culler, Robert Kaufman, Oren Izenberg, and Yopie Prins, among others. See also *The Lyric Studies Reader*, edited by Jackson and Prins, which includes canonical and more recent reflections on the lyric, including its intersections with avant-garde and sexuality studies.

3. Gillian White, *Lyric Shame: The "Lyric" Subject of Contemporary American Poetry* (Cambridge, MA: Harvard University Press, 2014), 2–3, 211.

4. For discussions of the documentary turn and the new "poetry of engagement." see Ann Keniston and Jeffrey Gray, *The News from Poems: Essays on the 21st Century American Poetry of Engagement* (Ann Arbor: University of Michigan Press, 2016).

5. Vernon Shelton, "The Poetry of Engagement and the Politics of Reading," in Keniston and Gray, *The News from Poems*, 26–46.

6. Lynn Keller, "'Just one of / the girls:— / normal in the extreme': Experimentalists-To-Be Starting Out in the 1960s," *differences: A Journal of Feminist Cultural Studies* 12.2 (Summer 2001): 47.

7. Ibid.

8. For examples, see chapters on Rankine in Christopher Nealon's *The Matter of Capital: Poetry and Crisis in the American Century* (Cambridge, MA: Harvard University Press, 2011); Andrew Epstein's *Attention Equals Life: The Pursuit of the Everyday in Contemporary Poetry and Culture* (Oxford: Oxford University Press, 2016); and Amy Moorman Robbins' *American Hybrid Poetics: Gender, Mass Culture, and Form* (New Brunswick: Rutgers University Press, 2014). Angela Hume describes Rankine's work as ecopoetry in "Toward an Antiracist Ecopoetics: Waste and Wasting in the Poetry of Claudia Rankine," *Contemporary Literature* 57.1 (Spring 2016): 79–120.

9. "The Vida Count," which "manually, painstakingly tall[ies] the gender disparity in major literary publications and book reviews," suggests that under pressure, major publications like *Harper's* and *Atlantic Monthly* have become more conscious about publishing more women writers. To view the results of their yearly tallies, see http://www.vidaweb.org/the-count.

10. Dorothy Wang, *Thinking Its Presence: Form, Race and Subjectivity in Contemporary Asian American Poetry* (Stanford: Stanford University Press, 2014), 117–18.

11. See, for example, Wang's chapters on Chin in *Thinking Its Presence*, as well as Steven Yao's chapter on Chin in *Foreign Accents: Chinese American Verse from Exclusion to Postethnicity* (Cambridge: Oxford University Press, 2010), and Xiaojing Zhou, *The Ethics and Poetics of Alterity in Asian American Poetry* (Iowa City: University of Iowa Press, 2006).

12. Geoffrey Treacle, "Annus Mirablis," *Chicago Review* 46.2 (Spring 2000): 136.

13. Ibid.

14. See Reginal Shepherd, ed., *Lyric Postmodernisms: An Anthology of Contemporary Innovative Poetries* (Boulder, CO: Counterpath Press, 2008), and Cole Swenson and David St. John, eds., *American Hybrid* (New York: W.W. Norton, 2009).

15. Leslie Scalapino, *The Public World/Syntactically Impermanence* (Middletown, CT: Wesleyan University Press, 1999).

16. For more on poethics, see Joan Retallack, *The Poethical Wager* (Berkeley, CA: University of California Press, 2004).

17. See her interview with Jay Hoppenthaler, "So Let It Be Like Rain: An Interview with Jean Valentine," *Arts & Letters* 3 (Spring 2000).

18. Martha Ronk, "A Foreign Substance: On Barbara Guest's 'Wild Gardens Overlooked by Night Lights.'" *Chicago Review* 53.4/54.1–2 (Summer 2008): 109.

MARILYN CHIN

POEMS

FROM *Rhapsody in Plain Yellow*

So, You Fucked John Donne

for MJW

So, you fucked John Donne.
Wasn't very nice of you.
He was betrothed to God, you know,
a diet of worms for you!

So, you fucked John Keats.
He's got the sickness, you know.
You *took precautions*, you say.
So, you fucked him anyway.

John Donne, John Keats,
John Guevara, John Wong,
John Kennedy, Johnny John-John,
The beautiful, the wreckless, the strong.

Poor thang, you had no self-worth then,
you fucked them all for a song.

Blues on Yellow

The canary died in the gold mine, her dreams got lost in the sieve.
The canary died in the gold mine, her dreams got lost in the sieve.
Her husband the crow killed under the railroad, the spokes hath shorn his wings.

Something's cookin' in Chin's kitchen, ten thousand yellow-bellied sapsuckers
  baked in a pie.
Something's cookin' in Chin's kitchen, ten thousand yellow-bellied sapsuckers
  baked in a pie.
Something's cookin' in Chin's kitchen, die die yellow bird, die die.

O crack an egg on the griddle, yellow will ooze into white.
O crack an egg on the griddle, yellow will ooze into white.
Run, run, sweet little Puritan, yellow will ooze into white.

If you cut my yellow wrists, I'll teach my yellow toes to write.
If you cut my yellow wrists, I'll teach my yellow toes to write.
If you cut my yellow fists, I'll teach my yellow feet to fight.

Do not be afraid to perish, my mother, Buddha's compassion is nigh.
Do not be afraid to perish, my mother, our boat will sail tonight.
Your babies will reach the promised land, the stars will be their guide.

I am so mellow yellow, mellow yellow, Buddha sings in my veins.
I am so mellow yellow, mellow yellow, Buddha sings in my veins.
O take me to the land of the unreborn, there's no life on earth without pain.

Rhapsody in Plain Yellow

for my love, Charles (1938–2000)

Say: 言

I love you, I love you, I love you, no matter
    your race, your sex, your color. Say:
the world is round and the arctic is cold.
    Say: I shall kiss the rondure of your soul's
living marl. Say: he is beautiful,
    serenely beautiful, yet, only ephemerally so.
Say: Her Majesty combs her long black hair for hours.
    Say: O rainbows, in his eyes, rainbows.
Say: O frills and fronds, I know you
    Mr. Snail Consciousness,
O foot plodding the underside of leaves.
    Say: I am nothing without you, nothing,
Ms. Lookeast, Ms. Lookeast,
    without you, I am utterly empty.
Say: the small throat of sorrow.
Say: China and France, China and France.
Say: Beauty and loss, the dross of centuries.
    Say: Nothing in their feudal antechamber
shall relinquish us of our beauty—
    Say: Mimosa—this is not a marriage song (epithalamion).
Say: when I was a young girl in Hong Kong
    a prince came on a horse, I believe it was piebald.
O dead prince   dead dead prince   who paid for my ardor.
    Say: O foot   O ague   O warbling oratorio . . .
Say: Darling, use "love" only as a transitive verb
    for the first forty years of your life.
Say: I have felt this before, it's soft, human.
    Say: my love is a fragile concertina.
Say: you always love them in the beginning,
    then, you take them to slaughter.
O her coarse whispers   O her soft bangs.
    By their withers, they are emblazoned doppelgangers.

Say: beauty and terror, beauty and terror.
    Say: the house is filled with perfume,
dancing sonatinas and pungent flowers.
    Say: houses filled with combs   combs   combs
and the mistress' wan ankles.
    Say: embrace the An Lu Shan ascendancy
and the fantastical diaspora of tears.
    Say: down blue margins
my inky love runs. Tearfully,
tearfully, the pearl concubine runs.
There is a tear in his left eye—sadness or debris?
    Say: reverence to her, reverence to her.
Say: I am a very small boy, a very small boy.
    I am a teeny weeny little boy
who yearns to be punished.
    Say: I can't live without you
Head Mistress, Head Mistress,
    I am a little lamb, a consenting little lamb.
I am a sheep without his fold.
    Say: God does not exist and hell is other people—
And Mabel, can't we get out of this hotel?
Say: Gregor Samsa—someone in Tuscaloosa
thinks you're *magnifico*, she will kiss
    your battered cheek, embrace your broken skull.
Is the apple half eaten or half whole?
    Suddenly, he moves within me, how do I know
that he is not death, in death there is

    certain / / caesura.

Say: there is poetry in his body, poetry
    in his body, yes, say:
this dead love, this dead love,
    this dead, dead love, this lovely death,
this white percale, white of hell, of heavenly shale.
    Centerfolia . . . say: kiss her sweet lips.

Say: what rhymes with "flower":
    "bower," "shower," "power"?
I am that yellow girl, that famished yellow girl
    from the first world.
Say: I don't give a shit about nothing
    'xcept my cat, your cock and poetry.
Say: a refuge between sleeping and dying.
    Say: to Maui   to Maui   to Maui
creeps in his petty pompadour.
    Day to day, her milk of human kindness
ran dry: I shall die of jejune jujune   *la lune la lune.*
    Say: a beleaguered soldier, a fine arse had he.
Say: I have seen the small men of my generation
rabid, discrete, hysterical, lilliput, naked.
Say: Friday is okay; we'll have fish.
    Say: Friday is not okay; he shall die
of the measles near the bay.
    Say: Friday, just another savage
day until Saturday, the true Sabbath, when they shall
    finally stay. Say:
                Sojourner
                        Truth.
Say: I am dismayed by your cloying promiscuousness
    and fawning attitude.
Say: *amaduofu, amaduofu.*
    Say: he put cumin and tarragon in his stew.
Say: he's the last wave of French Algerian Jews.
    He's a cousin of Helene Cixous, twice removed.
Say: he recites the lost autobiography of Camus.
    Say: I am a professor from the University of Stupidity.
I cashed my welfare check and felt good.
    I saw your mama crossing the bridge of magpies
up on the faded hillock with the Lame Ox—
    Your father was conspicuously absent.
Admit that you loved your mother,
    that you killed your father to marry your mother.

Suddenly, my terrible childhood made sense.
    Say: beauty and truth, beauty and truth,
all ye need to know on earth all ye need to know.
    Say: I was boogying down, boogying down
Victoria Peak Way and a slip-of-a-boy climbed off his ox;
    he importuned me for a kiss, a tiny one
on his cankered lip.
    Say: O celebrator   O celebrant
of a blessed life, say:
    false   fleeting   hopes.
Say: despair, despair, despair.
    Say: Chinawoman, I am a contradiction in terms:
I embody frugality and ecstasy.
    Friday Wong died on a Tuesday.
O how he loved his lambs.
    He was lost in their sheepfold.
Say: another mai tai before your death.
    Another measure   another murmur   before your last breath.
Another boyfriend, Italianesque.
    Say: Save. Exit.
Say: I am the sentence which shall at last elude her.
    Oh, the hell of heaven's girth, a low mound from here . . .
Say:
    Oh, a mother's vision of the emerald hills draws down her brows.
Say: A brush of jade, a jasper plow furrow.
    Say: ####oooooxxxxx!!!!

Contemplate thangs cerebral spiritual open stuff reality
    by definition lack any spatial extension
we occupy no space and are not measurable
    we do not move undulate are not in perpetual motion
where for example is thinking in the head? in my vulva?

    whereas in my female lack of penis? Physical
thangs spatial extensions mathematically measurable
    preternaturally possible lack bestial vegetable consciousness
lack happiness lackluster lack *chutzpah* lack love

Say: A scentless camellia bush bloodied the afternoon.
    Fuck this line, can you really believe this?
When did I become the master of suburban bliss?
    With whose tongue were we born?
The language of the masters is the language of the aggressors.
    We've studied their cadence carefully—
enrolled in a class to *improve our accent.*
    Meanwhile, they hover over, waiting for us to stumble . . .
to drop an article, mispronounce an R.
    Say: softly, softly, the silent gunboats glide.
O onerous sibilants, O onomatopoetic glibness.
    Say:
How could we write poetry in a time like this?
    A discipline that makes much ado about so little?
Willfully laconic, deceptively disguised as a love poem.

Say:
Your engorging dict-
atorial flesh
grazed mine.

Would you have loved me more if I were black?
    Would I have loved you more if you were white?
And you, relentless Sinophile,
    holding my long hair, my frayed dreams.

My turn to objectify you.
    I, the lunatic, the lover, the poet,
the face of an orphan static with flies,
    the scourge of the old world,
which reminds us—it ain't all randy dandy
    in the new kingdom

Say   rebuke   descry

Hills and canyons, robbed by sun, leave us nothing.

FROM *Hard Love Province*

Twenty-five Haiku

A hundred red fire ants scouring, scouring the white peony

•

Fallen plum blossoms return to the branch, you sleep, then harden again

•

Cuttlefish in my palm stiffens with rigor mortis, boy toys can't love

•

Neighbor's barn: grass mat, crickets, Blue Boy, trowel handle, dress soaked in mud

•

Iron-headed mace; double-studded halberd slice into emptiness

•

O fierce Oghuz, tie me to two wild elephants, tear me in half

•

O my swarthy herder, two-humped bactrian, drive me the long distance

•

Forceps, tongs, *bushi*, whip, flanks, scabbard, stirrup, goads, distaff, wither, awl

•

Black-eyed Susans, Queen Anne's lace, bounty of cyclamen, mown paths erupt

•

Gaze at the charred hills, the woe-be-gone kiosks, we are all God's hussies

-

I have not fondled the emperor's lap dog, whose name is Black Muzzle

-

Urge your horses into the mist-swilled Galilee, O sweet Bedlamite

-

Her Majesty's randying up the jewel stairs to find the pleasure dome

-

Ancient pond; the frog jumps in and in and in: the deep slap of water

-

The frog jumps into the ancient pond; she says, no, I am not ready

-

Coyote cooked his dead wife's vagina and fed it to his new wife

-

I plucked out three white pubic hairs and they turned into flying monkeys

-

Let's do it on the antimacassar, on the antimacassar

-

Little Red drew her teeny pistol from her basket and said "eat me"

-

Chimera: Madame Pol Pot grafting a date tree onto a date tree

-

His unworthy appendage, his mutinous henchman grazed my pink cheeks

•

He on top now changes to bottom, Goddess welcomes her devotee

•

Fish fish fowl fowl, mock me Mistress Bean-curd, I am both duck and essence

•

Don't touch him, bitch, we're engaged; and besides, he's wearing my nipple-ring

•

Sing sing little yellow blight rage rage against the dying of the light

Brown Girl Manifesto (Too)

Metaphor   metaphor   my pestilential esthetic
    A tsunami powers through   my mother's ruins
Delta   delta moist loins of the republic
    Succumb to the low-lying succubus   do!

Flagpole   flagpole   my father's polemics
    A bouquet of   fuck-u-bastard flowers
Fist me   embrace me with   your phantom limbs
    Slay me   with your slumlord   panegyrics

Flip over   so I can see your pastoral mounts
    Your sword   slightly parting from the scabbard
Girl skulls   piled like fresh baked loaves
    A foul wind   scours my mother's cadaver

Ornamental   Oriental   techno   impresarios
    I am your parlor rug   your chamber bauble
Love me   stone me   I am all yours
    Pound   Pound   my father's Ezra

Freedom   freedom   flageolet-tooting girls
Dancing   on the roof   of the *maquiladoras*

Black President

If a black man could be president
Could a white man be his slave?
Could a sinner enter heaven
By uttering his name?

If the terminator is my governor
Could a cowboy be my king?
When shall the cavalry enter Deadwood
And save my prince?

An exo-cannibal eats her enemies
An indo-cannibal eats her friends
I'd rather starve myself silly
Than to make amends

Blood on the altar   Blood on the lamb
Blood in the chalice
Not symbolic   but fresh

Beautiful Boyfriend

for Don Lonewolf (1958–2011)

My skiff is made of spicewood   my oars are Cassia bract
Music flows   from bow to starboard
Early Mozart   cool side of Coltrane   and miles and miles   of Miles
Cheap Californian Merlot   and my new boyfriend

•

My beautiful boyfriend   please shave your head
At the Miramar barbershop   take the tonsure
Bow toward the earth   prostrate and praise
Breathe in the Goddess'   potent citron

•

Bullet   don't shoot him   he's my draft-horse
Night scope don't pierce him   he's my love-stalk
Sniper   who are you   high on the roof
Stop for a slow cigarette   let him escape

•

If I could master   the nine doors of my body
And close my heart   to the cries of suffering
Perhaps   I could love you like no other
Float my mind   toward the other side of hate

•

The shanty towns of Tijuana   sing for you
The slums of Little Sudan   hold evening prayer
One dead brown boy is a tragedy
        Ten thousand is a statistic
So let's fuck   my love   until the dogs pass

•

All beautiful boyfriends are transitory
They have no souls   they're shiny brown flesh
Tomorrow they'll turn into   purple festering corpses
Fissured   gored   by myriad flies

•

My boyfriend drives up   in his late Humvee
Says: *We're going to   hunt Bin Laden*
We'll sleep in caves   and roast wild hare
And rise to praise   the bright red sun

•

I was once   a beloved spotted ox
Now I've become   a war-horse of hate
I pulled the lorries   of ten thousand corpses
Before   I myself   was finally flayed

•

Down the Irrawaddy River   you lay yourself to sleep
No sun   no moon   no coming   no going
No causality   no personality
No hunger   no thirst

•

Skyward   beyond Angkor Wat
    Beyond   Jokhanginlhasa
You were floating   on a giant stupa
    Waiting   for   Our   Lord

•

Malarial deltas   typhoidal cays
Tsunamis don't judge   calamity grieves no one
The poor will be submerged   the rich won't be saved
Purge the innocent   sink the depraved

•

You push down my hand   with your boney hand
The fox-hair brush   lifts and bends
There's no revision in this life   you sigh
One bad stroke   and all is gone

•

What do I smell   but the perfume of transience
Crushed calyxes   rotting phloems
Let's write   pretty poems   pretty poems   pretty poems
Masque stale pogroms   with a sweet whiff of oblivion

•

Three shots into the wind   according to the rites
Heaven's stealth caissons   confess nothing
Lotus cannot cry   Buddha feels no pain
Surrender   you must   to one love   one nation

Formosan Elegy

for Charles

You have lived six decades   and you have lived none
You have loved many   and you have loved no one
You wedded three wives   but you lie in your cold bed alone
You sired four children   but they cannot forgive you

Knock at emptiness   a house without your love
Strike the pine box   no answer   all hollow
You planted plums near the gate   but they bear no fruit
You raised herbs in the veranda   fresh and savory

I cry for you   but no sound wells up in my throat
I sing for you   but my tears have dried in my gullet
Walk the old dog   give the budgies a cool bath
Cut a tender melon   let it bleed into memory

The robe you washed   hangs like a carcass flayed
The mug you loved   is stained with old coffee
Your toothbrush is silent   grease mums your comb
Something's lost   something's made strong

Around the corner   a new prince yearns to be loved
A fresh turn of phrase   a bad strophe erased
A random image   crafts itself into a poem
A sleepless Taipei night   a mosquito's symphony

Who will cry for you   me and your sister Colette
Who will cry for you   me and your Algerian sister
You were a rich man   but you held on to your poverty
You were a poor man   who loved gold over dignity

I sit near your body bag   and sing you a last song
I sit near your body bag   and chant your final sutra
What's our place on earth?   nada   nada   nada
What's our destiny?   war   grief   maggots   nada

Arms   cheeks   cock   femur   eyelids   nada
Cowl   ox   lamb   vellum   marrow   nada
Vulva   nada   semen   nada   ovum   nada
Eternity   nada   heaven   nada   void   nada

Birth and death   the same blackened womb
Birth and death   the same white body bag
Detach   detach   we enter the world alone
Detach   detach   we leave the world bone lonely

If we can't believe in God   we must believe in love
We must believe in love   we must believe in love
And they zip you up   in your white body bag
White body bag   white   white   body   bag

POETICS STATEMENT

Brown Girl Manifesto, One Amongst Many

I. *A performative utterance*: each utterance of the first-person "I" as the speaking subject combats the history of oppression which extends to me. Through the spoken word, the "I" critiques, questions, corrects, annotates, examines, mocks, derides, offends, and talks back at the prevailing culture.

When I perform my poetry, the "I" speaks not only as the "poet" but also through enacted "difference"—through a body inscribed by historical determinations: brown (dirty), immigrant (illegal alien), girl (unwanted, illegitimate). An "I" as the brown-girl body who faces her audience, stands there vulnerable to the perennial history of pre/mis-conceptions, racism, and hatred. (If we think the brown-girl figure is no longer viewed through historical determinations, then, we are in denial of our role in her existence in the global situation.)

II. *Who is this "I" that is not "I"?* (the sex that is not one) she who is not allowed to speak. Like the old world feminist that I am (who represents something larger than myself—why should I not have greater ambitions for an art that is political?). Should I not want to speak on behalf of the marked brown-girl:

> the veiled "subaltern" from the (un) "Holy Lands"? the girl who is burned for a better dowry? the 24-year-old undocumented worker whom you both need and despise who died in the desert south of Dateland, Arizona traveling across the border? the nameless girl amongst thousands toiling in the factories in Gwangdong? a nameless girl murdered near the maquiladoras in Juarez? The perennial girl orphan, starving, crying, pushed from refugee camp to refugee camp. The most annoying of all, she is also your immigrant neighbor, the one with the screaming baby on her hip; the one you despise most of all, because her very existence, her moving into the neighborhood, has brought down the value of the real estate.

III. *The speaking subject is always an oppositional voice*. If the majority says "no dogs allowed," the speaking subject says, "grrr," and wags her tail and bites the man in the ass and won't let go.

If the majority says, we don't want you, immigrant, we'll send you back. The speaking subject writes on the walls of Angel Island: *I shall stay firm, I shall endure; I shall not be erased.*

IV. *Artistic subjectivity*: The "I" authorizes first-person subjectivity and enables artistic expression, which differs from autobiography. A brown-girl subject is not necessarily for sociological or ethnographical inquiry.

My grandmother is in the kitchen making dumplings. Yum, you say, what are the ancient ingredients—better yet, what ancient rites are you conducting? Don't you perform ancient rites in the kitchen?—let me bring my notepad, and my camcorder—this is important research (I'll get tenure).

But wait a minute, this is poetry. My grandmother is in the kitchen making dumplings out of General Iwane Matsui's liver; we have entered the realm of magical realism.

Perhaps you better not stay in that kitchen. Get the hell outta there!

Why should Maxine's "cutting the frenum" be forever subjected to the litmus test of an "authentic" autobiographical (ethnographical) experience when even Gregor Samsa gets to speak?

Why is a cockroach a speaking subject (laconic, nonetheless, decrying "mother, mother")? The ethnographers never question whether or not he is a descendent of other cockroaches. But seriously, why should you get to imagine yourself as Luke Skywalker while I can't imagine myself as the Woman Warrior? Aren't Chinese girls allowed to have a surreal imagination?

V. *The speaking subject is also the lyric poet*: Am I making art or only producing material for your ethnographical interest? Am I not also spewing out sonnets, palindromes, epigrams, rondeaus, haiku, renku, ballades, jueju, fu, ghazals, prophetic hallucinations and all the sweet and wild brilliant variations of the above? Am I not the poet of witness? Do I not take after Nelly Sachs and Paul Celan trying to describe the horrors of the Holocaust, meanwhile inventing a new lyric, which questions the possibility/impossibility of poetry after the most heinous episodes of history? Am I not a descendent of Qu Yuan, whose lyric intensity caused him to drown himself in the Mi Lo River in protest? And the descendent of the courageous feminist poet Qiu Jin who recited a poem on the path to her own beheading?

VI. *A Call for Unity*: Brothers and sisters of the revolution: contemplate for a moment, are we really now in a "post-identity, post-racial, post-feminist" era—and all is groovy and colorblind—equal work equal pay, equal justice for all? Having elected the first black president of the U.S.A. are we therefore all emancipated and free? Do we all have a stake in the American dream? Do we all have a place at the table? (Or do we still have to cook for you, serve and wipe the floor after you too—and sit quietly in the dark kitchen while you delight in that lush banquet?)

Why am I still standing here trying to answer to you: hegemonic economy, mordant philosophers! poebiz mongers! treacherous cognoscenti!

cultural flesh-traders, fascist (es)states! trickster patriarchs! pallid lease-
holders, cleaver-wielding grandmothers! erstwhile dreamers, readers, over-
lords: yeah you, you are never fucking satisfied!

NOTE

From Marilyn Chin, *A Portrait of the Self as Nation: New and Selected Poems*
(New York: W.W. Norton, 2018), 177–79.

MARILYN CHIN'S *HARD LOVE PROVINCE*
An Erotics of Grief

Catherine Cucinella

The poems in Marilyn Chin's *Hard Love Province* (2014), which won the
2015 Anisfield-Wolf Award for poetry,[1] explore, among other things, love
and grief. Love is *hard* precisely because, as Chin illustrates, it continually
circulates within overlapping registers of longing, desire, grief, absence,
and presence. The collection includes several elegiac love poems as well
as several longer poems that feature elegiac stanzas or quatrains. In these
poems and quatrains, heavy with the absence of lost lovers and filled with
the physical markers of their presence as well as with the sexual longing of
the female speakers, Chin places eroticism in tension with grief. Her explo-
ration of grief's terrain necessarily takes her to the boundary between life
and death and to love's place at that boundary. At this limit and beyond
it, time becomes a crucial element in what I identify as an erotics of grief.

Time provides the thematic thread running through the three major
contours that shape this erotics of grief. First, while denying solace to the
mourner, Chin offers a sense of permanence, linking the separated lovers
through the sexual desires the female speaker possesses and expresses for
her lost lover. Second, an excessive sexuality drives the speaker's grief and
actions, resulting in a sort of mourning that honors a woman's self-love
and, at times, sexual dominance. Third, an endless and unceasing desire for
the dead lover characterizes the expression of grief.

In *The Double Flame: Love and Eroticism*, Octavio Paz identifies love
and eroticism as "the double flame," a metaphor that reveals the dangers
and pleasures of both, and further suggests their fleeting nature. "There is

no remedy for time," Paz writes, "[o]r, at least we do not know what it is. But we must trust in the flow of time, we must live."[2] He names time "the greatest catastrophe" which "no love can avoid." Ultimately, the beloved succumbs to time's assaults—"age, infirmity, and death."[3] Yet, he offers hope. Although we can neither deny nor destroy time, we can transfigure it, which according to Paz, "the great artists, poets, philosophers, scientists, and certain men of action have done," and which, I would argue, Marilyn Chin has done throughout her career.[4] Indeed, this transfiguration of time proves crucial as she explores the spatial and temporal significance of both grief and love within the landscape of loss. The poems in *Hard Love Province* attest to the relationship between love and time—they, too, deal with death and eternity, and like Paz, Chin sees love as "an answer." She, however, poses different questions than Paz does, asking, "How can we mourn the dead from a place of embodied grief?" Her poetry does not ask the expected ontological or epistemological questions. Instead, Chin questions how love, loss, sexual desire, death, and time transform within the framework of an erotics of grief. Paz offers love itself as an "answer" because he sees "love as time and made of it, a consciousness of death and an attempt to make of the instant an eternity."[5] If Paz is right, then the elegy, specifically one overwritten with eroticism and sexual longing, proves a particularly apt poetic form for Chin's undertaking. The elegy, as Angela Leighton reminds us, "plays with tropes of distance, difficulty, even of unreclaimable absence, but it does not simply forget."[6] Chin insists on remembrance throughout *Hard Love Province*. She dedicates eight of its twenty-three poems to poets who have died or to her dead lovers; of the twenty-two stanzas in "Two Inch Fables," one is for Denise Levertov, one for Gwendolyn Brooks, June Jordan, and Sylvia Plath, another for Emily Dickinson, and yet another pays tribute to Don Lonewolf, Chin's deceased lover. As I will show, the elegiac soundings that reverberate throughout the pages of this volume mourn endless and continuous death, wrapping the keening in an anguish for the lost physicality of eroticism. The sexual yearnings pulse with both a felt bodily presence and the body's "unreclaimable absence." Although I focus on the elegies in *Hard Love Province* —including "Formosan Elegy," "Alba: Moon Camilla Lover," "Beautiful Boyfriend," and "Quiet the Dog, Tether the Pony"—I will also briefly discuss poems from Chin's previous collections, as well as other poems from *Hard Love Province*.

Working within and against the elegy, as well as other poetic forms, Chin's poetic longing, stark grief, and unabashed eroticism investigate female sexuality and desire.[7] Chin's elegiac voice mourns the violence women suffer through systemic gender bias, at the hands of damaged lovers, and in the name of nations. This voice also sounds outrage as it mourns the loss of "brown bodies," of lives shattered by wars, regimes, and pogroms.

Committed to recognizing the women and girls rendered silent by hegemonic systems (American and Chinese), Chin's erotics of grief allows women to mourn through their bodies, sexualities, and desires.

As she maps an eroticism of mourning throughout this province, Chin looks back to foremothers or invisible, nameless women. This looking back involves a play with what Andy Amato calls "poetic time" as these women of the past merge into the now of the poem, and the poems' speakers desire, love, and grieve as one. In "A Daring Hospitality: Towards a Poetics of Time," Amato describes poetic time as "a subjective phenomenon experienced in our moment-to-moment acceptance of our mutuality with others, our recognition that we, in an elemental sense are already ever sharing a middle world—a liminally conjoined world—with others."[8] In order to explain this "significant time" (poetic time), Amato links "theorizing, creativity, and ethics."[9] He offers the possibility that we can think of time as "poetic and ethical." The ethics arises from a shared world in which "[w]e find and make boundaries to transgress, materials with which to construct, and meanings to motivate and inspire us."[10] Chin seems to embrace the mutuality that Amato locates in poetic time, creating a poetry that operates in a "liminally conjoined world," fused by multiple poetic and cultural voices. Reconfiguring our notions of time, Chin conflates absence and presence, often merging absent lovers with present ones, allowing sexual longing to cross limits of space and time, and collapsing generational and historical timeframes. Within Amato's framework of poetic/ethical time, then, Chin finds and makes "boundaries to transgress." In addition, as I will show, the poetic time that she offers us in *Hard Love Province* filters through an erotics of grief which demands we reconsider notions of love and time, and, ultimately, *what it means to be in time.*

In representing mourning grounded in eroticism, Chin engages in what Elizabeth Grosz calls "writing *otherwise*," an endeavor that hinges on thinking in the "*future anterior*," or what will have been. Such thinking reconfigures our present moment while simultaneously changing our understanding of the past as "fixed, inert, given, unalterable and rock-solid."[11] Chin's elegies acknowledge that the past, including past love and sexual desire, "must be regarded as being inherently open to future rewritings, as never 'full' enough, or present enough, to retain itself as a full presence that propels itself intact into the future."[12] In most of Chin's elegies, *nothing* is full enough, and much depends on recognizing the paradox of an absent presence, of the spaces between words, the silences necessary to grieve. Instead of attempting to reinscribe an event, "producing it anew," Chin offers the elegy "as an opening up to a life that is not exhausted in its pastness."[13] The event that Chin presents in her elegies, generally, is not death itself; rather, she offers elegiac soundings of love interrupted and desire unfinished. Interruption and incompleteness open spaces in which the poet can share time—present and future—with the dead. In this book of elegies, she "[weaves] in and out of the quatrain, in and out of sorrow."[14] Consequently, the "pastness" of the beloved, and the speakers' sexual longing and love, manifest as extremely present but also empty *and* full, as the speakers' mourn "a life that is not exhausted in its pastness." Desire and love do not abate with death: "If we can't believe in god we must believe in love / We must believe in love we must believe in love."[15]

In Chin's poetry, love often depends on both absent and present lovers, proving extremely complex when linked to the erotics of grief and the aesthetics of the body that Chin utilizes throughout the poems in *Hard Love Province*. As Abigail Licad rightly notes, Chin "celebrates love in its multitude of forms and objects: for another, for oneself, for art, for language, for sex and sexuality"[16] and, I would add, for the dead. Further, according to Steven Yao, Chin's poetic eroticism "appears . . . in her tendency to approach her various concerns through the metaphorical armature and rhetorical scenarios of sexuality."[17] Looking at the first line in the following stanza from "Cougar Sinonymous," Licad identifies a conflation of "sexual and literary virility"[18] that exemplifies the eroticism so prevalent throughout Chin's work:

> Hell no   Dude-bro!   You think you own this poetry
> I see your lips trembling   counting syllables
> Cry epiphany   long before   the penultimate turn
> A dry cough   and a verse   smears the ceiling[19]

Clearly, Chin places the woman in control of poetic and sexual expression. The "dude" reaches "epiphany" prematurely ("long before the penultimate turn"). Paradoxically, his "dry cough" produces a viscous verse that "*smears* the ceiling." This dude fails to satisfy—sexually or poetically. He has come too soon, staining the ceiling with his "premature" poetry. The speaker goes on to call him "pretty boy supine and lazy." She tells him, "Die a third time we'll pen you an elegy."[20] Clearly evoking the metaphor of orgasmic death, Chin insists that this "pretty boy" has died twice but must die again to warrant a formal elegy. If the first two deaths were orgasmic, what then is that third death? Literal death? In these stanzas Chin plays with the trope of orgasm as "little death." However, she complicates this notion by lacing the eroticism with female dominance, challenging males' rights in the domains of poetry and sexual exchange.

An erotics of grief often overwrites, sometimes subtly and, at other times, blatantly, the sexual desire and freedom, as well as the politics of sex, that mark Chin's earlier poetry. In *Thinking Its Presence: Form, Race and Subjectivity in Contemporary Asian American Poetry*, Dorothy Wang examines Chin's poetic irony, identifying it as both a "means and strategy." For Wang, irony works to give Chin a voice within "the English tradition" and white America, and allows her to grapple "with questions of assimilation, miscegenation, [and] the psychic fallout from becoming 'American.'"[21] In her insightful reading of "Exile's Letter," a poem from Chin's first volume of poetry, *Dwarf Bamboo*, Wang tells us "[t]he Chinese American girl has begun to realize that her blossoming . . . sexuality can be 'profitable,' in terms of both sexual and economic payoff . . . [and can become] the material vehicle for border crossings and upward mobility."[22] Wang references the following lines from the poem:

> Life goes on, Mei Ling,
> Even I've bloomed lovelier, I think
> resembling you a little,
> but rounder where profitable.
> And behind that briared fence
> the boys are watching, even now,
> the white boys."[23]

Wang further suggests that this Chinese American girl "understands that her Asian female sexuality can be used as a means of entry into certain privileged domains of power usually barred to nonwhites."[24] This poem, whose full title is "Exile's Letter (Or: An Essay on Assimilation)," also contains images of death: a barren wife "dying of cancer," a "desiccated cactus," a "wasteland." Because the poem's speaker renders dying productive, Wang suggests that we should read these lines ironically: "'The dying are not unwise, / even the most desiccated cactus / issues a flower before death.' / Grandmother said this, gazing / at the vast cultivated wasteland."[25] However, these images of death—with a tone more elegiac than ironic—prepare us for what follows in the poem: a subtle eroticism in the image of the young girl ripening under the gaze of the white boys, mixing with the grief of barrenness and the implied loss associated with assimilation. In addition, the speaker mourns the exoticism of the Asian female as a kind of death, one that involves erasure of the female's desires. Erasure, however, does not translate into absolute absence because, in these political poems, the mourning and eroticism often continue to imply the presence of female sexual desire.

In both "Exile's Letter" and "The Barbarians Are Coming" (from *The Phoenix Gone, The Terrace Empty*, Chin's second volume of poetry), the speakers mourn the objectified female body and the violence enacted upon that body. In her analysis of "The Barbarians Are Coming," Wang argues that the women "are bodies/objects to be traded among different men [yet] they are also weighted with the heavy responsibility of shoring up national boundaries—their bodies expected to prevent the walls from being breached but also to be available to be penetrated at will."[26] Tellingly, the traded, nationally responsible, and penetrated female body in "The Barbarians Are Coming," begins with "young nubile women," moves to "only one woman," and then to the "I" of the poem:

> *The barbarians are coming:*
>   If you call me a horse, I must be a horse.
>   If you call me a bison I am equally guilty.[27]

This shift in perspective, in some sense, erases the female body from the poem. The repetition of the italicized phrase *"the barbarians are coming"* emits an elegiac tone. The repetitiveness also sounds a death knell for the women for whom the barbarians come, even as Chin, with her characteristic wit, follows one of these lines with "and how they love to come." The tone of mourning in this poem—for the degradation of women and their bodies—speaks to the fact that systems predicated on unchecked violence to women demand the female body be fully present in its erasure. Although I have argued elsewhere that Chin's poetic bodies are very often political ones—and, like Wang, see them as the sites where time, history, generations, and culture merge and/or intersect[28]—I also believe that these poetic bodies exceed their own physicality or absence when confronted with death and sexual longing within the register of an erotics of grief. Intriguingly, political or patriarchal erasure of bodies seldom occurs in the elegies in *Hard Love Province*; rather, it is death that destroys corporeal presence.

Despite this destruction, bodily absence and presence are tightly bound by the sexual longing of the mourner, or by the excessiveness of the eroticism, or by the overlapping of shared worlds that poetic time allows. In some sense, the body or bodies that circulate throughout the elegies in *Hard Love Province* function much like the body that Paz describes in "an erotic encounter," an encounter which "begins with the sight of the desired body."[29] In Chin's poetic eroticism of mourning, this encounter does not always begin with a literal sighting or involve physicality. However, the erotic encounters that she describes, regardless of how otherworldly, do emerge as fully embodied within registers of intense sexual longing. The body that Chin's elegies mourn is the one "that for an instant is every form in the world,"[30] thus possessed with an overabundance of presence. Paz insists that in an erotic encounter we see the desired body first as a presence and then as a myriad of parts: "Each of these fragments exist in and of itself yet refers to the totality of the body. A body which has suddenly become infinite."[31] Through this erotic encounter, we experience the body's immensity, and in the face of this immensity, "[w]e lose ourselves as persons and recover ourselves as sensations."[32] Chin's poetics of loss extends the possibility of the erotic encounter. The speakers of the elegies in *Hard Love Province*, as I will illustrate, recognize that mourning involves acknowledging themselves "as sensations," as if grieving through their bodies for an erotic encounter with a dead lover. Although Paz implies a loss of identity in a sexual/erotic encounter, he also reminds us that love does not deny the body nor the world. It "is bound to the earth by the body's gravitation, which is pleasure and death."[33] Aware of the earthly and earthy nature of love as it is grounded in the body, Chin's erotics of grief also cannot deny body or world, presenting both as receptacles of presence and absence.

The elegies in *Hard Love Province* that memorialize Chin's lovers represent presence and absence simultaneously, refusing to do the work of mourning as presented by Freud or by contemporary standards. There is no "working through." Certainly not the first poet to violate the "traditional elegiac model [which presents] the [mourning] process as a set of conventional tasks with preordained beginning, middle, and end," as described by Michael Moon,[34] or to refuse consolation, renewal, recovery, or transcendence, also associated with the traditional elegy, Chin does grieve the loss of the very things that traditional elegy *and* the Freudian model of mourning promise. Chin's elegies offer fleeting moments of resolution, of recompense, and of peace. They do not, however, offer lasting solace; like the "beautiful boyfriends," in the poem with the same name, the comfort is "transitory." Paz locates eroticism in "the realm of the imaginary, like celebration, representation, rites, and because it is ritual . . . [eroticism] intersects in places with violence and transgression."[35] Grieving, too, occupies this same realm, imaginary and ritualistic, and Chin's elegiac eroticism often manifests as violent and transgressive.

Although Chin, like most contemporary poets working with the elegy, rejects the Freudian paradigm of painfully confronting the loss, accepting it, and returning the ego to a "free and uninhibited" state,[36] she does, paradoxically, offer us an element of permanence—a permanent thread that connects living to dead. This permanence lies in the erotics of grief that permeates the most clearly marked elegies: those for Chin's dead lovers —in the speakers' sexual desires and in their refusal to relinquish sexual yearnings for these lovers. Chin herself has said that "[y]ou remember your beloved through sex as well . . . You can't have that physical presence."[37] In Chin's elegies, sexual longing connects living and dead lovers precisely because the living's yearning for the beloved's presence bespeaks an erotic aspect.

Many gay and lesbian scholars have, as Moon points out, "written evocatively on mourning and sexuality."[38] According to George Haggerty in "Love and Loss: An Elegy," this poetic form of mourning provides expressions of desire that "begin to defy the limits placed on male-male desire."[39] Sexual desire expressed in elegies also reconfigures cultural messages about lesbian/gay bodies, sexualities, and relationships, as Moon argues in "Memorial Rags."[40] Much is at stake for these scholars in their arguments, and

I do not wish to co-opt the eroticism that they identify in the elegy and overwrite it with notions of heteronormativity. However, I also believe that much is at stake for Chin as she traverses the geography of loss in *Hard Love Province*. Her elegies make clear that she grieves from the margins and mourns the lives of those on the margins: brown boys sold into slavery, female ancestors brutalized by their Chinese husbands, women poets scarred by their feminist and poetic battles, women killed in order to allow younger women to speak truth to power. Her elegiac eroticism is fierce, excessive and, at times, terrifying, even when it is most quiet. It often defies both cultural and patriarchal dictates regarding "acceptable" femininity, female desire, and perhaps, poetic decorum.

Indeed, excessive female sexuality and desire frequently underpin the erotic mourning that defines the geography of *Hard Love Province*. Chin will not deny her female sexuality—those deep cravings for the physicality of her dead lover. The speakers in her poems are most often women, and, in many cases, the speaker proclaims love for her own body. This self-love often emerges in longer poems that contain elegiac stanzas, constructing an excessive erotics of grief that recognizes a woman's sexual self. The speakers long not only for the touch of their lovers but also for passionate sexual encounters. Chin does not often evoke euphemisms in either her love poems or her elegies. Rather, words such as "vulva," "cock," "ovum," "semen," "breasts," "crotch," and "scrotum" appear in these poems. These words locate both desire and grief at the body's most vulnerable and "naked" level—fully exposed. Yet Chin also gives us the following images: a male lover "cradling // His own soft sacks," "His loveroot dangling before a crimson sack," and a female speaker proclaiming, "My yoni still tight my puma is on fire." These poems may softly murmur love for the beloved, or they may send up a howl for a loss of physical love. The speaker may not want to "face the wall" like the speaker's grandmother or be eaten and "bent backwards" like the speaker's sister in "Cougar Sinonymous."[41] Instead, she may want to "fuck until the dogs pass" or, as in "Two Inch Fables, "love [her] beautiful vulva."[42]

In "Formosan Elegy"—dedicated to a lover killed in a plane crash— Chin uses the caesura to foreground the bleakness of the fundamental yin and yang of the poem: unbearable presence and unreclaimable absence. These gaps, while providing unity to the poem, underscore the existential nothingness that the images of a fragmented body raise. As this poem is devoid of all other punctuation, these caesurae actualize the grieving process. The visual gaps on the page—the spaces in the poetic line—stop our progress; they suspend thought—meanings freeze: nascent, half-formed, fleeting, and elusive. Like the grief-stricken, we falter when confronted with the everyday objects of absence, the over-determined presence of the loved body forever gone:

Knock at emptiness   a house without your love
Strike the pine box   no answer   all hollow
You planted plums near the gate   but they bear no fruit
. . . .
The robe you washed   hangs like a carcass flayed
The mug you loved   is stained with old coffee
Your toothbrush is silent   grease mums your comb[43]

Chin undercuts the solidity of the house with the words "emptiness" and "without." The sturdiness of the pine box crumbles in the "hollow" silence as the speaker mourns the loss of the physicality of love. Because the speaker's lover cannot physically inhabit the house, all that remains are poignant reminders of both his presence and absence—the barren plum tree, the silent objects bearing witness to daily rituals: robe, mug, toothbrush, and comb. Simultaneously, these objects manifest as terrifying reminders of human decay: "a carcass flayed," the stains and grease that signify indelible marks of use and of filth.

These metonymic markers of a lived life lead the speaker to proclaim: "Something's lost something's made strong," at the end of one stanza.[44] Whereas the loss seems obvious, what is made strong seems less so. The following stanza, the fifth of ten, opens with a glimpse of a hopeful future, and perhaps the "answer" to what death has strengthened: "Around the corner   a new prince yearns to be loved."[45] Midway through this poem, the speaker seems to have found solace, and, having done the work of mourning, found a new love object. However, the image of a passive body —this "new prince"—waiting to be loved quickly evaporates, morphing into poetry itself: "A random image   crafts itself into a poem."[46]

These lines indicate the lessening of the speaker's inability to "speak" poetry—to sing her grief. Earlier in the poem, confronting a space empty of love, filled with markers of absence and reminders of presence, the speaker cried a soundless cry, but her "tears dried in [her] gullet." Unable to audibly mourn, she retreats from song and, by implication, from poetry, turning instead to mundane rituals—walking the dog, bathing the budgies, cutting melons. Only by focusing on the objects strewn throughout the house, reading them like scattered pieces of her lover's body, can she perform the mourning and poetic rituals that constitute an aesthetics of the body and an erotics of grief, both of which begin the return to poetry.

Sitting near her lover's body bag, the poet/speaker regains her voice. She "sing[s him] a last song" and "chant[s his] final sutra."[47] Thus, in "Formosan Elegy," grief, corporeal presence and absence, and eroticism become tightly bound, felt in the body. Haggerty suggests that "[t]he dying form of one so loved does not resist . . . eroticization . . . rather, death itself becomes a scene of unspeakable intimacy."[48] Referring here specifically to the body of a lover dying from AIDS, Haggerty nonetheless presents a framework through which to consider the moment in "Formosan Elegy" when the poet/speaker can utter her song of grief. She does so once she is near her lover's body, the physical closeness suggesting the erotic attachment that Haggerty describes. For Chin, it allows her simultaneously to reconnect with her lover, to share the intimacy of his death, and to ask and answer the age-old questions: "What's our place on earth?" "What's our destiny?" Her answers resound with paradox: "nada" // war   grief   maggots   nada."[49] How can one's place and destiny be nothingness? Perhaps both depend upon eroticism which, according to Paz, "evaporates, and evaporates, and all that remains in our hands . . . is a shadow, a gesture of pleasure or of death."[50]

In Chin's poetic rendering, the vapors of eroticism mingle with the bodies torn asunder by death—thrust into the nothingness that is death in this poem. By stanza eight, both body and poetic line fragment. Spaces appear between every word, causing us to linger over each separate image, most related to the body—and each severed from it:

Arms   cheeks   cock   femur   eyelids   nada
Cowl   ox   lamb   vellum   marrow   nada
Vulva   nada   semen   nada   ovum   nada
Eternity   nada   heaven   nada   void   nada[51]

No longer the body of the speaker's lover, the body in this stanza is both male and female, animal and human. The loss is personal and social, confined and all-encompassing, everything and nothing. In the following stanza, the speaker exhorts, "We must believe in love," yet this exhortation lacks conviction—it seems stark and empty when followed by the closing image of the "white   body bag   white   white   white   body bag."[52]

Although her elegies may not literally reclaim the lover's body, Chin hopes that the poems dedicated to Don Lonewolf, a lover who died in 2011, "will help his memory linger a little longer on earth."[53] The elegies dedicated to Lonewolf also memorialize Chin's grief and sexual longing for him. Whereas the love mourned in "Formosan Elegy" seems specific, the loss in "Beautiful Boyfriend," one of several poems dedicated to Lonewolf, takes on a more generalized form of mourning, grieving for all the lost beautiful boyfriends, even as the poem more overtly proclaims the speaker's sexual desires for her dead lover.[54] "Beautiful Boyfriend" opens with images of the speaker drifting in a skiff "made of spicewood," surrounded by sounds of "early Mozart," Coltrane, "and miles and miles of Miles, with [her] new boyfriend." It draws on water metaphors—floating, submersion, sinking—as the poem moves, at times swiftly and at times slowly, through geographies of space and time. In these spaces, Chin articulates a longing for forgetfulness as she simultaneously insists on remembrance, collapsing space/time/death/life/absence/presence.

In a 2012 interview for *Poetry Magazine*, Chin speaks at length about the opening quatrain of "Beautiful Boyfriend," admitting that it sounds "a universal message—it's about surrendering to love—a sunny afternoon adrift with music, wine, and love."[55] She goes on to speak about the "splendid[ness] [of] our short life on earth [and the] blissful[ness] [of] our human moment."[56] In this opening quatrain awash in sensuousness, "the skiff erotically signifies the woman's body."[57] But the splendidness, blissfulness, and sumptuousness, do not sustain. The woman's body can only send her lover off on his final journey, and the skiff becomes a funeral barge. Sorrow and sexual desire merge as the speaker beseeches, "Bullet don't shoot him   he's my draft-horse / Night scope don't pierce him   he's my love-stalk."[58]

Although the speaker attempts to identify the conditions that will allow her to love the seemingly ambiguous "you" that appears in the fourth quatrain "like no other" and "to float [her] mind toward the other side of hate," she appears unsuccessful. Either she cannot meet these conditions, or they prove inadequate to mastering "the nine doors of [her] body" and "clos[ing] [her] heart to the cries of suffering."[59] If the closing of the doors refers to dying, then clearly the speaker remains among the living; if it refers to gaining the highest state of consciousness, then the speaker suggests she cannot forsake her bodily desires. These desires emerge even as the poem seems to move from the personal to the social—from private to public mourning. In the following quatrain, the elegiac voice grieves not for one lost love but for many, and the mourning spans place and time:

> The shantytowns of Tijuana   sing for you
> The slums of Little Sudan   hold evening prayer
> One dead boy is a tragedy
>   Ten thousand is a statistic
> So let's fuck   my love until   the dogs pass[60]

This quatrain upends us by the ambiguity of the "you" once again, because that "you" can simultaneously be the speaker's dead lover, the "one dead boy," and Don Lonewolf. Whom does the speaker mourn? Whom does she wish to fuck? The ambiguous "you" invites interpretation: the poet/speaker mourns her dead lover and seeks forgetfulness in her new one, or she mourns her dead lover and voices her sexual desire for him. In this elegy, sexual longing and overwhelming desire for physical contact with a dead lover define the contours of mourning within the framework of an erotics of grief. Throughout *Hard Love Province*, Chin's speakers do not search for spiritual or transcendent intimacy with the lost lover. Instead, intimacy occurs when bodies touch. Chin makes very clear that death ends erotic encounters, and she mourns their loss. In seeking solace for his own loss, Haggerty hoped that the elegy might offer a way for him to "reach out to [his] lost lover," and he questions the efficacy of the form if his "loss is primarily physical."[61] Haggerty asks, "What if the terms of the communion I seek can be realized only by touch, rather than by a thought?"[62] "Beautiful Boyfriend" raises a variation of this question: What if the communion Chin seeks can be realized only by touch, rather than by poetic expression? In that case, perhaps these love poems—these elegies that express outrage, loss, pain, and desire through an erotics of grief—can serve only as consolation.

The eroticism, sexual longing, and anger in "Beautiful Boyfriend" abate in the ninth and tenth quatrains. Chin returns us to the water, and the grief is quiet. In the ninth quatrain, we are on the Irrawaddy, the River of Spirits, in Myanmar. Here the "you" of the poem—clearly the speaker's dead lover—floats away among the spirits. And yet, in Chin's rendering, we are also once again in the "nada," a space devoid of "sun," "moon," "coming," "going," "causality," "personality," "hunger," "thirst." The following quatrain contains markers of the beloved's journey as he floats on a giant stupa, past Hindu and Buddhist monasteries (Angkor Wat and Jokhang Lhasa), waiting for the Christian God. These two quatrains follow and precede ones depicting violence—images of both war and "calamity," events resulting in overwhelming numbers of death: a "Humvee," "a war-horse of hate," "ten thousand corpses," "Malarial deltas typhoidal cays." In the face of destruction by war, by nature, by God, the speaker's tone becomes cynical:

> Tsunamis don't judge   calamity grieves no one
> The poor will be submerged   the rich won't be saved
> Purge the innocent   sink the depraved[63]

Like the ten thousand dead brown boys who become a statistic or the ten thousand corpses in the eighth quatrain, the number of dead in this stanza seems too many to mourn.

Unable to mourn the many and needing to mourn the one, the speaker returns to her lover's body: "You push down my hand   with your bony hand // The fox-hair brush   lifts and bends."[64] The "you" remains ambiguous. Is this coupling that of the speaker and her new boyfriend, or a remembered encounter between her and her dead lover? Perhaps one between her and her lost lover in a shared world? Although the lover in "Beautiful Boyfriend" sighs, *There's no revision in this life / One bad stroke   and all is gone*," and although the speaker "smell[s] the perfume of transience," and longs to "mask stale pogroms with a sweet whiff of oblivion," the poem ends, once again, in a place of irresolution: "Surrender   you must   to one love   one nation."[65] Who is this "you"? The dead lover? All lovers? Must we all surrender, and what is the result of surrender? The end of grief, of desire, or of life? The poems for Don Lonewolf pulse with sexual yearnings as Chin explores these questions in the face of a numbing and paralyzing grief that simultaneously blunts and initiates the speaker's sexual desires.

Throughout "Beautiful Boyfriend," Chin also repositions us within time, a repositioning that often depends upon physical geographies, landscapes, disasters, or erotic encounters. In this poem and others, Chin's erotics of grief makes time overwhelmingly apparent and frustratingly elusive. As Elizabeth Grosz suggests in *In the Nick of Time*, intense moments of eroticism can allow for the direct observation of time; Chin's elegiac eroticism offers the "ruptures, nicks, cuts . . . [and] instances of dislocation" through which we can consider time, as time itself "contains no moments or ruptures and has no being or presences, function[ing] only as continuous becoming."[66] Eroticism in Chin's poetry, when linked to grieving, is also a continuous becoming. In these poems, a mourning that is overwritten with sexual desire for the dead both "stops" time—making us keenly aware of it—and collapses past, present, and future—disorienting us in time. In "Cougar Sinonymous," the speaker describes a twilight world where living and dead lovers meet:

> A flower   and yet not a flower
> A dream   and yet not a dream
> At midnight   he comes to my bed
> At daylight   he returns to the dead[67]

Here, elegiac eroticism makes living bearable, yet it also manifests as excessive. Past desires are continuously written onto present and future ones. Desire becomes endless, perhaps unbearable, ending in a place of oblivion, of nothingness—that gesture of pleasure or death that Paz says *is* eroticism.

In "Alba: Moon   Camellia   Lover," Chin uses the poetic form of the alba, or morning song, which expresses the longing of illicit lovers forced to part by the coming of day. Traditionally, a watchman or guard warns the lovers of the approaching sunrise, signaling that they must return both to their homes and to their "legitimate" lovers. By dedicating this poem to Lonewolf and including "Moon" in the title, Chin forewarns that this alba promises to circumvent tradition. Rather than a song of sunrise, this alba is one of night. Chin presents multiple layers of desire and writes a multi-layered love poem, locating the lust not only in the present moment with the new love but also in the past with the parted lovers. Ironically, the body most visible in "Alba: Moon   Camellia   Lover," is the male body rather than the female one. The speaker is not a male troubadour singing of his reluctance to part from his lover, but a woman yearning for an erotic encounter with a lost lover. The sexuality in this poem hinges on a refusal to deny the body's desires, intertwining grief and female power:

Last night through the camellia boles
I gazed, transfixed, at the moon—
Pale-faced, hook-nosed.
I know that she is my mother
Staring back from death, a dark matter.
For hours, we were one
With the earth's static blindness.
She did not envy the living
And I did not mourn the dead.[68]

The speaker seemingly finds comfort in "mother moon," communing with her in the night and with the sleeping lover lying next to her. The desire circulating in this poem is quiet; the female speaker lingers with the departed lover yet denies the grief that the dedication might suggest. She does appear, however, to admit to a temporary respite from grief as she and the moon are "one / with the earth's static blindness."[69] In the night hours, when time seems either endless or nonexistent, the speaker can occupy that liminally conjoined world that constitutes poetic time. In this space, she can linger with sexual yearnings for the body of her dead lover; she can sleep next to her lost love, and she can both mourn and not mourn him.

In "Alba: Moon　Camellia　Lover," the speaker tells us that she "did not mourn the dead," at least not at that moment with the moon shining on

The camellia tree and [her] lover
He, asleep on his side, cradling
His own soft sacks.[70]

In the tradition of the alba, lovers must part as night gives way to day. Chin transforms this alba into an elegy, however, complicated by a grief overlaid with sexual desire for the dead lover. Further breaking with this poetic tradition, the speaker does not dread the coming of light; instead, the speaker "witness[es] the ecstasy of the changing hour." The stanza continues with blatant sexual imagery as the sleeping lover becomes the speaker's "new love":

As the sun devours the moon's corona
And the camellia unfurls
In brilliant pinks and reds, and my new love,
With a sweet smile on his sour lips
Struggles toward the bathroom.
His flanks are glistening pearls.[71]

Traditionally, the parting lovers would be "illicit" ones, forced by dawn to part. In this poem, the parting lovers are old and familiar ones; they precede the speaker's new love. The sexual imagery of the open flower and the "glistening" male body hurl us to the speaker's present moment—and perhaps present sexual desire—mapped onto or obscuring her desire for the dead lover.

As previously mentioned, the alba often involves a third character —a watchman or someone else who helps the lovers. Although the trio in the title's "Moon   Camellia   Lover," suggests a third, identifying this character proves difficult. It could be the moon, or grief, or sexual desire. The difficulty arises because Chin, while insisting on the centrality of the body, maps sexual desire onto grief—which involves both the absent *and* the present male body. Even identifying the lovers in this poem is not as straightforward as a first reading might suggest. The female speaker might constitute one of a pair or, perhaps, the constant in two pairs. But Chin subtly suggests that the sleeping lover in the first stanza may not be the "new love" in the third stanza. Which "lover's swooning moans" does the speaker hear?

"Alba: Moon   Camellia   Lover" begins with the speaker temporarily relieved of her mourning—peaceful with a sleeping lover. Then her quiet communion with the moon breaks the certainty "of another tomorrow." The contemplative quality of the poem shifts as the speaker's awareness of the physical presence of her "new" lover increases. In the last stanza, the speaker pleads ("O my mother") that her quiet grief abate as the sunlight erases the moon's "final torso" and that "suffering / fade into the traffic's clean hum."[72] The eroticism in this poem relies on a grieving woman conjuring up the felt presence of her dead lover while in the physical presence of her new lover. The mourning process occurs in a shared bed, with the speaker in a seemingly altered state—in a distorted space where time collapses. Past, present, and future merge—and time stops—until the reminder of tomorrow's certainty puts time in motion once again. Chin offers an eroticism of grief that depends on midnight returns and daylight leave-takings, on the stillness and quietness of a moonlit night.

The achingly beautiful, "Quiet the Dog, Tether the Pony"—whose title comes from lines in Yeats's poem on silence, "Long-Legged Fly"—closes *Hard Love Province*. "Long-Legged Fly" freezes historical moments as Yeats insists on the importance of stillness of mind for leadership, beauty, and art. "Quiet the Dog, Tether the Pony" freezes human life, the moments of being. The silence in Chin's poem is the silence of death, the stillness brought about when desire transforms into an erotics of grief. "Quiet the Dog" circulates within the realm of unceasing desire as Chin maps endless sorrow and sexual longing onto a place of continual nothingness, a lover's search for the beloved, and a liminally conjoined world.

The first line directs our "gaze beyond the vermilion door"—a reference to a 1965 Chinese film about a complicated love triangle. From the opening line, the speaker tells us to see what we cannot—to recognize desire denied and unfulfilled, to look upon the tragedy of separated lovers, and to listen for the sound of grief in the reduplications and silences between words. As the stanza progresses, we must look far in time and space at the "road's interminable end," an oxymoronic task as *interminable* means endless, everlasting, ceaseless. Thus, the speaker asks the impossible. Our eyes prove inadequate to see that which never ends; our mind is incapable of comprehending the endlessness of eternity; our body and mind fail in the force of ceaseless grief. Yet we hear the weeping, the longing, "the inner self-condemnation, and the rages and wailing" in the silences between the words.[73]

Although relatively short (five stanzas of three lines), the poem itself seems like a dirge, heartbreakingly slow. Once again, Chin uses the white spaces between words and phrases to weight the lines with grief, with the mourner's paralysis in the physical world:

> Gaze   gaze   beyond the vermilion door
> Leaf   leaf   tremble   fall
> Stare blankly   at the road's interminable end[74]

Interminability and the speaker's unending desire for the beloved propel this poem. Desire and grief root deep in the body: "Tears   are   exhausted   now   shed   blood."[75] Addressing her use of spaces and silences, Chin says, "The silence, the breath, is where we hold both grief and forgiveness."[76] This poetry demands that we read it with our bodies. We, too, pause in the gaps, hold our breath as we endeavor to reach the end of Chin's poetic line. Chin, however, grants us little relief, because "the feeling that is 'grief grief,' that is 'deep deep' . . . is inexhaustible."[77] Because the speaker's body refuses or can no longer produce the external signs of mourning (tears), she turns to what she can shed—to what remains— the body's essence, blood. While this desire for death remains clear, the speaker's actions are not.

The next stanza opens with reduplications, doublings of adjectives or verbs, a practice common in Mandarin Chinese that occurs throughout "Quiet the Dog, Tether the Pony." There is a sense of slipping from consciousness: "Deep   deep   the baleful courtyards."[78] These reduplications, which generally add emphasis (with adjectives) or make the meaning softer (with verbs), do both in this poem, while simultaneously sending a deafeningly silent cry of grief. The harshness of the imperatives to "gaze beyond the vermilion door" or to "walk through waning meadows" softens in the reduplications of the verbs. The repeated adjectives ("cold," "long," "broad," "deep," "steep") and nouns ("leaf," "folds") emphasize the extremes of the speaker's journey to find her lover and to assuage her pain. We "hear" the grief in the "physical spaces between words . . . the water flowing between stones, . . . silent lute strings."[79] These reduplications, along with Chin's use of "physical spaces between words," combine with the images in the poem to suggest an ontological loss—a diminishment of self in the loss of love and in the emptiness of desire denied and unfulfilled: "Stare blankly," "cold cold mountains," "baleful courtyards," "waning meadows," "missing pronouns," and "are nothing." Regardless of the speaker's exhaustion, she continues her journey through an inhospitable physical landscape toward a province of either unceasing desire or forgetfulness.

Despite its slow dirge-like tone, the poem is full of movement; the speaker is restless in her exhaustion, looking past her present time, her immediate place. She searches for the world in which her lover exists; the one liminally conjoined with hers. She leads us up "cold cold mountains," down "long long valleys," across "broad broad waters." "Twilights become endless," as she climbs to the monastery of "ten thousand Buddhas," knuckles blue from gripping the railing. With the speaker, we too are restless, searching—for what? The lover? Solace? Death? Nada? Nothing suffices. The journey ends "in the land of missing pronouns." If these placeholders for persons, places, and things are missing, and we have no evidence that the things themselves populate "the land," Chin implies a double absence and places us once again in a void. However, in this void, "Sun is a continuous performance."[80] There is no night, no rest, no respite, no turning away from the glare. The glare, Chin suggests, is unremitting, "and we my love are nothing."[81] Unlike the you in "Beautiful Boyfriend," in "Quiet the Dog, Tether the Pony," this you is not ambiguous. This you is the speaker's lover. The you and I do not exist separately; rather, they are a continual being in nothing—in the fullness and emptiness of death. I suggest that nothing is both the moment of orgasm and death, a moment that has pulsed through these elegies in the sexual longing that delineates Chin's erotics of grief and that Paz implies in his ideas about the erotic evaporating into pleasure or death or, perhaps, nothingness.

The nothingness that haunts several of these elegies is a space of total embodiment *and* disembodiment, the instant when absence becomes a full presence, and the moment when we become fully aware of time *and* lost in timelessness. Both the living and the dead share the "nada" that manifests in many of the elegies in *Hard Love Province*. Through an eroticism of mourning, Chin tells us that love and death are tightly bound. In the elegies and elegiac stanzas in the longer poems, she offers both a poetics and an aesthetics of loss and desire that recognize women's sexual longings for their dead lovers. Chin presents desiring female bodies transgressing the boundary that separates living and dead. Her erotics of grief adds another dimension to her insistence that women speak—and speak their sexual and bodily desires. Thus, this eroticism extends Chin's body poetry beyond the limits of our physical world into a shared and "liminally conjoined one." In *Hard Love Province*, as in her other work, Chin challenges us to think beyond what we know, beyond our certainties, and beyond boundaries.

NOTES

Portions of this essay were presented at the 2015 Pacific Ancient and Modern Language Association Conference under the title "Love, Eroticism, Grief, and Time in Marilyn Chin's *Hard Love Province*." Following the conference, curators Brian Reed and Kornelia Freitag included my paper in the Stanford Arcade Colloquy, "Locating Contemporary Asian American Poetry," arcade.stanford.edu.

1. The Anisfield-Wolf Awards, presented by the Cleveland Foundation, focus on books that address racism and human diversity, thus enhancing our understanding of both. Chin was one of the first recipients of the award for *Hard Love Province*.

2. Octavio Paz, *The Double Flame: Love and Eroticism*, trans. Helen Lane (Orlando: Harvest Books, 1995), 263.

3. Ibid., 262.

4. Ibid., 264.

5. Ibid.

6. Angela Leighton, *On Form: Poetry, Aestheticism, and the Legacy of a Word* (Oxford: Oxford University Press), 127.

7. In a 2015 interview with Irene Hsiao, Chin explains her choice of the quatrain for *Hard Love Province*: "I wanted to write a book of elegies, and I was thinking of what form the elegy would take. The quatrain—the eastern quatrain, the *jue-ju*—is self-contained, but one could leave them open. I was studying the *jue-ju* from Li Bai and Tu Fu, but I was also looking at Emily Dickinson and Sylvia Plath, these women who wrote tight, vivid quatrains in the Western tradition. I wanted to meld the two worlds, and I thought the quatrain would work, so I tried to float them around in this book. One could read this book from beginning to end like one long poem, and one could also take a quatrain or two and contemplate it."

8. Andy Amato, "A Daring Hospitality: Towards a Poetics of Time," *KronoScope* 20.1–2 (2010): 61, 49–63; DOI: 10.1163/156852410X561844 (5 May 2015).

9. Ibid., 61.

10. Ibid., 58.

11. Elizabeth Grosz, "Histories of the Present and Future: *Feminism, Power, Bodies*," in *Thinking the Limits of the Body*, edited by Jeffrey Jerome Cohen and Gail Weiss (New York: State University of New York Press, 2003), 17.

12. Ibid.

13. Ibid.

14. Marilyn Chin, interview by Carleigh Takemoto, *Voices from the Master of Fine Arts Program in Creative Writing at Fresno State*, February 2015; fresnostatemfa.wordpress.com/2015/02/17/in-conversation-with-marilyn-chin/ (9 April 2017).

15. Chin, *Hard Love Province*, 20.

16. Abigail Licad, "Of Grievance and Grief: Marilyn Chin," *The Critical Flame*, 22 July 2014; criticalflame.org/of-grievance-and-grief-marilyn-chin/ (10 October 2015).

17. Steven Yao, *Foreign Accents: Chinese American Verse from Exclusion to Postethnicity* (Cambridge: Oxford University Press, 2010), 230.

18. Ibid.

19. Chin, *Hard Love Province*, 39.

20. Ibid., 40.

21. Dorothy J. Wang, *Thinking Its Presence: Form, Race and Subjectivity in Contemporary Asian American Poetry* (Stanford: Stanford University Press, 2014), 129.

22. Ibid., 136.

23. Marilyn Chin, *Dwarf Bamboo* (Greenfield Center: The Greenfield Review Press, 1987), 43.

24. Wang, 136.

25. Chin, *Dwarf Bamboo*, 43.

26. Wang, 143.

27. Marilyn Chin, *The Phoenix Gone, The Terrace Empty* (Minneapolis: Milkweed Editions, 1994), 19.

28. Catherine Cucinella, *Poetics of the Body: Edna St. Vincent Millay, Elizabeth Bishop, Marilyn Chin, and Marilyn Hacker* (New York: Palgrave, 2010).

29. Paz, *The Double Flame*, 253.

30. Ibid.

31. Ibid.

32. Ibid., 254.

33. Ibid., 257.

34. Michael Moon, "Memorial Rags," in *Professions of Desire: Lesbian and Gay Studies in Literature*, edited by George Haggerty and Bonnie Zimmerman (New York: MLA, 1995), 325.

35. Octavio Paz, *An Erotic Beyond: Sade*, trans. Eliot Weinberger (New York: Harcourt Brace, 1998), 69.

36. Sigmund Freud, "Mourning and Melancholia" in *The Standard Edition of the Complete Psychological Works of Sigmund Freud*, vol. XIV, trans. James Strachey (London: The Hogarth Press, 1916), 244–45.

37. Marilyn Chin, interview by Irene Hsiao, "Elegies, Allergies, and other Elusions: Marilyn Chin Talks Hard Love," *Los Angeles Review of Books*, 3 April 2015; lareviewofbooks.org/article/elegies-allergies-elusions-marilyn-chin-talks-hard-love/.

38. Moon, 235.

39. George Haggerty, "Love and Loss: An Elegy," *GLQ: A Journal of Lesbian and Gay Studies* 10.3 (2004): 388.

40. Moon, 236.

41. Chin, *Hard Love Province*, 37.

42. Ibid., 63.

43. Ibid., 19.

44. Ibid.

45. Ibid.

46. Ibid.

47. Ibid., 20.

48. Haggerty, 387.

49. Chin, *Hard Love Province*, 20.

50. Paz, *An Erotic Beyond*, 14.

51. Chin, *Hard Love Province*, 20.

52. Ibid.

53. Marilyn Chin, "Q&A," *Poetry Magazine* (December 2012); www.poetry foundation.org/poetrymagazine/articles/detail/69887 (25 March 2017).

54. Here is Chin's full response to being asked to talk about "Don to whom the poem is dedicated": "Don was my boyfriend, who died suddenly of an aneurysm during Thanksgiving week, 2011. He was the love of my life. He was only fifty-three. He closed his eyes, fell into a coma, and I didn't have a chance to say good-bye." Chin, "Q&A."

55. Ibid.

56. Ibid.

57. Ibid.

58. Chin, *Hard Love Province*, 73.

59. Ibid.

60. Ibid., 74.

61. Haggerty, 388.

62. Ibid.

63. Chin, *Hard Love Province*, 75.

64. Ibid.

65. Ibid., 76.

66. Elizabeth Grosz, *In the Nick of Time: Politics, Evolution, and the Untimely* (Durham: Duke University Press, 2004), 5.

67. Chin, *Hard Love Province*, 38.

68. Ibid., 17.

69. Ibid.

70. Ibid.

71. Ibid., 17–18.

72. Ibid., 19.

73. Chin interview by Hsiao.

74. Chin, *Hard Love Province*, 78.

75. Ibid.

76. Chin interview by Hsiao.

77. Ibid.

78. Chin, *Hard Love Province*, 78.

79. Chin interview by Takemoto.

80. Chin, *Hard Love Province*, 78.

81. Ibid.

BIBLIOGRAPHY

Works by Marilyn Chin

POETRY
Dwarf Bamboo. Greenfield Center: The Greenfield Review Press, 1987.
The Phoenix Gone, The Terrace Empty. Minneapolis: Milkweed Editions, 1994.
Rhapsody in Plain Yellow. New York: W.W. Norton, 2002.
Hard Love Province. New York: W.W. Norton, 2014.
A Portrait of the Self as Nation: New and Selected Poems. New York:
    W.W. Norton, 2018.

FICTION
Revenge of the Mooncake Vixen. New York: W.W. Norton, 2009.

TRANSLATION
The Selected Poems of Ai Qing. With Eugene Eoyang. Bloomington: Indiana
    University Press, 1982.

EDITED VOLUME
Dissident Song: A Contemporary Asian American Anthology. With David Wong
    Louie. Santa Cruz: Quarry West, 1991.

SELECTED INTERVIEWS
Hsiao, Irene. "Elegies, Allergies, and other Elusions: Marilyn Chin Talks Hard
    Love," *Los Angeles Review of Books*, 3 April 2012; lareviewofbooks.org
    /article/elegies-allergies-elusions-marilyn-chin-talks-hard-love/.
Parmar, Nissa. "'Double Happiness': An Interview with Marilyn Chin." *Contem-
    porary Women's Writing* 8.3 (November 2014): 241–51.
Takemoto, Carleigh. Voices from the Master of Fine Arts Program in Creative
    Writing at Fresno State, February 2015; fresnostatemfa.wordpress.com
    /2015/02/17/in-conversation-with-marilyn-chin/.
Weisner, Ken. "An Interview with Marilyn Chin." *MELUS* 37.3 (Fall 2012):
    189–214.
Worra, Bryan Thao. "Asian American Press Interview: Marilyn Chin." Voices
    from the Gaps, 2004; University of Minnesota Digital Conservancy, hdl.handle
    .net/11299/166379.

Selected Criticism

Cheung, King-Kok. "Slanted Allusions: Transnational Poetics and Politics of
    Marilyn Chin and Russel Leong." *Positions* 22.1 (Winter 2014): 237–62.
Cucinella, Catherine. "Writing the Body Palimpsest: Marilyn Chin." In *Poetics
    of the Body: Edna St. Vincent Millay, Elizabeth Bishop, Marilyn Chin, and
    Marilyn Hacker* (New York: Palgrave, 2010), 81–105.
Gery, John. "'Mocking My Own Ripeness': Authenticity, Heritage, and Self-
    Erasure in the Poetry of Marilyn Chin." *LIT* 12.1 (April 2001): 25–45.
Hsiao, Irene. "Broken Chord: Sounding Out the Ideogram in Marilyn Chin's
    Rhapsody in Plain Yellow." *MELUS* 37.3 (2012): 189–214.

McCormick, Adrienne. "'Being Without': Marilyn Chin's 'I' Poems as Feminist Acts of Theorizing." *Hitting Critical Mass* 6.2 (Spring 2000): 37–58.

Wang, Dorothy. "Irony's Barbarian Voices in the Poetry of Marilyn Chin." In *Thinking Its Presence: Form, Race, and Subjectivity in Contemporary Asian American Poetry* (Stanford: Stanford University Press, 2014), 115–61.

Wong, Sau-Ling Cynthia. "Staying Alive: Kingston's *Woman Warrior* Afterlife and Marilyn Chin's *Revenge of the Mooncake Vixen*." In *The Legacy of Maxine Hong Kingston: The Mulhouse Book*, ed. Sämi Ludwig and Nicoleta Alexoae-Zagni (Münster: LIT, 2014), 313–42.

Zhou, Xiaojing. "Marilyn Chin: She Walks into Exile Vowing No Return." In *Ethics and Poetics of Alterity in Asian American Poetry* (Iowa City: University of Iowa Press, 2006), 66–101.

FANNY HOWE

POEMS

FROM *The Lyrics*

From "Forty Days"

8.

When donkeys traveled
Without glancing to the side,
Long-lashed and buckled
Inside their own hide,
When they brayed for joy
Into the gray industrial clouds
And the cows replied
Like balloons deflating into moos,
The strain on the immaculate heart
Was as grave as it could get.
Awful pity.
To be so blessed
As to pound for happiness.

12.

Give me my shawl, my corkscrew
And my cloth bag.
Give me my hot water bottle and my book.
Give me my stick and my water.
One shoe for walking and one to dance.
No stability. Thirst.
The will to keep moving.
An instrument's heat.
Bald mountains and a spider that was a leaf.
The scheme is organic, it knows itself.
See that light across the enslaved sea?
Redemption time knows when.

13.

If I were Jesus, would you slap both sides of my face?
If I were Jesus, would you stamp on my hands?
If I was Jesus, would you lock me up?
Would you make me crawl down the prison hall?
Would you cover my head?
Stick my face in the pot? Would you rape me?
If I were Jesus, would you break down the door?
Would you wreck the house and terrify my family?
If I was Jesus, would you bomb my trees, my place
Of parables, the fig trees and the rivers of wheat?
If I were Jesus—

Well, I'm not. So please—go right ahead.

A Hymn

> When I fall into the abyss I go straight into it,
> head down and heels up and I'm even pleased
> I am falling in such a humiliating position,
> and for me I find it beautiful.
> And so in that very shame I suddenly begin a hymn.
>
> F. DOSTOEVSKY

I traveled to the page where scripture meets fiction.
The paper slept but the night in me woke up.

Black letters were now alive
and collectible in a material crawl.

I could not decipher their intentions anymore.
To what end did their shapes come forth?

To seduce or speak truth?

While birds swept over the water
like pot-bellied angels.

beautiful bells rang to assist the hoist.

Up they went to slake their thirst,
drinking from the mist

for the sound of bells seemed to free
as well as hold them.

Then down to scavenge the surf
and eat the innocent.

"I love God and the ferry too," wrote Kerouac.

Only that which exists can be spoken of.

•

I wonder, will our imagination
remain a temple burning with candles

against all odds?
Behind a nipple and a bone?

The simplest of glands laid in a circle
around skin and liquid

that stirs up imagery
winged and prismed, as if blood

were a wine inducing visions.

•

Some people cry when the characters die.

Then they kill themselves off-stage, away from the pages
that they are turning in the night.

Some people sacrifice themselves on a whim
and regret it later on paper.

Now I see you in the window.
Are you in the book I was looking for?

The one who traveled back to the happy days

when she could jump on a moving bus
and swing in the open air

clutching a worn novel in her purse . . . ?
A curtain, a knife, adoring eyes?

•

I watched the children running
and turned to Alyosha for a blessing.

He was sunk in the morass
of rural life

I like to sit with him in the grass.

Then we see the same thing at the same time,
and are one mind.

We two masses, one a book, one a hand.

When Alyosha spoke to the boys at the end
I anticipated their next question and his answer

For they formed a single gesture
of kindness.

"Will we?"   "We will."

•

It seemed evil to read about people
we would never meet.
We tested their fortitude as if in sleep.
They generally failed the challenge
being strangers in a strange brain.

They were baffled by the tools
handed to them and by the traffic's direction.
Frankly in a dream or story,
the goal is absolutely hidden
from the one to whom it matters.

•

Eons of lily-building
emerged in that one flower.
Eons, eons. Pins
and wool, thread and needle,
all material
made of itself and circumstance.

It was a terrible century:
consisting of blasted
oil refineries and stuck ducks,
fish with their lips sealed by plastic
and tar in the hair of cooks.
Filth had penetrated the vents.

Institutions moan from the bowels.
Balls of used cotton
from the hospital dumpster, redden.
Yawning on obsolescence
the computer wonders

who punched in such poor grammar.
First-padded virgins
graduate to this suffering drama
all by her-selves.
Who once were cells.

•

History is more than just another surmising
grandmother at a window

or a reminiscence twisted in the scrim of translation.

Some long-ago light is pulsating in a trout's heart
on a laboratory dish.

That light has entered all the holes,
no matter how small, because it is the light that wants to live.

•

Still waiting for you my sunshine
of justice and mercy.

If west is east of Moscow,
depending where you're going

then will you ever find me
coming from a northerly direction?

Are you even looking at the earth?
Remember the map is flat but everything else is not.

Is the newest child the oldest body in creation?

Does he carry more information than his mother?

Does her mother, his grandmother, do I seem redundant
by having arrived with less, though first?

Is that why I read at night with my lips compressed?

•

The fact is, I never knew if anyone felt me
the way Nijinsky knew how to feel.

Or Nastasya. Nothing could shock that woman
who had done so much wrong.

As if trained in a theater, multiple personalities
streamed from her tongue.

This made her an exemplar for our time.

She knew how others felt and became each one,
forgetting who she was before.

I remember her as a child.

Her skirt got tangled up
in a thorn bush when she watched the sky.

Shaking herself free,
she had to see the spiders, ants and dirt
around her skirt,

It was like peering into her own body
and she screamed in horror.

Later, consolation
would be extended by a man dark and handsome:

It came with his semen
(when she wanted hibernation.)

She didn't commit suicide this time, but ran
down Nevsky Prospect as it began to rain,

and paused to lift her umbrella.
For this moment

we were in our soul a child
rushing home to granny five floors up.

•

I dropped the book, wept and went to the movies.

It is here where I can forgive someone for his crime.

Poisoning babies for profit. Harry Lime.

I can actually forgive it when he is crawling in shit.

Otherwise we will stand on the ferris wheel together forever.
stuck in the fog and iron.

I just a witness to his ironic story

He will be a mix between Paul Celan and Oscar Levant
when we are at our happiest
and no forgiveness is asked.

Neurotic, pale, and drawn to the canals,
we will lean over the embankment like sister and brother

who are tempted to be actors.

It is here that his shoes and cat
will converge in the dark. Like fish in a secular city

flipping through sewers for a flash of Christ.

FROM *Second Childhood*

For the Book

Yellow goblins
and a god I can swallow.
Eyes in the evergreens
under ice.

Interior monologue
and some voice.

Weary fears, the
usual trials and

a place to surmise
blessedness.

The Garden

Black winter gardens
engraved at night
keep soft frost
on them to read the veins
of our inner illustrator's
hand internally light
with infant etching.
Children booked
on blizzard winds
and then the picture
is blown to yonder
and out of ink:
the black winter verses
are buds and sticks.

Parkside

Stone walls and chalk scratches
for different ages.
None of us could be sure now
how many we were or where.

There were hurtful pebbles,
cracked windows
and bikes. We cut the butter
and the day's bread evenly.

We were children and a metal bed.

Twelve loaves
and five thousand baskets.
Five baskets,
twelve pieces of dough.

Twelve times five and butter
for a multitude.
Bread made—that is—with
twelve thousand
inhalations of leaven.

Evening

Christmas is for children
on an English hill.

Simple, dismal,
and blissful,
a few little balls and crystal.

Dark by 4 p.m.
but you can ride your scooter
up the hill and down
in the arctic rain
each drop a dimple
on a—
and a silver handle
in a drain and a boy
can stand beside your hand
at the window
of a store full of cribs
and tinsel
before an icon
of the infant
with the news
rolled in his hand.

The Ninth Hour

At the ninth hour you want to be clear.
If you're sleeping don't wake up.

At the ninth hour it's always night
A few hours after four.

Why did the names of seasons
Depress you that year?

It was near the end but not quite there.
You had an hour to be happier

On either side of Massachusetts Bay.

But you were stricken at the word "summer."
I told you I couldn't turn around

Because I was going to Quincy
A place not a season the seasons are over.

You have no land to leave to your children.
Not even a square the size of paper.

That's why place-names are saddening.
Put them back in the drawer

And return to Back Bay Station
To the hour of your humiliation.

Only when it's over can you give the blessing.

POETICS STATEMENT

In the fiery year of 1968, I began reading Simone Weil, and after that I read Malcolm X, Frederick Douglass, W.E.B. Du Bois, Franz Fanon, the Boff brothers, Ivan Illich, Dorothy Day, and Gustavo Gutiérrez and other Catholic liberation theologians.

Any ideas I have held onto, began then.

I realized the whole person (gender and ethnicity included) *surpasses* the possibility of satisfaction. This is not quite Marxist but does eliminate identity issues and builds a politics out of necessities (for life) and the inclusion of the unknown with the need to know.

In the prose I read I would often find awareness of this overflow. Especially in Virginia Woolf, Joyce, Djuna Barnes, Zora Neale Hurston and others who wrote during the first half of the twentieth century.

My novels attempted to slip around the porousness of body, nature, mind, mind and more mind.

Virginia Woolf is always onto this: "Only the shadows of the trees, flourishing in the wind, made obeisance on the wall, and for a moment darkened the pool in which light reflected itself; or birds, flying, made a soft spot flutter slowly across the bedroom floor." She is inhabited by the world around her. It can be very refining and very distressing too.

My poetry was something else but not so far from prose, and now I can see it as a lot of looking around and many footsteps, taking notes and then examining them for a strangeness that was recognizable.

Because of certain childhood readings (Keats, Yeats) and a continuing adolescent longing for meaning, the world seemed to be hiding a secret that I must investigate, and expose. The person of my poems lives without many attributes, a bare figure outside of marriage. Imminent violence defines my life and poetry.

I was always strongly affected by the place I was in, and by the news, and went to the movies whenever possible.

Like most poets, I believed in the healing power of beauty and still do.

In his poem "The Acts of Youth," John Wieners of Boston writes some lines I understand:

> And with great fear I inhabit the middle of the night
> What wrecks of the mind await me, what drugs
> to dull the senses, what little I have left,
> what more can be taken away?
>
> The fear of travelling, of the future without hope
> or buoy. I must get away from this place and see
> that there is no fear without me: that it is within
> unless it be some sudden act or calamity
>
> to land me in the hospital, a total wreck, without
> memory again; or worse still, behind bars. If
> I could just get out of the country. Some place
> where one can eat the lotus in peace.

What I have learned then?
From learning Latin: the ethics
From learning French: the beautiful sound
From learning American: the song of conversation
From watching films: fleetingness & design
From the heroic woman poets of my time: perseverance

A PLACE APART

Sound, Silence, and Play in the Poetry of Fanny Howe

Meg Tyler

Whimsical, flickering, Fanny Howe's poems like to play, or playfully to ponder. In her syllables, phonemes, punctuation (or lack thereof), a sense of skirting around things and then suddenly alighting upon the thing itself marks her work, which is both serious and noncommittal. Her writing successfully resists categorization and canonization and it is in this liberated sphere where her life's great work has unfolded. I cannot help but think of Dickinson when I read Howe. Like Dickinson, Howe's playfulness sometimes incorporates irony and sometimes does not, especially when the language of spirituality appears. In what follows, I'll consider the ways in which Howe plays with sound and silence and, in turn, offers us adult forms of poetry, oblique but not confounding, mystical but not mystifying. My method is meditative and exegetical. Alongside readings of particular poems that have moved me, I try to bring into view the connections she has with readers and thinkers that matter to her. From early Celtic poetry to the ruminations of Simone Weil, Howe keeps wide-ranging company. She listens carefully, to both the sounds of other voices and the silences that bridge such sounds.

"By silence," Susan Sontag writes, "an artist frees himself from servile bondage to the world." Silence has always been vocal in poetry: the engulfing white spaces of the margins, the headers, the footers; the spaces between lines, words, letters, and even marks of punctuation. We think of Thomas Hardy's "The Voice," the last stanza of which seems increasingly consumed by the silence around it, the loss of the woman's living voice.[1] Poets carve words into the blankness, or the blankness arranges itself around our language, as snow settles onto the features of a landscape. Language supports or acts as a foil to the unsaid. As Howe says of her writing process: "You create a circle where you can focus your attention, the focus being the pad of paper, the pen. You have to stay fixed there until there is a reflected image rising up between your mind and the page."[2]

Such focus and silence turn our attention to neighboring sounds. Howe makes no declarations about what a poem should be or what it should or shouldn't do; she resists being hauled into the great machine of category. The poems themselves act out this resistance and are most effectively read in context with preceding and following poems, similar to the way in which a word gains meaning by the force of the surrounding words, the semantic context. Or the way in which an abstract painting might have a different or more noticeable expression when compared to others in a series. This is how her poems work. Daniel Kane perceptively writes that

> Howe builds on this notion of the poem as a field of various sonic and interpretative possibilities when she characterises her approach as a "kind of Cubist, or three-dimensional look at language. By stacking the independent clauses, and keeping them as free as possible from the chaining effect of the next lines, the words give an optical illusion of depth and clamour. The line stands alone, and in tandem, and in space."[3]

She is not alone in imagining the line as a figurative station of the cross. Elsewhere she writes that "a whole poem of mine is a sentence composed of sound-lines (bars), each line being the equivalent of a complex word. Each sound-line floats in tandem with the next one. Each one is a word. The group of 'sound-lines' or complex words forms a sort of sentence which is a poem."[4] What this looks like can be exemplified by her poem, "The Source."

> The source
> I thought was Arctic
>
> the good Platonic
>
> Up the pole
> was soaked film
>
> an electric elevation
> onto a fishy platform
>
> and waves on two sides greenly welcoming
>
> The sunwater poured on holy atheism
>
> It was light that powered out
>
> my ego or my heart
> before ending with a letter[5]

The poem ostensibly tries to determine the source of light, a metaphor for wisdom. As you can see, the lines aim at a series of associations: she thought the source was somewhere in the Arctic, then something Platonic, before it comes from an "electric elevation" and produces "waves that are "greenly welcoming." As for sound-lines, I read "sunlight pouring" in "sunwater poured on . . . light that powered out," which is her version of a complex word. "Poured" and "powered" chime. Sun wants to find another mate in "light." The "sentence" of the poem tells us that the source of light or insight is mysterious, not precisely unknowable.

Play of sound and play of light: from very early in Howe's work, the poems converse with objects and dazzle with sound. The 1988 volume *The Vineyard* delivers a characteristic instance of this, an enlargement of echo:

> One dreams of a land with vines
>
> In purple or shadows on hills
> Aren't pockets of mercy
> In a world mostly stone
> A constant elf—himself, herself—
> Elevates song
> To the day when birds will be angels
> Again all senses precious
> And light in the service of loneliness[6]

Using the collected nouns as guideposts for reading, this poem tells a somewhat-story of dreams, land, hills, shadows, stone, song, light, and loneliness, the connections between subjects teasing but not shallow. At the center of Howe's poem is an "elf," which appears inside "himself, herself," and then transmogrifies into "Elevates song." In "el" (a phoneme which echoes throughout—it has fifteen soundings) we might hear the Hebraic dimension, "of God." The poem's sense and sounds splinter in different directions, like thought, perhaps even like belief.

Note the lack of irony and the absence of punctuation in "Aren't pockets of mercy" (and I almost misread "mercy" for "misery"), which question finds no definitive answer (not that poems need to offer such things), but we know intuitively that "pockets of mercy" are not found with frequency in our world, in "a world mostly stone." We drift, bearing with us a sense of uncertainty and the harsh truth of things, edged by momentary beauty — "light in the service of loneliness." Fanny Howe's poems ask and answer questions and appeals through indirection. Her poems rely on image and metaphor, on metaphor's ability to draw us in and to insist upon associations and kinships and on an image's resonance, an image let be. Birds are perhaps the only "angels" we will ever know.

Howe's work celebrates the silence that amasses around an image. Silence, after all, is what we associate with heightened sensation, say, in a watchful child. A child's expressiveness often lies in gesture, in physicality, in performance of feeling and thought. Sun beams, rainstorms, and parents' tempers go to work on them without the interfering and mediating power of analysis. Every moment of every day, they are alive to all kinds of weather. Howe's work is deeply impressionistic, but she doesn't leave off there; tension exists between the thing that represents something else and our urge to use it to make meaning.

She thinks about what a poem at any given historical moment can or might or should offer: closure, maxim, solace, song, description, insight. She refuses these promises by going quiet. If ideals—and here I am thinking of something "conceived or regarded as perfect or supremely excellent in its kind" (*OED*)—keep us from facing the true, in what ways do her poems turn away from ideals, from the attempt to promise something? An iconoclast even amid the avant-garde branch of American poets, Fanny Howe has freed a poem from the limitations and expectations of discrete beginnings and endings, from romantic rhetoric, sometimes even from signs of human warmth.[7] For Howe, poetry is a habit of mind. Seeking her measure in poems that do not feel complete, that feel left off, casually accidental and incomplete, she is still as interested in the architecture of a poem as any other good poet. She needn't structure poems like her American or Irish forbearers (Lowell, Dickinson, Yeats) but her work is a way of distantly conversing with recognizable historical forms without echoing them. Silence is part of her statement. As the poet Maureen McLane, in "Song and Silence: My Fanny Howe," writes:

You find in Howe both an inward and an outward eye. Lyric may require solitude, but most often you find in Howe's poems not the bliss but the agony of solitude. Before her solitudes, behind them, lies a sundering, an impasse. . . . You find in these intimate lines an astonishing impersonality. Not the impersonality T. S. Eliot advised the poet to cultivate, but the impersonality of Zen.[8]

· · ·

The poems feel impersonal even when inhabited by a first person singular pronoun. In the spare couplets of a single lyric, "For the Book," from *Second Childhood* (2014), we surely find ourselves on both certain and unsure footing:

> Yellow goblins
> and a god I can swallow:
>
> Eyes in the evergreens
> under ice.
>
> Interior monologue
> and some voice.
>
> Weary fears, the
> usual trials and
>
> a place to surmise
> blessedness.[9]

Unlike Dickinson, there are no ellipses to suggest the unspoken, or the broken. The white spaces are instead "a place to surmise / blessedness" (in this case) or something else. Yellow goblins are flowers and yet when we read the expression glancingly, we take away something of our childhood associations with goblins, yellow eyes, nighttime colors. What role does narrative play here? The string of images creates a story of a kind but it resembles that found in non-figurative art. Yellow flowers, dark tips of pine shining behind ice like eyes. The poem suggests mood, sensory experience, but resists telling us or even showing us how to feel.

Even Howe's use of sound patterning is quiet: the end sounds of "goblins" pairs with "evergreens," "ice"" with "voice," "surmise" with both "ice" and "voice" and "blessedness." While Howe does not often directly use rhyming pairs, her sounds stitch a fabric together even when the semantic sense of a poem unfolds only partially, or briefly, as in "For the Book" above. Reading it can feel mildly disorienting if you are looking for a clearer view, as if we were walked into a film half-way through and only catch a few frames, some unattached statements, before we are marched out again. Fragments are what we are left with, what we must make sense of. As Kane notes, her poems are like a "fragmented score approaching the materiality of a sound-poem as it is a text that manifests an imaginative and melancholy thought unfolding in time."[10]

Howe thinks about how other forms have unfolded in time. She has expressed her love of early Celtic folk poems that use a spare form, the kind that she calls "central to being." These early poems, such as the following one by "Priscian, the Irish monk who stayed in Switzerland in the ninth century," limit the scope of their measurement in size but not in sense:

> A wall of forest looms above
>   and sweetly the blackbird sings;
> all the birds make melody
>   over me and my books and things.
>
> There sings to me the cuckoo
>   from bush-citadels in grey hood.
> God's doom! May the Lord protect me
>   writing well, under the great wood.[11]

Howe writes: "God's doom! Fear is everywhere and suddenly erupts. There is no containing it, not even from a poem by a contented monk."[12] Poems about meaningful objects (birds and books) and meaningful moments (writing, surrounded by forest) appeal to her, and one detects such an impulse in her work, a quest to find a form that rejects embellishment and pays tribute to "being."[13]

Being is ever a riddle, and in some respects her poems are like Anglo-Saxon riddles: they bewilder, create doubt, and embed their sounds in Anglo-Saxon syllables. But added up, the lines create a traceable thought-sentence, even though the parts feel a bit disparate. The separation between elements of the poem appears in the silences that exist between the worlds suggested—in "The Source," the arctic is a physical geographical space and the platonic an imaginative realm, for example. "Electric elevation" and "fishy platform" are not phrases one commonly yokes together. There is much connective tissue missing. However, like Sapphic fragments, the pieces have potency and resonance, like the image of light retained on the retina after the light is suddenly extinguished. As Howe admits, the poems are "written in one kind of fever or mood or they relate to one kind of experience, what the Arabs five centuries ago called a 'day,' a complete experience."[14] There is no returning to them, deliberating over meter or diction. To adhere to the logic of her poems, the lines are fairly short for the most part, except in prose-poem passages, and the page from a distance looks more like one of Dickinson's than Whitman's. The lines often extend to no more than six syllables, with variations, and they rarely take up a whole page.

Many but not all of her volumes are composed of these sound bars. In *Introduction to the World* (1986), each poem is ten lines and each line varies from five to twelve syllables in length, small enough to create a tight acoustic chamber. The volume *O'Clock* (1995) contains poems that are a mixture of couplets, tercets, quatrains, and one-line stanzas, each stanza divided by a white space. There appears to be no set pattern to the arrangements. The size of the stanza is determined by how much room the thought needs to find expression. For example:

> I was sick of my wits
> like the kids in *Landscape In The Mist*
>
> hammered down into a sequence
> like climbing onto a train
> and sitting down
>
> I had to keep moving the books around[15]

Her poems strain against the use of too much wit, almost successfully resisting their own intelligence. Simile becomes her way of both describing and understanding. (As Robert Hass says, "metaphor surprises us into self-awareness."[16]) Worth noting is that *Landscape in the Mist* is a Greek film about two children searching for their father; it is a symbolic quest for value in a world that has grown spiritually hollow. The children in the film feel compelled to keep looking, following the "sequence," getting on and off trains in search of their father. This kind of searching has steps to follow. Howe finds this fatiguing, the following of an expected sequence to obtain a desired end. She becomes "sick of" her "wits." Set patterns ask to be broken. Howe is drawn towards the architectural expression of spontaneity; she echoes this openness in her use of punctuation.

The tension between spontaneity and order plays out in her work indirectly. For the most part, she avoids end-stops and uses little ordinary punctuation. But we grow to expect certain movements of thought across the series or sequences, and know to listen for where they might pause. "The Nursery" finds her experimenting more with line breaks, indenting lines. This reflects an interest in breaking bounds:

> The baby
>   was made in a cell[17]

The baby, whose imagination will be limitless, is first made as a cell, a tiny unit of matter and an imprisoned space.

In Howe's volumes the forms do not remain consistently the same but they also do not change dramatically. This means that we notice, say, when *The Vineyard* (1988) introduces a pattern of arrangement in the stanza lengths (and each stanza is separated by a white space): 1 and 8, 1 and 1 and 7, 1 and 2 and 6. Then she returns for the most part to the 1 and 8 structure; there is also a nine-line poem and a ten-line poem. *O'Clock* contains several seven-line poems, broken into couplets or tercets and one-line stanzas. But there are also eight-line poems, and ones twice as long. The point is that as soon as a pattern appears to emerge, become established, it changes.

As William Corbett says, "[Howe] writes poems and throws them over her shoulder."[18] The verses are not reworked, refashioned into lasting edifices (what we feel with Yeats, for example). As Corbett related, her poems are like "Irish weather," always changing. In her is a desire not to make a certain kind of poem: the long-lasting monument to an established form. Her poems imitate the way she has led her life: peripatetic, always moving, traveling, not settling down. Her work has—like a lifetime of movement—an accumulative force. I do not sit down to read one of Howe's lyric poems to find solace, companionship, or whatever else it is I go to other poems for. I sit down with a volume and read through the series of poems, to alight upon her way of seeing, to catch her drift.

Silence is the structural force in the poems. Parts of the narrative are left unspoken, as in folk poems or ballads. "Joy Had I Known," a poem about the season's desolation and a glimpse of solace, reads:

> Outside snow decays the country
> Browns of fertile mud's lowliness
> Or the storms of Labrador
> Blow the doors of heaven closed
> The sunshine index drops to zero
> and electric light is solo
> Cheer along with other scientific things
> The wind brings
> Scattered flurries
> Freezing spray and I'm living
> When I hear your voice say *Joy*
> *Had I known before.*[19]

In sense and in spirit, it seems to be having a conversation with the anonymous fifteenth-century lyric "Western Wind":

> Western wind, when wilt thou blow,
> the small rain down can rain?
> Christ, if my love were in my arms,
> And I in my bed again.[20]

Notice how the first five lines of Howe's lyric begin with capital letters, the sixth is lowercase, followed by words beginning with uppercase letters. Logic might suggest that because "and" is a conjunction it does not need capitalization, but what of "Or"? The "electric light" is the poem's only unnatural image, and is ushered in without ado. In poems that rarely attribute phrases to others, the mention of a voice saying, and then what it says, stand out. If "joy" is something "known before," the suggestion is that it is now gone, which is similar to what the speaker of "Western Wind" experiences, a surge of longing for what one does not have, what one could not hold onto. Nature seems the focus of this lyric until the end of the third-to-last line, when a speaker's thinking erupts: "I'm living / When I hear your voice say *Joy* / *Had I known before*." Joy is an ideal, a form for which we long, are always trying to relocate. The suddenness of the entry of the voice forces the poem to swerve away from what we suspected was its direction, a disquisition on nature, and mood. But no more knowledge is offered; we are uncertain about what this joy is or was. As suddenly as the voice sounds out, it is gone, silence returning.

"Silence remains, inescapably, a form of speech," writes Susan Sontag in "The Aesthetics of Silence"; Sontag's title could offer a way of describing Howe's concerns.[21] Like Sontag, Howe understands that each historical era wrestles anew with questions of spirituality; spirituality encompasses an era's ideas and expressions which broach, as Sontag puts it, the "resolution of painful structural contradictions inherent in the human situation."[22] It is in this place of encounter that language becomes most fraught. The artist must interrogate her art in the same way a pilgrim might interrogate his heart. Howe is this kind of behind-the-curtain interrogator. (As Howe has voiced elsewhere, "Art was religion where I grew up."[23]) In a review of her *Selected Poems*, Corbett writes: "These are quiet poems, at times muffled to the point of obscurity, as if Howe had stifled her desire to speak in the very act of speaking."[24] The unwillingness to say too much is not quite akin to a vow of silence, but it approximates the gesture, a move toward a deeper spiritual communion. An engagement with spirituality is in part a quest for transcendence, a transcendence that broadens rather than narrows human consciousness.

. . .

Reigning in speech, reacting against garrulousness, could be one way to understand her impulse in the poems. It is not of course unusual for a poet to detect symptoms of illness in the way we commonly (mis)use, or overuse, language. Wry, clipped statements pepper Howe's work. Less said, for Howe, is better. In an early poem, we find "This America is a wonderful place, / one immigrant said. If it's a cage, then it's safe." Safe from what? We are not told. From whatever led them to emigrate. Is it that the immigrants are perceived as dangerous? Howe is interested in other kinds of cages, those of the mind, our complacency and the way we protect ourselves from unpleasantness. This has much to do with her formal aesthetic, which does not resemble a cage. Her poems lack clean endings and beginnings; each poem acts like a line, dangling there, suggestive of not only what has not been said but of what cannot be said.

In her most recent book of essays, *The Winter Sun: Notes on a Vocation* (2009), she quotes Simone Weil from "Human Personality":

> At the very best, a mind enclosed in language is in prison. It is limited to the number of relations which words can make simultaneously present to it; and remains in ignorance of thoughts which involve the combination of a greater number. . . . The intelligent man who is proud of his intelligence is like a condemned man who is proud of his large cell.[25]

Howe rattles against the cage, feeling no pride in or attachment to the cell of a poem (hence the throwing of them over her shoulder), or even to the idea of a mind isolate from others. In "Person, Place and Time," from *Winter Sun*, Howe discusses her interest in the "imitations" Robert Lowell was writing—of Baudelaire, Rimbaud, Montale, Sappho, etc.—"because they prove that there is a simultaneity of thought among poets." She continues:

> The dominant idea of "influence" has always been suspect to me, so these poems translated by Lowell fueled my belief in another process going on among poets. I saw this process as being horizontal and irrational. I still see it this way. There is a confluence of conditions that produces a movement among poets from the United States to China. We change together. And we change in a range of time that is like a great pond where we are born to swim in relation to each other.[26]

Howe sees herself as part of a group, a mass movement of people born during the Second World War who share communal ideas and values because of their common experience. Communal is her preferred term over "personal" and "political."[27] Part of this sensibility admires those who push language to its limit and engage in what her friend and sometimes mentor Edward Dahlberg called "ethical writing": "writing that is so conscious of potential falsehoods, contradictions, and sloppiness in its grammar, it avoids becoming just one more symptom of the sick State."[28] This ethical awareness is heightened by seeing what one does as an action in concert with others, as part of a community. Ego is quiet in her work. The sense of connectedness to others is related to the fact that the voice in Howe's poems is often seemingly impersonal. It is less an "everyman" voice than the voice of one trying to efface distinguishing characteristics, trying not to draw attention to the self (the ego) of the speaker. From *Gone* (2003), in a section entitled "The Passion":

> She put her hand
> inside of his
>
> and they held on
> two wings on a bird
>
> Then he let go
> willing the sacrifice

to a little nest
at a higher position

"Give me a bucketful of colors
And not this melancholy gray memory"

If a goldfinch can pick up
a bucketful of water

with a tiny string, her mind
can lift her hope again.[29]

The emotional remove of the poem displays a wariness of utterance that is smeared by subjectivity, too colored by the individual's well of feeling. The tonal distance—the "she" instead of an "I"—could potentially weaken a poem's rhetoric but here it does not act to diminish; the strength of the final metaphor is made pronounced because there is no "I" attached. Silence about the self, as identified by the "I" in a poem, makes a statement about what Iris Murdoch calls the insatiability of the "fat, relentless ego."

· · ·

Structural silences inform the poems too. Even though question marks do not adorn the pages of her books, a question pulses at the heart of each poem. The questions do not necessarily invite an answer, nor are there necessarily any answers to be had. She avoids declaration, but there are slight clues about her concerns along the way; in "Q," she writes: "If goals create content stealth creates form."[30] No comma disturbs the pacing of the line, as if she doesn't want to be caught being dogmatic, or declarative (which makes my mind dart to an early poem from *Introduction to the World* [1986]; of consciousness, she writes: "I'm just moving inside it, catch as catch can't.")[31] She leans towards puzzle here, a revision of a hypothetical statement, and plays with the edge of logic. Press at it too hard and it can fragment—such lines have the most force when they remain impressionistic. Her touch is painterly.

The poems offer puzzles that sometimes do not easily yield, but it is important to keep in mind what she is after: luminosity. She leaves all these unsolved puzzles along the way, like tracks in the dirt that suddenly end. Fragments have been employed by American poets for so long that they now seem commonplace. In describing poetry that appears to "bring one up short," John Ashbery writes of its value:

Eliot's and subsequent fragmentations in poetry have shown us how to deal with fragments: by leaving them as they are, at most intuiting a meaning from their proximity to each other, but in general leaving it at that. The poetry is complete as it stands, and to wish a further completeness for it would be to destroy its tough but fragile essence.[32]

In Howe we find just such a "tough but fragile essence." The poems are often not distinct pieces that remain aloof from others in the collection. Rather, in many volumes her poems are like individual needles on a branch of pine, suggestive of redolence when alone, intoxicating when taken in as a whole. The nature of the poems can be sketch-like, but as with the plastic arts, the "unfinished look" of a sketch becomes a finished product of its own. For example, here's a section from *O'Clock*, its dashes (ellipses) reminiscent of her distinctly New England foremother (but its place names become distinctly Irish):

> Rain—red rhododendron tree—
> whitethorn—drumlin—you and me—
> a hum of bees—teas—
> white milk—brown sugar—bread—honey—
> waterdrops—late afternoon sun—near Drum.
>
> Inside me, a pulse of desire.
> Inside me, the way elsewhere.[33]

Alliteration and repetition bring these seven lines into the realm of what we understand as a poem; she appears to take joy in the play or linking of the "r" sounds: rain, red, rhododendron, tree, whitethorn, drumlin, etc. And we observe the quiet mutation of "whitethorn" into "white milk," "drumlin" into "Drum," just as the speaker observes the pulsation of desire that broadens into a more zen-like perception that the mind/soul can carry one elsewhere. We don't arrive at the poem's place until the end of the first stanza. And the place is also an instrument of music-making, a sound-maker. It is worth knowing that the civil parish of Drum is in County Monaghan in the heart of Éire/Ireland. (The name Drum is an Anglicized version of the original Irish name, *An Droim*, from *Droim Dreastain*, meaning "Drestan's ridge"). An Irish reporter, Bibi Baskin, once described it as being "not a town, nor a village, but a place apart."[34] Howe's poems are like this, "a place apart" from other contemporary poems. Not anecdotal, not stridently Language poetry, not American, not Irish, but somewhere hovering in between all these traditions and categories.

The riddle of this poem from *O'Clock* is similar also to the riddles of haiku. Howe has written that:

> Often a poet will use repetition by *not* repeating the same word in one poem. Instead the poet will *almost* repeat or rhyme a sound but not quite. *Almost* suggests there is a margin of uncertainty around your thinking. It reminds you that there are echoes that bounce up and away and all is wildness.[35]

This is what the reader begins to do, almost unconsciously, when faced with a poem by Howe: listen for an echo of sorts, some hinge on which to hang the aural frame of the poem. *Poured, powered. Rhododendron, drum. Ice, voice, surmise.*

Note how the Dickinson-like dashes disappear in the second stanza, (echoes of) the past whisked away. Those ellipses suggest what has been left unsaid; once they are removed, what is said becomes somewhat louder: "Inside me, a pulse of desire, / Inside me, a way elsewhere." The sound correspondences—the anaphora and the off-rhyme of "desire" and "elsewhere"—give it a semblance of sound patterning. A few sections later in the poem, we find:

> Parent above, look down and see
> how far from you I've travelled.
>
> From the swell in your firmament
> you'll see the way that the light
> has diffused the location of home.[36]

The first couplet offers an observation most of us have about how our lives have carried us away, in many respects, from those of our parents. What once was solid proximity—a "swell in your firmament"—has now become diffuse, like light. Home is not a place but something spread out and malleable. The closing two lines divulge the characteristic Howe wit at work:

> I've lost it, roads wilden
> into an interstate between work and wine.

She has lost track of home, and with it the expression "roads widen" has lost track of itself by becoming "wilden." This kind of minute alteration often brings each poem its punch, one we experience again as she plays with the word "interstate" (logically following upon the mention of roads), which expands its meaning into an in-between state of mind, "between work and wine," labor and pleasure; within wine I hear "whine" too, which must have its place in any poem about the relationship between children and parents. This habit of picking up on a sound and repeating it in different contexts in these slight-seeming poems becomes a kind of aural theme that ties the poems together.

· · ·

Howe uses structural elements to complement her address of silence and belief most successfully in *Gone* (2003). Here she examines the remnants of belief and reassembles them, but not to aim for coherence. Continuing to eschew rigid poetic structures and fixed modes of thought, she remains loyal to her conventions: that of the open-ended, more often than not untitled poem, fragments shored against our ruin," as T. S. Eliot would have it.

Instead of filling in the gaps, she lets the gaps have their say. As in other Howe poems, the mental "click" that often takes place at the closing of a tightly punctuated poem finds indefinite postponement. The absence of closure means an extension of the sense of being rapt in the poem. The lack of commas, periods, and dashes faithfully imitates the way thoughts trail off without clear ending—how better to enact the music-making capacity of the mind? Yet *Gone* does not celebrate the open-ended as much as it dissects what remains when others—people, strictures of language, options for faith—have fled. At moments this reminds us, for example, of the efforts of H.D.'s *Trilogy* to distill the aftermath of World War II. H.D.'s work can falter, the distillation fail to compel. In a way, Howe is less ambitious. She works from line to line. When the eye lifts from the page, the sense of linguistic play does not dissipate but remains lodged in the ear. The sound patterning in such lines as "(the urge to hurt her emerges)"[37] is deliberate but perhaps without obvious intent. We are so busy attributing meaning to things; Howe's patterning tries to relieve us of this urge.

Gone consists of five sections, the second compiled of prose segments. As we have seen, the metrical contract Howe forms with her readers has more to do with sound patterning than accentual-syllabic measurement. We trust in the falling into place of knowledge that comes about through a careful placement of words on a line, each line representative of a "complex word." The volume opens with a journey that is determined not only by a frame of sound connection (the short "i" sounds blend into each other as "in" is repeated three times to emphasize the direction of the movement) but also by established visual parameters:

> When I was a child
>
> I left my body to look for one
> whose image nestles in the center of a wide valley
>
> in perfect isolation wild as Eden
>
> till one became many: spirits in presence[38]

An imaginative quest is taking place. The "I" begins to travel towards "one," the third line "nestles" close to the second. The "wide valley" is given girth by its following line break and space, as is the wildness of "Eden," allowing for the entrance of "many" spirits. The line organization enacts the drama it creates. I hear the ghost of heroic verse in "in perfect isolation wild as Eden."

Quiet gives structure to the verse. The first section, "The Splinter," closes with this untitled poem:

> Winter spears
> its buds of snow

until a white rose
bleeds gold and trembling
and barely visible
(artificial)
two at a windowpane[39]

The windowpane itself acts as a frame (an artificial frame, as the paren-
thetical remark suggests) for the poem. The imagery itself is layered, line
upon line, just as the phrases are layered by line-breaks. Instead of frozen
grass spiking through snow it is "winter" that "spears" the "buds of snow."
The ice has solidified or transformed the living element, just as doubt can
crystallize or paralyze faith. The precise number "two" saves this fragment
from the wintry despondency the setting evokes, clarity lifting the mood.

In "Doubt," a prose piece from *Gone*, Virginia Woolf, Edith Stein, and
Simone Weil are said to have "sought salvation in a choice of words."[40]
Their work and hers celebrate selectivity and, in Howe's case, paucity in
language. In *Gone* we get the sense of a mind seeking a place of rest,
but we know that if found, the station would be unsatisfactory, and the
mind would move on to perform more of its restless but necessary work.
Sorrow is the result of stasis, Howe's imagination seems to suggest. The
poems pay tribute to the continual shaping of a new vocabulary, not de-
void of sense, a different arrangement. She also does not shy from the
un-returnable purchases made by the heart. As much as this volume repre-
sents an investigation into doubt, which "emerges and magnifies the world
[and] eliminates memory," it also shows "what allows a single gesture to
have heart."[41]

Her language complements the logic of feeling, and yet there is nothing
sentimental here. What is uppermost in mind as one reads is her virtuosic
linguistic performance combined with telling messages about the complex-
ity of human impulses:

> She grew to dare herself to murder that
> Which worked to murder her
> And murder what was birthed to murder her as I also
> Aspired to murder
> Slaved and longed to murder her name
> My own murderous member.[42]

Howe conflates the words "murder" and "birth" and "member" so that
their meanings intertwine but do not dissolve. Although this poem depends
upon the past for its development, past-participle forms of verbs edge omi-
nously towards the present in the chilling final line, "My own murderous
member." What Howe achieves in her verse is not far from what Laura
Riding was after: "a work on language in which the relation between the
spiritual basis of language and the rational principles informing it is traced,

and the operation of those principles explored in the patterning of word meaning."[43]

·　·　·

What Ashbery says about Raymond Roussel could well apply to Fanny Howe; her poems can, "like Cubism, show us an object seen in its totality through a prismatic grill of fractured planes."[44] The experience of reading becomes kaleidoscopic; sound patterns appear, then disappear. Sound and then no sound. The logic of the thinking breaks down. The work is suggestive, not declamatory or exclamatory. And yet, her poem "2002" is an indictment against the Bush administration. *On the Ground* (2004) was written in the wake of September 11th, the invasion of Iraq, but before the terrorist bombings on the subway in London. Fear was in the air. It is a generative title. "On the ground" occurs in the final stanzas of *Paradise Lost* as Adam and Eve are led (or pushed) out of paradise by the cherubim:

> On the ground
> Gliding meteorous, as evening mist
> Risen from a river o'er the marish glides,
> And gathers ground fast at the labourer's heel
> Homeward returning.[45]

Hovering above the ground, not unlike stealth airplanes, military transportation. "On the ground" also hints at "on the grounds of" say, incompatibility, one seeks divorce. This volume responds to the violation of war: "Smoke of assassination / Burning of oil [. . .] In the rape robe of war?" ("Far and Near").[46] The poem "The World Bank" concerns the plane crash of "Americans for the World Bank" on the Dalmatian coast in 1996.[47] This is as direct as Howe gets. Her work is glancing but the glance pierces, then moves on to the next target, often an image from the natural world and usually not as laden with dark consequence:

> Satan says things that don't make sense
> Like "The planes were delayed and so they crashed."
>
> Now muddy starlings flock around
> The salt-sad lagoons[48]

This juxtaposition of claims, which are never long-winded but are more like sharp asides, and startling images from nature (because they suggest what is fleeting) is typical of her work. The politicized voice, the poet finding an image of relief (or sometimes not) in nature—these two sides to her thinking resonate in the stronger poems.

·　·　·

Why was I chained to these language problems that I myself had created?
Why all this scratching and erasing? It was more like drawing an invisible figure
than painting what was in front of me.[49]

Form for Howe does not have suggestions of permanence. (Not for her, "so long as man can breathe, or eyes can see.") She is interested in what is fleeting, and how we bear up under this pressure of nothing ever being the same for long, while always longing for this promise of sameness. Intriguingly, the more recent poems have titled sections, sometimes even titles for the individual poems, but also sometimes not. She rarely makes a tradition of certain maneuvers. In "The Sea-Garden," she writes:

The human is a thing

Who walks around disintegrating. Robins
Take turns in the birch. Lower down, hottentot figs
Burst green water

I've got to try touching
A cactus

Never happier in the world—that—am
Happy as yellow monochrome
The fragilest color among them[50]

Happiness is, after all, fragile, fleeting, like a flower. But there is nothing sentimental or predictable about her phrasing of this sentiment. She tells her truth and consistently tells it slant; the angle and not the outcome draws attention to itself. There is a patterning to the suggestiveness; even the oblique or the occult succumb to order. What Howe offers is a kind of relentless questioning of our interiority (and our surroundings), things both seen and unseen. Her poems never burst into full-throated song. Continually questioning, they resist the ideal. The escapism of song is not allowed for her. But the suggestion of song, a snatch of tune ("catch as catch can't") lingers. Silence informs and protests against too much noise in her poems; song breaks at what could be called, but is not, the heart of each one.

NOTES

1. *The Complete Poems of Thomas Hardy*, ed. James Gibson (New York: Mac-Millan Publishing, 1976): 346.
2. The Kenyon Review Conversations: Fanny Howe (2005); www.kenyonreview.org/conversation/fanny-howe/.

3. Daniel Kane, "Fanny Howe," *PN Review* 157 (May–June 2004): 32.

4. "Daniel Kane Interviews Fanny Howe." Poets Chat, March 2001, n.p.

5. Fanny Howe, *Gone* (Berkeley: University of California Press, 2003): 46.

6. Fanny Howe, *Selected Poems* (Berkeley: University of California Press, 2000): 107.

7. She is in many ways distinct from the "avant-garde" although she has spent most of her life associated with it. Because of her sense of play, of leaving off saying, Howe is more frequently associated with the Language/Post-Language/SF school crew than with poets like Jean Valentine or Donald Revell, with whom she also shares affinity.

8. Maureen McLane, "Song and Silence: My Fanny Howe," *Boston Review* 34.2 (March/April 2009): 50.

9. Fanny Howe, *For the Book* (Minneapolis: Graywolf Press, 2014), 4.

10. Kane, *PN Review*, 32.

11. Fanny Howe, "My Father Was White But Not Quite," *Poetry* (December 2008); www.poetryfoundation.org/poetrymagazine/toc/1139.

12. Ibid.

13. Andrew Patner, "Critical Thinking with Andrew Patner: Fanny Howe," WFMT Radio Chicago, August 31, 2009.

14. Patner, 2009.

15. Howe, *Selected Poems*, 22.

16. Robert Hass, "Tranströmer's Baltics," in *Twentieth Century Pleasures: Prose on Poetry* (New York: Ecco Press, 1984), 74.

17. Howe, *Selected Poems*, 33.

18. William Corbett, Telephone interview, July 6, 2013.

19. Howe, *Selected Poems*, 55.

20. *The Norton Anthology of Poetry*, Salter, Ferguson, and Stallworthy, eds. (New York: Norton, 2004), 84.

21. Susan Sontag, "The Aesthetics of Silence," in *Styles of Radical Will* (New York: Picador, 2002), 192.

22. Sontag, 190.

23. Patner, 2009.

24. William Corbett, Review of *Selected Poems* by Fanny Howe, *Boston Phoenix* (June 2000); www.bostonphoenix.com/archive/books/00/06/22/FANNY_HOWE.html.

25. Fanny Howe, *The Winter Sun: Notes on a Vocation* (St. Paul: Graywolf Press, 2009), 166.

26. Howe, *The Winter Sun*, 67.

27. Patner.

28. Howe, *The Winter Sun*, 73.

29. Howe, *Gone*, 73.

30. Howe, *Selected Poems*, 30.

31. Ibid., 9.

32. John Ashbery, "Olives and Anchovies: The Poetry of Thomas Lovell Beddoes," in *Other Traditions* (Cambridge: Harvard University Press, 2000), 42.

33. Howe, *Selected Poems*, 161.

34. See www.drum.ie.

35. Howe, *The Winter Sun*, 150.

36. Howe, *Selected Poems*, 163.

37. Howe, *Gone*, 14.

38. Ibid., 3.

39. Ibid., 20.

40. Ibid., 23.

41. Ibid., 25.

42. Ibid., 15.

43. Laura Riding, "Neglected Books," *Antaeus* 20 (Winter 1976): 155–57.

44. Ashbery, 65.

45. John Milton, *Paradise Lost* (New York: Longman, 1986), Book XII, 628–32; 640.

46. Howe, *On The Ground*, 3.

47. Ibid., 7.

48. Ibid., 8.

49. Howe, *The Winter Sun*, 6.

50. Howe, *Selected Poems*, 128.

BIBLIOGRAPHY

Works by Fanny Howe

POETRY

Eggs. Boston: Houghton Mifflin, 1970.

The Amerindian Coastline Poem. New York: Telephone Books, 1976.

Poem from a Single Pallet. Berkeley: Kelsey Street Press, 1980.

Alsace Lorraine. New York: Telephone Books. 1982.

For Erato: The Meaning of Life. Berkeley: Tuumba Press, 1984.

Introduction to the World. New York: The Figures, 1985.

Robeson Street. Boston: Alice James Books, 1985.

The Vineyard. Providence: Lost Roads, 1988.

The End. Los Angeles: Littoral Books, 1992.

The Quietist. Oakland: O Books, 1992.

O'Clock. London, UK: Reality Street, 1995.

One Crossed Out. Minneapolis: Graywolf Press, 1997.

Q. Cambridgeshire, UK: Paul Green Press, 1998.

Forged. Sausalito: Post-Apollo Press, 1999.

Selected Poems. Berkeley: University of California Press, 2000.

Gone: Poems. Berkeley: University of California Press, 2003.

Tis of Thee. Berkeley: Atelos, 2003.

On the Ground. Minneapolis: Graywolf Press, 2004.

The Lyrics. Minneapolis: Graywolf Press, 2007.

Emergence. London, UK: Reality Street, 2010.

Come and See: Poems. Minneapolis: Graywolf Press, 2011.

Second Childhood. Minneapolis: Graywolf Press, 2014.

SELECTED FICTION

Forty Whacks. Boston: Houghton Mifflin, 1969.
First Marriage. New York: Avon, 1974.
Brontë Wilde. New York: Avon, 1976.
Holy Smoke. New York: Fiction Collective 2, 1979.
The White Slave. New York: Avon, 1980.
The Blue Hills. New York: Avon, 1981.
Yeah, But. New York: Avon, 1982.
In the Middle of Nowhere. New York: Fiction Collective, 1984.
Radio City. New York: Avon, 1984.
Taking Care. New York: Avon, 1985.
The Race of the Radical. New York: Viking, 1985.
The Lives of a Spirit. Los Angeles: Sun & Moon Press, 1986.
The Deep North. Los Angeles: Sun & Moon Press, 1988.
Famous Questions. New York: Ballantine, 1989.
Saving History. Los Angeles: Sun & Moon Press, 1992.
Nod. Los Angeles: Sun & Moon Press, 1998.
Indivisible. Cambridge: MIT Press, 2000.
Economics. Chicago: Flood Editions, 2002.
Radical Love: 5 Novels. Beacon, NY: Nightboat Books, 2006.
What Did I Do Wrong. Chicago: Flood Editions, 2009.

SELECTED PROSE

The Wedding Dress: Meditations on Word and Life. Berkeley: University of
     California Press, 2003.
"The Pinocchian Ideal." In *The Grand Permission: New Writings on Poetics and
     Motherhood,* ed. Patricia Dienstfrey and Brenda Hillman (Middletown, CT:
     Wesleyan University Press, 2003), 263–66.
The Lives of a Spirit/Glasstown: Where Something Got Broken. Beacon, NY:
     Nightboat Books, 2005.
The Winter Sun: Notes on a Vocation. St. Paul: Graywolf Press, 2009.
"Incarnational." In *Jean Valentine: This World Company,* ed. Kazim Ali and John
     Hoppenthaler (Ann Arbor: University of Michigan Press, 2012), 111–15.
The Needle's Eye: Passing Through Youth. Minneapolis: Graywolf Press, 2016.

SELECTED INTERVIEWS

Corbett, William. "An Interview with Fanny Howe." *Brick* 72 (2003): 149–57.
———. "Fanny Howe on Race, Family, and the Line between Fiction and Poetry."
     Lit Hub, November 2016; lithub.com/fanny-howe-on-race-family-and-the-line
     -between-fiction-and-poetry/.
Jensen, Kim. "Fanny Howe." *Bomb Magazine,* Winter 2013; bombmagazine.org
     /article/6925/fanny-howe.
Kane, Daniel. "Fanny Howe." *What Is Poetry: Conversations with the American
     Avant-Garde.* New York, NY: Teachers & Writers, 2003.
Vigderman, Patsy. "The KR Conversations: Fanny Howe." *Kenyon Review* (May
     2004); www.kenyonreview.org/conversation/fanny-howe/.

Selected Criticism and Reviews

Chorier-Fryd, Bénédicte. "Secret du retournement dans Nord profond de Fanny Howe." In *Les Écritures secrètes*, ed. Michel Briand, Colette Camelin, Liliane Louvel, and Pascal Drouet (Rennes, France: Presses Universitaires de Rennes, 2009), 33–38.

Fan, Kit. "'Between the Blank Page and the Poem': Reading Simone Weil in Contemporary American Poets." *Cambridge Quarterly* 36.2 (2007): 129–54.

Field, Miranda. "On Fanny Howe." In *Women Poets on Mentorship: Efforts in Affection* (Iowa City: University of Iowa Press, 2008): 25–34.

Gelpi, Albert. "Emily Dickinson's Long Shadow: Susan Howe and Fanny Howe." *Emily Dickinson Journal* 17.2 (2008): 100–12.

Hinton, Laura. "Postmodern Romance and the Descriptive Fetish of Vision in Fanny Howe's *The Lives of a Spirit* and Lyn Hejinian's *My Life*." In *We Who Love to Be Astonished: Experimental Women's Writing and Performance Poetics*, ed. Laura Hinton and Cynthia Hogue (Tuscaloosa: University of Alabama Press, 2002), 140–49.

Huk, Romana. "'A single liturgy': Fanny Howe's *The Wedding Dress*." *Christianity and Literature* 58.4 (Summer 2009): 657.

Kane, Daniel. "Fanny Howe." *PN Review* 30.5 (2004): 31–35.

Keller, Lynn. "'Just one of / the girls:— / normal in the extreme': Experimentalists-To-Be Starting Out in the 1960s." *differences: A Journal of Feminist Cultural Studies* 12.2 (2001): 47.

Kriner, Tiffany Eberle. "Wary Grammar: Fanny Howe's Narrative Bewilderment." *Arizona Quarterly* 69.3 (Autumn 2012): 129–56.

McLane, Maureen. "Song and Silence: My Fanny Howe." *Boston Review* 34.2 (March/April 2009).

Sampson, Fiona. "The winter sun: notes on a vocation." *Times Literary Supplement* 18 (September 2009): 27.

Toussaint, Steven. "Fanny Howe's Revelation: A Review of *Emergence*." *Jacket* 2, May 2011; jacket2.org/reviews/fanny-howes-revelation.

Vickery, Ann. "Finding Grace: Modernity and the Ineffable in the Poetry of Rae Armantrout and Fanny Howe." *Revista Canaria de Estudios Ingleses* 37 (November 1998): 143–63.

ALICE NOTLEY

POEMS

FROM *165 Meeting House Lane*

Dear Dark Continent

Dear Dark Continent:

                          The quickening of
the palpable coffin
                fear so then the frantic
doing of everything experience is thought of

but I've ostensibly chosen
                    my, a, *family*
so early! so early! (as is done always
as it would seem always) I'm a two
now three irrevocably
                I'm wife I'm mother I'm
myself and him and I'm myself and him and him

But isn't it only I in the real
whole long universe? Alone to be
in whole long universe?

But I and this he (and he) makes ghosts of
I and all the *he*s there would be, won't be

because by now I am he, we are I, I am we.

We're not the completion of myself.

Not the completion of myself, but myself!
through the whole long universe.

FROM *Songs for the Second Unborn Baby*

Untitled

My little boy's sick tonight
Oh get well while you're asleep
Honey, and we'll go out
Together at noon
Everything as always

FROM *Parts of a Wedding*

I the People

I the people
to the things that are were &
        come to be.
We were once what we know
        when we
make love   When we go away
        from each other because
we have been created
        at 10th & A, in winter &
of trees & of the history of houses
        we hope we are
notes of the musical scale of
        heaven—I the
people so repetitious, & my
        vision of
to hold the neighbors loose-
        ly here in

light of gel, my gel, my vision
         come out of
my eyes to hold you sur-
         round you in
gold & you don't know it
         ever. Everyone
we the people having our
         visions of
gold & silver & silken liquid
         light flowed
from our eyes & caressing
         all around all the
walls. I am a late Pre-
         in this dawn of
We the people
to the things that are & were
         & come to be
Once what we knew was only
         and numbers became
It is numbers & gold & at 10th
         & A you don't
have to know it ever. Opening
         words that show
Opening words that show that we
         were once
the first to recognize
         the immortality of numbered
bodies. And we are the masters
         of hearing & saying
at the double edge of body &
         breath
We the lovers & the eyes
All over, inside her
         when the wedding
is over, & the Park "lies cold &
         lifeless"

I the people, whatever is said
        by the first
one along, Angel-Agate. I wear
        your colors
I hear what we say & what
        we say . . . (and I
the people am still parted in
        two & would cry)

FROM *The Descent of Alette*

"A car" "awash with blood" "Blood at our feet" "& I
& others" "have small springs" "of blood from our"
"feet & knees" "There is an inch or two" "of blood"
"all over" "the car floor" "Replenished" "periodically"

"by our body springs" "of blood" "And trickling out"
"the door" "when it opens" "at stations." "The
tyrant" "sends a hologram" "a life-sized hologram" "of
himself" "into our car" "He stands mid-car" "& says:"

"'The blood at our" "feet" "has cost me" "so much"
"The blood" "at our feet" "has cost us so" "much"
"To clean" "the blood" "is difficult" "to clean the
car.'" "There is a litter" "of things" "in the

wash of blood" "I see sanitary" "pads," "kleenex,"
"black-blood encrusted" "old bandages" "An old black
suitcase" "spills out" "torn men's clothes" "& frayed towels"
"The hologram tyrant" "says, 'Here" "are my tears'" "Holds

up his palm" "His tears are" "small drops of jade"
"Red" "& white jade" "His tears have turned to jade"
"They will be placed in" "a National" "Museum" "There is
something in" "my ear" "I pull it out a" "white cord"

"a long" "silk cord" "I pull it out &" "hear our blood"
"It hums" "a unison one" "note loud a" "sheet of sound"
"It hangs there" "sad insect noise" "insect-like"
"Our blood."

FROM *Mysteries of Small Houses*

Flowers

I was there because of the poetry
I thought it only grew in really dirty dirt
And there was so much of it everywhere
Ugly-beautiful red rag petals, folksongs of agitation elation
Waving streaming or floating in or through bad air

I lived in a lovely redpetal slowly burning house
On fire because
I lived in a situation which would end
With someone who would die because
Ill-health, excess, poverty, neglect
Are a common sight along roadsides
Orange to scarlet then deep blue as I always say

And so some of it we did and some was done to us
Of the so-called negative characteristics and happenstance
Some of the flowers were ugly and leathery
Swamp-stink brown-spotted fights
I'm not being clear, we had inappropriate emotions
The American poetry vacant lot's small and overgrown

So you squabble with everyone
That can be healthy or vicious
When someone's dying for years

He does and doesn't say so: We sip at our sweet poisons
Jewel-colored legendary chemicals
At our emotions splenetic and ecstatic
We are used for various purposes in return for subsistence
But it's always hoped that one
Will contain oneself . . .
Will you not overflow into the lot
As anything beyond your dirt as
Prophecy cry-for-help cry-of-rage cry-of-too-much-
Love cry-of-knowledge, not overflow?

I feel that the others don't want to know.
Speaking even now as a later presence.
But in order to be honest
I must change my poem
Drastically, can't get there this way—
I am now the poet in this story

I have a headache in a burning house for years
Hardly know that it's burning
Then after the death-event itself
There's threat of flood and drowning
Scatter marijuana on the waters
To quieten them—is Atlantis sinking?
Nothing so grand as that dream in our lot
Where I'm still choked in dense clusters
I must leave the lot of flowers
To find a purple female cunt-lipped tree
"Drink of the spring inside me"
Water in a tree . . .
This water's really dark and purple
Deathlike and dangerous and free
And drink of it if you can; she says, "I'm
The laurel tree"
But if I drink of her who knows it
If I've drunk from the actual tree
Who can tell except her and me?

Laurel's not for the public head it's a
Secret intoxication
I wonder if this is an obnoxious poem
I wonder if it's really understood that
Poetry and I are its subject, not
The death of a husband in neglect
It's my neglect I'm entranced by
And my garland of the everlasting laurel leaves
Evergreen darkgreen elliptical thick and bunched

FROM *Reason and Other Women*

Growth of the Light Flat upon Her

if there were a tunnel between the two worlds only poetry would matter in it if there
were that dark tunnel some say of a passage between life and death what would be of
service only poetry which deals in the resonance the connection between the pieces of
its the feeling for we bring to things. if there were a tunnel between the two only
poetry would matter there some say of a passage between the states life and death
would be only knowledge of poetry of how to connect the parts as of dreams but i dont

believe in tunnel except as piece of poem itself except as poem when everything to me
manifestly overlaps a machine made of tubes sending messages all night all night but
thats i think we're erasing poetry with a movie or video camera which shows nothing
shadows it seems i have a lot c a lot of cash in my pocket but we will buy bees instead.
in exchange for chips of coral and jade which i have earned along my lifeline and all
night i the two bodies i lie in bed and create the real body which is light its where i life
exactly its i and next to its the other body this white body is the real body and is really
there this is a body and that i participate in its construction lying there in the dark. all
night i lie in bed and create the real body which i see as light layer on me its exactly i
body its where i lie and next to its the other the other body aside there this they are
bodies and i participate exactly in the construction of this the real body me where i am
lying in bed in the dark. am i always hes holding up the building which is the library

must walk me home its so late but the sky is full of the most brilliant constellations bursting with light out of their patterns against the dark morning sky and yet i have seen a subtler sky which was a whole wide light cloud a pearl sky pearl with light behind it all of light. the sky of constellations is the best sky of the first world the sky of stars but stardom vanish i have to sleep in a basement and i dont know how my mail will get delivered because the mailbox is inside the room so where does my real

mail come from. i sleep in the basement room of a house and my mailbox isnt outside near the door its inside the room so how will my mail be delivered. why does the young poet type all his stressed words in caps its because he thinks stress is absolute but it but it is a puddle of stress a pool small of light from the live one up all night and in the back and forth between the two worlds. must bursting see a subtler sky a sky pearl the other body which is the real that i am there are two bodies not a body and soul there are two bodies as there are two skies two worlds two lying in bed in the dark and i participate exactly in the construction of this the real body sending messages to the inside of my basement the basement of the house my mother has insisted that he walk me home to home but i have to go back go back to his for three books and wake up a girl. there are two babies two girls and the one has been awake all night is home sleeping im holding the other one at the poetry conference

someone complains about the stress poet the caps one but i like him this is a body with poetry to take into the tunnel the tubes which send messages are everywhere theyre everywhere cant get away from bursting with small light under the layer under the level where live from a light depth of poetry how he holds up object at dream table we arent really there. it isnt exactly a language a set of living relations which arent so known of stress a mud puddle all li light with extr t extras syllables the mess

of it spilling out into the life or death worlds of but what words can tell when your cleanliness has been of no use small mud puddles full of light. i didnt have to walk across to there because my there wasnt that. to take into a tunnel there are on reed across question two babies girls and one all asleep all night waiting growth of the light flat upon her as second body the construction of the body beneath from which we can speak to o each other in the real sequence what is that in the second that here and there are nev havent been named. he didnt want us to live there it wasnt as he. but i could do no other after the body had been constructed and i had become this other who i am now a second one yet is that a thing. im enjoying this a great deal this body faith what some what white light and flat and flat its where i am in the body bed in the way you know where you are and that i construct it myself i have chips of mother of pearl in my pockets jeans pockets stealing on back im happy about that if there were a tunnel only poetry would matter is the first time more like a thought of it and in the grand hotel theres room for everyone with womb fresh red carpet and long curtain gold braid and star. theres something that happens twice about everything happens happens an echo from when the golden amoeba first first split night in a sort of arena what are the names of the first what are the nonnames of the real relations between what are right and some that are not wrong but wrong exclusive too old being taken by

a young to some clubs but i didnt want to go it was the wrong body the prevailing topography of female sex but that is no seeing an iconic painted face like the second body under construction with blue light blue paint the face of reason leaping at me snake to bite my hand and ensure the second world the second body the second line or poem which is frayed it isnt really its that it isnt entirely formed because its the second or real body under construction the public library is just a dream. i will be just and happens. between any several things the life permits choosing but not choice i mean leaps at me bites me to take into the real there is no accidental here you are making making your judgment on body with golden oz oozing from womb of wrong exclusive too old and yet what to some clubs faith what i am faithful forgetting the path because there is no and on on other either side of the question but there is no question at all not from here from this body which i am real.

FROM *Songs and Stories of the Ghouls*

City of Ghostly Festivals

Try to find
the center of night. this city

A hear break, I can't *hear* it.

Dido the appropriated victim
sets all the bottles rattling
in the wind of our agains.

I wanted a different again.

It's different.

————

The syllabary
      of my
sins
a
thing Maat
flicks
      into
the river
running
judgment

a million literal years of.
I'm sick of judging your carnage,
      she says,

you are all left alone
      with it.

————

Dido's job
for two thousand years
has been to
      commit suicide

after
her death, and after
the Romans destroy her
      foundation.

————

The witch's job. is to change
        time
which runs in short lines
        between
events like innumerable
        falls of cities

is watching me. But it isn't.

If you change the nature of
        events
do you change time?

Event: I sat down to
talk to everyone
        who had ever lived.

————

'My country
is broken and it can't be fixed'

time loved so
femina-hating Rome
        always falling

I, the witch, pardon no one

instead, I change Dido's job.

————

Man with whom everything is
        boring
everything he does and that one
        does with him
is boring. One is condemned
to be part of his
        boring world.

There is another man
with whom one's condemned
        to be
duplicitous
Everything's a cheat a scam
in the big-guy road-house world
Help him tell lies. wear special
        clothes
for that.

————

THIS WAS HOW I BROKE IT

They told me I couldn't have
        it—time—so
I took it.
I put him
        away
who had withered to a doll.

————

We ghouls waiting outside of time . . .

Dido to poem: Do all my remembering
    now
so city continues.
Do we accept it says voice
He became too old to be wise; we
had to step outside him
and into knowledge
of poetry, the ghoulish, timeless state.

————

This poem, the poem,
always
my real country

Carp Shoals and Tules

Marie goes down to the river to fish for a carp. She has an old
mended net; she stands in the shallows and nets one, in a little
backwater from the big current, back here in the ugly shady trees.

Once she caught a chuckawalla with a sharp stick, rammed it
into its big airy torso. Flat fatty. She roasted it. Everything
tastes like chicken—rattlesnake does, cottontail does. Marie
doesn't own a gun. You can eat caterpillars and grasshoppers

Why not? But don't let the girls see you. Or anyone else.

She's thinking about a daughter, a house on fire—
she feels her scars—But she's not really thinking; she doesn't
have to think about it, does she? Not like in thinking,
you don't have to face everything. Every time someone burns
down her shack. It's like they know; but they don't.

Standing in the river cools off the scars. No one sees me
You don't have to get over it. You don't have to do anything.
I'm never going to get over it. I'm never going to think
about it. Oh standing in iced sapphires in this heat,
catching a fish. Haul it up in the net; and take it home.

POETICS STATEMENT

The Responsibilities of Poetry

Poetry has absolutely no responsibilities as an abstract noun. It is an ancient art, the closest to reality if not coincident with it. It is measurable, layered, and vibrates across itself, like one does; what you should ask is, what are your responsibilities to it? Shouldn't you pay more attention than you do to an art that doesn't flatten everything out, like the novel, creating endless distracting stories that are in no way like us really, rather than being, really being, life? Or take a one-sense art like painting or music, music that mostly makes you drunk; or for god's sake film, the nothing art, with a haphazard product—"product"—of all that money can arrange. These being the "moneyed" arts that are never accused of needing to live up to their responsibilities, since they are always part of the economy, bought and sold; there would be no point in complaining or accusing. Poetry is everyone's patsy when one wants one.

I do sometimes think I *owe* the writing of a particular kind of poetry—but I owe it to an ideal society that bothers about my art. But I also owe, when I owe something vis-à-vis poetry, to poetry itself and to my own talent. And to the voices that speak to me while I write. I have given up most of what the world thinks one should have, for poetry, to be a poet. I don't feel responsible to anyone for anything now; I possess very little and am free. I don't even have a credit rating.

Poetry itself tells me what to do when I write; society has no idea what it wants from poetry, because it doesn't know what it is. It seems to me that people have lost all sense of a connection to the art. I feel this is in no way my fault. People are delighted with stories and with a representation of themselves as character and emotion—love, rage, desire. They are always caught in time; poetry offers timelessness—it is condensed and in one time, always folding back into itself. Its music isn't pelvic or to the heart, though it also isn't just cerebral. It's more of an all-body experience asking you to think with rhythm and stress, with the intellect active. Poetry is spooky—the soul as spook: what does the soul sound like?

I am responsible to my talent, which tells me what to write next and always has. I didn't recognize that I had this talent for some time, because poetry is not generally known as an aptitude; but I know that I am a genius of it. I repeat, largely I won't do anything *it* doesn't tell me to do. That may sound Nineteenth Century Romantic; believe me it isn't, it's scary as hell. And I have risked being called indolent, irresponsible, and *poor*—everyone's worst insult—all my life. I don't see any bigger artistic risk—for as we all know, you will want to say, poetry achieves nothing and probably doesn't help. Is there something to be achieved? Do only politicians and soldiers help? Do teachers really know any valid thing to teach?

I perpetually hear voices; I cultivate them and am responsible to them. They ask me to speak to and for them; particularly the dead do. Who, it seems to me, are still caught in the sadness of their lives. I am trying to help *them* let go of their melancholy; and by talking to the dead I am exposing the metaphysics of the universe, to anyone who wants to know it. This is, finally, a very large responsibility, either poetry's or mine.

NOTE

Alice Notley's Poetics Statement was written for Responsabilités de la Poésie, a conference held at the University of Rouen, France, on March 14, 2016.

RESIST, REFRAME, INSIST

Alice Notley's Poetics of Inclusion

Elline Lipkin

On the first page of Alice Notley's *Culture of One*, in the poem "At the Beginning Stop Suffering," she writes "I have no understanding of who I am; / though, with my thousand arms, I have written of my own / nature since writing began. I inhabit you and you write about me again."[1] She continues: "I'm here inside when / you need me; I can come to you when you've forgotten my / name."[2] These lines—with their evocation of a permeable self and resistance to the rational—serve as a précis of a poetics of inclusion that Notley has insisted upon throughout her prolific (and ongoing) career, resisting the traditional expectations associated with the singular lyric "I" in order to create a more "collective poetry." The speaker's fluid boundaries allow Notley to realize an aesthetic that supports a collage of lyrical voices, as in these lines where the "I" inhabits another speaker, and the "you" writes about the speaker. This exchange is representative of Notley's project—to diversify or split the solitary "I" by incorporating others' voices into her work—a move that is often political and feminist. Acknowledging "no understanding of who I am" is also emblematic of Notley's vision: one that abnegates the restrictions created by a traditional, singular voice in favor of a more communal poetics.

By rejecting singularity and fixed meanings, Notley resists the stagnation of being enclosed within set terms, or even cultural systems, that don't represent her or, even worse, oppress her subjectivity. To reach with her "thousand arms" is central to Notley's aesthetic, which maps the movement of her mind and strategically uses un-fixedness or the possibilities of more porous boundaries (both poetic and personal) in order to admit more into the poem than had been previously allowed. This tenet becomes explicit early in Notley's career when she writes about the need to invent a poetry that can encompass the experience of being doubled during pregnancy, and then split into many selves while raising young children. Refusing to relegate the realities of her life as a mother to the margins, Notley deliberately writes poems that address the expansiveness of containing more than one self, physically as well as psychically. As I will show, pregnancy, childbirth, and motherhood are experiences that inspire Notley's development of a poetics of inclusivity born out of a resistance to the constrictions she has felt as a female writer.

In this essay I look at Notley's earliest work, first published in the early 1970s, as her voice as a poet emerges concurrently with her identity as a new mother, delineating her early, instinctive attempts to contain and represent multiplicity within the poem (as her writing mirrors her life), and then turn to her further development of this trait twenty years later in her book-length epic, *The Descent of Alette*. There, Notley again invents a poetic form that breaks with expectations of the solitary "I" in order to include a panoply of voices that offer polysemous meanings. Challenging on multiple levels, this strategy distorts the singular, and expected, frame placed around meaning(s), and advocates for a pluralistic experience in both the writing and reading of Notley's work.

The Expanded "I"

Notley's resistance to the aesthetics of the New York School and her steadfast position outside a specific school or movement makes visible the silenced or even taboo subjects within the poetry world at the time she began writing—something echoed powerfully in the anthology *The Grand Permission: New Writings on Poetics and Motherhood*, which includes Notley's essay "Doublings." In this essay, she is explicit about the struggles she underwent to forge her new aesthetics in the face of the (sometimes unspoken) censure she experienced as a female writer—a topic that informs many of the essays in *The Grand Permission*. In an earlier essay, the foundational "The Poetics of Disobedience," Notley notes that in her early writing life she wanted to "disobey" the status quo and instead focus on "what was going on most literarily around one, the pregnant body, and babies for example. There were no babies in poetry then."[3] She revisits some of these ideas in "Doublings," further tracing her personal and poetic histories and their concomitant goals: "I became a poet somewhat coincidentally to becoming a mother. I wrote my first 'good poems' in early '71 and bore my elder son in '72."[4] Her husband, poet Ted Berrigan, realizing the impact having children would have on her ambitions, suggested that she put off writing seriously for a long while and plan on being a "late bloomer," without, it seems, giving thought to how new fatherhood might demand his own sacrifices or impact his career.

It was clearly a galvanizing moment, prompting the anger and resistance that is a hallmark of Notley's work. Rather than letting pregnancy and motherhood impede her creative life, she decides they will form a nexus of co-creativity for her: "It was how I got to be the poet, [and] got to be born, too," she comments.[5] As she goes on to explain, pregnancy, motherhood, and childrearing led to the rendering of an expanded "I" and fundamentally shaped her aesthetics. In addition, within "Doublings," Notley emphasizes the implosion of the singular "I" in her body and in her consciousness when pregnant and, postpartum, as mother to first one child, and then two children. Over the years, poets and critics have commented that Notley's inclusion of pregnancy and her young children within her work gave *them* implicit permission to write about these subjects and, in *The Grand Permission*, many of the writers included echo Notley's ideas about the ways motherhood changes one's understanding of writing and even language. The need to find a way to integrate having children with one's writing life is a unifying theme in the collection, with several writers touching on the sense of division they experienced once they had children —sometimes in terms of a psychic splitting of the self, sometimes more pragmatically in terms of the bifurcation of their ambitions and their time. Several poets express ideas about motherhood that resonate with Notley's sense that the demands of a child-centered life dictate first understanding and then inventing a new rhythm and inclusiveness within the poems— one that can reflect the realities of their lives.

In her essay in *The Grand Permission*, Maureen Owen describes the profound nature of the need for new forms and new ways of writing, of "having no choice but to almost make [her]self 'one' with [her] children" and "include them in the moments when [she] pulled out [her] notebooks and wrote."[6] Of her own sense of perpetual fracturing she says, "Suddenly, I wasn't one person, but three." Owen concludes, "I had my children and my writing. They were interwoven. The boys were part of my poems, they surfaced and resurfaced in them. And my poetry made it possible for me to be the kind of mother I wanted to be."[7] Mary Margaret Sloan writes of realizing, with horror, that her newborn daughter was a "guest that would not be leaving,"[8] and mentions years of trying to write a lyric poem with "line breaks, regularized rhythm, a melodious pattern of sound . . . the entire work unified by means of a central 'I' which progresses toward a moment of revelation at the conclusion of the poem, at which point its intended meaning becomes clear."[9] This is contrasted with a sense of her own subjecthood now disrupted by this "alien." When she realizes she cannot occupy a singular point alone, the revelation calls for a reordering—literally—of her idea of what a poem is and can be.

A number of the contributors to *The Grand Permission* mention needing to assimilate their children's voices into their creative work—an idea that also comes up in "Doublings"—not only as a strategy for writing at all, but also in order to convey the joys in hearing the prelinguistic babble and original locutions of their offspring, which provides an experience that reroutes their relationship to language and their perspectives on their own poetry. Susan Griffin comments on the linguistic possibilities that can accompany raising small children, noting that "the voice[s] of the children [are] . . . madcap, zany, as if teetering over the edge of impossible meanings."[10] Carolyn Forché writes about discovering new levels of connection through pregnancy: "With [my son] I experienced a radiant interdependence of sensation and thought; he was of me but he was not 'mine.'"[11] She too waxes on about her son's pre-linguistic state, "He was at the gates of language, where only the invisible is obvious. Or so it seems to me now."[12]

Previously unexplored perspectives in poetry become a focus of Gillian Conoley's *Grand Permission* essay:

> What motherhood is teaching me, in relation to identity is the rapidity with which [my] selves can come and go, how fiercely they are erected and erased. For me, one of the least understood and discussed aspects of motherhood has been the extent to which our own children shape and alter our identities, and we theirs, each of us demanding of the other a constant shifting of reality.[13]

Like Sloan, Conoley writes about her resistance to traditional understandings of both poetry and motherhood, grappling with the differences between her own experience of childbirth, and the observations of the great Modernist poet William Carlos Williams, who as a physician specialized in obstetrics. Williams wrote about witnessing "the domains of birth and of the mother, of one body leaving another," which Conoley explains is described as "an actuality, a physical, psychological, and spiritual actuality of extreme unity, followed by extreme separation."[14] Conoley takes issue with this "blur[ring]" and Williams' idea of mother and child as "together as one," commenting that she experienced "more of a splitting off, molecule by molecule; something more like a 'together, as many,'" a concept that suits her better.[15] Together, the essays in *Grand Permission* make the case that motherhood affects, informs, and initiates a poetics of motherhood;

the writers propose that motherhood instantiates "a third space" that is forged by new identity.

Notley has consistently written about her awareness of a negative or third space surrounding certain subjects, which ignited her desire for greater inclusion of these topics within poetry. "Where is the [poetic] form for this as yet unidentified meaning growing inside me?" she writes in "Doublings,"[16] and of her pregnancy: "In 1972 it seemed obvious that my subject was what I was carrying, because he signified enormous change and because . . . there was little poetry that dealt with this change."[17] In an interview in *3AM Magazine*, Notley explains "there were hardly any poems with pregnancy and childbirth as their subject, . . . so I proceeded to invent a Modernist poetry of motherhood, which was simultaneously being initiated and echoed by other women of my generation. I was then widowed: where was that poetry? I wrote it."[18]

As she parses the fracturing of the self that results from her new role as a mother and begins to cultivate a taxonomy for the multiplicity she is experiencing, Notley also insists on addressing postpartum depression, a topic not commonly acknowledged. She writes, "I was two people, the one that I had always been and the new one that was suffering. The strangeness of being one suffering, being one so other, coexisted alongside a happiness with and a fascination with my son. How could being be so double? Giving birth was about doubling, and marriage was, and poetry was."[19] While eschewing any kind of essentialized stance about what it means to write as a mother, Notley is explicit about the physical changes she experienced that necessitated changes in her writing, one that reflected a need for larger containment of collective moments. Of this period, she says, "the poetic forms I used were often either thick slablike shapes or swirlings, influenced by painting and designed to hold a lot of thoughts and feelings and observations in one suspension, just as the contradictions in me were united in my selfhood."[20] A full-time mother to two young children, Notley facilitates their needs as well as her own and is profoundly aware of the interconnection and interdependency of their bodies and thoughts. The "forms" she chooses necessitated a "thickness" to hold the layers of meaning she is trying to express—not just through her mind's perceptions, but a collective depiction of their day and their myriad shared interactions.

In a strategic move toward multivocality within her poems, Notley begins to incorporate her sons' voices in collage-like poetic forms, the "thick slablike shapes" she references. She explains that she did this, in part, as a way to keep writing in the midst of endless conversation:

> I invented forms which included all this talking [because] . . . I had to write while people were around. And in the midst of active mothering, I invented conversational poetic narratives and diaries spun out of outer talk and inner mental narration in prose-like verse and verse-like prose separate and mixed.[21]

The "non-room-of-one's-own" position in which Notley found herself (quite literally, and on the page), allowed her to expand the number of speakers and the dimensions of her poems: "[the children] were as inventive in conversation as all the poets who visited were . . . their feelings were cleaner and there was a pure clean light around their talk which I liked to be near and which I liked to include in my work."[22]

Notley's development of a shifting or permeable "I" that can encompass the other subjectivities in the room, and even inside her own body, can be seen within the earliest work written during this period of intense child-centric life. In the poem "Dear Dark Continent," published in one of her first books, *165 Meeting House Lane*, Notley chronicles her interchanging roles: "I'm a two / now three irrevocably / I'm a wife I'm mother I'm / myself and him and I'm myself and him and him,"[23] she writes, as she tries to integrate a sense of multiplicity. Her pronouns continue to intermingle in the lines, "But I and this he (and he) make ghosts of / I and all the *hes* there would be, won't be // because by now I am he, we are I, I am we."[24] "We're not the completion of myself," is a phrase that repeats in almost fugue-like rhythm as the speaker tries to gather a shifting self from a panoply of identities.

When her children are young, their daily activities together become subjects, often signified by the quoted remarks of others who are unidentified, but who surround them, such as in the poems "Three Strolls" and "3 Postpartum Exercises." Notley is unafraid to include details about laundry, the voices of strangers who join in to tell her "your baby's crying," and commentary about her clothing in relationship to losing postpartum weight.[25] There is a sense of fluidity between Notley's day, her observations, and her deeper frustrations and desires, and all are given equal importance. This passage from "Three Strolls" reflects the swirling interchange that she feels:

> and the baby stares & stares at the
> maroon cushion
> the vast space of the maroon
> soon to become more myriad
> a more
> myriad space a more myriad maroon
> he swoons at it
> I swoon at him
> who's also it.[26]

Throughout the sections of this poem, Notley narrates her day with her infant son—his observations (as she perceives them), her observations (sometimes of him perceiving her), and the intermingling of their consciousnesses. In the passage above she triangulates their interaction (of swooning) to include the maroon pillow, which joins them as an entity of equal value. The boundarylessness of her life at this stage—body continually demanded by a child, child out in a stroller available for commentary from any passerby, porousness of a new mother aware of the world now through her child's reactions to it—is reflected in this excerpt as Notley expands the poem's boundaries. "The form of the day keeps slipping away / from my control," she writes in another section, continuing, "and he wants food & play awake at / constant irregular intervals / the day now it's him now it's me again him,"[27] mirroring the sense of permeability that she shares with her child.

In a section entitled "(Cleaning the House)" within the poem "Splashes of Yellow," Notley intermingles levels of thought again, revealing a floating consciousness that won't create a hierarchy of ideas or hide the domestic:

> Here are the sandals gum clouds on soles
> Here is C.P. Snow, white
> with orange and an abbey
> Here is Edinborough green and dusky
> Here is Anselm asleep with his thumb his alcove flesh
> Here is <u>he</u> asleep bearded big idée fixe
> Here am I a blue morning integer.[28]

This thread continues within the numbered sequence "Songs for the Unborn Second Baby," in which Notley addresses herself—pregnant for a second time—as well as her unborn child and the constellation of thoughts that surround the multiple states she inhabits. She writes: "I ingeminate // I dream / of a compost / into whose composition paper / can go // and which itself / composes the paper" as a unified "I" deliberately disassembles.[29] Throughout the sections that follow, Notley's forms are very mixed: she intersperses short, vertical columns of text with longer, more expansive lines that visually echo her rumination about her expanding body, mental state, and her need to include the voice of her older child. In a series of epigrammatic statements within "Songs for the Unborn Second Baby" she addresses her in utero child and her interior self that now includes his consciousness, and then shifts to include the voice of her older child and the moments she is aware of as exterior to her thoughts.

Later in the poem she writes, "O rose-like cluster course, / state of organs which marks / the resemblant rose, / it is perfect to trust / him, to drop from your stem / comb form / in names of salts strewn / . . . / I'm mashed on you. You're my diaphanous, my / slip [. . .] / you set of rays meeting at my point / that's constantly natal."[30] This is followed by a subsection entitled "January," which draws from her older son's utterances, particularly those marked by "child-speech," with the attendant (and poetic) lack of logic and often mystical qualities these word-patterns contain. In the opening section she includes the conversation, "Mommy what's this fork doing? / What? / It's being Donald Duck. / What could I eat this? / Eat what? / This cookie. / What do you mean? / What could I eat it?"[31] Later, in another exchange, she writes, "Do you remember when you were like Edmund? / Yeah. / What did you do? / crawled with him. / Do you remember last year? / Yeah, Mommy what did you / do when you be Anselm?"[32] By integrating the children's lack of fixed selves into her poems, the space of the poem becomes shared, deliberately receptive to many voices.

Elsewhere in "January," Notley sets out a vertical column of text that includes a mix of child-logic with parental wonderment, intermingling consciousnesses in a manner that becomes characteristic of her writing:

> I walk.
> I am big.
> I can say
> what they
> say. It's
> fun to
> sound. I
> walk. I am
> big. I finally
> get the blue
> and red container
> of [. . .]
> sneezes![33]

Notley's insistence on including her children's speech, complete with nonsensical child-logic that defies linear thought, demonstrates her concept of creating a poem that includes others—revealing how the voices she hears can join with the speaker and remake the lyric from the concentrated voice of one consciousness in the "I" to a union of voices. In another section of the poem, she comments directly from a singular perspective about the sense of interchange she has with her children, and movingly reveals her own sense of blurred edges with them: "They're beautiful / Bodily they're incomprehensible. I can't tell if they're / me or not. They think I'm their facility. We're all about / as comprehensible as the crocuses. In myself I'm like a / color except not in the sense of a particular one."[34]

The poem "The Howling Saint T-Shirt" reiterates these senses of exchange and inclusiveness, and their purposefulness for her writing: "My kids are like me superficially so I watch them / or, writing, ignore them, until they say something I like / I need their words for my poems, to speak for a / house we make together that's fragile and strong / shaky in an American wind contrary to poetry."[35] Years later, in her *Grand Permission* essay, Notley reflects: "From the age of six Edmund in fact wrote his own poems, and I early on become a voice in *his* poems, since I collaborated with him on poems that appeared in *his* books."[36] This spirit of exchange and inclusion, which generates transparent integration of her family life into her poetry, ultimately fosters stronger poetic community, as both of her sons are now practicing poets, creating an even closer fusion of poetry and family within her life. Of this regeneration, she says: "Thus mothering's culminating effect on my poetics has involved the emergence of new poetry colleagues for me to interact with and to be influenced by."[37]

In "That Awkward Grace," Eric Selinger describes the general impact of Notley writing about her children. Focusing on the poem "January," Selinger emphasizes how Notley refuses to exclude her children as valid subject matter and then traces the resulting effects. The playfulness in her young children's language and speech patterns, he writes, "recalls the freedom with language that lies at the heart of her art, even as their demands for her time keep her from writing, except in jots and scraps, quick musings and diary entries of muddled, free-associative spills."[38] For Selinger, Notley stands apart from the "two most obvious models for feminist poetry in the early 1970s: the fierce, resistant mythologizing handed down from Plath; and the feminist exploration of women's 'essential connection' to each other, to their mothers, and to their children, sponsored by Rich."[39] While both Plath and Rich write about their children, their similar position is that their children are very separate from them and their poetic practices. They are subject(s), but not subjectively present. Notley's approach is markedly different in seeking to make her children not just subjects but subjective voices within her work. While some of Plath's most well-known poems are about her children, they reflect her feelings about motherhood, and her children, specifically, in brief moments. A sense of separation is always present, while Notley seeks to erase that line and integrate her relationships.

This is where Notley's work around identity and dislocation of a singular "I" swarms within her poetry—and she falls within a tradition of other women poets who acknowledge this fracturing as a result of the corporeal experiences of pregnancy, motherhood, and their interactive effects. In her essay entitled "Voice," Notley affirms again a sense of self that is enclosed within her body and also more amorphous. She writes of sensing her poetic voice being outside of her forehead ("on the right side"[40]) though it has since traveled to different locations on her body. The idea that a poetic voice floats or hovers can be linked to her perspective on identity as free-floating and unmoored, unfixed. She writes, "I think the poet's voice takes on a life of its own, but that it's from the poet; it's as if it has to get free of the pieces, the mess, of the real person and regroup as a unity. Then suddenly the poet is there not the person, not thinking anything but the poem being written, in her voice and in her style."[41] This openness, begun while concurrently launching as a poet and as a mother, becomes a central tenet that deepens as her oeuvre develops.

Writing such as Notley's, which is often considered "difficult," offers a way to experience reading differently—as a form of engagement that turns away from reading as a solitary experience and instead invites a collective experience of meaning-making. As Juliana Spahr suggests in *Everybody's Autonomy: Connective Reading and Collective Identity*:

> when we tackle literary criticism's central question of what sort of selves literary works create, we should value works that encourage connection. By "connection" here I mean works that present and engage with large, public worlds that are in turn shared with readers. I mean forms of writing that well represent and expand changing notions of the public, of everybody.[42]

Spahr's emphasis is on looking at "works that encourage communal readings."[43] I have been suggesting that Notley is also interested in offering others the experience of joining into the intention of her poem and, as an extension of her paradigm shift while writing and mothering, in co-creating meaning as a way to free the lyric from the restrictive expectation of serving a singular consciousness. By not putting the reader at a remove, Notley intends for her writing to join with the community she inhabits as she creates, whether that community is made up of her children, her household or, more broadly, those she affiliates with through her political convictions. This is the impetus for creating a more permeable space so that the "I" does not emerge from a solitary consciousness, but rather is inclusive—of her family, of others' voices both heard and imagined, and of a sometimes paradoxical mind. The reader is invited, without hierarchy, into these spaces, in order to fulfill a poetic vision that Notley situates in a more democratic or inclusive space.

Much as Notley's insistence that patriarchal and corporate environments are pervasive, horrible, and must be resisted, if not dismantled, her poetry and personal agenda are inseparable. Spahr notes that the writers she focuses on in *Everybody's Autonomy*, such as Gertrude Stein and Harryette Mullen, are often labeled "opaque," and yet these writers "engage the complicated claims around identity that come to the forefront of large social concerns in the late 1960s."[44] The entrenched sexism that Notley encountered, both within the literary world and outside of it, has fiercely goaded her own insistence on poems that include gender and class as both direct and implicit subject material. In "But He Says I Misunderstood," from *Not For Mothers Only*, Notley recounts what seems to be a fight with her then-husband Ted Berrigan in which they argue over money, power, and status within their relationship (Berrigan forgets to put "[her] name on [their] checks"). Notley writes that Berrigan is "older & successfuller & teaches,"[45] to which she responds, a few lines later, "So I got pregnant / . . . / I'm a slave, well mildly, to a baby / Though I could teach English A or / type, no bigshot (mildly) poet-in-residence like him / Get a babysitter never more write any good poems / Or, just to / Scrounge it out, leave him."[46] She concludes the poem with the lines, "All I can say is // This poem is in the Mainstream American Tradition,"[47] insisting that her poem —in which she describes her lack of status as a mother and wife, and as the less recognized poet in a marriage of professional hierarchy—deserves its place as well. It's a bold ending to a poem that reflects her insistence that she must be explicit about the gendered inequities she faces, something she lays out (literally) on the line and that her experience (of mothering)—so often discounted (not only as subject but in general value)—is worthy of the "Mainstream American Tradition." Notley is frank about money and gender equity as a wife earning less than a husband, about the realities of status within a hierarchical literary world, about her meager job prospects, and about the potential difficulties associated with leaving her marriage— subjects not regularly lauded within the "Mainstream American Tradition" of poetry, and yet she names them as subjects that belong in this tradition and insists on their legitimacy and that they not be excluded.

The Descent of Alette

Witnessing the evolution of Notley's oeuvre, book to book, is akin to try- ing to gather the ineffable. The quality of voice found within the range of content has a steadying effect that holds the reader's mind with a sense of intimacy and anchors the often free-floating subjects Notley glances upon, observes, and then might either stay to explore, or flit away from associa- tively. Critic Joel Brouwer writes that a "stream-of-consciousness style . . . both describes and dramatizes the movement of the poet's restless mind, leaping associatively from one idea or sound to the next without any irri- table reaching after reason or plot." Her goal, he suggests "is to establish or continue no tradition except one that literally can't exist—the celebration of the singular thought sung at a particular instant in a unique voice."[48] This ambition becomes evident the more one reads her work: its effects sink in on conscious and unconscious levels, accessing the subliminal, emotive, and instinctive layers far beyond the cognitive. Her writing explores a per- spective both iconoclastic and idiosyncratic, one that flees structure as soon as it is sensed yet leaves a lingering shape or imprint in the reader's mind, traced by the movement felt, rather than clearly tracked or fully revealed.[49]

The inclusive "I" and Notley's rupturing of the singular voice continues within her extensive oeuvre and is developed in a particularly important way in her book-length poem, *The Descent of Alette* (hereafter referred to as *Alette*). Originally published in 1996, *Alette* has received wide attention for both its content as well as the form that Notley invents. One of Not- ley's most innovative recastings of the poetic line is the manipulation of the quotation mark, dramatically repurposed within *Alette*. She encloses

every written phrase in the book within a set of quotation marks, with ap-
proximately four sets of quoted phrases per line, a structure she first exper-
imented with in the final poems in *Beginning with a Stain*.[50] By enclosing
every phrase within quotation marks, the poem jars visual expectations as
Notley reassigns what these punctuation marks signify. The poem assem-
bles a panoply of unspecified, dialogic voices in conversation, disrupting
readerly expectation on deeper syntactic and literal levels as well. Another
reading of this choice is that its odd effects mark diverse or divergent inten-
tions as Notley creates an innovative way to enter what has traditionally
been a masculine form—the epic tale.

A number of critics have approached *Alette* and Notley's inventive use
of the double quotation mark through a feminist lens. Susan McCabe has
suggested that *Alette* overtly combines "experimental use of epic form
along with an unabashed feminism." Notley's poem calls attention to the
"pervasively masculinist discourse" of the epic and simultaneously reimag-
ines it, having it "reflect women's particular and erased concerns and iden-
tities."[51] Notley herself has suggested that *Alette* was "an immense act of
rebellion against dominant social forces. . . . It begins in pieces and ends
whole, narrated by an I who doesn't know her name and whose name
when she finds it means appendage of a male name."[52]

Acts of rebellion and resistance can be seen throughout the poem, as
Alette comes into contact repeatedly with a *materfamilias* character who
serves as an earth mother or progenitor figure. Disturbingly headless, this
First Woman figure's "most marked quality," Notley writes, "is that she's
a storyteller: . . . she can speak from the throat, and she has the ability
to make you *be in* her stories."[53] By emphasizing the ways in which the
female figures in the text derive power both from their bodies and from
the stories they tell, Notley conflates women's sexuality and the ability to
bear life. *Alette* consistently emphasizes the mutability of the human body,
and the interdependent permeability between physical bodies that can be
taken apart, manipulated, and then inventively reconstituted. This physi-
cal shape-shifting can be understood as an extension of Notley's interplay
with others which, as I have shown, is also present in her earlier work
and signals her interest in the mutability of the human voice, rendered in
Alette through highly changeable bodies and deliberate obfuscation of a
singular voice. *Alette* also includes many pregnant figures, as well as the
mention of babies, which as I have noted above links to one of Notley's
central concerns and undergirds her conceptualizations around multiplic-
ity. Transmuting gender identity through phantasmagoric shape-shifting
also continues throughout the text with Notley's characters exploring the
permeability of form connected to bodily agency.

Characters are "entered" on multiple occasions and then reemerge or
are "reborn" in new form. In Book One, Alette notices, "I saw" "a black

flower" "growing" "from the platform" which enlarges and then she enters it, becoming one with it: "I was it, for a time" "was that black blood crushed velvet" "velvet / womb, I guessed" "womb of Hell" / "I was womb."[54] After this passage, the sense of internal telescoping continues as she writes about being inhabited by a "seed that was" "an eye" "a small eye" "a blue eye"[55] and then inside that, a pupil, and then inside that the "black flower," "again."[56] The cyclic exploration circles around until Alette is unsure of who or what she really is and states:

> "who" "would I be?" "Did it matter" "to me?" "Since really I"
> "was womb?" "blood-black" "And would always" "again"
> "become that."[57]

By inventing a new usage of quotation marks, Notley can reject the expectations that already exist for these marks (" "), a gesture that has gendered implications as well. As McCabe suggests, Notley's use of quotation marks "reflects her double position as a woman poet: she reveals how quotation usually signals citational authority, but here it ruptures the line, thus fragmenting image and narrative, unsettling epic voice and legitimacy."[58] In another feminist reading of the poem, Susan Rosenbaum suggests that Notley's resistance to naming or "un-naming within this poem" is the condition for imagining possibilities of self-hood not constrained by patriarchy."[59] For Rosenbaum, Notley's use of quotation marks "serves to defamiliarize everyday uses of language, [and] to resist the cultural weight of inherited meanings so as to open up the possibility of resignification."[60]

In the preface to *Alette*, Notley makes explicit that, for her, quotation marks function to slow down reading. She writes that they are "poetic feet," and a measure of her own invention. She also makes the point that the quotation marks are meant to distance the narrative from herself—to emphasize that she is not Alette—and that "each phrase is a thing said by a voice," reiterating that she wants to reclaim narrative for the long-form poem. Forced to notice each phrase in isolation, there is a break with expected linearity and a dislocation from ordinary syntax and punctuation that the reader must learn to "read" in order to understand this new recasting of the quotation mark. The inundation of their repetition forces each mark to be noticed and to stand out, as well. Notley writes: "If I had simply left white spaces between the phrases, the phrases would be rushed by the reader—read too fast for my musical intention. The quotation marks make the reader slow down and silently articulate—not slur over mentally —the phrases at the pace, and with the stresses, I intend."[61]

Traditionally, of course, the use of quotation marks indicates a spoken phrase. By making every word part of a quotation, Notley creates a shift to more permeable boundaries yet controls the effect of all the phrases being understood as overheard, a "thing said by a voice," as she writes in her author's note.[62] The panoply of voices intermingled through this method de-centers the authority of one voice and refuses a central narrator. There is also a sense of continuous interruption as phrases are set off by themselves, rather than constituting complete sentences, not unlike the cadence of conversation with a small child. Notley constructs a multi-vocal text in which there is no single all-knowing speaker. This has the effect of disorienting the reader, a deliberate choice on Notley's part as she works to reject centralized authority and power. The visual effect of the repetitive marks also distinguishes the text as constructed, as punctuation evades its "normal" purpose of invisibility, marking and "scoring" the printed text. The unexpected visual repetition strikes the eye and forces a rereading of the words enclosed.

The urge to read each phrase surrounded by quotation marks as divorced from an identified speaker creates a universality that opens up a range or chorus of voices that echo and defy specific identification or location. The reader is taken away from linear expectation, which mirrors the perambulations of Alette as she navigates her way through a subterranean system of challenges to conquer the "Tyrant"—a decidedly patriarchal figure at the center of the book. McCabe also sees Notley's innovative use of quotation marks as a feminist strategy: "This device scores her work as a made thing . . . part of her interruptive strategy, as if what lived between segments were as significant as what speaks within them. The marks become dismaying, halting signals for the fact that we can't hope for an intact, cohesive narrative (why would we want to?) that assures and comforts."[63] Notley's use of the quotation mark can be viewed in the context of other contemporary women poets who have reclaimed punctuation for their own inventive purposes, often to imbue their poetry with a visual marker for what cannot be said or fitted into words, such as Chelsey Minnis's use of the ellipses in *Zirconia*. Adrienne Rich's use of the double colon (::) in her later work, and particularly Alice Fulton with her "double-bride sign" used throughout her book *Sensual Math* with its (deliberately unpronounceable) poem entitled "==". For her part, Notley has said that her "experiments" with *Alette* led to other evolutions in her later writing as she thinks of the lengthier phrases joining together "like harpsichord runs which can't keep from getting faster and faster."[64]

Blank areas in the poem also serve as a productive space—one that Notley leverages through the re-inscription of emptiness as not blank, but as holding possibility. Although it is jarring to encounter a page that provides the reader with little guidance, Notley clearly signals through the use of blank space that she eschews expectation and will demand that the reader relate to the text in a way that flouts singular authority. The reader must grapple with the disruption of continuous narrative, alongside the promotion of a sense of collage. The poems appear to have been constructed from separate phrases or units of speech; the voices and phrases are patched, rather than seamlessly integrated into an ongoing conventional narrative. Beyond her early incorporation of her sons' voices and the desire to capture their interdependency, Notley masterfully demonstrates inclusion in *Alette*, a joining achieved through the deprioritization of a singular speaker, the enfolding of narratives from dreamscape and waking, and characters who can transmute physically and psychically as well.

But there is also clear evidence in *Alette* that Notley continues to be inspired by, and to conspire with, the voices of others—particularly members of her family. Plumbing the origins of *Alette*, she has written that she "discovered that [her] brother was behind the poem," and when she figured it out, "[she] went back and built him more into it. Though [she] was writing it because of him, all along, [she'd] forgotten, because the poem isn't personal, it's public. Though feminist it includes everyone."[65] In a later essay, "Thinking and Poetry," Notley reflects on her understanding of joining the "I" in a poem with a sense of community—that the usefulness of the singular has a power, even obligation, beyond a solitary function. She writes (of the book she is then writing and future books she envisions): "I have a preconception in the book I'm writing, that there is a unified self and that the pronoun 'I' is a word which should be given back to people, who need it, but deepened."[66] Notley cites her realization that the epic could represent others' voices beyond those who are involved as an impetus for writing *Alette*. She comments, "Suddenly I, and more than myself, my sister-in-law and my mother, were being used, mangled, by the forces which produce epic, and we had no say in the matter, never had, and worse had no story ourselves. We hadn't acted. We hadn't gone to war. . . . We got to suffer, but without a trajectory."[67] Hence, she decides on using "singing, dialogic, quarreling voices"[68] to represent the presence of others' voices and stories within the epic she constructs.

In her earlier work (written during the 1970s and '80s), Notley herself has said she "used peoples' voices verbatim, from the room and also from the street and from the media," in poems that contained many voices. At the time, she thought she was being "practical about writing in a crowded apartment" but has come to see that she "created a unified work, out of various peoples' voices and words, which reflected [her] individual self and situation."[69] This beginning, of writing through amalgamation or a harmonizing of disparate voices, propels Notley toward a poetics of gathering and of inclusion. In *Culture of One*, a more recent work, this idea still resonates as fugues of interchange play throughout the book with the presence of a few central characters. The poem "A Tale of Mercy" opens with the line "I told you she is I, though I myself call on her."[70] Her prescient questioning continues, "I'd touch anyone to give them relief. If I can. But my definition / is that I can. . . . I am a unique culture of one, from everywhere. / I am her map and her self. I am everyone in the story; I / am the story."[71] The intermingling of selves and plurality of bodily occupation perseveres for Notley and, as her work develops, deepens into a more lateral or even formless level of connection through which to establish community.

Notley's persistence and insistence on fully realizing her political and poetic vision has been recognized by many critics. In "Alice Notley's Disobedient Cities," Zoe Skoulding remarks that Notley has described "one of her goals as a poet as being to take up as much literary space as any male poet."[72] It is fair to say that Notley has done this—through her prolific (and ongoing) output, the recognition she's garnered from the academy (however ambivalently received on her part), and even more so in forging a poetic tradition in which her voice, and the voices she chooses to include, will not be denied. In a 2013 interview in the *Boston Review*, Notley comments on several manuscripts in progress that have yet to be published. She comes back, full circle, to where she started in terms of hearing others' voices, and knowing that she can, and in fact must, admit them into her work. "The ghouls let me speak for them because only I will,"[73] she says. "I'm at the mercy of my poetic voice and of their voices. No choice in the matter. . . . I'm trying to speak for everyone."[74] "To speak for everyone," her interviewer suggests. "Speak for everyone," Notley reiterates. "Yes. I make myself available."[75] While Notley's work tracks the vastness of her mind, her ongoing writing reveals a commitment to move boundaries—to join with others through her writing—to mingle subjectivities within the space on the page in order to expand the solitude of the traditional speaker and create a more democratic shift, a move that is a hallmark of her poetic oeuvre and vision.

NOTES

1. Alice Notley. *Culture of One* (New York: Penguin Group, 2011), 3.
2. Ibid.
3. Alice Notley, "The Poetics of Disobedience," Poetry Foundation website, accessed June 20, 2012; www.poetryfoundation.org/learning/essay/238698.
4. Alice Notley, "Doublings," in *The Grand Permission: New Writings on Poetics and Motherhood*, ed. Patricia Dienstfrey and Brenda Hillman (Middletown, CT: Wesleyan University Press, 2003), 137.
5. Ibid., 138.
6. Maureen Owen, "When as a Girl on the Plains of Minnesota," in Dienstfrey and Hillman, eds., *The Grand Permission*, 11.
7. Ibid., 16.
8. Mary Margaret Sloan, "Elaborations of Between: The Interpolation of a Child into a Writer's Poetics," in Dienstfrey and Hillman, eds., *The Grand Permission*, 95.

9. Ibid., 94.

10. Susan Griffin, "And the Motherhood of Poetics," in Dienstfrey and Hillman, eds., *The Grand Permission*, 87.

11. Carolyn Forché, "Emergence," in Dienstfrey and Hillman, eds., *The Grand Permission*, 64.

12. Ibid., 62.

13. Gillian Conoley, "Language and the Gaze of the Other: A Poetics of Birth," in Dienstfrey and Hillman, eds., *The Grand Permission*, 205.

14. Ibid., 206.

15. Ibid.

16. Ibid., 137.

17. Ibid.

18. Sophie Erskine, "Unique and Splendid, Compressed and Layered, Sonic and Cognitive: Alice Notley," accessed June 26, 2012; www.3ammagazine.com/3am /unique-and-splendid-compressed-and-layered-sonic-and-cognitive-an-interview -with-alice-notley/.

19. Notley, "Doublings," 138.

20. Ibid.

21. Ibid., 140.

22. Ibid., 141.

23. Alice Notley, *Grave of Light: New and Selected Poems 1970–2005* (Middletown, CT: Wesleyan University Press, 2006), 8.

24. Ibid.

25. Alice Notley, "Three Strolls," in *Not for Mothers Only: Contemporary Poems on Child-Getting and Child-Rearing*, ed. Catherine Wagner and Rebecca Wolff (Albany: Fence Books, 2007), 86.

26. Ibid., 89.

27. Ibid., 87.

28. Ibid., 93.

29. Ibid., 98.

30. Ibid., 102–3.

31. Ibid., 103.

32. Ibid., 105.

33. Ibid., 107.

34. Ibid., 105.

35. Ibid., 114.

36. Notley, "Doublings," 142.

37. Ibid.

38. Eric Murphy Selinger, "That Awkward Grace," *Parnassus: Poetry in Review* 21.1–2 (1996): 311.

39. Ibid., 313.

40. Alice Notley, *Coming After: Essays on Poetry* (Ann Arbor: The University of Michigan Press, 2005), 155.

41. Ibid.

42. Juliana Spahr, *Everybody's Autonomy: Connective Reading and Collective Identity* (Tuscaloosa: The University of Alabama Press, 2001), 4–5.

43. Ibid., 5.

44. Ibid., 6.

45. Notley, *Not For Mothers Only*, 97.

46. Ibid., 98.

47. Ibid.

48. Joel Brouwer, "A State of Disobedience," *New York Times*, October 14, 2007, accessed March 15, 2012; www.nytimes.com/2007/10/14/books/review /Brouwer-t.html.

49. Ibid.

50. Notley, *Coming After*, 137.

51. Susan McCabe, "Alice Notley's Experimental Epic: 'An Ecstasy of Finding Another Way of Being,'" in *We Who Love to Be Astonished: Experimental Women's Writing and Performance Poetics*, ed. Laura Hinton and Cynthia Hogue (Tuscaloosa: University of Alabama Press, 2002), 41.

52. Notley, "The Poetics of Disobedience."

53. Notley, *Coming After*, 177.

54. Alice Notley, *The Descent of Alette* (New York: Penguin Books, 1992), 29.

55. Notley, *Alette*, 29.

56. Ibid.

57. Ibid.

58. McCabe, "Alice Notley's Experimental Epic," 41.

59. Susan Rosenbaum, "Anonymous Outside the Museum: The Poetry of Mina Loy and Alice Notley," *How2* 1.3 (February 2000), accessed June 20, 2012; www .asu.edu/pipercwcenter/how2journal/archive/online_archive/v1_3_2000/current/ readings/rosenbaum.html#8.

60. Ibid.

61. Notley, preface to *Alette*, i.

62. Ibid.

63. McCabe, "Alice Notley's Experimental Epic," 51.

64. Notley, *Coming After*, 137. In some later poems, Notley again uses ellipses to notate or mark phrases, indicating separation beyond just the white spaces between words.

65. Ibid., 178.

66. Ibid., 164.

67. Ibid., 172.

68. Ibid., 173.

69. Ibid., 148.

70. Notley, *Culture of One*, 35.

71. Ibid.

72. Quoted in Zoe Skoulding, "Alice Notley's Disobedient Cities," *Feminist Review* 96 (2010): 90.

73. Lindsay Turner, "'At the Mercy of My Poetic Voice': An Interview with Alice Notley," *Boston Review*, November 12, 2013, accessed September 12, 2014; boston review.net/poetry/lindsay-turner-alice-notley-interview-feminism-mojave-collage.

74. Ibid.

75. Ibid.

BIBLIOGRAPHY

Works by Alice Notley

POETRY

165 Meeting House Lane. New York: 'C' Press, 1972.
Incidentals in the Day World. New York: Angel Hair, 1973.
Phoebe Light. Bolinas: Big Sky, 1973.
For Frank O'Hara's Birthday. Cambridge, England: Street Editions, 1976.
Alice Ordered Me To Be Made. Chicago: The Yellow Press, 1976.
A Diamond Necklace. New York: Frontward Books, 1977.
Songs For the Unborn Second Baby. Lenox, MA: United Artists, 1979.
When I Was Alive. New York: Vehicle Editions, 1980.
Waltzing Matilda. New York: Kulchur Press, 1981; reissued Cambridge, MA:
    Faux Press, 2003.
How Spring Comes. West Branch, Iowa: Toothpaste Press, 1981.
Sorrento. Los Angeles: Sherwood Press, 1984.
Margaret & Dusty. St. Paul: Coffee House, 1985.
Parts of a Wedding. New York: Unimproved Editions Press, 1986.
At Night the States. Chicago: Yellow Press, 1988.
From A Work In Progress. New York: DIA Chapbook Series, 1989.
Homer's Art. Canton, New York: The Institute of Further Studies, 1990.
The Scarlet Cabinet, with Douglas Oliver. New York: Scarlet Editions, 1992.
Selected Poems of Alice Notley. Hoboken: Talisman House, 1993.
To Say You. Riverdale: Pyramid Atlantic, 1994.
Close to me & Closer . . . (The Language of Heaven). Oakland: O Books, 1995.
Désamère. Oakland: O Books, 1995.
The Descent of Alette. New York: Penguin, 1996.
Etruscan Reader VII, with Wendy Mulford and Brian Coffey. Newcastle under
    Lyme: Etruscan Books, 1997.
Byzantine Parables. Cambridge, England: Poetical Histories No. 45, 1998.
Mysteries of Small Houses. New York: Penguin, 1998.
Disobedience. New York: Penguin, 2001.
From the Beginning. Woodacre, CA: The Owl Press, 2004.
Grave of Light: New and Selected Poems 1970–2005. Middletown, CT: Wesleyan
    University Press, 2006.
Alma, or The Dead Women. New York: Granary Books, 2006.
City of. Minneapolis: Rain Taxi, 2006.
In the Pines. New York: Penguin, 2007.
Reason and Other Women. Tucson: Chax Press, 2010.
Songs and Stories of the Ghouls. Middletown, CT: Wesleyan University Press,
    2011.
Culture of One. New York: Penguin, 2011.
Manhattan Luck. Oakland: Hearts Desire Press, 2014.
Negativity's Kiss. Rouen: Presses Universitaires de Rouen, 2014.
Certain Magical Acts. New York: Penguin, 2016.

SELECTED PROSE

Dr. Williams' Heiresses. Berkeley: Tuumba Books, 1980.

Tell Me Again. Santa Barbara: Instant Editions, 1981.

"Doublings." In *The Grand Permission: New Writings on Poetics and Motherhood*, Patricia Dienstfrey and Brenda Hillman, eds., Middletown, CT: Wesleyan University Press, 2003.

Coming After: Essays on Poets and Poetry. Ann Arbor: University of Michigan Press, 2005.

SELECTED INTERVIEWS

Baker, David. "Alice Notley." Kenyon Review On-Line (October 2009); www .kenyonreview.org/conversation/alice-notley/.

Dewhurst, Robert. "Alice Notley." *Bomb* 133 (Fall 2015); bombmagazine.org /article/4331827/alice-notley.

Dick, Jennifer. "Alice Notley Interviewed by Jennifer Dick." *Doublechange* 3; www.doublechange.com/issue3/notleyint-eng.htm.

Gzemski, Sarah. "Dreaming This World Into Existence: An Interview With Alice Notley." *1508 Blog*, University of Arizon Poetry Center (November 2016); poetry.arizona.edu/blog/dreaming-world-existence-interview-alice-notley.

Keelan, Claudia, and Alice Notley "A Conversation: September 2002–December 2003." *The American Poetry Review* 33.3 (May/June 2004): 15–19.

Olidort, Shoshana. "Between the Living and the Dead: An Interview with Alice Notley." *Los Angeles Review of Books* (December 2016); lareviewofbooks .org/article/between-the-living-and-the-dead-an-interview-with-alice-notley/.

Rogers, Damian. "Interview with Alice Notley: Part One." January 28, 2010; damianrogers.wordpress.com/2010/01/28/interview-with-alice-notley-part -one/.

———. "Interview with Alice Notley: Part Two." February 23, 2010; damian-rogers.wordpress.com/2010/02/23/interview-with-alice-notley-part-two/.

Shamma, Yasmine. "Alice Notley in Conversation with Yasmine Shamma: Paris, 18 March 2009." *Jacket 40* (2010); jacketmagazine.com/40/iv-notley-ivb -shamma-2009.shtml.

Stefans, Brian Kim. "Brian Kim Stefans Interviews Alice Notley." *Jacket Magazine*, July 15 and 16, 2001; jacketmagazine.com/15/stef-iv-not.html.

Turner, Lindsay. "At the Mercy of My Poetic Voice," *Boston Review* (November 2013); bostonreview.net/poetry/lindsay-turner-alice-notley-interview-feminism -mojave-collage.

Selected Criticism and Reviews

Birkbeck Contemporary Poetics Research Centre. "Constellation: Alice Notley." Website; www.bbk.ac.uk/cprcevents/alicenotley.html.

Brouwer, Joel. "A State of Disobedience." *New York Times*, October 14, 2007; www.nytimes.com/2007/10/14/books/review/Brouwer-t.html.

Dubois, Page. "'An Especially Peculiar Undertaking': Alice Notley's Epic Differences." *A Journal of Feminist Cultural Studies* 12.2 (Summer 2001): 86–97.

Dunagan, Patrick James. "Culture of One." Review of *Culture of One*, by Alice

Notley. *Switchback* 13 (Spring 2011); www.swback.com/issues/013/review
-iculture-onei-alice-notley.html.

Erskine, Sophie. "Unique and Splendid, Compressed and Layered, Sonic and
Cognitive: Alice Notley." *3AM Magazine* (February 19, 2009): www.3am-
magazine.com/3am/unique-and-splendid-compressed-and-layered-sonic-and
-cognitive-an-interview-with-alice-notley/

Kossinets, Gueorgi, and Duncan J. Watts. "Origins of Homophily in an Evolving
Social Network." *American Journal of Sociology* 115 (2009): 405–50.

McCabe, Susan. "Alice Notley's Experimental Epic: 'An Ecstasy of Finding
Another Way of Being.'" In *We Who Love to Be Astonished: Experimental
Women's Writing and Performance Poetics*, ed. Laura Hinton and Cynthia
Hogue (Tuscaloosa: The University of Alabama Press, 2002), 41–53.

McSweeney, Joelle. "Byzantine Mind." Review of *Reason and Other Women*, by
Alice Notley. *American Book Review* 31.6 (September/October 2010): 19–20.

Ponsot, Marie. "Her Field Is Her Consciousness." *The Nation*, April 7, 2008;
www.thenation.com/article/her-field-her-consciousness.

Rosenbaum, Susan. "Anonymous Outside the Museum: The Poetry of Mina Loy
and Alice Notley." *How2* 1.3 (February 2000); www.asu.edu/pipercwcenter
/how2journal/archive/online_archive/v1_3_2000/current/readings/rosenbaum
.html#8

Selinger, Eric Murphy. "That Awkward Grace." *Parnassus: Poetry in Review*
21.1–2 (1996): 298.

Sikelianos, Eleni. "On Alice Notley." In *Women Poets on Mentorship: Efforts &
Affections*, ed. Arielle Greenberg and Rachel Zucker (Iowa City: University of
Iowa Press, 2008).

Skoulding, Zoe. "Alice Notley's Disobedient Cities." *Feminist Review* 96 (2010):
90.

Stefans, Brian Kim. "Notes from the Underground." Review of *Disobedience*, by
Alice Notley. *Boston Review* (December 2002–January 2003); bostonreview
.net/BR27.6/stefans.html.

CLAUDIA RANKINE

POEMS

FROM *Citizen*

The new therapist specializes in trauma counseling. You have only ever spoken on the phone. Her house has a side gate that leads to a back entrance she uses for patients. You walk down a path bordered on both sides with deer grass and rosemary to the gate, which turns out to be locked.

At the front door the bell is a small round disc that you press firmly. When the door finally opens, the woman standing there yells, at the top of her lungs, Get away from my house! What are you doing in my yard?

It's as if a wounded Doberman pinscher or a German shepherd has gained the power of speech. And though you back up a few steps, you manage to tell her you have an appointment. You have an appointment? she spits back. Then she pauses. Everything pauses. Oh, she says, followed by, oh, yes, that's right. I am sorry.

I am so sorry, so, so sorry.

•

Not long ago you are in a room where someone asks the philosopher Judith Butler what makes language hurtful. You can feel everyone lean in. Our very being exposes us to the address of another, she answers. We suffer from the condition of being addressable. Our emotional openness, she adds, is carried by our addressability. Language navigates this.

For so long you thought the ambition of racist language was to denigrate and erase you as a person. After considering Butler's remarks, you begin to understand yourself as rendered hypervisible in the face of such language acts. Language that feels hurtful is intended to exploit all the ways that you are present. Your alertness, your openness, and your desire to engage actually demand your presence, your looking up, your talking back, and, as insane as it is, saying please.

•

To live through the days sometimes you moan like deer. Sometimes you sigh. The world says stop that. Another sigh. Another stop that. Moaning elicits laughter, sighing upsets. Perhaps each sigh is drawn into existence to pull in, pull under, who knows; truth be told, you could no more control those sighs than that which brings the sighs about.

•

The sigh is the pathway to breath; it allows breathing. That's just self-preservation. No one fabricates that. You sit down, you sigh. You stand up, you sigh. The sighing is a worrying exhale of an ache. You wouldn't call it an illness; still it is not the iteration of a free being. What else to liken yourself to but an animal, the ruminant kind?

•

You like to think memory goes far back though remembering was never recommended. Forget all that, the world says. The world's had a lot of practice. No one should adhere to the facts that contribute to narrative, the facts that create lives. To your mind, feelings are what create a person, something unwilling, something wild vandalizing whatever the skull holds. Those sensations form a someone. The headaches begin then. Don't wear sunglasses in the house, the world says, though they soothe, soothe sight, soothe you.

•

The head's ache evaporates into a state of numbness, a cave of sighs. Over the years you lose the melodrama of seeing yourself as a patient. The sighing ceases; the headaches remain. You hold your head in your hands. You sit still. Rarely do you lie down. You ask yourself, how can I help you? A glass of water? Sunglasses? The enteric-coated tablets live in your purse next to your license. The sole action is to turn on tennis matches without the sound. Yes, and though watching tennis isn't a cure for feeling, it is a clean displacement of effort, will, and disappointment.

•

The world is wrong. You can't put the past behind you. It's buried in you; it's turned your flesh into its own cupboard. Not everything remembered is useful but it all comes from the world to be stored in you. Who did what to whom on which day? Who said that? She said what? What did he just do? Did she really just say that? He said what? What did she do? Did I hear what I think I heard? Did that just come out of my mouth, his mouth, your mouth? Do you remember when you sighed?

●

Memory is a tough place. You were there. If this is not the truth, it is also not a lie. There are benefits to being without nostalgia. Certainly nostalgia and being without nostalgia relieve the past. Sitting here, there are no memories to remember, just the ball going back and forth. Shored up by this external net, the problem is not one of a lack of memories; the problem is simply a lack, a lack before, during, and after. The chin and your cheek fit into the palm of your hand. Feeling better? The ball isn't being returned. Someone is approaching the umpire. Someone is upset now.

●

You fumble around for the remote to cancel mute. The player says something and the formerly professional umpire looks down from her high chair as if regarding an unreasonable child, a small animal. The commentator wonders if the player will be able to put this incident aside. No one can get behind the feeling that caused a pause in the match, not even the player trying to put her feelings behind her, dumping ball after ball into the net. Though you can retire with an injury, you can't walk away because you feel bad.

•

Feel good. Feel better. Move forward. Let it go. Come on. Come on. Come on. In due time the ball is going back and forth over the net. Now the sound can be turned back down. Your fingers cover your eyes, press them deep into their sockets—too much commotion, too much for a head remembering to ache. Move on. Let it go. Come on.

•

Words work as release—well-oiled doors opening and closing between intention, gesture. A pulse in a neck, the shiftiness of the hands, an unconscious blink, the conversations you have with your eyes translate everything and nothing. What will be needed, what goes unfelt, unsaid—what has been duplicated, redacted here, redacted there, altered to hide or disguise—words encoding the bodies they cover. And despite everything the body remains.

Occasionally it is interesting to think about the outburst if you would just cry out—

To know what you'll sound like is worth noting—

•

In the darkened moment a body given blue light, a flashlight, enters with levity, with or without assumptions, doubts, with desire, the beating heart, disappointment, with desires—

Stand where you are.

You begin to move around in search of the steps it will take before you are thrown back into your own body, back into your own need to be found.

The destination is illusory. You raise your lids. No one else is seeking.

You exhaust yourself looking into the blue light. All day blue burrows the atmosphere. What doesn't belong with you won't be seen.

You could build a world out of need or you could hold everything black and see. You give back the lack.

You hold everything black. You give yourself back until nothing's left but the dissolving blues of metaphor.

•

Sometimes "I" is supposed to hold what is not there until it is. Then what is comes apart the closer you are to it.

This makes the first person a symbol for something.

The pronoun barely holding the person together.

Someone claimed we should use our skin as wallpaper knowing we couldn't win.

You said "I" has so much power; it's insane.

And you would look past me, all gloved up, in a big coat, with fancy fur around the collar, and record a self saying, you should be scared, the first person can't pull you together.

Shit, you are reading minds, but did you try?

Tried rhyme, tried truth, tried epistolary untruth, tried and tried.

You really did. Everyone understood you to be suffering and still everyone thought you thought you were the sun—never mind our unlikeness, you too have heard the noise in your voice.

Anyway, sit down. Sit here alongside.

•

Exactly why we survive and can look back with furrowed brow is beyond me.

It is not something to know.

Your ill-spirited, cooked, hell on Main Street, nobody's here, broken-down, first person could be one of many definitions of being to pass on.

The past is a life sentence, a blunt instrument aimed at tomorrow.

Drag that first person out of the social death of history, then we're kin.

Kin calling out the past like a foreigner with a newly minted "fuck you."

Maybe you don't agree.

Maybe you don't think so.

Maybe you are right, you don't really have anything to confess.

Why are you standing?

•

Listen, you, I was creating a life study of a monumental first person, a Brahmin first person.

If you need to feel that way—still you are in here and here is nowhere.

Join me down here in nowhere.

Don't lean against the wallpaper; sit down and pull together.

Yours is a strange dream, a strange reverie.

No, it's a strange beach; each body is a strange beach, and if you let in the excess emotion you will recall the Atlantic Ocean breaking on our heads.

•

Script for Public Fiction at Hammer Museum

On the train the woman standing makes you understand there are no seats available. And, in fact, there is one. Is the woman getting off at the next stop? No, she would rather stand all the way to Union Station.

The space next to the man is the pause in a conversation you are suddenly rushing to fill. You step quickly over the woman's fear, a fear she shares. You let her have it.

The man doesn't acknowledge you as you sit down because the man knows more about the unoccupied seat than you do. For him, you imagine, it is more like breath than wonder; he has had to think about it so much you wouldn't call it thought.

When another passenger leaves his seat and the standing woman sits, you glance over at the man. He is gazing out the window into what looks like darkness.

You sit next to the man on the train, bus, in the plane, waiting room, anywhere he could be forsaken. You put your body there in proximity to, adjacent to, alongside, within.

You don't speak unless you are spoken to and your body speaks to the space you fill and you keep trying to fill it except the space belongs to the body of the man next to you, not to you.

Where he goes the space follows him. If the man left his seat before Union Station you would simply be a person in a seat on the train. You would cease to struggle against the unoccupied seat when where why the space won't lose its meaning.

You imagine if the man spoke to you he would say, it's okay, I'm okay, you don't need to sit here. You don't need to sit and you sit and look past him into the darkness the train is moving through. A tunnel.

All the while the darkness allows you to look at him. Does he feel you looking at him? You suspect so. What does suspicion mean? What does suspicion do?

The soft gray-green of your cotton coat touches the sleeve of him. You are shoulder to shoulder though standing you could feel shadowed. You sit to repair whom who? You erase that thought. And it might be too late for that.

It might forever be too late or too early. The train moves too fast for your eyes to adjust to anything beyond the man, the window, the tiled tunnel, its slick darkness. Occasionally, a white light flickers by like a displaced sound.

From across the aisle tracks room harbor world a woman asks a man in the rows ahead if he would mind switching seats. She wishes to sit with her daughter or son. You hear but you don't hear. You can't see.

It's then the man next to you turns to you. And as if from inside your own head you agree that if anyone asks you to move, you'll tell them we are traveling as a family.

•

In Memory of Jordan Russell Davis
In Memory of Eric Garner
In Memory of John Crawford
In Memory of Michael Brown
In Memory of Laquan McDonald
In Memory of Akai Gurley
In Memory of Tamir Rice
In Memory of Walter Scott
In Memory of Freddie Gray
In Memory of Sharonda Coleman-Singleton
In Memory of Cynthia Hurd
In Memory of Susie Jackson
In Memory of Ethel Lee Lance
In Memory of DePayne Middleton Doctor
In Memory of Clementa Pinckney
In Memory of Tywanza Sanders
In Memory of Daniel L. Simmons, Sr.
In Memory of Myra Thompson
In Memory of Sandra Bland
In Memory of Jamar Clark
In Memory of Alton Sterling
In Memory of Philando Castile
In Memory
In Memory
In Memory
In Memory
In Memory
In Memory
In Memory

because white men can't
police their imagination
black people are dying

POETICS STATEMENT

Lately, when I think about this question of genre (which, in my under-
standing, is a literary category characterized by a particular style, form,
and content), my mind immediately turns to the essay, "Tradition and the
Individual Talent" by T. S. Eliot, and to the book, *Signifying Monkey: A
Theory of Afro-American Literary Criticism*, by Henry Louis Gates Jr.
Both works, in different ways, argue for a text's inevitable communion/
community with other texts.

For Eliot, there exists an historical connection, a consciousness of the past,
that the contemporary text cannot escape. He writes: "no poet, no artist of
any art, has his complete meaning alone" — a history of allusions informs
and brings meaning to any language use.

For Gates, the black text is double-voiced. It talks to other texts. A quick
example of this is the relationship among Richard Wright's *Black Boy* and
Native Son, James Baldwin's *Notes of a Native Son*, and Ralph Ellison's
Invisible Man. Another example Gates offers is "Favorite Things" from
The Sound of Music (as sung by Julie Andrews) alongside John Coltrane's
instrumental rendition of the song. There is a self-conscious engagement
with what came before, often with the intent to revise and shift a percep-
tion the earlier text asserted.

Both Eliot and Gates agree that artists come to the table with knowledge
and expectations and the work enters into an intertextual conversation
with their own literary history. In both theories the artist's communication
and communion with other texts happens on the level of style, form, and
content. Sometimes, however, form is disrupted so radically that we feel
genre as a ruptured category.

This rupture happens when the text engages with texts outside of its partic-
ular genre. I would argue that it is here that certainty and authority break
down, and in the words of the literary theorist and cultural critic Gayatri
Spivak, "habitual forms of imagination have to be retrained." Then we can
no longer over-identify with a particular form and its particular history.
The conversations still exist but they exist in areas not so easily catego-
rized or contained. The text that extends its conversation across genres
both embraces and resists the history of its genre in order to accommodate
its marriage to another way of seeing. Its conversations must be constantly
renegotiated between distinct sets of expectations, both in terms of form
and content.

Muriel Rukeyser, in her poem "The Book of the Dead," includes twenty sections of testimony from Washington hearings, stock market reports, x-ray analysis, and letters. Regarding her formal break with lyric conventions, Rukeyser writes: "I think very strongly that this is the material of poetry for us now, that it is our business to extend the document." The activity of extending the document beyond the limit of its genre contains, in my view, contaminated fields of possibility (contaminated because the habits of that genre are disrupted and generative because the perceived sense of unity contained in the habits of that genre are disrupted). Reading, as defined by Juliana Spahr (in her "connective poetics"), becomes "a negotiation rather than a conquering, an exchanging rather than a fixing," when one is willing to navigate the broken form.

I have always tried to keep in mind Barthes' notion of the text as plural in my own writing. The idea that speech acts have double destinations, and that words are alive in their proximity to other words and images, makes working across genres generative for me as an artist.

THE ATLANTIC OCEAN BREAKING ON OUR HEADS

Claudia Rankine and the Whiteness of the Lyric Subject

Kamran Javadizadeh

At its midpoint, Claudia Rankine's *Citizen: An American Lyric* (2014) asks us to recall the violence of the Middle Passage. Rankine's words cast the poem's lyric subject as an unspecified second person: "if you let in the excess emotion," she writes, "you will recall the Atlantic Ocean breaking on our heads."[1] This image—of the oceanic violence of the Atlantic slave trade—returns in *Citizen*'s final pages, which reproduce the seascape in J.M.W. Turner's painting *The Slave Ship* (1840) and then zoom in on a detail from the painting's foreground: the shackled limb of an enslaved person, breaking the surface of the water, a human body preyed upon by fish and fowl. This, then, is an image of "the Atlantic Ocean breaking on our heads"; this is what Rankine's poem, at its midpoint, asks us to recall.

But another echo can be heard here, too, one whose connection to the book's ostensible topic—racism's role in the circulation of self in contemporary public life—seems less obvious: lines from one of twentieth-century poetry's most intimate scenes.[2] Rankine's phrase, "the Atlantic Ocean breaking on our heads," directly alludes to the conclusion of "Man and Wife," a poem in Robert Lowell's *Life Studies* (1959), in which Lowell addresses his wife, Elizabeth Hardwick, in bed: "your old-fashioned tirade— / loving, rapid, merciless— / breaks like the Atlantic Ocean on my head."[3] What is Lowell's phrase—and the scene of marital disharmony it figures as oceanic collapse—doing in the middle of Rankine's book? Why should Lowell's lines about a private argument have given Rankine the language she adapted to describe the injuries of the Middle Passage? The answers to these questions yield insight not only into Rankine's reconfiguration of Lowell's poetics but also into the theoretical underpinnings and racialized formations of the poetic traditions—call them confessional and experimental—whose reconciliation she has, for some time, sought.

Rankine has been open about the challenge that she has set herself in fashioning this reconciliation. In a recent interview, she invites us to think about her project as the consequence of the literary historical contingencies of her education: "You have to remember that I was in graduate school during the Language poetry movement, but that I also came out of an orientation that was based on autobiography, so these two modes started to come into conversation during that period."[4] Rankine goes on to cite Louise Glück's influence on her while she was an undergraduate, suggesting that, through Glück, she inherited an autobiographical model whose immediate source was the confessional poetry of Lowell and John Berryman.[5] For Rankine, Lowell especially has seemed representative not only of confessional poetics but also of a (mostly white, mostly male) post-Romantic lyric tradition for which confessionalism has long seemed the denouement; *Life Studies*, in particular, serves as one important site through which Rankine navigates her relationship to the long history of the expressive lyric.[6] But the premises that authorized the apparent ease of Lowell's autobiographical turn—"Yet why not say what happened?" he had asked —seemed suddenly shakier, for Rankine, when she began to read Charles Bernstein, Lyn Hejinian, and the Language movement's modernist poet of choice, Gertrude Stein.[7] Harder, after all, to "say what happened" when the sovereignty of the subject (the *whom* that "what happened" had happened *to*) had been called into question, when the poet's self was thought of not as an internally coherent reservoir of Wordsworthian memory but instead as a linguistically—and therefore, in Rankine's view, socially and politically—contingent and shifting site.

Moreover, for Rankine, experimental poetry offered an aesthetic intervention that resonated with something her experience of being black in

America had required: "As a black person, it's difficult *not* to understand that you are part of a larger political and social dynamic, but those writers made me pay closer attention to the materiality of the language itself."[8] Described in these terms, what experimental poetics had diagnosed as the naivete of the post-Romantic lyric begins to sound like a literary form of white innocence.[9] In the last decade, Virginia Jackson and others working in the field of historical poetics have used the term "lyricization" to describe the process by which a century and a half of reading practices collapsed the various genres of *poetry* into an anachronistically narrow conception of *lyric*. Jackson describes that process—and its product—this way: "the progressive idealization of what was a much livelier, more explicitly mediated, historically contingent and public context for many varieties of poetry had culminated by the middle of the twentieth century . . . in an idea of the lyric as temporally self-present or unmediated."[10] Race has not, so far, been a central preoccupation of "the new lyric studies," but Jackson's account of the historical consolidation of a normative lyric as "temporally self-present or unmediated" resonates with whiteness's implicit claims to universality and unmediated identity, where to be white in America is to be, apparently, without race and without a role in the erasure of whiteness's racialized others.[11] To make visible the historical formation of the confessional subject is, then, to add a chapter to the violent history of whiteness itself.

When Jackson dates the high-water mark of lyricization as "the middle of the twentieth century," she has in mind the broad dissemination of the New Criticism, which gave institutional harbor to the idea of a context-less lyric. Particularly as it was developed out of a reading of T. S. Eliot's early essays by the Southern Agrarians, the New Critical emphasis on formalist reading practices might also seem like a rearguard action in the shoring up of whiteness.[12] That is the position taken up by Jericho Brown, whose contribution to *The Racial Imaginary* (2016)—a volume edited by Rankine, Beth Loffreda, and Max King Cap—offers a series of letters to writers past and present. Here Brown writes to the author of *The Well Wrought Urn*:

> Dear Cleanth,
>   I'm sorry, but seeing the poem as artifact without seeing the history and culture embedded in the poet suggests we read without any history at all. This may be a convenient way of reading for those who have a history they can't face.[13]

In Brown's reading of Brooks, whiteness is the (unspoken) name both for a history that can't be faced and for the privilege that enables its effacement. In their introduction to this same volume, Rankine and Loffreda write:

> White writers often begin from a place where transcendence is a given—one already has access to all, one already is permitted to inhabit all, to address

all . . . For writers of color, transcendence can feel like a distant and elusive thing, because writers of color often begin from the place of being addressed, and accessed.[14]

Once the idea of a transcendent lyric subject—the end result of a century and a half of lyricization—has been exposed as a form of white innocence, how can a poet retain the intimacy allowed by the lyric tradition without replicating its pernicious political effects? Why even try?

Those questions have been urgent for Rankine because, despite the skepticism she has maintained about the lyric, she has nevertheless remained invested in its capacity for the staging of interiority. As Rankine puts it, in the same interview quoted above: "How do you keep the intimacy of the language that is afforded the first person in the meditative, introspective lyric, and yet make it democratic and aware of its political investments?"[15] How, in other words, can poetry continue to offer the opportunities for mutual recognition once thought of as lyric's purview after the very idea of the lyric has been revealed as theoretically naïve, even politically suspect? The briefest consideration of the alpha and omega in the arc of the titles Rankine has so far chosen for her five volumes of poetry suggests that she has long been wrestling with this very question. Her first book, *Nothing in Nature is Private* (1994), makes a titular declaration that both gestures towards the familiar terrain of lyric intimacy and insists upon its permeation by the political, while her most recent, *Citizen: An American Lyric*—which shares a subtitle with the book that precedes it, *Don't Let Me Be Lonely* (2004)—announces the paradoxical achievement of a project at once public (American) and private (lyric).

Though they are both "Atlantic," the oceans that break on the heads of the lyric subjects in *Life Studies* and *Citizen* carry starkly different freight. Rankine's recasting of Lowell's lines reveals something in them that had been hidden in plain sight: what underwrites the autobiography of confessional poetry is its construction of whiteness, an identity that assumes its universality even as it anxiously apprehends its sovereignty to be under threat (whether from madness, familial dysfunction, a shifting racial order, or some combination of all three). Confessional poetics reifies the white subject whose identity it began by assuming. In attending to the racialized formation of the lyric tradition for which Lowell has seemed representative, Rankine inhabits a mode of writing that feels both intimate (which is to say, born of and habitable by particular experiences of subjectivity) and yet also alert to the historical formations that impinge upon and undergird such feelings. She does so by rerouting the Lowellian investment in the singular self, discovered in established lines of American genealogy, into a sustained and historicizing attention paid to dispersed and ad hoc networks of kinship. Rankine's Atlantic carries the weight of what Lowell's had worked to erase, a living knowledge of what Saidiya Hartman has called "the afterlife of slavery."[16] The lyric subject discovered in the wake of Rankine's breaking Atlantic remains open to the knowledge that those waters bear.

The Congo in the Heart of Boston

I want first to give an account of what Rankine has seen in the confessional model; my aim is to show how Rankine allows us to reimagine Lowell's paradigmatic example, a reimagining that has played an important role in the formation of Rankine's own lyric subject. Asked to address her approach in *Citizen*, she began by naming what has been, so far, an unremarked-upon source: "Lowell's *Life Studies* was in the back of my mind, with its poems and prose and portraits. . . . It's difficult to find critical work on the construction of whiteness in Lowell, but that is what I am reading in there—a struggle with that."[17] Rankine is right to say that there's not much work on the construction of whiteness in Lowell; her citation of him thus opens a door to an underexplored aspect of confessional poetics and, in doing so, helps better define the ambivalent nature of Rankine's confessional inheritance.[18] I begin by tracing the genealogy of Rankine's reference to Lowell's *Life Studies*—and then back further still, into that text's prehistory. I'll ask what *Citizen*'s recasting of *Life Studies* has to teach us about Lowell's "struggle with the construction of whiteness" and what that struggle can illuminate about the relationship between modernist poetics and the construction of racial identity in midcentury American culture, before turning, in the remainder of this essay, to consider more directly the new forms of lyric subjectivity that are allowed by Rankine's reconfiguration of Lowell's late-modernist poetics.

Where in the conclusion of "Man and Wife" might Rankine be reading Lowell's struggle with the construction of whiteness? It's not what the poem is known for. Lowell's poem opens with a couplet whose first line layers confessionalism's paradigmatic disclosures one on top of the other: sex, drugs, and overdetermined Freudian psychodrama: "Tamed by *Miltown*, we lie on Mother's bed; / the rising sun in warpaint dyes us red."[19] Marjorie Perloff, in her review of Lowell's *Collected Poems*, asks, "Who can forget the shock waves generated by these lines?"[20] Those shock waves resulted from the extent to which Perloff's expectations of contemporary poetry circa 1959 had been shaped by the decorousness of the New Critical lyric in the style of Richard Wilbur—and, it should be said, of the younger Robert Lowell. Both in the degree to which taboo subjects are disclosed and in the colloquial *ease* of those disclosures, the line violates the norms of the New Critical lyric. Or, rather, it dramatizes its own swerving away from those norms even as it gestures, residually, towards the prevailing aesthetics of the mid-50s lyric. Here, that residual presence can be heard in the poem's initial heroic couplet, a formal attribute that contrasts ironically with the scandalous disclosures of those lines—and with the rest of the poem's relative metrical irregularity.[21]

The opening of this poem also shores up the whiteness of this married couple. Consider the second line, which completes the opening couplet: "the rising sun in war paint dyes us red." The lassitude of the first line modulates at daybreak into the anger that will fill the stage by poem's end—and what figures that modulation is the sun's simulation of the racialized transformation of their skin. Lowell and Hardwick's pallor indexes their initial enervation; to be roused from their tranquilized stupor is also to become, for the moment, "red." The poem's drafts make clear that Lowell had been thinking about Philip Rahv's 1939 essay, "Paleface and Redskin," which diagnosed American literature as suffering from a "split personality" and which depended on a racist characterization of the Indian as noble savage to fill out its binary with cerebral, all too cerebral, New England refinement.[22] Rahv's essay, which ends by speculating about a reconciliation between these two "fatal antipodes," was mostly about the novel; two decades later, Lowell worried about what he considered an analogous split in American poetry—between the "cooked" verse of poets like Wilbur and the "raw" effusion of the Beats.[23] Both Rahv and Lowell attempt to reconcile these split halves in anxious consolidations of whiteness.

Of course there's another split here, one whose description is the more explicit burden of Lowell's poem: the fraying of the bond between husband and wife. When the Atlantic crashes on Lowell's head at the poem's conclusion, it does so in the form of his wife's tirade. The reader of *Life Studies* understands what might have provoked such frustration from Hardwick; the next poem, a companion to "Man and Wife" (they grew out of the same draft material, called "Holy Matrimony"), gives Hardwick a chance to speak: "My hopped up husband drops his home disputes, / and hits the streets to cruise for prostitutes, / free-lancing out along the razor's edge."[24] Lowell's "free-lancing," in an early draft of "Holy Matrimony," leads him to a surprising expression of affiliation:

> On warm spring night though, we can hear the outcry,
> If our windows are open wide,
> I can hear the South End,
> The razor's edge of Boston's negro culture. They as we
> Refined past culture's possibility,
> Fear homicide,
> Grow horny with alcohol, take the pledge[25]

The wide-open windows in Lowell and Hardwick's Marlborough Street brownstone make it possible for him to hear, in this draft account, Boston's midcentury racial transformations from the privacy of his own bedroom.

Lowell identifies with what he calls "the razor's edge / Of Boston's negro culture," claiming, in a curious phrase, that both he and the South End's black population are "refined past culture's possibility." Lowell's phrase is drawn from the following passage in Rahv's essay:

> As for the paleface, in compensation for backward cultural conditions and a lost religious ethic, he has developed a supreme talent for refinement, just as the Jew, in compensation for adverse social conditions and a lost national independence, has developed a supreme talent for cleverness. (It might be pertinent, in this connection, to recall T. S. Eliot's remark about Boston society, which he described as "quite uncivilized, but refined beyond the point of civilization.") Now this peculiar excess of refinement is to be deplored in an imaginative writer, for it weakens his capacity to cope with experience and induces in him a fetishistic attitude to tradition.[26]

Rahv cites a quip Eliot reportedly made about Boston while an undergraduate at Harvard, and Lowell adapts the formulation, "refined beyond the point of civilization," to describe the terms of his own (Bostonian) identification with the South End's black culture. In the passage above, Rahv both articulates an anxiety that Lowell would feel throughout the writing of *Life Studies* (anxiety about succumbing to a form of refinement that would preclude vitality) and models a kind of interracial affiliation that, just as it allowed Rahv to collapse the figure of "the Jew" into the category of "the paleface," would likewise lead Lowell to hear, through his open window, an echo of his own identity in the voices he assigned to a racialized subculture.

In other drafts, and even here scribbled in Lowell's block letters, he would imagine the culture conjured by the sounds that entered his open window as the "Congo in the heart of Boston." That shocking phrase put Lowell, in the compositional process, in a tradition of modernist poetry inaugurated by Vachel Lindsay's once wildly popular poem, "The Congo: A Study of the Negro Race" (1914). Rachel Blau DuPlessis has shown that Lindsay's poem was a crucial text for the construction of whiteness in the poetry of Eliot and Wallace Stevens. For these modernists, she writes, "'Whiteness' is not a clean construct holding an impure Other at bay but a desire to distance *and* confront its own creolized or miscegenated markers."[27] A similar ambivalence is at work in Lowell's poem. Whatever freelancing out on the razor's edge Lowell himself had done, within the space of this poem, he never leaves the bedroom he shares with Hardwick. The blackness Lowell apprehends in the world outside his window is allowed in only long enough to figure the mania that has strained his domestic tranquility. And then it's gone. The published poem contains no mention of "Boston's negro culture," much less of the "Congo" that had once filled Lowell's imagination.

I have written elsewhere about Lowell's autobiographical poetics as a form of hygienic sincerity; in his self-representations, I argue, Lowell anxiously grooms his face until it appears blank.[28] What Rankine has helped me see is that this blankness has always also been a form of whiteness. In the drafts of "Man and Wife," Lowell sets his evocation of the "Congo in the heart of Boston" in ironic opposition to something else happening far from "hardly passionate" Marlborough Street:

> Though now the South is casus belli for
> A civil war,
> My Nashville Tennessee Agrarian
> Masters are teaching metrics in the Middle West.[29]

Those "masters" were John Crowe Ransom and Allen Tate, both centrally involved in the work of the Indiana School of Letters (formerly the Kenyon School of English). Lowell had come to study with them both—first at Vanderbilt and then following them to Kenyon—after his first and only year as a Harvard undergraduate. When Ransom died in 1974, Lowell wrote, "The kind of poet I am was largely determined by the fact that I grew up in the heyday of the New Criticism."[30] What Lowell learned from Ransom and Tate was their version of Eliotic impersonality, seen through the lens of Agrarian nostalgia. Form, for Ransom and Tate, became both the repository of appropriately calibrated veneration of tradition and a bulwark against the excess emotion of the individual talent. Lowell experimented, in drafting this poem, with intricate stanzaic forms and metrical regularity. Ultimately, those commitments surface only residually: the occasional rhyme, a loosely iambic rhythm. What does the work of metrics by other means, though, what holds the lyric subject's excessive emotion at bay, is the equally old-fashioned remonstrative tirade from his wife, now figured as the ocean that crashes on Lowell's head, connecting New England to old.

In their introduction to *The Racial Imaginary*, Rankine and Loffreda describe the anxiety suffered by white people in America as a state of "unknowing":

> they know that they are white, but they must not know what they know. They know that they are white, but they cannot know that such a thing has social meaning; they know that they are white, but they must not know that their whiteness accrues power. They must not call it whiteness for to do so would be to acknowledge its force.[31]

When the Atlantic crashes on Lowell's head, it does so as punishment and cleansing bath. It washes away, according to the poem's logic, the desires that had threatened to lead him away from home, away from the nuclear family he had made there with his wife, and away from the historical structures within which his family name had accrued power. Lowell's Atlantic renders him mute, unknowing, even as it reaffirms the power of his identity. It produces, in other words, the condition of white innocence.

You Don't Really Have Anything to Confess

When Elizabeth Bishop first read the autobiographical sequence in *Life Studies* in manuscript, she wrote to Lowell with her own confession:

> I am green with envy of your kind of assurance. I feel that I could write in as much detail about my Uncle Artie, say—but what would be the significance? . . . Whereas all you have to do is put down the names! And the fact that it seems significant, illustrative, American, etc., gives you . . . the confidence you display about tackling any idea or theme, *seriously*. . . . In some ways you are the luckiest poet I know![32]

Bishop worries that, without Lowell's claims to centrality in American history (and without his gendered security in patrilineal institutions), she must give up the possibility of writing like him, since Lowell was uniquely positioned to tell a story that was at once personal and historically visible. What Bishop registers as Lowell's immense "luck," Rankine would have us recognize as his whiteness. In *Citizen*, in lines that address both the poem's speaker and Lowell (whose Brahmin status authorized his "life study"), Rankine offers her own version of Bishop's worry:

> Maybe you are right, you don't really have anything to confess.
> Why are you standing?
> Listen, you, I was creating a life study of a monumental first person,
> a Brahmin first person. (72–73)

Rankine's recognition of the "social meaning" of Lowell's whiteness leads her to experiment with reconfigurations of the lyric subject that avoid replicating the structures upon which Lowell's self-assurance was built, while maintaining the possibility that the lyric might serve as a space for the intimate relationality Lowell's poetry so memorably explored. These reconfigurations guide Rankine's deployment of the pronouns "I" and "you."[33]

To see, as Rankine suggests, Lowell's "representativeness" or "centrality" as "whiteness" allows us to recognize the terms both of his autobiographical claims to universality and of the unavailability (indeed the insufficiency) of that particular first-person mode to Rankine. I'll have more to say about *Citizen*'s unique negotiation of that problem shortly, but Rankine has long been worrying over her access to the lyric first person. In 2001, Rankine wrote, "when I use the first person, my wish is to expose the implications of what it means to speak from the seeming coherency of that position."[34] Those "implications" were profound:

No "I" in my mind's eye is the whole of anything. I am a part and so, torn apart by the aggression of the uninterrupted . . . I look around and see the illusion of wholeness and surety inciting the Crusades, slavery, the Battle of Little Big Horn, *Shoah*, Hiroshima, Pearl Harbor, Vietnam, etc. . . . We cannot be committed to any version of the first person to the extent that we are unwilling to interrupt, diverge, or reroute in the name of known and unknown truths. This attempt, the constant investigation of subjectivity, should be what it means to be human.[35]

The imperative Rankine feels to attend to "known and unknown truths" doesn't so much foreclose the possibility of the "I" as it requires a shift in awareness of the pronoun's deployment. In *Don't Let Me Be Lonely*, Rankine focalizes her "constant investigation of subjectivity" under the banner of an "I," but that book's first person functions not to create an illusion of wholeness but instead as a placeholder that lays bare the porousness of the subject it names.[36] That ruminative awareness announces itself explicitly from within the book: "Is 'I' even me or am 'I' a gearshift to get from one sentence to the next?"[37]

Citizen, the book that followed *Lonely*, extends this awareness—a capacity to hold in attention and to regard with curiosity what the voice doesn't already (and may never) know—to the second person of lyric address. Just as the "I" in *Lonely* allows a critical exploration of the claims made by the pronoun's everyday use, so too does the "you" of *Citizen* remain skeptical of its ability to locate a stable referent in the reader who holds the book in hand. For Anthony Reed, such skepticism makes *Citizen* a prime example of the tradition he calls "post-lyric," which, he writes, "chafes at the confidence that the other is a surrogate self, 'the' reader, reliably thinking and feeling in ways identical or even 'kindred' to the self in the poem."[38] *Citizen* manifests and makes productive this lack of "assurance" in two ways: first, by distributing its use of the second person across such a wide range of anecdotes that no single reader could reliably identify with each "you" and, second, by muting the emotional range within the experience of subjectivity claimed by this "you." Both of these features are carried over from the voice Rankine adopted in *Lonely*; both volumes gather together the stories of a number of Rankine's friends and colleagues under the name of a single pronoun, and both render these stories in a voice notable for its emotional flatness.

Those aspects of *Citizen*'s "you"—the collectivity of its sourcing and the flatness of its tone—figure crucially in Rankine's reconfiguration of the confessional lyric. If, as Bishop noted, what made Lowell's autobiography meaningful for readers was the extent to which his family name had already been interwoven with the history of the United States (and if, as Rankine has suggested, this fact indexed the power of Lowell's whiteness), then what Rankine's American lyric inhabits is a subject position that has

been rerouted from those well-established lines of genealogy and discovered, instead, in circuits of contemporary friendship and revisionist historiography. Rankine has testified to the importance of grounding *Citizen* in collective experience: "It took longer to collect incidents of microaggressions from friends and colleagues than it would have to simply use my own experiences, but it was essential to me that it be a collective and researchable document."[39] *Citizen* is researchable in the sense that its recounting of public events—e.g., the racism directed at Serena Williams during the 2004 U.S. Open—can be tested by the skeptical reader against an archive streaming online. But the book makes itself democratically available in another way: keeping in mind that Rankine has collected the material for the stories here from her friends and colleagues, we might imagine the "you" in each episode to be addressed, in the first place, directly to the friend who provided the anecdote, telling each story back to its original teller. That would be an especially significant service to provide to friends whose race renders them either invisible or hypervisible within the structures of white supremacist ideology, and who therefore may be made to feel like they barely exist. Rankine's book works to register and record such stories, to grant such testimony the ontological solidity of lyric telling, and to give that telling (and, with it, a durable sense of belonging) back to the teller.

But then that specific invocation of a "you" (and, since Rankine was the source for at least *some* of these stories, the "you" is sometimes a name for Rankine herself) is always also a platform for a more general address, so that *any* reader of the book is invited, however provisionally or imperfectly, to fill the role of the anecdote's original teller.[40] Here, then, is where the general flatness of the book's tone becomes especially operative. Heather Love has written of the "coldness of [Rankine's] gaze" in *Citizen*, noting, "rather than create a live scene of identification, the second person renders affect diffuse and featureless."[41] One consequence of this muted affect is that even if Rankine's second person invites a reader's identification with the poem's lyric subject, the experience of such identification is unlikely to feel epiphanic or cathartic. As Love, following Reed's earlier argument about *Lonely*, describes *Citizen*'s episodic descriptions of racist microaggressions, "these experiences are not meant to be universal; they are staged not as epiphanies but as object lessons."[42] The effect is not one of transcendence but instead of groundedness; the reader is put in contact not with truths so shocking that they have been hidden from view but instead with experiences so common that we have become inured to seeing what shocks they regularly deliver.

Rankine revises the confessional tradition by making visible the privilege upon which its self-disclosures depended for their power and by repurposing its tropes of breakdown so as to animate her own representations of durably social—and not merely provisional or private—incoherence.

In *Citizen*, this move is less invested in dismissing the subject position of *Life Studies* than in decentering it: "Your ill-spirited, cooked, hell on Main Street, nobody's here, broken-down, first person could be one of many definitions of being to pass on" (72). Rankine rattles off a sequence of phrases Lowell used to describe himself in "Skunk Hour," the final poem in *Life Studies*.[43] In this case, the identity of Rankine's "you" seems clear: the "you," for the moment, is Lowell. But the rapidity of her citation of Lowell's phrases recontextualizes them—and, with them, the stability of Lowell's position—aggressively. Unlike Bishop, who merely marveled at Lowell's "assurance"—that is, at the factors that authorized his autobiographical poetics—Rankine extends *her* critical intervention to include the capacity of whiteness to have silenced a first person like her own: "Drag that first person out of the social death of history, then we're kin. / Kin calling out the past like a foreigner with a newly minted 'Fuck you'" (72). Lowell's family, in Bishop's account, makes his autobiography "significant, illustrative, American"; Rankine writes from a recognition that *her* place in national history has been occluded by the Middle Passage, by antebellum slavery, by Jim Crow, by white supremacist ideology writ large. Both installments of her "American Lyric," *Don't Let Me Be Lonely* and *Citizen*, discover meaningful ways to say "I" and "you" that don't rely on the "assurance" whiteness provides.

Traveling as a Family

Let me now extend the conclusions drawn from this juxtaposition of Rankine and Lowell to argue that *Citizen* has reconfigured another of the methods by which confessional poetry made its lyric subject legible: embedding that subject in recognizable familial structures. For Lowell, this allowed the subject to be seen in terms both Freudian and national-historical —even as the subject in *Life Studies* had strayed from the traditions of the family whose name he bore, his cycle of poems offered a narrative of recuperation. Observe, then, another scene of injury and familial recuperation, this one from *Citizen*:

> A man knocked over her son in the subway. You feel your own body wince. He's okay, but the son of a bitch kept walking. She says she grabbed the stranger's arm and told him to apologize: I told him to look at the boy and apologize. Yes, and you want it to stop, you want the child pushed to the ground to be seen, to be helped to his feet, to be brushed off by the person that did not see him, has never seen him, has perhaps never seen anyone who is not a reflection of himself.

> The beautiful thing is that a group of men began to stand behind me like a fleet of bodyguards, she says, like newly found uncles and brothers. (17)

Rankine's second person is at one diegetic remove from the episode, as if to dramatize the transferability of such injury ("You feel your own body wince"). But just as pain circulates casually in the crowded space of the subway and in the telling of this story, familial networks respond by forming spontaneously. The men who gather behind the mother telling this story are "*like* newly found uncles and brothers." Near the end of the book, on another train, Rankine's "you" sits next to a man other passengers avoid and silently decides, "if anyone asks you to move, you'll tell them we are traveling *as* a family" (133, emphasis added). What the two moments in *Citizen* share is a conception of family as constituted by "like" or "as"; "family" is the name given to a horizontal, ad hoc arrangement that makes visible the human beings who constitute it.

But is Rankine's apparent reliance on this notion of family as a mode of redress in danger of replicating the bourgeois structuring of subjectivity that she'd been wary of? After reading the passage that I cited above at Harvard University in 2015, Rankine confessed ambivalence:

> I was discussing that piece with Lauren Berlant, and she said to me, "Why are you positing the family as some kind of solution to this?" And I fear she's right, but it was one of those moments where, because it *happened*, I thought, well, it *did* happen—which, you know, is no reason for anything. But I feel it's my duty to erase the ending, even as I speak it.[44]

Without getting into the merits of *Citizen*'s suggestion that "traveling as a family" offers some restitution for the injuries inflicted by anti-black racism, let me just observe here that Rankine's thinking-aloud at the Harvard reading guides her back to the question of whether "what happened" will survive the threat of "erasure." It seems, in this case at least, that it will. Whether or not "your" resolution to form an ad hoc family with the solitary black traveler on her train could ever be a "solution," the arrangement has a reality that persists—"it *did* happen." Again and again, *Citizen* records precisely the kinds of social arrangements that threaten to flicker from view.[45]

The spontaneity and tenuousness of such familial arrangements in *Citizen* mirrors the precarity in its representations of black life. That precarity is discernible not only in the book's anonymized descriptions of microaggressions but also in its engagement with stories that have entered the public record. The Harvard reading described above took place on the same day as the funeral of Freddie Gray; noting that coincidence as she addressed the audience, Rankine began her reading with this selection from *Citizen*:

> My brothers are notorious. They have not been to prison. They have been imprisoned. The prison is not a place you enter. It is no place.
> My brothers are notorious. They do regular things, like wait. On my

birthday they say my name. They will never forget that we are named. What is that memory? (89)

The reader of Rankine's book who sees, on the page before these words appear, that the section is "In Memory of Trayvon Martin" might well assume that the "name" alluded to in the passage above belongs to that particular teenager. But if that reader hears this voice as Martin's, an audience member at Rankine's 2015 Harvard reading may have heard the voice as Gray's. The passage's language makes such ambiguities possible, even unavoidable; though this voice says, "They will never forget that we are named," no proper names appear within the passage. Instead, Rankine moves slowly through an iterative process whereby certain key words feel both specific and general at once: "And as yet I do not understand how my own sorrow has turned into my brothers' hearts. The hearts of my brothers are broken. If I knew another way to be, I would call up a brother, I would hear myself saying, my brother, dear brother, my dearest brothers, dear heart—" (89). Fraternal bonds work both synchronically and diachronically; they extend from Martin to his biological brothers and living friends, to contemporary victims, like Gray, of the same racism that ended Martin's life, and backwards to the "years of and before me and my brothers, the years of passage, plantation, migration, of Jim Crow segregation, of poverty, inner cities, profiling, of one in three" (89).

Rankine's distribution of voice within such familial networks alters not only the nature of her lyric subject, dislodging it from any innocently claimed sovereignty, but also the relationship her "American lyric" establishes with its reader. As Rankine's script for Martin modulates from words *about* his brothers to an apostrophe *to* them, the poem's reader slides into the role of the addressee in the telephonic connection:

> If I called I'd say good-bye before I broke the good-bye. I say good-bye before anyone can hang up. Don't hang up. My brother hangs up though he is there. I keep talking. The talk keeps him there. The sky is blue, kind of blue. The day is hot. Is it cold? Are you cold? It does get cool. Is it cool? Are you cool?
>
> My brother is completed by the sky. The sky is his silence. Eventually, he says, it is raining. It is raining down. It was raining. It stopped raining. It is raining down. He won't hang up. He's there, he's there but he's hung up though he is there. Good-bye, I say. I break the good-bye. I say good-bye before anyone can hang up, don't hang up. Wait with me. Wait with me though the waiting might be the call of good-byes. (90)

"Don't hang up," we hear. In a sense, that is the message behind the entirety of this section of *Citizen*. This is the function of language that Roman Jakobson describes as "phatic," characteristic of "messages primarily serving to establish, to prolong, or to discontinue communication, to check whether the channel works ('Hello, do you hear me?'), to attract the attention of the interlocutor or to confirm his continued attention."[46] The sustained attention demanded of us is expected to withstand the attenuations of the repeated words that comprise it, attenuations that figure the forms of violence ("It is raining down. It was raining. It stopped raining. It is raining down") that threaten to end the life of the lyric moment's speaker. The image on the page that follows this "waiting [that] might be the call of good-byes" makes visible both the white supremacist ideology that is exerting such pressure on Rankine's script for Martin and the stakes—disappearance—of that pressure. Rankine reproduces the 1930 photograph of the public lynching of two black men, Thomas Shipp and Abram Smith, but erases their bodies from her reproduction. What remains in the wake of that erasure is a plain view of the whiteness that produced it.

In response to the ubiquitous threat of such anti-black violence, we find, in *Citizen*, the presence of familial care in dispersed and anonymous networks.[47] Near the end of the book, we are invited to watch along with a father supervising an ordinary scene:

> Closed to traffic, the previously unexpressive street fills with small bodies. One father, having let go of his child's hand, stands on the steps of a building and watches. You can't tell which child is his, though you follow his gaze. It seems to belong to all the children as it envelops their play. You were about to enter your building, but do not want to leave the scope of his vigilance. (149)

The "you" who watches wants to connect the father's protective gaze to the lost object of its vigilance, but that project is futile. And yet this futility isn't registered as loss; it is rerouted, instead, into a dispersed form of loving attention: "It seems to belong to all the children as it envelops their play." The father, "stand[ing] on the steps," taking in his view of children whom he regards as family, recalls the speaker of Lowell's "Skunk Hour," who "stand[s] on top / of [his] back steps and breathe[s] the rich air" and observes, from that vantage, the ordinary doings of "a mother skunk with her column of kittens."[48] Edward Brunner has argued that the mother skunk offers the manic, transgressive Lowell "an example of family solidarity," one whose "domesticity shelters him as well."[49] The protection of such domesticity seems out of reach in Rankine's scene. The father has let go of his child's hand, he stands on the steps of "a" building (not *his*, as it had been for Lowell), and the duration of his vigilance, now extended to include all of the "small bodies" who fill the street, invites even the "you" who watches—and you who read—to dwell in the public intimacy of the scene and to delay, thereby, your eventual reentry into the privatized space of "your building."

Open Lyric

The "you" who lingers outside, who watches another's watching, who wants to be included in the form of care that is the duration of that watching, insufficient as it may be—this "you" is the lyric subject of *Citizen*. Towards the end of her book, Rankine describes a scene in which "you," in a car with your partner, receive some insult from the driver of another car. Your partner wants to get out of the car and confront the other driver, but "you" resist:

> Trayvon Martin's name sounds from the car radio a dozen times each half hour. You pull your love back into the seat because though no one seems to be chasing you, the justice system has other plans.
>
> Yes, and this is how you are a citizen: Come on. Let it go. Move on. (151)

This section of *Citizen* is dated "July 13, 2013," the date of George Zimmerman's acquittal for Martin's murder. That news event, relentlessly broadcast into the couple's car, provides a reminder of the racism that polices black life in America. In this essay's brief final section, I want to describe the openness with which Rankine meets such experience, for that openness is the most salient characteristic of her reconfigured lyric subject. While "you" prevent your partner from confronting the potential violence that lurks outside the car, that danger is evidently not reason enough for you to cut yourself off from the world: "Despite the air-conditioning you pull the button back and the window slides down into its door-sleeve. A breeze touches your cheek. As something should" (151).

Rankine's "Come on. Let it go. Move on" lifts and rehearses those phrases from the book's earlier voicings of tennis self-talk: watching a televised tennis match on mute in a narcotic response to the litany of injuries so far recounted, only to see the apparently ordinary sociality of the match punctured by an another racist disruption, Rankine's "you" had borrowed the professional athlete's language of self-address: "Feel good. Feel better. Move forward. Let it go. Come on. Come on. Come on. In due time the ball is going back and forth over the net" (66). As in that example, what Rankine is finding here, as her "you" pulls her partner back into the car, is a mode of both attending to the injury delivered by the world and maintaining a durable sense of living, beyond the event of injury. Rankine's lyric subject does not so much consist in the supersession of vulnerability as it holds such injury in its imperfect attention—what Angela Hume has called its "dwelling *within* a problematic mode in order to expose how the duration of the wasting of life becomes a way of life."[50] In her *Paris Review* interview, Rankine described her response to a reader who wondered why there weren't "hopeful moments" in *Citizen*: "The book is full of people living their lives, and even if it focuses on the interruptions to those lives, around the interruptions there are still lives."[51] The mode of attention Rankine describes practicing as a member of an audience earlier in the book accounts for the vulnerability that makes such interruptions possible and suggests the forms of life that makes them endurable:

> Not long ago you are in a room where someone asks the philosopher Judith Butler what makes language hurtful. You can feel everyone lean in. Our very being exposes us to the address of another, she answers. We suffer from the condition of being addressable. Our emotional openness, she adds, is carried by our addressability. Language navigates this. (49)

Rankine calibrates her language to meet and recognize the language that surrounds and indeed permeates her own sense of being.[52] The very form of her book is open to the recording of such injuries: in one of its most striking features, a page is given to memorializing a list of names of black victims of police violence. The words "In Memory of" stream down the left-hand margin, and space has been left for the names of young victims to match that elegiac gesture, whose flexibility is emblematic: the names that appear in any given printing of the book ground the lyric in a documentary record just as the space left for more names in subsequent printings suggests an openness to and mournful foreknowledge of the injuries whiteness will inflict.

Rankine's model of the open lyric is most clearly manifested in the moment of intertextuality with which this essay began, in her direct citation of Lowell. There, she reverses the stern injunctions of Eliot's early essays. No longer must the poet turn away from emotional excess; instead, Rankine invites an unblinkingly open form of "letting in":

> Yours is a strange dream, a strange reverie.
> No, it's a strange beach; each body is a strange beach, and if you let in the excess emotion you will recall the Atlantic Ocean breaking on our heads. (72–73)

What had been, for Lowell, a simile ("your old-fashioned tirade— / loving, rapid, merciless— / breaks like the Atlantic Ocean on my head") becomes, for Rankine, a memory whose content is both literal and collective. Whereas the vector of the displacement of "the Atlantic Ocean" from the scene of Lowell's poem was figurative, in Rankine's poem that vector is historical. And while Lowell's ocean has its own historical resonances, evoking the transatlantic genealogy mythologized by his work, that history is, as ever, summed up in his singular identity ("on *my* head"). Even as Rankine's evocation of "the Atlantic Ocean breaking on *our* heads" asks us to imagine not the impersonalizing (and yet singular) wash of Lowell's poem but instead the particular (and plural) injuries of the Atlantic slave trade, its gesture is finally not towards a universalizing form of history but towards the strangeness of the particular. "Each body is a strange beach," positioned between land and sea, an interface between the world and the injured self, shaped by and attending to that positioning in time and place.

Those lines anticipate the book's final image: Turner's *Slave Ship*, where the breaking of the Atlantic upon the human body is a matter of historical representation. On the previous page, Rankine prefaces the book's concluding anecdote by writing, "I don't know how to end what doesn't have an ending" (159). When do we notice that Rankine's voice has slipped into the first person? The next line, "Tell me a story, he says, wrapping his arms around me," returns us to the scene of a marital bed (159). Is this a reprise of the confessional scene of Lowell's "Man and Wife"? What follows is recognizable as one of *Citizen*'s episodic microaggressions; in this one, a white woman decides to find a different parking spot once she notices that she has parked across from the speaker. Again the implications of this encounter are registered but not pursued; again tennis serves as a figure for the sociality whose demands eventually draw the subject from a more sustained inquiry into the racism that structured the experience. Come on. Let it go. Move on. The speaker's partner asks, "Did you win?" Rankine's answer suggests that she is determined to end this book without closure: "It wasn't a match, I say. It was a lesson" (159). The injury is not to be transcended but instead to be studied. A kind of life study, after all. When we turn the page and see the Turner painting, we are being asked to extend that life study to the most dehumanizing of white supremacy's injuries, chattel slavery. We are being asked, finally, to know, as we look, how it is that the injuries represented in Turner's seascape endure here and now, in our bodies, in our shared and strange lives.

NOTES

For their generous attention to this essay as it took shape, I thank this volume's editors as well as Joe Drury, Travis Foster, Brooke Hunter, Mary Mullen, and Megan Quigley. The essay has also greatly benefited from the attention it received from editors and anonymous reviewers at *PMLA*, where a slightly different version appeared. I also wish to thank two research assistants, Ann Marie Jakubowski and Brian Borosky, for their help at every turn.

1. Claudia Rankine, *Citizen: An American Lyric* (Minneapolis: Graywolf Press, 2014), 73. Subsequent references will appear parenthetically in the text.

2. *Citizen*'s success (its reception as the most culturally significant book of American poetry of the last several years) has, at times, obscured its recognition *as* poetry. One of my aims here is to lay bare the logic behind this obfuscation.

3. Robert Lowell, *Collected Poems*, ed. Frank Bidart and David Gewanter (New York: Farrar, Straus and Giroux, 2003), 189.

4. David Ulin, "The Art of Poetry No. 102," *Paris Review* 219 (Winter 2016): 156.

5. Ibid., 157.

6. Understanding Lowell as modernism's anointed heir and *Life Studies* as the culmination of an expressive lyric tradition that connected Romanticism to Modernism is as old as the essay that gave confessional poetry its name: M. L. Rosenthal, "Robert Lowell and the Poetry of Confession," in *Robert Lowell: A Portrait of the Artist in His Time*, ed. Michael London and Robert Boyers (New York: David Lewis, 1970), 45–49. For a reappraisal of Rosenthal's genealogy in the context of recent academic work on the lyric, see Gillian White, *Lyric Shame: The "Lyric" Subject of Contemporary American Poetry* (Cambridge: Harvard University Press, 2014), 31–37.

7. Lowell's question, which appears in the final poem, "Epilogue," in *Day by Day* (1977), was posed to him by Hardwick during his completion of the *Life Studies* manuscript (*Collected Poems*, 838, 1148n).

8. Ulin, "The Art of Poetry No. 102," 157.

9. To say that the avant-garde critique of the post-Romantic lyric could diagnose white innocence shouldn't imply that experimental poetics has been alert to its own replications of racism. See Cathy Park Hong, "Delusions of Whiteness in the Avant Garde," *Lana Turner* 7; Erica Hunt, "Response to Race and the Poetic Avant Garde," *Boston Review*, March 10, 2015. See also the response to Kenneth Goldsmith's performance of "The Body of Michael Brown" in CA Conrad, "Kenneth Goldsmith Says He Is an Outlaw," *Harriet: The Poetry Foundation Blog*, June 1, 2015. For responses to Perloff's defense of Goldsmith, see Jen Hofer, "If You Hear Something Say Something, Or If You're Not At the Table You're On the Menu," *Entropy*, December 18, 2015; and Fred Moten, "On Marjorie Perloff," *Entropy*, December 28, 2015.

10. Virginia Jackson, *Dickinson's Misery: A Theory of Lyric Reading* (Princeton: Princeton University Press, 2005), 9.

11. See two review essays on *The Lyric Theory Reader*, co-edited by Jackson and Yopie Prins: Eric Hayot, "Against Historicist Fundamentalism," *PMLA* 131.5 (2016): 1417–20; Lytle Shaw, "Framing the Lyric," *American Literary History* 28.2 (Summer 2016): 405. For an example of work that takes up Jackson's account of lyricization, but with respect to race (and for which Rankine is a central example), see Anthony Reed, *Freedom Time: The Poetics and Politics of Black Experimental Writing* (Baltimore: Johns Hopkins University Press, 2014), 96–122. Reed has continued that work more recently in Reed, "The Erotics of Mourning in Recent Experimental Black Poetry," *The Black Scholar* 47.2 (2017): 23–37: "Lyricization corresponds with and provides an aesthetic basis . . . for the emergence of Man" (26).

12. For more on the role played by Tate and Warren in constructing an Agrarian version of racialized modernism, see Aldon Lynn Nielsen, *Reading Race: White American Poets and the Racial Discourse in the Twentieth Century* (Athens: University of Georgia Press, 1988), 102–122. See also Andy Hines, "Why Critics Wait," *Public Books*, August 1, 2015, which explores the relationship between Agrarian New Criticism and race.

13. Jericho Brown, "Love the Masters," in *The Racial Imaginary: Writers on Race in the Life of the Mind*, ed. Claudia Rankine, Beth Loffreda, and Max King Cap (Albany: Fence Books, 2013), 232.

14. *The Racial Imaginary*, 16.

15. Ulin, "The Art of Poetry No. 102," 157.

16. Saidiya Hartman, *Lose Your Mother: A Journey Along the Atlantic Slave Route* (New York: Farrar, Straus and Giroux, 2007), 6. Later in *Lose Your Mother*, in sentences that might serve as an alternate-epigraph to *Citizen*, Hartman writes: "I, too, live in the time of slavery, by which I mean I am living in the future created by it. It is the ongoing crisis of citizenship" (133).

17. Sandra Lim, "Interview with Claudia Rankine, 2014 National Book Award Finalist, Poetry," National Book Foundation, accessed June 1, 2017; www.nationalbook.org/nba2014_p_rankine_interv.html.

18. One exception to Rankine's statement about the lack of work on whiteness in Lowell comes in Christopher Grobe, *The Art of Confession: The Performance of Self from Robert Lowell to Reality TV* (New York: New York University Press, 2017). Grobe builds, in part, on Marsha Bryant, "The Confessional Other: Identity, Form, and Origins in Confessional Poetry," in *Identity and Form in Contemporary Literature*, ed. Ana Maria Sanchez-Arce (New York: Routledge, 2014), 177–94. The only academic notice that I have discovered of Lowell's presence in *Citizen* is in Michael LeMahieu, "Robert Lowell, Perpetual War, and the Legacy of the Civil War Elegy," *College Literature* 43.1 (Winter 2016): 91–120. LeMahieu notes Lowell's presence among Rankine's list of "Works Referenced" and considers his "For the Union Dead" an antecedent for Rankine's memorializing. His reading is persuasive, although, curiously, he also claims, "Rankine does not refer to Lowell . . . explicitly in her poetry" (115–16).

19. Lowell, *Collected Poems*, 189.

20. Marjorie Perloff, "The Return of Robert Lowell," *Parnassus* 27.1–2 (Winter 2004): 76–102.

21. See Deborah Nelson, *Pursuing Privacy in Cold War America* (New York: Columbia University Press, 2002) on "the ghost of formality" (45) in *Life Studies*.

22. Philip Rahv, "Paleface and Redskin," *Kenyon Review* 1.3 (Summer 1939): 251–56; 253.

23. Robert Lowell, "Robert Lowell, Winner of the 1960 Poetry Award for *Life Studies*," National Book Foundation, accessed June 1, 2017; http://www.nationalbook.org/nbaclassics_rlowell.html. See also Langdon Hammer, *Hart Crane and Allen Tate: Janus-Faced Modernism* (Princeton: Princeton University Press, 1993), where Hammer discusses *Life Studies* in the context of Rahv, "Paleface and Redskin," 214.

24. Lowell, *Collected Poems*, 190.

25. Robert Lowell, MS Am 1905, Folder 2204, Robert Lowell Papers, Houghton Library, Harvard University.

26. Rahv, "Paleface and Redskin," 255.

27. Rachel Blau DuPlessis, "'HOO, HOO, HOO': Some Episodes in the Construction of Modern Whiteness," *American Literature* 67.4 (December 1995): 667–700.

28. I make an extended version of this argument in my current book manu-

script, in which I see Lowell's writing as a central example of the period's "institutionalized lyric," a poem born simultaneously of the *institutional* structuring of poetry at midcentury and of the experience of psychiatric *institutionalization* central to so many of the period's poems.

29. Robert Lowell Papers, Houghton Library, Harvard University.

30. Lowell quoted in Ian Hamilton, *Robert Lowell: A Biography* (New York: Random House, 1982), 57.

31. *The Racial Imaginary*, 20.

32. Elizabeth Bishop and Robert Lowell, *Words in Air: The Complete Correspondence Between Elizabeth Bishop and Robert Lowell*, ed. Thomas Travisano and Saskia Hamilton (New York: Farrar, Straus and Giroux, 2008), 247.

33. While I haven't the space to unpack Rankine's connection to the *other* confessional poet, Berryman, whose influence she cites, his experiments with pronouns and blackface minstrelsy in *The Dream Songs* provide another version of confessional subjectivity. See Berryman, "One Answer to a Question: Changes," *The Freedom of the Poet* (New York: Farrar, Straus and Giroux, 1976), 326. Her primary citation of him in *Citizen*— "Someone claimed we should use our skin as wallpaper knowing we couldn't win" (71)—refers to Dream Song 53: "Gottfried Benn / said: —We are using our own skins for wallpaper and we cannot win," in Berryman, *The Dream Songs* (New York: Farrar, Straus and Giroux, 1969), 60. For more on Berryman's minstrelsy, see Peter Maber, "'So-called Black': Reassessing John Berryman's Blackface Minstrelsy," *Arizona Quarterly* 64.4 (Winter 2008): 129–49.

34. Claudia Rankine, "The First Person in the Twenty-First Century," *After Confession: Poetry as Autobiography*, ed. Kate Sontag and David Graham (St. Paul: Graywolf Press, 2001), 134.

35. Ibid., 135–36.

36. Claudia Rankine, *Don't Let Me Be Lonely* (Minneapolis: Graywolf Press, 2004). For a related argument about Rankine's use of the first person in *Lonely*, see Reed, *Freedom Time*, 99, 114–15.

37. Rankine, *Don't Let Me Be Lonely*, 54.

38. Reed, "Erotics of Mourning," 27.

39. Ulin, "The Art of Poetry No. 102," 144.

40. See Evie Shockley, "Race, Reception, and Claudia Rankine's 'American Lyric,'" in "Reconsidering Claudia Rankine's *Citizen: An American Lyric*. A Symposium, Part I," *Los Angeles Review of Books*, January 6, 2016. Shockley argues that *Citizen*'s "you" "thrusts every reader into the position of speaker and addressee simultaneously," and that "[w]hat results may be less of a challenge to the coherence of the lyric speaker than to the coherence of many readers" (np). Coherence, I have argued, is one of those New Critical values that confessional poetics tended to rely upon, worry over, and finally to reconstitute; I'm arguing here that the very idea of lyric "coherence" is something that Rankine unsettles.

41. Heather Love, "Small Change: Realism, Immanence, and the Politics of the Micro," *Modern Language Quarterly* 77.3 (September 2016): 439.

42. Ibid., 437.

43. Rankine rehearses these self-descriptions from "Skunk Hour": "I hear / my ill-spirit sob in each blood cell"; "I myself am hell; / nobody's here—"; as well as a

description of the titular skunks, who "march on their soles up Main Street" (*Collected Poems*, 192). Her use of the word "cooked" refers to Lowell's 1960 National Book Award acceptance speech, discussed above.

44. Claudia Rankine, "The Making of 'Citizen': Claudia Rankine," April 27, 2015, Woodberry Poetry Room, Harvard University; hcl.harvard.edu/poetryroom /listeningbooth/poets/rankine.cfm.

45. The provisional formation of family in *Citizen* recalls what Fred Moten names the "material reproductivity of black performance": "that transference, a carrying or crossing over, that takes place on the bridge of lost matter, lost maternity, lost mechanics that joins bondage and freedom, that interanimates the body and its ephemeral if productive force, that interarticulates the performance and the reproductive reproduction it always already contains and which contains it." Moten, *In the Break: The Aesthetics of the Black Radical Tradition* (Minneapolis: University of Minnesota Press, 2003), 18. Hartman writes: "Racial solidarity was expressed in the language of kinship because it both evidenced the wound and attempted to heal it" (*Lose Your Mother*, 6).

46. Roman Jakobson, "Closing Statement: Linguistics and Poetics," *The Lyric Theory Reader*, ed. Virginia Jackson and Yopie Prins (Baltimore: Johns Hopkins University Press, 2014), 238.

47. Rankine's investment in the idea of dispersed care can also be found in *Lonely*, where, as Christopher Nealon argues, she responds to the catastrophes of twenty-first-century capitalism by finding "a medium for the mutuality that risk-sharing, securitization, mocks: linked vulnerability." Nealon, *The Matter of Capital: Poetry and Crisis in the American Century*, (Cambridge: Harvard University Press, 2011), 153.

48. Lowell, *Collected Poems*, 192.

49. Edward Brunner, *Cold War Poetry: The Social Text in the Fifties Poem* (Urbana: University of Illinois Press, 2001), 252.

50. Angela Hume, "Toward an Antiracist Ecopoetics: Waste and Wasting in the Poetry of Claudia Rankine," *Contemporary Literature* 57.1 (Spring 2016): 79–110.

51. Ulin, "The Art of Poetry No. 102," 164.

52. Rankine's lyric subject would thus be well described by Christina Sharpe's theorizing of black life: "To be in the wake is . . . to recognize the ways that we are constituted through and by continued vulnerability to overwhelming force though not *only* known to ourselves and to each other *by* that force." Sharpe, *In the Wake: On Blackness and Being* (Durham, NC: Duke University Press, 2016), 16.

BIBLIOGRAPHY

Works by Claudia Rankine

POETRY
Nothing in Nature is Private. Cleveland: Cleveland State University Poetry Center, 1994.
The End of the Alphabet. New York: Grove Press, 1998.
Plot. New York: Grove Press, 2001.

Don't Let Me Be Lonely: An American Lyric. Minneapolis: Graywolf Press, 2004.
Citizen: An American Lyric. Minneapolis: Graywolf Press, 2014.

EDITED VOLUMES

American Women Poets in the 21st Century: Where Lyric Meets Language. With
 Juliana Spahr. Middletown, CT: Wesleyan University Press, 2002.
American Poets in the 21st Century: The New Poetics. With Lisa Sewell. Middle-
 town, CT: Wesleyan University Press, 2007.
Eleven More American Women Poets in the 21st Century: Poetics Across America.
 With Lisa Sewell. Middletown, CT: Wesleyan University Press, 2012.
The Racial Imaginary: Writers on Race in the Life of the Mind. With Beth
 Loffreda and Max King Cap. Albany, NY: Fence Books, 2016.

SELECTED PROSE

"The First Person in the Twenty-First Century." In *After Confession: Poetry as
 Autobiography*, ed. Kate Sontag and David Graham (Minneapolis: Graywolf
 Press, 2001), 132–36.
"Our Sons Know They Could Be the Next Michael Brown. But They Should
 Never Surrender." *Guardian*, October 12, 2014; www.theguardian.com
 /commentisfree/2014/oct/12/sons-michael-brown-two-months-later-ferguson.
"The Image of the Black in Western Art." *New York Times Book Review*,
 December 4, 2014; www.nytimes.com/2014/12/07/books/review/the-image-of
 -the-black-in-western-art.html.
"Amiri Baraka's 'SOS.'" *New York Times Book Review*, February 11, 2015;
 www.nytimes.com/2015/02/15/books/review/amiri-barakas-s-o-s.html.
"The Condition of Black Life Is One of Mourning." *The New York Times
 Magazine*, June 22, 2015; www.nytimes.com/2015/06/22/magazine/the
 -condition-of-black-life-is-one-of-mourning.html.
"The Meaning of Serena Williams: On Tennis and Black Excellence." *The New
 York Times Magazine*, August 25, 2015; www.nytimes.com/2015/08/30
 /magazine/the-meaning-of-serena-williams.html.
"Teju Cole's Essays Build Connections between African and Western
 Art." *New York Times Book Review*, August 9, 2016; www.nytimes
 .com/2016/08/14/books/review/teju-cole-known-and-strange-things.html.

SELECTED INTERVIEWS

Adewunmi, Bim, and Lynzy Billing. "A Conversation with Claudia Rankine."
 Buzzfeed, August 7, 2015; www.buzzfeed.com/bimadewunmi/a-conversation
 -with-claudia-da-gawd-rankine.
Alvarez, Connie, and Alan Howard. "Claudia Rankine: Citizen, An American
 Lyric." KCRW Bookworm, March 12, 2015; www.kcrw.com/news-culture
 /shows/bookworm/claudia-rankine-citizen-an-american-lyric.
Anderson, Kurt. "How Does Racism Actually Feel? Claudia Rankine's 'Citizen'
 Gives an Unblinking Look." PRI Studio 360, February 20, 2015; www.pri.org
 /stories/2015-02-19/how-does-racism-actually-feel-claudia-rankines-citizen
 -tells-us.
Asokan, Ratik. "I Am Invested in Keeping Present the Forgotten Bodies." *Believer*

Magazine, December 10, 2014; www.logger.believermag.com/post/2014
/12/10/i-am-invested-in-keeping-present-the-forgotten.

Berlant, Lauren. "Claudia Rankine." *BOMB Magazine*, Fall 2014; www
.bombmagazine.org/article/10096/claudia-rankine.

"Claudia Rankine in Conversation." Poets.org, September 15, 2009; www.poets
.org/poetsorg/text/claudia-rankine-conversation.

Cocozza, Paula. "Poet Claudia Rankine: 'The Invisibility of Black Women Is
Astounding.'" *The Guardian*, June 29, 2015; www.theguardian.com
/lifeandstyle/2015/jun/29/poet-claudia-rankine-invisibility-black-women
-everyday-racism-citizen.

Coleman, Aaron. "The History Behind the Feeling: A Conversation with Claudia
Rankine." *The Spectacle*, September 23, 2015; www.thespectacle.wustl.edu
/?p=105.

Dodd, Philip. "Community, The Amber Collective, Poet Claudia Rankine." BBC
Radio Free Thinking, June 24, 2015; www.bbc.co.uk/programmes/b05zhbdj.

Flescher, Jennifer, and Robert N. Caspar. "Interview with Claudia Rankine."
Poetry Daily, 2006; www.poems.com/special_features/prose/essay_rankine
.php.

George, Lynell. "Writer Claudia Rankine on White Blindness, The Black Body,
and Freedom to Live." KCET, September 3, 2015; www.kcet.org/shows
/artbound/writer-claudia-rankine-on-white-blindness-the-black-body-and-the
-freedom-to-live.

Kachka, Boris. "Claudia Rankine: Serena, Indian Wells, and Race." *Vulture*,
March 18, 2015; www.vulture.com/2015/03/claudia-rankine-serena-indian
-wells-and-race.html.

Schwartz, Claire. "An Interview with Claudia Rankine." *TriQuarterly*, July 15,
2016; www.triquarterly.org/issues/issue-150/interview-claudia-rankine.

Sharma, Meara. "Claudia Rankine on Blackness as the Second Person." *Guernica*,
November 17, 2014; www.guernicamag.com/blackness-as-the-second-person/.

Ulin, David. "The Art of Poetry No. 102." *Paris Review* 219 (Winter 2016):
139–166.

Zucker, Rachel. "Episode 4: Claudia Rankine." *Commonplace Conversations
with Poets (and Other People)*, July 15, 2016; www.commonpodcast.com
/home/2016/7/15/episode-4-claudia-rankine.

Selected Criticism and Reviews

Bass, Holly. "Claudia Rankine's 'Citizen.'" *New York Times Book Review*,
December 24, 2014; www.nytimes.com/2014/12/28/books/review/claudia
-rankines-citizen.html.

Bedient, Calvin. "Review: The End of the Alphabet." *Boston Review*, June 1,
1999; www.bostonreview.net/poetry/calvin-bedient-review-end-alphabet.

Bell, Kevin. "Unheard Writing in the Climate of Spectacular Noise: Claudia
Rankine on TV." *The Global South* 3.1 (Spring 2009): 93–107.

Chiasson, Dan. "Color Codes: A Poet Examines Race in America." *The New
Yorker*, October 27, 2014; www.newyorker.com/magazine/2014/10/27/color
-codes.

Epstein, Andrew. *Attention Equals Life: The Pursuit of the Everyday in Contemporary Poetry and Culture*. Oxford: Oxford University Press, 2016.

Flynn, Nick, Mark Nowak, Ruth Ellen Kocher, and Carmen Giménez Smith. "Roundtable on '*Citizen: An American Lyric*,' Part One." *The Los Angeles Review of Books*, December 14, 2014; www.lareviewofbooks.org/article /roundtable-citizen-american-lyric/.

———. "Roundtable on '*Citizen: An American Lyric*,' Part Two." *The Los Angeles Review of Books*, December 15, 2014; www.lareviewofbooks.org /article/roundtable-citizen-american-lyric-part-ii.

Gilbert, Alan. "The Ethics of Language: A Review of *Don't Let Me Be Lonely*." *Boston Review*, February 1, 2005; www.bostonreview.net/archives/BR30.1 /gilbert.php.

Hume, Angela. "Toward an Antiracist Ecopoetics: Waste and Wasting in the Poetry of Claudia Rankine." *Contemporary Literature* 57.1 (Spring 2016): 79–120.

Hunt, Erica. "All About You." *Los Angeles Review of Books*, December 8, 2014; lareviewofbooks.org/article/all-about-you/.

Kellaway, Kate. "Citizen: An American Lyric by Claudia Rankine; Review—The Ugly Truth of Racism." *Guardian*, August 30, 2015; www.theguardian.com /books/2015/aug/30/claudia-rankine-citizen-american-lyric-review.

Kimberley, Emma. "Politics and Poetics of Fear after 9/11: Claudia Rankine's *Don't Let Me Be Lonely*." *Journal of American Studies* 45.4 (November 2011): 777–91.

Laird, Nick. "A New Way of Writing about Race." *The New York Review of Books*, April 23, 2015; www.nybooks.com/articles/2015/04/23/claudia -rankine-new-way-writing-about-race/.

Lee, Felicia R. "A Poetry Personal and Political: Claudia Rankine on 'Citizen' and Racial Politics." *New York Times*, November 28, 2014; www.nytimes .com/2014/11/29/books/claudia-rankine-on-citizen-and-racial-politics.html

LeMahieu, Michael. "Robert Lowell, Perpetual War, and the Legacy of Civil War Elegy." *College Literature* 43.1 (Winter 2016): 91–120.

Love, Heather. "Small Change: Realism, Immanence, and the Politics of the Micro." *Modern Language Quarterly* 77.3 (2016): 419–45.

Nealon, Christopher. *The Matter of Capital: Poetry and Crisis in the American Century*. Cambridge: Harvard University Press, 2011.

Newcomer, Caitlin. "Casting a Shadow from Flesh to Canvas: Claudia Rankine's Plot and the Gendered Textual Body." *Genre* 47.3 (September 2014): 357.

Phillips, Siobhan. "Claudia Rankine's *Citizen*." *ArtForum* (February 2015); www .artforum.com/inprint/issue=201502&id=49793.

Rader, Dean. "The Poetry of Politics, the Politics of Poetry: On Claudia Rankine's Citizen." *Huffington Post*, December 11, 2014; www.huffingtonpost.com/dean -rader/the-poetry-of-politics-the-politics-of-poetry_b_6278798.html.

Reed, Anthony. *Freedom Time: The Poetics and Politics of Black Experimental Writing*. Baltimore: Johns Hopkins University Press, 2014.

———. "The Erotics of Mourning in Recent Experimental Black Poetry." *The Black Scholar: The Journal of Black Studies and Research* 47.1 (April 2017): 23–37.

Robbins, Amy Moorman. *American Hybrid Poetics: Gender, Mass Culture, and Form*. New Brunswick: Rutgers University Press, 2014.

Siraganian, Lisa. "Don't Let Me Be Universal: Or, the Postwar American Poem." *nonsite.org*, June 22, 2015; www.nonsite.org/article/dont-let-me-be-universal.

Spillman, Rob. "Yes, It's about Racism." *Guernica*, November 10, 2014; www .guernicamag.com/rob-spillman-yes-its-about-racism/.

Tracy, D. H. "Reviewed Work(s): *Don't Let Me Be Lonely: An American Lyric* by Claudia Rankine." *Poetry* 185.6 (Winter 2005): 471–72.

Welch, Tana Jean. "Don't Let Me Be Lonely: The Trans-Corporeal Ethics of Claudia Rankine's Investigative Poetics." *MELUS: Multi-Ethnic Literature of the U.S.* 40.1 (Spring 2015): 124–48.

MARTHA RONK

POEMS

FROM *In a Landscape of Having to Repeat*

In a landscape of having to repeat

In a landscape of having to repeat.
Noticing that she does, that he does and so on.
The underlying cause is as absent as rain.
Yet one remembers rain even in its absence and an attendant quiet.
If illusion descends or the very word you've been looking for.
He remembers looking at the photograph,
green and gray square, undefined.
How perfectly ordinary someone says looking at the same thing or
I'd like to get to the bottom of that one.

When it's raining it is raining for all time and then it isn't
and when she looked at him, as he remembers it, the landscape
    moved closer
than ever and she did and now he can hardly remember what it
    was like.

Trying

When I raise my arm I do not actually try to raise it.
WITTGENSTEIN

Trying to find out what one thinks is approximate
at best, trying on one thing and then another
or trying to think of what to say
as in *up the Oregon coast or in a fine spray of mist.*
Trying is not something anyone can do, he says
so we go for a walk in the fog as it happens
a coincidence not to do with trying.
The morning's simply overcast for the third day in a row.
Anyone can add the blue of the distant sea.
Anyone can color in the sky.
But the expanse of gray extends beyond what else is there to say.

A Photograph of a Plate Glass Window

We come to know ourselves through these photographs
as if they were memories yet to come.
An act of mortification looking at the boy in his arms
not the essay about the light off the plate glass (the bird flying into it)
not learning to keep quiet.
The face out there is the one I used to walk by the store
near where I lived. The items in the window, the curtains I'd
forgotten.
The boy in his arms was a boy.
The way one no longer has anything to say looking at (the bird flying
    into it).
The wings expand, we say, the wings are expanded in a blue light.
He writes an essay about it and disappears into the future
of photography where the boy used to lie in his arms.

"I cannot remember anything about this journey other than this"

A moment of inattention brought it all back as in the dream
it catches in your throat and you jerk back from the edge or
hear the cry from someone else although the scene is eerily
quiet almost everywhere. The more images I gathered from the past
the more unlikely it seemed that the past had actually happened
in this way or that, but rather one had pulled back from the edge
and for that moment it all came rushing in.
Events that might have happened otherwise play themselves out
in ways that begin to seem familiar as if the sentence itself
by the one word turned the stream as a jutting rock might do.
I see a man fishing and I see the line spooled out
over his head in beautiful figure eights as if I were practicing
my hand in the school my mother went to before I was born.

"It is only a question of discovering how we can get ourselves attached to it again"

—a drawing by Vija Celmins

I practice interruption to get used to it, get up to get the cup
and sit down, go out to look at the sign on the corner, sit
down, open the book to 37, *Moon Surface (Luna 9)*, close
it, open my mouth to get used to what it says and then
in some weathers, it's offered up freely and you have to
cover the books in plastic, remember to take it with you just in case
and you have to be grateful not to think things up.
Her surface drawings put one squarely on the moon
and there's nothing to take your mind off it, no one brings coffee,
and she's reminded of a scene where the actor talks about how
he's scared to leap off a balcony and then finally leaps.
Someone keeps coming to the door, someone makes a mark
like graphite until it builds up slowly on the surface.

"The shadows of clouds scudded across the steep slopes and through the ravines"

An almost theatrical obscurity seems to have settled on
the adjacent area usually described as ordinary and plain.
The field of weeds is overtaken by the constriction of one's chest,
concealed by rhapsodies. In these cases,
despite the numbers of internal distractions
it is usually best to move about and although everywhere
there are great effusions of feeling, it is nonetheless
recommended to follow the last of the sunlight into that very field
even if the darkness itself is overtaking.
After a passage of time a light breaks on the scene
and allows one to exit in favor of the highly unusual display of clouds.

The

When having finished   the

                the beginning again, the article

in the root of Water fern, every eye may discern the form of a Half Moon

everyone, every eye, every age disappears

                a dissolving moon, nothing to be seen through the smoke and ashes

the sentence itself an integument of flexible green, evoking

beginning and end

a half mirrored   a whole   a half and beginning again—

and discernment, the quiet of parsing

the streets stilled

ruins one's ancestors recall and filmic versions of the same

the   root   of a water fern and time enough   for the

Remembrance

You have to write what you don't yet know and hope

that in another time you might.

But there will be no French

even if he translates some few words to help.

He's ordered more birds to replace those lost

and the few scatter, leaving bits of white.

No one can free himself from the manner of his time

and even he didn't believe he was invited where he received invitations to go.

The yellow bird was up the road and took off quickly

though not so quickly as the swallows skimming the field at the end of the day—

I couldn't believe there were so many and couldn't see what they were after.

Underneath the crescendo the sounds of footsteps

although he'd gone up hours ago.

Even in another tongue, it's something like the thing itself.

> *For the subject in existence is logically constituted only by*
> *the object for which and to which and by which he lives.*
> HENRY JAMES

A Glass Bowl

You enter the room in which each item has been carefully placed, not perfectly or according to any specific aesthetic rules, but certainly, obsessively. Each has to be where it is, exactly here or exactly there. The verbena sticks up out of its vase just as it should at the far edge of a table bought years ago on a street of junk shops and panhandlers. The blackened Chinese jar arches its handle next to the black arch of a companion bowl, a photographic memory never remembered until intruded upon.

Someone has come in the room and moved the chartreuse glass bowl so chartreuse as to seem a gigantic smudge, and suddenly the room begins to swim. The bowl floats in a wobbly arc into the foreground, the rest of the room dims and you feel suddenly and uneasily intimate with the glassy and sickly surface, glazed over by displacement.

Corroded Metal

What I found was a flat piece of metal, corroded, pocked, and shaped quite like a cloud. I hung it over the sink in lieu of a window and looked at it. We wonder what, if anything, objects want, if our rearranging satisfies some hidden need not only of ours but of theirs. Things found in the gutter and rescued, we say, are given another life, but as what—to be looked at, handled, to be made into what one wills, as if one were still a child and had no sense of the so-called value of a thing, but could find in a coil of wire, a bit of cardboard, a flat piece of metal all the possible worlds one might want, given time enough to conjure. So perhaps it is this— this time of seeming eternity that objects want and have no way of requesting, just as we have no way of guaranteeing either for them or for ourselves.

The Window

The window is both a thing in itself and a transparency that obliterates itself by being itself. The thing itself is the wooden frame and cross pieces, the smudged glass panes. The frame creates both an exact view—a tree cut off at the right edge, a corner of roof and jacaranda blooms—and also a frameless view that pulls one off the seat one is sitting in, towards the walls on the other side of the room and out into the blinding white of the morning. It is between inside and outside, between every picture one has seen of trees and these trees, between stasis and movement, between the certainty of the keyboard beneath the fingers and possibility, both the slight noise of tapping and the tapping of branches on the window, creating an illusion, belied by the weighty body, of a weightless glide into the California light that seems the absence of all light, transparency itself.

From "The Book"

1.

The word in the sentence has been smudged, the ink blotted, the paper overfolded, the meaning derailed; the sentence now pale, missing its force and import, languishing as the characters in *La Bohème*, sickly as music without words. The others, the ones intact, try to make up for the missing word and proliferate a range of meanings consistent with the vocabulary and syntax, yet still it is the realm of guesses, guesses as to the missing, as to the alteration in meaning, as to the endless possibilities contained in what would otherwise have been a quite mundane sentence leading to the next in the paragraph, but which now has taken over completely given the aggressive force of the uninvited guest.

2.

For a writer, the intimacy of the image is in submitting completely to what one has imagined and put on the page, to oneself one might say and yet not oneself, an onanism without guilt, the subsuming embrace of an image abstract enough as not to flush the skin, yet vivid enough to cause a collapse into the lilies as if trying to remember the names of the angels and archangels and all the company of heaven, although one never can, just the overwhelming smell of them at the side of the greenhouse door—so much white odor, dusty stamens, the moment of her modest rapture as she saw him appear in the archway with the single flower, the ceiling a complex mosaic of blue and stars, *ave gratia plena dominus tecum*.

3.

The book lies open and prone but keeps closing itself like an irritating fan if the body beneath shifts position from side to side. The paper is there; the fingers are there, and they slip in and out of one another. Yet immersion in one of these things is not, one first thinks, an encounter with the material and restless thing on one's lap. It is rather an encounter with a tyranny of sorts, a haunting into the next hours as a character whom one has never met comes closer, not inhabiting exactly, not taking over thoughts and gestures, but warmer than a fictional character ought to be, standing too close and breathing hard in an internal landscape that was once your own and through which you are both walking where the fictional snow is a kind of snow closer to paper confetti than rain, its texture not unlike the feel of the page underneath your fingers.

FROM *Ocular Proof*

A Blurry Photograph

The tree azalea overwhelms evening with its scent,
defining everything and the endless fields.

Walking away, suddenly, it slices off and is gone.

The visible object blurs open in front of you,
the outline of a branch folds back into itself, then clarifies—just as you turn away—

and the glass hardens into glass

as you go about taking care of things abstractedly
one thing shelved after another, as if they were already in the past,

needing nothing from you until, smashing itself on the tile floor,
the present cracks open the aftermath of itself.

No Sky (after Robert Adams's *California: Views*)

No sky a gray backdrop merely
and below: the straggle of dusty fronds, the scrub oak and scrub jay
whose abrasive noises sharpen in response.

Shadows proliferate in deep furrows no sky above
merely a scrim registering conical thrusts, a heightened flurry &
outlines of branches, the dead ones slowly petering out.

magnificent ruin   the cut through the field   blasted chaparral

As I understand my job, it is, while suggesting order, to make things
appear as much as possible to be the way they are in normal vision.

An unvoiced series of sentences, without articulation,
with gray shapes, formulating a syntax loosening and then tightening from edge to edge.

The frame sets a border down from which a thin straggle hangs at random
like purposeful intrusion, and so unlike

and the interstate (in the title) missing from the photograph itself
merely a dry riverbed, the density of shadows trapped in the confusion
of bush and bush-like tree

except from higher up than the rest, its thin trunk arched against
no sky

colorless, less often remarked upon, appositely emotionless these days,
a relic, like the fan palm living at the edges of water.

> *Ultimately, photography is subversive not*
> *when it frightens, repels, or even stigmatizes,*
> *but when it is pensive, when it thinks.*
> ROLAND BARTHES

Elegy (and a photograph by Robert Adams)

Headlights light up a weed, then a cone of blossoms lifting off into shadows
driven by the demarcation of time
and they stay with us as we go forward in undifferentiated dark.

Part of the trouble is an echo of objects just past and those about to arrive.

They fade out slowly
those conical bright shapes out from the field and across the dashboard.

He had walked into/fallen into the truck crossing the road.
Later he had fallen into the water near the pier.
Earlier he had decided or he hadn't decided or it had shaped itself around him.

It's hard to see sunflowers in the dark but the dark center surrounded
by many gray petals is immediately clear, despite shadows,
despite tricks played on the eye.

It seems more than obvious that nothing particular is about to happen.

When the painters paint the white line down the middle of the road do they see
how it shines in the near dark nearly upon us.

> *Now, everywhere, in the street, the café,*
> *I see each individual under the aspect*
> *of ineluctably having-to-die, which is*
> *exactly what it means to be mortal.*
> *—And no less obviously, I see them*
> *as not knowing this to be so.*
> ROLAND BARTHES

POETICS STATEMENT

Poems often arise from efforts to think through confusions. I once wrote a series of poems for my book *Why/Why Not* called "in the perplexities." I return again and again to what knowing might look like, to how to make sense of what is seen or said, to the vagaries of time—and so my repeated effort to write about memory and the failures necessarily bound up with memory—even of the quotidian, even moments just past. In his book, *In Quest of the Ordinary*, Stanley Cavell writes, "The everyday is what we cannot but aspire to, since it appears to us as lost to us." Poetry often acknowledges this loss, reaching for the missing by means of a language outside the normative; it can make the familiar unfamiliar, edgier, more vivid, in a shifted frame. Or it can offer a way of finding words for the unfamiliar, inexplicable. One is drawn to poetry, in part I believe, as it articulates the uncanny nature of both language and representation, a kind of thinking that allows for the silences and confusions, both private and public, in which we live.

I come to poetry from a parallel career in Renaissance literature, committed to a practice in which they interpenetrate and influence rather than oppose one another. For me, poetry often opens a space that includes both the visual and verbal, as in the plays of Shakespeare: his ability to create a visual spectacle in words and simultaneously to erase it as "only a play," or his way of revising a character like Viola in act 3 of *Twelfth Night* by means of an emblematic image: "Patience on a Monument." Or the strange and metaphysical images in Donne's poetry that work to express the ambiguous and yoke heterogeneous ideas together. The use of the verbal to encounter and coax the visual into being creates a particular frisson for me as it both succeeds and fails. The juxtaposition of images and poetic language enacts a kind of failure since a writer can never bring the visual into language and since the alternation of the visual and verbal seems to shatter each, to acknowledge the failure of congruity—even at the moments of greatest success and enrichment. The shattering affects me internally, on the spine. I am also drawn to the work of W.J.T. Mitchell, who describes the friction between the visual and verbal in which the ekphrastic image acts like a sort of unpresentable "black hole" in the verbal structure, absent but shaping the poem. As a writer I am always aware not only of transience, the melancholy of loss, but also of the melancholy of impossibility. Barbara Guest also addresses images in work I greatly admire, seeing them as disruptive. Extending the work of her chosen predecessors, Guest radically changes the ways in which images are used, not as ways to complement an idea or scene, but as foreign substances that run counter to or athwart much that they seem to be connected to. As she says in "H.D. and the Conflict of Imagism," the image is a "foreign substance," and as such it causes a dislocation that creates movement, vitality, elusiveness, and realms Guest refers to as mysterious. Images work as the energy that propels or attracts, that initiates thinking and creates movement.

Poetry for me specifically means thinking in relation to the words of others, so that memory functions as my own memories in conjunction with other writers as a way of moving away from, or at least modifying, the personal and habitual, a way of acknowledging the imbedded nature of all verbal expression, the fluid nature of a first-person pronoun.

Whatever I write seems intertwined with the language of others, an adopted and temporary internalization, once writing as the mad Ophelia. I write in specific league or conversation with other writers, as if I stood in the same arena, constrained by another's subject matter, line length or diction or framing or images. In *Vertigo* (an homage to W. G. Sebald) I follow out long lines that shift in the middle or segue into a new direction following out the vagaries of memory as he does. His rearranged sentences serve as titles to my own poems.

In *Partially Kept*, I immersed myself in Sir Thomas Browne's *Garden of Cyrus* (1658) in order to think about the disappearance of his view of nature—divinely ordered—and also his amazingly rich vocabulary and sentence structure—so arcane to us today. I used broken lines, small segments of quotations and fragments of lines floating in white space in order to suggest loss, including loss of my own past and self. I've gathered myself close to other figures and hoped for some shift of language, diction, perspective —windows to the world, enlargements.

Incorporating others, the writers I have frequently read and taught, I often feel as if I am ventriloquizing. I often envy poets who belong to a community of other poets sometimes carved out in MFA programs or by working on literary journals or by theoretical persuasion; my own community has often been located in the literary past somewhere, uncannily distant. I returned to reading the poetic prose of Henry James while thinking about the mysterious nature of objects—silent, tropic, unspeaking, evocative—in my book, *Transfer of Qualities* (his phrase). The book tries to enact the uncanny way in which people and things transfer qualities back and forth from one to the other. Standing in the space of *The Spoils of Poynton*, I created a series of prose poems focused on vases, frames, seashells, albums, found objects, photograms.

One way into "the poetics of memory" that so interests me is through the dual image of writing and being written upon as happens in *Hamlet* when Hamlet encounters the ghost of his father, who commands Hamlet: "Remember me." Hamlet's response refers not only to his mental efforts ("Ay, thou poor ghost, while memory holds a seat / In this distracted globe"), but also to writing. Hamlet images his memory as a "table" or tablet that can be wiped clean and written on again:

> Yea, from the table of my memory
> I'll wipe away all trivial fond records,
> All saws of books, all forms, all pressures past
> That youth and observation copied there,
> And thy commandment all alone shall live
> Within the book and volume of my brain. (1.5.98–103)

This conjunction in the play helps locate the ways in which memories are both beyond one's grasp—received from the beyond one might say —and also a product of one's own efforts: to write something down and also to erase and revise and write over it. This particular moment in the play also captures for me the ways in which being written upon necessarily includes both "private" incursions from one's own memories—indeed one's own forgettings—and also public ones. In the play Hamlet takes in his father's vivid description of his own murder, the poison in his ear, the poison and corruption of the kingdom; he may also remember something the culture itself has forgotten: purgatory, for example, which Protestant England had excised a generation before. Central to the question of the poetics of memory is the bifurcated, ambiguous image of memory as unmediatedness and transparency, on the one hand, and as writing, mediation, and opacity, on the other hand. Memory as a digging up and making visible objects from a buried storehouse is thus in tension with practices of writing and reading.

For me questions of memory are very often associated with photography, partly as a result of happenstance, my own childhood Brownie camera and subsequent albums, but more importantly, my immersion in the art world of photography when I first moved from the east coast to Los Angeles in 1971. I collected books, went to shows and galleries, took photographs with my old Leica and printed them, took part in discussions about various aspects of the meaning of such images. My introduction to photography happened at the same time as my own dislocation and loss of a familiar world and introduction to a foreign one of desert, earthquakes, cactus, and culture, and so photographs also became associated for me, as for many others, with questions of memory, documentation, the authentic and the inauthentic, representation. Photographs are both proofs and failed proofs of what was there. They are evocative of the missing and past; perhaps this is too great a reach, but the dialogue between photograph and word seems to me analogous to negative capability, putting one in a realm in which the insistence of each unsettles and produces uncertainties, including a lessening of the self. Photographic images have been allied, by Barthes, Benjamin, Blanchot, and others, with absence and death, presenting the ghosts of what is past. So again, I find myself drawn to ideas and objects that continue an obsession with the transient and melancholy, with an alternating vivid specificity and its concomitant loss. (One way I wrestled with the idea of obsession was to create obsessive and rather comic narrators in my book of short stories, *Glass Grapes*.) It is difficult to know why certain ideas take hold; years ago I belonged to an academic group reading about ekphrasis. It has been with me ever since in my academic work with ekphrastic images of female characters in Shakespeare's plays, through most of my books of poetry, and certainly in *Ocular Proof*, my recent poetic work with photographs. All of us are eager to know "why." But for me this is another question without answer that calls for more poetry, the most intense practice I know.

MARTHA RONK'S DISTRESSED LYRICS

Brian Teare

Introduction: The Lyric's Distress

It's an interesting time for the lyric. Since the 2005 publication of Virginia Jackson's *Dickinson's Misery: A Theory of Lyric Reading*, New Lyric Studies has emerged as a challenge to the orthodox narratives of contemporary American poetics recycled and reified by scholars, poets, and poet-critics whose sometimes acrimonious, often public arguments fueled the Poetry Wars of the '80s and '90s and structured critical discourse well into the new millennium.[1] This was a time in the United States when Language poetry's Marxist-inflected poststructuralist critiques had filtered out of the talk series and small journals of the Bay Area and New York City and into English departments and creative writing programs nationwide, sweeping up scholars, poets, and students alike in a conflict whose rhetoric, to some, conjured echoes of faith-based arguments.[2] This either-you're-for-us-or-against-us era caused many to feel asked to choose: between critically vaunted avant-garde poetries and what Language poet Ron Silliman pejoratively called "the School of Quietude," formally conventional poetries with "a consistency of viewpoint, narrative or expository lines that are treated as unproblematic, language that integrates upwards to meta-levels such as character, plot, or theme."[3]

Language poetry's critique of the "mimetic" and "expressive" language of so-called quietist poetry eventually helped critics to collapse these qualities (and more) into a reductive, polemically expedient idea of the lyric that was then either promulgated by what poet-critic Charles Bernstein calls "official verse culture,"[4] or abjected by avant-gardists as aesthetically complacent, individualist, bourgeois, and politically naïve (at best).[5] But for Jackson and other literary critics currently revitalizing theories of the lyric,[6] the genre has ceased to serve as a polemical object in aesthetic and political debates between poetry's avant-garde and protectors of official verse, and has instead become a figure in the study of how twentieth- and twenty-first-century Anglo-American poetry critics have deployed the generic term. In helping to foment what many experienced as a crisis of affiliation, as Rei Terada writes in "After the Critique of the Lyric," "Language poetry . . . helped lyric studies arrive at this juncture"[7] where the suspicion targeting the lyric has been turned, instead, toward the entire critical discourse that served the Poetry Wars as armory and supplied its heavy weapons.

From the 1980s to the present, Los Angeles poet Martha Ronk has made a career out of cultivating such suspicions, writing apparently lyric poems that self-consciously elaborate on the myriad possible misprisions at play between a reader and the object being read. "Since all that we capture in language is destined to be 'merely' a representation," she writes in the short essay "Poetry and Photography and the Transitory," "what interests me is the ways in which a writer might make that explicit and suggestive."[8] Indeed, from her first book—*Desire in L.A.* (1990)—to her most recent—*Ocular Proof* (2016)—Ronk has consistently allowed the lyric to register the epistemological contingency it has gained in the context of postmodernism, a fact that makes her already remarkable body of work seem both critically canny and remarkably prescient.[9] During the Poetry Wars and in the years since, avant-garde poets have continued to disrupt normative capitalist reading practices through parataxis and disjunction and to free poetic language from conventional semantic meaning and mimetic duties, while more traditional poets have continued to practice poetry as a kind of specialized and heightened speech act, utilizing the generic tropes of "speaker" and "voice" to create the feel of a lyric subject. Meanwhile Ronk has issued book after book whose postmodern lyrics refuse to choose between paratactical disjunction and tropes of voice, frustrated mimesis and stylized representations of speech. As she argues, "poetry can simultaneously document scenes, thought processes, images, emotions, and also acknowledge or demonstrate the artificiality of its presentation."[10] In a genre that has long been characterized by critics like Northrop Frye as depending on "an internal mimesis of sound and imagery" to achieve the feel of being overheard speech, to demonstrate the artificiality of mimesis presents a serious revision of lyric tradition.[11] Indeed, it's her work's *apparent* lyricism—its continual acknowledgement of the artificiality of its images and emotions—that posits Ronk's oeuvre on the major fault line of late twentieth century poetic practice and literary critical discourse about poetics.

Under the scrupulous focus of Ronk's critical intelligence, the lyric appears to flaunt the wear and tear of having been made an object abjected in recent decades after being a genre vaunted for over a century. In light of this literary critical history, it makes sense to read genre as a device that mediates our reading of it, and to see lyric as *technology* in its most etymological sense: *techne* (art, craft) + *logia* (the study of). Though each of Ronk's poems "attempt[s] to be itself an event rather than the representation of an event," as Jonathan Culler writes of the lyric, Ronk takes pains to make each poem read like *both an event and the representation of the poem's attempt to be an event*, one that may or may not succeed.[12] In other words, Ronk's poems highlight their artificiality through the ways they fail to capture "an internal mimesis of sound and imagery" even as they continue to employ some aspects of what Frye, Culler, and other critics call lyric. Half *techne*, half *logia*, Ronk's art employs the lyric as a primary technology precisely because it has traditionally assisted poets in representing consciousness and philosophical interpretations of perception. Thus it would be fair to say that Ronk's most representative poems study their own craftedness, a *poiesis* that performs a theory of making obsessed with the way language always already mediates individual consciousness.

"When I raise my arm I do not usually try to raise it," Wittgenstein writes in entry 622 of *The Philosophical Investigations*, one in a series of passages meditating on the relationship between will and knowledge.[13] Ronk uses this sentence as an epigraph to "Trying," from *In a Landscape of Having to Repeat* (2004), a poem that questions the causal relationship between action and intention in a Wittgensteinian manner. "Trying to find out what one thinks is approximate / at best," Ronk writes, "trying one thing and then another / or trying to think of what to say / as in *up the Oregon coast or in a fine spray of mist*."[14] But by showing us the philosophical attempt to try "to find out what one thinks," Ronk's also trying out the powers of the lyric itself, borrowing what Culler calls "the enunciative apparatus" and the "relation to voice and voicing" for which the genre is famous.[15] "So we go for a walk in the fog as it happens," Ronk writes "a coincidence not to do with trying." As in so many of Ronk's poems, the fog of mediation haunts the linguistic event as self-consciousness about representation, thereby marking the mimetic limits of lyric language. But it is through showing us the *attempt* to try "to find out what one thinks" that Ronk examines the generic technologies by which representation comes to be while enacting a disavowal of representation's mimetic powers.

Indeed, "Trying" dares descriptions of sea and sky inscribed with the awareness of their blasé status as tropes in the history of both landscapes and lyrics. "Anyone can add the blue of the distant sea. / Anyone can color in the sky," the poem asserts before adding, "But the expanse of gray extends beyond what else there is to say." Even as Ronk points to description as a nonfigurative act "anyone" can do, she points fog's more figurative role in the poem, allowing the image to evoke an obscure linguistic space that extends out beyond "what else there is to say." It's worth noting that Ronk reserves for herself the power to point to this fog—it's *not* something "anyone" can do—thus underscoring her signature gift for seeing the limits of representation intrinsic to the technology of the lyric.

Martha Ronk's Distressed Lyrics

Although Ronk has been publishing for over thirty years, her poetics has remained relatively consistent, a virtuoso set of formally deconstructed variations on classic lyric themes like love, perception, grief, and the passage of time. In a 2016 interview with Andy Fitch about the elegies of *Partially Kept* (2012), she speaks of her poetics in terms of linguistic fragility, of failures "based on the limits of language":

> One of the things I've always thought is that if I were to write a poetics, it would have to do with the poetics of failure, and the way in which all the things that you claim or that you try for are already based on the limits of language. I hope that this comes through, maybe in the sense of fragility— the sense that language is as fragile as the little alpine plant. . . . Maybe that's why the elegiac always gets in there. People have said to me "Your poems are so melancholy." For me, failure has to be acknowledged, needs to be faced in some way.[16]

One of the salient qualities of Ronk's oeuvre is that it often appears to employ the technology of the lyric in an unproblematized manner by utilizing many of the formal generic conventions of modern lyric poetry, including brevity, sonic and syntactical compression, ekphrasis, and allusions to canonical literature. Upon closer inspection, however, her oeuvre reveals itself to be simultaneously performing the failure to embody many of the formal qualities most valued by traditional critics of the lyric. "The essential structure of a poem . . . resembles that of architecture or painting," Cleanth Brooks writes in that chestnut of New Criticism, *The Well Wrought Urn*, "it is a pattern of resolved stresses . . . a pattern of resolutions and balances and harmonizations, developed through a temporal scheme."[17] Given that, as I have argued, Ronk has played out her "poetics of failure" as formal variations upon that theme, it should come as no surprise that the temporal schemes of her most characteristic poems undercut any "pattern of resolved stresses," leave "balances" unresolved, and offer cognitive dissonance its prime place in their theory of harmony. Thus my strategy in this essay will be to read poems drawn from across the career in which Ronk has employed the conventions of the lyric to expose how language always already fails, perhaps *especially* in those moments of deepest intimacy we've come to expect from the genre so often defined as "an utterance in the first person, an expression of a personal feeling."[18]

For instance, "Odi et amo 4," from *Why/Why Not* (2003), offers itself as a reading, and thus also as a reiteration, of Catullus's famous epigram, one of lyric poetry's most concise statements about the crucible of romantic love. Catullus 85 perfectly dramatizes Anne Carson's sense of the dilemma of early Greek lyric poets: "in the lyric poets, love is something that assaults or invades the body of the lover to wrest control of it from him, a personal struggle of will and physique."[19] Catullus, of course, was himself a close reader and translator of Sappho, and his love poems often enact the same dynamic Carson describes at work in the Sapphic canon:

> I hate and I love. You wonder, perhaps, why I'd do that.
> I have no idea. I just feel it. I am crucified.[20]

"I hate and I love," Catullus writes, what a dumb thing to do. It's not logical —"You wonder . . . why I'd do that"—though the poem attempts to subject the speaker's feelings to a kind of analysis before simply giving up. He doesn't get far; instead of ideas, he has feelings, *Odi et amo*, the most odious couple. Feeling opposite emotions at once simply exhausts the speaker's intellectual resources, and there's nothing to do but let them work upon the self as a form of suffering. Catullus 85 records the generic lyric situation that Carson characterizes as a "struggle of the body as a unity of limbs, senses and self, amazed at its own vulnerability."[21] Though his poem attempts to proceed logically, it shows us that linear logic only gets us so far when faced with one of the central paradoxes of human experience.

Though Ronk's "Odi et amo 4" clearly recapitulates the drama of subjective experience central to Catullus's famous couplet and the lyric poetry of early Greece, its methods are very different than those of conventional lyrics in the Anglo-American tradition. Catullus 85, as an elegiac couplet, can easily be read as an example of Brooks's well-wrought "pattern of resolved stresses," but Ronk's "Odi et Amo 4" does not resolve the stresses it inflicts upon traditional grammar, though its compact design *does* give it a curiously balanced imbalance, one achieved by duration. Where Catullus proceeds logically—stating his predicament, inquiring into its nature, and then giving up thinking he'll ever understand it—"Odi et amo 4" asserts an argument in the first line that the poem refuses to prove or refute in any discursive way:

Allegory is the only way to conclusion.
Dubious with the growing grass I miss you.
You turned out to be long past the event.
Each geranium leaf lent itself to the morning.
The amount of time spent counting.
Lifted out of herself and over the fence.
Several birds and several more birds.
Some things are quiet and others resolved.
When you became what I couldn't stop thinking.[22]

If "Allegory is the *only* way to conclusion," then this poem is never going to get anywhere, evoking as it does the attention span of the alienated lover waiting for some sign that the beloved returns their affection. Each end-stopped line closes a line of thought that the next line may or may not re-open; each end-stopped line is a measure of "The amount of time spent counting," a pastime, we know from Shakespeare's sonnets, that's a favorite of anxious lovers. Ronk uses the paradox at the heart of Catullus 85 as the generative seed for a poem that seems to explore desire's divisive effect on mind—where Catullus uses logic to clearly explain his painful situation, Ronk only *appears* to use structures of grammar and logical proposition, instead undermining them and demonstrating desire's talent for creating instability even within structures that are supposed to hold true. Catullus explains the irrational rationally; Ronk *shows* us how the irrational feels as it breaks the conventions of grammar.

Ronk's restaging of Catullus 85 brings the central dilemma of Greek lyric poets into the twenty-first century by integrating into the lyric the kinds of breakages with grammar Language poetry made possible, transforming parataxis and fragment into the mimesis of an individual psychology. Ronk has made the fragmented *form* of the postmodern lyric an allegory for the stuck state of loving and hating at once; the end-stopped lines recreate the frustration of circling around a subject, a somewhat dithery movement countered by the fact that their fragmentariness stutters to a conclusion that doesn't end in the traditional sense. The lines feel barely controlled, their detached tone comes across as hard won, and their pinched syntax everywhere betrays the proximity of the uncontrollable, thus marking the many ways love and hatred are a bad fit, out of sync with event, with narrativity. And while the poem indeed makes room for some things that "are quiet"—that geranium leaf, for instance—nothing seems quite resolved or harmonized; the speaker remains painfully obsessed with the "you," a state that in the final line indeed seems to border on the erotic possession Carson describes as central to Greek lyric poetry. By the end of "Odi et amo 4," it's fair to say that we've gotten no allegorical resolution in the narrative sense of the word: no pilgrim, no progress. Rather than effecting a poetic closure that makes us aware of "a pattern of resolutions and balances and harmonizations," the last line leaves us in the grip of irrational passion, but it also keeps *Odi et amo* going, the ancient integrated into lyric's contemporary iteration.

While Ronk's work obviously derives a large part of its charm and power from its commitment to thematic and formal conventions borrowed from the lyric, this commitment is also one of its greatest risks. On the one hand, the conventional lyric with its emphasis on personal inwardness, linguistic poise, and formal unity poses a serious challenge to the disruptive editing techniques and the philosophical questions Ronk's poetics of failure traffics in. On the other hand, the lyric has been critiqued and rejected by the west coast avant-garde with whom Ronk has sometimes been associated; orthodox definitions of the lyric have even been thoroughly questioned by the critics of New Lyric Studies. But I'd argue that in a poem like "Odi et amo 4," lyric has become what poet-critic Susan Stewart has called a "distressed genre," one in which the lyric "appears as a process of appropriation, manipulation, and ultimately transformation" of both precursor and current text.[23]

Indeed, one of Ronk's signature techniques is to resist the generic expectations produced by lyric technology by playing up the inherent structural tension of free verse, flaunting how line and line break threaten the integrity of sentences, and vice versa, thus creating a "distressed" syntactical and prosodic texture instead of the "pattern of resolved stresses" that characterizes a New Critical vision of the lyric. And though distressed genres, Stewart argues, are marked both by "a desire to escape mediation" by returning to the tropes of an earlier mode and a concomitant "inauthenticity of presentation" because of those very tropes, Ronk's distressed lyrics employ "outdated" notions of lyric *because* of their need to *contrast* literary historical modes of knowledge and knowing's contemporary contexts.[24] Thus *distress* in Ronk's lyric poems is not "a desire to escape mediation," but rather the admission of mediation's omnipresence in all literary language, perhaps especially in the lyric. Likewise, techniques that would create "inauthenticity of presentation" in a traditional lyric become in Ronk's oeuvre the *only* means of experiencing, in language, experience of any kind.

In other words, Ronk uses disjunction and fragment to effect a rather literal "distressing" of the lyric, subjecting the well-wrought urn to epistemological duress while largely maintaining the illusion of the lyric's formal integrity. Such distress is as much a marker of the lyric's travel through time as it is a marker of its contemporary situation, reminding us of the fact that *travel* and *travail* share a root. And in certain of Ronk's more recent poems, the lyric's tight syntactical weave gives way, leaving the resulting fragments to scatter like the ashes of their source text. As Ronk writes in "Below the moon, above the sun," from *Vertigo* (2007), a poem selected from the text of Sir Thomas Browne's *Selected Writings*,

In vain   , or

    below the Moon

        above the Sun

            con -

trived   is lost in

    a folly of   memory

There is no antidote against the *Opium* of time, which temporally
considereth all things;[25]

Throughout this erasure-based collage, Ronk foregrounds not illusionistic
joinery and montage but text giving way to fragment under the weight of
history—this is especially apparent in the punctuation, the comma and
semicolon that cling to the phrasing like residue of a former context. In
"Below the moon, above the sun," the lyric indeed appears *distressed*, both
in the sense of being broken-in and of having the appearance of an "an-
tique" fabricated recently, its remnants deliberately contrived "in vain." "I
find myself constantly drawn to the fragility of things in the face of time,"
Ronk writes in her 2008 essay "Poetics of Failure," "I want to catch the
threads of transitory things, to acknowledge the dislocation we all suffer
and count on."[26] In its emphasis on the wounds dealt to language by its
temporal and historical situation, Ronk's relationship to conventional crit-
ical accounts of the lyric resembles the relationship to conventional read-
ings of the Modernist fragment Ann Lauterbach describes in her essay "As
(It) Is: Toward a Poetics of the Whole Fragment":

                                    . . . This
            fragment is not
    one in which one laments a lost whole, as in Stein, Eliot and Pound, but
            which acknowledges the fact
    of our *unhandsome condition*, where we suffer from having been being,
            and in that
    acknowledgment foreground, or privilege, what is: the abraded and indefinite
    accumulation of an infinite dispersal of sums. In this construction, meaning
            abides
    or arises exactly at the place where "use" appears, "use" here meant both as
            pragmatics
    and as wear.[27]

Ronk's *distress* is likewise an aesthetics of duration and wear, and, like
Lauterbach's whole fragments, her lyrics propose the peculiar mode of
"having been being" as their ontological ground. Deeply pragmatic in

many senses of the word, Ronk's work also grounds itself in an investigation of "use" not unlike that of the ordinary language philosophy associated with Wittgenstein. So at times she highlights the wear accumulated by a genre game whose conventions, according to critical histories of the lyric, are centuries old, and, at other times, she frames the lyric as a language game whose tropes she must scrutinize in light of the postmodern. In both cases, Ronk employs fragment, collage, and various ingenious nonce forms of joinery to create a syntax that is as capable of confronting the folly of memory as it is of critical reflexivity. Her lyrics are *distress* as both noun and verb, a situation and an action, a kind of context and its effect on its content, all of its meanings originating in the root feeling of being pressed, vexed, or strained. The magic of Ronk's oeuvre is its ability to inquire into this uncomfortable feeling with rigorous intelligence and tender wonder.

An Epistemology of Distress

I could certainly argue that the epistemological distress found in Ronk's poems is symptomatic of postmodernism in general, given that "for us today," as Frederic Jameson writes in *Postmodernism, or the Cultural Logic of Late Capitalism*, "art does not seem in our society to offer any direct access to reality, any possibility of unmediated representation or of what used to be called realism."[28] I could also argue that Ronk's poetics of failure measures the distance from the aesthetics that inform a traditional lyric (with its illusion of unmediated access to a speaking subject) to those that inform a Language poem (with its emphasis on the always already mediated nature of language), and that this distance is measured by the work of other poets as well.[29] As Reginald Shepherd writes in his introduction to *Lyric Postmodernisms: An Anthology of Contemporary Innovative Poetries*, postmodern lyrics like Ronk's tend to

> integrate the traditional lyric's exploration of subjectivity and its discontents, the modernist grappling with questions of culture and history and language's capacity to address and encompass those questions, and the postmodernist skepticism toward grand narratives and the possibility of final answers or explanations, toward selfhood as a stable reference point, and toward language as a means by which to know the self or its world.[30]

By moving in an arc from "traditional lyric" through "modernist grappling" to "postmodernist skepticism," Shepherd does a beautiful job of describing the work not only of Ronk and the other poets he includes in his anthology, but of a particular poetics that emerged in the United States both alongside and in the fractious wake of Language poetry. Thus between the Poetry Wars and the advent of New Lyric Studies came a time in the late '90s and early aughts when some critics, in the attempt to describe and advocate for this new work, disrupted the false but controlling binary of "Language" vs. "Lyric" with a series of third terms: while Stephanie Burt controversially suggested "elliptical,"[31] and David St. John and Cole Swensen offered "hybrid,"[32] Michael Palmer also dubbed these lyrics "analytic"[33] before Shepherd characterized them as "postmodern." The inspiration for such gestures was not merely exasperation with the current state of affairs, nor were these epithets prescriptive the way the terminology favored by Language poetry often seemed to be. Terms like "elliptical poetry" or "lyric postmodernism" or "analytic lyric" were descriptivist, attempts to characterize and catalogue work that was already being published, work that seemed to transgress the polemical divide between Language and lyric poetries.

And while labeling Ronk an elliptical poet or a lyric postmodernist may at first usefully orient us toward her poetics of failure, such epithets largely serve to suggest a zeitgeist rather than describe the specifics of Ronk's own poetics.[34] Because her poems concern themselves with illusory access to a speaking subject's perceptions, thoughts, and feelings, *and* the failures of such illusions due to the always already mediated nature of language, Ronk remains unique among elliptical poets and lyric postmodernists in her career-long commitment to using the technology of the lyric as the primary means to mark its limits. To enact this contradiction at the heart of her work, she uses an array of signature techniques that a) test the limits of lyric language without destroying the musicality and affective effects of the lyric, b) create the *affect* of knowing we have no unmediated access to reality, c) demonstrate how difficult it is to untangle what we think about reality from the mediated images we've internalized, and d) create the further uncanny affect of knowing how difficult it is to have access to *any* unmediated thoughts about reality. Using the disjunctive techniques of postmodern poetics to set up provisional structures in the distance between *seems* and *is*, Ronk's poems distress their own epistemology by worrying the boundary between perceiving and knowing.

The unstable landscape of uncertainty is a residence poetry and philosophy have increasingly shared since the twentieth century, when both practices experienced a heightened awareness of the troubled and troubling relationship between perception, language, representation, and the real. "From its *seeming* to me—or to everyone—to be so," Ludwig Wittgenstein writes in *On Certainty*, "it doesn't follow that it *is* so. What we can ask is whether it can make sense to doubt it."[35] The radical doubt Wittgenstein asks us to cultivate in relation to seeming, Ronk brings to bear upon the lyric and to knowing the world in and through language. Like Wittgenstein's propositions, like the epigraph to "Trying" she draws from *The Philosophical Investigations*, Ronk's lyrics find infinite sensible occasions for doubt in the space between seeming and being, appearance and certainty. Ronk is as interested as Wittgenstein in the language game of representation as she is in interrogating the hidden logics and limits it depends upon. For instance, a poem from *Desire in L.A.* (1990), "Rhetoric No. 3," begins:

> Why does "it" rain, it's raining, or it's wet
> everywhere, why does "it" hurt, displacement
> away from the center of what can't be
> conceived—self, sky, what's up there somewhere
> bringing to or toward . . .[36]

This early poem demonstrates Ronk's career-long propensity for building a complex poem out of a simple question: to what does the pronoun "it" refer when we say "*It* is raining"? For Ronk that *it* becomes an occasion for philosophical inquiry, a sign for "the center of what can't be / conceived," an abstract feeling as particular as William James's famous "feeling of *and*, a feeling of *if*, a feeling of *but*, and a feeling of *by*," feelings that exist because of grammar and because emotions are both held by and derived from it.[37] But we can't individuate and name those feeling states until we inquire into the grammar with which we build our relation to the world. "My work exists in the interrogative mode," admits Ronk in her essay "Poetics of Failure," "whether or not a question mark appears at the end of a line."[38] And in the same way Wittgenstein's propositions depend upon conventional semantics even as he examines how meaning gets made through conventional usage, so Ronk subjects the lyric to a scrutiny of the artifice it traditionally depends upon. "Is meaning really only the use of the word?" Wittgenstein asks in *Philosophical Grammar*, "Isn't it the way this use meshes with our life?"[39] In "Paraphrase," a poem from *State of Mind* (1995), Ronk seems to answer Wittgenstein's questions: "How close to the original they could get / was more to the point."[40]

Concerned both with how we experience perception and with what role art and language play in our interpretation of the real, Ronk also often returns to how our experience of reality is always already inflected by artistic and technological media and scaffolded by structures inherent in language. Ronk especially hones in on "the tension between the visual and verbal," she argues in "Poetics of Failure," in an attempt to show how "they belie one another, shatter one another" and "also, potentially, suggest and enhance."[41] Her 2004 poem "Photography Loves Banal Objects" exemplifies the contradictions that underlie that tension between our experiences of the visual and the verbal, contradictions that become especially exaggerated by technological meditation:

> The words remained the same despite the variation in scale
> manipulated by the program she was using for graphic design
> of how much she wanted to tell her.[42]

For Ronk, the tension between the verbal and the visual is best articulated in the lyric, as it is in film, by technique. This excerpt demonstrates Ronk's characteristic methods, particularly her use of line break as an equivalent to the film editor's razor and tape. In her hands, lines join but in slightly off-kilter ways that suggest montage, a form of joinery characterized by a cut that splices two images or scenes into forced relation. For all of its initial smoothness, her editing is subtly disorienting because her expert splicing relies on the *illusion* of grammatical logic maintained despite the obvious disjunction inside its syntax. At her most paratactical, Ronk refuses the montage effect of enjambment, and leaves each line a fragment whose final period claims a kind of completion, as in "Odi et amo 4." Given that these "complete" fragments often consist of obviously collaged phrases, such end-stops raise the same questions posed by the word *cleave*: does the hard cut of the end-stop join the lines? Does it refuse such joinery? Or does the cut join and refuse simultaneously? A poem from *Eyetrouble* (1998), "Collage," deploys both enjambment and end-stop, both joinery and fragment, and seems to suggest several answers to my several questions:

> What's missing's been cut out and for a number of years.
> A question is rows put in yesterday. What can't be won't change.
> If you have a number of them you can choose each time
> a different shape or face you can make an arrangement in a jar.[43]

As is clear from this excerpt, Ronk's practice of collage allows for a variety of textural gestures, from the end-stopped fragment of the first line to the collage logic of the first sentence of line two, to the simultaneously enjambed and collaged joinery of lines three and four. Her signature technique is to pit the lyric mode against itself by playing up the inherent structural tension of free verse, flaunting how the line and line break threaten the integrity of the sentence, and vice versa, thus creating her signature "distressed" syntactical textures. Throughout her work, clearly articulated dependent and independent clauses brush up against sentences and lines that persist in some liminal grammatical state between dependence and independence. Rather than asking us to rest purely in certainty or uncertainty, or to choose between *is* and *seems*, ambivalence and doubt make possible a plurality of possible relationships to meaning. "If you have a number of them," she reminds us, "you can choose each time / a different shape or face."

The Lyric Subject's Distress

Jonathan Culler reminds us in *Theory of the Lyric* that lyric subjects enact a both/and situation: lyrics grant readers provisional access to the interior lives of their authors at the same time that they present fictional subjects speaking out of invented dramas. A form of mediation that depends on the generic trope of a lack of mediation, lyric "can tell truths," Culler writes, "and can also lie."⁴⁴ Allowing the lyric this kind of latitude allows us to treat the genre "as a linguistic event of another type, an act of poetic enunciation which one can attribute—why not?—to the poet, but a poet who remains in a biographically indeterminate relation to the claims of the poem itself."⁴⁵ Culler's version of the lyric here describes the dynamic between Ronk's lyric subjects and the scenes of distress they both create and suffer from, while also anticipating Michael Palmer's desire "to address the problematics of the purely private utterance" in the postmodern era. "An entire body of work . . . built on an anxiety about the fragility of signification," Palmer reminds us, "leads to the lyric voice, the problematics of self-expression" because "the self comes dramatically into question if one is going to face the actual condition of the individual."⁴⁶

In the same way that Ronk's postmodern lyrics take for granted the both/and truth/lie situation that Culler outlines, Ronk's oeuvre seems less interested in questions of selfhood *per se* than in how language does and does not communicate an individual self experiencing itself knowing and perceiving. Ronk is, after all, the author of a book of short autobiographical essays, *Displeasures of the Table* (2001), subversively subtitled *Memoir as Caricature*. The linking of these genres—memoir, which largely presents autobiographical experience as immersive, realist narrative; and caricature, which deliberately aestheticizes, exaggerates, and falsifies facts for critical purposes—alerts us immediately to a genre situation whose aestheticized relationship to the author's biography is similar to that of Culler's indeterminate "act of poetic enunciation." And though its critical history largely suggests otherwise, lyric poetry isn't bound by the same "autobiographical pact" as autobiographical prose, a pact that Philippe Lejeune describes in *On Autobiography* as the structural equation of the author with the protagonist of her narrative, a pact signed into effect by the fact of the author and protagonist bearing the same name. "The autobiographical pact is the affirmation in the text of this identity," Lejeune writes, "referring in the final analysis to the *name* of the author on the cover."⁴⁷ Neither Ronk's "memoir as caricature" nor her poetry make the structural effort to link author and narrator or lyric subject through this kind of affirmation. And though there are biographical continuities across her oeuvre—such as a childhood in Ohio, and an adulthood spent among the landscapes of Los Angeles and Vermont—these generally do not carry the same weight as the autobiographical pact made by the structural equation of author and narrator. Rather, if and when we read Ronk's postmodern lyrics as representative of her life, it's with the weaker agreement of the lyric's critical history in mind, an agreement not so much structural as cultural, an agreement whose contractual vagueness Ronk mines for all it says—and, more importantly, *doesn't* say—about lyric language and its relationship to self-hood and subjectivity.

For if, as Culler argues, the lyric poet is in a "biographically indeter-minate" relation to the lyric subject of her poems, it's fitting that Ronk's lyrics utilize techniques that simultaneously create the illusion of auto-biographical presence and undermine that illusion, often in ways that are quite playful and witty. The resulting lyrics never seem to raise the ques-tion of whether or not they are true to Ronk's own experience; rather, they raise the question of whether or not language can ever get close to *anyone's* experience. "Closer to My Natural Voice," from *In a Landscape of Having to Repeat* (2004), is one such lyric:

> I keep a lot to myself although as you say
> I am always giving pointed answers to pointed questions
> what others kinds are there you say I said what's kept
> is a kind of where I was yesterday for example
> or a certain whine as I am quoting
> although it seems otherwise than it might
> but closer to my natural voice as you say isn't
> a crucial event but the actual words I've kept for
> such an occasion when what I've kept to myself
> as if anyone would want to hear for any reason
> except you sound so like yourself again.[48]

This wickedly knowing poem deploys two critically canonical aspects of the lyric in a sharp-edged exploration of their limits: 1) the supposedly "natural voice" of the lyric subject, and 2) apostrophe, whose lyric address has the effect of replacing "narrative temporality with [the] temporality of the poetic event."[49] The "poetic event" here is classic lyric: an overheard conversation with another, possibly a beloved, whose presence is conjured through the vocative. But the execution of this event is classic Ronk: every-where the lines break against phrasal completion and semantic meaning; clauses are fused at awkward moments within the lines so that who speaks and what is spoken become confused; and the "naturalness" of the voice is undermined by the artifice of poetry, though not by the lyric's tone or dic-tion. This tension between "my natural voice" and poetic artifice stages a drama crucial to the lyric: "one of the central features of the lyric," Culler argues, "is the tension between enchantment and disenchantment."[50] This also happens to be one of the tensions central to romantic love. As Susan Stewart argues in *Poetry and the Fate of the Senses*, voice plays a central and analogous role in both lyric and romance because "The beloved's voice is untouchable. It is that which touches me and which I cannot touch. Yet the one who 'owns' it—that is, the one who belongs to it—cannot touch it either."[51] In "Closer to My Natural Voice," Ronk's use of an apostrophe in which "my natural voice" and the voice of the addressed become some-what indistinguishable through artifice seems to speak simultaneously of the postmodern lyric's disenchantment with voice *and* the enchantment of coupledom, that place where touch and the untouchable merge and own-ership isn't singular.

Thus it's fitting that Ronk's lyric claims that "closer to my natural voice as you say isn't / a *crucial* event" (my emphasis). In fact, this voice is "what I've kept to myself / as if anyone would want to hear for any reason." There is in this poem a kind of hilarious pull between a suspicious with-holding—"I keep a lot to myself"—and a begrudging intertwining—"I am always giving pointed answers to pointed questions / what other kinds are there *you say I said*" (emphasis mine). In stark contrast to most apos-trophic lyrics, the "you" is not only addressed, but is also reported to have talked back, and in fact acts as a repository for things the I has said in the past, phrases that become present in the poem as implied dialogue. This spiky intimacy refashions apostrophe as a kind of enchanted disen-chantment, a place where interior experiences such as memories—"what's kept / is a kind of where I was yesterday for example"—meet voice—"a certain whine as I am quoting"—and both of these meet the other of lyric address in a reported address to the lyric subject. The poem's final four lines—and in particular its final line—exemplify the complexity of this meeting, given that the grammar leading up to them suggests they are spo-ken to the I before the I repeats them: "but closer to my natural voice *as you say* isn't / a crucial event" (emphasis mine). The rest of the poem can then be read as the voice of the addressed rendered by the I, an act that ren-ders the final line a surprising inversion of apostrophe: through the mouth of another, the lyric turns to address its own author!

That the phrase that completes this turn is "you sound so like yourself again" has the further delightful irony of suggesting that in order to get "closer to my natural voice," this lyric subject has to hear their own words echoed back to them through another. This witty mediation not only points toward Michael Palmer's sense of "the problematics of a purely private utterance" by suggesting even such utterances are always already medi-ated events, but also underscores Susan Stewart's sense of voice as a me-dium through which "the beloved . . . gives witness to what is alive in our being."[52] In the case of Ronk's lyric subject, we find a lively sense of humor animating the deep skepticism about language that's native to postmodern aesthetics: "closer to my natural voice as you say isn't / a crucial event but the actual words which I've kept for / such an occasion" emphasizes that it's not "my natural voice" but "actual words" that are the crucial event here in the space between self and other, poet and reader, the natural and the actual. And yet words aren't off the hook; they could in fact be said to *be* the hook the speaker's on.

Ronk so thoroughly infuses her lyric subject with a distrust of language's power to represent voice that the resultant first person could be said to be the words it claims to say in the same way that the lyric is the way its words are arranged. "Language games are the forms of language with which a child begins to make use of words," Wittgenstein writes."[53] Like a word in one of these language games, like the word "it" in the clause "it's raining," Ronk's lyric subject is both a basic function of grammar and a set of philosophical and literary critical problems. It consists of how it has been deployed by and used in both the critical history of the lyric and her own lyrics—indeed, "Closer to My Natural Voice" insists that neither I nor the lyric are separate from the way grammar works, or lines break, or how the generic fiction of a "natural" voice addressing another succeeds and fails. Ronk's lyrics turn Culler's "poetic event" into a high stakes language game. So what kind of game is the lyric and what kind of speaker is this, exactly? These questions are inextricable from "Closer to My Natural Voice," in which "naturalness" and artifice, voice and words, coexist without offering a single answer. Typically, the poem seems to suggest that both the lyric and its erstwhile speaking subject are both/and. Indeed, Ronk's postmodern lyric insists on a productive blur between spoken and written discourse, speakerly fiction and language, while tacitly acknowledging that speaking and writing, and person and words, exist in the world as very different facts all mutually implicated in each other.

For these reasons, it ultimately seems inaccurate to call the "I" of Ronk's poem a speaker or subject in the traditional senses of those words. "If I do speak of a fiction," Wittgenstein writes in *The Philosophical Investigations*, "then it is of a *grammatical* fiction."[54] Indeed, Ronk's lyric subject is much closer to a *narrator* than a speaker, and her lyrics are more like diegetic worlds in which language literally serves as setting, syntax serves as character, and grammar lays out the plot. It makes sense, then, that Ronk's lyrics are as likely to be in first person as third (and often combine elements of the two), and that the obsessions of her speaker-narrators remain consistent across all the genres in which she's published. One short story from *Glass Grapes* (2008), "Her Subject/His Subject," opens with the same Wittgenstein epigraph as "Trying," and both texts concern the relationship between description and perception, language and landscape, willful effort and "just" being:

> Her subject is people in landscapes of estrangement; his subject is the landscape. *You are never looking out the window*, he says to her. *Here you are driving through the most beautiful section of the California coast, and you are talking to me about a novel you are reading, the words on the pages, the characters' clothes. I am in the scotch broom*, he says, and yes, he seems to be as far as I can tell, and he is right and I am not.[55]

Of course it's hard not to notice an intertwining of voices and dueling perspectives similar to those in "Closer to My Natural Voice." But what this passage also reveals is that perhaps the character of Ronk's narrator-speakers just happens to be similar to the character of postmodern skepticism about representation: for her, the mediated nature of textuality is perhaps more immediate, seductive, and absorbing than reality. But it is a useful and fruitful habit, this being in the wrong, this palimpsest of text over perception, because, as Ronk writes in "Poetics of Failure," in "writing by means of analogy or even juxtaposition," "the whole seems to teeter and to fail, certainly to defy logic, but in the most satisfying moments, in the failure of absolute congruity, to create new constructs."[56] Thus our narrator's "landscapes of estrangement," like the landscapes of Ronk's own lyrics, bear the strains and traces of interpreting them and rendering those interpretations in language, and, in bearing such traces, become something twice seen anew. One thing Ronk's story does, however, that her lyrics steadfastly refuse to do, is to describe the process of perceptual estrangement and to hazard a psychological analysis of the narrator's preference for mediation and textuality over the fiction of an unmediated real:

> To me the foggy blur over the tops of trees is a mental affair. You hold in your mind another time and live there in that other imagined time while the present time, new and raw in some way, presses for attention . . . I can't remember when I haven't done this. Being in two places at one time. This is my definition of a person, I say . . . It began, no doubt, as a protective device.[57]

Rather than extrapolate from this passage a psychological theory with which to read the lyric subject of Ronk's oeuvre, we might instead note that the speaker's "definition of a person" ultimately has to do with certain techniques of mind, the very things that we as readers are asked to do when we read Ronk's lyrics: "You hold in your mind another time . . . while the present . . . presses for attention." And while Ronk goes on to speculate, briefly, about the reasons these techniques developed, what gets analyzed in her prose fiction gets deployed in its purest form in her lyrics as technique. Indeed, her lyrics restlessly and relentlessly enact the same gestures of superimposition, collage, and palimpsest again and again, a characteristic formal repetition we might associate with the lyric writ large—the return of a lyric poet to a singular idiom with an attendant set of seemingly inexhaustible techniques. Like Dickinson, for instance, Ronk discovered her preferred techniques early on, and has since her second book, 1992's *Desert Geometries*, explored these preferences, which she describes in "Poetics of Failure":

> I try for language that is familiar and yet in which words are juxtaposed in unusual ways, for sentences that seem quite ordinary, but veer off in new

directions, take up unexpected threads, omit transitions. I jam two sentences together so that certain words fall out, leaving a trace despite their absence . . . It is complex syntax that must do most of the work, the articulation between one sentence and another; I am not interested in single words in white space, but in joinery.[58]

Ronk's description of her aims is notable not only because it demonstrates that she thinks of the words, sentences, and syntax she works with as the primary materials of writing. It's also notable because, though she doesn't root her poetics in personal narrative or psychology, she omits them from her account of her poetics without totally disavowing them either. "Like others I am wary of narration, but am also interested in the complex integuments of a line, and in music as part of that complexity," she writes. "Or perhaps I'd be more honest to say I can't help it."[59] What psychologizing Ronk does is spent on her aesthetic preferences, which for her, like words and sentences and narration, are ultimately materials to be manipulated for effect, not their autobiographical truth-value, though autobiographical and true they may helplessly be. And her description also accounts with remarkable accuracy for the way her lyrics actually work: despite sentences that veer, transitions that get omitted, words that fall out of sentences jammed together, and the resulting traces of such waywardness, absence, and collision, Ronk's lyrics hold together through her interest in joinery, an interest so highly refined and finely practiced that it reminds us all joints are exacted from cuts fashioned to fit and carry the weight of use.

But it's the fact that this joinery persists and succeeds *despite* the myriad ways her lyrics court and perform an epistemology of distress and failure that makes them so remarkable and so indubitably hers. Judging by the philosophical and aesthetic terms they set up, they *successfully* fail: to be representational and not to be representational, to be lyrics and not to be lyrics, to be speakerly and not to be speakerly. And if Ronk's lyrics are written under the sign of a habitually unmarked interrogative, it is not because asking inherently gets us anywhere in a teleological sense. Indeed, the recursive quality of reading her oeuvre underscores the sense that inside the larger questions are only the same questions writ smaller. "Explanations beside the point," her lyrics don't answer the questions they pose but instead reproduce the anxieties of not knowing, of asking and then worrying over the resultant knowledge.[60] And if the interrogative mood assumes a speaker and an interlocutor—not unlike the apostrophe of "Closer to My Natural Voice"—her lyrics usually avoid narrating any stable dyadic Q&A relation in favor of creating a diegetic world of generalized, shared unknowing.

It's this world of unknowing that we too inhabit while reading Ronk's oeuvre, and the lyric as it is redefined through her work has everything to do with the labor of knowing that we as readers share that unknowing. Her lyrics again and again remind us that *all* forms of knowledge are provisional and contingent, from genre to perception to our own subjectivity. "You have to write what you don't yet know," she writes in a poem from *Partially Kept* (2012), "Remembrance," "and hope / that in another time you might."[61] Marking as they do the gaps between writing, knowing, and knowing you know, Ronk's lyrics remind us that critical discussions of the contemporary lyric have for too long implicitly separated professional readers of the lyric (i.e., critics) from practitioners (i.e., poets) much in the same way they've separated criticism from the lyric itself. But in Ronk's lyrics the lyric subject *is* a reader and critic of her own existential and linguistic situations, and thus her lyrics themselves constitute a readerly and critical practice. Though the lyric subject of her poems never explicitly situates itself as a teacher or scholar,[62] the poems nonetheless everywhere bear the influence of "literary sources and . . . a firm belief in dialogue with the language of others—in the interdependence of reading and writing."[63] Fittingly, Ronk's books are filled with allusions to the Renaissance literature on which she wrote her dissertation, but they are just as likely to allude to novelists Henry James and W. G. Sebald and to visual artists like Eva Hesse or Hannah Hoch as they are to Shakespeare and Sir Thomas Browne. And though many poems dialogue with literary sources or the techniques of other arts, Ronk's lyrics allows this dialogue to constitute neither narrative situations nor allusions that can be reduced to easily legible critical narratives of intertextuality; instead, this dialogue produces further questions, each an instance of shared unknowing that suggests to readers a critical framework to use in interpreting this shared epistemological situation.[64]

In the end, it is this interdependence of reading and writing in the lyrics of a working contemporary poet that most potently challenges the critical orthodoxies of both New Lyric Studies and proponents of the avant-garde, the former of which privileges criticism over the lyric itself, and the latter of which devalues lyric without interrogating the inherited critical assumptions its critiques of lyric depend upon. Virginia Jackson's claim that "lyrics can only exist theoretically" seems to deny their actual existence, and indeed tacitly privileges the theory and theorists that "make" them exist.[65] But Ronk destroys the critical fiction of the lyric's putatively theoretical existence by writing lyrics that produce and deploy their own critical framework intra-lyrically. Rather than requiring critics to frame and decode them extra-lyrically, Ronk's lyrics school critics in the critical issues most pertinent to their own workings. Ronk also refutes Language poetry's equation of lyric with "modest tones intended to argue one's case in a voice just loud enough to be overheard. Propriety is the rule."[66] Rather than helplessly reproduce a genre that uncritically employs the fiction of a subject issuing transparent communication intercepted by an overhearing reader, Ronk's lyrics instead produce a lyric subject whose textual presence is marked both by a postmodern aesthetics of epistemological distress and a deliberate ambivalent wavering between textuality and speakerliness. Indeed, her emphatically lyric poems boldly employ some of the same assumptions of Language poetry: like the work of Ron Silliman et al., they "intend to 'lay bare language's inherent capacity to construct belief' by 'disrupt[ing] its convention as communicative transparency.'"[67] This is the power and gift of Ronk's lyrics: by insisting on both/and, on lyric *and* language, they force us to abandon our habits of reading for Ronk's own habitual, signature estrangement from knowledge. As much episteme as aesthetic, as much critical as existential, this shared unknowing becomes a place where, "In the midst of all uncertainty . . . assurance was unwelcome," a landscape whose frank rejection of certainty proves a welcome respite from having to know anything else.[68]

NOTES

1. Gillian White, *Lyric Shame: The "Lyric" Subject of Contemporary American Poetry* (Cambridge: Harvard University Press, 2014), 16–26.

2. Joel Bettridge, *Reading as Belief: Language Writing, Poetics, Faith* (London: Palgrave, 2009).

3. Ron Silliman, *Silliman's Blog*, "Saturday, June 14, 2003," ronsilliman.blogspot .com/search?q=school+of+quietude. Accessed 13 August 2018.

4. Charles Bernstein, "The Academy in Peril: William Carlos Williams at the MLA," in *Content's Dream* (Los Angeles: Sun and Moon Press, 1986): 248–49. Bernstein's description of "official verse culture" is nuanced and open in a way that generally gets closed down after the term enters critical discourse at large: "Official verse culture is not mainstream, nor is it monolithic, nor uniformly bad or good . . . What makes official verse culture official is that it denies the ideological nature of its practice while maintaining hegemony in terms of major media exposure and academic legitimation and funding. At any moment its resiliency is related to its ability to strategically incorporate tokes from competing poetry traditions and juggle them against one another while leaving for itself the main turf." It should further be noted that Bernstein's description is not at all about poetic form per se, but rather about the accumulation and hoarding of cultural capital and power.

5. Marjorie Perloff, "Safety First," *Boston Review* (18 May 2012); www.boston review.net/forum/poetry-brink. Here is a sample from Perloff's inflammatory introduction to "Poetry on the Brink: Reinventing the Lyric": "the poems you will read in *American Poetry Review* or similar publications will, with rare exceptions, exhibit the following characteristics: 1) irregular lines of free verse, with little or no emphasis on the construction of the line itself or on what the Russian Formalists called "the word as such"; 2) prose syntax with lots of prepositional and parenthetical phrases, laced with graphic imagery or even extravagant metaphor (the sign of "poeticity"); 3) the expression of a profound thought or small epiphany,

usually based on a particular memory, designating the lyric speaker as a particularly sensitive person who really *feels* the pain, whether of our imperialist wars in the Middle East or of late capitalism or of some personal tragedy such as the death of a loved one." Rather than the care and relative nuance of Bernstein's earlier analysis of literary ideology, this passage beautifully articulates the conceptually sloppy end result of the eventual conflation of Official Verse Culture with the lyric: *American Poetry Review* = irregular lines of free verse = imagery and metaphor = "poeticity" = profound thought = "lyric" speaker.

6. In 2008, Jackson curated a selection of essays on "New Lyric Studies" for the *PMLA* and Robert Von Hallberg published *Lyric Powers*; these publications were followed in 2012 by "Poetry on the Brink: Reinventing the Lyric," a much-discussed forum in *Boston Review* featuring Marjorie Perloff and eighteen poets and critics; in 2014 Jackson and Yopie Prins published *The Lyric Theory Reader: A Critical Anthology*; later in 2014, Gillian White added *Lyric Shame: The "Lyric" Subject of Contemporary Poetry* to the field; and most recently, in 2015, Jonathan Culler released his long-awaited *Theory of the Lyric*, and in 2016 Nikki Skillman published her innovative interdisciplinary study *The Lyric in the Age of the Brain*. These, among other scholarly and editorial projects, have posed serious challenges to the critical orthodoxies of the academic study of poetry and poetics, particularly the assumption that when we study poetry, we "naturally" study the lyric (or its recent antagonists).

7. Rei Terada, "After the Critique of the Lyric," *PMLA*, 123.1 (January 2008): 198.

8. Martha Ronk, *Ocular Proof* (Richmond: Omnidawn Books, 2016), 71.

9. Even Ronk's earliest work anticipates Frederic Jameson's claim in *Postmodernism, or, The Cultural Logic of Late Capitalism* (Durham: Duke University Press, 1991) that "it is generally the case that what looks like realism turns out at best to offer unmediated access only to what we think about reality, to our images and ideological stereotypes about it" (150), and in that sense she could be said to typify a postmodern attitude toward the real.

10. Ronk, *Ocular Proof*, 72.

11. Northrup Frye, "Theory of Genres," in *The Lyric Theory Reader: A Critical Anthology*, ed. Virginia Jackson and Yopie Prins (Baltimore: Johns Hopkins University Press, 2014), 32.

12. Jonathan Culler, *Theory of the Lyric* (Cambridge: Harvard University Press, 2015), 35.

13. Ludwig Wittgenstein, *The Philosophical Investigations*, trans. G. E. M. Anscombe (New York: MacMillan, 1968), 161.

14. Martha Ronk, *In a Landscape of Having to Repeat* (Richmond: Omnidawn Books, 2004), 10.

15. Culler, 34.

16. Andy Fitch, "An Interview with Martha Ronk," *Rain Taxi Review of Books* (2016); www.raintaxi.com/an-interview-with-martha-ronk/.

17. Cleanth Brooks, *The Well Wrought Urn: Studies in the Structure of Poetry* (New York: Harvest Books, 1956), 203.

18. Jackson and Prins, 1.

19. Anne Carson, *Eros the Bittersweet* (Normal: Dalkey Archive Press, 1998), 45.

20. Gaius Valerius Catullus, *The Poems of Catullus*, trans. Peter Green (Berkeley: University of California Press, 2005), 191.

21. Carson, 45.

22. Martha Ronk, *Why/Why Not* (Berkeley: University of California Press, 2003), 12.

23. Susan Stewart, "Notes on Distressed Genres," *The Journal of American Folklore* 104.411 (Winter 1991): 7.

24. Ibid.

25. Martha Ronk, *Vertigo* (Minneapolis: Coffee House Press, 2007), 48–49.

26. "Poetics of Failure," in *Lyric Postmodernisms: An Anthology of Contemporary Innovative Poetries*, ed. Reginald Shepherd (Denver: Counterpath Press, 2008), 182.

27. Ann Lauterbach, *The Night Sky: Writings on the Poetics of Experience* (New York: Viking, 2005), 42.

28. Jameson, 150.

29. Exemplary practitioners of this kind of postmodern lyric include, among many others, Rae Armantrout, Mei-mei Berssenbrugge, Kimiko Hahn, Brenda Hillman, Harryette Mullen, Evie Shockley, Juliana Spahr, and Elizabeth Willis.

30. Reginald Shepherd, "Introduction," in *Lyric Postmodernism*, xi–xii.

31. Stephen Burt, "The Elliptical Poets," *American Letters & Commentary* 11 (1999): 46–54. The editors of *American Letters & Commentary* commissioned responses to Burt's essay and collected them in the issue, including one from erstwhile Ellipticist Cole Swensen. In "Elliptical Poetry: A Response," Swensen suggests that her major reservations with Burt's "school" are: 1) its fairly arbitrary historical context, 2) its erasure of aesthetic difference between its alleged members, 3) its capacity to be endlessly inclusive. "Does it include," Swensen asks, "Martha Ronk, Sam Truitt, Martine Bellen, Malinda Markham or many, many others?" *American Letters & Commentary* 11 (1999): 66. Swensen would go on to include Ronk in her 2009 anthology, *American Hybrid: A Norton Anthology of New Poetry*.

32. *American Hybrid: A Norton Anthology of New Poetry*, ed. David St. John and Cole Swensen (New York: W.W. Norton, 2009).

33. See "Lyric Practice (Analytic Lyric?)," the second section of Michael Palmer's essay "Counter-Poetics and Current Practice" in *Active Boundaries: Selected Essays and Talks* (New York: New Directions, 2008), 247–58.

34. Similarly, I could also situate Ronk's oeuvre in her longtime home of Los Angeles, particularly in relation to Douglas Messerli's Sun & Moon and Green Integer Presses (both of which published Ronk as well as many of the Language poets), and as part of a loose group of poets and writers that includes, among others, Paul Vangelisti, Standard Schaeffer, and Dennis Phillips. The Los Angeles in which Ronk first began publishing poetry was close enough to San Francisco to feel the aftershocks of Language poetry, but far enough away to produce its own brand of avant-garde poetics. This scene was shaped not only by Messerli's Language-oriented editorial vision, but also by the aesthetic breadth of Leland Hickman's great magazine *Temblor*, which, as Bill Mohr writes in *Hold-Outs: The Los Angeles Poetry Renaissance, 1948–1992* (Iowa City: University of Iowa Press, 2011),

"remains a destabilization of the usual categories of avant-garde communities" (150) and in which Ronk published many poems from her first book.

35. Ludwig Wittgenstein, *On Certainty*, trans. Denis Paul and G.E.M. Anscombe (New York: Harper and Row, 1969), 2e.

36. Martha Ronk, *Desire in L.A.* (Athens: University of Georgia Press, 1990), 24.

37. William James, *Principles of Psychology* (New York: Henry Holt and Company, 1890), 282.

38. Ronk, "Poetics of Failure," 181.

39. Ludwig Wittgenstein, *Philosophical Grammar*, trans. Anthony Kenny (Berkeley: University of California Press, 1978), 9.

40. Martha Ronk, *State of Mind* (Los Angeles: Sun and Moon Press, 1995), 14.

41. Ronk, "Poetics of Failure," 182–83.

42. Ronk, *In a Landscape of Having to Repeat*, 24.

43. Martha Ronk, *Eyetrouble* (Athens: University of Georgia Press, 1998), 64.

44. Culler, 108. Culler's description of lyric subjectivity owes much, as he notes, to "Käte Hamburger's discussion of 'The Lyric Genre' in *Die Logik Der Dichtung*" (105).

45. Culler, 109.

46. Palmer, *Active Boundaries*, 253–54.

47. Philippe Lejeune, *On Autobiography*, trans. Katherine Leary (Minneapolis: University of Minnesota Press, 1989), 14.

48. Ronk, *In a Landscape of Having to Repeat*, 15.

49. Culler, 229.

50. Ibid.

51. Susan Stewart, *Poetry and the Fate of the Senses* (Chicago: University of Chicago Press, 2002), 108.

52. Ibid.

53. Ludwig Wittgenstein, *The Wittgenstein Reader*, ed. Anthony Kenny (Oxford: Blackwell Publishers, 1994), 46.

54. Wittgenstein, *The Philosophical Investigations*, 103.

55. Martha Ronk, *Glass Grapes and Other Stories* (Rochester: BOA Editions, 2008), 77.

56. Ronk, "Poetics of Failure," 182–83.

57. Ronk, *Glass Grapes*, 78.

58. Ronk, "Poetics of Failure," 182.

59. Ibid.

60. Ronk, *Why/Why Not*, 61.

61. Martha Ronk, *Partially Kept* (Callicoon: Nightboat Books, 2012), 57.

62. Like many poets of her generation (she was born in 1940), Ronk has long been a college professor, though unlike many poets of her generation, she earned her PhD from Yale as a scholar of Shakespeare rather than an MFA as a student of writing.

63. Rusty Morrison, "A Brief Interview with Martha Ronk," www.omnidawn .com/product/transfer-of-qualities (accessed 26 June 2019).

64. For instance, Ronk's most recent collection, *Ocular Proof*, collects ekphrastic poems dedicated to photography, particularly the way we read photographs

simultaneously as artifice and proof. "We have learned to question them," Ronk writes, "yet photographs also carry with them the status/strain of document" (71).

65. Jackson, *Dickinson's Misery*, 11.

66. Ron Silliman, Carla Harryman, Lyn Hejinian, Steve Benson, Bob Perelman, and Barret Watten, "Aesthetic Tendency and the Politics of Poetry: A Manifesto," *Social Text* 19–20 (1988): 266. Quoted in White, 19.

67. White, 19. Quoted phrases are from Ron Silliman, et al. "Aesthetic Tendency and the Politics of Poetry: A Manifesto," 266–67.

68. Ronk, *In a Landscape of Having to Repeat*, 75.

BIBLIOGRAPHY

Works by Martha Ronk

POETRY

Desire in L. A. Athens: University of Georgia Press, 1990.

Desert Geometries. Collaboration with visual artist Don Suggs. Los Angeles: Littoral Books, 1992.

State of Mind. Los Angeles: Sun & Moon Press, 1995.

Eyetrouble. Athens: University of Georgia Press, 1998.

Why/Why Not. Berkeley: University of California Press, 2003.

In a Landscape of Having to Repeat. Richmond: Omnidawn Publishing, 2004.

Vertigo. Minneapolis: Coffee House Press, 2007.

Partially Kept. Callicoon: Nightboat Books, 2012.

Transfer of Qualities. Richmond: Omnidawn Publishing, 2013.

Ocular Proof. Oakland: Omnidawn Publishing, 2016.

Silences. Oakland: Omnidawn Publishing, 2019.

PROSE

Displeasures of the Table: Memoir as Caricature. Los Angeles: Green Integer, 2001.

Glass Grapes & Other Stories. Rochester: BOA Editions, 2008.

EDITED VOLUME

Place as Purpose: Poetry from the Western States. With Paul Vangelisti. Los Angeles: Green Integer, 2002.

CHAPBOOKS

Emblems. Saratoga: Instress, 1998.

Allegories. Collaboration with visual artist Tom Wudl. Italian translations by Paul Vangelisti. Castelvetro Piacentino: Michele Lombardelli & NuovaLitoEffe editori, 1998.

Quotidian. San Francisco: a+bend press, 2000.

Prepositional. Los Angeles, Mindmade Books, 2004.

SELECTED CRITICAL PROSE

"Embodied Morality in *The Duchess of Malfi*." *Pacific Coast Philology* 23.1–2 (November 1988): 47–59.

"Representations of 'Ophelia.'" *Criticism* 36.1 (Winter 1994): 21–43.

"Locating the Visual in *As You Like It*." *Shakespeare Quarterly* 52.2 (Summer 2001): 255–76.

"Desdemona's Self-Presentation." *English Literary Renaissance* 35.1 (Winter 2005): 52–72.

"Poetics of Failure." In *Lyric Postmodernisms: An Anthology of Contemporary Innovative Poetries*, ed. Reginald Shepherd (Denver: Counterpath Press, 2008), 181–83.

"A Foreign Substance: On Barbara Guest's 'Wild Gardens Overlooked by Night Lights.'" *Chicago Review* 53.4/54.1–2 (Summer 2008): 109–112.

"Ferocious Friendship: On Elena Ferrante's *Those Who Leave and Those Who Stay*." *Los Angeles Review of Books*, 2 September 2014; lareviewofbooks.org /article/ferocious-friendship.

"*Model City* by Donna Stonecipher." *The Constant Critic*, 16 May 2015; www .constantcritic.com/martha-ronk/model-city.

"Ashes to Ashes: On Laird Hunt's *Neverhome*." *Los Angeles Review of Books*, 4 January 2015; lareviewofbooks.org/article/ashes-ashes.

"*The Albertine Workout* by Anne Carson and *Loom* by Sarah Gridley." *The Constant Critic*, 15 January 2015; www.constantcritic.com/martha-ronk/the -albertine-workout-by-anne-carson-and-loom-by-sarah-gridley.

"*Lazy Suzie* by Suzanne Doppelt (trans. Cole Swensen)." *The Constant Critic*, 10 November 2015; www.constantcritic.com/martha-ronk/lazy-suzie.

"*Some Worlds for Dr. Vogt* by Matvei Yankelevich." *The Constant Critic*, 28 February 2016; www.constantcritic.com/martha-ronk/some-worlds-for -dr-vogt.

"*The Poet, the Lion, Talking Pictures, El Garolito, a Wedding in St. Roch, the Big Box Store, the Warp in the Mirror, Spring, Midnights, Fire & All* by C. D. Wright." *The Constant Critic*, 17 October 2016; www.constantcritic.com /martha-ronk/the-poet-the-lion-talking-pictures-el-garolito-a-wedding-in-st -roch-the-big-box-store-the-warp-in-the-mirror-spring-midnights-fire-all.

"*Archeophonics* by Peter Gizzi." *The Constant Critic*, 4 January 2017; www .constantcritic.com/martha-ronk/archeophonics.

SELECTED INTERVIEWS

Fitch, Andy. "An Interview with Martha Ronk." *Rain Taxi* Online Edition, Summer 2016; www.raintaxi.com/an-interview-with-martha-ronk.

Morrison, Rusty. "Rusty Morrison with Martha Ronk." *The Conversant*, 21 December 2013; theconversant.org/?p=5865.

Selected Criticism and Reviews

Doxsee, Julie. "Review of *In a Landscape of Having to Repeat*." *Double Room* 5 (Winter/Spring 2005); doubleroomjournal.com/issue_five/Martha_Ronk _Review.html.

Hass, Robert. "Poet's Choice: Review of *State of Mind*." *The Washington Post*, Book World, 3 August 1997, Sunday ed., p. X02.

Hecht, Jennifer Michael. "Review of *Ocular Proof*." *American Poets*, Fall/Winter 2016; www.poets.org/poetsorg/book/ocular-proof.

Kelsey, Karla. "Review of *Transfer of Qualities*." *The Constant Critic*, 1 February 2014; www.constantcritic.com/karla_kelsey/transfer-of-qualities/.

Landry, Benjamin. "*Transfer of Qualities* by Martha Ronk." *The Rumpus*, 15 March 2014; therumpus.net/2014/03/transfer-of-qualities-by-martha-ronk/.

Mazur, Gary. "*eyetrouble*: poems by Martha Ronk." *Harvard Review* 15.1 (September 1998): 171–73.

Muratori, Fred, "Microreview of *In a landscape of having to repeat*." *Boston Review* 30.2 (April/May 2005); bostonreview.net/archives/BR30.2/microsmore.php.

Reed, Brian. "Grammar Trouble." *boundary 2* 36.3 (2009): 133–58.

Roig, Denise, "Review of *Displeasures of the Table*." *Gastronomica* 6.1 (Winter 2006): 112.

Silliman, Ron. "Friday, August 01, 2008." *Silliman's Blog*, 1 August 2008; ronsilliman.blogspot.com/2008/08/there-is-exactness-both-of-vision-and.html.

Teare, Brian. "'In Quest of the Ordinary': On Martha Ronk's *In a landscape of having to repeat*." *Poetry Flash* 296/297 (Winter/Spring 2006): 18–19.

Waldie, D. J. "Our New Jerusalems: *Recent Terrains: Terraforming the American West*, Photographs by Laurie Brown, Poetry by Martha Ronk." *Los Angeles Times Book Review*, 24 December 2000, p. 3.

Zembal, Christine. "What So Cal Poets Are Reading: Review of *Displeasures of the Table*." *Speechless: The Magazine*, Spring 2007; www.speechless themagazine.org/magazine/in_review_1203.htm.

LESLIE SCALAPINO

POEMS

FROM *way*

Floating Series 1

the
women—not in
the immediate
setting
—putting the
lily pads or
bud of it
in
themselves

a man entering
after
having come on her—that
and the memory of putting
in
the lily pad or the
bud of it first,
made her come

having put
the
lily pad in herself—
encouraging the man
to
come inside
her

a man to
come on the woman
gently—her
having
put the lily pad in
herself
with him not
having entered
her yet

people who're
there
Already—though
the other
people aren't
aware of that

not
being able to
see the
other people—and
to be sticking the
lily pad
in
themselves

the man—though
the woman had

come
with
the bud of it
in her
—not having done
so on
that time

or her not
having
put it in—and
the man
coming on her
gently
lying on her
in that
situation

people having
been
there—being
from
the city—already
—and
others not
aware of them

or
having
put in the bud of
it
and
the man not
having
entered her
coming first

that in
the city as in
the middle—to

someone who's
death comes from
age

having
nothing to
do in
a place
—as having
been crazed in
his life-
time

and
having been
aware
before
of others
—who'd
been in
the setting
all along

a man
putting
the lily pad
in her—
after he'd
come—and
she hadn't
on that time

that in
the city as in
the middle—to

someone

the thought
that
they—should be
treated
well—if they'd
paid
their money—or
not

a man's
sense—of—when
he'd come and
she had
the
lily pad in her
and
hadn't come then

the man—on
whom the boy
spit—from him riding his
bicycle by over and
over—was lying on
the sidewalk

not
having
anything to do
as
his having a blockage
with others around
in
the setting

having the
high rents
with
an attitude that
they
shouldn't live in
this
place—who're poor

Notes to Waking Life

The Present*

1

Why the form of the detective novel as if it were a certain thing known which is about finding corpses.

it is out before.

Seeing (our) actual in reality dying in that the (other) finds the corpses after they're dead.

Other reflects only him, which is why he is isolated.

Bob doesn't like it when it is lovely as being convention. Or if there's suffering. Convention can be made without suffering.

(It appears to be convention only and is lovely.)

The fake canned sense of happiness we're supposed to have in our culture, which isolates one, is not the same as the lovely images.

A book is calm because it is serial. which is a form unrelated to suffering.

The black gardenia in the mouth of the running dog is the inner man. it seems. as it is shallow, which is this loop.

---

* "The Present," given here only in its prose form, is also a play. The play includes passages from *Notes to Waking Life*.

2

REALISM:

Moving in a real terrain that is thought of as simply itself, having no shape or view given to it. a city. so if one is in that can see it. the viewer is in the center of it, moving. beggars. cars. Someone comes by. It is an actual historical event though with a wide loop that separates one from it.

It is so that one is a mannerism in the terrain which is simply itself. The intense blue water on the desert with cattle coming to it. The loop is there.

that the nature as such of the person is romantic is given as such if it is. in the same place. people's suffering or such, there is the loop that separates from it. so that it really is close.

the separation (for someone) isn't being alienated.

3

This is the present time in that it is inner.

There is a similarity to our innocent, provincial nature.

That enabled the war recently. There are the individuals but they are simple and innocent.

Qualified, relative, not centralized.

It is before the area of apprehension, or behind it or alongside. The center is empty. Everything is always present-time. therefore there is no content. there is no present. One doesn't see there's a center or that it's empty until later or ever know where this occurred. One has to read the whole thing, of the various parts in it to know this.

Being past the center of each of the various parts later: the events of the pulp or detective novel/B movie meet and are our culture. The latter exists less than the life.

They simply go out, where they find corpses; and come back home again. That's the only action.

so there's no 'life,' really no distance between it. in that space has been compressed. conventional/supposed 'actual' life has been eliminated that is content so one is calm. one is in it and it is still.

Other cannot reflect only him; he cannot be isolated, in the form.

The detective novel/B movie is a copy like a Xerox; that is why it is so beautiful.

4

In the Midwest, there is no other. A line
is separate, this is the only life there is.

isolation

Other reflects only him, which is why he is isolated.

The child has no sense of the flowering bum. then suffering isn't anything as it's oneself.

The Midwest is nothing but suffering.

That speaking is a copy supposedly of life, which it resembles not at all, or others and inner and historical events at the same time is its actual present-time.

5

and not figure out how it unfolds

Wheeling on the sled—having slept in the indentation—
deer simply have ticks which become huge until they drop off.

a huge tick in the side of having waded.

they begin singing—soldiers she meets on the road are a choir and they began singing.

into the area of just pulp—only that

One realizing I have to do this myself.

the leg is soaked. She goes on the sled. There's a sandbar out along stretching on which are corpses the buzzards sapping it whirling. It's far gone. in the light air.

The content of life can be seen only from our culture's suffering which is only what we see. but really one is roaming and playing.

It defeats our isolation in the present-time reality by being that.

There's a stream of one-line phrases that go past that. it is a sheet.

because it actually does not resemble oneself. or a dream. so it has to be as close to that actual real-time as possible.

such is a new way of seeing not because the individual has created that but because they see it. everyone sees that, which is plainly visible. it is not willed and is thus calm, inner as seeing the original imposition on it.

of our saying. so one roams and plays, when one is past the sheet that's our saying it.

FROM *Day Ocean State of Stars' Night*

DeLay Rose

Occurrence of one's is without one once

      at once   two people

      in conversation—in outside's motion
            as Creeley thought
                 words
      and speaking
            as catching up to being in
            that motion outside
                (at) once

DeLay corrupts   to

money launder   falling out of

    intimidate lobbies so they're only being   on
one side while government rule is tied to favors on both sides of
floatation for their huge corporations' con   tracting and

officials on the take when they know nothing en   events acting

one sun and moon at once by each other day at night *then* and
wrecked Iraq   Occur's first   with dome floating our penned
                                           starving moved

also then   '   our'

    president'd   for photos kiss the green corpses swim

    ing in the flood   than the living transported in

outside's motion—the occurrence between—as Creeley thought
                                          words

    one's to catch up to being (in) one's events   at all? I

'd wake at night having dropped out of being in that event *then*
hav having terror that having to be in one's events and *not* being

in them then *when that*—is that like his in which   occur's *first*—

                          where? one is first too/two not
                          caused anywhere they're only once/
                                    at once
outside of occurrence is _____? not.   Occur's first
                          is therefore also two—he'd
have
sentiments be actions, outside's motion *there* too. To occur first
                          is outside's motion
                                    of one

    In Memory of Robert Creeley

•

DeLay's   corrupt decussation between the outside
                                     and one still aleatory mazarine elands run
                                                           viewed
                                               as on, that is, single line that's
an isobath   imaginary   line   throughout flooded cities in the oce
ans   the govt's DeLay's Atlantis
waves everything's   one
's   outside the mazarine elands are two too a
                                          hierarchy has to be more than one
man speaking of one man/hierarchy as acting on an ecstatic
single basis (words)   speaks as if no one else knows of that
or had (known) ever   Is an ecstatic basis as one's young only
when young? (by this time that one's dead) a basis isn't caused
                                          outside isn't caused
            there US soldier said they're told to kill prisoners rather
                                          than
return with them to base, slaughtered them until Fallujah filled
                                                      with
numbers are transported
floated soldier says naked Iraqi corpses tied as a deer on a Hum
                                          vee's hood,
sport   *Occur's first*   a corpse killed driven on the hood through
the streets dome floating ours penned starving moved—The
worst thing is—of the flooded poor here, left corpses swimming
—some of these people (will) want to *stay* in Texas, as if they
                              already do will want, the mother
            of 'our' president says who's from Texas.   penned have
been   transported
            from the   flood   crowd not on isobath   each
                  enters by speaking it

Set at a certain place is or comes in only *there* at our sides so
blae sky our rubble on isobath float one drops any line; that is,
also   in one that one line so there could be anything occurring
there   ocean   together (without it)

a split in being one and that's being in language also words are
          occur's   first   ec
                                                              static two
Are things a being in ecstasy are first together—not caused there

                          one's here split between day and night is a
one's structure *for*/to be its it's anti-structure being outside only

one no longer able to catch up to one separated   a delay

for roses first on a roar

     •

                                   Occur's first

the mazarine elands are two heard the split between day and
                                                        night
one's (my) having the split in one—so ecstatic basis single is not
                                                        caused
there—soldiers are still and run   there's no isobath as line in o
                                                        ceans
                                                        begin

FROM *The Front Matter, Dead Souls*

Dead Souls

(I sent an early version of this to six or so newspapers, though it wasn't published, during the election campaign.)

> Lyrical horror is our "participation in democracy" at the level of violence of compulsory voting in El Salvador. Taken as an assertion, then, such lyricism no longer works even as a form of bondage between writers.   BARRETT WATTEN

Invisible, not that they're not real, actions occur so that one's seeing has to change to be realistic.

These actions are constantly denied by those in them, though sometimes they are not denied and are corroborated exactly.

So that seeing on the rim one could be free one feels but must see actions on the rim with or as where we live. One links them diverging because that is how to see it.

Unable to walk, there's no way for them to get to work. Infants don't need to be born.

The eye in the sky floats, liquid, blue.

Silent reading is inner so that it is centralized appearing.

A child is born for delight as its nature. Take fragments of the present. They are not shreds as newspaper text already but modulations of fragments in one.

Extreme is subjective and so not visible in them.

In adolescence in 'extreme' conflict, not a child, one was simply out there. Not needing rebellion even, government not even existing, one was in immunity where the 'extreme' conflict later unfolds and is seen serene outside. Later, as adult one's physical state is endless.

Even greed in the bureaucracy has sunk retentive not appearing to be a motive.

The deaths of infants of a hundred and seventy thousand maybe in the aftermath of the war are not shown while they force children to be born.

On the edge of the flat, the figure fills the bright blue air. One doesn't have to figure out writing.

The hyenas swarming for scraps are seen on the news, they're the anchormen.

The images do not reflect back. They are only themselves, which is not in relation to existence.

Yet that is existence everywhere. This is to isolate the shape or empty interior of some events real in time so their 'arbitrary' location to each other emerges to, whatever they are.

This is a serial written to be chapters printed in installments in the newspaper, like Dickens' novels. The reader of the newspaper sees in current time. An arbitrary present time image exists in time here. Mimicking here in writing isn't representation.

The leering of the president's mouth on a bulging torso is twisted on pinched haunches as he runs away.

He's going to shoot at them again just to renew his popularity for his reelection campaign.

Thinking is having our original inferior nature. Only sentimentality is communing here. One can't know anyone that way so it isn't communing either. We sentimentalize our killing by wearing yellow ribbons. Not conforming here is the worst mark, being worthy of violence, ridicule for not being valued.

POETICS STATEMENT

Creeley's continual dislocation from himself (typified in *Pieces*)
trying to only *be* in that—a struggle to be intensely one with
someone as love a terror of not being one ever as falling out of being
there had to be constant striving driven to move as action—"*so as not to
know what I am doing" (before I do it)—it cannot be in future if known before.* not
in anything to undo one reinterpreted to oneself continually *as social*—
writing to be *only* actions disbands separation 'outside'/one

"Writing simply has no connection to reality. The actual event is entirely
absent" (*Defoe*, 1994)—there is only the writing because representation
or description of event is as such separation from it. Language is separate
from one's sensational phenomenal action (such as walking) though it is
another phenomenal action itself (consciousness). If writing were not this
separation, it would falsify: Therefore it must *be* the *no*-connection to (so-
cially) 'formed reality'/representation in order to *be* reality (be its process).
Starting with streams of actions, in the *second* half of *Defoe*, I was writ-
ing a way of having motions be *before* they're conceived in/be *before* their
entirety. Motions without/before becoming entity, the writing is a spatial
conceiving of motions not determining these no thing already settled but
forming. One is to be seeing ahead of there being event (an 'event' as such
would already be concluded), is to let go description that creates detach-
ment of the individual from outside (let go the misconception that the
outside is pre-formed). War is not 'reporting that's political'—as if a phe-
nomenon is separate from its description, seen—any more than memory
seeing a starving dying man lying in the street where one was walking as
a child. 'Society saying' these are separate, I'm trying to break down those
defined categories of seeing/being. The categories are our seeing—as and
in—our social autism. "When Rage Affects the Flesh" (a section title in
Defoe). The flesh is the text as if the 'experience' is inside of all the people,
(as in) the returned soldiers who are met on the street.

In *Defoe*, prose that is a flood of events (of war, and paragraphs as
sheets of actions at once, such as motorcyclists flying in the air flown up
in the midst of fighting with other people) that are to be proliferation in-
enarrable outweigh the reader's processing to separate. Actions are to be
phenomena one takes in, attention, as reading, experiencing one's mind
and space (as text) as if these are the same, *until mind comes into the
text.* One's attention, conceptual seeing and *optical* seeing, description of
an action and the action (that which is being described) are *felt* as the
same. That is, description is an action, by the mind being 'on' the object it

is describing, tracking it describing is not separate from mind/*its* action; therefore there is no mind-body split, no divergence from attention. So, *no divergence from live action takes place* by *description being act of thought itself.* This passage is from the 'commentary' chapter of *Defoe*; it follows interpreting the first half of the book that is action scenes (the two, action/commentary at once, now united):

> Action collapses on itself and is compressed, in that it describes itself. It is thus in the present-time, still and calm.   It does not diverge from itself, supposedly. That's a conception which people already know. Therefore speaking enables one to see the diverging of separation that is this present. These actions occur as if to make the pupil of an eye (some other's) dilate, and be held open. The present takes place as 'some other.'
>
> Life is dilated.
It does not diverge because description
> cannot be separate. as it is of itself. (*Defoe*, 125)

My construct in *Defoe* was an imagined horizontal line, like a horizon line, all phenomena 'seen' (imagined) as coming up meeting this line as if above it, below it, on it; then these actions (as in action scenes) as thoughts dissipating, bursting, are replaced by other actions continually (as one reads). I also wrote two poem-plays (*The Present* and *The Weatherman Turns Himself In*) using the text of *Defoe* as a basis. Description-commentary (in the plays as well as in *Defoe*) is separate from action (a way of writing *having nothing to do with reality*)—yet *being*—yet it *is* the action also, later. The actors in *The Present* speak the motions they are doing as they do these (speaking also being an action) and also have periods of commentary during the play in which the prior physical motions/memories suddenly impinge into the description *as* mind (of viewers/actors' previous or simultaneous motions) the seers' minds being the same as the sight of—occurrence of—description of—(and)—these enacted *together with/as* physical movements. Yet the intent is *not* the social illusion as the cliché of "wholeness" either. I always write sequences as these are segments in series.

Any way of making event's occurrence a singular *subject* or an argument of discourse outside of its language as its action (discourse as looking at event by separating oneself from *being* it, not seeing such separation is creating being the social schism as perceiving): is *writing* reproducing customary mind-body split that is inherently hierarchy-authority, to place perception/writing back in same social autism unknown to one when/because doing 'being that autism.' As dismantling hierarchy-authority (and that of the outside thoroughly embedded *as one self*), there can be no general dictum as the poetry's tactics or purpose except to find as its language mind-shape sound/mystery of being a gyration that can be 'heard' even silently at points in a sequential poem. In *way*, I had a sense of/heard a syntax gyration as if mystery of being occurring somewhere in the sound as duration of the poem sequence that is the rendition of motions of the outside's-events (as sound in the poem's line breaks). This 'gyration' may be a gap, emptiness where word/reality face or abut each other, a whirr between word-based and experience-based idea, as apprehension. Gyration, as measure, is shape emptiness of name/word, and reality/named, the sense that neither is existent there. *Both* (word/reality) are being constructed at once, by the reader. This experience and description is akin to Buddhist emptiness theory in regard to language apprehension—unknown to me at the time of writing *way*.

Tracking is the reader's mind's gesture itself in any instant of attention. Attention is an action, whose content *is attention*—apprehension as motion. Sometimes in a poem sequence an instant can occur 'between' apprehension-space-motion, is one's/outside's 'being.'

> the mind is action literally, not departing from that—being events or movement outside, which is inside, so the mind is collapsing into and as action.—I can't rest, at all now.

> this is despair. *for Dante.* If action of events (my mind) were the same as resting, brought to that, in the way the physical body rests outside

> one is not having a rim—'understanding' rather than 'just get rid of one's mind and body—in traveling'—at all—
> the physical body, inner, must continue to move only (*New Time*)

My poems are not "autobiography" (implying one's completed view about one's formed life) in the sense that the category, as now conceived, separates from phenomenal relation in the way the word "personal" *means* separation from 'the world.' In *way* (1988) real-time historical outside's-events in series or sequences are imitated *as* the syntax sound-shape of one's mind-shape, the supposition being that the outside is one's mind/*as* writing. Event (as in *way*) being the instant of its sound-shape only—is why I would not want anyone to rewrite my language, to tell readers the plot of individual segments as if these events were not multiple always, to say what the event supposedly is that's happening as 'plot of one segment' as if fixed in time replaces my sound-shape/mind-shape whose events as exactly imitated motions simultaneous are rendition of these events new in formations. A sound *configuration* in any case doesn't occur in the plots of isolated events, but in their *relation*. A replacement omits instant of gyration.

I had the sense of dropping out of my events even while in them, in their real-time then (for a while in my life, as when I was writing *way*). Real-time event *only one's* subjective trace of/as mind/text (sound-shape, sensory), there—is 'being' that's 'between' apprehension's motions.

LESLIE SCALAPINO'S ANARCHIC MOMENT

Michael Cross

Can writing test the limits of space—in terms of organic bodies moving in "real" time—if the text opens an autonomous realm while concomitantly occupying a collective social environment? And what might time *be* if, rather than mere linear progression, we understand it *affectively*: the *feeling* of occupying space as attention, in which "attention" means cognition watching itself watch itself? Could we consider Leslie Scalapino's writing not as poetry or prose or drama or detective fiction (or any of the other instantly discernable genres she deftly moves through—often in the space of a stanza), but rather as a conceptual practice tracking the limits of space and time in order to, finally, test the limits of consciousness: scrutiny-cum-praxis pitting the two-dimensional tensile strain of the word against a mind *making* experience fictional—a writing in which the nexus reader-writer-word is the burden of the testing ground itself? In this sense, the telos of her writing is the recovery of what recoils amidst and against the habitual—its goal is to make the space of the page the *unconcealment* of the "anarchist moment," which we might understand as the experience of time itself: "no authority anywhere or in one."[1]

Scalapino's testing-space is precarious as both interior(s) and exterior(s) conform to structures of legibility (often through the habit of "making sense"), and the mind struggles against the gravitational pull toward recognition, fighting to free itself from "mind formation" while acknowledging that mind formation itself is the very apparatus by which we come to know anything at all. If "One 'has to' leave formation, not be in formation,"[2] the writing swallows itself at the tail, flipping in and out like a Möbius strip as it reifies into brief glimpses of legibility only to *evolve* into chaos. It accomplishes the impossible: to *be* mind formation as the destruction of mind formation, and this, of course, is why Leslie Scalapino's writing is often described as "challenging."

Testing Space

In *hmmmm*,[3] a poem Scalapino refers to as "the first time (she) was writing,"[4] the text is its struggle to remain anarchic, to "be only disjunction itself." It does so by blurring the boundaries that partition known from unknown from unknowable while steering clear of Dadaist "non-sense." For Scalapino, one must occupy the "rim" of cognition to track how the mind fools itself, and, as such, attention weaves in and out of legibility in order to witness its own response. In order to inhabit this testing-space, the mind watches itself watch itself watch itself, and for Scalapino, what happens outside happens inside (and vice versa) since everything happens *in* mind (*as* mind). She writes in her experimental "Autobiography":

> 'thought' for me is entwined with early events/actions and geographical place: sense of utter freedom (my older sister and I riding all over Rangoon in rickshas—our parents away in northern Burma; our wandering walking around Bombay by ourselves and going to Indian movies; my older sister and I staying, while our parents were away, in a missionary boarding house in northern Thailand, my reading while there about Buddhism (had visited temples in Japan), our bicycling by rice fields racing Thai girls) . . . reading about Buddhism there was no 'God' and we have to die. There is no authority anywhere or in one.
>
> In the process, I've created this memory track. Yet had the sense that I had to make fixed memories move as illusion, that they move as illusions. . . . For me, writing's experimentation of mind formation. One "has to" leave formation, not be in formation.[5]

The terror of Vietnam, the poverty and abjection on the streets of Calcutta, the scars of collective subjectivation: these somatic facts happen in the body, just as internal desire is externalized through masturbation or intercourse—how the biological fact of mastication and digestion is made abjectly tangible through excretion. Rather than a reified somatic sheen, the skin is a porous threshold of movement, a fluid partition between a thinking-writing and a writing-thinking in which the text is always more and less than the body itself.

This work of disjunction entails unsettling both the reader's and writer's attempts to land in the text and preen in the comfort of insouciance. Both the body, seat of the mind, and the page, seat of thought, act as the intercutaneous layer in which interior and exterior become interchangeable, so that writing is, as Charles Olson held, the projective movement from thought-to-page-to-reader—what Frank O'Hara once called, in his characteristic irreverence, "Lucky Pierre."[6] "Space" for Scalapino is not the open maw by which and through which one wakes and eats and sleeps, any more than it is the white space of the page or the reader's mind by which the work is "digested." Then what is "space?" And further, when is the "time" of writing if it is written-read in composition and read-written in reception?

Her earliest work begins to ask these questions, or at least to acknowledge them, but it does so through the construction of "illusion." By dismantling the reality of both exterior and interior "fact," the writing *is* dismantling itself. Here the action is deferment. Nothing is ever what it is, and in so being is always more (and less) than how it's understood. Take, for example, the very first poem in *hmmmm*:

> Consider certain emotions such as falling asleep, I said,
>
> (especially when one is standing on one's feet), as being similar
> to fear, or anger, or fainting.   *I* do.   I feel sleep
> in me is induced by blood forced into veins
> of my brain.   I can't focus.   My tongue is numb
> and so large it is like the long tongue of a calf or
> the tongue of a goat or of a sheep.   What's more, I bleat.
> Yes. In private, in bed, at night, with my head
> turned sideways on the pillow. No wonder I say that I *love* to sleep.[7]

Scalapino asks her interlocutors to "consider certain emotions," but to do so we must follow a deeply fraught syntactical unit through an opaque logic puzzle. Rather than "consider" a *specific* emotion, she asks us to consider "certain" of them "such as" (not *this* in particular, but something like it) "falling asleep," which of course is not what we normally think of as "emotion," and to complicate things, we're to do this "especially" when "standing on (our) feet" (versus sitting? recumbent?). If this weren't difficult enough to follow, the logic twists at the end of the first line due to the interrupter "I said" (to whom? us, the readers?). We leave the second person for the first, only to take another detour when the speaker asks us to consider sleep next to "fear, or anger, or fainting," a fairly dissimilar grouping. While we could rearrange syntactical units to make comprehension more linear (for instance, "I would like you to consider, while standing, emotions like falling asleep as similar to fear, anger, or fainting"), parsing the sentence does little good on behalf of barefaced comprehension. By the end of the third line, the subject's integrity is drawn into question altogether by the italicized *I*, and the line ends with the phrase "I feel sleep" (an eye-rhyme for "I fell asleep") which we might take to suggest affective change (I feel sad), only to find that we should read over the line break: "I feel sleep / in me." In these three short lines the reader's mastery of content, her firm grasp on legibility, is relentlessly undermined as Scalapino ratchets sense, pulling the carpet out from under the reader, only to reveal a trap door below.

While the modifiers "such as" and "especially" pull us *away* from the particulars of fact, her use of simile is what makes this particular experiment so interesting. Almost every one of the twenty-eight sections of the poem hinges on a haywire epic simile at the heart of its disjunction. Take the following lines from across the poem:

> My tongue . . . is like the long tongue of a calf
> . . . .
> . . . my disease is like rabies
> . . . .
> . . . the same face . . . like the man who loved a woman for her sheared hair
> . . . .
> . . . she was like a hyena. Or, like a mongrel or like a short-haired dog
> . . . .
> . . . the nod . . . like the bob of a head
> . . . .
> . . . she walks as if she were loping in slow motion.[8]

Here, simile serves a particular purpose in that it creates a rhythm of presentation: its use becomes so deeply formalized that it establishes a percussive rhythm—something of a sonorous pulse—similar to the way Gertrude Stein uses repetition as a rhythmic device. Further, the simile's over-determination begins to hinder its aim of fabricating amplified visual specificity. Rather than illuminate a thing by insisting on its particularity, its autonomy—that is, it was red like a fire truck . . . *that* kind of red —the over-determination draws us away from particularity to a universal equivalence—from *haecceity* to *quiddity* (this-ness to what-ness): she is not simply *like* a hyena, but also like a mongrel and a dog and any number of other things, so she is ultimately *not* like herself (is not herself) nor is she *really* any of the things with which she is compared. In other words, as Nietzsche has it, "every name in history is I":

> Isn't it interesting how a woman like me
> pursues in man after man
>
> the same face or even the same foot or hand. Like the man
> who loved a woman for her sheared hair.   Sure. Loved her,
> he said,   because she was like a hyena. Or, like a mongrel
> or like a short-haired dog. i.e. When in bed, the man said,
> while calling her pet names by whistling, he like to nip her
> with his lips. And once, during intercourse, when he told her
> what he would like most from her,   the man said facetiously:
> I want you to say the word yip, as in the yelp of a young dog[9]

The breakneck torque keeps us falling through trap doors: the address at the beginning draws attention to the absent "me," especially as we are immediately asked to question the identity of the interlocutor (is it the reader?). And then face becomes foot becomes hand *like* a man (which one?) who loved a woman for her hair who was *like* a hyena or mongrel or dog, which is exemplified by a man (which one?) who, when in bed ("the man said"? to whom?) likes to nip and asked "her" (who?) to yip *like* the yelp of a young dog (my italics).

The constant shifting of attention and emphasis curtails the standard action of mining the poem for objective meaning—as the reader finds herself transformed into a mere voyeur watching *particular* strangers (*this* man we don't know). We are witness to phenomena we might not otherwise see (thoughts, desires, the slow internalized process of subjectivation), and what we see is not quite *this* or *this* but is more like *this* or *this* or *this*. The entire poem becomes a kind of shifting deictic marker, and as a result, it induces a percussion of sound and movement that is somehow synonymous with the rhythmic alternation between being, being-me and being-toward-death.

Punching a Hole in Reality

The rhythm of deferral and defamiliarization in Scalapino's testing-space is particularly unsettling as it functions mimetically to deterritorialize the nature of epistemology and hermeneutics. When inhabiting Scalapino's experiments, we find ourselves questioning how we gain knowledge, how we evaluate the veracity of what we've gained, what it *means* to "gain" in the first place. As we have seen in *hmmmm*, the more we "learn" about the subject, the more and less we know: if this person is *not this* or *this* or *this*, but is *like this* and *this*, we only know about the subject and her web of relations negatively (in the way we "know" the sacred thanks to apophatic theology). We ultimately gain "nothing" in market terms: because she's like so many things, she's ultimately not like any of them.

The movement of disequilibrium, the product of the distance created by metaphor and deixis, is tempered by the sonic *push* of measure, a push and pull eroding the stability of the reader's point of view. The poem tips back from the counterthrust of a visual score of movement, particularly of gesture. While the nature of the subject is defamiliarized through simile, the *image* of these particular generalizations, these quiddities (employing Scholastic terms), are made uncanny by the alienation of familiar gestures—another rhythmic or percussive device. Take, for instance, "Dog," which is also from *hmmmm*:

> Suppose I *was* thinking something, say, not knowing I was thinking it,
> one day when I saw this dog before a house on the sidewalk,   he
> not really sidling toward me,   but more like loping sideways?
> Well, his tongue was lolling. And he was whining the way human heads
> loll forward in sleep and whinny.   Something so hesitant and low
> More so, because it was a nasal sound, a neigh, the way

we neigh, not thinking, when we are nervously mimicking a horse.
So I mimicked him, the dog, right back. Really I was being flippant
by pretending to gallop; and all the while not moving,
and letting my tongue slip forward between my lips, really laughing.[10]

This poem is a blur of movement: thinking, knowing, thinking, seeing, sidling, loping, lolling, whining, lolling, neighing, thinking, mimicking, being, pretending, (not) moving, letting, laughing—but it's not solely the poem's motion that establishes rhythm: it's really the movement between legibility and illegibility as we grasp the familiar with a white-knuckled grip—the motion of semiotic collapse establishes its own rhythm until it too reaches a kind of "lolling": a "whining the way human heads loll forward in sleep and whinny." It's remarkable how Scalapino sharpens the point of attention so that a single motion demands the entirety of our attention; however, once we are drawn *through* the motion, its significance is stripped and reterritorialized.

Interestingly, it's particularly the face that becomes the palate of this movement of reterritorialization in the early work. Throughout *hmmmm* our eyes are drawn to lips, teeth, mouths, tongues; the pursing of lips, swelling or slipping of tongues, biting of teeth:

. . . I wanted to put my fingers
between my lips; so that, by pretending to be sullen and by
pulling my lip down into a grimace, I would actually be saluting him
(in the sense of someone making a gesture such as   raising
the hand   in a certain way   to the head) .[11]

While the movement here is gestural, a kind of rhythm of signs, the semiotic is restrung through an animal defamiliarization: that which is most familiar, animality, is what shocks us out of the present. The face and its praxis—mastication, orality, tenderness, spirit—are rendered profane by what makes us most human—attention, thought, passion. It's precisely our ability to pay attention that jolts us (in terms of the equivalence of gesture): the mouth bleats or yips, tongue slipping in and out of lips, kissing and barking, teeth clenched into the skin, body sidling or lopping; we are suddenly aware again of the materiality of the mouth and its teeth and lips—they lose their functionality, if only briefly, and are isolated *not* as a metonymy for the body, but as organic and autonomous things, attached to (but separate from) the body's functions. The gestural rhythm is made fuller by the rhythms of semiotic collapse.

If by "punching a hole in reality"[12] Scalapino means impeding the habitual effort to make phenomena mean as singularities, then as the sculptor Carl Andre writes about his own artistic praxis, "a thing is a hole in a thing it is not."[13] The poem is a transparency laid on experience (actual and imagined) so that the palimpsest of experience is always seeing through seeing—obstruction can't become part of the singularity of experience without drawing attention to how the experience of one layer conditions the next. We might gather generic stock experience as a kind of base color —assuming that most generic experience is organized in our minds telically (with beginning, middle, and end, even if these segments don't exist in the experience of their real temporality). By placing the poem on top of this experience, the mouth that at once seemed only a stroke or detail of a consolidated phenomenon becomes a rupture point: imagine here a model from an advertisement, with Scalapino's mouth pasted over the figure's pixilated lips—disembodied, bleating, fingers pulling at the lips, making them move, tracing the teeth. While we are conditioned to "make" sense, we will never reconstruct the image seamlessly. Like plastic surgery used to improve a prior botched cosmetic operation, the rupture point cannot be made to join the surface of experience without drawing attention to its endemic lawlessness.

In this way, Scalapino's writing is a *kartageo*, an active disengagement through a state of radical passivity: a deactivation or state of inoperativity that makes experience fuller through isolation, amplification, and subsequent reterritorialization.[14] Each element of our experience is made to mutually arise with everything else, both by itself and as a member of an assemblage. Thus, even the Deleuzian model of the rhizome is not flexible enough for this work, as it still implies a fixed dimension, often horizontal (like the rhizomatic root system). In relation to Scalapino's writing, a more proper visual representation would break the roots of the rhizome apart, connecting them to every other leg of the system so that phenomena and our experience of phenomena mutually arise together.

In short, Scalapino's poetry demonstrates that if it's true that experience is mutually arisen, as Buddhist practitioners claim, the potential of the poem (and our engagement with it) is the potential of a reader's attention. As every element is and is not connected to every other element, our experience of the work is always understood in terms of its micropolitics, and as a result, we *become* our attention. We make meaning or pay attention to this web of relation, and the poem is that reading each and every time; reading, then, is a process of subjectivation in which the poem and our selves enter an assemblage Scalapino calls "writing," and this writing serves as a testing-space for each and every element of consciousness drawn into its nexus.

His Organ and Flesh Were Also a Leopard's

The movement of the body in Scalapino's work is another "texture" or "rhythm" of writing—oscillating bodies enlivened by the stroke of her pen—and yet these bodies are always conditioned by their animality—

profane subjectivity coupled with mammal mobility—lopping, lulling, panting:

> but (maybe because of the way he pulled his neck back—
> with his shoulders heaving in time to the music—which is the way a dog
> bites down on a stick when it's being yanked out of his mouth)   ,
> I immediately had the idea that the man was   hungry[15]

For Scalapino, erotic desire is both figured and conditioned by its baseness: one's "ipseity" or individuality is made paradoxically commonplace and generic as the speaker further fetishizes what makes bodies unique. While coupling bodies retain their "this-ness" (haecceity) through the intimacy of perspective and the duration of attention, sexual union is also portrayed as anonymous and animalistic. Rather than the particulars of specific bodies—the details readers often crave in erotic passages—we find "she" and "he," "him" and "her," "adults," "a man," "a woman," giving and receiving a kind of impassive pleasure, isolated from one another, disaffected and anonymous. "In Sequence"—a longer serial piece from Scalapino's second full-length collection, *That they were at the beach* (1985)—begins,

> She heard the sounds of a couple having intercourse and then getting
> up they went into the shower so that she caught a sight of them naked
> before hearing the water running. The parts of their bodies which
> had been covered by clothes were those of leopards. During puberty
> her own organs and skin were not like this though when she first had
> intercourse with a man he removed his clothes and his organ and
> flesh were also a leopard's. She already felt pleasure in sexual activity
> and her body not resembling these adults made her come easily which
> also occurred when she had intercourse with another man a few
> months later.[16]

While the voyeuresque narrative has an affinity with erotic fiction as genre —as does the fetishization of the particularities of bodies—the terms of sexual engagement are flat and anonymous as "arousal" seems peripheral to these passages. The "viewer" in the poem makes the primal quality of the sexual act erotic, and reduces bodies to animal reproductive organs. For example, "she" is aroused by difference since "her body not resembling these adults made her come easily."[17] She continues:

> She had intercourse with the man who had the features and organ of
> a leopard and whom she had first seen with the group of men who
> lacked these characteristics. The other men were attractive as he was.
> Yet having the sense of the difference between him and the others, she
> found it pleasant for him to come and for her not to come that time.
> The same thing occurred on another occasion with him.[18]

If the viewer does experience arousal in these passages at all, it is a product of difference alone—that someone could experience subjectivation differently. Later, she is "excited" by an incestual relationship between brother and sister because she does not have a brother—excited by a pregnant woman because she herself is not pregnant and because "the woman (does not receive) attention or remarks on the pregnancy."[19] In other words, pregnancy becomes "erotic" when this obvious paragon of difference is publicly ignored. The viewer is pushed away from her subjectivity, is in some ways made alien by her commonality and the "common sense" of her interpretive faculties. Identity politics are rendered inoperative as individuals are reduced to generalizations, to the middle terms of relations (never singular, always like . . . like . . . like), to animals devoid of social decorum, to elemental bodies moving as terms of significance and signification —"marks" in motion, oscillating between words to make action. These are not real people (even if they *are* real people) because, as mind formation, they are simply projections: the brain's effort to sort out the waves of data washing over the subject.

When Scalapino reduces subjects to the materiality of their sexual organs, she does so past the point of pat sexual recognition, juxtaposing human genitalia with the stems and stamens of plants:

> The couple are seen then—by these people—without any clothes, lying on each other. The pink or rosish tip of the man's stem—the pink long slender stem pointed out—is not in the young woman.
> The young man's stem is pointed out—he has an erection though it is not in her yet with him sitting up bending toward her, him innocently unexpectedly, though having no interest in them. The flower opens. . . .
> The mature large bull-man with his stem extended—who's out some time, legs planted apart—coming when rutting but which is not theirs who're foreign. Not that culture. Either.
> The mature large bull-man puts his stem in her.[20]

This segment from *The Return of Painting*, published over a decade later in 1997, retains many of the characteristics from "In Sequence": the voyeuresque, the anonymous, the erotics of difference. Further, the animal and elemental, flora and fauna, draw the particulars of subjectivity further from haecceity to quiddity, from this-ness to what-ness. The reader works through a set of contradictions: a young couple, the man's "pink long slender stem" is erect, the flower opens, and the male is suddenly recast as a mature minotaur, "legs planted apart," sporting the monstrously grotesque sexual organ of a bull. This antinomy draws the reader away from the particulars of sexual copulation and figures the erotic as a series of movements universalized by difference.

The attention paid to the defamiliarization of sex acts certainly jars the reader from settling into a prosaic relationship with "love-making" as social signifier. The portrayal of romantic copulation on television, coupled with the anonymity of non-signifying (because stripped of signifying power) pornographic images, produces a general numbness of affect different in kind from that produced in Scalapino's stanzas. While we are often unfazed by images of sexual copulation in culture, this disinterested perspective does nothing to fundamentally change our relationship to the images we live amongst. In fact, if anything, we continue to fetishize the body and its sexual affectations while further obscuring the particulars of *this* person and *this* body. Scalapino's treatment, however, draws us radically to ourselves—to the fact of our own bodies—in part because of the anonymous yet hardly *disinterested* subjects in her writing.

The Disinhibiting Ring

To better understand how Scalapino troubles the contours of the human's animality in her testing-space, we might turn to German biologist Jakob Von Uexküll, heralded by many as the founder of biosemiotics. For Uexküll, animals occupy "as many worlds as there are subjects,"[21] worlds built around, and protecting, each animal like soap bubbles containing individual environments "filled with the perceptions accessible to that subject alone."[22] Uexküll was among the first of his colleagues to imagine the world from the perspective of the animal in contradistinction to the anthropomorphic view of human science. There is, he claims, a difference between the *umbebung*, the "world" as we humans know it, a *supposedly* shared phenomenal space, and an *umwelt*, a "surrounding-space" or personal "environment-world" that surrounds each animal like a translucent cocoon. Uexküll imagined the ecosystem as a three-dimensional musical score in which each animal, each note, exists autonomously in-itself while contributing to the symphony of the whole—playing off, and corresponding with, other musical phrases. Consequently, according to Uexküll, there are "an infinite variety of perceptual worlds that, though they are uncommunicating and reciprocally exclusive, are all equally perfect and linked together."[23] As a result of this perspective, the animal is merely able to comport to its "carriers of significance," those "marks" made legible through the shield of its respective ring of significance: it can only identify those "marks" that successfully secure its desired telos—say, its "desire" to identify a sufficient host, to feed, to reproduce. In fact, according to Uexküll, the animal's receptive organs are perfectly matched to its marks, and it is only through these carriers of significance that it can comport at all; as a result, the animal only enters into relation with its desire, not with the *object* of its desire.

Martin Heidegger latched on to this idea to insist that the radical break between humanity and animality lies specifically in our ability to abstract from this "captivation," to *know* our ring of significance as such. According to Heidegger, the animal is "encircled by this ring constituted by the reciprocal drivenness of its drives. . . . [It] surrounds itself with a *disinhibiting ring* which prescribes what can affect or occasion its behaviour. . . . Or more precisely—the life of the animal is precisely the struggle to maintain this encircling ring or sphere within which a quite specifically articulated manifold of disinhibitions can arise."[24] Consequently, while the human too encircles itself with a ring of desire, what we might call subjectivity or ideology, the human is *less animal* (according to Heidegger) due to the abstraction from captivation, the turn toward the ring of disinhibition itself.

It is precisely here that Scalapino's poetry troubles the relationship between humanity and animality. In Scalapino's testing space, there are "as many worlds as there are subjects" (as Uexküll has it), each subject occupying both *umwelt* and *umbebung*—moving between the intimacies of one's ontic disinhibiting ring while simultaneously navigating and contributing to a collective social milieu. Part of the effort of attention (for both reader and writer) is placing our own carriers of significance in contrast to the details of the poem, if only to paralyze them in inoperativity. In some ways, the subject of the poem is this activity: the tension between various and often contradictory realities, both external and internal, as the subject builds a temporarily legible self, only to abstract away from this fiction as the self becomes a note in another subject's score. In other words, Scalapino's animal-focused writing lead to *umwelts* penetrating fictional *umbebungs*, drawing attention to the made-ness of our selves as we view our identities from the alien territory of another's subject position. As a result, the constructivist nature of human subjectivity rests loosely atop the animal contours of *bios*, or bare life, forcing us to abstract away from our made-ness in order to hold firm in Scalapino's testing-space.

This experimental ground functions, then, as its own critical ecology in Felix Guattari's sense, in which a "nascent subjectivity," "a constantly mutating socius," and "an environment in the process of being reinvented"[25] play with one another's emergence. "Reducing" the human to its animality makes it possible to concentrate on these marks of significance in terms of nascent subjectivity and the interplay between subject and social, and part of the shock of Scalapino's passages comes from the realization that we hold ourselves in these chrysalides of significance for the benefit of our own understanding of ourselves.

As a result, Scalapino denudes individuals by making them "relations" and out of relations come what we understand as "subjects." In this sense, "affective bodies" are the agents in these poems, and their anonymity serves to make them more animal, more universal, and more particular as doppelgangers of our "truer" selves. The ecology of the poem, then, serves as an *umbebung* within an *umbebung*, world within world, where the gos-

samer threads of our *umwelt*, our "surrounding-environments" punctu-
ated (punched out?) by an ontic core, are cleaved to shreds by competing
pressures. The reader enters the sphere of conflicting desires to find one
fragile bubble threatening another, the lip of one universe closing in on
(and swallowing) another. As readers, we track and interpret our "marks,"
use them to respond in kind—and yet, what if the marks are so tangled,
ultimately, that the *umbebung* reads like a monstrous miscreation of parts,
a patchwork of wholly divergent microclimates? In such an ecosystem,
readers warily interpret the signs of their surrounding climes, and we're
left with the disinhibiting ring of the page distorting the frequency of our
own fragile *umwelt*, leaving us to return to the *umbebung* outside the page,
circumspect, leery, one element among others, mutually arisen.

Waking Life

If Scalapino's testing-space is the site of the subject's rupture, in which the
poem acts as a corrosive, stripping away cultural calcification (of text,
image, sound, subject) from what's left of the living tissue of engagement,
through this process we come to see ourselves in a provisional "present"
as ourselves. However, this process only sets the stage for another kind
of "anarchist moment" in which the testing space itself is drawn into the
nexus of dissolution. As such, Scalapino also challenges the materiality of
the poem itself in an effort to undercut the stability of the reader, deacti-
vating the tyranny of word and image by using both as primary tools to
release imagination from the rigid grasp of capital—making the mystifica-
tion of poetry inoperative through a complex negotiation between over-
amplification and underdetermination (of time, space, and subject, yes, but
also word and image).

A careful reader of Walter Benjamin, Scalapino saw the image embed-
ded within cultural tensions and aporias that determine how we come to
know who we are and what we see. For Benjamin, "the place where one en-
counters [dialectical images] is language."[26] It is in and through language,
because it is in and through *thinking*, that we discover the veiled aporias
that populate the representations we use to historicize ourselves. For Ben-
jamin, a clear picture of the cartography of "now-time" depends on the
acuity of our interactions with these dialectical images, as they flash forth
in fits and starts from lines of rupture marked by the reader's "awakening."

The crepuscular—that threshold between dusk and dawn—is particu-
larly fertile ground in Scalapino's writing—because it serves as the zone
between a dream state of hidden (but very real) values and the "waking
life" in which those values come to signify (or not)—what she calls an
"antilandscape" in which the subject comes to doubt the totality of lived
experience as absolute. In other words, Scalapino juxtaposes, as she writes

in *R-hu* (2000), "disparate images . . . so as to create an antilandscape that no longer 'refers' to a recognizable world."[27] By insisting on the legibility of our images, we are drawn back into the comfortable axiom in which what we see is really, truly what we get. Benjamin called this overcodification "myth": where the diurnal trumps the sur-real of dream, we occupy the present in a dream-state we mistake for authentic experience. Benjamin's "myth time" is "unsplit," "empty, homogenous time" or "critical naiveté,"[28] whereas the dialectical image "marks out a limit or blind spot in the visual field of the present."[29]

For Benjamin, the dialectical or "thinking" image "blasts" the object out of "the continuum of historical succession,"[30] so that thinking stops "in a configuration pregnant with tensions."[31] Scalapino uses nearly identical language to frame the image in her first poems: "I intended this work to be the repetition of historically real events the writing of which punches a hole in reality. (As if to void them, but actively)."[32] "Blasting" or "punching a hole" means to rupture or awaken from a string of over-codified "events" that frame the content of our lives in a supposedly meaningful way (or at least in a manner we've come to understand as meaningful), but what might it mean to write a poetry in which seeing and seeing *not seeing* exist next to each other as a continuum?

In Scalapino's testing-space, "one is seeing constructing, and seeing 'not seeing constructing' by 'seeing' being 'visual' which is actually only-language"[33]—a tortuous construction that sounds remarkably close to Benjamin's notion of awakening in dialectical images, or what he famously called "the dissolution of 'mythology' into the space of history."[34] The act of seeing is "visualized" in the deactivation of its overdetermination; images that retain the *disjecta membra* of cultural currency are subtracted from fields of causality and reactivated in a plethora of signifying modes that shake our faith in what we see (while further imbricating the movement between prehension, apprehension and comprehension). Image no longer "illustrates" or links meaning in causal chains or signifies a particular sign. Instead, the image is a nomad, a variable, roaming aim-lessly (not "randomly," but "without taking aim") through the work, signifying here, only to act as syntactical shape (or visual fact of color or sonic plateau of sound) there. Take for instance the following line from Scalapino's now classic "novel" *Defoe* (1994): "Snorts smoke holding in his lung cage, of man in loose suit jacket, and then releases the fume."[35] Rather than employ the traditional model of filmic gaze, in which the camera pans to the man's hand and then zooms in for a close-up on the cigarette, Scalapino isolates the movement of the fumes, presenting the image from inside the "sealed" body as a constellation of actions: snorting, holding, and releasing the putrid fumes. The "man in loose suit jacket" becomes a recurring "character" in *Defoe*, but here I mean to emphasize character as a written mark with a related significance. The virtuality/potentiality that is "the-man-in-loose-suit-jacket" is only recognizable as a flurry of activity, and enters the text as a variable, giving shape to the actions around it. Rather than relate to this "subject" as a human actor with desires that determinately alter the events of the "novel," this "character" enters the text as a visual and aural signifier that adds color to the action around "him" while the environment itself comes to life as it swirls around the "action" of the "characters":

> The vegetation becomes the color of henna. With inlets running through it and swans. The swans are on a dazzling plateau of blue. Some are in the inlets in the thick red grass. There are these flaming trees surrounding the maze of inlets on which these swans float. A streak in the sky.[36]

Here the image is an undulating visual texture of movement and color; even the swans forfeit their currency as symbolic cultural capital (viz. "beauty" and "grace"). As the eyes move over this "antilandscape," or rather, as *it* washes over the eyes, the function of sight is suddenly conspicuous as it feeds the brain's crossed signals.

> Slick against the knotted white bulbs in the air writhing. The bulged muscles feel hard to her touch. That's a spine, so that he's running. Out there as his knotted bulbs that are slick and wet. The foot of thick red leaves has been sent up floating behind him. He's still, but being just before there so that the street is like gills opening and then flattening— with him running in it.
> The cold invades the flesh so that one feels the frame from the feet up as empty. Forward in the gills that are narrow and flattening. The gills open are filled with the red leaves.[37]

Isolated, the "slick white bulbs" retain a hint of the organic, drawing to mind fresh-peeled onions, only to begin writhing, slowly morphing into grotesquely determinate muscles "hard to the touch." This movement from the organic to the erotic just as quickly evaporates as the body begins to move, first with the spine's undulation, only for the eyes to travel to the feet "running." But even this moment of "continuity" (can we even call it that?) erupts as the feet turn to "thick red leaves" floating in stillness, hovering, gills opening and closing, only for the figure to move again.

Scalapino's writing is the struggle to occupy a perpetual state of *awakening*—even if being "awake" feels like dreaming—because to occupy and produce this awakening is the dissolution of the real as "myth." She writes, "Yet for (Walter) Benjamin of course 'idea' *was* its rupture: that *is* the action. That was the occurrence I wanted in *hmmmm*, both."[38] However, she continues, "Now we've become inurned to either integration or disruption as filmic illusion, one's translation of film image as disruption having become inurned to be *only* image again. That is, disruption of image requires continual change as introduction of a new medium."[39] The act of writing has to *be* this shock, with the understanding that "undoing the accepted 'reality' is continual as it is constantly being reestablished"[40]—that mystification is often an *optical* phenomena in the "real world," so rehabituation is most facile when images are the catalyst. In the introduction to *Sight*, a collaboration between Scalapino and fellow west coast poet Lyn Hejinian, the authors write that they wished to "turn seeing up to an extreme in order to see it," and as a result create a poetry that feels "as if dreaming being suppressed were bursting out as luminous seeing in the waking state."[41] Elsewhere, Scalapino calls this the "extinction of images" after Danielle Collobert, "'not continuing' the chain of images which constitutes being, and writing"[42] by creating a new chain of images that deconstitute being as stasis.

Scalapino uses the image amplified to profound effect in *Defoe* (the first section of which is called "Waking Life"), but it is really in *The Front Matter, Dead Souls* (1996) where this tactic is pushed to its limit. In *Front Matter*, "The writing is scrutiny of our and 'one's' image-making, to produce extreme and vivid images in order for them to be real"[43]—which means, of course, in order for them to have *content*. The writing is *only* content, completely devoid of framing devices, a play on the Language writing scene in the early 1980s that claimed that writing should "have no content."[44] The writing's content is itself seeing *seeing* itself. Writing about *The Front Matter, Dead Souls* (1996) in *Zither and Autobiography* (2003) —an autobiography of her writing life—Scalapino insists: "The images are to be bulbous, 'extreme' vivid in the sense of their being 'of' eyesight only, as if existing apart from any 'event' that is written-meaning"[45]:

> The thin day with the greyhound coagulating in it barely exists. Dead Souls on her way to the race track the officer on the long slender limbs floats by the coagulating dog. His slender black hands drifts in the air to open the car door for her.
> He had been in the previous day with the fleck emerging to him when the limousines wallowing in the air with the sumos emerging coming in for the funeral grieving were rubbed by the crowd.
> Dead Souls in the little high-heels comes to the car when there's only thin air with the greyhound floating in it.[46]

The writing bears the characteristics of this "blasting" or "punching out" of the myth of homogenous time, because the images are disassociated from their context in such a way that they become grotesquely out of scale. As images pass sequentially before the readers' eyes, one begins habitually to construct a scale or narrative to frame the percussive rupture of this antilandscape. But the writing undercuts the reader's desire to frame the images, and forces her to watch—to see the patterns of mythologizing that allow for the present to be separated from the "now." But as Scalapino has shown time and time again, for the image to retain the "extremity" of its presentation—for it to act as a rupture or shock in her testing-space —she must alter the strategies that allow the image to remain exterior to the codification that makes language rhetoric. The result is an incredibly intense barrage of detail that begins to visually shape the terrain of this antilandscape as a kind of musical score:

> The rose light so that he's on the rim holding the man, the sumo picks him up in the black air but begins moving bounding like a vast bulb floating on it.
> A worm flies to them on the street. The air unfolds in the silk suit softly billowing to them faintly in it. As it meets them, the man held by the sumo swims out slashing it. His projecting from the arms of the sumo, they're buoyed so not from each other.
> The green hump lies peacefully so eyes floating on the sky.[47]

As the images pass by, they begin to act more like texture, rhythm, percussion—synonymous with trees and rocks and bushes in a visual landscape —and as the eyes pass over the ridge, the reader begins to watch herself reading, like a tourist self-conscious of those behaviors that define her *as* tourist.

Because nothing is actually "happening," "one's seeing it is its sole occurrence," and this rim of observation as negative space becomes the truly dialectical image. While Scalapino is certainly interested, as is Benjamin, in a dialectical image capable of blasting the object *and* subject out of the continuum of history, unlike Benjamin, Scalapino is not interested in the possibility of a redeemable future. Scalapino's writing is patently "anti-allegorical," "being (instead) only occurrence/actions."[48] While her images are mined from the sources around her—often those images that populated her morning paper—they are not "symbolic." In fact, while they certainly signify, they do so in often dramatically disparate ways in any given line. It's tempting for readers to assign signifying parts to the image, but in so doing we fall back into the effort to contextualize in order to understand. Each image is the rim of occurrence where reader meets the antilandscape of visual texture. There she watches the self struggle to occupy Benjamin's "now-time" in which the production of subjectivity mutually arises with the present as it "attain(s) to legibility."[49] But for Scalapino, to occupy the now of recognizability, one must understand the "now" *through* what makes it legible.

Whereas Benjamin arranges objects to reveal the hidden truth of the social, Scalapino rearranges the subject to reveal the truth of sociability itself, because we risk losing ourselves if we can't recognize ourselves in every moment. The secret of the object is the subject—how the subject chooses to frame the object in history, and that the subject, too, is merely an object. When Benjamin "unlocks" the secret of the object, he is only unlocking the object *for himself* and his reading of the particular moment of recognizability. That's why every interpretation of the present is devoid of emergence. *Seeing* seeing leaves a reverberation or gyration—an after-image or lightning strike—that helps the reader recognize the construction of subjectivity in the "now of recognizability."

Scalapino's interest in the hand-painted movie posters of Ghana is an interesting illustration of how this works in her practice. The "by product" of the short-lived but extremely popular "video clubs" of Ghana, hand-painted movie posters were used to advertise nomadic sites of Western popular culture, where VHS copies of popular American movies were shown in impromptu "cinemas"—popular gathering sites similar to the domestic family room.[50] These posters, while ostensibly "advertising" the films at hand, speak less to the particular fleeting moment of western culture and more to how that culture is made fungible overseas. Drawn in incredibly vivid colors with details verging on the grotesque, the posters detach themselves completely from their antecedents: rather than provide a mimetic representation, artists often interpreted or modified the subject matter, mostly because they had often yet to see the film. The image then becomes misrecognition through mistransmission, positively framing the cultural value of the signifiers *themselves* rather than the content they purport to deliver. The grotesque figures signify particular elements of American culture that are both attractive and repulsive—violence and sex are amplified and in so doing draw our attention to their codification. While the movie poster is designed to deliver content—a mimetic representation of a determinate thing—it is precisely in how these posters rework their content that the images slip from overdetermination into the nomadic life of polysemy. Emphasis on the "accuracy of representation" seems less valuable than the artist's ability to construct images that arrest the viewer's attention.

Scalapino's writing is similarly very much about how it transmits or mistransmits, depending on where you're sitting. It skirts mimesis or interpretation for misrecognition. "Turning the volume up" serves to detach images from cultural currency while signifying through difference. The "bulbous" can only signify by what it is not (or can no longer be) and in so doing marries "seeing" with social obsession and desire. In terms of Uexküll's "disinhibiting ring," the vivacity of her writing draws our attention to how desire enters into our field of disinhibition, allowing us to read and interpret "marks" (words) as culturally significant signs. For Scalapino, the act of misrecognition, coupled with overamplification and underdetermination, creates a scenario by which writing is reactivated as the very tool for understanding emergence. And as a result, her testing-space serves as a tool to make and understand ourselves, if only temporarily, before we watch our fictions dismantle under the competing pressures of both poem and world.

NOTES

1. Leslie Scalapino, *Zither & Autobiography* (Middletown, CT: Wesleyan University Press, 2003), 2.
2. Ibid.
3. Originally published as the opening gambit of Leslie Scalapino's first book *Considering how exaggerated music is* (San Francisco: North Point Press, 1982).
4. Scalapino, *Zither & Autobiography*, 34.
5. Ibid., 1–2.
6. See Frank O'Hara, "Personism," *The Collected Poems of Frank O'Hara*, ed. Donald Allen (New York: Knopf, 1971), 499.
7. Scalapino, *Considering how exaggerated music is*, 3.
8. Ibid., 3–8. Interestingly, this swarm of similes marks one of the final appearances of this convention in Scalapino's writing (aside from very rare exceptions). By ultimately doing away with figurative comparisons in her work, she further blurs the line between illusion and objective "reality." Insistence on *a priori* fact or fiction disappears completely (or, at least, the firm conviction that a subject can distinguish the difference *a posteriori*).
9. Ibid., 6.
10. Ibid., 4.
11. Ibid., 7.
12. Scalapino writes, in "Note On My Writing: On *that they were at the beach —aeolotropic series*," "I intended this work to be the repetition of historically real events the writing of which punches a hole in reality. (As if to void them, but actively)." Leslie Scalapino, *How Phenomena Appear to Unfold* (Elmwood, CT: Potes & Poets Press, 1989), 21.
13. Carl Andre, *Cuts: Texts* (Boston: The MIT Press, 2005), 84.
14. Giorgio Agamben, *The Time That Remains: A Commentary on the Letter to the Romans* (Stanford: Stanford University Press, 2005), 95.
15. Ibid., 37.
16. Leslie Scalapino, *that they were at the beach* (San Francisco: North Point Press, 1985), 57.
17. Ibid.
18. Ibid., 61.
19. Ibid., 58.
20. Leslie Scalapino, *The Return of Painting, The Pearl, and Orion: A Trilogy* (Jersey City: Talisman House, 1997), 21–22.
21. Brett Buchanan, *Onto-Ethnologies: The Animal Environments of Uexküll, Heidegger, Merleau-Ponty, and Deleuze* (Albany: State University of New York Press, 2008), 22.
22. Ibid., 1.

23. Giorgio Agamben, *The Open: Man and Animal* (Stanford: Stanford University Press, 2004), 40.

24. Ibid., 255.

25. Felix Guattari, *The Three Ecologies* (New York: Continuum, 2005), 68.

26. Walter Benjamin, *The Arcades Project* (Cambridge: The Belknap Press, 1999), 462.

27. Leslie Scalapino, *R-hu* (Berkeley: Atelos, 2000), 93.

28. Tom McCall, "'The Dynamite of a Tenth of a Second': Benjamin's Revolutionary Messianism in Silent Film Comedy," in *Benjamin's Ghosts: Interventions in Contemporary Literary and Cultural Theory*, ed. Gerhard Richter (Stanford: Stanford University Press, 2002), 79.

29. Ibid., 75.

30. Benjamin, *The Arcades Project*, 475.

31. Walter Benjamin, *Illuminations* (New York: Schocken Books, 1976), 262.

32. Scalapino, *How Phenomena Appear to Unfold* (1989), 21.

33. Scalapino, *Zither & Autobiography*, 36.

34. Benjamin, *The Arcades Project*, 458.

35. Leslie Scalapino, *Defoe* (Los Angeles: Sun and Moon Press, 1994), 54.

36. Ibid., 81–82.

37. Ibid., 120–1.

38. Scalapino, *How Phenomena Appear to Unfold* (New York: Litmus Press, 2011), 205.

39. Ibid.

40. Leslie Scalapino, *Objects in the Terrifying Tense Longing from Taking Place* (New York: Roof Books, 1993), 26.

41. Lyn Hejinian and Leslie Scalapino, *Sight* (Washington, DC: Edge Books, 1999), Introduction.

42. Scalapino, *Objects in the Terrifying Tense Longing from Taking Place*, 8.

43. Leslie Scalapino, *The Front Matter, Dead Souls* (Middletown, CT: Wesleyan University Press, 1996), 2.

44. For more on this claim, see Scalapino's essay "Disbelief" in *How Phenomena Appear to Unfold* (2011).

45. Scalapino, *Zither & Autobiography*, 36.

46. Scalapino, *The Front Matter, Dead Souls*, 40.

47. Ibid., 70.

48. Leslie Scalapino, *Green and Black: Selected Writings* (Jersey City: Talisman House, 1996), 70.

49. Benjamin, *The Arcades Project*, 462.

50. For examples, see *Extreme Canvas: Hand-Painted Movie Posters from Ghana* (New York: Dilettante Press, 2001), a book Scalapino owned in her personal library.

BIBLIOGRAPHY

Works by Leslie Scalapino

POETRY
O and Other Poems. Berkeley: Sand Dollar Press, 1976.
The Woman Who Could Read the Minds of Dogs. Berkeley: Sand Dollar Press, 1976.
Instead of an Animal. Kensington, CA: Cloud Marauder Press, 1978.
This eating and walking is associated all right. Bolinas, CA: Tombouctou, 1979.
Considering how exaggerated music is. New York: North Point Press, 1982.
That they were at the beach. New York: North Point Press, 1985.
way. New York: North Point Press, 1988.
Crowd and not evening or light. Brooklyn: O Books, 1992; reprinted 2010.
La Foule et Pas Le Soir ou La Lumiere. French translation. Royaumont, 1992.
Sight. With Lyn Hejinian. Washington, DC: Edge Books, 1999.
New Time. Middletown, CT: Wesleyan University Press, 1999.
The Tango. Text and photographs by Scalapino, collaboration with artist Marina Adams. New York: Granary Press, 2001.
It's go in/quiet illumined grass/land. Sausalito, CA: The Post-Apollo Press, 2002.
Zither & Autobiography. Middletown, CT: Wesleyan University Press, 2003.
'Can't' is 'Night.' New York: Belladonna, 2003.
Day Ocean State of Stars' Night. Los Angeles: Green Integer, 2007.
It's go in horizontal: Selected poems, 1974–2006. Berkeley: University of California Press: 2008.
The Animal is in the World Like Water in Water. Text by Scalapino, images by Kiki Smith. New York: Granary Books, 2010.

FICTION/INTER-GENRE
The Return of Painting. New York: DIA Foundation, 1990.
The Return of Painting, The Pearl, and Orion: A Trilogy. New York: North Point, 1991; reissued Northfield, MA: Talisman, 1997.
Defoe. Los Angeles: Sun & Moon Press, 1995; 2002.
The Front Matter, Dead Souls. Middletown, CT: Wesleyan University Press, 1996.
Orchid Jetsam. Berkeley: Tuumba, 2001.
Dahlia's Iris—Secret Autobiography and Fiction. Salt Lake City: Fiction Collective Two, 2003.
Floats Horse-Floats or Horse-Flow, a novel. Buffalo, NY: Starcherone Press, 2010.
Dihedrons-Gazelle, Dihedrals-Zoom. Sausalito, CA: The Post-Apollo Press, 2010.

ESSAY COLLECTIONS/INTER-GENRE
How Phenomena Appear to Unfold. Elmwood, CT: Potes & Poets Press, 1989; second expanded edition, Brooklyn: Litmus Press, 2011..
Objects in the Terrifying Tense/Longing from Taking Place. New York: Roof Books, 1994.
Green and Black, Selected Writings. Northfield, MA: Talisman Publishers, 1996.

The Public World/Syntactically Impermanence. Middletown, CT: Wesleyan
University Press, 1999.
R-hu. Berkeley: Atelos Press, 2000.

PLAYS

Goya's L.A., a play. Elmont, CT: Potes & Poets Press, 1994.
The Weatherman Turns Himself In. Tenerife, Spain: Zasterle Press, 1999.
Stone Marmalade (the Dreamed Title). Collaboration with Kevin Killian.
Philadelphia: Singing Horse Press, 1996.
The Belladonna Elders Series 1. Collaboration with E. Tracy Grinnell. New York:
Belladonna Books, 2008.
Flow—Winged Crocodile & A Pair/Actions Are Erased/Appear. Tucson: Chax
Press, 2010.

SELECTED PROSE

"Re-Living." *Poetics Journal* 4 (1984).
"Poetic Diaries." *Poetics Journal* 5 (1985).
"Aaron Shurin's *Elsewhere*." *Poetics Journal* 8 (1989).
"Robert Duncan's H.D. Book." *Talisman: A Journal of Contemporary Poetry and
Poetics* 7 (1991).
"'Thinking Serially' in For Love, Words and Pieces." *Talisman: A Journal of
Contemporary Poetry and Poetics* 8 (1992): 42–48.
"The Canon." *American Poetry Review* 27.3 (May–June 1998): 9–12.
"Pattern—and the 'Simulacral.'" In *Artifice and Indeterminacy: An Anthology of
New Poetics*, ed. Christopher Beach (Tuscaloosa: University of Alabama Press,
1998), 130–39.
"War/Poverty/Writing." *Poetics Journal* 10 (1998).
Introduction to Philip Whalen's *Overtime, Selected Poems*. New York: Penguin,
1999.
"Interior Scrutiny: Example of H. D." In *H.D. and After*, ed. Donna Krolik (Iowa
City: University of Iowas Press, 2000), 203–10.
"Fiction's Present without Basis." *Symplok_* 12.1 (2004): 35–52.
Introduction to Philip Whalen's *Collected Poems*. Middletown, CT: Wesleyan
University Press, 2008.
"Thinking and Being/Conversion in the Language of *Happily* and *A Border
Comedy*." *Aerial 10: Lyn Hejinian* (2010).
"The instant is the giant lamp we throw / our shadows by," preface to *Of Indigo
and Saffron, New & Selected Poems*, by Michael McClure. Berkeley: Univer-
sity of California Press, 2010.

SELECTED INTERVIEWS

Brewster, Anne. "'We're always at war': the Worlding of Writing/Reading, An
Interview with Leslie Scalapino." *How2* 2.2 (2004); www.asu.edu
/pipercwcenter/how2journal/archive/online_archive/v2_2_2004/current
/feature/brewster.htm.
Foster, Edward. "An Interview with Leslie Scalapino." *Talisman: A Journal of
Contemporary Poetry and Poetics* 8 (Spring 1992): 32–41.

Frost, Elizabeth. "Interview with Leslie Scalapino," *Contemporary Literature* 37.1 (Spring 1996): 1–23.

Golston, Maggie. "Interview with Leslie Scalapino." *University of Arizona Poetry Center Newsletter* 22.1 (Fall 1997); poetry.arizona.edu/blog/interview-leslie -scalapino.

Lederer, Katherine. "PW Talks to Leslie Scalapino." *Publishers Weekly* 247.44 (October 30, 2000): 72.

Rosenthal, Sarah. "Leslie Scalapino in Conversation with Sarah Rosenthal." *Jacket2* 23 (August 2003); jacketmagazine.com/23/rosen-scal-iv.html.

"What Person?" Exchange with Ron Silliman. *Poetics Journal* 9 (1991).

Selected Reviews and Criticism

Bedient, Calvin. "Breath and Blister: The Word-Burns of Michael Palmer and Leslie Scalapino." *Parnassus: Poetry in Review* 24.2 (2000): 170–96.

Bremmer, Magnus. "Out of Site: Photography, Writing, and Displacement in Leslie Scalapino's 'The Tango.'" In *The Future of the Text and Image: Collected Essays on Literary and Visual Conjunctures*, ed. Ofra Amihay and Lauren Walsh (Newcastle upon Tyne: Cambridge Scholars, 2012), 169–97.

Campbell, Bruce. "Neither In nor Out: The Poetry of Leslie Scalapino." *Talisman: A Journal of Contemporary Poetry and Poetics* 8 (Spring 1992): 53–60.

Cazé, Antoine. "Alterna(rra)tives: Syntactic Spaces and Self-Construction in the Writing of Lyn Hejinian and Leslie Scalapino." In *Ideas of Order in Contemporary American Poetry*, ed. Diana von Finck and Oliver Scheiding (Würzburg, Germany: Königshausen & Neumann, 2007), 197–214.

Ellis, Stephen. "Lock-Step Chaos: Leslie Scalapino's Multiples of Time." *Talisman: A Journal of Contemporary Poetry and Poetics* 8 (Spring 1992): 53–60.

Emerson, Jocelyn. "What's Love Got to Do with It? A. R. Ammons, Leslie Scalapino and Chaotic Poetics." In *Restoring the Mystery of the Rainbow: Literature's Refraction of Science*, ed. Valeria Tinkler-Villani and CC Barfoot (Amsterdam, Netherlands: Rodopi, 2011), 601–626.

Frost, Elizabeth. "Signifyin(g) on Stein: The Revisionist Poetics of Harryette Mullen and Leslie Scalapino." *Postmodern Culture: An Electronic Journal of Interdisciplinary Criticism* 5.3 (1995 May); doi:10.1353/pmc.1995.0023.

———. "Splayed Texts, Bodily Words: Handwriting and Seriality in Feminist Poetics." In *The Contemporary Narrative Poem*, ed. Steven Schneider (Iowa City: University of Iowa Press, 2012), 221–44.

———. "'Time-less or Hieroglyph': Self and Simulacrum in H.D. and Leslie Scalapino." In *H.D. and Poets After*, ed. Donna Krolik Hollenberg (Iowa City: University of Iowa Press, 2000), 211–24.

Gilbert, Roger. "Textured Information: Politics, Pleasure and Poetry in the Eighties." *Contemporary Literature* 33.2 (1992): 243–60.

Hinton, Laura. "Formalism, Feminism, and Genre Slipping in the Poetic Writings of Leslie Scalapino." In *Women Poets of the Americas: Toward a Pan-American Gathering*, ed. Jacqueline Vaught Brogan and Cordelia Chávez Candelaria (Notre Dame: University of Notre Dame Press, 1999), 130–45.

———. "The Return of Nostalgia: A Fetishistic Spectator in Leslie Scalapino's

The Return of Painting and the Hudson River School of Art." *Textual Practice* 42.2 (April 2010): 223–53.

———, ed. "Critical Feature on Leslie Scalapino." *How2*, 2.2 (2004); www.asu .edu/pipercwcenter/how2journal/archive/online_archive/v2_2_2004/current /feature/index.htm.

Lagapa, Joseph. "Something from Nothing: The Disontological Poetics of Leslie Scalapino." *Contemporary Literature* 47.1 (2006): 30–61.

Myk, Ma_gorzata. "'One's Mind Makes Fictions as Its Function': Writing as Experimentation in Mind Formation in Leslie Scalapino's *Defoe*." In *Novelistic Inquiries Into the Mind*, ed. Grzegorz Maziarczyk and Joanna Klara Teske (Newcastle upon Tyne: Cambridge Scholars, 2016), 59–76.

Nash, Susan Smith. "Magic and Mystery in Poetic Language: A Response to the Writings of Leslie Scalapino." *Talisman: A Journal of Contemporary Poetry and Poetics* 14 (Fall 1995): 90–100.

Ratcliffe, Stephen. "Listening to Reading." *Talisman: A Journal of Contemporary Poetry and Poetics* 8 (Spring 1992): 61–62.

Robbins, Amy Moorman. "Affective Identification, Critical Production: Leslie Scalapino's 'hmmmm.'" *Studies in the Humanities* 41.1–2 (2015): 143+.

Samuels, Lisa. "If Meaning, Shaped Reading, and Leslie Scalapino's *way*." *Qui Parle: Literature, Philosophy, Visual Arts, History* 12.2 (Spring–Summer 2001): 179–200.

Simpson, Megan. "Poetic Jouissance: The Subject-in-Process in American Women's 'Language-Oriented' Poetry." In *Critical Studies on the Feminist Subject*, ed. Giovanna Covi (Trento: Dipartimento di Scienze Filologiche e Storiche, Università degli Studi di Trento, 1997), 185–208.

Tan, Kathy-Ann. *The Nonconformist's Poem: Radical "Poetics of Autobiography" in the Works of Lyn Hejinian, Susan Howe and Leslie Scalapino*. Trier, Germany: Wissenschaftlicher Verlag Trier, 2008.

Watten, Barrett. "Political Economy and the Avant-Garde: A Note on Haim Steinbach and Leslie Scalapino." *Talisman: A Journal of Contemporary Poetry and Poetics* 8 (Spring 1992): 49–52.

COLE SWENSEN

POEMS

FROM *Such Rich Hour*

May 21, 1420: The Signing of the Treaty of Troyes

And thus we give up: This and this and

In a ceremony in which hands are severed, it's traditional to hire a choir, to blind
the neighbors, to refuse all letters

or you could simply pluck out my eyes, serve them up on a plate (some saint
already tried this) and I'll walk around reciting "Ok, I get it

Said Charles VI
and in signing found
that when he went to pick up the pen he couldn't remember whether he wrote
with his right hand or his left. It's permanent. They delivered a black granite
cube ten feet high and stood it on his toe.
You get a great view from here; it just isn't yours anymore.

December 25, 1456: Je Françoys Villon escollier

It's snowing
                                bitter
                    ground
        to dust
        and salt
                    will shudder in the heel:
                                a broken window

"It's I who steals from churches
                                        who reaps the learnèd sequence
                                                    who says

            (I was made for loving
        my only
        Joan of Act)
        here in my hand
                    (*I bequeath the beautiful theft*
                    La Lanterne de la rue Pierre-au-Lait
        all my names
                    tooth after tooth
                                phalanxed to snow   no

                                            night
                        boned
        black
        (they say) (no, it was I)
        who said when wolves live on wind they get fat.

FROM *The Book of a Hundred Hands*

Shadow Puppets

The First Movies

Then, all hands touched. Hands shone. The hand was a public thing.
A tool that rang when dropped. The two hands moved across
What moves between a screen and a match
awakened in the cold
                              (The smaller the light, the more enormous
the hands will live) by a sound
will be gone. Enormous trees, a castle, a pond
and no sky
in the broken ray
into birds on the opposite wall.

Birds

Most shadow puppets are birds. This all depends on darkness. Birds prefer darkness.
Cockatoo, parrot, and lark have in common
you can see through them; a density based on ambient light. They must live inside
any number of things. Things without number. Name them:
                                               two flying birds
                              two flying birds
                    require both hands as
hands are more supple than the rest of the body
because they don't belong to it.

Advances in the Form

The latest work in shadow puppets is being done on verbs. Make the form of a soar, of a veer. Make the tense clear. Distinguish the past perfect from the simple past. Neither was. And on into conditionals. Would have found, etc. Would have gone
myself, but I wasn't home. Bird lovers often use sign language because, though birds are fond of the human voice, they are downright hypnotized by the swaying hands and will walk right into them.

FROM *The Glass Age*

And so began the Age of Glass, the first one named
for a thing man-made, and the first one made to
break. Anemic ghost that lives on salt, it was an
accident of silicate that neatly held its own until it
suddenly exploded around 1800.
                                        For

instance,
the earliest arcades, the glass-ceilinged passages interlaced across Paris,
were constructed from the
beginning of the 19th century on
                and on, all gallery. Adapted from the
grand houses of Italy and France, with their long
halls in which their owners' treasures lay exposed
under glass.

        •

The great conservatories took off at about the same
time—Chatsworth, Chiswick, and from there to the
public garden. A palm house, an aviary, a passion
for orchids swept the country.

        •

While in France, they built whole mansions of glass;
called *orangeries* or *serres* or *vies*, a conservatory can

be made, paned, claimed

I grew a lemon from a forest of thieves. I grieve

still for the infinitesimal

difference between
what you can see and what you cannot see.

•

"I see no difference," he said, sifting from the right
hand to the left. I am deep within the house where,
after all these doors, there is only glass and someone
coming down the hall whistling a tune that sounds
like someone walking down a spiral stair.

A Garden is a Start

Because the kings of France loved Tivoli
                           these windows bearing oranges
                                         globed,
glowed, and that's how night becomes day without taking your eyes off their palaces
in winter.

A garden is a mirror
                   he said stepping back to get a larger view
                                     he knew
a globe upon a table, that's containable,
                         whereas an orange will seem
                to expand in the dark—
                we've trained our explosions to slow down. We thought
the world was warm, was orange, and hung
                     ripe among the leaves all around us.

From the French: *garder*: to keep as well as to tend: *gardien*,
garde bien, keep well, guard them
within
the horizon stepping back, dropping off—
                here,
                he opens his arms, spreads out his hands, now off the map,
"You will see

A garden is a window: A garden starts, of course, in the eye, which is looking out a window, which starts geometry on its rounds, each pane
recording the faceted plantings
that a single finger traces
in the crisp veil of late frost,
some fortunes turn dust to dust.
André Le Nôtre spent his childhood among the gardens of the king and his gardeners studying
to be a painter

who paints "This lives"

who paces trees
who sees:

André Le Nôtre spent his childhood.

Everything he ever planted now is dead.

André Le Nôtre died a rich man.

"Le Nôtre couldn't stand views that end"—Saint-Simon

Half a century earlier, his grandfather had undertaken, on his own and at his own expense, to replace all the dead trees in the Jardin des Tuileries.

We
who were born in 1613
are we who remain here in the garden as it leads outward
an owl of all edging
and compass inciting
obeisance and trust us—
we left for the forest
through a grand avenue of oaks
all leaning inward, they
leaned over as we spoke:

four rows of elm
all bordered in hawthorn
four huge coffers
of shadow in flower
for four kilometers of one
can only hope
for a good handful
of the restless
coming down to earth.

And to you we leave these trees.

If it were to curve

he said, the earth

and it turned
        as things turn to stone with a word spoken
at a given angle to the wind.
You measure the angle with an astrolabe and needle,
                  the needle balanced
          on the middle finger and the eye aligned
to the eye   around which it glides.

He dreamed of a spherical garden
and listened to the spring tighten
as he wound the clock

counting slowly
as it slowly, unknowing, comes into view
reciting:
      But I'm an astronomer,
I lose things.

FROM *Gravesend*

A Ghost

erodes the line between being and place   becomes the place of being time   and so
the house turns in the snow   is why a ghost always has the architecture of a storm

The architect tore down room after room   until the sound stopped.   A ghost is one
among the ages at the edge of a cliff   empty sails on the bay   even when a ship

or the house moves off in fog   asks you out loud   to let the stranger in

Kent

In the grounds of Bayham Abbey   in a garden designed by Repton
a procession of monks just about dusk   or just after darkness has fallen
go walking.

Or there was no sadness, just a simple fold in time.

One must be for others a reason to live.

Often, it is said, the presence of a ghost is signaled by illogical cold.

Lord Halifax noted it when investigating "the Laughing Man of Wrotham,"
who strode into his brother's room and murdered him   night after night

to the horror of the maid who, a century later, wedged a chair against the door and
watched him disappear.

There is no cure

for anything, and that cough you have, Madam, once

there was a fire every Friday the 13th, and once there was a death
that seemed to deserve it, but that was an illusion. Once there was a

death, but that was illusory, too. And all over Kent, someone is still
heading up the stairs, lighting the way with a match.

One No

When this it goes.   She said winnow winnow   Why come thou   Watch now
My latch was its watchspring   My love was an eland   And I that hypnotic

am knocking on tables   unmarrowed in craving   the chant won't ungiving   a knuckle
a breastbone   a light switch, an ibis   They say that wherever   bird enter—when there

as it happens, a bird comes into the house uninvited   (most often through a window)
someone will die soon. My lover, that eon   My watcher, that whiteness   That bone there

an icon   I stumble to seem like   I stutter and bleach eye   and sinew on farther
which unlike further   means a distance you can measure   and my boat such a small one

Gravesend

My   ended   grove   my threaded shriek   drawn   along
by swans straining at the same   Did you fall off the edge

and which   home carved from an egg   as if a little

trap door slowly spread through every room   ever this ready
the dead are hauling   a circus behind them in flames

Who Walked

across water   who gathered   there over   a gathering mist
is a migration.   They went down just off the coast   and sometimes almost

an army balanced out there on the waves   but in rags   and flagrant in wind
Legend claims that on calm nights   you can hear their footsteps from the cliff   a soft

howl, the children are wading   out past the horizon   he was sailing alone   returning late
when he saw an army of children dressed in rage   walking over the sea on their hands

FROM *Landscapes on a Train*

The light is an accident because the trees are old. So and without wind with grain.
Orchard grain on light. Orchard lined the heart. A spire, a forest, a village made
By hand. And another stand of trees, of hay in rolls in fields. In every distance is
Sieved and moves off slowly, a long thin line that trains the eye. A line of hills that
Pulls away.

Shore as it pulls away. There's a grey lake below the grey sky. Hundreds of grey
Trees lining the banks of a stream. Stream down sun in little coins. A bigger town.
A church too big for its hill. And cows easing down the slope. Slows its calm, and
More little sun goes on among selves.

A window opens a train. Now on whiter air. Other measures drift. Quick, hasp
And fast the green comes back, innumerably strong. Swung the sky off light. Light
The one comes down. To a single ray in a single field. Divides and buries on. A
Train across open land opens night. (A train lands all night across an open field.)

A church in the middle of a field is a tree. Poplar poplar. Hundreds of swans. White
Is a tiny gash. All over the swan is light striking an arc. Or any animal that adamant.
Emphatic crows in a field. Three. And then dozens are the dark. Are the traveling
Folded. Intricate folding apart.

Planes of migrating geese. The geese are hundreds, they are sheets, hundreds of
Feet up there are two sheets of geese only barely each other and shifting screens,
The infinite splitting of finite things.

Quiet lights the fog, washes the grey. Grey, the green that could have been rain.
A long line of greenhouses and boats tied up to the bank, young plants under canvas
Arches another river passes, fewer boats and a house built for summer whose rain
Rains down upon rain.

And orchard on. Trees count. One more house. Fallen down. Goes falling on. One
More canal tearing the clear. And the singular way that trees take over a meadow.
All that walking. All it calls. I heard something call. One if animal. And horses once
More a plain cut by a rivulet. A house stands alone in a field.

A white cow stands alone in a field. A white horse stands alone among trees. A
Line of trees stands alone. In sheaves of green. As the eye strikes a far thing, a
Small thing, a thing at this distance becomes distance alive all alone.

Paysage à Céret, 1920

if the house entered the wind or rather
if the wind is in fact or becomes the windows
or in what order wind and house arrange
themselves there is a shroud
to find or lace or veil at times the whole town
wearing out, wearing down
to the face of the animal beginning to show
the procession of white walking out of itself, not
at all as violent as one would have thought or
it was not the wind

Soutine painted some 200 landscapes around Céret in the three years he
spent there between 1919 and 1922. His first dealer, Zborowski, took
him down to the south to give him the time and the means to paint. First
to Cagnes, just west of Nice, but Soutine was restless, and so moved on
to Céret, a small town just above the border with Spain and some 20
miles from the sea.

Many of the landscapes are houses, and many others are trees. *Les modes
de la vie.* The rooms into which. We move through rooms, whole in the
air, which is open, opening doors, a house on a hill that spins on its own,
undone. This is the case with *The Oak*, c. 1939, which is mostly sun, and
The Tree, c. 1939, with houses the size of dice somewhere down below.
                              Is a painting of a tree a landscape or
a portrait? He painted so vigorously that he one day dislocated his thumb.

Paysage à Céret, 1921

> For someone loved a forest and someone loved the trees
> on the side of a hill falling home. Another home
> and their curving green. We always seem
> to be drifting back, back past the paint where the world
> looks just like this and because an object is
> as it is loved—a road, a house, a sun—it comes
> to join the trees in their unlikely light.

FROM *On Walking On*

Wordsworth

Dorothy walking from Kendal to Grasmere and Grasmere to Keswick, a mere 33 miles, from Alfoxden to Lynmouth and back again for the sake of a landscape, an internal painting, refining in brushstrokes a new form of breathing. She could breathe again, and wrote it up, notational: *March 30: Walked I know not where. March 31: Walked. April 1: Walked by moonlight.* Walked till blind. Walked by wind. Walked into time. Hunkered woman, dove-shaped   as the hand takes on   the size and shape of a bird across the pages of a journal: Walked in silence.   Walked inside.   And was neither heard nor herded   although I sensed the gathering forces trying to gather up the indeterminate group of all things headed forward. I will sort them.

George Sand: *Promenades autour d'un village*

They set off along the river literally on white horses, G. Sand and two friends, listing
shades of green, counting leaf by leaf, tree, sheen, and a translucent insect almost

invisible at the tip of a blade of grass. One friend was an entomologist in search
of certain cocoons, while the other, although an artist, was also looking for an insect,

a common blue butterfly, but a perfect one. They walked on, late June, 1857.

The insect as pearl, the insect as chime, the insect as amethyst gilded in mica.
This is what it's like to take a walk with an entomologist. A flight of crickets

suddenly ignited by a hand brushing across the top of the reeds and into
the studded sky we breathe through the branches, we filtered through grasses

we occupy. Butterflies, he claims, though migratory, never cross a sea, never still
a step beyond, yet said

that only something small could I believe. An antelope the size of an earring
is nibbling a maze through the long grass down the long hill.

Sand had a particular affection for this particular village and chose it
as a starting point for a series of radiating walks that wound along

through gorges, past mills, down the river, a keen observer,
she watches across the mirrored water, four people in a boat in the

very act of crossing, is an act of gliding slowly, barely parting. The mirror
is green and almost touching. The oar drawing the boatman holding it

a moment playing with the light on its edges breaking. Sand walked
as a way of engraving in and then on the mind outside, landing farther,

a stone tower overtaken by a flowering vine, a pencil tracing the entire route
there and back, themselves overtaken by dusk and thus erring, errant,

wandered all evening to find it suddenly late at night and the village asleep,
picking their way down the steep stone street, each a candle in hand.

Debord

à la dérive   de la Bièvre   de Guy Debord who could sweep through any city
on a curve   could river aloft   even an old river knotted   in the middle
of the night   can be traced by its heat   Debord who refused to follow
the meticulous scent   only a city could in such debt   could a city disarticulate
its flickering grid   in walking is   the destruction of city planning   the de-
Haussmannization of the mind on an October afternoon   filtered light   fingering
a break in the seal   cast aside   decades later   a group of young people
got into the habit of walking a straight line across Paris   no matter what buildings
rivers or other obstacles happened   to refuse the pattern   they unlocked
the genetic sequence   and not without effect   on the English Inclosure Acts of
the 18th and 19th centuries   though this is difficult to document   which is one
of its principal strengths.

POETICS STATEMENT

As Mallarmé said in 1896, there's a crisis in poetry. His remark was in-
tended for that moment, but, in fact, it's a statement that's always appro-
priate. There's always a crisis in poetry because poetry simply *is* language
in crisis—it doesn't exist any other way, and it's this aspect of it that al-
lows it to do what it, socially and culturally, needs to do, which is to be
agitated, and then, in turn, to agitate. For a "crisis in poetry" doesn't mean
that something is happening *to* poetry, but that poetry is itself happening
something to language—i.e., it makes "to happen" into a transitive verb.
    In that light, the word "crisis" re-encounters and extends its root in the
Greek word *krinein*, "to decide," and its noun form *krisis* or "decision."

Not only does this downplay the drama, but it also underscores the deliberate decision by poets to use poetry to act upon language in very specific, directed ways. It's this sense of the crisis inherent in poetry that allows it to play the role of a minor literature in relation to prose in the way that Deleuze and Guattari developed the concept—a literature that coexists within another, dominant, one that it constantly disturbs, continually forcing the major literature to rethink itself, regroup itself, and reassert itself—necessarily changed.

Though Deleuze and Guattari were talking about minor and major literatures in very specific linguistic and cultural contexts, their concept is applicable to generic contexts as well; i.e., all poetry acts as a minor genre to all prose, regardless of the language, and its ability to do this is based on its capacity to remain indefinitely in a state of active disequilibrium. Poetry's disturbances, both on the surface of language and within its deeper structures, consist in its constant, subtle erosion of the principles of clarity and stability that define and direct prose. To the prosaic dream of a 1:1 relationship of word to meaning, poetry proposes any other ratio—and therefore has many more compositional options than prose, while yet, in the mind of the culture at large, always remaining subordinate to it.

One of the many current crises in poetry (there are always many, carrying out a variety of agendas) is directly engaged with this "minorist" activity in that it addresses the informational language that is usually solely the territory of prose. Grappling with the relationship of information to art, this crisis is emerging in movements as diverse as documentary poetry and spoken word, as well as in countless other works that seek to interfere with the seemingly seamless production of information.

One way that has come increasingly into play is a reconsideration of statement, which amounts to a reconsideration of the relationship of language to fact, in which non-semantic aspects of language are consciously used to pressure the semantic in a variety of ways. The prominence of this approach and this project has everything to do with an ongoing interrogation of truth in philosophical and critical contexts. A rigorous and necessary philosophically driven project to explore the inevitable multiplicity of truth with all its ramifications devolved into popular culture through what Stephen Colbert recognized in 2005 as "truthiness" and then into the culture at large as what we all—despairingly or gleefully, depending—have come to recognize as the "post-truth" world. "Post-truth," as I'm sure everyone reading this knows, was the OED's word of the year for 2016.

And such a shift from philosophical query to new world order occurs, of course, first in language—a commons so fluidly shared that no one ever thinks about who's responsible for maintaining it. If not properly addressed at the level of linguistic invention, such a shift then goes on to affect all realms, from the domestic to the judicial to the economic to the military, with often horrible results that could have been, if not avoided, at least mitigated if due pressure had been put upon its earliest emergences in language.

Fact is always two-fold: it first exists as an event in the world, and then as an act of language, and no one doubts that the second determines, and *in fact*, irremediably alters the first. A time-based event in the world necessarily and instantaneously vanishes, and a statement takes over—with no one having any way of determining or proving its veracity. And thus the statement becomes the "truth," overwriting that of the event. This is rarely questioned. We say that one *tells* the truth—not that one sees the truth or hears the truth or feels the truth. Of course one does, initially, see and hear and feel it, but only if one happened to have been present, and even then, once the moment has passed, language necessarily takes over, and telling becomes the only body that truth can adopt. And it is an adoption—i.e., there is a disruption in the line of descent. That doesn't necessarily mean that it's therefore unfaithful, but a difference is inevitably and irrevocably inscribed.

One of poetry's most promising crises is also focused in a disruption of a line, in this case, the poetic one, through disruptions of syntax and syllogistic logic that implicitly query how event gets transformed into language, and then how manipulations of language, including ambiguity, parataxis, and other interruptions of sense as normally understood can thwart a blithe acceptance of truth-as-offered by constantly forcing people to consider how what is handed off as fact, as truth, is constructed and, above all, by whom.

This is nothing new. It's just newly again re-important. Only worse. And the only thing that poets and poetry can do about it is to remain its minor, to remain an element of constant irritation, resisting the apparent transparency and "naturalness" of language through consistently asserting the evidence of its always partisan construction.

The minor in this sense plays a role not dissimilar to that played by the minor key in many traditional musics in the western world. It's a key that resists resolution, that registers restlessness, and as such, it's analogous to poetic strategies such as off-rhyme, syntactic scrambling, and *non sequitur*. The minor keys in music are often said to have a "dark" sound, and they do—of the sort of darkness that illuminates the invisible, analogous to linguistic elements, such as those listed above, that carry meaning without carrying it semantically.

There is endless speculation on and many theories about why the minor key in music is experienced as dark and brooding; many of them claim that it's simply cultural conditioning, but others suggest that it's at least in part because the middle note of a minor chord is a half-step closer to the tonic than it is in a major chord, creating frequencies that are less synchronized, and are therefore more dissonant. In other words, they are literally less re-solved, physically more ambiguous, continuing much longer, perhaps for-ever, in an unsettled state.

The parallels here with poetry leap out—dissonance, dissolution, and darkness as modes of demanding an accounting. So much traditional west-ern music—the blues and the English ballad, just to name two—implic-itly and insistently *demand*—everything from revision to restitution. They *brood*; they plan; they plot.

The minor keys are also often said to convey a sense of loss and/or yearning. In the United States certainly, and, arguably, globally, we are at a moment of critical loss, and perhaps, therefore, at a moment at which sound arts, from poetry to performance to music, can offer ways to con-struct meaning that, by circumventing the strictly semantic, can also cir-cumvent the dominant reduction of multiplicitous and labyrinthine truths into the eminently commodifiable "post-truth" object.

TRUTHS SURPASSING FACT

Cole Swensen's Research-Based Poetics

Lynn Keller

Cole Swensen's work displays a longstanding fascination with the *be-tween*, with what can bridge oppositions or break up the established terms of a binary. Ron Silliman acknowledges one manifestation of this enduring investment in his blog response to *American Hybrid: A Norton Anthology of New Poetry* (2008), which Swensen edited with David St. John. Noting that hybrid poetics, "[r]ather than representing a revolt" within either of the competing poetry traditions of the second half of the twentieth cen-tury, instead "seeks to ameliorate the borders betwixt the two, to operate perhaps as if no chasm in aesthetic & cultural values gave rise to these traditions," Silliman quotes a passage from Swensen's introduction that includes the following:

This anthology springs from the conviction that the model of binary oppo-sition is no longer the most accurate one and that, while extremes remain, and everywhere we find complex aesthetic and ideological differences, the

contemporary moment is dominated by rich writings that cannot be catego-
rized and that hybridize core attributes of previous "camps" in diverse and
unprecedented ways.

Silliman adds: "I don't know about 2009, but I do know that this is a po-
sition very close to the one that Cole Swensen took as my student in 1982
at San Francisco State University. It's a belief long & deeply held. And she
was already an awesomely talented young writer, capable of adapting from
one form to the next, regardless of the mode's origins." One may or may
not agree with her assessment of the dynamics operating in the current po-
etry scene; Silliman, as when he gestures toward a "chasm," suggests that
such a perspective erroneously imagines a healing of the "cultural and po-
litical rupture between aesthetic conservatives & progressives."[1] But there
can be little question that in Swensen's own writing and thinking, this in-
terest in what may be found or produced *between* has been persistently
generative, crucial to the production of a remarkable body of poetry.

Despite her having entered the poetry scene at a time and place where
Language poetry was coming into full force and re-charging the divisions
of the midcentury anthology wars, the oppositions of primary interest to
Swensen are not those between poetic camps. Dyads more fundamental to
her thinking—extensively explored in the essays collected in *Noise that
Stays Noise* as well as in her volumes of poetry—include: reading and see-
ing (or the legible and the visible), the seen and the heard, the referential
and the performative, the language of information and language as art,
image and text, abstraction and representation, information and noise, art
and daily life, the living and the dead, the spiritual and the material, pres-
ence and absence.

Swensen insists that the "betweens" she explores are not compromises
between poles, not syntheses that locate a middle ground, but rather trans-
formations that expand the terrain in new directions.[2] For instance, in dis-
cussing the fractal motion she admires in the poetry of Susan Howe and
Anne Marie Albiach (and which, I have argued elsewhere, is evident in
her own writing as well),[3] she explains that just as fractal geometry cre-
ates a "new zone" of fractal order "between the domain of uncontrolled
chaos and the excessive order of Euclid" (as Benoît Mandelbrot put it), in
literature "the fractal offers an opening onto a space between the utterly
unstructured and structures whose fixity restricts the possibilities of the
language they support. . . . This new form is neither a third pole nor a com-
promise between (combination or rearrangement of elements of) the two
original poles; rather, it is something new that breaks up a binary entrench-
ment by stepping outside of its terms."[4] Similarly, when considering poet-
ry's unique fusion of the visual and verbal, she claims "poetry that works
to maximize these two modes can deliver an experience that is 100 percent

aural and 100 percent visual, which results in an overload, an overflow, which spills into another zone of perception, creating an active hybrid between the two senses. And it is above all the 'between' itself that is created and that is full of cultural and creative promise" (*NSN* 32–33). Discussing those liminal creatures, ghosts, in another essay on Howe's writing, Swensen asserts, "Ghosts are neither living nor dead, and so offer a third state, one whose territory is the periphery. And here the periphery is not so much a relative position as it is a different quality, requiring different senses, such as a different kind of seeing" (*NSN* 36). In "The Fold," a short piece on *La prose du Transsibérien* by Blaise Cendrars, known as the first "simultaneous book," Swensen celebrates the text's having "exploded" the "rigid division" between the worlds of the verbal and the visual by "using a number of moves to fuse text and image and in so doing, creat[ing] a third, hybrid object that was neither visual nor verbal, but an intricate interfolding of the two" (*NSN* 91). The fold, she goes on to argue, opens the text to motion; by making a moving part of a single thing, the fold is in fact "raw motion" (*NSN* 95).

As these examples suggest, Swensen repeatedly emphasizes the motion generated in or out of spaces of betweenness, the expansion or excess that emerges from the interrelation of conventionally dichotomized elements, and the potentially molten quality of language itself. As she does so, she sometimes recruits figurations of biological, cybernetic, or mathematical complexity such as the rhizome or noise or the fractal to supplement terms like *hybrid* and *between* that are difficult to release from the strictures of binarization. Her interest lies ultimately in what exists beyond the reach of any language, often suggested in her poetry through what is evanescently glimpsed only from the corner of one's eye or in the motion of turning one's head. At the same time, she joins other experimental poets who deliberately push against the limits of language, seeking to open up "the territories of the previously unexpressed" or previously inexpressible (*NSN* 10).[5] Although Swensen's chosen subject matter, which remains largely within the artistic and cultural history of Western Europe between the Middle Ages and the late nineteenth century, has registered for some readers as hermetic,[6] the stakes of this shared enterprise are huge and politically charged: "enlarging the field of the sayable, and thus of the thinkable, the imaginable, for the culture as a whole" (*NSN* vii).

In this essay, I will focus on one particular opposition (through which some of the others will filter), examining the ways in which Swensen in her works of "research-based poetics" negotiates and undoes the gap between the language of information and language as art—the latter being strongly linked to "the unquantifiable qualities of sound relationship, word associations, and innate rhythms" she terms "poeticity" (*NSN* 7). These project-based volumes, precisely because they all push at the same dichotomy, provide a telling demonstration of the continuing innovation evident in Swensen's work. They represent her expression of an impulse shared by many U.S. poets in the twenty-first century: to enhance poetry's cultural importance by expanding and developing its handling of public material. Often, as is the case in Swensen's writing, this involves both some kind of muting or redistribution of the "I" and some incorporation of documentary elements; Swensen's approach is one that emphasizes maintaining beauty and aesthetic richness, the material pleasures and the sensory and imaginative presentness of the poetic.

At least since her 1997 collection, *Noon*, Swensen's books have been loosely unified in their preoccupations, with repeated terms and gestures acting as threads tying together the individual lyrics. The nine nine-part poems in *Noon*, for instance, are repeatedly concerned with seeing and apperception, with the limits of our senses ("The human body is blind except for the minute exception of the eyes") but also their access to the spiritual realm (as in its repeated references to a verse from the Koran declaring "Everywhere you turn you see the face of God").[7] Written in short, sometimes asyntactic units usually arranged as prose, the poems make of repetition an explicit motif ("Repeat after me:" "Repeat:") and a constant practice via recurring actions or words such as *face, body, hand, blind, forest, river, shadow*. Almost all Swensen's subsequent volumes, however, have had definite unifying projects, most of which have depended upon scholarly research and have therefore involved elaborated investigations of what might be generated in interactions between "poeticity" and information.

Swensen's essay "News that Stays News" offers her fullest theorization of "the problem of how to reconcile the language of information with the language of art" (*NSN* 53). Its consideration of documentary poetry illuminates the issues because documentary and poetry are so fundamentally at odds. Poetry, Swensen argues, does not represent the outside world so much as it creates its own alternate worlds that operate according to their own logics and laws; a "true act" in itself, the poem is "absolved from the truth test." Documentary, however, is devoted precisely to "present[ing] as accurately as possible events in the outside world" (*NSN* 54). Documentary's truthfulness, moreover, raises issues about speaking for others; avoiding appropriation of the voice or experience of others often requires repression of the artist's imagination. Happily, this sacrifice entails some gains: "A shift away from imagination and toward what is in this case its opposite—the truth—presents a shift in what we usually think poetry can and should do, revealing that it can be an effective part of civic life and can bring the news in a way that no other form can." Swensen adds, "If poetry can do this, its ability to do so must be bound up with poeticity (defined here as the poetic function in Jakobson's sense—putting the focus on the message for its own sake—along with figurative language, image, ambiguity, and juxtaposition). This amounts to bringing language as art into the heart of the language of information" (*NSN* 55).

Although Swensen obviously admires the documentary volumes she analyzes by Mark Nowak and Claudia Rankine, one senses her discomfort with limiting the poetic to the extent that they have. Because these documentary poets have urgent truths to convey, both carefully restrict the poetical dimensions of their work (though what poetic elements they subtly introduce, Swensen makes clear, are artfully employed to imaginatively engage the readers' responses); they do so in order to establish credibility with an audience who assumes that poetic language, because it is "not . . . liable to the truth test," is "incapable of conveying truth" (*NSN* 58). Swensen recognizes the prudence of such an approach, but in her own practice her interest lies in the distinctive role played by the poetic, and her inclination seems to be to expand it:

> poetry—amid all its ambiguity and ornamentation—is not only perfectly capable of conveying truth; it can also attain a unique relationship to truth because it implicitly acknowledges and interrogates the limitations of language. The truth of a human situation can't fit into language (contrary to the tacit assumption of journalism) because human truth surpasses fact. However, through interstices opened up by figurative language, ambiguity, juxtaposition, sound relationships, and rhythmic patterns, room can be made for those aspects of truth that can't be articulated. (*NSN* 58)

To close "News That Stays News," Swensen turns from documentary poets who adopt a clear, flat voice and generally limit themselves to transparent language, in whose work the subject matter is foremost and a call to action is implicit, toward one whose aesthetic is much closer to her own, Susan Howe. Taking *Pierce-Arrow* as her example, Swensen presents Howe's poetry as representing another kind of documentary work in which "language . . . is more at the service of art, and its writers have devised ways of making the language of art even more aesthetically complex by augmenting it with the language of information. . . . Such texts are not calls to action but calls to reflection. . . . Such texts are often no less socially oriented, but they operate in a different time frame" (*NSN* 64). Swensen does not use the term "research-based poetics" here; that I took from a videotaped interview in which Swensen discusses a seminar she was teaching on the subject in the fall of 2010.[8] In "News that Stays News," she does, however, attend to Howe's reflexive consideration of her own acts of research as she discusses the roles of both documentation and invention in the constitution of knowledge. Swensen calls attention to lines from *Pierce-Arrow* ostensibly written in the language of information that swerve into other forms of language use "in which poeticity rules and the visual qualities of language are maximized" (*NSN* 65). Such lines cease to participate in "the economy of truth, even though they use its vocabulary and syntax" (*NSN* 65). Swensen's description of Howe's aims aptly summarizes Swensen's own poetics in her research-based works: "She embarks on a vertiginous balance between rigorous inquiry and the recognition that normative language necessarily reduces truly new thinking—that normative language, by its very normativity, cannot accommodate the act of thinking; it can only accommodate thought, its prepackaged past tense" (65). Rather than following the kind of documentary writers who, for political goals she admires, adjust their language to accommodate the widespread distrust of poetic language, Swensen is eager to change her readers' attitudes toward poetic language by expanding their appreciation of the distinctive forms of knowledge that language as art allows. In what follows, I will trace the development of Swensen's research-based poetics, identifying the strategies by which she opens up its between spaces and examining what she accomplishes by so doing. After having demonstrated the growing confidence and sense of play evident in Swensen's research-based art, the essay will close with a demonstration of the interpretive possibilities and challenges offered by such hybrid texts.

Swensen's 1999 volume *Try* enacts her initial foray into research-based poetics. Unlike some of her later collections, this one contains no scholarly bibliography or critical explanation of historical backgrounds, but it obviously rests on substantial study of artworks and art history. Its nine three-part poems along with its prologue and epilogue are all ekphrastic, and this ekphrasis has a scholarly surface; the artworks to which the poet responds are usually named and dated within the poem titles or texts, where fragments of critical commentary sounding like voices of art critics sometimes appear as well.[9] One could accurately observe that the volume's predominant subject is an epistemic shift registered in European visual arts with the emergence of landscape in paintings of religious subjects at the beginning of the Renaissance. Yet such a summary would not do justice to the imaginative and temporal freedom evident in the text, nor to all the multiple dimensions of knowledge and apprehension that are woven into the book through the poet's deployments of language as art. These would include her explorations of eroticized touch—only some of which are tied to art history—of the objectified female within and outside of art, and especially of shifting perspectives and subject positions through which she undermines the gap between writer and artwork conventional to ekphrasis.[10] In her view, that gap limits the kind of knowledge one can have of the work of visual art. Consequently, she, like Howe, invokes the language of information and the associated objective stance but then allows them to dissolve, as in this passage from the "Prologue" in which a characteristically mobile subjectivity moves among proliferating perspectives and temporalities both within and outside the painting:

>   My angel of Giotto, MADONNA
> OGNISSANTI, 1310: the right eye
> traveling, planned, fled and
> the left fixing forward like a pin.
> He who watched him who wings
> world without end and where
> were you when she spun around and stared
> and my God what on earth
> has happened to their eyes?[11]

The first three lines in a lively but accurate way describe the eyes of Giotto's Madonna. As subsequent enjambed lines flow on, however, the identity of those referenced (he, him) becomes more elusive, while the introduction of a "you" draws the viewer/reader into an ambiguous time and space of either the painting or Mary's life. By the last few lines quoted, the speaker, no longer an objective recorder, seems to have entered the scene to respond with shock to a transformation that has taken place in an uncertain temporal and spatial location: perhaps in the lives of the figures Giotto represented, or perhaps in the art of painting in Giotto's time. The powerful sense of presence enabled by ambiguities and instabilities is more the point than any specific "true" information about the painting.

At times, the language of information is entirely suspended, but more often the poems weave among different registers, shifting, sometimes seamlessly and sometimes quite abruptly, among purely lyrical presentation, narrative associated particularly with the Biblical scenes depicted, and the informational language of art-historical description or scholarship. In all of these modes, Swensen tends to use syntax in a way that opens multiple possibilities; this is not simply the syntactic doubling that many poets use as meaning shifts over a line break. Rather—or in addition—syntactic gestures remain incomplete, so that they reach into an expansive semantic space. Here, for instance, is the opening of "The Flight into Egypt," a key story for artists developing an interest in landscape:

> Reach me to
>   new all other
>   land
> That flees
> Known. Recognized though
> you can't remember what
> the house looks like it's huge
>
> And carried in her arms
> and in her arms held
>
>   and stopped a moment to sit

where the cells coalesce
exchange address

           though it's huge

and does not walk alone.

"From the fourteenth to the eighteenth centuries, we find in the
painterly obsession with the Flight into Egypt a recognition of . . .
as being . . . who focus . . . here on earth, though without . . . and
the function of the metaphor (Fly! Fly!) in setting the stage for the
nineteenth-century fabrication of Orientalism."[12]

Occasionally, the reader can simply fill in what has been left out: what she
carries or holds in such scenes is undoubtedly the Christ child. But most of
these lines, employing what I have elsewhere termed Swensen's lacework
aesthetic,[13] leave spaces for imaginative elaboration, as they suggest that
the Flight to Egypt is an archetypal scene for any flight from the familiar to
the vastness of an unknown. Sometimes fragmentation itself is what is gen-
erative since units remain incomplete or broken in ways that make connec-
tions uncertain; at other times it's the absence of punctuation that opens up
the syntax (is it the house that's huge, or something else, such as the space
of the new landscape, the exchanged address?). Holes are torn even in the
scholarly passage placed in quotation marks, so that while it employs the
language of information and important information is to be gleaned here
(that this painterly obsession involves a focus on "here on earth" as op-
posed to the heavenly divine, and that its metaphor of flight anticipated
the Orientalist fascination with the Other), space is deliberately opened for
imaginative speculation (recognition of what? without what?).

When she deploys the language of scholarship in *Try*, Swensen's meth-
ods suggest a combination of respect and impatience, demonstrated in the
opening of the second poem in "Triptych," titled "There":

"an implicit assumption that the concrete world is inaccessible"

"an implicit assumption that the concrete world is more lovable"

Love me and you love the world
he said while over his shoulder
or through a little window just to the right
of the picture

blue and green
this haze will never falter
"Throughout the Middle Ages and for several centuries thereafter, the
eye was
continually directed toward a scene of moving people, but
and in intricate detail

sometimes down to leaf by leaf
it's spring and a farmer
who shall remain nameless, no more than half an inch tall
plows a world we will not enter[14]

On the one hand, the materials in quotation marks—or marked with open quotes—help focus the reader's attention on historical questions of real interest to Swensen concerning particular eras' or particular paint-ers' relations to the concrete world. Yet the presentation of two diver-gent interpretations of "implicit assumptions" encourages readers not to equate scholarship with truth. Moreover, the slippage from the seemingly art-historical notation of "intricate detail" to a kind of participation in the painting's world—"it's spring" (even though that world is one "we will not enter") suggests the speaker's preference for the vibrant concrete realms of either trees and fields or green and blue paint over the abstrac-tions of critical discourse. On one level, this may not differ much from Swensen's handling of informational language in *Noon*, where factual propositions tend to dissolve in near-surrealist image: "Close observation of the black beetle reveals an inverted architecture in which the subterra-nean vaults flay themselves against noon. While inside, a different night takes over."[15] However, precisely because it calls attention to research, *Try* manifests a much clearer desire to position poetry as a significant—and significantly alternative—source of reliable information and as a medium in which intellectual debates may be furthered. This is a position more con-fidently occupied by subsequent volumes that expand the space between the language of information and language as art.

Swensen's most ambitiously researched book to date and one of her longest collections, *Such Rich Hour*, appeared in 2001, just a few years after *Try*. Where *Try* called attention to ways of interacting with paintings that challenge the conventions of art-historical discourse and enlarge the parameters of traditional ekphrasis, *Such Rich Hour* adds to these projects a supplementation, via language as art, of the historian's ways of knowing and representing the past. Always preoccupied with ways of seeing, Swen-sen here seems particularly interested in investigating the perspectives of an era of upheaval—the literal perspectives employed in its artworks as well as the cultural and religious perspectives discerned and imagined for its inhabitants. Doing so involves bringing to the realm of information the distinctive resources of poetry.

Such Rich Hour opens not only with a poetic prologue, as the earlier vol-ume did, but also with a "Preface," an explanatory prose "Introduction," a "Foreword," and a poem titled "Forward." Half-mocking academic schol-arship, the poet calls attention to the excesses of her own apparatus. The opening "Prologue," which I quote in full, begins *in medias res* with very specific historical information but also with an unsettled temporal perspective and shifting address:

> And ten days later, the locks and keys
> to the city of Paris were changed (1405) you will die
> eleven years later of plague)
>   were made
>   Captains of the city of Paris
>   Mes Sieurs de Berry et de Bourbon
> entièrement dit   You
> (toi aussi)
> that death is an angle with grey eyes
> I read it somewhere;
> therefore,
> come true.
>
>   (if you only)   le least idée   of that qui doit arriver
> (mon âme)
> it is said
> "it is sown" though there is no
> reason, particularly,
> that it had to happen/will happen (circle one) this way.[16]

This conveys a lot about Swensen's approach to history in what she calls a "story of a hundred years." The inclusion of dated historical facts, along with the casual bits of French that suggest her fluency in the language of the history to be explored, are gestures that establish her scholarly authority. The predominant message of the poem, however, is that while people tend to see what happens as destined or in some way determined ("that qui doit arriver"), and while death is indeed inevitable, the particular ways in which things have happened, or will happen in the future, are not in fact determined. That Swensen shares the historian's interest in how people at different times have made sense of their experience is evident from the other introductory poems' focus on historicized attempts to understand the universe in terms of mathematical or religious structures. While the historian would be interested in rationally tracing causes for events moving through time, however, "Prologue" makes clear that the poet is intrigued by coincidence and chance and by the inner experience (present and past) of living where loss and death are inevitable but events remain radically unpredictable; rather than illuminating causality or chronology, the shifting subject positions and perspectives of Swensen's poems produce a multifaceted, compound-eye vision of these areas.

As the "Introduction" explains, the poems are based on the *Très Riches Heures du Duc de Berry*, a fifteenth-century book of hours—that century being one in which the "rate, magnitude, and variety of change look extreme even from a post-twentieth century point of view" (*SRH* 4). The fabulously illuminated manuscript was originally designed to "allow individuals to observe religious ritual outside the strict format of the mass" (*SRH* 4). Swensen explains that because the poems respond especially to the calendar section of the book, which lists the principal saints' days and other important religious holidays, the poems follow the sequence of days and months "and not necessarily that of years." Although some poem titles include specific years (not in order) and mark notable historic events—births or deaths of particular individuals, the first book printed in Paris, etc.—many poem titles identify only days of the month. One does not get from reading the volume a sense of historical chronology, an understanding of the Hundred Years' War, or even a consistent sense of the illustrations in the *Très Riches Heures*. Deflecting such expectations, Swensen's "Introduction" carefully qualifies the extent to which the work is conventionally ekphrastic as well as the role played by historical knowledge. Those poems titled for the first day of each month, which "bear a relation" to the medieval monthly calendar illustrations,

> like all the other pieces here—soon diverge from their source and simply wander the century. And finally, they are simply collections of words, each of which begins and ends on the page itself.

> Similarly, references to the Hundred Years' War and other specific events do not require a run to the encyclopedia, but will instead, I hope, contribute to the life-in-lore of these events, a life that gives another, parallel life to all that occurs. However, those interested in pursuing the history of the period and/ or the images themselves will find a list of sources at the end [in a "List of Sources" that concludes the volume]. (*SRH* 5)

Despite Swensen's disclaimer, in my own experience a little historical research (for which Wikipedia will usually suffice) often makes the poems more accessible and interesting. Basic information about the lives of the saints whose days are registered in the volume's calendar or about named historical figures can lend meaning to numerous details in the corresponding poems. Even when the poems themselves provide relevant background, a bit of online exploration can add further illumination; thus, while "The Invention of Equal Hours" contains this declaration, "*And not until the end of the Middle Ages and the advent of societies of commercial basis came the genesis of the equal hour and its mechanical registration*"(*SRH* 25), it's helpful also to understand that canonical hours, in not being spaced evenly, supported a concept of time as something that varied with place and season. And, of course, viewing reproductions of pages from *Très Riches Heures* provides insight into the poems' ekphrastic dimensions. But these are quibbles; Swensen's overriding point about wanting to contribute not to historical knowledge but to "life in lore" significantly clarifies this volume's relation to the language of information. The poet, though working from the foundation of substantial historical knowledge, is not aiming to teach facts or preach an airtight argument about them. Thus, "June 15, 1416: The Death of Jean, Duc de Berry" conveys the information that the Jean "had fallen in love in prison (1363)" and that he was predeceased by his three sons, but what's most memorable in the poem is its imagining of what an imprisoned nobleman might have seen from his prison cell:

> The swans migrate past the cell window
>   (the window narrow
>   so the huge birds cross it
>   one by one
>   frame by frame   (almost growing)
> or it's the same one passing   (enormous)   and in between
>   the sky. (*SRH* 60)

Invited into fifteenth-century life and lore, the reader may well come away from the volume with an intensified sense of the brutality of the times (in, say, the ways in which those who displeased authorities were tortured), the hardships people endured (famine, plague, attacks by wolves and hostile human invaders), and the remarkable ingenuity and inventiveness evident in this era of transformation and expanded trade (the development of techniques of gilding or navigation, of particular pigments or of movable type, for example). But because language as art flows in and out of—or sometimes fragments and disrupts—the language of information, it deflects closed structures of logic while it opens emotive and sensory insight into medieval life or into thinking within the period's conceptual structures, its literal and figurative perspectives.

Even more significant than Swensen's comment about historical research in the passage quoted above is her emphasis on poems ultimately being collections of words, for she frequently identifies the materiality of language as one of the key resources of language as art, essential to the ways in which poetry can be "an alternative mode of knowledge" (*NSN* 65). *Such Rich Hour* extends explorations evident in *Try* (and also in *Oh*, which, though not published until 2000, was a finalist for the National Poetry Series in 1998) into the expressive possibilities of page space and textual arrangement and the mobilizing effects of play with patterns and relations of sound. The opening of one of the calendar poems, "June 1: Reaping" can demonstrate:

> Sickle one, scythe two and sweep and sheaf and sign
> in the rocking field and the river whole
>   in its own   (what hold
>   what
>   boat

of the errance of a spire (despite appearance
    it's miles

  (at the door of the river) (that curves into harvest

Choir: Let us
    harbor in this witness

                      a man
       with an oar
shreds a surface

(at the door he calls a river) (*SRH* 57)

Here a strong iambic rocking precedes the announcement of a "rocking field," while the echoing long *o* sounds of *whole, own, hold, boat* bind these lines into the proclaimed wholeness. The music of *s*'s flows from "sickle" and "scythe" through the near-rhyming "spire" and "miles," to "shreds" and "surface," while the slight modification from "at the river" to "he calls a river" gives a kind of aural curve to that nearly repeated line. The short lines "what hold / what / boat" and "it's miles," gracefully centered in the midst of open space, slow the poem's motion and momentarily suspend the imagined craft on a page otherwise filled with reminders of time's motion and death's approach.

Sound and sense are closely bound here, but the role of both sound and visual effects is not merely mimetic. These sensory aspects of language add other kinds of meaning associated with the semiotic, even as they obstruct more formulaic ways of processing linguistic information; "the visual aspect of language is always poetic because it obstructs transparency. As soon as we are seeing language, we are no longer seeing through it" (*NSN* 56). Both aural and visual effects are part of poetry's distinct defamiliarizing "noise" that, by interfering with the usual process of denotation, keeps the imagination active and pushes the reader to construct new meanings. In addition, the richly immediate sensory pleasures generated insure a valuable presentness that Swensen sees as one of the gifts of the aesthetic: "aesthetics is always concerned with achieving presence, and recognizes that it is the *arrangement* of the present that makes presence possible—not in the sense of re-creating a scene or event so well that you feel like you're there, but by creating a new, entirely separate event right where you actually are" (*NSN* 78). Her decision to use "hour" in her title rather than translating the plural *heures* may speak to the value she places on experiencing the singular moment.

In subsequent volumes Swensen seems increasingly comfortable with the language of information, or perhaps more accurately, more confident that allowing it more room or fullness in her poems need not mean ceding to it more power. Her next volume, *Goest* (2004), coheres around whiteness and light; its middle section, "A History of the Incandescent," contains twenty poems based on a mid-nineteenth-century book, *A History of Inventions, Discoveries, and Origins*. Frankly announcing their researched subject matter, these poems have titles like "The History of Streetlights," or "The Invention of the Mirror," or "The Exploration of Fluor-Spar," and many of these appear to stay quite close to their source. The fact that their perspective is a nineteenth-century one gives them a quirkiness or anachronism that itself adds a kind of poeticity: "The Development of Natural Gas," for instance, points slantedly toward the present era of fracking precisely through its striking distance from contemporary scales of development, lending the information it conveys surprising emotional resonance:

> There's a button factory in Birmingham using it to solder
> A single cotton mill in Manchester
>   with over a thousand burners
>   in a detailed account
>   of the coal fields of China
>   while drilling even deeper
>   the flames some 20 or 30 feet high
> once harnessed, boiled the water from the salt, while
> what remained, remained as light, a lucent fringe
> to the hand that turned
>   the valve to red[17]

What happens to the language of information in such contexts is comparable to what happens, according to Swensen, when poets use scientific terminology. Seen by scientists as misusing such language, poets in fact are "reaching out to scientific language for its precision, and taking it from there as raw material to be worked through metaphor, metonymy, and ambiguity until it expresses something that can't be expressed otherwise" (*NSN* 17).

Experimentation with giving the informational fuller range is particularly evident in *The Glass Age* (2007). As in *Such Rich Hour*, Swensen again depicts an era of cultural transformation largely by contemplating selected art of that time. This more streamlined text, however, which focuses primarily on one (again French) artist—Pierre Bonnard—and a single material—glass—explores clearer conceptual patterns and is more evidently about the coalescing of perceptions involved in a shift that defines and distinguishes a particular age. While the language of information still frequently dissolves into suggestive fragmentary images and gestures that open toward mystery and possibility, Swensen frequently incorporates informational propositions as complete syntactic units in this volume; sometimes the only text on a page will be a coherent informational paragraph. As if to emphasize the inclusion of this nonpoetic material, now rarely signaled as a distinct tonality by quotation marks and instead comfortably integrated into the speaker's voice, *The Glass Age* arranges text predominantly as prose.

Language as art sometimes enters very subtly; for instance, in the following passage (which occupies a page early in the text), the only element of poeticity is the absence of a final period; this invites the reader to "see" the space on the rest of the page—not to "see through" it as a blank, but to experience its expansiveness as palpable:

> Bonnard's work implicitly asks what is it to see, and what it is to see through. We think of the arguments for the materiality of language that have played such an important role in philosophy and poetry of the 20th century. Bonnard argued for a similar materiality of the window. There is nothing you can see through. You see[18]

Sometimes, however, as in the following passage (again, all the words on that page), prose arrangement of text creates an appearance of normativity that proves illusory:

> So often in Bonnard's work, the window is where we actually live, a vivid liminality poised on the sill, propped against the frame, he turns and speaks for the first time that day. The window, ajar, swings fully open in the breeze, and you watch his face glide away. (*GA* 18)

With "propped against the frame" as a hinge, the first sentence itself swings open: initially the reader understands the window—that vivid embodiment of liminality—to be propped against the frame, but then, as "he" suddenly is added, "he" becomes the one who was propped. Invited in the first sentence to identify with a universalized human "we," by the end, the reader is situated as a singular "you" left behind by the movement of the man's (Bonnard's?) reflection. The reader experiences unsettlement as a kind of aftertaste.

On most of the pages of *The Glass Age*, however, it's quite apparent that what one is reading is not informational prose but rather an art form in which a high level of poeticity emerges from and around facts and the language usually used to convey them. The opening page establishes that kind of expectation at the moment when an intellectual battle with high emotional stakes is unexpectedly likened to a cardinal and a surprising first-person possessive darts in:

> Pierre Bonnard, 1867–1947, painted next to a north-facing window. The battle over just what constitutes realism was at that moment particularly acute—an emotional thing, such as a cardinal out my window. Could streak away and shatter the composition of the world into a vivid wind in which the world goes astray. (*GA* 3)

On the next page the cardinal (along with the "my") reappears in more thoroughly poetic, visually textured lines that continue to explore, in the open-ended ways available through poeticity, the idea of changing understandings of order:

> most
> facing north, a cardinal first
>
> is a color and might if
> flight is
>
> spliced into the eclipse outside my window, igniting patterns,
> parterres, some gardener
> amiss. (GA 4)

It's not a coincidence that "I" and "we" appear more frequently here than is generally the case in Swensen's research-based work; with such a strong counterbalancing weight of public informational discourse in the volume as a whole, the private I—though still elusive and possibly unstable—can have more latitude.

The Glass Age, while it explores late-nineteenth-century ideas of realism and perception, of seeing in, out, and through—along with such historical developments as the increased reliance on trains or the construction of arcades—also encourages readers to think about language as itself timelessly analogous to glass. Glass functions as a solid but in fact possesses a different molecular structure, comparable to that of a supercooled liquid; Swensen accurately refers to it as a "non-crystalline rigid." Its being neither a liquid nor a solid is one of the ways in which glass is a substance of betweenness; its forming windows, which are at once openings and closings off, is another. Similarly, humans most commonly use written language to fix understandings and perceptions, aiming to communicate with maximum clarity and decisiveness; but language is inherently more fluid. Bonnard "managed, through adamant insistence, through window after window, through sheer repetition" (GA 65) to bring the world of his window paintings to life. According to Swensen, "The space in paintings is not paint; it is space" (GA 15). In similar fashion, Swensen invites us to use language in ways that depart from conventional meaning in order to expand and enliven our lives: "A life-sized window is the size of a life" (GA 65).

In her early volumes that employed research-based poetics, Swensen established the strategies she has continued to use in comparable projects published since. The language of information often leads the way into a poem or a volume, but the logic and certitude it drives toward are undermined as that discourse is made to interact with other kinds of language that convey alternative perspectives, often through embodied gesture or vivid sensory data (such as color). As conventional semantics are additionally disrupted through fragmentation or opening of syntax, through the intensification of sound patterns, as well as through the opening up of page space, language in the poem gains mobility, and linkages among or beyond a poem's parts, and behind or beyond its presented facts, multiply. Yet even though Swensen's hybridization of research and poeticity quickly assumed recognizable shape, the ways in which she fleshes out that form have varied significantly from volume to volume. This variation follows no linear path; as one reads from *The Glass Age* (2007) to *Ours* (2008) to *Greensward* (2010) to *Gravesend* (2012), the emphasis on scholarly precision waxes and wanes, while the subject matter of interest moves forward and backward in history. The works vary in length, in degree of unity, in the balance of prose with poetry, in the proportion of left-justified passages. They don't, however, vary radically in tone or procedure, and a coherent set of interests threads throughout. Even the interrelations among many of her volumes' titles point to the intellectual coherence and formal harmony of her oeuvre: near homonyms, "ours" and "hour," appear in the titles of volumes that take similar approaches to history, one through the art of gardening and the other through an illuminated manuscript; illumination of another sort is subject of *Goest*, in which we hear "ghost," the subject of *Gravesend*. *Greensward*'s focus on gardens echoes the focus of *Ours* (itself a play on the name of the seventeenth-century garden designer of most interest in the book, Le Nôtre, who originally designed for the elite but whose gardens are now "ours" as public parks). "Ours," moreover, is a word with considerable resonance for research-based poetics, where the emphasis on information and public discourse underscores the communal nature of language.

Within the graceful coherence of Swensen's work, there also is always continuing invention. This can be demonstrated by pointing to significant developments in her practice of research-based poetics evident in her two most recent collections, *Gravesend* and *Greensward*. Perhaps a function of steadily increasing confidence in this mode of writing, these two volumes demonstrate a greater sense of play (and of humor) in their methods, bringing together the language of information and language as art, while also incorporating new techniques.

The obvious new addition to *Gravesend* is the inclusion of informal interviews. This device gives a concreteness to the dispersal of the "I" operating in most of Swensen's writing; here, multiple voices, often repeating what they have heard from others, generate communal speech that sheds light on the culturally shared fears, griefs, and repressions reflected in a society's ideas about ghosts. These sources add diversity to Swensen's research archive, which is more usually limited to arcane texts, scholarly studies, and materials housed in museums or galleries. As a research technique employed in academic disciplines, interviewing is governed by extensive regulation designed both to protect the rights of those interviewed and to insure the reliability of the information gleaned. In Swensen's volume, however, the interviewees are either friends of the poet, whom she questions about their experiences with ghosts, or residents of Gravesend, apparently encountered in pubs, who are asked how their city got its name. That both groups constitute a statistically insignificant sampling of not necessarily reliable informants is of no concern to the poet—or to the reader—though it would be to the scholar. Serious ideas about the significance of ghosts circulate through the volume, since these liminal entities (often associated with grief or fear) occupy several of the between spaces that most fascinate Swensen—between material and immaterial, living and dead, the known and the unknowable, the present and the past (or, in one poem, the past and the future), presence and absence, and, in the case of Gravesend, New and Old Worlds. But the poet is clearly having a great deal of fun here, as she recounts—and explores the differences between—literary and folk versions of the ghost story, and as she records the sometimes stirring and sometimes laughable responses of her informants. There's no insistence on avoiding the cliché or familiar. Even in sober meditations, she sometimes takes playful freedom with her sources, as in "According to Scripture," where she modifies the Bible's recounting of the words of Samuel's ghost (in the King James version, "Why hast thou disquieted me, to bring me up?") as follows:

> had been trying to forget   as had the ghost
> in I Samuel 28:13 who said "I have been torn   from the touch   I am blind, and I flinch
>
> and had forgotten how the world in which you live is so limited in its range of visible light"[19]

In this volume, the characteristic ways in which Swensen's syntax fades into mystery or is interrupted (here, lines usually run the full width of the page but are broken by spaces into several parts), seem a bit of a ghostly game though, ultimately, the game is very seriously that of mortality: the ghost is, among other things, "a rip in the air   through which the endless endlessness   that replaces us   calmly stares."[20] Although I find this volume less dazzling in its language and imaginings than some of Swensen's other research-based collections, the multiple contemporary voices that fill its pages enrich the writing's texture, while its tonally unpredictable meditations, which sometimes reach toward the humorous, achieve a lively range.[21]

Swensen's 2010 volume *Greensward* is playful in at least three senses. The very first page—appearing even before the one that bears the name of the press and date of publication—sets up the volume as if it were a staged play, locating the action in a particular time, social class, and nation: "The following takes place in 18th century England; the scene is the garden of a manor house." This announcement of the performativity of the text—perhaps bringing to mind the comedy of manners—shapes my reading, particularly as it distances the voice of the poet from the perspectives of the voices in the text. Secondly, the volume also acquires a playful cast—as well as conceptual depth—through its incorporation of visual images. Most of these derive from etchings and engravings of estate or palace gardens by the eighteenth-century cartographer John Rocque. The selection and arrangement of these images contribute significantly to the poeticity of the text, as the interaction of text and image precludes any reading of verbal text as transparent. And thirdly, the volume plays with ironic perspectives on the goals and beliefs of the eighteenth-century garden designers and cartographers whose vision and skill it at the same time respectfully honors.

Although so many of her collections have responded to visual art, *Greensward* is Swensen's first widely available volume to include visual images, here generated through "graphic collaboration by Shari Degraw."[22] This inclusion is an important addition to the resources of her research-based poetics. Each set of facing pages in this volume contains some intriguing combination of text and black-and-white image; the images are often aerial perspectives, frequently enlarged details excised from the astonishingly detailed maps that were the plans for estates of the very wealthy, though sometimes non-aerial landscapes appear, with humans and dogs or cutout human figures, perhaps in coaches or boats. Sometimes the image occupies one page, the text the other; sometimes text is superimposed on the image; and sometimes, usually with small snippets from a larger image, the two are separate but appear on the same page. Thus, an enlargement of a drawing of "The New River" curves across one page, facing a text arranged in couplets whose lines are broken into short, widely spaced units. Turning the page, one sees a gray textured surface covering the top two-thirds of both facing pages, below which run a few lines of text in which each word is widely separated from the next. On close examination, the textured field proves to be full of drawings of (deciduous?) trees, spaced with slight irregularity, about a dozen per square inch; it's an aerial view of a forest! Turn the page again, and the verso contains three versions of a single circular cluster of eight trees, again tiny in aerial view, each with a shadow, located among straight vertical lines of either decorative or crop plants and accompanied by the number 54. Two rectangles of text are inserted between the square visual images, one extending below the images, and the other extending above. On the facing recto, there is only text, arranged in three long lines extending from margin to margin, with a larger space before the fourth long line. And so on; each set of pages has a unique design. This enthralling, varied material is in one sense part of the language of information: it constitutes a key part of the data on which Swensen draws in order to consider eighteenth-century aesthetics as manifest in gardens, and what garden drawings of the time suggest about human/animal relations. Images in the book provide evidentiary support for informational passages like the one that begins "William Kent's trademark was the dog. Dogs fill all his garden sketches—they bound on ahead, or they chase a rabbit; they race back to their people, they leap around the children, and are always shown 'taking off,' which is to say, their back feet are always on the ground while their front leap into the air and stop there."[23] Images containing Kent's dogs on page 39 and below the colophon demonstrate this. But of course, the artful interplay of text and image here also alters the information radically because it so heightens one's awareness of arrangement and construction; our words, like our maps, are projections of our desires.

Swensen's focus on the animal in this volume is, by and large, new to her work.[24] The gifted critic Brian Reed argues in a review that

what truly distinguishes *Greensward* from *Ours* and its other antecedents is its underlying argument that humans and animals not only take aesthetic pleasure in their surroundings but, under the right circumstances, can also share that pleasure with each other. The volume begins by asserting that "whatever aesthetics is, it can only be transmitted to other species—and it can be transmitted along with other higher cognitive functions—through gardening." Swensen explains that a "garden is . . . an open link . . . a line between humans and other species" that allows them both to experience and respond to the "aesthetic principles of balance, rhythm, motion, etc., and the ethical principles inherent in them." This act of communication, moreover, goes "in both directions," since gardening gives animals and humans opportunities to observe each other and learn from each other.[25]

My own reading differs from Reed's, however, because I think he has to some extent been taken in by what appears to be the language of information but actually is a more in-between substance with a different relation to fact. I also think he is overlooking the importance of the framing of the text as a performance, and the extent to which it implicitly comments on the views of a particular century without necessarily sharing them. Admittedly, the epigraphs are from the twentieth and twenty-first centuries: one from a scientist of animal behavior, pointing to the not yet understood but, in the speaker's perspective, quite possibly real aesthetic sense in animals, and the other from Wallace Stevens—"And nothing is left except light on your fur"—functioning as a reminder that humans are animals. Swensen does have a genuine interest in the possibility of non-human animals possessing or being able to acquire an aesthetic sense, but there's also a playfulness to her exploration that Reed doesn't take sufficiently into account. Moreover, there's an anthropocentrism to the presentation of animal intelligence here that renders quite problematic the reading that Reed puts forward: What he identifies as Swensens's "ecological sensibility" would be buying into the anthropocentric way in which animal intelligence is registered here, when in fact the art of this text pulls it away from the anthropocentric information and complicates the book's message. I'd say the "underlying argument" is that, as eighteenth-century garden drawings demonstrate, westerners tend to think of both animals and plants as part of a natural world to be altered and ordered for human convenience and pleasure, so that even our thinking about (non-human) animal intelligence, what little there has been of it, has occurred through a distorting lens in which the human being is dominant and in control.

Aware that *Greensward* is a work of research-based poetics, when I read the statement on the opening page, "That whatever aesthetics is, it can only be transmitted to other species—and it can be transmitted along with other higher cognitive functions—through gardening"—I take this not as a statement of fact, but as the premise to be imaginatively explored in the world of the poem. That world operates under different laws than the world outside, though what one learns there may be of great relevance to the extra-poetic world; gardens are indeed "an open link" between humans and other species, but what we discern from an expansive consideration of gardens and their representations reveals more about human than non-human intelligence. Although the opening statement employs the language of fact, its last phrase in particular ("through gardening") may well be one of those swerves one sees so often in Swensen's poetry as factual information dissolves into something else. And in this text set up as a play, we should not incautiously equate propositional assertions with the views of the author.

Moreover, Reed has omitted from consideration what I take to be a few crucial details in the passage from which he quotes. Here's the entire original, the text on the volume's second page:

> And less alone there, a garden is, in short, an open link bent on forming more, ever outward, a line between humans and other species, falling open, a following thinned to an horizon with all its attendant aesthetic principles of balance, rhythm, motion, etc., and the ethical principles inherent in them, and in both directions, i.e., it comes back to us. [*Gr* 9]

The phrase "bent on" emphasizes the human will expressed in gardens; the line of connection is imposed in human terms, and ultimately "it comes back to us" humans. The next page of text is the first of many to introduce an animal, this time a deer, and explore its intelligence or aesthetic sense. The deer that emerges from the patterned imagery of a drawing, no less an aesthetic artifact than the "cropped / tree," is given a voice here, and it's a voice that resists imposition of a human aesthetic: "And I, the (here give the Latin name), was / nonetheless cognizant that watches it shrinken am tell'em / refuse'm: a tree is a part of the sky and will therefore not be / moving any time soon, thank'u'em. I hoof'en" (*Gr* 11). The animal, it would seem, has an aesthetic sense of its own, involved in an ecological perception of trees as part of the sky, not as autonomous objects to be arranged and rearranged at will. It's not at all clear that the animal needs to *learn* aesthetics, though deer and human aesthetics do not coincide.

The book contains some fascinating anecdotes in which animals do learn from humans and particularly from gardens; among the more striking is one Reed discusses in which a hawk returns for several days to fly over a labyrinth of boxwood, until finally the observer around noon "saw that the shadow of the bird / was tracing a steady path to the heart of the maze" [*Gr* 28]. This story has, for me, the same degree of authenticity as the other mysterious narratives in Swensen's oeuvre, particularly those with the flavor of urban legend. (One thinks, for instance, of the story in *Try* of the man who'd begun dating a woman and, after some warm embraces and kisses, they "were getting nearer and nearer to a physical intimacy, so one day she said, there's something I think I should tell you: I have no left hand.")[26] Such tales raise questions about the limits and biases of our perceptions; they need not pass "the truth test." Admittedly, some of the examples Swensen presents—of ravens learning to count to nine, of elephants recognizing themselves in mirrors, of sheep remembering human faces or cows distinguishing among a hundred human voices—may be genuine demonstrations of animal intelligence. But it's also striking that the measures of intelligence underlying such findings are human-centered. Ultimately, they seem versions of domestication, about which Swensen offers this passage:

> And the dog keeps her eyes locked on the vanishing point, which alone is what is pulling them (dog and man) silently, smoothly, inexorably into the heart of the 18th century. It's the future that vanishes, not thinking, and the dog sets off at a run, as it is, as it always has been, her gift and her wish to bring it back to him. (*Gr* 35)

It all comes back to us. We've trained dogs to retrieve, and they have indeed come to take pleasure in that activity and in pleasing humans, but the environmental crises of the twenty-first century may follow quite directly from the insistence on dominance fundamental to domestication. Although Kent's eighteenth-century drawings, as Reed notes, could "suggest that animals instruct humans in how best to experience a garden,"[27] *Greensward* offers no evidence of humans trying to learn from animals' knowledge of the environment, however much the human desire for connection to nonhuman animals is apparent. The problem is that the human-animal connection has been imagined (and conducted) so much on our terms:

Toward the end of the 18th century, many of Humphry Repton's drawings also seem to advocate for animals—cows, sheep, deer appear quite prominently, so apparently he, at least, had faith in their aesthetic sense, was confident that, once invited in, they would know just how to pose in order to contrast nicely with a stand of oaks, add texture to a shoreline, or strike a silhouette atop a gentle rise to call to mind the understated majesty inherent in every horizon. Perhaps he hired them. [Gr 45]

Happily, however seriously problematic the orientations behind such a vision of "advocacy" may be, the poet is again having fun as well as making fun here, just as she is when she announces, "The squirrel, after observing topiary, started using its entire body as a shadow puppet" [Gr 24–25].

Reed asserts something fundamental to Swensen's research-based poetics when he notes: "Science and analytic philosophy continue to valorize rational thought; the aesthetic thinking of poets and gardeners brings us closer to the beasts of the field."[28] Research-based poetry is one way in which Swensen at once challenges and supplements rational thought. My reading of *Greensward* diverges less thoroughly from Reed's than I may have suggested, since, like him, I do not see the book's explorations of animal intelligence as entirely fanciful. Moreover, like Reed, I see in the book "the deconstructive insight that humans are forever trying to speak as if the world were full of what it manifestly lacks—namely, value, purpose, and intent."[29] My purpose in presenting the differences between our readings is to demonstrate that "research-based poetics" present particular reading challenges, precisely because they unsettle the conventional truth-value associated with language as information. That the between space such unsettling generates is not another fixity, not some kind of solid middle ground, becomes evident precisely in the way that two experienced critics reading a single work in this mode can hear differently what emerges from the interrelation of language as art and language as information.

NOTES

1. June 24, 2009; ronsilliman.blogspot.fr/2009/06/american-hybrid-is-important-book-but.html.

2. In "Response to Hybrid Aesthetics and its Discontents," Swensen has this to say to those who mistakenly see *American Hybrid* as making a case for a homogeneous middle ground and as replacing a binary with a unity: "The work gathered in the *American Hybrid* anthology is not a collapsing-towards-the-middle, not a center-between-extremes, but is exactly the contrary; each poet's work is a different deviation from the linear continuum that runs from the conventional to the experimental; taken together they form an errant field that explodes that narrow, linear path into a three dimensional space in which the unique nature of each body of

work is discernable, and tidy groupings are difficult or impossible to make." In *The Monkey and the Wrench: Essays into Contemporary Poetics*, ed. Mary Biddinger and John Gallaher (Akron, OH: University of Akron Press, 2011), 152.

3. Lynn Keller, "Singing Spaces: Fractal Geometries in Cole Swensen's *Oh*," *Journal of Modern Literature* 31.1 (2007): 136–60.

4. Cole Swensen, *Noise that Stays Noise: Essays* (Ann Arbor: University of Michigan Press, 2011), 23. Subsequent references will appear parenthetically in the text, using the abbreviation *NSN* followed by the page number.

5. Her extensive work as a translator of contemporary French poets and publisher of others' translations from French also contributes to such a project because, through translation, "[t]he foreign enters any given language's literature . . . importing values and perspectives that gradually estrange a language from itself" (*NSN* 98). In addition to having published well over a dozen books that she herself translated, one of which was awarded the PEN Center USA Literary Award for Translation, Swensen is founder and editor of La Presse. For more information see www.lapressepoetry.com.

6. "One might wish for a topic less hermetic," Celia Bland says in a review of *Glass Age*, and others have voiced similar responses to the high-cultural Eurocentric focus of Swensen's interests. Bland goes on, however, to observe that even if "removed from the chaos of today's news," these poems "say / an entire world" and to praise their "argumentative sweep." Especially relevant to this essay is her characterization of Swensen's analysis as "gestural, not argumentative." *Boston Review*, November 1, 2007; bostonreview.net/bland-the-glass-age-cole-swensen.

7. Cole Swensen, *Noon* (Los Angeles: Sun & Moon Press, 1997), 11, 9.

8. "Cole Swensen," "On the Fly: Writers on Writing." Uploaded December 16, 2010; www.youtube.com/watch?v=yJMvErGPTHE.

9. While one might assume that these quoted fragments come from art criticism, they are not unattributed appropriations of others' words. The quotation marks signal a shift in voice or tone, a splitting of Swensen's own voice, and appear most often when the register shifts to the academic.

10. For more consideration of Swensen's ekphrasis, see Lynn Keller, "Poems Living with Paintings: Cole Swensen's Ekphrastic *Try*," *Contemporary Literature* 46.2 (Summer 2005): 176–212, which appears in slightly revised form as chapter 5 of *Thinking Poetry: Readings in Contemporary Women's Exploratory Poetics* (Iowa City: University of Iowa Press, 2010); Barbara Fischer, "Noisy Brides, Suspicious Kisses: Revising Ravishment in Experimental Ekphrasis by Women," in *In the Frame: Women's Ekphrastic Poetry from Marianne Moore to Susan Wheeler*, ed. Jane Hedley, Nick Halpern, and Willard Spiegelman (Newark: University of Delaware Press, 2009), 72–90; Ashby Kinch, "The Broken Mirror of the Book: Cole Swensen's *Such Rich Hour* and the *Très Riches Heures de Jean, duc de Berry*," *Word & Image* 27 (June 2011): 175–89.

11. Cole Swensen, *Try* (Iowa City: University of Iowa Press, 1999), 3.

12. Ibid., 33.

13. Keller, "Poems Living with Paintings," 190.

14. Swensen, *Try*, 39.

15. Swensen, *Noon*, 70.

16. Cole Swensen, *Such Rich Hour* (Iowa City: University of Iowa Press, 2001), 1. Subsequent citations of this volume will appear in parentheses within the text, using the abbreviation *SRH* followed by the page number.

17. Cole Swensen, *Goest* (Farmington, ME: Alice James Books, 2004), 52.

18. Cole Swensen, *The Glass Age* (Farmington, ME: Alice James Books, 2007), 7. In the first line of this quotation I have, at the poet's request, substituted the word "see" for "look." "Look" was accidentally introduced in the production of the book, and Swensen did not at the time catch the error. Subsequent citations of this volume will appear in parentheses in the text, using the abbreviation *GA* followed by the page number.

19. Cole Swensen, *Gravesend* (Berkeley: University of California Press, 2012), 15.

20. Ibid., 11.

21. Humor is not unprecedented in Swensen's oeuvre—though of course it's a quality that different individuals locate differently. I, for one, am amused by the parts of *Oh* where the text highlights opera's outrageous excesses of passion and drama. *Oh*, which rests on extensive knowledge of the operatic repertoire and its history, is another one of Swensen's research-based works. None of the volumes she has produced since *Noon* is without some element of research, though the majority of the poems in *The Book of a Hundred Hands* are not obviously research-based, and the 2012 chapbook *Stele* seems not to participate in this poetics.

22. This collection was preceded the year before by a collaborative limited edition publication, *Flare*, where Swensen's poems appear in conjunction with Thomas Nozkowski's images, and a book from 2011 collecting "image + text work" by women artists and writers includes an "excerpt" from *Greensward* in which some of the text/image combinations are significantly altered.

23. Cole Swensen, *Greensward* (Brooklyn: Ugly Duckling Presse, 2010), [34]. Printed page numbers appear infrequently in this book because of its design. Subsequent citations of this volume will appear parenthetically in the text using the abbreviation *Gr*; inferred page numbers appear in brackets.

24. These are not her first poems on animals; *Noon*, for instance, contains a section of animal poems titled "Bestiary." However, animal intelligence and human/animal relations have not been among Swensen's prominent preoccupations before this.

25. Brian M. Reed, "*Greensward*," *Chicago Review* 56.2/3: 209–210.

26. Swensen, *Try*, 75.

27. Reed, 210–11.

28. Ibid., 211.

29. Ibid., 213.

BIBLIOGRAPHY

Works by Cole Swensen

POETRY
It's Alive She Says. Cedarville, CA: Floating Island Press, 1984.
New Math. New York: William Morrow & Co., 1988.
Park. Inverness: Floating Island Press, 1991.

Numen. Providence: Burning Deck Publications, 1995.
Noon. Los Angeles: Sun & Moon Press, 1997.
Try. Iowa City: University of Iowa Press, 1999.
Oh. Berkeley: Apogee Press, 2000.
Such Rich Hour. Iowa City: University of Iowa Press, 2001.
Goest. Farmington, ME: Alice James Books, 2004.
The Book of a Hundred Hands. Iowa City: University of Iowa Press, 2005.
The Glass Age. Farmington, ME: Alice James Books, 2007.
Ours. Berkeley: University of California Press, 2008.
Flare. Collaboration with visual artist Thomas Nozkowski. New Haven: Yale
    University Art Gallery, 2009.
Greensward. Brooklyn: Ugly Duckling Presse, 2010.
Gravesend. Berkeley: University of California Press, 2012.
Landscapes on a Train. New York: Nightboat Books, 2015.
On Walking On. New York: Nightboat Books, 2017.
Gave. Berkeley: Omnidawn, 2017.

CRITICAL PROSE
Noise That Stays Noise: Collected Essays. Ann Arbor: University of Michigan
    Press, 2011.

EDITED VOLUME
American Hybrid: A Norton Anthology of New Poetry. With David St. John.
    New York: W.W. Norton, 2009.

CHAPBOOKS
O. New York: Beautiful Swimmer Press, 1999.
And Hand. San Francisco: a+bend Press, 2000.
Reading Robert Ryman. Erratum Press, 2002.
Thy Versailles. Boise: Free Poetry, 2006.
Ghosts are Hope. St. Louis: Observable Books, 2006.
Stele. Sausalito, CA: Post-Apollo Press, 2012.

SELECTED INTERVIEWS
Anderson, Maria. "The Rumpus Interview with Cole Swensen." *The Rumpus*
    (May 2016); therumpus.net/2016/05/the-rumpus-interview-with-cole-swensen.
"Cole Swensen." *Kenyon Review On-Line: The KR Conversations* (December
    2015); www.kenyonreview.org/conversation/cole-swensen/.
Dick, Jen. *Continental Review* (Summer 2007); www.thecontinentalreview.com.
"Discussion with Cole Swensen." *The Form Our Poetry Takes: A Pedagogy
    Conversation*. Essay Press Listening Tour 13 (June 2014); www. essaypress
    .org/ep-13/.
McLennan, Rob. "12 or 20 Questions." November 2007; 12or20questions
    .blogspot.com/2007/11/12-or-20-questions-with-cole-swensen.html.
"On the Fly: Writers on Writing." December 2010; www.youtube.com/watch?v=
    yJMvErGPTHE.
Scisco, Mason. "The Lit Show" on KRUI, September 28, 2012; www.litshow.com
    /archive/season-06/cole-swensen-interview/

Thompson, Jon. *Free Verse* (Spring 2004); english.chass.ncsu.edu/freeverse /Archives/Winter_2003/Interviews/interviews.htm.

SELECTED TRANSLATIONS

Alferi, Pierre. *Natural Gaits*. Los Angeles: Sun & Moon Press, 1995.
———. *OXO*. Providence: Burning Deck, 2004.
Cadiot, Olivier. *Art Poetic'*. Los Angeles: Green Integer Books, 1999.
———. *Future, Former, Fugitive*. New York: Roof Books, 2004.
———. *Colonel Zoo*. Los Angeles: Green Integer, 2005.
———. "Fairy Queen." *Lana Turner* 2 (Fall 2009).
Doppelt, Suzanne. *Ring Rang Wrong*. Providence: Burning Deck, 2006.
———. *The Field is Lethal*. Denver: Counterpath Press, 2011.
Dubois, Caroline. *You're the Business*. Providence: Burning Deck, 2008.
Frémon, Jean. *Island of the Dead*. Los Angeles: Green Integer Books, 2003.
———. *The Real Life of Shadows*. Sausalito, CA: Post-Apollo Press, 2009.
———. *The Posthumous Life of Robert Walser*. Richmond, CA: Omnidawn Press, 2012.
Hoquard, Emmanuel. *The Invention of Glass*. Co-translated with Rod Smith. Ann Arbor: Canarium Press, 2012.
Lespiau, David. *Ouiji*. Geneve: Editions Héros-Limite, 2009.
Monnier, Pascalle. *Bayart*. New York: Black Square Editions, 2002.
Pesquès, Nicolas. *Physis*. Anderson, SC: Free Verse Editions, 2007.
———. *Juliology*. Denver: Counterpath Press, 2008.

Selected Criticism and Reviews

Fischer, Barbara K. "Noisy Brides, Suspicious Kisses: Revising Ravishment in Experimental Ekphrasis by Women." In *In the Frame: Women's Ekphrastic Poetry from Marianne Moore to Susan Wheeler*, ed. Jane Hedley, Nick Halpern, and Willard Spiegelman (Newark: University of Delaware, 2009), 72–90.
———. "Someone (A Woman) Watching: Site-Specific Ekphrasis by Three Feminist Innovators." In *Museum Meditations: Reframing Ekphrasis in Contemporary American Poetry* (New York: Routledge, 2006), 143–186.
Keller, Lynn. "Singing Spaces: Fractal Geometry in Cole Swensen's *Oh*." *Journal of Modern Literature* 31 (Fall 2007): 136–60.
———. "Poems Living with Paintings: Cole Swensen's Ekphrastic *Try*." In *Thinking Poetry: Readings in Contemporary Women's Exploratory Poetics* (Ames: University of Iowa Press, 2010), 97–123.
Kinch, Ashby. "The Broken Mirror of the Book: Cole Swensen's *Such Rich Hour* and the *Très Riches Heures de Jean, duc de Berry*." *Word & Image* 27.2 (2011): 175–89.

NATASHA TRETHEWEY

POEMS

FROM *Bellocq's Ophelia*

Bellocq

—April 1911

There comes a quiet man now to my room—
Papá Bellocq, his camera on his back.
He wants *nothing*, he says, but to take me
as I would arrange myself, fully clothed—
a brooch at my throat, my white hat angled
just so—*or not*, the smooth map of my flesh
awash in afternoon light. In my room
everything's a prop for his composition—
brass spittoon in the corner, the silver
mirror, brush and comb of my toilette.
I try to pose as I think he would like—shy
at first, then bolder. I'm not so foolish
that I don't know this photograph *we* make
will bear the stamp of his name, not mine.

Theories of Time and Space

You can get there from here, though
there's no going home.

Everywhere you go will be somewhere
you've never been. Try this:

head south on Mississippi 49, one-
by-one mile markers ticking off

another minute of your life. Follow this
to its natural conclusion—dead end

at the coast, the pier at Gulfport where
riggings of shrimp boats are loose stitches

in a sky threatening rain. Cross over
the man-made beach, 26 miles of sand

dumped on a mangrove swamp—buried
terrain of the past. Bring only

what you must carry—tome of memory
its random blank pages. On the dock

where you board the boat for Ship Island,
someone will take your picture:

the photograph—who you were—
will be waiting when you return

Myth

I was asleep while you were dying.
It's as if you slipped through some rift, a hollow
I make between my slumber and my waking,

the Erebus I keep you in, still trying
not to let go. You'll be dead again tomorrow,
but in dreams you live. So I try taking

you back into morning. Sleep-heavy, turning,
my eyes open, I find you do not follow.
Again and again, this constant forsaking.

•

Again and again, this constant forsaking:
my eyes open, I find you do not follow.
You back into morning, sleep-heavy, turning.

But in dreams you live. So I try taking,
not to let go. You'll be dead again tomorrow.
The Erebus I keep you in—still, trying—

I make between my slumber and my waking.
It's as if you slipped through some rift, a hollow.
I was asleep while you were dying.

Elegy for the Native Guards

Now that the salt of their blood
Stiffens the saltier oblivion of the sea . . .
ALLEN TATE

We leave Gulfport at noon; gulls overhead
trailing the boat—streamers, noisy fanfare—
all the way to Ship Island. What we see
first is the fort, its roof of grass, a lee—
half reminder of the men who served there—
a weathered monument to some of the dead.

Inside we follow the ranger, hurried
though we are to get to the beach. He tells
of graves lost in the Gulf, the island split
in half when Hurricane Camille hit,
shows us casemates, cannons, the store that sells
souvenirs, tokens of history long buried.

The Daughters of the Confederacy
has placed a plaque here, at the fort's entrance—
each Confederate soldier's name raised hard
in bronze; no names carved for the Native Guards—
2nd Regiment, Union men, black phalanx.
What is monument to their legacy?

All the grave markers, all the crude headstones—
water-lost. Now fish dart among their bones,
and we listen for what the waves intone.
Only the fort remains, near forty feet high,
round, unfinished, half open to the sky,
the elements—wind, rain—God's deliberate eye

Incident

We tell the story every year—
how we peered from the windows, shades drawn—
though nothing really happened,
the charred grass now green again.

We peered from the windows, shades drawn,
at the cross trussed like a Christmas tree,
the charred grass still green. Then
we darkened our rooms, lit the hurricane lamps.

At the cross trussed like a Christmas tree,
a few men gathered, white as angels in their gowns.
We darkened our rooms and lit hurricane lamps,
the wicks trembling in their fonts of oil.

It seemed the angels had gathered, white men in their gowns.
When they were done, they left quietly. No one came.
The wicks trembled all night in their fonts of oil;
by morning the flames had all dimmed.

When they were done, the men left quietly. No one came.
Nothing really happened.
By morning all the flames had dimmed.
We tell the story every year

From "Before Katrina"

Hegel wrote, "When we turn to survey the past, the first thing we see is nothing but ruins." As I contemplate the development of the coast, looking at old photographs of once new buildings—the pride of a growing city—I see beneath them as if in palimpsest, the destruction wrought by Katrina. The story of the coast has been a story of urban development driven by economic factors and a much-less-than-needed awareness or consideration of the effects of such development on the environment. It can be seen in all the concrete poured on the coast—impervious to rainwater, a strip of parking lots and landfill. It can be seen in the changing narrative, since 1992, of the landscape of historic buildings into a casino landscape of neon and flashing lights and parking decks.

The past can only be understood in the context of the present, overlapped as they are, one informing the other. The present imagery of the devastated Mississippi Gulf Coast is, of course, what forces me to see the palimpsest of ruin in the "before" photographs, and yet turning to survey the past, I did not expect to find what I did. I was going back to read the narrative I thought was there—one in which gambling and the gaming industry, responsible for so much recent land and economic development on the coast, was a new arrival, not something already ingrained in the culture of the place. I expected a narrative in which the seafood industry had simply been replaced by the gaming industry, not one in which they operated side-by-side in many ways until competition from other places, and perhaps indirect environmental effects of the gaming industry, helped foment the seafood industry's decline. I expected to find a story that would tell me that everything had been fine until 1992, when legalized offshore gambling returned, not that the losses to wetlands because of development had already begun as long ago as 1950—and had continued.

Seeing my own need to believe one narrative, I think again of the words of Flannery O'Connor, *Where you thought you were going to never was there.*

FROM *Thrall*

Elegy

For my father

I think by now the river must be thick
        with salmon. Late August, I imagine it

as it was that morning: drizzle needling
        the surface, mist at the banks like a net

settling around us—everything damp
        and shining. That morning, awkward

and heavy in our hip waders, we stalked
        into the current and found our places—

you upstream a few yards and out
        far deeper. You must remember how

the river seeped in over your boots
        and you grew heavier with that defeat.

All day I kept turning to watch you, how
　　　first you mimed our guide's casting

then cast your invisible line, slicing the sky
　　　between us; and later, rod in hand, how

you tried—again and again—to find
　　　that perfect arc, flight of an insect

skimming the river's surface. Perhaps
　　　you recall I cast my line and reeled in

two small trout we could not keep.
　　　Because I had to release them, I confess,

I thought about the past—working
　　　the hooks loose, the fish writhing

in my hands, each one slipping away
　　　before I could let go. I can tell you now

that I tried to take it all in, record it
　　　for an elegy I'd write—one day—

when the time came. Your daughter,
　　　I was that ruthless. What does it matter

if I tell you I *learned* to be? You kept casting
　　　your line, and when it did not come back

empty, it was tangled with mine. Some nights,
　　　dreaming, I step again into the small boat

that carried us out and watch the bank receding—
　　　my back to where I know we are headed.

Miracle of the Black Leg

*Pictorial representations of the physician-saints Cosmas and
Damian and the myth of the miracle transplant—black donor,
white recipient—date back to the mid-fourteenth century,
appearing much later than written versions of the story.*

1.

Always, the dark body hewn asunder; always
    one man is healed, his sick limb replaced,
placed in another man's grave: the white leg
    buried beside the corpse, or attached as if
it were always there. If not for the dark appendage
    you might miss the story beneath this story—
what remains each time the myth changes: how,
    in one version, the doctors harvest the leg
from a man, four days dead, in his tomb at the church
    of a martyr, or—in another—desecrate a body
fresh in the graveyard at Saint Peter in Chains:
    there was buried just today an Ethiopian.
Even now, it stays with us: when we mean to uncover
    the truth, we dig, say: *unearth.*

2.

Emblematic in paint, signifier of the body's lacuna,
    the black leg is at once a grafted narrative,
a redacted line of text, and in this scene a dark stocking
    pulled above the knee. Here the patient sleeping,
his head at rest in his hand. Beatific, he looks as if
    he'll wake from a dream. On the floor
beside the bed, a dead *Moor*—hands crossed at the groin,
    the swapped limb pocked and rotting, fused in place.
And in the corner, a question: poised as if to speak
    the syntax of sloughing, a snake's curved form.
It emerges from the mouth of a boy like a tongue—slippery
    and rooted in the body as knowledge. For centuries,
this is how the myth repeats: the miracle—in words
    or wood or paint—is a record of thought.

3.

See how the story changes: in one painting
    the *Ethiop* is merely a body, featureless in a coffin,
so black he has no face. In another, the patient—
    at the top of the frame—seems to writhe in pain,
the black leg grafted to his thigh. Below him
    a mirror of suffering: the *blackamoor*—
his body a fragment—arched across the doctor's lap
    as if dying from his wound. If not immanence,
the soul's bright anchor, blood passed from one
    to the other, what knowledge haunts each body—
what history, what phantom ache? One man always
    low, in a grave or on the ground, the other
up high, closer to heaven; one man always diseased,
    the other a body in service, plundered.

4.

Both men are alive in Villoldo's carving.
    In twinned relief, they hold the same posture,
the same pained face, each man reaching to touch
    his left leg. The black man, on the floor,
holds his stump. Above him, the doctor restrains
    the patient's arm as if to prevent him touching
the dark amendment of flesh. How not to see it—
    the men bound one to the other—symbiotic,
one man rendered expendable, the other worthy
    of this sacrifice? In version after version, even
when the Ethiopian isn't there, the leg is a stand in,
    a black modifier against the white body,
a piece cut off—as in: origin of the word *comma*—
    caesura in a story that's still being written.

Calling

Mexico 1969

Why not make a fiction
        of the mind's fictions? I want to say
    it begins like this: the trip
       a pilgrimage, my mother
kneeling at the altar of the Black Virgin,
      enthralled—light streaming in
     a window, the sun
    at her back, holy water
in a bowl she must have touched.

What's left is palimpsest—one memory
    bleeding into another, overwriting it.
      How else to explain
       what remains? The sound
of water in a basin I know is white,
      the sun behind her, light streaming in,
     her face—
as if she were already dead—blurred
    as it will become.

I want to imagine her before
    the altar, rising to meet us, my father
      lifting me
    toward her outstretched arms.
What else to make
    of the mind's slick confabulations?
     What comes back
is the sun's dazzle on a pool's surface,
    light filtered through water

closing over my head, my mother—her body
    between me and the high sun, a corona of light
      around her face. Why not call it
  a vision? What I know is this:
I was drowning and saw a dark Madonna;
      someone pulled me through
  the water's bright ceiling
    and I rose, initiate,
    from one life into another.

Enlightenment

In the portrait of Jefferson that hangs
    at Monticello, he is rendered two-toned:
his forehead white with illumination—

a lit bulb—the rest of his face in shadow,
    darkened as if the artist meant to contrast
his bright knowledge, its dark subtext.

By 1805, when Jefferson sat for the portrait,
    he was already linked to an affair
with his slave. Against a backdrop, blue

and ethereal, a wash of paint that seems
    to hold him in relief, Jefferson gazes out
across the centuries, his lips fixed as if

he's just uttered some final word.
    The first time I saw the painting, I listened
as my father explained the contradictions:

how Jefferson hated slavery, though—out
    of necessity, my father said—had to own
slaves; that his moral philosophy meant

he could not have fathered those children:
     would have been impossible, my father said.
For years we debated the distance between

word and deed. I'd follow my father from book
     to book, gathering citations, listening
as he named—like a field guide to Virginia—

each flower and tree and bird as if to prove
     a man's pursuit of knowledge is greater
than his shortcomings, the limits of his vision.

I did not know then the subtext
     of our story, that my father could imagine
Jefferson's words made flesh in my flesh—

the improvement of the blacks in body
     and mind, in the first instance of their mixture
with the whites—or that my father could believe

he'd made me better. When I think of this now,
     I see how the past holds us captive,
its beautiful ruin etched on the mind's eye:

my young father, a rough outline of the old man
     he's become, needing to show me
the better measure of his heart, an equation

writ large at Monticello. That was years ago.
     Now, we take in how much has changed:
talk of Sally Hemings, someone asking,

How white was she?—parsing the fractions
     as if to name what made her worthy
of Jefferson's attentions: a near-white,

quadroon mistress, not a plain black slave.
     Imagine stepping back into the past,
our guide tells us then—and I can't resist

whispering to my father: This is where
    we split up. I'll head around to the back.
When he laughs, I know he's grateful

I've made a joke of it, this history
    that links us—white father, black daughter—
even as it renders us other to each other.

POETICS STATEMENT

From "'Why I Write': Poetry, History, and Social Justice"

In his 1946 essay, "Why I Write," Orwell begins by describing the conditions of his early childhood that inculcated in him the notion that he would be a writer. He mentions seeing his father very little, and this causing him to be lonely, to develop the lonely child habits of making up stories and holding conversations with imagined characters. "I think," he writes, "from the very start my literary ambitions were mixed up with a feeling of being isolated and undervalued. I knew that I had a facility with words and a power of facing unpleasant facts, and I felt that this created a sort of private world in which I could get my own back for my failure in everyday life." In Orwell's words I hear the suggestion that the creation of that private world was a way to triumph over the circumstances of one's daily life, and I recognize in his experience some hint of my own. . . .

I can see now how much of my own early development as a writer was linked to my circumstances—the condition, place, and historical moment into which I was born and raised. For the nine months of the school year, I lived in Georgia with my mother. In my home I was a kind of outsider, isolated by my stepfather who was envious of my mother's previous relationship with her former husband and contemptuous of me, the product of that relationship. Because my stepfather was reading my diary regularly, I began to write knowing that he would see it. He was, in a sense, my first audience—and I carried on a difficult conversation with him that could not be spoken aloud. For him to challenge me on what I wrote would be for him to admit what he was doing—invading that private world of words I was setting down on paper. I began to think, then, that nothing I wrote could be private, and that my words—like Anne Frank's—might speak not just for me, but also to and for other people.

During the summer months, I went back to Mississippi and stayed with my maternal grandmother. In her neighborhood there were no children my age, and I spent my days turning inward, like Orwell—as the lonely child does—reading, making up stories and writing them down in the form of poetry or prose, musing upon my own self and my position in the world mostly in the form of a racialized inquiry, a speculation supported by a kind of rudimentary research. For example, I spent countless hours reading the encyclopedia and one day came upon the section, in the 1967 edition, on Races of Man. There I learned what were supposed to be distinguishing racial characteristics—that if you were white, the ratio of femur to tibia was different than if you were black: in one race (the editors asserted), the femur is longer, in the other the tibia. I sneaked into my grandmother's workroom to steal away with her tape measure thinking it would finally reveal to me who and what I was. I was, after all, growing up black and biracial in Mississippi and Georgia, having been born on the heels of the Civil Rights movement, and I had begun to come face to face with notions of difference and how various aspects of my existence were often subjects of curiosity or contempt to many white people I encountered. Indeed, because of this, my father had begun telling me at an early age that I had to be a writer because of the very nature of my experience: that I had something important to say. I had no idea what it was, but I wanted to believe that what my father said was true. . . . It would have been impossible then, as it is now, to say I am going to sit down and write a poem about social justice—though I see now how the hope for and commitment to it pervades every word I write, and it is the lens through which I see the world. . . .

It makes sense to me now that I was headed here all along: everywhere around me in the late sixties and early seventies of my childhood I saw evidence of injustice—a cross burned on my family's lawn, the poor segregated neighborhoods with sub-standard grocery stores and higher prices, the clothing stores where my grandmother was not allowed to try on the hats as white women did, all the everyday slights commonplace in people's lives—not to mention the threat of real danger that loomed around us. The list goes on. An overly sensitive child, I committed to memory King's words: "Injustice anywhere is a threat to justice everywhere." . . . As I grew older, it occurred to me that the world was changing, gradually, and that some of the more insidious forms of injustice were beneath the surface of what I could see around me. Along with the atrocities and overt injustices that came to us nightly on the world news report, the injustices of day-to-day life and the various forms of institutional injustice (in housing or education or the courts, for example) were the quiet, ongoing injustices— stunningly apparent—in the pages—and in the absences in the pages—of history. And the history of the place from which I'd come, intimate and personal as well as public and collective, was evidence to me of Heraclitus's axiom: Geography is fate.

I had been born to the geography of the Deep South, the state of Mississippi whose name means "great river"—that river a metaphor suggesting all the hidden history in its murky depths, troubling the surface from underneath. I was born in the land of King Cotton, land of a brutal history of slavery, racism and injustice, land of violence, of lynchings and murders, one of the poorest states in the nation.

But also, I was born to a place of rich delta soil, one of the most fertile regions on earth; birthplace of the blues; home to a tradition of writers like William Faulkner, Eudora Welty, Richard Wright, Margaret Walker Alexander, and Tennessee Williams. I have inherited from this geography both great cultural richness and great suffering. I am guided by the words of Henry James: "Be tethered to native pastures even if it reduces you to a backyard in New York." I am tethered to a place whose Jim Crow laws rendered my family, my people, second-class citizens, whose laws against miscegenation rendered my parents' marriage illegal, my birth illegitimate not only in the customs but also in the constitution of the state. Thus, I write to claim my native land even as it has forsaken me, rendered me an outsider. I write so as not to be a foreigner in my homeland. I write from a place of psychological exile. I take up the burden of history. I am guided by King's words: "No lie can live forever."

Social justice depends on social awareness, not blindness, an awareness rooted in both historical knowledge and a contemporary reckoning with the past and its ongoing influence on the present. I write to tell a fuller version of American history, to recover the stories and voices of people whose lives have been marginalized, forgotten, erased, overlooked. I write in order to redress the omissions and errors in history, to confront the willed forgetting that haunts our interactions with each other and to create a vision of a more just society based on reckoning with our troubled past rather than forgetting it. I write because I believe, as historian Michael Vorenburg has written in describing the ongoing study of the Civil War, that "a better, more humane civilization can be forged in the smithy of painful memory." And that by restoring to our collective memory "the savagery, heartlessness and racism" of our past, "we can allow for the possibility of a civilization based on justice rather than amnesia."

How could I not, having been a product of my own tumultuous age—the fate of my geography, its history—how could I not find a sense of purpose in the beautiful idea of social justice for all human beings? I can say that in my life writing poetry has been a necessity. But I am reminded, and so must also say, that inasmuch as the language of poetry is about a kind of play, it has also been a privilege, a luxury that countless people in the world do not have. I have always been more concerned with people than with words. . . .

Certainly there are many poets and critics out there who believe that all personal experience is passé—my famous poet professor said as much on many occasions—though I have never heard anyone simplistically admonish white poets by saying they'll write better poems when they stop writing from personal experience. Often, when poets who are from groups deemed "other" write about personal experience, some readers assume that the poems can't speak to universal human experience, thus imparting the work with a "message" some readers would rather not encounter. Saying this, I am reminded of the young white woman I met while visiting a small college in South Carolina. Her professor had assigned a book of mine to the class, and when the student read the blurbs on the back informing her that the book was by a black woman and was about—among other things—black workers in the Jim Crow south, she dreaded reading it because, as she told me: "I didn't think it would speak to me because it didn't have anything to do with my experience." She wasn't referring to the fact that the book was about work she'd never done, but that it was about black people. What she initially believed underscores the notion that the experiences of black people can't speak to universal, human experience. It's implied on each book jacket that describes the poems inside it as "transcending black experience" in order to praise them for rising to the level of plain old human experience—as if the two are mutually exclusive. It also implies the notion that only black people and people from groups termed "other" experience race. It forgets or ignores that the experiences of white people are also experiences of race and that they too write from within a particular racialized experience of the world. Fortunately, that young woman came away from the book with an entirely different view.

This, I think, is why so many poets are "accused" (and it is often an accusation) of writing about political issues, of being too concerned with message, whether they intended to or not. I have been described many times as a poet who writes about race—though I can assure you that not only have I never sat down to write a poem on the theme of race, but also that I don't consider my poems to be about race at all. That some of them have racial implications or come out of my racialized experience goes without saying. Geography is fate.

The implication that certain subjects (thus certain messages) belong in poems and that some do not is present each time I am asked—why poetry? This question usually comes after I have discussed my obsessions—the motivations that I believe deserve to be followed—as though I should have chosen some other vessel for my content, for that which I have been given to write. To that I ask, why not? I believe, after all, that poetry is the best repository for our most humane, ethical, and just expressions of feeling. This is because poetry ennobles the human soul, that it opens—not closes—our hearts. Poetry matters not only because of its aesthetic beauty, but also because of the possibility of humane intelligence—its ability to teach us what we have not known, to show us what we have been blind to, to ask of us the most difficult questions regarding our own humanity and that of others. Across time and space, it shows us how we are alike, not that we are different. It asks of us that we approach the world with more openness than we might employ in our daily lives. It asks that we be more observant, more compassionate, empathetic. I write because I cannot stand by and say nothing, because I strive to make sense of the world I've been given, because the soul sings for justice and the song is poetry.

NOTE

This essay was excerpted from a transcript of a lecture delivered by Natasha Trethewey in Emory University's Distinguished Faculty Lecture series on February 3, 2010. For the complete lecture, visit archived.waccamawjournal.com/pages .php?x=323.

NATASHA TRETHEWEY'S PALIMPSESTIC POETICS

Khadijah Queen

Natasha Trethewey's poetry takes on the essential task of defining the self in relation to public history and collective life—a task made more difficult by the labyrinth of exclusions and denials that racism and its resultant traumas impose. Rita Dove, in her introduction to *Domestic Work*, offers a quote from James Baldwin that resonates across Trethewey's books —"People are trapped in history, and history is trapped in them"—and notes Trethewey's "challenge: to bear witness and give face to the legions of nameless men and women who cooked, scrubbed, welded, shoveled, hauled and planted for an entire nation."[1] In traditional and received forms as well as free verse, Trethewey's poems peer through the lens of history to give life to anonymous people in the past, as Gwendolyn Brooks's poems, such as "The Anniad" and "Ballad of Chocolate Mabbie," do for the "nameless" in Chicago. Trethewey animates and elegizes those "Whom the higher gods forgot / Whom the lower gods berate"[2] with a sharp visual attention and an eye for the subtle.

Trethewey's approach to poetry involves writing, palimpsestically, a new history on top of accepted versions of history. The term "palimpsest" is often used to describe a deliberately layered literary work, but in Trethewey's hands, the palimpsest serves as a kind of methodic erasure. Trethewey's work erases previously accepted misconceptions in order to assert the speaker's memories and observations and thus redefine image, memory, or history. Sometimes Trethewey's palimpsestic poetics works through ekphrasis—that is, through poems that describe or reflect on visual art. For example, she endows anonymous prostitutes in E. J. Bellocq's photographs with rich inner lives and dramatizes eighteenth-century *casta* paintings that chart racial hierarchies in colonial Mexico. At other times, Trethewey turns official history and poetry's formal traditions themselves into surfaces upon which to record unwritten histories, as when she inscribes the lives and deaths of unsung black soldiers onto a Confederate monument.

Critics have recognized Trethewey's use of ekphrasis as central to her poetics. Meta DuEwa Jones defines ekphrasis as "art that feeds on another art form, especially forms of image making. As a poetic figure, ekphrasis is principally concerned with vision." In Trethewey's hands, Jones argues, ekphrasis serves to "push readers beyond the traditional enclosures encompassing the body of visual, racial and sexual 'knowledge' of women raced as black."[3] Like the multilayered palimpsest and like memory itself, "Ekphrasis repeats and remembers; it reassembles in words what was already assembled as image," maintains Jones.[4] In his essay on "racial-spatial phototexting" in Trethewey's work, Thadious Davis also notes that "she puts her extraordinary range in accessing vision to excellent use in her formal poetic strategies."[5] Davis suggests that Trethewey layers her poems with personal and family history: "The most apparent of these strategies is her use of ekphrasis in linking vision in a poem directly to a photograph or a painting. . . . But she also pushes the expected limits by enfolding into her poetic representation her own social autobiography and familial history."[6]

As Jones and Davis imply, ekphrasis is itself a palimpsestic device: one of its key powers is its ability to layer an image with story. The significance of Trethewey's ekphrastic work within the American poetic tradition lies in its palimpsestic effect: her poems inscribe personal stories and perspectives onto the larger historical and cultural landscape, using ekphrasis as a vehicle for emotional re-envisioning on individual and sociopolitical levels, as the subjectivity of art, history, and memory coincide. Trethewey confronts and reshapes historical events and individual stories by using both visual documents and often-faulty remembrances. Here ekphrasis extends the act of looking. By reframing visual art, photographs, and historical documents from the point of view of those who have been silenced or are otherwise unable to speak for themselves due to class, race, gender, educational, or other sociocultural factors, Trethewey writes stories that have been hidden at the same time as she rigorously interrogates ways of seeing that deny or obscure those stories.

If her palimpsestic poetics functions in part through effacement that leaves traces of the original, Trethewey's poems do more than take up space atop those traces; instead, they revise dominant, accepted versions of history. In fact, Trethewey treats history itself as a canvas for ekphrastic reflection. Her literary reimagining favors the textual, even as the poems rely on the visual as source material. Palimpsestic poetics and ekphrasis work in tandem not only to invite the reader into the speaker's reimagining or retelling of an event, but also to enable the reader to see that event differently. Trethewey's palimpsestic poetics has a twofold function: first, through her telling of hidden stories, the past comes alive for her readers, the inheritors of a history whose consequences we continue to navigate; and secondly, traditional poetic forms become a connective tissue that both links readers to the past and revises that past as Trethewey subverts expected subject matter.

The impact of Trethewey's palimpsestic poetics strikes hardest on the subject of race. Trethewey's work uniquely explores that fact as she engages with history via ekphrasis. The complexity of her work builds with each new collection, presenting the local "self" of the speaker inside collective African-American and indeed American identity as stronger and more powerfully asserted, resilient, and aware of the myriad truths buried beneath the routine misperceptions, willful ignorance, and violent erasure that characterize institutional racism. By using the Southern slow reveal as pacing style and borrowing from both the oil painter's layering of color and the photographer's focused aperture, Trethewey pays keen attention to the unfolding American narrative around race and captures the unmistakable, variegated, and yet indefinable music of blackness itself, creating deep parallels between content and craft.

Overall, Trethewey's poems move beyond ekphrasis to become standalone textual portraits—visual, tactile, and revelatory. These qualities are pronounced not only in her first volume, *Domestic Work* (2000), but also in her second, *Bellocq's Ophelia* (2002), as the contradictions of the tragic mulatto story are re-envisioned by an eye that sees not only outwardly, but inwardly. Here, Bellocq's photographs work as both gateway and mask for Trethewey's personal story. In *Native Guard* (2006), Trethewey elevates black soldiers from the Mississippi Delta into legend, making evident the irony of fighting for a land in which one is not safe. Her palimpsestic approach entwines personal tragedies with the national racial conflict that shapes citizens of all colors. As a body of work, Trethewey's poems track that tumultuous brew, where "[w]hat matters is context— . . . how suddenly / everything can go wrong."[7] The respite is often not a respite. Even God may have an answer too devastating to beg for. In *Beyond Katrina*

(2010), Trethewey tackles the way the tragic hurricane and its aftermath affected her home state of Mississippi, which, with all the attention on New Orleans, was somewhat neglected in terms of aid, media coverage, and recovery.[8] Here devastation serves as an entry point into Mississippi before, during, and after the storm in the slow motion of a page that mirrors the lasting moment it describes, becoming a palimpsest of seeing. Finally, ekphrastic poems are integral to *Thrall* (2012), her most recent collection. In each poem, Trethewey relates a story based on an image while relentlessly excavating what lies beneath the surface, as she declares in "Calling": "What's left is palimpsest—one memory / bleeding into another, overwriting it."[9]

Palimpsestic Re-inscriptions: Family Documents, Historical Personae, and Objects

In Trethewey's palimpsestic poetics, family, photographs, historical documents and even objects serve as surfaces for re-inscription. "History Lesson" from *Domestic Work*, for example, charts the historical distance between two family photos. As a racially charged anti-pastoral, "History Lesson" not only inverts the idyll of the pastoral, but also works palimpsestically using what Katherine Henninger calls "ekphrastic overlay technique."[10] The subversive inversion is subtle but clear. The first half of the poem describes a photograph of the speaker as a child posing "on a wide strip of Mississippi beach, / my hands on the flowered hips // of a bright bikini" (*DW* 45). The sensory details are vivid but violent: "my toes dig in . . . The sun cuts . . . Minnows dart at my feet / glinting like switchblades." The violence underlying these lines emphasizes the precarious position of the speaker—"I am alone"—as the poem shifts, midway through, from the speaker to her grandmother: "except for my grandmother, other side // of the camera, telling me how to pose." The figure of the grandmother operates as a hinge of both social history and personal identity. In the second half of the poem, we learn that the speaker can only pose on the beach because it had been desegregated two years before: "It is 1970, two years after they opened / the rest of the beach to us." The grandmother's instructions about "how to pose" hint at the politically significant performance of being present and visible in that particular time and place.

The speaker then turns to another family photograph, this one of the grandmother on another section of that same beach four decades prior:

> where she stood on a narrow plot
> of sand marked *colored*, smiling,
>
> her hands on the flowered hips
> of a cotton meal-sack dress. (*DW* 45)

This is another kind of pose; the smile is perhaps one of resignation, in a nod to "the mask that grins and lies" in Paul Laurence Dunbar's classic poem, "We Wear the Mask."[11] The repetition of "flowered hips" underscores the contrast between the speaker's "bright bikini" and the grandmother's shabby "cotton meal-sack dress." Such continuity despite change highlights history's twisted trajectory: the desegregation of the beach is supposedly a sign of progress, but it still feels perilous—the speaker cannot trust this improvement because of past betrayals and ongoing persecution. Indeed, as Dunbar writes, "with torn and bleeding hearts we smile, / And mouth with myriad subtleties,"[12] the African-American subjects of the poem internalize difficulty, enduring oppression while outwardly smiling or, through "subtleties," signaling pain, anger, and other emotions that are unsafe to express publicly. The grandmother's pose in Trethewey's poem intimates visually that she sees integration of the beach as progress. But between the lines lies a keen awareness of the history that progress might obscure without the pointed remembrance the photograph engenders. Susan Sontag writes, "Photographs had the advantage of uniting two contradictory features. [. . .] Yet they always had, necessarily, a point of view. They [. . .] bore witness to the real—since a person had to be there to take them."[13] In "History Lesson," Trethewey gives voice to the camera's point of view through the grandmother who bears witness to the four-year-old speaker's presence in a new reality. Her granddaughter can stand on a "wide strip of Mississippi beach," not a "narrow plot / of sand." The line break after "plot" underscores the pun on both conspiracy and death, as in burial plot. While charting sociopolitical and economic progress, Trethewey also shows her reader how the two photographs are part of the same through-line, connected by family and a deeply political geography in the idyllic landscape that yet retains thinly veiled perils, from the sun to the tiny minnows.

Indeed, in "History Lesson," Trethewey not only uses family photographs to complicate a progressive historical narrative about race in the United States, but also subverts formal modes, using the apparent constraints of formalism to frame her rewriting of history. Henninger maintains that "in Trethewey, the pastoral is never pastoral, particularly not in the Romantic sense"—i.e., it is not characterized by a pervading nostalgia.[14] Rather, Trethewey's pastoral is an anti-pastoral where "nature is everywhere shot through with the detritus of the built world, and the sweat of labor," and further, is "tempered by the history and memory of that past"—a problematic past fraught with trauma. In her anti-pastorals, "images of natural beauty often belie or distract from the human reality just outside their frames. . . . Opposite to the Romantic tradition of childhood's pastoral revealing or embodying lost innocence, the 'green world' in Trethewey's poetry tends to conceal repressed violence" in an apparent inversion of traditional pastoral scenes.[15]

In other ekphrastic poems, the historical persona as mask serves as another kind of palimpsest—a physical and psychic vehicle that acts as a catalyst for the inscription of a new narrative. In "Photograph of a Bawd Drinking Raleigh Rye" from *Bellocq's Ophelia*, for example, Trethewey aligns the reader's gaze with that of a viewer of the photograph and, ultimately, with that of the photographer E. J. Bellocq. His subjects are a black woman, with skin so light as to make her appear Caucasian, and the objects that surround her in a New Orleans brothel. The viewer's surveying gaze is circular and attends to motion: "The glass in her hand is the only thing moving— . . . / She raises it toasting, perhaps, the viewer you become / taking her in." In implicating readers in the viewer's gaze and indeed Bellocq's act of photographing, the poem challenges us to think about not only what we see but also *how* we see it. Trethewey implicitly asks why some people remain in the background or confined to surface consideration, continually silenced in their stillness, reduced to aesthetic collectibles of sorts: "On the wall behind her, the image again—women in paintings, in photographs, and carved relief."[16]

Trethewey flips the perspective in the persona poem "Bellocq," one part of the serial poem "Storyville Diary." In "Bellocq," the woman-as-subject becomes the speaker who reflects on the photographer and the resultant photograph. Her underlying thought process is made visible: "I try to pose as I think he would like—shy / at first, then bolder." The speaker's intelligent affect renders her all the more tragic. She is aware of her relative powerlessness, even as she recovers a measure of power through that awareness itself: "I'm not so foolish / that I don't know this photograph *we* make / will bear the stamp of his name, not mine" (*BO* 39). Through "the stamp of his name"—a personal, standardized, visible mark—Trethewey performs a palimpsestic meta-ekphrasis: the speaker in the photograph reflects on a visual aspect of it that was not part of the scene depicted, but instead was stamped on the finished product. By layering the images with a deeper history and multiple perspectives, Trethewey makes the reader-viewer a co-witness to what the poems represent.

The poem "Photography," in the same "Storyville Diary" series, goes even further, as the speaker tries to understand the art form itself. The poem depicts a lesson in seeing: "Bellocq talks about the light, shows me / how to use shadow, how to fill the frame / with objects—their intricate positions." But instead of taking him as the final authority, and even as she "thrill[s] to the magic of it," the speaker also thrills at her own wisdom and vision:

> I look at what he can see through his lens
> and what he cannot—silverfish behind
> the walls, the yellow tint of a faded bruise—
> other things here, what the camera misses. (*BO* 43)

By using the invented-yet-real (black) speaker's voice to draw attention to details unseen by Bellocq, Trethewey points to the limits of photography itself. Trethewey remains mindful of realities under the surface of cultural and personal memory as she palimpsestically re-surfaces visual art and historical documents with hidden narratives.

Not even objects escape palimpsestic re-inscription in Trethewey's work. Even in poems that are not technically ekphrastic, gesture often takes on the same role it plays in painting, capturing the full meaning of a moment and making an object emblematic. In "Hot Combs" from *Domestic Work*, for instance, Trethewey inscribes memory onto an object found at "the junk shop." While "Hot Combs" is not overtly ekphrastic, this portrait of a commonplace object used to transform black women's hair from its natural state to a texture closer to that of white women's hair, via an often painful ritual, allows Trethewey to showcase the pervasiveness of racism's effects, from small gestures to significant violence. This grooming object —a metal comb heated on the stove and subsequently run through the hair to straighten it—has been common to African-American households since its invention. The comb is "black with grease, / the teeth still pungent / as burning hair" (*DW* 29). The self-immolation entailed in "Hot Combs" may seem trivial to some, but in describing the object, Trethewey recounts a history of pain that plays itself out in the grooming process for black women. Presenting childhood reflection from an adult point of view, Trethewey explores the painful contortions racism imposes on the body and mind. Contending with standards of beauty that her own mate and community subscribe to, a black woman thus may choose to straighten her hair even if she burns tender parts of the skin—typically the back of the neck, forehead, or behind the ear—in the process.

Finding hot combs at "the junk shop" prompts the speaker to recall her own mother pressing her hair:

> . . . The heat in our kitchen
> made her glow that morning I watched her
> wincing, the hot comb singeing her brow,
> sweat glistening above her lips,
> her face made strangely beautiful
> as only suffering can do. (*DW* 29)

Those closing two lines deliver a punch that makes the speaker's personal history communal. Here "suffering" has multiple meanings: even the making of beauty for black women involves a small, self-inflicted violence. The hot comb itself becomes slightly menacing ("teeth still pungent / as burning hair") and contrasts with the delicate rendering of the mother's "slender wrist." The need to look more white has encroached upon the mother's body and the poem's speaker sees that effort, the "eyes shut as she pulled /

the wooden handle and laid flat the wisps / at her temples." The mother feels the pain but closes her eyes to it, as the daughter watches more than just the hot comb "singeing her [mother's] brow." Here the mother's dance between pain and beauty in an effort to fit into another's paradigm parallels black efforts at integrating into white society. The process is often futile and can produce scars—and even the scar is a palimpsest, inscribing pain onto the body and making memory physical.

Ekphrasis and Histories of Racism and Sexism in Thrall and Bellocq's Ophelia

In the ekphrastic poems that are central to *Thrall* and *Bellocq's Ophelia*, Trethewey turns her palimpsestic poetics to the task of excavating the intertwined histories of racism and sexism as recorded and refracted in visual art. In *Bellocq's Ophelia*, as we have seen, she attends to nineteenth-century photographs of mixed-race women in New Orleans brothels, while, in *Thrall*, she often turns her attention to fourteenth- through seventeenth-century European and colonial Mexican paintings. Trethewey uses these paintings as an entrée into an examination of her own mixed-race heritage, histories of racial categories, and, whether consciously or unconsciously, the marriage of African-American and European sensibilities in her poetics.

Trethewey's headnote to "Miracle of the Black Leg" tells us that the poem is based on "pictorial representations of . . . the myth of the miracle transplant—black donor, white recipient—[that] date back to the mid-fourteenth century" (*Thrall* 9). The poem reflects on several European paintings and carvings that depict the amputation of the lower leg of "*an Ethiopian*" who lies prone on the floor next to a white man's gilded bed; sometimes the amputee is depicted as dead, but sometimes he is alive to watch a surgeon sew his (former) limb onto the white man's body: "In version after version, even / when the *Ethiopian* isn't there, the leg is a stand in, / a black modifier against the white body" (*Thrall* 12). In section 4, these problematic images juxtapose opulence with the grotesque and stratify two men bound together by body and experience:

> Both men are alive in Villoldo's carving.
>   In twinned relief, they hold the same posture,
> the same pained face, each man reaching to touch
>   his left leg. . . .
>   . . . How not to see it—
>   the men bound one to the other, symbiotic—
> one man rendered expendable, the other worthy
>   of this sacrifice? (*Thrall* 12)

Trethewey's use of these images highlights that physical connection, an underreported aspect of the oppressive relationships between the races: "If not for the dark appendage, / you might miss the story beneath this story— / what remains each time the myth changes" (*Thrall* 9). Indeed, the amputee left alive on the floor to witness the surgical collage underscores the macabre way in which "the men [are] bound one to the other . . . in a story that's still being written" (*Thrall* 12).

Far from being relegated to history, the poem suggests from its very first line that racist violence is ongoing and no accident: "Always, the dark body hewn asunder; always / one man is healed, his sick limb replaced, / placed in the other man's grave" (*Thrall* 9). The word "always," used twice, leaves no argument about the historical reality and present-day continuation of violence in the name of preserving the kind of racial hierarchy that the Villoldo carving depicts. One early twentieth-century example of such violent bodily "hew[ing] asunder" is the lynching of Mary Turner in Georgia in 1918: her unborn child was sliced from her hanging body and crushed under the boots of his mother's killer.[17] Another is James Byrd, Jr., who was dragged through rural Texas streets until all that was left of him was, as Lucille Clifton wrote in her poem "jasper texas 1998," "a man's head hunched in the road."[18] Beyond lynching, one may also consider the enslaved women Dr. J. Marion Sims used in gynecological experiments, their bodies publicly and painfully invaded in the name of science.[19] Such more recent examples are implicit in the first line of Trethewey's poem, beginning in the gloomy past but bleeding into the present. The truth is buried in gruesome and unnatural ways, as the "sick limb" of racism is "placed" and hidden in the graves of those killed by racists (*Thrall* 9). But, despite the apparent anonymity of the figures it depicts, the fact that Trethewey's poem exists means that such truths do not remain silenced. Text resurrects, even in its incompleteness: "the black leg is at once a grafted narrative, a redacted line of text" (*Thrall* 10). Trethewey's poem not only gives the mythic leg and the "Ethiopian" from whom it was taken elegiac due, but also redacts its meanings so that this "*piece cut off*" is transformed into a "*comma*: / caesura in a story that's still being written" (*Thrall* 12).

As *Thrall* progresses, Trethewey's use of ekphrasis becomes more personal. "Knowledge" is based on a Civil War–era chalk drawing by J. H. Hasselhorst and also details the cutting of a body—this time via the autopsy of a woman, "young and beautiful and drowned," that occurs in "a temple of science over which // the anatomist presides. In the service of beauty." After a description of the objectification of "*Mary* or *Katherine* or *Elizabeth* / to *corpus, areola, vulva*," the speaker says, "and yet how easily / the anatomist's blade opens a place in me, // like a curtain drawn upon a room in which / each learned man is my father." The speaker thus becomes both a witness to the autopsy and the body dissected on the table, palimpsestically re-inscribing this historical document with her own experience, recognizing that she has endured a racial dissection by her own father: "I hear, again, his words—*I study / my crossbreed child*" (*Thrall* 28–30, italics in original). While the poem reflects on the father's implanted narrative, which could define how the speaker sees herself and paralyze self-discovery, it also shows the speaker searching for a truer story, a personalized palimpsest that reexamines images in memory in order to rewrite that memory. As Trethewey writes in "Calling," "Why not make a fiction / of the mind's fictions" (*Thrall* 66)?

In contrast to the more imaginative ekphrasis of the two previously discussed poems, "Taxonomy" is based on a series of eighteenth-century *casta* paintings that schematically represent racial categories in colonial Mexico and deliberately verges on the explanatory. In slow-paced, short-lined couplets, section 3 outlines the hierarchy of miscegenation encoded in the *casta* paintings. In one particular painting, the child of a Spanish father and a *mestiza* mother

> turns toward the father,
>   reaching to him
>
> as if back to Spain,
>   to the promise of blood
>
> alchemy—three easy steps
>   to purity:
>
> *from a Spaniard and an Indian,*
>   *a mestizo;*
>
> *from a mestizo and a Spaniard,*
>   *a castizo;*
>
> *from a castizo and a Spaniard,*
>   *a Spaniard.* (*Thrall* 22–23, italics in original)

The white space of the page and the lines' lack of density attenuates logic, perhaps mirroring the scattered logic of categories of miscegenation themselves. Across "Taxonomy," the repeated themes seem concerned with justifying a rewrite or an overwrite—in other words, the poet's palimpsestic treatment of the history of racial hierarchies in Mexico. The poem elaborates "the typology of taint" in section 4, "*The Book of Castas*":

> of stain: blemish: sullying spot:
>
> that which can be purified,
>   that which cannot—Canaan's

black fate. How like a dirty joke
　　it seems: *what do you call*

that space between
　　the dark geographies of sex?

Call it the *taint*—as in
　　T'aint one and t'aint the other—
　　　　　　(*Thrall* 24–25, italics in original)

Trethewey's play on words layers "Taxonomy," which focuses on paintings about the "taint" of "Indian" heritage in colonial Mexico, with an American idiom that evokes racial categories and concepts of miscegenation in the United States.

In a poem later in the volume, "*De Español y Negra; Mulata*," Trethewey turns to another eighteenth-century *casta* painting by Miguel Cabrera that categorizes blackness in colonial Mexico. The speaker's gaze is captured by a mixed-race child in the "center / of the painting, then the word nearby: *Texocotes*, / a tiny inscription on the mother's basket" (*Thrall* 39). Also known as a manzanita, the *tejocote* is related to the hawthorn. It serves as a focal point as the poem fans out to include the white father, "the dominion / of his touch," as he holds the fruit up to the darker face of the mother, "the black cloak making her blacker still." In this instance of ekphrasis, Trethewey combines unmistakable Christian imagery alongside the "contrast— / how not to see it?"—of skin color. The fruit and the child stand in for one another, and the mother's "body [is . . .] / like spilled ink spreading on a page, / a great pendulum eclipsing the light" (*Thrall* 40).

In the context of *Thrall*, with its poems about Trethewey's relationship with her father, this particular poem reads as a slant autobiography and thus showcases her palimpsestic poetics. "*De Español y Negra; Mulata*" examines visually the obliteration of the child's whiteness by the mother's darkness and what that suggests—the "pendulum" of history swinging toward the visibility of darker-hued people and their stories, which are no longer reduced to "flat outline" (*Thrall* 40). Though Trethewey does not rely on a link to white writers for agency or legitimacy, her work undeniably engages with Eurocentric traditions in poetry and painting. At the same time, one cannot deny the inherent blackness of Trethewey's poems and poetics. That the two coexist, however precariously or beautifully, seems a uniquely American problem that should position Trethewey's work at the heart of a definition of American poetics and poetic history.

In a 2012 review in *The New Criterion*, critic and poet William Logan skewers *Thrall* for its focus on histories of race and racism: "Trethewey . . . has a gift for elaborating the perfectly obvious, . . . with stale adjectives and battery-depleted language" which "is as dull as a dirty mirror," and further, "if she can't think of a better adjective, she chooses 'dark.'" Logan adds: "Trethewey can barely see beyond race and subjugation—she ignores the transcendence that would spoil her slightly privileged sense of injustice. The workmanlike prose of the poems too often succumbs to artsy poeticizing," and he refers to the *casta* paintings as "portraits displaying the bewildering variety of mixed-race children," bemoaning the content as well as the "bland, passionless verse," wherein "the images are already like encyclopedias."[20]

It is telling that Logan doesn't engage with "Miracle of the Black Leg," or indeed with any of the poems in *Thrall* that depict more explicit atrocities, other than to call "lurid" a three-part poem, "The Americans," that examines three images whose common thread is blood. Its first section, subtitled "*Dr. Samuel Adolphus Cartwright on Dissecting the White Negro, 1851*," describes "the body's diminishment— / blood deep / and definite" as the presumably mulatto corpse is defiled for scientific evidence of race: "we still know white from not" (*Thrall* 33). Cartwright, a physician who practiced in both Natchez and New Orleans, wrote numerous articles attempting to scientifically prove the inferiority of African Americans. He argued specifically that African Americans are suitable for slavery and coined the term "drapetomania" as a psychological diagnosis for the urge to run away.[21]

Given Logan's hostile response to work that addresses racism, perhaps stating the obvious is a necessary and deliberate part of Trethewey's strategy. Logan's dismissive refusal to participate in this conversation and his stated bewilderment smack of the kind of disengagement and lack of compassion for nonwhite experiences that shut down thoughtful exchanges about racism and its impact on individuals, families, and society as a whole. The same wall of blatant bias, unconscious or not, has traditionally confronted contemporary black women writers from Toni Morrison to Ntozake Shange. Logan even casts aside Trethewey's personal poems about her father, infantilizing them as the whining of an "oversensitive [daughter], so quick to view the world through the narrow lens of race."[22] Far from aiming to elicit sympathy, Trethewey's clarity and insistence means to educate and elucidate instead.

In a group interview, "Interchange: Genres of History," Trethewey discusses her motivations for choosing her subject matter. Trethewey describes her approach as both ekphrastic and palimpsestic, aiming for a visceral experience: "I want imagery vivid enough to invite them into the world of the poem as participants who experience the emotional context of it rather than as distant observers who are told what to think or feel about the historical material I am presenting. This is, of course, all about empathy."[23] Thus, to reject wholesale her poems' perceived or actual literality without approaching the difficult content with openness to new understandings and different points of view is to deny or overlook, as Walt Hunter writes, that Trethewey's poems clearly "capture the violence of capital and of colonization."[24]

At that violent intersection, in *Bellocq's Ophelia* as in *Thrall*, Trethewey's poetry might also be considered "in thrall to a word"—specifically, mulatto (*Thrall* 26), a word that connotes the complex relationship between race and the male gaze for the women depicted in the photographs and poems. As Trethewey imagines the interior and daily lives of the often-mournful women in Bellocq's images, she palimpsestically conflates the observer and the observed. The speakers' fictive speculations in Trethewey's persona poems blur the line between personal feelings and a sense of historical location, bringing the photographic subject's presence to life in a visceral way for the reader. Further, Trethewey constructs poems in which it seems that the poet discovers a truth in the process of the writing, the poem having taken on a life of its own.

Trethewey's "Vignette," for example—and perhaps *Bellocq's Ophelia* in general—represents a photographic encounter in such a way that it becomes a new encounter between text and reader. Such meta-ekphrastic poems—that is, poems that examine photographs in which the photographed subjects in turn seem to examine their visual representation—cannot be anything but complex, despite the deceptively simple language of the poem. "Vignette" looks at the scene Bellocq interpreted photographically and speculates on what the subject, once a living woman, may have experienced. In planning how to capture the woman in the photo, Bellocq "waits / for the right moment, a look on her face / to keep in a gilded frame, the ornate box / he'll put her in" (*BO* 47). His act of framing her in his lens becomes a trap, however "ornate." The poem suggests that the woman in the photograph is aware of having to fit in that "box" as her mind wanders:

> . . . she must be thinking
> of her childhood wonder at seeing
> the contortionist in a sideshow—how
> he could make himself small, fit
> into cramped spaces, his lungs
> barely expanding with each tiny breath.
> She thinks of her own shallow breath—
> her back straining the stays of a bustier,
> the weight of a body pressing her down.

The reader first witnesses Bellocq's construction of her image, then her thoughts on that constrictive framing, and then, in the final lines, the possibility that she might break free from it all, "stepping out / of the frame, wide-eyed, into her life" (*BO* 47–48).

Indeed, the poem reflects Trethewey's deep interest in having the woman in the photograph "inscribe her own presence."[25] Trethewey describes how she approached writing about the Bellocq photographs: "I didn't want other voices, particularly the voice of Bellocq, getting in the way of her story. I wasn't interested in his story. . . . We know much more about him than we know about the anonymous women that appeared in his photographs."[26] In doing the work of imagining the hidden or untold thoughts and stories of the women in *Bellocq's Ophelia*, Trethewey creates a palimpsest of different kinds of vision, a fictive history upon which Bellocq's narrative, then the woman's, and finally the reader's become inscribed.

Layering History, Geography, and Memory in Beyond Katrina and Native Guard

If Trethewey's layering of historical documents with personal experience is especially evident in her many ekphrastic poems, the same palimpsestic poetics shapes her non-ekphrastic poems as well. In an interview with *Interchange*, Trethewey declares: "in my work I have a goal of trying to place my own experience, my personal history, within the larger context of public history."[27] Her personal narrative is perhaps most contextualized by public history in her 2010 book *Beyond Katrina*, a hybrid text of poetry and nonfiction prose that together offer a winding narrative of Gulfport, Mississippi, Trethewey's home territory. She focuses on the devastating effects Hurricane Katrina had on her family—effects that particular towns and people, including her brother, still contend with. The prose sections take special notice of the man-made damage done by corporations, even as many of her poignant memories include those corporations: "Gulfport is *me* at the Woolworth's lunch counter . . . listening to the sounds of shoes striking the polished tile floor of Hancock Bank, holding my grandmother's hand . . . *me* riding the elevator of the J. M. Salloum Building—the same elevator my grandmother operated in the thirties."[28] Trethewey points out how much people rely on the agents of their own destruction when she reveals that casinos eroded the coastline, making the area that much more vulnerable to hurricane damage. She laments Governor Haley Barbour's decision to allow onshore gaming while recognizing that people in the area could sorely use the jobs the gaming industry provides (*BK* 58). Likewise, the poems reflect the bond between the South and its inhabitants, taking a wide sweep across the Mississippi landscape and through centuries, decades, and moments with the simultaneity and overlap characteristic of Trethewey's palimpsestic poetics. The opening poem in *Native Guard*, "Theories of Time and Space"—which is reprinted in *Beyond Katrina*—has a circular arc, a cinematic pan:

Everywhere you go will be somewhere
you've never been. Try this:

head south on Mississippi 49, one-
by-one mile markers ticking off

another minute of your life. Follow this
to its natural conclusion—dead end

at the coast, the pier at Gulfport where
riggings of shrimp boats are loose stitches

in a sky threatening rain. (*BK* 5)

The sense of futility in these lines not only underscores the fact that the speaker cannot escape the past or her identity, but also drives her to confront both. Once again, an image—this time one associated with a memory rather than shown in a photograph—serves as a marker of both past and present. The "pier at Gulfport" becomes a site for the unraveling of —"loose stitches"—that occurs when the speaker confronts her past. The lack of punctuation in that line denotes the continuousness of this unraveling, and yet even the eroding landscape and its inhabitants remain alive in memory, the vivid image available for recall in Trethewey's telescopic text.

During a panel discussion at the 2012 Dodge Poetry Festival, Trethewey and the poet Patricia Smith, author of the Katrina-based poetry collection *Blood Dazzler*, called the storm "a human event."[29] Trethewey and Smith agreed that one has to let go of wanting to be an insider or to be approved by insiders—i.e., those who witnessed and survived Katrina—in order to tell the story that needs telling. Trethewey discussed George Orwell's *The Road to Wigan Pier* as an influence: she realized she couldn't help but impose an outsider's perspective because she no longer lived in Mississippi and did not witness the storm, but she challenged herself not to "otherize" Katrina victims.[30] In *Beyond Katrina*, Trethewey walks the fraught line between her Mississippi subjects and herself as speaker with a certain grace, confronting her own outsider status as one who was physically safe from the storm but nevertheless felt its impact emotionally. That emotional vulnerability gives her the authority to write stories that seem not to belong to her directly; in fact, the strong sense of alienation that underlies the book belongs to many more than just Trethewey.

Like Smith—who, in *Blood Dazzler*, takes on the varied personae of Katrina victims and, repeatedly, of Hurricane Katrina herself—Trethewey tends to revisit speakers in *Beyond Katrina*. These speakers often maintain a certain observational distance that is self-concerned but melancholy, grieving not only for a personal past framed by tragedy, but also for places devastated by the storm. In section 6 of the poem "Congregation," subtitled "*Prodigal*," the details underscore not only the speaker's long-standing connection to particular people and places, but also her current disconnection from them: "Once, I was a daughter of this place: / daughter of Gwen, granddaughter / of Leretta, great of Eugenia McGee." That lineage imbues the speaker with an authority that is modified by the word "Once"—as in, no longer. "As a child," the speaker "was baptized . . . behind / the drapes my grandmother sewed," further emphasizing her separation. This tragic difference becomes "a white bloom pinned to my chest —the mark of loss," singling her out as "a motherless child" (*BK* 79). The prodigal daughter, returning as an adult, must muck through difficult memories, the inescapable past, and their effects on the present in order to move forward. To do so, the speaker palimpsestically rewrites accepted facts from her point of view and uses visual cues to reach a new understanding. Indeed, she cannot proceed until she is *seen*. The speaker, back "home" as "witness" or "pilgrim," goes into "the rebuilt church / across from my grandmother's house":

> I got as far as the vestibule—neither in,
> nor out. The service went on. I did nothing
> but watch, my face against the glass—until
> someone turned, looked back: saw me. (*BK* 81)

In *Beyond Katrina*, both the poetry and prose describe Trethewey's sense of feeling apart from a place that is so much a part of her. But instead of shying away from those complex feelings, Trethewey addresses them, unraveling the endless stitch of memory's internal and external machinations. What does it mean when home is a reminder of deep loss? Rather than a place of comfort, the speaker in "Congregation" sees "home" as "a cradle / of the past . . . a narrative of rust" (*BK* 79). Both her discomfort and her bravery are understood through the act of seeing:

> I wanted to say I have come home
> to bear witness, to read the sign
> emblazoned on the church marquee—
> *Believe the report of the Lord*—
> and trust that this is noble work, that
> which must be done. I wanted to say *I see*,
> not *I watch*. I wanted my seeing to be
> a sanctuary, but what I saw was this:
> in my rearview mirror, the marquee's
> other side—*Face the things that confront you*. (*BK* 81)

Here, the rearview mirror itself becomes a palimpsest, inscribed with the past, with the speaker's intentions and aspirations, and with the place that pushes back against her presumptions through church signs and returned glances.

In *Native Guard* Trethewey extends this exploration of areas where Mississippi history and her personal memories overlap. The opening poem, "Theories of Time and Space," sets the tone for the recollection of a Southern experience riddled with habitual fears and hurt that is both expected and accepted. Many poems in the book inscribe individualized pain onto presumed national narratives. Indeed, micro- and macroaggressions happen so many times that they become one continuous act of psychological violence whose warped normalcy is captured, aptly, in the pantoum "Incident," which creates a palimpsestic loop of fear and remembrance. As in Countee Cullen's poem of the same title, a single incident redefines an entire season. In Cullen's poem, racism ruins the speaker's joy at visiting Baltimore on vacation. Encountering another child his age and smiling, he was met with an epithet—"he poked out / His tongue, called me, 'Nigger'"—that colored the entire experience. Matter-of-factly, the speaker recalls: "I saw the whole of Baltimore / From May until December; / Of all the things that happened there / That's all that I remember."[31] Rhyme in Cullen's "Incident" serves chillingly as an echoing device, as does repetition in Trethewey's pantoum. The twin opening and closing lines in her poem, "We tell the story every year," highlight the repetition both of the terrorist act of cross-burning and of the family's act of remembering it. Yet another repeated line—"Nothing really happened, / the charred grass now green again"—denies the significance and severity of this violence. "No one came" for the "white men in their gowns," presumably Klansmen who terrorized African-American families for decades with impunity (*NG* 41). The image of the "charred grass" that makes way for new green implies a palimpsestic renewal, but not in a positive way: instead, the green lawn offers a blank slate for new cross-burnings. Further, the twisted "angels" exude a quiet and incendiary hate that clashes with the holiday season ("the cross trussed like a Christmas tree"): "a few men gathered, white as angels in their gowns." Here angels, understood as godly and innocent protectors, are recast as persecutors. A harsh reality turns a celebratory time into a new kind of normal characterized by fear ("the wicks trembling in their fonts of oil"), destruction ("charred grass"), and resigned acceptance ("No one came. Nothing really happened").[32] The pantoum form, with its insistent repetition, lends itself to the palimpsestic re-inscription of memory. The image of the cross burning on the front lawn remains just as haunting with each retelling. Beginning and ending with "We tell the story every year" works against silence, implying both warning and remembrance. To forget, to not tell the story, is to deny both history and reality, a denial Trethewey makes it her mission to avoid.

Like history, geography can also be a kind of messy palimpsest, as the literal ground is re-inscribed by each new inhabitant of a place and, sometimes, as with disasters like Hurricane Katrina, is obliterated or radically reshaped. In *Native Guard*, Trethewey inscribes traces of her own refusal to forget on both land and memory. She does this in part through conversation with literary tradition: the book has thirteen notes and epigraphs from sources ranging from singer and activist Nina Simone to seventeenth-century English poet Robert Herrick. "Elegy for the Native Guards" and "Genus Narcissus" elegize unsung heroes both historic and personal. "Genus Narcissus" has an epigraph from Herrick: "*Faire daffadills, we weep to see / You haste away so soone.*" Significantly breaking at "see," these lines set up both the poem's seasonal performance of grief through the "short spring" of daffodils, and actual grief at the foreshadowed death of the poet-speaker's mother (*NG* 7).

Trethewey-as-speaker writes of a childhood landscape "dense with trees and shadow, creek-side / and lit by yellow daffodils, early blossoms // bright against winter's last gray days," again overwriting the bucolic pastoral scene with something more sinister. Her palimpsestic approach inscribes a sorrowful personal history onto that traditionally lighter genre. While Herrick reflects on the literal loss of "daffadills,"[33] for Trethewey daffodils are additionally associated with grief and "childish vanity." The daffodils presage her mother's death in the final line—"*Die early*, [they said] to my mother"—and, since Trethewey's mother was killed by her second husband, one might easily extrapolate that the poem's speaker considers women killed in domestic violence to be unsung figures, their stories untold except for the sad facts of their murders.[34] Indeed, Trethewey mentions in an interview that *Native Guard*'s three sections serve as "document, monument, and testament," and that the poems themselves reinscribe, through elegy and history, certain narratives that "intersect with the lives of people in my family."[35]

The formal qualities of "Elegy for the Native Guards" also put Trethewey in conversation with literary traditions and historical personae. Rather than intersecting with family, though, "Elegy for the Native Guards" tells a forgotten story of Trethewey's native Gulfport. The speaker addresses the "black phalanx" of Union soldiers who served in the Civil War in Mississippi—"tokens of history long buried," their names absent from the honorific "plaque" at the fort she visits (*NG* 44). In recounting this "half reminder" of their existence—a harrowing existence, to be sure, detailed thoroughly in the book's title poem—Trethewey ultimately shows the civic and human responsibility both to stake a claim to the "weathered monument" where "fish dart among their bones," and to celebrate the experiences and sacrifices of all Americans. Indeed, "God's deliberate eye" watches not only over the ruined monument, but also over those who have neglected it. The palindromic rhyme scheme (ABCCBA) that Trethewey uses reads the same backward and forward, suggesting that the history of the Native Guard continues to be disremembered in the moment of the poem's composition. Thus, like the "casemates, cannons, the store that sells / souvenirs," the poem itself becomes a "token of history long buried." Further, the monument to Confederate soldiers who also died there also serves as a palimpsest—a partially erased surface upon which Trethewey can write the lives of the Native Guard. In inscribing and describing the Native Guard's missing history onto a monument already memorializing "some of the dead," the speaker's detailed and layered seeing becomes an enhanced remembrance (*NG* 44).

A more recent poem by Trethewey, "We Have Seen," performs a reverse architectural ekphrasis, with its speaker looking outward from a church. The act of seeing a building and understanding its meaning and function in community and history is described from inside of the building, framed by the church's choice of "stained glass: Christ the Good Shepherd / facing east."[36] The poem could serve as a distillation of Trethewey's palimpsestic poetics that both sees and sees beyond "the ruined tableau" and "what should have been"—in this case, the bombing of the 16th Street Baptist Church in Birmingham, Alabama, on September 15, 1963, as stated in the headnote. Though the speaker is unable to change what happened, the poem nevertheless provides the reader with an alternate understanding of the tragic and politically galvanizing event that killed four little girls. History might allow for this alternate understanding imaginatively or continue to deny it through repeated brutality. Trethewey invites the reader to imagine an alternate history in which the girls live: "If you could look beyond it—the palimpsest of wreckage." But further, "and in the middle ground, / a man raising a camera to capture / something we might have never had reason / to see." Once again, she layers an event, palimpsestically, with a fictional photograph, masterfully linking history with imagination and fact with a futile longing for a possible safer future for black parishioners. But even the images of Jesus are not spared here: "his body left nearly intact / but faceless, after the blast."[37]

"It is commonplace that the landscape is inscribed with the traces of things long gone," Trethewey writes in *Beyond Katrina* (*BK* 33). With both land and memory as palimpsestic surfaces, the parallels consistently drawn, her oeuvre contains carefully tended and boldly asserted personal and political histories, rendered with a fiercely intelligent attention to "the lives of people that history and public memory often forget,"[38] marking Trethewey as one of the finest stewards of collective memory in contemporary letters.

NOTES

1. Rita Dove, introduction to Natasha Trethewey, *Domestic Work* (Minneapolis: Graywolf Press, 2000), xi. Hereafter I will refer to this work with in-text citations as *DW* followed by the page number.

2. Gwendolyn Brooks, "The Anniad," *Blacks* (New York: Third World Press, 1994), 99.

3. Meta Duewa Jones, "Reframing Exposure: Natasha Trethewey's Forms of Enclosure," *English Literary History* 82.2 (2015): 411.

4. Ibid., 413.

5. Thadious M. Davis, "Enfoldments: Natasha Trethewey's Racial-Spatial Photo-texting," *Southern Quarterly: A Journal of the Arts in the South* 50.4 (2013): 38.

6. Ibid., 39.

7. Natasha Trethewey, "What the Body Can Say," *Native Guard* (Boston: Houghton Mifflin, 2006), 9. Hereafter I will refer to this work with in-text citations as *NG* followed by the page number.

8. "In Mississippi, A Feeling of Neglect." NBCnews.com, September 4, 2005 (accessed August 26, 2013); www.nbcnews.com/id/9190498/ns/us_news-katrina _the_long_road_back/t/mississippi-feeling-neglect/.

9. Natasha Trethewey, *Thrall* (Boston: Houghton Mifflin Harcourt, 2012), 66. Hereafter I will refer to this work with in-text citations followed by the page number.

10. Katherine Henninger, "What Remains: Race, Nation, and the Adult Child in the Poetry of Natasha Trethewey," *Southern Quarterly* 50.4 (2013): 59.

11. Ibid. See also full text of "We Wear the Mask," by Paul Laurence Dunbar at the Poetry Foundation; www.poetryfoundation.org/poems-and-poets/poems /detail/44203.

12. Ibid.

13. Susan Sontag, *Regarding the Pain of Others* (New York: Farrar, Strauss & Giroux, 2003), 26.

14. Henninger, 58.

15. Ibid.

16. Natasha Trethewey, *Bellocq's Ophelia* (Minneapolis: Graywolf Press, 2002), 34. Hereafter cited in the text as *BO*, followed by the page number.

17. The Mary Turner Project. www.maryturner.org (accessed July 28, 2013).

18. Lucille Clifton, "jasper texas 1998," *The Collected Poems of Lucille Clifton 1965–2010* (Rochester, NY: BOA Editions, 2012), 552.

19. L. L. Wall, "The Medical Ethics of Dr. J. Marion Sims: A Fresh Look at the Historical Record," *Journal of Medical Ethics* 32.6 (2006): 346–50; doi.org/10 .1136/jme.2005.012559.

20. William Logan, "Song & Dance," *New Criterion* 31.4 (December 2012): 74–75; www.newcriterion.com/articles.cfm/Song---dance-7511 (accessed August 22, 2013).

21. Dr. Samuel Adolphus Cartwright, "Diseases and Peculiarities of the Negro Race," *De Bow's Review, Southern and Western States*, vol. XI, New Orleans, 1851 (New York: AMS Press, 1967); www.pbs.org/wgbh/aia/part4/4h3106t.html (accessed December 20, 2016).

22. Logan, 75.

23. "Interchange: Genres of History," *Journal of American History* 91.2 (September 2004): 581–85; jah.oxfordjournals.org/content/91/2/572.extract (accessed August 14, 2013).

24. Walt Hunter, "The No-Prospect Poem: Lyric Finality in Prynne, Awoonor, and Trethewey," *Minnesota Review* 85 (2015): 146; minnesotareview.dukejournals.org/content/2015/85/144.full.pdf+html (accessed December 18, 2016).

25. Rowell, 1031.

26. Ibid.

27. "Interchange," 586.

28. Natasha Trethewey, *Beyond Katrina* (Athens: University of Georgia Press, 2010), 63. Hereafter cited in the text as *BK* followed by page number.

29. Natasha Trethewey and Patricia Smith, "Conversation: In the Path of the Storm," Panel, Dodge Poetry Festival, North Star Academy Great Room, Newark, New Jersey, October 13, 2012.

30. Ibid.

31. For the whole poem, see "Necessary Utterance: On Poetry as a Cultural Force," *VQR-on-line* (Winter 2014); www.vqronline.org/necessary-utterance.

32. Natasha Trethewey, *Native Guard* (Boston: Houghton Mifflin, 2006), 41. Hereafter cited in the text as *NG* followed by page number.

33. "Robert Herrick: 1591–1674"; www.poetryfoundation.org/poems-and-poets/poets/detail/robert-herrick (accessed December 20, 2016).

34. Charles McGrath, "New Laureate Looks Deep Into Memory," *The New York Times*, June 6, 2012; www.nytimes.com/2012/06/07/books/natasha-trethewey-is-named-poet-laureate.html.

35. Charles Henry Rowell, "Inscriptive Restorations: An Interview with Natasha Trethewey," in *Callaloo* 27.4 ("Contemporary African-American Poetry: A New Wave," Autumn 2004): 1033; www.jstor.org/stable/3301000 (accessed December 20, 2016).

36. Natasha Trethewey, "We Have Seen: View from the Window of the Sixteenth Street Baptist Church, September 15, 1963," *Smithsonian Magazine* 47.5 (September 2016): 53–54.

37. Ibid.

38. Rowell, 1027.

BIBLIOGRAPHY

Works by Natasha Trethewey

POETRY
Domestic Work. Minneapolis: Graywolf, 2000.
Bellocq's Ophelia. Minneapolis: Graywolf, 2002.
Native Guard. New York: Houghton Mifflin, 2006.
Thrall. Boston and New York: Houghton Mifflin Harcourt, 2012.

EDITED VOLUMES
Best New Poets 2007: 50 Poems from Emerging Writers. With Jeb Livingood. Charlottesville: University of Virginia Press, 2007.
Best American Poetry 2017. With David Lehman. New York: Scribner, 2017.

PROSE

Beyond Katrina. Athens: The University of Georgia Press, 2010.

SELECTED INTERVIEWS

Chang, Jennifer. "The Public Life of Poetry: An Interview with Natasha Trethewey." *Los Angeles Review of Books*, June 11, 2013; lareviewofbooks .org/article/the-public-life-of-poetry-an-interview-with-natasha-trethewey/.

Hall, Joan Wylie, ed. *Conversations with Natasha Trethewey*. Jackson: University Press of Mississippi, 2013.

Magee, Rosemary, and Joan Wylie Hall. "'The Larger Stage of These United States': Creativity Conversation with Natasha Trethewey and Rosemary Magee." *Southern Quarterly* 50 (Summer 2013): 17–28.

McKee, Mark. "A Conversation with Natasha Trethewey." *Missouri Review* 33 (Summer 2010): 144–59.

Petty, Jill. "An Interview with Natasha Trethewey." *Callaloo* 19 (Spring 1996): 3–17.

Pfefferle, W. T. "Decatur, Georgia." *Poets on Place: Interviews & Tales from the Road* (Logan, UT: Utah State University Press, 2005), 163–67.

"Poet Laureate: 'Poetry's Always A Kind Of Faith.'" *Fresh Air*, June 8, 2012; www.npr.org/2012/06/08/154566358/natasha-trethewey-poetrys-always-a -kind-of-faith.

Rowell, Charles Henry. "Inscriptive Restorations: An Interview with Natasha Trethewey." *Callaloo* 27 (Autumn 2004): 1021–34.

Schwartz, Claire. "Natasha Trethewey: Language and Ruthlessness." *Oxford American*, January 8, 2016; www.oxfordamerican.org/item/745-natasha -trethewey-language-and-ruthlessness.

Solomon, Deborah. "Native Daughter." *New York Times Magazine*, May 13, 2007.

Wright, William. "Speak Against the Silences: An Interview with Natasha Trethewey." *Atlanta Review* 20 (Fall–Winter 2013): 11–17, 31.

Selected Criticism and Reviews

Birdsong, Destiny O. "Memories That Are(n't) Mine": Matrilineal Trauma and Defiant Reinscription in Natasha Trethewey's *Native Guard*." *African American Review* 48 (Spring/Summer 2015): 97–110.

Davis, Thadious M. "Enfoldments: Natasha Trethewey's Racial-Spatial Photo-texting." *Southern Quarterly* 50 (Summer 2013): 37–53.

George, Courtney. "Revisiting Place, the Memorial, and the Historical in Tom Piazza's Why New Orleans Matters and Natasha Trethewey's Beyond Katrina." In *After the Storm: The Cultural Politics of Hurricane Katrina*, ed. Simel Dicken and Evangelia Kindinger (New York: Columbia University Press, 2015), 113–30.

Goad, Jill. "Throwaway Bodies in the Poetry of Natasha Trethewey." *South: A Scholarly Journal* 48 (Spring 2016): 265–82.

Hall, Joan. "'I shirk not': Domestic Labor, Sex Work, and Warfare in the Poetry of Natasha Trethewey." *The Mississippi Quarterly* 62 (Winter 2009): 265–80.

———. "Guest Editor's Introduction: 'The Necessary Utterance': Natasha Trethewey's Southern Poetics." *Southern Quarterly* 50 (Summer 2013): 7–13, 22.

Henninger, Katherine. "What Remains: Race, Nation, and the Adult Child in the Poetry of Natasha Trethewey." *Southern Quarterly* 50 (Summer 2013): 55–74, 223.

Hopkins, Chandra Owenby. "The Robert A. Schanke Award-Winning Essay Whispers from a Silent Past: Inspiration and Memory in Natasha Trethewey's *Native Guard*." *Theatre History Studies* 35 (2016): 287–300.

Hoyt, Alex. "How Poet Laureate Natasha Trethewey Wrote Her Father's 'Elegy.'" *The Atlantic*, August 4, 2012; www.theatlantic.com/entertainment/archive /2012/08/how-poet-laureate-natasha-trethewey-wrote-her-fathers-elegy /261126/.

Hunter, Walt. "The No-Prospect Poem: Lyric Finality in Prynne, Awoonor, and Trethewey." *Minnesota Review* 85 (Fall 2015): 144–52.

Jones, Meta Duewa. "Reframing Exposure: Natasha Trethewey's Forms of Enclosure." *English Literary History* 82 (Summer 2015): 407–429.

Leahy, Anna. "Natasha Trethewey's White Lies." *The Explicator* 69 (July 2011): 113–16.

Logan, William. "Song & Dance." *New Criterion* 31 (December 2012): 69–76.

MacArthur, Marit J. "Monotony, the Churches of Poetry Reading, and Sound Studies." *PMLA: Publications of the Modern Language Association of America* 131 (January 2016): 38–63, 239.

McGrath, Charles. "New Laureate Looks Deep Into Memory." *New York Times*, June 6, 2012; www.nytimes.com/2012/06/07/books/natasha-trethewey-is -named-poet-laureate.html.

Millichap, Joseph R. "Photography and Southern Literature in a New Century." In *The Language of Vision: Photography and Southern Literature in the 1930s and After* (Baton Rouge: Louisiana State University Press, 2016), 114–32.

Ramsey, William M. "Terrance Hayes and Natasha Trethewey: Contemporary Black Chroniclers of the Imagined South." *The Southern Literary Journal* 44 (Spring 2012): 122–35.

Russell, Richard. "The Black and Green Atlantic: Violence, History, and Memory in Natasha Trethewey's 'South' and Seamus Heaney's 'North.'" *Southern Literary Journal* 46 (Spring 2014): 155–72, 225.

Turner, Daniel Cross. "Lyric Dissections: Rendering Blood Memory in Natasha Trethewey's and Yusef Komunyakaa's Poetry of the Black Diaspora." *Southern Quarterly* 50 (Summer 2013): 99–121.

Ward, Jerry W. Jr. "Beyond Katrina: A Meditation on the Mississippi Gulf Coast." *Southern Quarterly* 49 (Fall 2011): 128–33.

JEAN VALENTINE

POEMS

FROM *Dream Barker*

First Love

How deep we met in the sea, my love,
My double, my Siamese heart, my whiskery,
Fish-belly, glue-eyed prince, my dearest black nudge,
How flat and reflective my eye reflecting you
Blue, gorgeous in the weaving grasses
I wound round for your crown, how I loved your touch
On my fair, speckled breast, or was it my own turning;
How nobly you spilled yourself across my trembling
Darlings: or was that the pull of the moon,
It was all so dark, and you were green in my eye,
Green above and green below, all dark,
And not a living soul in the parish
Saw you go, hélas!
Gone your feathery nuzzle, or was it mine,
Gone your serpentine
Smile wherein I saw my maidenhood smile,
Gone, gone all your brackish shine,
Your hidden curl, your abandoned kill,
Aping the man, liebchen! my angel, my own!
How deep we met, how dark,
How wet! before the world began.

The Child and the Terrorist, The Terrorist and the Child

The globe's on fire in his hands
and everyone's asleep.

What will we feed him when he comes?
Just getting to know his step, his voice,

my step, a way back in the dark
to where I go without telling lies

or leaving anyone, will take a lifetime,
and it's going slowly,

                              and there's that blue-
white shell I turned my back on at my back,

cracked, stuck to me bone by bone,
turning to stone, wanting to drop,
wanting to turn in a cool globe,
wanting to call

—You, how is it with you?
Archaically cut off. Antarctic miles.

Pilgrims

Standing there they began to grow skins
dappled as trees, alone in the flare
of their own selves: the fire
died down in the open ground

and they made a place for themselves.
It wasn't much good,
they'd fall, and freeze,

some of them said
Well, it was all they could,

some said it was beautiful, some days,
the way the little ones took to the water,
and some lay smoking, smoking,

and some burned up for good,
and some waited,
lasting, staring
over each other's merciful shoulders,
listening:
        only high in a sudden January thaw
or safe a second in some unsmiling eyes
they'd known always

whispering
Why are we in this life.

Trust Me

Who did I write last night? leaning
over this yellow pad, here, inside,
making blue chicken tracks: two
sets of blue footprints, tracking out
on a yellow ground,
child's colors.

Who am I?
who want so much to move
like a fish through water,
through life . . .
                         Fish *like* to be
underwater.

Fish move through fish! Who
are you?

And Trust Me said, There's another way to go,
we'll go by the river which is frozen under the snow;

my shining, your shining life draws close, draws closer,
God fills us as a woman fills a pitcher.

The First Station

The first silver work of kindness,
my hand, your hand and your eye, and then the gold play
of watery car lights across the child's white quilt
was slept under and on top of, that February . . .

The rude walnut smell of the hibernation nest.
Sleeping I thought

If there was a hole through you
and a hole through me
they'd take the same
peg or needle
and thread us both
through the first station
and there we'd lean
and listen and listen . . .

The River at Wolf

Coming east we left the animals
pelican beaver osprey muskrat and snake
their hair and skin and feathers
their eyes in the dark: red and green.
Your finger drawing my mouth.

Blessed are they who remember
that what they now have they once longed for.

A day a year ago last summer
God filled me with himself, like gold, inside,
deeper inside than marrow.

This close to God this close to you:
walking into the river at Wolf with
the animals. The snake's
green skin, lit from inside. Our second life.

FROM *Growing Darkness, Growing Light*

World-light

Do well in the world.

If you do well
we'll throw you away.

We'll put you in the state asylum
like we did your grandfather.

(He did well then fell.)
("The drink." "But harmless.")
    But if you fall

we'll never say your name.
They'll think you're dead.

You will be one of the
Disappeared.

(We too, although we live
on a certain street, have certain jobs,

we too, we were
the Neverhere.)

Home

Breath entering, leaving the leaf,
the lion tense on the branch luxuriant,

the ten-foot drop to
the water-hole, the God-taste

—*that's* what lights it up,
Nature, and Art: your skin feather to feather
scale to scale to my skin

and the airy sleep, like wine . . .
two soft old children's books
with the red and blue and green crayons still warm on us.

FROM *The Cradle of the Real Life*

Little Map

The white pine

the deer coming closer

the ant
in my bowl
—where did she go
when I brushed her out?

The candle
—where does it go?

Our brush with each other
—two animal souls
without cave
image
or word

The Blue Dory, The Soul

But what about the blue dory—the soul

—*Thief the sun*   *Thief the rain*

Into love
the size of a silver dollar
[the soul] disappeared
to a pencil point then
nothing.
                Left
his nails
and his hair.

FROM *Break The Glass*

In prison

In prison
without being accused

or reach your family
or have a family   You have

conscience
heart trouble

asthma
manic-depressive

(we lost the baby)
no meds

no one
no window

black water
nail-scratched walls

your pure face turned away
embarrassed

you
who the earth was for.

Even all night long

Even all night long while
the night train

pulls me on in my dream
like a needle

Even then, down in my bed
my hand across the sheet

anyone's hand
my face anyone's face

are held
and kissed

the water
the child

the friend
unlost.

A Child's Drawing, 1941

A woman ladder leans
with her two-year-old boy in her arms.
Her arms & legs & hands & feet
are thin as crayons.

The man ladder
is holding his glass of bourbon,
he is coming out of the child's drawing
in his old open pajamas—

he's in the war. The sky
is blackest crayon-canyon.
When does he leave again? When he leaves,
I leave.   I like that river in the sky.

[The ship] is slowly giving up her sentient life. I cannot write about it.

> *I cannot write about it.*
>   SHACKLETON, diary

Next to where their ship went down
they pitched their linen tents.

You, mountain-climbing,
mountain-climbing,
wearing your dead father's flight jacket—

My scalp is alive,
love touched it. My eyes are open water. Yours too.

Sitting in the dark Baltimore bar
drinking Coke
with you with your inoperable cancer
with your meds

no tent
no care what we look like
what we say

Later that night, in my room
looking into the mirror, to tell the truth I was loved.
I looked right through into nothing.

Song

I was asking pardon, who am I?
Of them who I am: pardon.

Of the slow wearing down
of the window, the sun, I was asking forgiveness,

of the crocodile, that good hider,
of the heron, that good feeder,

& of Christ the pelican.
                              Christ said,

Over a thousand pages of Scripture,
& I was not reading, but dreaming.

It's the same right now, he said.
                              He just stood there.

I, I was not painting, but watching the animals.
I was not copying, but dreaming.

Over one thousand newborns in this clearing. We started
to lick them clean, dreaming, one by one.

Icebergs, Ilulissat

In blue-green air & water God
you have come back for us,
to our fiberglass boat.

You have come back for us, & I'm afraid.
Great sadness at harms.
But nothing now
can be like before.

Even when the icebergs are gone, and the millions of suns
have burnt themselves out of your arms,

your arms of burnt air.

POETICS STATEMENT

Excerpt from "An Interview with Jean Valentine" by Michael Klein

Alberta Turner said in her review of Home. Deep. Blue. in Field, that your new poems are in response to the threat of an empty universe. You've more defined, opened out in a way with that work, the questions you'd been asking all along. True?

In my first book, *Dream Barker*, I was paying attention to the form of poems and to language for its own sake—just delighting in language. I was very much influenced by my education by the male poets that I was reading at that time, although I had begun to read Bishop, and of course, Marianne Moore. But Bishop got to me more, and so did Adrienne Rich's earlier work, which was all she had written by that time!

Looking back, I see that I had the same preoccupations, but the book is written more in an apprentice sort of way—the way most poets' first books are. I was actually in an unhappy period of my life when I wrote the next two books and I was having more success as a poet but didn't really have the confidence in communicating that I have now.

When did that confidence reveal itself to you?

I think it began to change in *The Messenger*. Part of the reason, although I didn't know it at the time, was that I was drinking a lot less and began to turn outward more towards the world again, towards other people. For some years, and with the writing of two books I was in a lot of pain and my words were spoken to somebody, but it was hard for me to speak to lots of people. I see more openness in the poems, and I hope I can be more open than I am today. The poems before *The Messenger* are not less faithful poems, but I've turned more toward the everyday and towards the physical world. But I'm not the person to judge.

How were you able to actually write when you were in that pain?

Well, writing was my lifeline. It was one of the only ways I had of speaking and that was true, even as a child. Writing was like having an imaginary friend. There was the page I was speaking to, but it wasn't only the page; I was speaking to a person. I think speaking *means* you're speaking to somebody—to speak means there's somebody hearing you, whether it's God or an imaginary friend or a real friend, in the flesh. Being in pain didn't mean I wasn't speaking, but it certainly colored the way I spoke.

What about therapy and its effect on your writing, if any?

I remember having a therapist who said "write every day. Don't even take Christmas off." He thought that writing was my health. I used to be scared of the writers who went ahead of me—so many of them were alcoholic or mentally ill or suicidal. They were not a heartening model.

It must have affected how you thought of yourself as an artist; having made that choice in life.

I had a deep feeling, a deep fear, about being an artist, that it would lead me right off the edge of cliff into death, not just into alcoholism or mental illness, but that I wouldn't survive. And I had young children. Dr. Shea helped me enormously by telling me that writing was my health, that for artists, art was their health.

Isn't it more than just health?

I suppose it is. We were also talking earlier about how art is a gift from God, and I believe that. I don't believe God would give you a gift that's going to cost you your life, because that isn't God's business—death. That would be a puritanical nightmare, which I lived with for some years; that in order to write, I would have to die, or at any rate, suffer. I don't believe that anymore. Shea helped me a lot in the seventies to see that that wasn't true. Writing saved me.

Assuming art is a gift from God, do you see a connection between poetry and prayer?

I feel that all poetry is prayer, it's just as simple as that. Who else would we be talking to? I think the intensity in a poem may be because it's so prayerful—it's intense in the way that a song is, but in a way that prose isn't, and doesn't attempt to be. Plays sometimes are, though—like Beckett's plays, they're all prayers to me. They're just very moving prayers spoken by people walking across the stage. In his case, not very much walking across the stage!

What do dreams give your poems?

I feel more and more as if my poems are almost all from dreams, or written as if from dreams. I don't want to sound falsely modest or self-deprecating or say that I just write down what I dream—that's not true. The way another poet might write from an outward experience is the same way that I would write from a dream. Our dreams are universal; our emotional and spiritual life is universal. Because of that, it's just as much a communication, from one person to another, as if you were describing a landscape. This is where I think it's similar to what movies can do. Dreams are a connection to the movies because you see them in the dark.

Could you relate that to prose, if it does relate?

I think in poetry you are receiving information in a different way. Prose isn't less spiritual by any means, but poetry has a kind of intensity in *our* time. You can't sustain that kind of intensity throughout *Paradise Lost* or *The Iliad*. They have different intents. The cry of the heart of modern poetry, for the most part, is more like prayer. Prose, at its best, is more like the old narrative poems. You're going to learn history, and how people are with one another. I think we learn meanings from poetry. I like both poetry and prose, but I like poetry more. Prose makes another world, and I think it takes another gift. I wish I had them both, of course.

When you say "prose makes another world . . ." I was finishing that statement in my mind with ". . . out of the one we have." Could poetry be making another world out of the one we seek?

Maybe that's it. You know, this quote comes to my mind which may not be an answer, but it's a good joke. Mark Twain said, introducing Kipling to the reporters: "Mr. Kipling knows everything there is to know about this world, and I know all the rest." I sometimes think that the poets that I love are like Twain, they want to know all the rest. Maybe the prose writers do too. But I don't think that poets are that interested in recording things. I think they're interested in going through them, going through them like doors. Maybe it is to a world we're seeking, not a world we already know.

How much do you feel you have to give readers in order for them to understand what you are saying?

I think I do everything I can to be understood but after a point there's nothing more I can do. When I say to my students, "be clear, be clear, be clear," they say to me "you're asking something of us that you don't give to your own work." Well, that's one thing I can do as a reader, is say when I'm with you and when I'm not. But there's a point where you can't change a poem any more, or the poem becomes not itself anymore. There's nothing left, there's no poetry left. It just becomes an explanation or something.

Sometimes you can lose what was poetry, even if it wasn't explicable —and that is where I would hold out for mystery, where another person might say "to hell with it, I don't understand it." It's a very thin line for me because I don't have any liking at all for obscurity, but I do love mystery.

NOTE

From Michael Klein, "An Interview with Jean Valentine," *American Poetry Review* 20.4 (1991): 39–44.

SKIRTING HEAVEN

Jean Valentine's Late Dream-Work in *Shirt in Heaven*

Lisa Russ Spaar

> . . . I found two books: the Window and the Door.
> All I did was wait & sleep & write. *Please change. Please open.*
>
> Another hundred years,
> The Window opened me.
> The Door said, *More.*[1]

I.

Fifty years have passed between the publication of Jean Valentine's first book of poems, *Dream Barker* (1965), winner of the Yale Younger Poets Prize, and the appearance of her most recent collection of poems, *Shirt in*

Heaven, with Copper Canyon Press in 2015. In that half-century, Valentine has been widely lauded for her more than fifteen full-length collections and chapbooks of poetry, as well as for her work as a translator, essayist, and editor. Her many major awards include the National Book Award for Poetry (for *Door in the Mountain: New and Collected Poems, 1965–2003*), the Wallace Stevens Award of the Academy of American Poets, and a prize for exceptional literary achievement from the American Academy of Arts & Letters. She has served as the Poet Laureate of New York and taught at a number of universities, including Sarah Lawrence College, becoming a beloved teacher and mentor for generations of writers.

Yet despite this significant recognition, Valentine remains in many ways a "poet's poet," riding a bit below the radar with a small legion of loyal readers of all ages. Certainly her poems' dendritic, dream-fueled image systems, temporal vexations, pronominal slippage, and resonant thematic ambiguities may account for both their irresistible attraction and their perceived inaccessibility. "I'm always trying to hear the sound of the words, and trying to take out everything that doesn't feel alive," Valentine has said about her own poems. "That's my goal: to take out everything that doesn't feel alive. And also to get to a place that has some depth to it. Certainly I'm always working with things that I don't understand—with the unconscious, the invisible. And trying to find a way to translate it."[2] It is possible that Valentine's daring dedication to working with "what [she herself doesn't] understand"—with the difficult act of translating (and also of refusing to translate) "the unconscious, the invisible" dream-logic—is what perplexes some readers and fascinates others, challenging even the most articulate and astute of admirers. Often non-linear, eschewing the mechanics of plot, exposition, and expected rhetorical signatures in favor of physical observations and thought fragments that often feel as numinous as consciousness itself, her poetry might be easy to dismiss as slight, on the one hand, or hermetically remote on the other. As Philip Booth puts it in an essay on *The Messenger*, her poems are "so apparently transparent that it takes a most caring kind of close reading to honor their emotional and spiritual depth."[3]

The "transparency" Booth speaks of does not refer to the kind of "windexed" window that narrative, plain-speech poems offer into their subjects and plots. Rather, it refers to Valentine's atmospheric resistance to expected logical adherences, temporal sequences, and groundings in place, so that the reader, attracted by the dream ether of a given poem, might at the same time feel excluded, frustrated, or silenced by its ephemeral elusiveness. "Perhaps the reason there has been little critical discussion on the work of Jean Valentine should be obvious," writes Kazim Ali in *Jean Valentine: This-World Company* (2012), a collection of essays paying tribute to Valentine. "What do you say about work that traffics so sublimely in the half-said, the unsaid, more than that (or less than that?) the half-thought-of, the still unarticulated, ever evanescent?"[4] To make the partially under-stood or articulated one's primary subject is risky business for a poet; the writer dwelling too much in the oneiric hazards losing the earthbound reader, while a writer who grapples only with the physical and quotid-ian chances dullness. Adrienne Rich suggests that what makes Valentine unique is her ability to involve the reader in her vision. Anyone who works hard and is attentive enough to a Valentine poem becomes integral to its completion. "Looking into a Jean Valentine poem," Rich writes, "is like looking into a lake: you can see your own outline, and the shapes of the upper world, reflected among rocks, underwater life, glint of lost bottles, drifted leaves. The known and familiar become one with the mysterious and half-wild, at the place where consciousness and the subliminal meet. This is a poetry of the highest order, because it lets us into spaces and meanings we couldn't approach in any other way."[5]

In speaking of Valentine's work in terms of "halves" ("half-said," "half-thought-of," "half-wild"), both Ali and Rich touch the nerve—the source of Valentine's poems' power and beguilement—which resides, at least in part, in an attempt to speak the ineffable, to make manifest, despite the trappings of body and language, what Emily Dickinson called the "Cos-tumeless Consciousness"[6] that we associate with dreams and, by extrapo-lation, with any "reality" that feels inaccessible to intellection: emotion, subjectivity, heaven. In *Jean Valentine Abridged: writing a word, chang-ing it* (2011), C. D. Wright articulates the ambiguity of this Dickinsonian "Double Estate"[7] of body and mind: "When I read Jean Valentine's poems, I fill up with questions, spill over with emotion. I cease, in some way, to think. At least the din of thinking dies back. . . . A great silence is ante-rior to what gets said, so that what is said, must by necessity be put down, expressed."[8]

What Wright describes—a kind of spell-inspired, entranced writing, in which the "great silence" of the unconscious is mined for its "anterior" or prior ineffabilities, its nerve, its élan vital (a praxis which, in a Valentine's poem, the body has a significant share in translating)—might be a way to characterize Valentine's work in general. But it might also be said of Valentine's work that the body itself—balky, a nuisance, a source of plea-sure and ruin—is also plumbed in order to express "dream" states: truth, mystery, death, heaven. For reasons worth exploring, these paradoxes and their possibilities come into particular, scintillating, and arresting clarity in Valentine's late work, the work of her old age.

In addition to shedding light on Valentine's poetry, Adrienne Rich's ideas about the body in her groundbreaking book *Of Woman Born: Moth-erhood as Experience and Institution* (1976), can help further pin down Valentine's aesthetics:

Thinking is an active, fluid, expanding process; intellection, "knowing," are recapitulations of past processes. In arguing that we have by no means yet explored or understood our biological grounding, the miracle and paradox of the female body and its spiritual and political meanings, I am really asking whether women cannot begin, at last, to *think through the body* [my italics], to connect what has been so cruelly disorganized—our great mental capacities, hardly used; our highly developed tactile sense; our genius for close observation; our complicated, pain-enduring, multipleasured physicality.[9]

Perhaps Rich's distinction between *knowing* as a matter of "recapitulation," of stasis, and *thinking* as a process, animated and restive, provides a key to understanding Valentine's work, particularly as it has evolved over time. Never particularly interested in answers, in solving for X, so to speak, Valentine has been more engrossed in a restless shuttling among and around the perimeters of the realms of dream and waking in an often vexed, tense, nervy negotiation of mind and body. Alan Williamson, remembering Robert Lowell's appreciation for Valentine's early poems in *Pilgrims*, which Valentine was composing when she sat in on Lowell's infamous "secret" office hours at Harvard in the sixties, writes that "on one occasion [Lowell] compared [Valentine's poems] to Plath's *Ariel*. One could see why; though less tough (in both senses, resilient and aggressive), they had the same perfectly attuned ear to how the world impinged on one nerve-strung sensibility."[10] Williamson is not speaking so much here about *nervosa* (though Valentine is open, in interviews, about her bouts with depression, alcoholism, therapy, and one five-year hiatus in the 1980s when she did not write)[11]; instead, he's talking about her very particular ability to inhabit bodily and mental space in a uniquely vital way: "only Jean Valentine's [poems]," Williamson writes, "aside from Lowell's own, put me back inside [their subjects'] *nerves*."[12]

What the poems in Valentine's most recent collection, *Shirt in Heaven*, reveal—as they grapple forthrightly with their speaker's aging body and her attempts to engage with and "hold" onto an ever-growing host of loved ones lost to time and death—is that more than attempting to "think *through* the body," as Rich admonishes, Valentine's work has been about how to think, intuit, or know anything *without* a body—or, perhaps more to the point, with how to acknowledge the body's share *at all* when we are confronting our most raw, un-costumed feelings, the sort of grief or anguish or loss that might create a sense of ex-stasis, of being beside or without a body. These extremes become italicized the closer we draw to the deaths of our parents, our partners, our friends, ourselves. The sick and dying body is both receding and aggressively progressing in relation to whatever unfathomability lies beyond this mortal coil, and as her recent poems confront this fact, Valentine's at times uneasy relationship with the bodily and the mysterious comes into striking focus.

A brief look at two exemplary poems, one from Valentine's early years as a poet and one from her mid-career—"Woods" from *Pilgrims* (1969) and "At the door" from *The River at Wolf* (1992)—helps to trace Valentine's evolving struggle with the body/mind, physical/spiritual conundrum, an endeavor at first primarily erotic and then increasingly spiritual in its exploration of what it means to inhabit a human body flooded with God-hunger and incorporeal longings. As I shall show, the exigencies and inexorabilities of old age, in which the body, approaching the end of life, is italicized in a way that differs from the body in the flush of youth and middle age, adds a new dimension to Valentine's dream/waking, body/being dance. Kazim Ali writes that "with each passing year, [Jean Valentine] seems more and more the poet of exactly our moment—one concerned with material immediacy, the physical experiences of the body, and the uncharted ineffable realms equally."[13] As twenty-first-century "realities" become more vexed and virtual, there is much to be learned from a poetry that is both cerebral and embodied, that avoids high volume rhetoric in favor of a concentrated listening, and which confronts the paradox, risk, and consequences of living either too much or too little in any one claustral realm of extremity.

This recalibrating of extremes, apparent in *Shirt in Heaven*, warrants close attention, not only for the book's intrinsic record of the inner life of a poet in late career, but for the ways in which its project suggests—through poems of surprising directness—that Valentine's life-long "dream-work" has always represented a dedication, however unsettled, to the body as the most important source of knowledge and truth. In their relative boldness, these new poems suggest, by contrast, that thinking through, or out of, or in spite of the body is something Valentine has been presciently engaged with skirting and revealing—in strikingly different ways—from the very beginning of her career.

II.

Born in 1934, Valentine's long, prolific career affords readers of poetry the privilege of witnessing the evolution of a unique talent over time. As the title of her first book, *Dream Barker*, suggests, Valentine has been tapping into oneiric, "unconscious, invisible" territory from the very beginning. "I dreamed you and he / Sat under a tree being interviewed," she writes in "Sasha and the Poet."[14] The titles themselves reflect her obsession —"The Second Dream," for instance, and, of course, "Dream Barker." Valentine's more traditional side is demonstrated in "To My Soul," a whimsical, highly formal poem from *Dream Barker* that riffs on her own name in the lines "Scattered milkweed, valentine, / Moonlighting darling, leonine," and closes with:

Hypnotizing, gemmy toad,
My generation's cameo,

Symplegadês of every road,
Closet bones, unflowered sod,
Laugh, my little nuncio! (*DM* 72)

While strictly adhering to rhyme and meter, even in this early work, Valentine quickly moves into what have remained characteristic stylistic moves: inverted, splintered, or interrupted syntax, elliptical and figurative bodily suggestiveness, and an intensity of attention both lapidary and fluid. The "thinking" in these early poems is often gestural and sexual, as in the nervy, winter-threaded imperative eroticism and immediacy of "Woods," from *Pilgrims*:

Dearest darling woodenhead
I love you

I can taste you
in bed laughing (*DM* 80)

From the outset, the poem arrests the reader with an apostrophic, almost voyeuristic glimpse into a scene of playful intimacy that is at once lucidly direct ("I love you"), mysteriously figurative ("woodenhead"), and synesthetic ("I can taste you / in bed laughing"). The setting is decidedly located ("in bed") but also dreamy in its sensory flux. As Valentine's speaker presses on, imperatives ("come" and "feel"—and then, later, "Look" and "Wait") and interrogatives ("feel me . . . ?") follow the opening apostrophic exclamation, and all of this moves into almost dithyrambic invocation.

The speaker argues that even the world is softening, its wooden-headed trees "ready to fuzz"—and in this manner pitches her woo:

come Teach I love your
hair

Penseroso,
crab, you angel!

feel me on the palm of your hand?

Look

all the thin trees
are hanging this morning ready to fuzz,

high birds I can't see are whistling,
winter's dripping down

faster and faster and
faster. And not to death.

Wait.

The thought, the dream, the "heaven" this speaker is skirting and flirting with the edges of is, of course, sexual fulfillment. What is exciting about this early poem—in its own way a blason—is the means by which it shows us its "invisible" subject not by announcing it but by dancing all around it, displacing into brushstroke details of the thawing winter world and enacting through quick jumps in perspective the speaker's own amorous designs. Valentine's slippage among rhetorical modes (declarative, interrogative, exclamatory) and her cinematic agility distorting space and time give the poem a breathless urgency. In a way, reading an early Jean Valentine poem is a lot like listening to music, specifically to the improvisatory riffing of jazz. It requires close listening to hear, for example, how a particular theme or "melody" might be subverted and recomposed through tangential soloing, changes of key, or shout-out quotations as a given poem proceeds. Her resonant syntactic fluidity, as in the line "come Teach I love your / hair," where "Teach" reads as both imperative and nickname, her whimsical allusiveness (the speaker calls her lover "Penseroso," evoking Milton's *Il Penseroso*, "The Serious Man," trapped by melancholia in his own head), and her fleet leaps between contraries (the speaker follows "Penseroso" with seemingly contradictory appositives, in the agitated way of lovers: "crab, you angel!") all conspire to create a poem of mental persuasiveness ("penseroso" < pensive, OF "think", L "ponder") and bodily, specifically sexual, urgency: "winter's dripping down ," she closes, "faster and faster and / faster. And not to death. // Wait."

The command to listen at the close of this poem, to attend to silence, reflects Valentine's move not only into a poetry of compression, proximal attention, and strange, wondrous soundings that are both interior and exterior, but to a "thinking through the body" in poetic ruses that create a text both bodily and mysterious at once, as though listening at nerve's end for consciousness and the body, word and world, to exchange their secrets, even if those secrets must be delayed or cannot be "worded." The speaker's jumpy restlessness suggests a disquiet about the body, to which she attends synesthetically and by displacing sentience into the natural world—so that the incipient budding of trees or whistling birds embody the speaker's sexual desire. Afraid to look for too long or too closely at any one thing, this poem exemplifies Valentine's early engagement with somatic intellection, a frisson so charged that, after skirting it, she forces herself to stop. That final "wait" is directed as much to the speaker as it is to her lover.

In his essay on *The Messenger*, a book that might be said to mark Valentine's move to mid-career, Booth suggests: "Jean Valentine's poems understand tragedy, loneliness, uncertainty, as given; the joy of her work lives in how she turns to transcend anguish by writing not merely 'out of' tragedy but (in a Freudian sense) *through* it."[15] The erotic skittishness and playfulness of the mind/body dance in the early work is, in the work of Valentine's middle period, replaced by poems that confront with more physicality and duration the difficulties posed by mortality and the loss of love. As intimated above, however, this is often less a matter of thinking "through" the body but rather of wondering what role the body can possibly play in contemplating the roil created by big questions in the inner life. The complexity (the difficulty, the depth) of the poems Valentine writes in the thirteen or so years between *Messenger* (1979) and *The River at Wolf* (1992) is something different from, say, the heavily damasked linguistic obscurity of Hopkins or the cryptic metonymies of Dickinson. In these poems of middle age, the difficulty comes from the at once oneiric and bodily terror of the biggest questions. In "Sanctuary" (from *The Messenger*), she writes: "What do you dread? / What happens when you die?" (*DM* 148). Is shelter possible for the unsheathed nerves of the bereaved, the survivors of all manner of losses: marital, parental, literary, sexual, historical, spiritual? Is it possible to know God? to hope? to heal?

Valentine's sensory and emotional preoccupations in this period move —as children age, loves end, and parents die—from the predominantly erotic to the increasingly elegiac, and are more and more charted (and enlarged) with spiritual questing and questions. They move, tentatively, toward something akin to Keats's "negative capability": "I have begun, so late," she writes in "Lines from a Story," "to trust what I love!" (*DM* 159). One result is that the poems from this time begin to feel like epistolary prayers, always leaning in from anguish or pain—quietly electric—to heed from a distance what the closely attended-to silence might, *or might not*, speak in return. "Not to invade," she writes in "Actuarial File," but to "Wait, here in the quiet" (*DM* 157).

A mid-career example of Valentine's non-invasive skirting of and delving into each poem's particular "alive," as she puts it, is the poem "At the door" from *The River at Wolf* (*DM* 212–13). Doors and windows provide, for Valentine, liminal portals of possibility, where the interior and exterior can provocatively mingle, the physical and the emotional/spiritual cross back and forth across a membrane. The poem opens with the speaker outside of a house, looking in:

> Seeing my daughter in the circle of lamplight,
> I outside:

> It is not *I*,
> It is *Mother*.
> (But it is *I*.)

Almost immediately, the poem deepens from physical observation (seeing with the eye) into metaphysical musing on the constructed, myriad self (the "I"). The effects of Valentine's movement from outside to in, inside to out, from the personal to the un-gendered pronoun in any one moment, and her mix of sensory perception and dialectic argument, are disorientingly compelling; the text feels both physically located and philosophically fugal. The poem takes an even deeper plunge in the next stanza:

> It is the first tableau, the first
> red wellspring of *I*.

So much thinking and feeling happens in these two lines. "Tableau" evokes Madonna-and-Child and Pietà, alike. Even as the reader takes in this conflation of birth and death, the phrase "red wellspring" suggests that the circle of lamplight holding the daughter inside the house is both womb, blooded by birth, and tomb. The poem ends with fierce, talismanic force:

> Chimpanzee of longing,
> outside the light,
>
> wrap your long arms
> around the globe of light,
> hold your long haunches
> wide open: be
> ungodly I.

"Chimpanzee of longing" is a brilliant example of Valentine's particular mind-body frisson. On the one hand, the image is charged with an awareness of our humanimal evolution. This pan-species thinking through or beyond the human body is evident in the earlier poem, "Woods," as well, in which the lover and speaker are conjured in images inseparable from the flora and fauna around them. But the genitive link metaphor in "At the door" suggests that longing has primal origins that extend back, forward, and across species, time, and place. And of course in this prayer/ petition, the speaker, watching from "outside the light" (skirting heaven, as it were) is *herself* the "chimpanzee of longing," wrapping her long arms of wished-for protection "around the globe of light"—around the daughter, perceived in an instance of birth and death. In what is perhaps the poem's boldest move, the haunches of yearning open as well, and the "chimpanzee of longing" merges with the "daughter in the circle of lamplight" in the inimitable, "wide open" and humbly "ungodly" site that is the creation of the poem itself.

In this poem, and others from this period, Valentine continues to write out of both body and dream, keeping "alive" a slightly unsettled relationship to both sources of gnosis. The "eye"/"I" interdependency is confronted, however, in poems like "At the door" with an intensifying—if still inchoate or tentative—sense of poetic agency, the promise of which finds raw clarity, even radiance, in the later poems to come.

III.

The lyric poems Valentine writes in her sixties, seventies, and, with *Shirt in Heaven*, into her eighties, are suffused with a new equipoise and tensility, hard-won by her ongoing, daring, open-minded working through the neural mesh, the ligatures, tendons, and sinews of oneiric liminality—where image and thought, dark and light, dream and waking permit one another to deepen and speak—and by her tipsy balancing in the "cradle" that hangs, as Nabokov writes in *Speak, Memory*, over the abyss.[16] In an interview for Poetry Society of America, Valentine responds to interviewer Eve Grubin's remark that "[w]ith each book your poems seem more overtly spiritual," by saying, "It's because I'm getting older. I am going towards the spiritual rather than away from it."[17] And if Valentine has evolved into one of the most important living North American "spiritual" poets, she is spiritual in the way that Dickinson was religious, eschewing oversimplification and binaries in favor of a searching, analogic, and—to return to Rich —"multipleasured" acuity of perception and openness to the unknowable. As with Dickinson, in Valentine's late work there is always the float, in any one poem, of Eros, Thanatos, God-Hunger, and Poetry itself. It is impossible to talk about any one of these without the others.

In an essay concerning Valentine's unique manner of embodying consciousness, "'This Close to God this Close to You': Incarnation in Jean Valentine," Amy Newman writes about how Valentine's poems "attend to the unfinished, the layered, and the wandering . . . the openness and the division . . . [and to how] these divisions are implied [by] imperceptible attachments—invisible lines, like radio signals between the entities."[18] Newman's paradigm for understanding as invisible sight-lines or radio-signals what might be called Valentine's skittering or shuttling among perceptions physical and oneiric provides a useful way into just what has changed in Valentine's mind/body, dream/waking, "thinking through the body" nexus over time. Perhaps because Valentine is "going towards the spiritual" as she ages (and these poems are more and more full of illnesses—AIDS, alcoholism, anorexia, cancer—deaths, nostalgia, and what Charles Wright calls, in "A Journal of English Days," the "homesickness / When what you are sick for has never been seen or heard / In this world or even remembered"),[19] Valentine is more and more willing to refuse complete "translation" of dream to body, and vice versa, but rather to allow the sight-lines of what Newman calls her "gaps, stops, half-utterances, and . . . gestures toward separations, breaches, interims, limits" to emphasize these connections even as she maintains their mystery.[20]

The title *Shirt in Heaven* is itself a brief, koan-like meta-poem, which places, without editorial comment, a costume of the body (perhaps the shirt of a lost loved one, still redolent with the bodily fragrance of the physical world) right into the dream-context of the afterlife, the ether, the unfathomable, the unreachable prior or beyond. We see this image of a shirt in heaven, this "un-translation" of two seemingly incongruous worlds, writ large in nearly all of the poems in the collection. For Valentine, the distinction between dream and waking has always been fluid, but in *Shirt in Heaven* it is almost impossible, and unnecessary, to tell the worlds apart, particularly as Valentine's speakers lose to the Big Sleep what every night's little sleep portends. "I'm going to sleep now," she writes in "I'm going to sleep," "in case you visit my dream" (*SH* 38). In "You're gone," she writes, "You're gone in the daytime, but you're still here at night" (*SH* 42).

In "Bardo," (*SH* 18), for example, the speaker begins with something concrete, something she sees (or thinks she sees), in this case a possibly homeless person on the street:

> You were picking through a trash bag,
> taller than you.
> Taking out anything worth something.
>
> Our eyes met. I thought
> What keeps us here? Two-legged?
> You looked right through me.

These opening stanzas are electric with the sight-lines, the invisible radio signals, Newman speaks of, currents coursing between the bodily, the not-embodied. Valentine sets up a specular moment ("Our eyes met"), which she then subverts ("You looked right through me"). Neither the expected Valentine portal connection nor the peripheral, watch-and-wait skirting happens. The moment is not "translated." In an earlier poem, "At the door," for example, Valentine might attempt to "translate" the world of inside and out, dream and waking, even if that translation comes in the form of an admonition to stop, circle, and wait (as in her use of the neologism "woodenhead" in the early poem "Woods") or to displace longing into another entity (as in the "Chimpanzee of longing"). In "Bardo," by keeping the peripheral details unspecific ("anything," "something"), Valentine makes central her question: "What keeps us here? Two-legged?" The word "bardo," Tibetan for "intermediate space" or "liminal space," refers, in Buddhism, to the state between death and a being's next incarnation, and the speaker in the poem responds to this destabilizing moment of sensory doubt by recalling what the practice of Zen has taught her about the "now" and about how, paradoxically, to *exist* in a moment in which human existence is interrogated or even obliterated:

> My teacher says, just say to yourself,
> Something will happen.
> Something happen.
>
> I could take off my clothes
> and leave them on the ground,
> I could walk off into the snow
>
> out of human sight, out of
> all the northern evening's gold brocade.

As the speaker turns her teacher's advice ("say to yourself, / Something will happen") into a wish/command ("Something happen"), the dream-poem yields up a conditional re-imagining/inversion of the notion of "shirt in heaven," in which the narrator sheds her own garments and steps, mendicant and naked, off and away, still two-legged, but perhaps not for long, into "the snow / out of human sight"—into whatever heaven, paradise, nirvana, nada, purgatory, or other incarnation awaits. Who or what is walking at this point? And who is watching? Again, without editorializing or translating the gesture, Valentine raises a large question—is "heaven" (dream, emotion) an ulterior, unreal, abstract concept only suggestible by its absence? Or is heaven actually this earth itself, and the costumes of our bodies, including achievements, relationships, soma, poems, things we paradoxically shed there in order to die into, to enter new embodiments? Valentine doesn't feel compelled to annotate the zigzag "map" created by these movements toward and away from the body, toward and away from heaven. She doesn't feel the need to answer her questions; she lets them hang there. But by ending her poem with the richly damasked phrase "all the northern evening's gold brocade," the speaker suggests that any consciousness of the mystery of what is "out of human sight" is always going to come, for her, in part, from her body's attachment to the costume, the fabric, the brocade, of sensory perception and its possibilities, including the proxy embodiment of poetry.

A related engine of the poems in *Shirt in Heaven* is desire in old age, the desire of the aging body that has lost loves to death but which is not yet done with love. Valentine explores this late-life yearning in "*[The ship] is slowly giving up her sentient life. / I cannot write about it.*" (*SH* 31), which takes for its title a phrase from the diary of Arctic explorer Ernest Shackleton, before dilating into a personal memory that could be real or dreamed:

Next to where their ship went down
they pitched their linen tents.

You, mountain-climbing,
mountain-climbing,
wearing your dead father's flight jacket—

Valentine starts this poem with a screen memory of sorts, a depiction of the historical demise of Ernest Shackleton's doomed ship, which veils, briefly, the real subject of the poem: two aging friends who meet when one of them is sick, when each is so nakedly real and present to the other that vanity falls away, making room for erotic reciprocity and, more important, the kind of brave self-love that allows a person to gaze into a mirror and look "right through into nothing"—another kind of thinking through the undenied and dying body.

My scalp is alive,
love touched it. My eyes are open water. Yours too.

Sitting in the dark Baltimore bar
drinking Coke
with you with your inoperable cancer
with your meds

no tent
no care what we look like
what we say

Later that night, in my room
looking into the mirror, to tell the truth I was loved.
I looked right through into nothing.

The poem is replete with exchanges that blur worlds between the tented/jacketed realm of the living/waking and the inoperable nothing/nakedness of the dreamer, the dead. The former lover, "you," comes, implausibly, "mountain-climbing" up into the opening scene of Shackleton's shipwrecked men, tents pitched beside the dying ship. He is "wearing [his] dead father's flight jacket," a detail that merges past and present, the real and imagined. Valentine shifts from these external observations to her speaker's own perceived, proximate, physical sensations, writing, "My scalp is alive, / love touched it," an image that then takes another dreamlike, cross-phenomenal tack: "My eyes are open water. Yours too," a trope which stereoscopically evokes both real-time tears of reunion and the wild, open wintry waters of the scene of destruction that opens the poem. Age, time, and illness have brought these two old friends into new territory. The poem closes with another subverted specular moment—"Later that night, in my room / looking into the mirror, to tell the truth I was loved. /

I looked right through into nothing." It is in exchanges like these, which occur throughout *Shirt in Heaven*, that sentience—feeling, bodily intelligence, the capacity to see, weep, have sex, break out in gooseflesh—makes credible the otherwise inaccessible ("I cannot write about it") and impossible to articulate mysteries: love, death, loss, beauty, truth.

In Valentine's earlier work, notions of "heaven"—among them dream, paradise, fulfillment, nothingness, and all the big "invisibilities," such as truth, love, god—have tended to be skirted around and "defined," if at all, through physical indirection, suggestion, displacement, and projection. As suggested earlier, the effect is often one of being washed over by a piece of music whose "head," or melody, is elusive. Something that the French critic André Hodier said about saxophonist Charlie Parker's method of soloing is illuminating here: "[Whereas] Louis [Armstrong] transfigures the original melody by subtly distorting it rhythmically and by adding some extra figures, Bird encloses it and leaves it merely implied in a musical context that is sometimes fairly complex. . . . [and] it can only be guessed at behind the garland of notes in which it is embedded and which, far from being useless embroidery, form by themselves a perfectly articulated musical discourse of which the theme, hidden or expressed, is merely one of the constituent elements."[21] The poems in *Shirt in Heaven* evince a willingness not only to wait, watch, listen, and "think," *around* what lies beyond the "gold brocade" of the physical body, but instead to walk right out of it, or to look right into and through it. Whereas in earlier poems, a dream memory might jump-start a poem into a skitter of displaced or gestural bodily awareness or experience, in these late poems, the foibles and vulnerabilities of the aging body propel us the other way across the threshold. They permit the gaze into the dream, into the unconscious, into "nothing." The body's (the eye/I's) direct gaze into nothingness is also a direct look into the otherwise unknowable reader as well, implicating the reader in a very visceral way in the experience of the poem; rather than feeling outside Valentine's vision, warily, even admiringly watching with her from the umbral margins, the reader is allowed access into the gnawing gnosis of the poem and is in fact essential to its (in)completion. The "heaven" Valentine has often skirted is in fact, inside our own shirts. It is within us.

As "Bardo" and the Shackleton poem attest, writing out of the aging body has made Valentine particularly sensitive to all manner of obliteration and erasure. To return to Kazim Ali's suggestion that Valentine is more than ever a poet for our imperiled moment, it may be Valentine's ability not just to embroider and encircle and imply what can't be said or recovered or intellectually known, but to gaze directly into extinction ("extinction" in its fullest array of meanings), that marks her late work as especially relevant. For Valentine, the engine of this bodily thinking is largely personal, but her experience of it expands, empathically, into a fuller spectrum of the populous, human and not human. By resisting distinctions between body/mind and waking/dream with more authority, Valentine has also become with age more political.

A late poem from *Shirt in Heaven*, "You rope that pulls them where they do not go" (*SH* 22), is concerned with personal experiences of erasure and border-crossing, and this allies it radically with pressing political issues. The poem opens onto a world awry, an apocalyptic spectacle of crisis and attempted rescue, dealt out with the fragmentary, mythic clarity of trauma:

> horse running sideways
> on only water
>
> no school   no teacher   fire
> made out of fire
> poison houses
>
> children in a rough line
> holding onto a rope
>
> a man with a cell phone pulling the rope
> the reception breaking up

Things are not moving how or as they should; even the terrified animal, a horse, is "sideways" on untrustworthy footing. All structures of shelter (school, teacher, houses) are negated by an excoriating, toxic "fire / made out of fire," and any hope for the children, holding on to life's "rough line" resides with one man whose portal of communication is "breaking up."

There is no "I," no "you," in this passage, which makes the reader both anxious witness and panicked participant. Typical of Valentine's work in *Shirt in Heaven*, this vividly rendered but untranslated and unannotated moment of terror could be pure dream or pure fact; it could be a threatening domestic scenario or a scene from a war zone. That the distinction does not matter is part of this poem's significant power. Despite the cell phone and the suggestion of electronic "reception," the poem is ghosted by the attempted flights of imperiled innocents and refugees across centuries of time and space: past, present, and future, at once.

In the second half of the poem, Valentine's tone and mode shift. In the manner of a sonnet crown, she begins part two with the "man" who ends part one, explaining to herself, the reader, the children, perhaps even to the "you" (the rope) mentioned in the title, that whatever move he began in part one (toward rescue? obliteration? sacrifice? death?) necessitated a leaving behind of not only the precious things of life and culture ("books") but even the cycles of earth-bound life itself. And into the conversation, now, come persons, pronouns: the "I" and the "you" that are missing from part one:

> The man had to leave the books behind
> Leave night behind   I know you don't use words there
>
> sleepwalking a word-scrap   Day-walking my Redeem'
>
> I'm lifting something very light   a blanket
> Outside the window you're lifting something very heavy
>
> Pat the rope then
> chew the rope apart
>
> I know you don't have teeth there
> I know you don't have hands there

The identity of the "you" in this passage is resolutely ambiguous. On the one hand, it could be "the man" from part one, who is now on the other side of life and the scene of destruction in which he may have failed to rescue the children clinging to the rope. The title of the poem suggests that we at least entertain that the "you" is the "rope" itself that pulls "them" (the children, those requiring rescue, redemption)—a "you" who is a god or god-like entity. Again, less important than pinning a single reading of the identity of these players is noting the speaker's urging to surrender to what has happened. The rope here resembles images we've seen in other Valentine poems—sight-lines, doorways, thresholds, umbilici. It transforms from an agent of possible escape in part one to a vestige of a transaction (a failed rescue?) in part two. The only way to escape the "heavy," burdened limbo purgatory of word-scrap "sleepwalking" and abbreviated redemption ("Redeem'") is to sever the rope. To "Let be," as Hamlet would say. The assertive agency of the speaker here is something different from the waiting and tentative watching from the shadows in earlier poems. The speaker urges tenderness toward the rope ("pat the rope then") but is also primally, ruthlessly imperative ("chew the rope apart"). Perhaps the most moving part of the poem occurs in the final couplet, where the speaker acknowledges that the "you" (whether departed human or divine being), who is no longer embodied and who is, perhaps, in heaven, possesses neither teeth nor hands with which to do the severing. That action falls to her, on this side—a survivor carrying the "very light" blanket of language, and who is depicted in the act of convincing herself that, for now, this severing is something she must do herself in order to honor the incendiary chaos and losses of part one. By conflating images of birth (cutting the umbilicus) with suggestions of failed life-lines, of losses personal, cultural, and global, Valentine emerges as a poet working simultaneously at the very height of awareness and responsibility while also at the very limits of the human body. This is "thinking through the body" at its most urgent and extreme and, wherever the rope was meant to go (or should have gone) with its precious load, it must, for now, be embodied in the surrogate that is language, Valentine's poem itself, in which her notions of dreaming and waking allow for a vision blurring and binding inextricably both personal and political exile, obliteration, responsibility, and tenderness.

"Icebergs, Ilulissat," the poem that closes *Shirt in Heaven*, is an elegy for a "future-present" global scenario that is at once dire and strangely beautiful:

> In blue-green air & water God
> you have come back for us,
> to our fiberglass boat.
>
> You have come back for us, & I am afraid.
> Great sadness at harms.
> But nothing now
> can be like before.
>
> Even when the icebergs are gone, and the millions of suns
> have burnt themselves out of your arms,
>
> your arms of burnt air. (*SH* 65)

As with many Valentine poems in *Shirt in Heaven*, this final poem has a location both real and fabular, in this case Ilulissat, a town in western Greenland, some 200 miles north of the Arctic Circle, and at the same time a place both anterior and future ("In blue-green air & water God / you have come back for us"). The "self," the speaker in the poem, is both singular and plural ("I" and "us"), which suggests a culpability both individual and collective. The speaker, addressing God, is "afraid" and sad about "harms." God evokes here "the man" in "You rope that pulls them where they do not go." Deliberately ambiguous, the damage referred to in "Icebergs" could be something for which the speaker and her cohort are responsible, or the language may reflect a fear of retribution, or both. In any case, the change wrought by these harms is acknowledged as irreparable ("nothing now / can be like before").

The penultimate stanza makes clear that these harms and fears relate to the environment, the destruction of which has caused permanent change not just for the stranded and returned-for human denizens. (And returned-for why? in a moment of rescue, of second-coming, of rapture? or in an act of divine intervention/revenge?) God, Valentine implies, will also be changed, "[e]ven when the icebergs are gone, and the millions of suns / have burnt themselves out of your arms," the "arms" of the unknowable/ unnamable force of the universe will remain open. But open to what? Again, note the reversals here—it is not the speaker's own "ungodly" embodied arms opened talismanically, as in "At the door," but rather "godly," un-bodied arms that open to the burnt perfume of the once corporeal, now unpeopled earth.

Shirt in Heaven is a book of wakings. "I woke up," she writes in "Both you & he" (*SH* 36). Or "when I woke up" ("The Window," *SH* 51). Sometimes what the speaker wakes to *is* a dream, or might as well be one, as in "you came in a dream yesterday" ("Friend," *SH* 55) or "I was not copying, but dreaming" ("Song," *SH* 64). More than in any of Valentine's other books, the distinction matters little. In these poems of old age, Valentine brings into fresh clarity the interdependence of both worlds. In "The Window," she writes:

> . . . When I woke up
> my clothes were covered with writing,
> my hair was sentences, full of twigs,
>
> Lines ran between my fingers.
> Open, Window, Look, it's
> time to fly now.
>
> The owl looked back to me a minute
> from the sill: stiff feathers stood
> around his eyes: his book. (*SH* 51)

These stanzas imply that the dream world may have been, after all, the "real" world—the realm of twigs and sentences and writing—and that the world of waking is the fugal world of spirit, flight, and animal beyonding. In the rhyme of "look" and "book" we see the achievement of *Shirt in Heaven*. Valentine's poems have always been visionary, involving close bodily perception and inward dream-gazing. The word "mysticism," after all, derives from the Greek *muein*, "to close the eyes," a practiced, deliberate blindness effected to better focus on the spiritual experiences of the inner "I" and on the unfathomable beyond. The liminal, portal economies of the exchanges between dream and waking have taken many forms in Valentine's poems, but in her late work the movements have been concerned less with a shuttling back and forth across the asleep/awake threshold, or with embroidering the periphery of bodily and dream-fueled suggestions, and more with a generous motion out—into what both depends upon and is beyond either somatic or mental intelligences: that is, with the "afterlife" of creation, the poem itself. What is a poem, after all, if not a "shirt in heaven"?

Dream-work, then—from her first book, *Dream Barker*, through her most recent poems—is soul-work for Valentine. It constitutes the central nervous system of her oeuvre. How dream without a body? How be in a body and not dream? Working that threshold territory, in which imagination, emotion, thought, and the material facts of the physical world conspire, has been for Valentine a life-long engagement. Her late work reveals that Valentine has long used dreams to understand human yearning, and acknowledges more and more the ways in which the body, particularly the aging body, awakens us to new freedoms, new realms of consciousness, surrender, understanding, revelation, and agency that are related to poem-making itself. The transom across which many of her poems have worked their liminal body/mind magic ("I found two books: the Window and the Door") has, in late life, demanded something further: "The Window opened me. / The Door said, More" (from "Could it be heat?" in *SH* 47).[22]

Writing for the July 2015 issue of *The American Poetry Review*, Anne Marie Macari says that "the lyric impulse [of Jean Valentine and others] crosses, even erases, boundaries, [and] connects us to the other and to other worlds, helping us enter the ineffable, to let go briefly our false sense of dominion or safety. The lyric brings us into the moment, brings us to the place of—*Let it*—."[23] The body doesn't just allow us to "skirt" the big unfathomabilities, defining them by their absence; the body *is* the heaven in which we take off the garments, the trappings, of what we make of our lives—our sensations, our words—in order to step away from them into new ways of thinking and knowing. The significance both of what has been and of what will be, finally, lost could not be more humanly felt, on every level—intellectual, emotional, bodily, aesthetically—than in Valentine's final somatic image of "Icebergs, Ilulissat," with its sillage of an entire planet, and in Valentine's inimitable vision of the lyric poem itself, her "shirt in heaven": the courage, the nerve, of its singing, singed embrace.

NOTES

1. Jean Valentine, "Could it be heat?" from *Shirt in Heaven* (Port Townsend, WA: Copper Canyon, 2015), 47. *Shirt in Heaven* hereafter cited in the text as *SH* followed by the page number.

2. Poetry Society of America, www.poets.org/poetsorg/poet/jean-valentine.

3. Philip Booth, "On Jean Valentine's *The Messenger*," in *This-World Company*, eds. Kazim Ali and John Hoppenthaler (Ann Arbor: The University of Michigan Press, 2012), 63. *This-World Company* hereafter cited in the text and endnotes as *TWC* followed by the page number.

4. Ali, *TWC*, 1. This collection of essays helps to trace Valentine's trajectory and goes a long way to remedy the dearth of Valentine criticism; it includes pieces by such discerning readers as Brenda Hillman, Mark Doty, Brian Teare, Amy Newman, and Dorothy Barresi, engaging with Valentine's individual collections as well as with her thematic and formal issues, among them dreams, mythology, mysticism, politics, compression, gender, religion, and desire.

5. http://alicejamesbooks.org/ajb-titles/the-river-at-wolf/.

6. Emily Dickinson, *The Poems of Emily Dickinson: Reading Edition*, ed. R. W. Franklin (Cambridge: The Belknap Press of Harvard University Press, 1998), Fr 1486, 558.

7. Dickinson, Fr 1050, 429.

8. C. D. Wright, *Jean Valentine Abridged: writing a word changing it* (Philadelphia: Albion Books, 2011).

9. Adrienne Rich, *Of Woman Born: Motherhood as Experience and Institution* (New York: W. W. Norton, 1976), 283–84.

10. Alan Williamson, "For Jean Valentine, Out of Thirty-five Years," *TWC*, 160.

11. Amy Newman, "About Jean Valentine," *Ploughshares* 107 (Winter 2008–2009); www.pshares.org/issues/winter-2008–09/about-jean-valentine. Of this hiatus, Newman writes, "Later Valentine would experience another watershed moment, and stop writing for five tough years, from 1982 to 1987. 'My beloved therapist had at first moved away and then died [says Valentine, and] . . . [t]hat was an echo of loss and a real loss, an echo of loss from childhood that was really very strong.' During this difficult, instructive time, Valentine shed several of what she perceived as her 'identities,' among them drinking and smoking." Throughout these years of radio silence, Valentine was also living without a partner, and her grown children had left home. For Valentine, this shedding of identities was, as Newman relates using Valentine's words, "a very positive thing. I realized that my 'identity things' were not there, but I was still there. You could take away all my identities, and I was still there. That kind of knowledge has really been a beautiful thing." It is possible to see in this temporal hiatus a version, writ large, of the ellipses, the silences, a reader experiences in a given Valentine poem. As Valentine describes it, this period of not writing, of casting off of various prior identities in a spell of waiting, seems not unlike the waiting and wary watching/listening of the speakers in many of her poems, who lean into silence for possible translations of identity and meaning. It is a fertile not a sterile silence.

12. Williamson, *TWC*, 160.

13. Ali, *TWC*, 1.

14. Jean Valentine, *Door in the Mountain: New and Collected Poems, 1965–2003* (Middletown, CT: Wesleyan University Press, 2004), 50. Hereafter referred to in the text and notes as *DM* followed by the page number.

15. Booth, *TWC*, 61.

16. Vladimir Nabokov, *Speak Memory: An Autobiography Revisited* (New York: First Vintage International Edition, 1989; first published by Harper & Bros., 1951), 19.

17. "A Conversation: Jean Valentine & Eve Grubin," www.poetrysociety.org/psa/poetry/crossroads/interviews/2009-09-04_2/.

18. Amy Newman, *TWC*, 127.

19. Charles Wright, *The World of the Ten Thousand Things: Poems 1980–1990* (New York: Farrar, Straus and Giroux, 1990).

20. Newman, *TWC*, 127.

21. Ira Gitler, *Jazz Masters of the Forties* (New York: Collier Books, 1966), 37–38.

22. For an insightful biographical/historical reading of "Could it be heat?" and other work in *Shirt in Heaven*, see "Into Openness," an interview with Jean Valentine by Brian Teare, published in the *Los Angeles Review of Books* on November 28, 2015.

23. Anne Marie Macari, "Lyric Impulse in a Time of Extinction," *The American Poetry Review* 44.4; www.aprweb.org/poems/lyric-impulse-in-a-time-of -extinction.

BIBLIOGRAPHY

Works by Jean Valentine

POETRY

Dream Barker. New Haven: Yale University Press, 1965.
Pilgrims. New York: Farrar, Straus & Giroux, 1969.
Ordinary Things. New York: Farrar, Straus & Giroux, 1974.
The Messenger. New York: Farrar, Straus & Giroux, 1979.
Home. Deep. Blue: New and Selected Poems. Farmington, ME: Alice James Books, 1989.
The River at Wolf. Farmington, ME: Alice James Books, 1992.
The Under Voice: Selected Poems. Dublin, Ireland: Poolbeg Press Ltd., 1995.
Growing Darkness, Growing Light. Pittsburgh: Carnegie Mellon Press, 1997.
The Cradle of the Real Life. Middletown, CT: Wesleyan University Press, 2000.
Door in the Mountain: New and Collected Poems 1965–2003. Middletown, CT: Wesleyan University Press, 2004.
Little Boat. Middletown, CT: Wesleyan University Press, 2007.
Break the Glass. Port Townsend, WA: Copper Canyon Press, 2010.
Shirt in Heaven. Port Townsend, WA: Copper Canyon Press, 2015.

CHAPBOOKS

Lucy. Louisville, KY: Sarabande Books, 2009.
[the Ship]. Red Glass Books, 2012.
Friend. Philadelphia: Albion Books, 2015.

TRANSLATIONS

Marina Tsvetaeva. *Dark Elderberry Branch: Poems of Marina Tsvetaeva.* With Ilya Kaminsky (Farmington, ME: Alice James Books, 2012).

SELECTED PROSE

The Lighthouse Keeper: Essays on the Poetry of Eleanor Ross Taylor. Geneva, NY: Hobart and William Smith Colleges Press, 2001.
Papers of Jean Valentine 1952–2004 (inclusive), 1970–2004 (bulk). Arthur and Elizabeth Schlesinger Library on the History of Women in America, Harvard University; oasis.lib.harvard.edu/oasis/deliver/~sch00369.
"Preface to Three Poems," *Kestrel* 15 (2000): 14.

SELECTED INTERVIEWS

Akbar, Kaveh. "'The prayer is always that the words might help someone:' An Interview with Jean Valentine." *divedapper*, 27 October 2014; www .divedapper.com/interview/jean-valentine/.

Grubin, Eve. "A Conversation with Jean Valentine." *Poetry Society of America* (2009); www.poetrysociety.org/psa/poetry/crossroads/interviews/2009-09 -04_2/. Originally published in *Crossroads* 59 (Fall 2002).

Gudas, Eric. "An Interview with Jean Valentine." *The Marlboro Review* 4 (Summer/Fall 1998).

Hoppenthaler, Jay. "So Let It Be Like Rain: An Interview with Jean Valentine." *Arts & Letters* 3 (Spring 2000).

Jackson, Richard. "The Hallowing of the Everyday." *Acts of Mind: Conversations with Contemporary Poets* (Tuscaloosa: University of Alabama Press, 1983), 27–31.

Klein, Michael. "An Interview with Jean Valentine," *American Poetry Review* 20.4 (1991): 39–44.

McEwen, Christian. "Interview with Jean Valentine: Under the Surface." *Teachers & Writers Magazine*, 20 April 2015; teachersandwritersmagazine.org/under -the-surface-1251.htm.

Mitchell, Nancy. "Jean Valentine: To Stay Open." *Plume*, June 2016; plumepoetry .com/2016/07/featured-selection-jean-valentine/.

Rheannon, Francesca. "Jean Valentine: Poetry from the Right Brain." *Writers Voice* (podcast), 2011; www.writersvoice.net/2011/03/poet-jean-valentine/.

Teare, Brian. "Into Openness," an interview with Jean Valentine. *Los Angeles Review of Books*, 28 November 2015.

Selected Criticism and Reviews

Ali, Kazim, and John Hoppenthaler, eds. *Jean Valentine: This-World Company*. Ann Arbor: The University of Michigan Press, 2012.

Booth, Philip. "On Jean Valentine: A Continuum of Turning." *American Poetry Review* 9.1 (1980): 13–16.

Carter, Michael. Review of *Growing Darkness, Growing Light*. *Provincetown Arts* 12 (1996).

Fitts, Dudley. "Foreword." *Dream Barker*, by Jean Valentine (New Haven: Yale University Press, 1965).

Fuhrer, Erik. "'The Bodies Were Like Charred Trees': (re)Visions of Violence in Jean Valentine's Lyric Dreamscapes." *PN Review* 192, 36.4 (March–April 2010): 64–66.

Gibson, Lydia Lyle. "Lines of Friendship: Jean Valentine on Her Career and Literary Companions." *Harvard Magazine*, November–December 2016; harvardmagazine.com/2016/11/lines-of-friendship.

Goldberg, Beckian Fritz. "Under the Room of What We Say." *How2* 1.4 (September 2000); www.asu.edu/pipercwcenter/how2journal/archive/online_archive /v1_4_2000/current/alerts/golberg.html.

Miller-Mack, Ellen. "Review of *Break the Glass*." *Rattle* 5 (November 2010); www.rattle.com/break-the-glass-by-jean-valentine/.

Newman, Amy. "About Jean Valentine." *Ploughshares* 107 (Winter 2008–2009); www.pshares.org/issues/winter-2008–09/about-jean-valentine.

Phillips, Carl. "Reading Jean Valentine: 'About Love' as One Example." *Field: Contemporary Poetry and Poetics* 73 (October 2005): 38–44.

Rivard, David. "Review of *The River at Wolf*," *Ploughshares* 19 (Fall 1993): 246–47.

Spaar, Lisa Russ. "Second Acts: A Second Look at Second Books of Poetry by Peter Streckfus and Jean Valentine." *Los Angeles Review of Books*, 22 November 2014; lareviewofbooks.org/article/second-acts-second-look-second -books-poetry-peter-streckfus-jean-valentine/.

Upton, Lee. *The Muse of Abandonment: Origin, Identity, Mastery in Five American Poets*. Lewisburg, PA: Bucknell University Press, 1998.

Van Buren, Ann. Review of *Shirt in Heaven. The Rumpus*, 5 August 2015; therumpus.net/2015/08/shirt-in-heaven-by-jean-valentine/.

Wright, C. D. *Jean Valentine Abridged: writing a word / changing it* (Philadelphia: Albion Books, 2011).

CECILIA VICUÑA

POEMS

K'isa, alangó

A word moves
a bit of air
NACHMAN OF BRATZLAW

God is the essence of the written letters
concealed in the dust of the poet's pencil
SUMANA SANTAKA

To read a text in Thai is *tibot tack*: to smash it to pieces.

Tayil, a song is "the only material manifestation of the invisible reality," the Mapuche say.

"A song melts the boundaries between the worlds," Lawrence Sullivan says.

A vibratory disorder, an incantation bends time itself.

An image too, is an "interference pattern," a rhythm born at the meeting point of light and eye.

"We don't see light, we see with the light," someone says.

A word in the air
          lets you
                    hear the image
                              see the sound.

In the Andes people say an image hears, a textile sees.
(You don't put on a mask to be seen, but to see with
different eyes)

But there is no word for "beauty" (a song must never strike
a right note.)

> You say *K'isa* instead,
>> the slow power to
>>> transform.

El suave endulzar de una fruta secándose al sol. A slow
drying fruit.

The spectrum at work.

A color gradation is an effort of light to unite shadow and light.
Hate and anger becoming peace and love.

"The rainbow has a motor," they say.

To weave gradations is to weave an illusion, a destello that hits
the eye.

"Not to mystify with illusion, but to clarify the role of illusion
in our perception of reality."

Alangó, "beauty" in Java, is not a noun, but a god, a divine
manifestation.

Simultáneamente arrobado y arrobante, being in ecstasy creates
the state.

K'isa, alangó.

Solitude

> We would lose more than half
> our union
> if I stop
> being your friend
>
> There was no way out
> I was feeling gentle
>
> Do you want to make me see the sky?
> touch that space
> white
> between my thighs
> softly
> with no other intentions
> almost without wanting to

Mastaba

> I had the feeling I was
> leaning into a waterfall
> in the forest
> while you pushed your hand
> between my buttocks.
>
> I thought I was flying,
> dismounting from a horse,
> your hand on my sex
> impelled me
> like a humid bird.

I floated joyously
on the occasion,
was wet down to my knees
and two tears
blackened my cheeks
from being upside down so long.

Mawida

Since they started exterminating the puma
or American lion,
and since women were stripped of
their gardens of smoke
some have turned savage
and abandoning all
return to the mountain range.

They have been seen
roaming solitary cities
by the side of friendly lions,
swift leopards
guide their steps.
Haggard, innocent men
hoping to overtake them
have found shiny motorcycles
in cliffs and glaciers.

Fleeting, intractable she-wolves
threaten their lovers
with animal habits
wielding the lipstick
as their central symbol.

Teresa the Idiot

In reality my loves
are the strange box of a Polish doll
The blonde's eyes appearing
fixed to her hips long after midnight
the garret always singular to loosen
a massive mane
across her back, its strands
thick and fine draping
her otter-like chin
Deliberately she'd peer out from the wall
and nothing could be seen but the shadow of her breasts
hidden beneath marmots of hair
And lovely was her skin's radiance
at that unusual hour
Her waist's digressions
easily discerned
as bees through grass
the window neither open nor closed
What I saw, yellow like crystal,
rose from sleepy thighs
amassed in unseemly tourniquets
Everything before me, a pale shimmer
of hairs fanning delicately
to reveal the pink or green skin I no longer know
of hips a million centimeters
from my gaze.

Translated by Rosa Alcalá

Librarian Expedition

It's difficult to understand to what degree
minuscule species have survived
in the leaves of books
and even to imagine a reader
for each of these books is absolute chimera
There are volumes that have never been read
and others that have to wait decades
for someone to open them
The destiny of pages full of beauty
is not known
Who would dare dictate a deletion?
Who would dare propose a giant bonfire?
Some think that nowadays
more books than children are born
There are also more butterflies
than people
To visit a library is harder
than entering a virgin jungle
Some atrociously beautiful volumes
lay abandoned
nobody could ever classify those!
If anybody wishes to find a book
of the sixteenth century
she must leave her family
purchase supplies for a three-month-long journey
clothe warmly and enter the books
If she emerges alive
and doesn't get lost in the maze
she can consider herself very fortunate
Contrary to what people think
these difficulties can't but magnify
the interest in poetry
And though foolhardy adventurers
are rare
when one appears
she could only be a serious person

There are several rooms in the library
into which none have entered
Who knows whether in these places
the characters of a twentieth-century novel
and philosophic treatises of the eleventh
century are up to no good
It's possible that ideas have a concrete shape
unknown until now
and that a romantic woman immersed in an essay
or an epistolary from the last years
of the eighteenth century
may have fallen in love smitten
with a religious idea from the Middle Ages
Even mythological animals could have come
from these pages to join twelve-year-old virgins
It's terrible how manipulated
these unknowns are
When a woman decides to enter
these fields she must be stoned and forthwith
shrink from landscapes never before seen
Those who return let loose incoherences
into the dust the sounds the networks woven
by uncounted tiny creatures
Watch this intense warmth!
To voyage will allow
alcohol to vaporize

From "fables of the beginning and remains of the origin"

Silence
      turns the page
            the poem begins
                  alba del habla,
dawn of speech.

alquimia   del   nombre   alchemy   of   names

                el   instan

palabra   fantasma   sin   abrevar

"*The soul co-authors the instant,*" Humberto Giannini says.

Time undone by the instant!

Time is "tem": to cut.   A continuum contradicted by name.

An instant is present,
                it "stands,"
                        a filament of sta, a state of being, stamen,
a thread in a warp,
                a web in ecstasy.

"Being" is a compound of three forms: "to grow," "to set in motion" and "yes, it may be so."

Hedda Sterne said: "*Art is not in the object, nor in the eye of the beholder, but in the meeting of both: the ambrosia that feeds the gods.*"

Let the fable begin:

El comienzo es el *com*, being "with."

The "*uni* verse" wants to *con*verse,
"Verse" is to turn.

Galaxies and blood
breath and sound.

Ibn Arabi dreamt he made love to the stars.

Words are stars, the night sky I see.

"Justice" began as a ritual form.

Así lo veía mi corazón embelesado en la *con* templación,
the temple of *con*

           sciousness
                the fulcrum of change.

A possibility contained in the name.
Com: a pre-verbal form becoming the handiwork of peace, the search for
a common ground,

join   with,   mutually   comic,   c o l l e c t i v e l y.

Time
        is language and love,

a flowing of milk
           a gr*amma*r
                  in *amma*,
                            la leche manando,
la lengua y el trans.

Hipnótico manar
           the music of *am*,
                    morning and mother.

El *am*

      del *am*

           or

                                      not an abstract idea

but a *con*

          ti nui

               ty.

                                    "the love that gathers"
                                         say the Guarani

We are only exiled from the inner star.

Migrate and migrate to a way of being.

                                    Love in the genes, if it fails
                                    We will produce no sane man again.
                                         —George Oppen

The Quasar

Light of sound, or sound of light?

Its not-yet-being, its "no ser nada aún" is what attracted me.

Being "almost" a border, an "about to happen."

It kept me there looking for a form
before the form.

Form was not born from an idea.

It was an idea vanishing.

At its birth, the "no" understood and soothed it,
allowing it to be in its undoing.

A poem looking for its being, the quasar can only search
for the sleep of dreams.

A poem only becomes poetry when its structure
is made not of words but forces.

Force is poetry.

Everyone knows what poetry is, but who can say it?

Its nature is to be felt, but never apprehended.

Translated by Rosa Alcalá

The Undoer Doing (Muhammad Ali)

Transcript from an oral performance at The Poetry Project at St. Mark's Church, New York, May 15, 2002[1]

Last night I was a little sick
and they were watching *Ali*
they were watching, I said
did you notice that? hmmm
They. Who was that?
All my Mes
All my Cecilias, you know
Lying sick in bed, watching Ali
Do you remember Ali?
The little dancing feet?
Do you remember him?
I remember we were in Santiago
watching him
all of us gathered
hundreds of people
gathered just to watch
one little TV set
this was the origin of the TV set
And I was there
We was there
watching *Ali*
the little dancing feet
The unboxing boxer
The unhitting hitter
The undoer doing
My *GO-o-o-o-D*
And when he said
IIIII am pret-ty,
we felt *WE* were pretty
When he said *I* am Black,
we felt *we* are Black
It was a shock to come to the U.S. and realize
that we were not Black

after all (audience laughter)
hmmm
I wonder who narrowed it down (audience laughter)
We were him, certainly, that's for sure

And now I wanted to tell you this story
that's around the Internet
I've no idea whether this is true or not
this is what the web does:
it undoes the web,
doesn't it?
A message came
it said Guaicaipuro Cuahtemoc[2]
had been speaking
to the European
Community
on February the 8th, 19—sorry
18—sorry
2002.
He said
Usura[3] brothers
you who ask us to pay you
our debt
you are asking us to pay YOU our debt
in reality I loaned you millions and millions and millions and
ME ME ME ME ME
ME-LEE-YONS
of goold and silver
as a friendly gesture
of the Americas towards the development
of Europe
this was our "Marshalltesuma plan"[4] (audience laughter)
plan for the reconstruction
of the barbaric Europe.
Poor them.
But it failed—look (audience laughter)—
In its irrational capitalistic ways

they are still at it.
Europe always wants more
they need more
More more from us
But time has come for Eur Eur
I can't even say it—
Eu You You You Your
Your-UP.
To return to us
To return to us
the gold and silver
we so generously loooaned
We ask you to now sign a letter of inn-tent
as a way to discipline YOU.
. . .
And then I thought
of this Ino moxo
This Ino moxo is a black panther
It's impossible.
It is not a black panther
It's a person becoming
a black panther
How can it be?
There are no black panthers
in the Amazon
and this is an Amazon man
He says
"Cuando pienso en Fitzcarraldo
y en sus mercenarios
cuando pienso
que esos genocidas
eran hombres
me dan ganas de nacionalizarme
cuuu le bra"
I don't know how to do this
but this is Ino moxo
and he's saying

when I'm thinking of Fitzcarraldo
and his mercenaries
when I think that those people committing genocide
that they were people
I want to nationalize myself
into a snake   hmmm

That's César Calvo.
. . .
Mundo fronterado
in voluto de sierpe negra

y blanca
Vida hora
en tu revés

línea de muerto
línea de vivo
en tu insTANtez

They call her mother of sound
the mother of voice in the ear,
ayawhuasAAA
The thread of the dead
is speaking alive
when you hear them, they say
"El primer hombre
no era hombre
era mujer."
The first man
was not a man
was a woman—
didn't you see that?
Suenan los pasos, they say
and when I go outside every morning
I go greet the sun
because my place here is dark
dark as a cave

I go down to the street
I open the door
and let the sun in
and I watch the shadows
pass by
on Hudson street
these shadows are just as it says
in the poem
In the poem it says
the shadow is from the animal
you used to be
the shadow is from the one
you will be
The shadow is not from you,
from them
from the one who passes,
it's not a shadow at all,
it is the sound of a shadow
It is the shadow of sound.

WHERE is that silence
between words?
WHERE
has it gone?

The pax,
the peaks,
the peace

movement.
Where is it?

Transcribed by Rosa Alcalá

Clepsydra

I embroidered on my head long ago
the signs of abandonment and failure
no one had the fortune of knowing
to which galaxies I allude
with my smile.
I opted for wild trails,
the object of poetry
was always to create
spiritual and collective rings
where conjecture,
Juno, and Aristotle
dance among new shrubs.
From the beginning
I relied on my stupidity
and general lack of talent.
Always I shipwrecked among
nouns and verbs.
I continue to feel I am
a shitty preacher:
I enlighten no one
more than me.

Translated by Rosa Alcalá

POETICS STATEMENT

Three Notes

1

Poetry is a supreme affinity with the world's speech.
Speech meaning a secret breath.
Inhalation and exhalation, the world's heart beat
in a common language of perception.

Translated by Rosa Alcalá

2

> *Poetry is the notation of an answer*
> JOSÉ LEZAMA LIMA

I search for a *com*munal syntax arising from the space between *com* (together)
and *un* (one): the seed of language in dissonance, a clash, or double sound.
Not a denial of the individual, but its double realization: in solitude and togetherness.

I seek a way of being in language, listening to the tongues within tongues.

. . .

Light desires sound and sound desires light. Desire is light, a tuning of attention.
Sound and light speak to each other.
All forms emit light. Language is an enlightened form.

The heart of memory is resurrection. A cord responds to the touch of sound.
Our body re*cords*, remembers its core, a longing for togetherness.

Language dreams a po*ethical* ground of equity and exchange.

3

My sense of *com*position comes from the violent interaction between history and art. The day before my first exhibition opened in Santiago de Chile (*Otoño/Autumn*, June 9, 1971), a political murder took place unleashing the violence that led to the military coup that killed Salvador Allende on September 11, 1973. The beauty of our collective spirit, the historic chance to create a peaceful democratic revolution was undone. From that day forward, my art became invisible and inextricably woven into the violent history of Chile. *Autumn* was a poem in space, a participatory piece, dedicated to the construction of socialism. It was performed collectively as a contemplative act by family, friends, and the gardeners of the great urban parks of Santiago, who gathered leaves to fill a room of the museum. When people walked into the gallery, they found an ocean of leaves and this text at the end:

```
       everybody has only 70 years to live (more or less). most
    of the people coming to see the piece are between 15 and 50
    years old; some have only 45 years left, some only 20. keep
    this in mind. people aware of their own death are more likely
    to become revolutionaries.
       the "new being" is one who has a new perception of time and
    knows it can't be wasted. . . .
       joy could make people aware of the need to fight for joy. the
    urgency of the present is the urgency for revolution.
                                          Autumn Journal, June 1971
```

But this work, and the joyous spirit of the time, was erased in Chile and Latin America by U.S. intervention. Both our democratic movement and my work had emerged from an indigenous imagination that perceives death and the body as instruments for enlightened activity.

Why is the indigenous female imagination so threatening?

Who or what creates the *com*position, when democratic movements, people's rights, languages, species, and cultures are erased around the world?

Com is "with" in Latin, and *com*position is to position yourself with.
> *To dream is to speak with air.*
> say the Ashaninka
*Com*position is aware of itself. To *com*pose is to participate in *its* awareness.

The true performance is that of our species on Earth: the way we cause suffering to others, the way we warm the atmosphere or cause other species to disappear.

. . .

I come from an oral culture that "writes" with the body, inscribing its memory in the land through ritual and dance. For us, the poem is a performance, an *act* as Octavio Paz said.

. . .

The act of writing is a shadow, a filament or trail of the self-aware universe.
The Maya learned how to write from the trail of the snail.
From the start, I saw writing as an extension of the body and menstrual blood.

That's why I write by hand, to see the black thread, the shadow of my breath on the page.

NOTES

1. Transcribed from an audio recording. An earlier transcription was published in "Global New York," *The Literary Review* 46.2 (Winter 2003): 325–29.

2. At the time of this performance, Vicuña was unaware that, in 1990, Venezuelan writer Luis Britto García had published a fictional text titled "Guaicaipuro Cuatemoc cobra la deuda a Europa" in a Caracas newspaper. She read a version circulated on the Internet years later that omitted his name and, like many others, wondered whether it was a true account of a cacique addressing the heads of state of the European Union. See note by Rosa Alcalá, editor and translator of *New and Selected Poems of Cecilia Vicuña* (Kelsey Street Press, 2018), 266.

3. *Usura* is Spanish for usury.

4. Marshalltesuma is a combination of Montezuma, the sixteenth-century Aztec emperor, and the Marshall Plan, also known as the European Recovery Act. Named after Secretary of State George C. Marshall, the Marshall Plan was designed to provide financial help to post-World War II Europe.

RETURN OF THE DISAPPEARED

Cecilia Vicuña's *Saboramis*

Julie Phillips Brown

> Universes, cosmoses, unfinished winds raining down in thousands
> of pink baits onto the carnivorous sea of Chile. I heard plains of love
> never said, infinite skies of love sinking into the carnivorous tombs
> of the fish.   RAÚL ZURITA[1]

> Appearing as it does two months after Chile was carefully raped by
> starry striped militarists, *Sabor a Mí* is the very first howl of pain to
> emerge from the rubble under which Chile's conscience lies stunned.
>   FELIPE EHRENBERG[2]

Introduction

On September 11, 1973, Chileans at home and abroad bore witness to the
untimely death of their first democratically elected president, Salvador Al-
lende, and with him, the representative government of the Unidad Popular.
Allende's final address, delivered from within La Moneda at the height of
the coup, spoke of both history and the future at once:

> Placed in a historic moment, I will repay the loyalty of the people with my
> life. . . . the seed that we have sown in the dignified conscience of thousands
> and thousands of Chileans cannot be destroyed definitively. They have the
> force, they may overcome us, but social processes cannot be stopped, neither
> by crimes nor with force. History is ours and people make it."[3]

For Allende, the future is already a *fait accompli*, and only history remains
to be written. He asserts a vision of revolutionary time, of *future-as-history*,
when seeds sown in the "stunned" conscience of Chileans will have already
taken root. That communal conscience must flourish, Allende reasons, as
the inevitable and natural consequence of the "social processes" initiated
in his time, the time of the Unidad Popular.

Within a year of the coup, General Augusto Pinochet had assumed ab-
solute control of Chile. Pinochet's dictatorship ushered in an era of terror,
violence, and for artists and writers especially, heavily enforced censor-
ship. Like so many of his fellow Chileans, songwriter and poet Víctor Jara
was abducted, tortured at the Estadio Chile (now Estadio Víctor Jara),
and executed. Still others were "disappeared," their bodies dropped from

airplanes onto the mountains and into the sea like so many "thousands of pink baits."[4] According to current estimates, as many as 38,000 Chileans were tortured, and 3,065 killed or disappeared.[5] For survivors like the poet Raúl Zurita, the threat of state-sponsored violence gave rise to a fugitive poetics: "we had to respond to the terror with a poetry that was just as powerful as the pain being delivered, but at the same time you had to try to avoid being punished."[6] Publication was a matter of life or death, and few poets risked incurring Pinochet's wrath; indeed, only five books of poetry were published in Chile in the period from 1973 until 1978.[7]

Cecilia Vicuña, then a twenty-four-year-old postgraduate student in London, suddenly found herself exiled from the only motherland she had ever known. Spared from any immediate threat of violence, Vicuña mourned from a distance, memorializing the irrevocable losses of country and culture in the first of her published books, *Sabor a Mí* (1973).[8] As Ehrenberg implies, it is a cruel irony that in her exile, Vicuña was able to voice an immediate and unbridled response to the coup that would have been all but impossible within Chile's borders. As an artist's book, *Sabor a Mí* documents the poet's experience of the coup through its compelling arrangement of visual, verbal, and tactile materials, including drawings, collages, paintings, photographs, diary entries, letters, poems, and essays. With respect to both its content and its form, *Sabor a Mí* is one of the most important poetic representations of this most traumatic era in Chilean history, and yet, it continues to receive little critical attention.[9] The book was published by Beau Geste Press, a small artist's collective in England, with a print run of only 250 copies,[10] which explains, in part, the book's absence from the canon of literary responses to the coup.[11] But if the book has struggled to find its audience, it is also because its unruly poetics confound conventional reading practices with every turn of the page.

In the decades since the coup, Vicuña has continued to rework and republish the content of *Sabor a Mí* in numerous subsequent books.[12] The most notable of these books, published by ChainLinks in 2011, might be called a "semi-facsimile" edition, since it both reproduces and significantly expands and recontextualizes the original book. Unlike its predecessor, *Saborami* (2011) was published not under military dictatorship, but during the years of the Occupy Wall Street movement, when the streets near Vicuña's home in New York teemed with organized protests and communal actions. In the intervening years, Vicuña has also become a poet, visual artist, and filmmaker of international renown, with works that combine elements of poetry, visual and performance art, and film. Thus *Saborami* embodies a lifetime of Vicuña's complex, multi-dimensional poetics, and it gains new relevance in the company of other groundbreaking works by contemporary women poets. Collage techniques in both *Saborami* and Theresa Hak Kyung Cha's *Dictee* (1982), for example, evoke a sense of disorientation and cultural alienation through disjunctive arrangements of text and image. In *Muse & Drudge* (1995) and *things of each possible relation hashing against one another* (2003), Harryette Mullen and Juliana Spahr realize, respectively, radically pluralized poetic identities, echoing the complex relations between individual and communal subjectivities in the poems of *Saborami*. Other recent collections, such as Susan Howe's *The Midnight* (2003), Anne Carson's *Nox* (2010), and Marta Werner and Jen Bervin's *The Gorgeous Nothings* (2012), share Vicuña's elegiac mining and re-membering of materials from their respective archives. Most recently, the richness of the textual and visual materials in *Saborami* is rivaled only by Claudia Rankine's *Citizen: An American Lyric* (2014). Like *Saborami*, *Citizen* preserves and makes visible the identities of those who have been "disappeared" by institutional racism.[13]

As my title suggests, we ought to think of *Sabor a Mí* in the plural, for it is most certainly not a singular historical artifact. Together, the original artist's book and its various reincarnations form a *corpus* of works —a corpus that refuses to disappear. Rather, the books insist on their own materiality, evoking at once both the presence and the absences of history. History in the *Saboramis* is visible, tangible, and real, and is it also fugitive, flawed, and vacant. The books serve as memorial sites, intimate portals through which Vicuña returns to a Chile that no longer exists. Such an aim might seem simply impossible. Perhaps it is. That Vicuña returns to the material of *Sabor a Mí*, time and again, might indicate a fundamental failure in the original. And yet, the failures of the *Saboramis*—all those instances in which the books' visual and tactile elements reveal themselves as vacant simulacra—are what drive the renewal and expansion of the corpus. The poet's dogged reworking of the *Saboramis* suggests faith, and something to be salvaged. Like Allende, Vicuña conceives the *Saborami* corpus as a future that has already been fulfilled, as well as a history to be rewritten and redeemed by that future. As I will show, the act of *return*—as pilgrimage, as making, and as remaking—is the fundamental strategy through which Vicuña works toward redemption in her artistic and poetic practices.

As part of Vicuña's larger, open-ended project, each new *Saborami* recuperates, expands, and revises the corpus according to the exigencies of the present. Each new present in each new edition re-opens the possibility of redemption—for Vicuña, for Allende, and for their vision of radical social democracy. The transformative power Vicuña seeks, in all the manifold manifestations of the *Saboramis*, relies upon a fluid, non-linear concept of temporality:

> I was a young girl, studying architecture in Santiago when I had the sudden realization that "time" as we know it didn't exist. I experienced time as a fluid transforming movement, realizing I could be simultaneously in what

we call "past" or "future" at once. Consciousness moves not just in time, but through it, as through water. Time became a great mystery to explore, one of many dimensions available to being.[14]

Here Vicuña seems to move toward indigenous models of time; in Aymara, for example, the spatial metaphors for time imagine the future at our backs, with the past laid out directly before us.[15] For the *Saboramis*, Vicuña's strategy of return depends upon her ability to traverse and invert temporal boundaries: "simultaneously in what we call 'past' or 'future' at once," the poet may rewrite histories, both future and past.

If Vicuña's project sounds messianic, it may well be. In "Theses on the Philosophy of History," Benjamin invokes Klee's *Angelus Novus* to illustrate the "catastrophe" of history:

> His eyes are staring, his mouth is open, his wings are spread. This is how one pictures the angel of history. His face is turned toward the past. Where we perceive a chain of events, he sees one single catastrophe which keeps piling wreckage upon. . . . The angel would like to stay, awaken the dead, and make whole what has been smashed. But a storm is blowing in from Paradise; it has got caught in his wings with such violence that the angel can no longer close them. This storm irresistibly propels him into the future to which his back is turned, while the pile of debris before him grows skyward.[16]

For Benjamin, as for the Aymara, the past lies before us, directly at hand and mutable. Benjamin argues that it is the task of the historian to cultivate the porous openings between the past and the present. He calls for a "historian who . . . stops telling the sequence of events like the beads of a rosary," and instead "grasps the constellation which his own era has formed with a definite earlier one. Thus he establishes a conception of the present as the 'time of now' which is shot through with chips of Messianic time."[17] Thus both Benjamin and Vicuña conjure constellated, coeval temporal dimensions. The promise of historical redemption lies precisely in this temporal co-implication, figured here as shrapnel embedded in the present moment. It remains only for the historian—or poet—to reconcile both present and past by cultivating a consciousness that cuts through temporal boundaries like "water."

Featured among the paintings in *Sabor a Mí* is Vicuña's *Angel of Menstruation*, the poet's own unwitting answer to Klee's famous painting. A fitting counterpart for Benjamin's narrative, Vicuña's angel embodies her concept of temporal co-implication: the angel's torso is contorted—her right shoulder and left breast turn forward, and her left shoulder and right breast turn backward—so that she faces both past and future at once. Exposed with legs parted, the angel menstruates freely, her blood running into a thread that she spins around her leg and torso.

In Vicuña's description of the painting, she associates the angel's woven menstrual blood with her ability to birth a new socialist reality: "If she does not recapture the thread she may . . . accept a role within perfectly established structures, filling exactly into the place allotted to her and thus becoming a powerless creature . . . If she recaptures the thread she will make her unconscious active and discover the secret functioning of reality, following her own nature. She would work beyond the regular channels, or against them, recovering her joy, her visions."[18] Thus Vicuña represents the angel as a feminine, indigenized agent for social democracy in Chile and beyond, and she anticipates, rather uncannily, the radical feminism and forms of Carolee Schneemann's *Interior Scroll* (1975), as well as Vicuña's own later installation, *Quipu Menstrual* (2006).

The *Saborami* corpus also depends upon the ancient Andean concept of *pachacuti*, or world-reversal: "Andean cosmogony revolves around oscillations of time/space in which periodic catastrophes define moments of transition separating different epochs. This concept was expressed by the Quechua term *pachacuti*, derived from *pacha* (world, time and space, or state of being) and *cuti* (change, turn, or something that comes back on itself)."[19] With each new *Saborami*, Vicuña works toward *pachacuti*—within political realities and collective conscience. Together the books become both a memorial for social democracy in Chile and an open-ended ritual toward its redemption. But redemption is uncertain, and thus the *Saboramis* continually return to their origins, mourning what has been lost, but they also spiral outward, carrying their histories into the present, and the balm of the present back to the wounds of the past.

Precarious Origins

Though fabricated in England, *Sabor a Mí*'s true place of origin is Concón, the beach in Chile where Vicuña first began her work as an artist. As Lucy Lippard describes, Vicuña's intimate relationship with the site "began in 1966, when she arranged the refuse found on Con-cón, a stony beach in Chile where two waters met, a natural gathering place for rubbish, which she called her 'mine.' Beginning with sticks, stones, and feathers, later she added plastic detritus, drawings on the sand, powdered pigments, and objects made in the studio from beach finds."[20] Vicuña's use of the term "mine" indicates not only the intimacy of her claim to Con-cón, but also the site's richness as the mother lode for her art. Con-cón is home to many of Vicuña's earliest artworks, including *Casa Espiral* (1966) and *Guardian* (1967), which represent, respectively, two of the most integral aspects of Vicuña's artistic lexicon: sculptural drawings in the landscape,[21] and the *precarios*, a group of fragile, temporary objects constructed from found local materials. Both bodies of work are deeply site-specific: the drawings are inscribed into the earth, and the *precarios* always seem poised to return to their original environment. Both forms figure prominently in *Sabor a Mí*, as well as in Vicuña's later work.

In *Casa Espiral*, the minimalist arrangement of raw materials suggests a kind of altar or otherwise sacred space. A permeable border of vegetation and upright driftwood encloses a delicate interior composed of two circles —one, a braided hoop, and the other, a spiral drawn in the sand, with two upright feathers at its edge. The spiral is a persistent motif throughout Vicuña's poetry and artworks, from *Casa Espiral* to her *gramma kellcani* in *Instan* (2002)[22] to the recreated spirals at Con-cón for the film *Kon Kon pi* (2010). For Vicuña, the spiral's implications are manifold: the potential energy of spun wool, the Nazca spiral in Peru, and the swirl of galaxies. The spiral also embodies Vicuña's complex, bi-directional conception of temporality, as well as the reciprocal relationship between past and present realities: a spiral that spins outward and forward must also turn inward toward its origin, and backward in time.

Traced in the sand at Con-cón, the spiral of *Casa Espiral* suggests the inward folding of an ear, formed from the very earth itself. As Vicuña writes in her book-length autobiographical poem, *QUIPOem* (1997):

> The ear is a spiral
> > to hear
> a sound within
>
> An empty furrow
> > to receive
> A standing stick
> > to speak[23]

In these lines, the earth's speech remains imminent, and the poet anticipates the dual acts of listening and speaking through the "empty furrow" and "standing stick" of *Casa Espiral*. For Vicuña, both listening and speaking must be reciprocal: as the earth listens, the human voice spirals inward and down into the earth, while the two feathers at the edge of the spiral amplify the earth's voice outward toward the human listener. Thus *Casa Espiral* is a site of dialogue, of mutual exchange, between human and terrestrial planes. As the title implies, *Casa Espiral* is also the poet's home —a mythical origin, both material and immaterial, present and absent. Over the years, Vicuña's returns to the site of *Casa Espiral*, both in person and through her artworks, have been too numerous to count. With each of these returns, she revisits the memory of this first, originary artwork, renewing her relationship with her "mine," her Con-cón.

Like the spiral, the feather is an important motif that recurs throughout Vicuña's oeuvre, from her earliest precarious works, to the cover of *Sabor a Mí*, to her poem "Pajarito o Parejito," which first appeared in Spanish in

1. *Guardian* installed at the shore's edge at Con-cón in 1967.

Sabor a Mí. The feather evokes flight, of course, but it is also fragile, tenuous, and light, turning with the wind that carries it. The feather is, by nature, the first and essential *precario*. Like so many of the later *precarios*, *Guardian* (figure 1) is slight in scale, a diminutive figure easily lost within the landscape. A cross of driftwood and dun-colored rope, accented with colored yarns, feathers, and other detritus, *Guardian* appears half-bird, half-human. Its arms stretch into feathers spread wide, parallel to the horizon, as though in flight, or perhaps to protect the expanse of ocean behind it. And yet we also anticipate the figure's ultimate dissolution with the rising of the tide.

In her poem "Con Con," Vicuña seems to evoke *Guardian*, or a *precario* very much like it. She describes the *precario* at the moment before its making, when its "raw material" beckons the poet to fulfill her role as maker:

> The raw material
> waited
> to be seen
> as a way of hearing
> an interior sound
> asking us to
> create
> this or that union
>   a feather leaning
>   a trophy flying.[24]

As in *Casa Espiral*, the voice of the earth (here, "an interior sound") rests in the detritus Vicuña finds on the beach, and the poem implies an intelligence in the natural world that precedes human presence. The invocation of the plural first person "us" suggests that Vicuña shares the work of poiesis with her readers. Later in the poem, the speaker ponders the origins of the *precarios* and, revealingly, her complicated relation to her own indigenous identity:

> And the objects—where did they come from?
> From the soul of all the Indians I have been?
> From my shaman heart?
> I heard them dancing on the beach,
> setting something in order,
> an offering to the sun and sea.[25]

In this passage Vicuña lays claim to a simultaneously individual and communal identity. Her "shaman heart" locates her as a specific and individuated speaker, and yet she bears "the soul of all the Indians [she has] been" within her. In a more figurative sense, of course, this image invokes the speaker's indigenous roots, but if taken at face value, it also illustrates Vicuña's complex relationship with time: she is at once present and past, an ever-increasing thread of identities woven through the boundaries of time.

In Vicuña's later work, each new *precario* or drawing in the landscape constitutes a return in form, materials, and most importantly, location. If the act of return—to an earlier era, to her origins at Con-cón—forms the vital core of her artistic practice, as I have suggested, what would the coup and her subsequent exile mean for Vicuña? As we will see, in the *Saborami* corpus, the poet revisits Con-cón and the Unidad Popular, continually reinvesting in the material and spiritual specificity of that place and time. And yet, much as her returns are a demonstration of love, they are also an act of mourning.

Rupture

After years of working on the beach at Con-cón, Vicuña left Chile to pursue postgraduate studies at the Royal Academy of Art in London. She would not return until decades later. When the coup came, Vicuña's exile was immediate and complete. Her sense of her own losses—of family, friends, and home—became inextricably bound with the sufferings of her nation. As she described years later in, "The Black Page of a Black Book," the coup wrenched Chileans awake from their collective dreams of participatory democracy:

> The coup fell like a drop of blood into the void.
> If Chile had the power of collectively dreaming another
> possibility,
>   the coup interrupted that dreaming.

> Of the world that had been there remained only
> a few photos, the books burned,
> the bodies disappeared[26]

The description of the coup's violence is strangely subdued in this poem, represented as a single, diminutive "drop of blood into the void," and its aftermath evidenced only by scant photos, the burned remains of books, and the conspicuous absence of the bodies of the disappeared. The poem suggests that the coup's true rupture is not one of the body, but the imagination, and the death that cuts most deeply is that of "the world that had been," the Chile of the Unidad Popular. In this void, there is no body to mourn. Unlike the human body, which proves far too vulnerable, photographs and books, though fugitive and scarred themselves, still persist, offering up their wounds for the reader's inspection. The material remains of the coup, perhaps collected in a book, will have to serve as the site for mourning—and remembering—all that has been lost.

Return: 1973

The first *Sabor a Mí* was completed in October, just weeks after the death of Salvador Allende. In his introduction, Felipe Ehrenberg calls the book "sheer irony" and explains, "it collects nearly ten years of work by Cecilia and was planned as a celebration. Now it symbolizes the contained fury and the sorrow of her country's present."[27] Still, "the joyous optimism of Chile," to use Niall Binns' phrase,[28] remains apparent, as seen in the exuberant sensuality of poems like "Mastaba":

> I thought I was flying,
> dismounting from a horse,
> your hand on my sex
> impelled me
> like a humid bird.[29]

The speaker expresses an unfettered delight in the body, and performs—publicly, acrobatically—a spectacle of intimate contact. Magda Sepúlveda has called these early poems "counter-canonical," in large part because they represent women not as passive sexual objects, but as self-possessed sexual agents. She notes that the dissonance between the everyday imagery and the "obscene" content of "Mastaba," in particular, challenges the reader's sense of propriety.[30] For Vicuña, the obscenity and joy of these "counter-canonical" poems stood for all that the coup sought to extinguish, and she rushed to preserve them in the pages of *Sabor a Mí*:

> the coup took place only a few days before production. I had to change plans
> and create a new work, and do it fast. I decided to include the poems, the

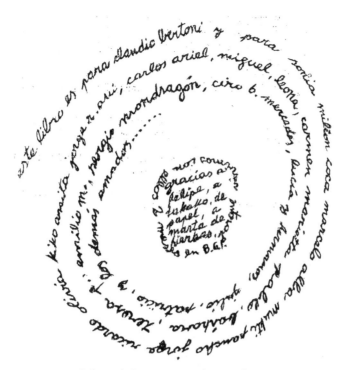

2. Acknowledgments page from *Sabor a Mí*
(Beau Geste Press, 1973).

paintings and the Autumn narrative, sensing that they would disappear. In fact these poems . . . were censored in Chile for the next 37 years.[31]

Thus *Sabor a Mí*, as precarious as it was in its own right, became a tangible time capsule, ensuring the survival of the poems and the paintings in the face of ongoing exile and censorship. Each of the 250 copies bore witness to the very existence of her art and manifested—through their drawings, photographs, and poems, as well as unique elements like hand-tipped leaves, insects, and letters—a self-contained, portable art exhibition. As with the *precarios*, many of these materials were gathered from the poet's immediate environs and paid homage to the Beau Geste collective.[32] But many other materials, like the envelope and letter, came directly from Chile, materializing an otherwise impossible connection between the present and Con-cón.

The acknowledgements page of *Sabor a Mí* (figure 2), as well as two unmarked sections of the book, "Diary of Objects for the Resistance" and "Otoño," bear distinct connections with Vicuña's earlier artworks, *Casa Espiral* and *Guardian*. The acknowledgements page features a large spiral composed from handwritten names, with an interior circle of handwritten text printed in the center. Vicuña's inclusion of the spiral form at the opening of *Sabor a Mí* invokes *Casa Espiral* in the same way that other poets might invoke the muse: the spiral is a sort of ear through which we might speak to, and hear, the book. The names in the spiral are written in dedication and thanks to other members of the Beau Geste collective, including Claudio Bertoni, Vicuña's then-partner.[33]

Vicuña's handwritten spiral is a visual metaphor for her complex conceptions of authorship and audience. The spiral begins with Bertoni, and many of the poems collected in *Sabor a Mí*, including "Mastaba," "Ease," and "Radiance of the Orifices," figure Bertoni as the speaker's erotic other, as both audience and muse. "Radiance of the Orifices," for example, offers a careful accounting of Bertoni's physical attributes, including this telling description of his ears:

> They are called THE ENTRANCES OF MUSIC
> and are somewhat wrinkled;
> commonly called ears
> they are the softest tools of love
> and which my boyfriend never washes
> for fear of damaging or scratching them,
> like when a record is destroyed,
> thus ending a source of miracles.

If the spiral in *Sabor a Mí* is the ear of the book, then it is a source of sensual delight, as well as of "miracles." As I have argued elsewhere, Vicuña moves easily between personal and communal intimacy in other poems from this same period,[34] and the folds of this spiral implicate the entire collective community at Beau Geste in the intimate and communal origins of the book. The spiral gathers Vicuña's loved ones into a close formal connection with *Casa Espiral*, thereby investing them and the subsequent pages of *Sabor a Mí* with the memory of Con-cón.

The first section of *Sabor a Mí* documents *A Diary of Objects for the Resistance*, a series of *precarios* that Vicuña originally made in support of Salvador Allende's Unidad Popular government, but later reworked "to support armed struggle against the reactionary government" following the coup.[35] In their forms and materials, the objects recall *Guardian* and the *precarios* of Con-cón, though their purpose is sharpened by the trauma of the coup. The objects, Vicuña states, are intended to function against Pinochet's regime on three levels at once: "politically, magically and aesthetically."[36] Among the objects in the *Diary* is a *precario* woven from incense sticks, strings, feathers, and beads. *Sabor a Mí* reproduces a grayscale photograph of the *precario*, with a poem typeset in and around the edges of its form (figure 3). The diminutive object carries Vicuña's plea for "a miracle":

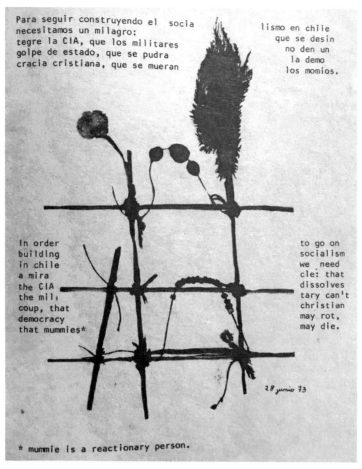

Para seguir construyendo el socia lismo en chile
necesitamos un milagro: que se desin
tegre la CIA, que los militares no den un
golpe de estado, que se pudra la demo
cracia cristiana, que se mueran los momios.

In order to go on
building socialism
in chile we need
a mira cle: that
the CIA dissolves
the mili tary can't
coup, that christian
democracy may rot,
that mummies* may die.

28 junio 73

* mummie is a reactionary person.

3. *Precario* woven from incense sticks for *A Diary of Objects for the Resistance* in 1974.

that "the CIA dissolves," that "the military forces" in Chile "can't coup," and that "[C]hristian democracy" at large in the Global South will "rot." Such a prayer might seem futile, and yet it is precisely the abject powerlessness of the object that reveals the monstrosity of the forces it opposes. As Juliet Lynd has noted, many of the *precarios* from the *Diary* also appear in *QUIPOem*,[37] some twenty-five years after the publication of *Sabor a Mí*. By the time this particular *precario* reappears in *QUIPOem*, the accompanying poem simply reads, "Weft of incense sticks: maximum fragility against maximum power." Thus the recent poem is no longer historically specific and violent in its aims, instead describing the materials of the *precario* like a caption in a catalogue raisonné. And yet Vicuña maintains her essential, underlying argument: that the weak will overcome the strong, or as Allende would have it: history belongs to the people, and neither "crimes" nor "force" will overwhelm them.

Approximately halfway through *Sabor a Mí*, the reader encounters a single glassine page with a dried, pressed leaf in the center. The leaf stands alone, without any contextual information, and the reader is invited to contemplate the look, the touch, and even the sound and smell of the thing itself. This minimalist collage acts as a frontispiece for the section dedicated to *Otoño*, an art installation Vicuña staged in Santiago prior to her departure for England. Like much of Vicuña's other work from the period, the installation celebrated socialism in Chile, and the task of gathering and installing the leaves in the gallery was a collective effort. Vicuña's artist's statement, reproduced in *Sabor a Mí*, presents a kind of manifesto for her revolutionary poetics:

> the "new being" is one who has a new perception of time and knows it can't be wasted. the new being will work to accelerate revolution, to metamorphose her mind and relationships . . . joy could make people aware of the need to fight for joy. the urgency of the present is the urgency of revolution.[38]

Vicuña urges both herself and her readers toward new conceptions of self and time. They must fight, collectively, to preserve "joy," a term Vicuña associates with the freedoms and pleasures of the Unidad Popular. As Vicuña's first major exhibition, *Otoño* ought to have been just such a joyous occasion, and yet its opening was overshadowed by the assassination of Chile's minister of the interior, Edmundo Pérez Zujovic. With her entire country in mourning, Vicuña recalled, *Otoño* "opened three days later with no one around to see it."[39]

Sabor a Mí recounts the history of *Otoño*, thus offering some consolation to the poet and to those who would fight for joy. Jill Kuhnheim argues that the leaf operates simultaneously as a reference to Chile, as self-referential pun, and as literal object: "The leaf synecdochically represents this piece; it stands for Chile, for another moment. In the context of the book, it makes reference to the page (hoja is both 'leaf' and 'page' in Spanish), but it is also simply a leaf."[40] I want to build on Kuhnheim's reading here and suggest that the leaf's being "simply a leaf" is more than a mere reminder of the original installation in Chile; rather, the leaves in *Sabor a Mí* recreate, in miniature, the *Otoño* exhibition within its pages. That the leaves come from Devon, rather than Chile, suggests that *Otoño*, like the *Saborami* corpus, can be remade at any time from locally available materials. While there is no gallery of leaves through which we might now wade, *Sabor a Mí* offers us its leaves—its pages—so that we might remember, or imagine.

The ChainLinks edition of *Saborami* registers the unresolved tensions of its predecessor, but it also shifts its focus toward documentation and dissemination. No longer a hand-fabricated artist's book, the 2011 *Saborami* anticipates a broader contemporary audience, and it demonstrates both the costs and the advantages of improved print production. Missing from the newer edition are the sensory delights of the original's hand-tipped found materials and dingy mimeograph reproductions. There are no real leaves pasted on glassine pages, and there is no envelope from Chile with its letter tucked neatly inside. Rather, the leaf appears only in silhouette, and the glassine page is printed on an opaque, coated stock. The transparency, texture, and sound of the glassine pages, like the rustle of *Otoño*'s leaves, are lost. The leaf still stands in for the 1971 exhibition, but it also historicizes *Otoño* as it appeared in *Sabor a Mí* in 1973. Like the leaves that filled the Salon Forestal, the history of *Otoño* is now layered with the sediment of documentation, and our access to those first leaves—of the exhibition, of *Sabor a Mí*—grows increasingly mediated and tenuous.

Each copy of *Sabor a Mí* contained an original envelope, with a mimeographed letter inside. Like the leaf, the envelope of the 1973 edition is reproduced photographically in *Saborami*, but the letter itself is absent—it has not been reproduced, nor has it been transcribed. Unless the reader can find one of the few extant copies of *Sabor a Mí*, the letter's contents remain unknown.[41] The text from the previous page, "(SIGUE DENTRO DEL SOBRE),"[42] or "continue inside the envelope," now points the reader to an envelope that can never be opened, haunted by a letter that has been disappeared. Refused by the sealed simulacrum of the semi-facsimile, the reader feels most palpably the rupture Vicuña suffered in 1973, as the lines of communication with Allende's Chile, and with *Sabor a Mí*, are cut.

From *Sabor a Mí* to *Saborami*, the loss of the original edition's most tactile elements is somewhat balanced by the inclusion of crisp, full-color scans of *El Cuaderno Café* (Vicuña's artist's-book-within-an-artist's-book), as well as the addition of an afterword, "Fragments of Memory." The full-color reproductions of *El Cuaderno Café* reveal, better than any mimeograph possibly could, the intricacy and fragility of its pages. Vicuña notes that *El Cuaderno Café* was originally made as a celebration of Chile during the period of Allende's presidency:

> During 3 years (1970–1973) chile was the most extraordinary place on earth . . . this notebook is to celebrate these three years, it is my way of reading chile and it was done in june 1973. it is handmade with cardboard and velvet. everything should be the result of a caress. a touched object is a charged object.[43]

Vicuña speaks of "reading" Chile, even from her distant exile, not by vision, but by touch. She implies that to handle the book is to charge its pages with affective energy—as though a reader's presence or caress might bring the book's memories back to life. It is difficult to read this passage in the 2011 edition without feeling somehow bereft—for if "a touched object is a charged object," what is left to caress in this later edition? We may find some satisfaction in the enhanced detail of the full-color reproductions; the photographs of Allende and Violeta Parra are more easily recognized, and the texture of *El Cuaderno Café*'s materials is at least visible, if not tangible. But these glossy, full-color pages repel any actual touch, as if to remind the reader that she is still farther from *El Cuaderno Café* than ever before. These tactile failures dramatize Vicuña's experience of exile, recalling a Chilean homeland she and her compatriots could only ever grasp at arm's length. If the original *Sabor a Mí*, in all its conspicuous materiality, served as a touchstone, a way of returning home to Con-cón, then the later edition falters, and the reader's own experience of loss and distance echoes that of the exiled poet.

While the ChainLinks edition of *Saborami* reproduces much of the content of *Sabor a Mí*, with varying degrees of accuracy, it also includes entirely new content in "Fragments of Memory: An Afterward." The new material historicizes the production of *Sabor a Mí*, but it also restores to the historical record several important elements that were absent or impossible in the 1973 edition: a painting of Salvador Allende's death, Vicuña's personal account of the losses she and her fellow Chileans suffered, and a poster picturing her disappeared uncle, Carlos Enrique.

The Beau Geste edition of *Sabor a Mí* contains reproductions of Vicuña's paintings, paired with brief explanatory texts. The singular exception is Vicuña's 1973 painting, *Salvador Allende's Death*, of which no image appears. Instead, Vicuña offers this textual placeholder:

> The Coup d'Etat is the red stain, the crime, the flying arbitrariness and this is the blood and the wounds of Salvador. The Coup is the Black Smoke killing all forms of life, transforming gardens into deserts. From the paradise of invention Chile was, there is nothing left but bones, stones, skeletons. . . . His death kills all my suns, my corners, my union, my velocity. Socialist Chile was all my energy; finally I was not *I* anymore, I was *US* for the first time!
>
> And whether his death will fertilize the ground for revolution or will mean the end of our one and only possibility, his death is my own death, and I will only come back to life when the revolution does, when the deserted plain which is fascist Chile now germinates again with revolution.[44]

Vicuña's reference to germination alludes to the "seeds" of Allende's final address, and her fierce declaration—that Allende's death is her own—offers back to him his own sentiments: she will repay his loyalty to the people with her life. The intense intimacy of this connection is haunted, however, by the conspicuous absence of the painting—as though the horror of Allende's death were too overwhelming to represent, as though it, too, must be disappeared. Indeed, even in *Saborami*, the explanatory text above remains as it was in 1973, placed with the other paintings and their descriptions, while the image of the painting now appears on the first page of the newly added afterword. This persistent separation of text and image suggests that while the explanatory text is historically bounded, Allende's death remains an open wound, still "afterward" and in the present.

The recuperation of the painting in the 2011 edition marks the first time that Vicuña's visual representation of the trauma of the coup—Salvador Allende's death, and the figurative death of the poet, too—appears in the *Saborami* corpus. The painting returns, unbidden and haunting. Its imagery is unsettling: a wide, red gash spills droplets of blood into a dark maw, and a plume of dark smoke rises from the barren landscape of Chile. The concentration of red pigment in the center of the canvas, and its juxtaposition with the jagged edges of the broken land, and with the sea below, make for a vertiginous focal point. The viewer cannot help but stare into the senseless unfoldings of the scarlet stain, and to pitch forward into the abyss with the spilled blood. Here there is no trace of the revolution's germination, only the stones and the bones, and a human heart, severed from the body and emptied of its blood. In an uncannily prophetic coincidence, the painting makes visible what the text alone could not: the blood of Allende, and, as we now know, the bodies of so many of the disappeared dropping into the sea. Thus the painting resurrects Allende and predicts, metonymically, the bodies of the disappeared, only for readers to remember and witness their loss once more. Like other audiences before them, readers of the contemporary *Saborami* cannot escape their place in history, nor help but perpetuate the melancholic returns of the coup's trauma.

Later in the "Afterward," in the passages "What we lost" and "The Dream," Vicuña attempts to explain the losses she and her fellow Chileans suffered as a result of the coup:

> In the Chile before the coup, the "I" was experienced simultaneously as individual and collective. We felt it when a million people marched together in Santiago (a city of only 3 million people) to salute Salvador Allende. We felt it as we chanted "ahora somos nosotros" "now we are us." Not the American "us versus them," but a collective us, including us all, even those who were against Allende.[45]

These statistics and translations accommodate an American readership —a readership less likely to understand the import of collective identity in pre-coup Chile. The passage clarifies that Chileans understood the pronoun "us" as an inclusive collective, rather than the more divisive meaning familiar to American readers (i.e., "us versus them"). Vicuña's explanations seem particularly shaped by the rhetoric of the Occupy Wall Street movement, which gathered nearby Vicuña's home in New York during the year of *Saborami*'s publication. In their critiques of income inequality, Occupiers often relied on an opposition between "us" (i.e., "the 99 percent") and "them" (i.e., "the 1 percent"). Thus Vicuña's language in this passage, couched in the lived history of the *Saboramis*, seems to challenge the Occupiers to adopt an ethos of reciprocal engagement with the opposition: they must remember that even the most distant "other" remains part of "nosotros," of the collective. For Vicuña, at least, nothing less than a complete, inclusive social body suffices to fulfill the democratic vision of the Unidad Popular.

The Future Past

In the *Saborami* corpus, the twin forces of mourning and remaking drive the poet's repeated acts of return. To return, to recover, to resurrect what has been lost might seem a failed project from the very outset—a melancholia born from a process of mourning that never completes—and yet, the *Saborami* corpus is also an open-ended project that continually evolves in response to its present moment. The trajectories of Vicuña's returns are ever in search of that "chip of messianic time," the smallest object or act that, in its "maximum fragility," will unleash the power of *pachacuti*. Within this indigenous idea of momentous change, Vicuña finds a model of revolution for redressing the trauma and the failures recollected in the *Saborami* corpus.

Vicuña's faith in woven incense sticks, a spiral in the sand, or the *Saboramis*—in *Guardian*, or even one of its single feathers—persists precisely because these works form part of a much larger, lifelong ritual for the revolution. Each small gesture of devotion to social democracy brings Vicuña closer to the moment when the present will open onto the past, when history might be rewritten and redeemed. Vicuña describes this incremental, precarious process in "Pajarito o Parejito," an early ars poetica first published in *Sabor a Mí*:

> And if I devoted my life
> to one of its feathers
> to living its nature
> being it understanding it
> until the end
>
> Reaching a time
> in which my acts
> are the thousand

tiny ribs of the feather
and my silence
the humming the whispering
of wind in the feather
and my thoughts
quick sharp precise
as the non-thoughts
of the feather.[46]

The intricacies of a single feather are such, Vicuña muses, that they exceed
even a lifetime's devoted contemplation. The poem meditates on the literal
feather, that slight material object that figures so integrally in *Casa Espi-
ral*, *Guardian*, and on the covers of both *Sabor a Mí* and *Saborami*. If the
feather is an emblem for the *Saboramis*, and for Vicuña's poetics in general,
it is because its "thousand / tiny ribs" gather into a precarious, but mirac-
ulous form—a single feather, the foundational element of flight, a fetish
object that turns as easily in the wind as the shift in consciousness the poet
seeks. The Spanish for "feather"—*pluma*—is, of course, also the word for
"pen." Any chance gust, any small poetic act, might be enough to turn the
feather just right, to tip our collective conscience toward participatory de-
mocracy and the redemption of history. Thus the speaker projects herself
into the messianic moment: at the edge of time and human understanding,
her "acts" of devotion become the barbed ribs of the feather itself.

At this final, imagined edge, Vicuña's returns to Con-cón, to the mere
raw materials of her *precarios*, might seem complete. And yet this final
transformation is only imagined, framed by the conditional "if" in the
opening line: there is no "then" to conclude Vicuña's proposition. The eli-
sion of the poet's thoughts and the non-thoughts of the feather also re-
mains tantalizingly incomplete; her thoughts are still *her* thoughts, as the
simile indicates: "precise / as the non-thoughts / of the feather." Thus the
true time of redemption is still in the offing. With no immediate resolution
for the trauma endured in Chile, nor for the continual emergence of new
forms of political violence and oppression, the *Saboramis* both memori-
alize and enact Allende's deferred hopes for social democracy. So long as
readers return to Con-cón and to *Sabor a Mí*, the project of the Unidad
Popular lives on. With each incremental act of devotion, one may still hope
for redemption, like so many feathers adrift and turning in the wind to-
ward Paradise.

NOTES

1. Raúl Zurita, "Excerpt from *INRI*: The Sea / El mar," in *The Oxford Book
of Latin American Poetry*, ed. Ernesto Livon-Grosman and Cecilia Vicuña (New
York: Oxford University Press, 2009), 494.

2. Felipe Ehrenberg, "A few explanatory words," in *Sabor a Mí* (Cullompton, Devon, UK: Beau Geste Press, 1973), 1.

3. Translated from the Spanish in Victor Figueroa Clark, *Salvador Allende: Revolutionary Democrat* (London: Pluto, 2013), 127.

4. The "Rettig Report," produced in 1991 by The National Commission for Truth and Reconciliation, and the "Valech Reports," produced in 2004, 2005, and 2011 by The National Commission on Political Imprisonment and Torture, serve as the primary records of the atrocities committed under Pinochet's dictatorship. For more on the politics of collective memory in post-coup Chile, consult Alexander Wilde, "Irruptions of Memory: Expressive Politics in Chile's Transition to Democracy," *Journal of Latin American Studies* 312 (1999): 473–500, and Macarena Gómez-Barris, *Where Memory Dwells: Culture and State Violence in Chile* (Berkeley: University of California Press, 1999).

5. Gideon Long, "Chile Recognises 9,800 More Victims of Pinochet's Rule," *BBC News*, August 18, 2011 (accessed November 18, 2016); www.bbc.co.uk /news/world-latin-america-14584095.

6. Raúl Zurita, "Written on the Sky," interview by Daniel Borzutsky, August 26, 2010 (accessed November 20, 2016); www.poetryfoundation.org/features/articles /detail/69577.

7. Ricardo Gutiérrez-Mouat, "The Politics of Contemporary Chilean Poetry," *The American Poetry Review* 18.5 (1989): 15–22.

8. The poems collected in *Sabor a Mí* derive from an earlier manuscript of the same title, but the remainder of that manuscript was unpublished until recently, with the Spanish-language release of *El Zen Surado* (Santiago, Chile: Editorial Catalonia, 2013). Hereafter I will distinguish the 1973 Beau Geste edition, *Sabor a Mí*, from the 2011 ChainLinks edition, *Saborami*. I use "the *Saborami* corpus" or "*Saboramis*" when referring to all of the editions together, including the 2007 edition from Ediciones Universidad Diego Portales and the 2015 edition from Galería Patricia Ready.

9. The most extensive critical responses to *Sabor a Mí* include Soledad Bianchi, "Pasaron desde aquel ayer ya tantos años, o acerca de Cecilia Vicuña y la 'Tribu No,'" *Hispamérica* 17.51 (1988): 87–94, and Magda Sepúlveda, "Cecilia Vicuña: la subjetividad poética como una operación Contracanónica," *Revista Chilena de Literatura* 57 (2000): 111–26. While making final preparations for this essay's publication, I discovered Candice Amich's unpublished dissertation, "Performing Future Memory: A Critical Poetics of Globalization" (doctoral dissertation, Rutgers University, 2012), which provides an excellent overview of the rich political history surrounding *Sabor a Mí*'s production in 1973. Amich anticipates some aspects of the argument I develop in this essay, calling *Sabor a Mí* "an artist's book that mourns the present and looks back on the immediate past longingly as it strives to imagine a future." Other English-language sources are scarce, but José Felipe Alvergue addresses the *Saboramis* in "Twentieth-Century Experiments in Form: A Critical Re-reading of Cecilia Vicuña's Indigenism as Episteme," *Comparative Literature* 68.3 (2014): 1, 10. However, Alvergue describes the 2011 edition as a "reissue" of the Beau Geste edition, rather than a distinct version, and mistakenly notes that "[a]ll text from the Chainlinks Press reissue of *saborami*, also cited as

Saboramí, appears in both Spanish and English." Although *Sabor a Mí* was always a bilingual text, several of the poems and other texts in the 1973 edition, including "Pajarito o Parejito," as discussed in this essay, appear only in Spanish. Conversely, certain contents in the 2011 edition, like the afterword, appear only in English and clearly target North American readers, as I explain later in this essay. These exceptions suggest that more attention is needed to understand the ways in which distinct editions of the *Saboramís* target and shape their audiences through language.

10. Cecilia Vicuña, *Saboramí* (Philadelphia: ChainLinks, 2011), 160.

11. Notable literary responses include Fernando Alegría's novel, *El Paso de los Gansos* (New York: Ediciones Puelches, 1975); Gonzalo Rojas' *Oscuro* (Caracas: Monte A_vila Editores, 1977); and Raul Zurita's first two books of poems, *Purgatorio* (Santiago de Chile: Editorial Universitaria, 1979) and *Anteparaíso* (Santiago de Chile: Editores Asociados, 1982). Several literary journals dedicated to Chilean literature flourished in exile, including *Literatura Chilena en el Exilio* (founded by Fernando Alegría and David Valjalo in Los Angeles) and *Araucaria de Chile* (edited by Volodia Teitelboim in Paris).

12. Other books in which elements of *Sabor a Mí* reappear include *Precario / Precarious* (New York: Tanam Press, 1983), *QUIPOem* (Middletown: Wesleyan University Press, 1997), *Saboramí* (Santiago, Chile: Ediciones Universidad Diego Portales, 2007), *Otoño* (Santiago, Chile: Museo Nacional Bellas Artes, 2007), and most significantly, a second semi-facsimile edition, *Saboramí*, published in 2015 by Galería Patricia Ready in Santiago, Chile. Unlike the 2011 edition from Chain-Links, this newest edition recreates the appearance of the Beau Geste edition more convincingly, from its dimensions to its gold- and tan-colored interior pages.

13. Unlike the original *Sabor a Mí*, *Citizen* has enjoyed a broad public audience, suggesting that contemporary readers may now be better prepared not only for *Saboramí*'s narrative and visual complexities, but also for its cries for vengeance and redemption. Regarding *Citizen*'s reception, see "Citizen in the Classroom, Citizen in the World," on the website of Graywolf Press, n.d. (accessed November 20, 2016); www.graywolfpress.org/resources/citizen-classroom-citizen-world.

14. "Cecilia Vicuña at the UA Poetry Center's Poetry Off the Page Symposium," University of Arizona Poetry Center, April 4, 2012 (accessed June 30, 2012); www.arizona.edu/features/cecilia-vicuñ-ua-poetry-center's-poetry-page-symposium.

15. Rafael E. Nuñes and Eve Sweetser, "With the Future Behind Them: Convergent Evidence from Aymara Language and Gesture in the Crosslinguistic Comparison of Spatial Construals of Time," *Cognitive Science* 30.3 (2006): 401–450.

16. Walter Benjamin, Hannah Arendt, and Harry Zohn, *Illuminations* (New York: Harcourt, Brace & World, 1968).

17. Ibid., 263.

18. Vicuña, *Sabor a Mí*, 142.

19. Paul R. Steele and Catherine J. Allen, *Handbook of Inca Mythology* (Santa Barbara: ABC-CLIO, 2004), 226.

20. Lucy Lippard, "Spinning the Common Thread," in *The Precarious: The Art and Poetry of Cecilia Vicuña*, ed. M. Catherine de Zegher (Hanover: University Press of New England, 1997), 6–15.

21. Like Vicuña, Raúl Zurita is known for his large text-drawings in the land-

scape. A fellow Chilean poet, artist, and survivor of the coup, he is perhaps best known for the poem he "bulldozed into the sand of the Atacama Desert." For more, see Forrest Gander, "Into the Mouths of Volcanoes," *Harriet*, January 1, 2008 (accessed January 1, 2014); www.poetryfoundation.org/harriet/2008/09/into-the-mouths-of-volcanoes/.

22. See Alvergue, "Twentieth-Century Experiments in Form," for analysis of *Casa Espiral* and Vicuña's *gramma kellcani*.

23. Cecilia Vicuña, *QUIPOem* (Middletown: Wesleyan University Press, 1997), 12.

24. Cecilia Vicuña, *Precario/Precarious* (New York: Tanam Press, 1983), 3.

25. Ibid.

26. Vicuña, *QUIPOem*, 44.

27. Ehrenberg, "A few explanatory words," 1.

28. Niall Binns, "Saborami," *Review: Literature and Arts of the Americas* 45.2 (2012): 260–61.

29. Vicuña, *Sabor a Mí*, 142.

30. Sepúlveda, "Cecilia Vicuña: la subjetividad poética como una operación Contracanónica," 123–4.

31. Vicuña, *Saborami* (Beau Geste, 1973), 159–60.

32. Ibid., 159.

33. In *Saborami*, there is also a photograph placed just above the spiral, a small group portrait with Vicuña and Bertoni in the first row, surrounded by other members of the Chilean activist art collective, the Tribu No. For more on Vicuña's involvement with the Tribu No, see Bianchi, "Pasaron desde aquel ayer ya tantos años, o acerca de Cecilia Vicuña y la 'Tribu No,'" 87–94.

34. See my discussion of Vicuña's poem, "Research Project," in "Introduction to Cecilia Vicuña," in *Angels of the Americlypse: An Anthology of New Latin@ Writing*, ed. John Chávez and Carmen Giménez-Smith (Denver: Counterpath, 2014).

35. Vicuña, *Sabor a Mí*, 10.

36. Ibid.

37. Juliet Lynd, "Precarious Resistance: Weaving Opposition in the Poetry of Cecilia Vicuña," *PMLA* 120.5 (2005): 1588–1607.

38. Vicuña, *Sabor a Mí*, 74.

39. Ibid, 159.

40. Jill Kuhnheim, *Spanish American Poetry at the End of the Twentieth Century* (Austin: University of Texas Press, 2004), 53.

41. The contents of the enclosed letter are a continuation of the text printed on the previous page of *Sabor a Mí*, rendering a fragmentary view of Vicuña's conversation with Francisco Rivera.

42. Vicuña, *Saborami*, 88.

43. Ibid., 43.

44. Ibid., 102.

45. Ibid., 161.

46. Cecilia Vicuña, *Unravelling Words & the Weaving of Water* (Minneapolis: Graywolf Press, 1992).

BIBLIOGRAPHY

Works by Cecilia Vicuña

POETRY

Sabor a Mí. Cullompton, UK: Beau Geste Press, 1973.

Siete Poemas. Bogotá: Ediciones Centro Colombo Americano, 1979.

Precario/Precarious. Trans. Anne Twitty. New York: Tanam Press, 1983.

Luxumei o El Traspié de la Doctrina. Mexico City: Los Libros del Fakir 33, Editorial Oasis, 1983.

PALABRARmas. Buenos Aires: Ediciones El Imaginero, 1984.

Samara. Valle del Cauca, Colombia: Ediciones Embalaje del Museo Rayo, 1986.

La Wik'uña. Santiago, Chile: Francisco Zegers Editor, 1990.

Unravelling Words & the Weaving of Water. Trans. Eliot Weinberger. Minneapolis: Graywolf Press, 1992.

PALABRARmas/WURWAPPINschaw. Edinburgh: Morning Star Publications, 1994.

La realidad es una línea. Kortrijk, Belgium: Kanaal Art Foundation, 1994.

Word & Thread. Edinburgh: Morning Star Publications, 1996.

The Precarious: The Art & Poetry of Cecilia Vicuña / QUIPOem. Ed. Catherine de Zegher. Trans. Esther Allen. Middletown, CT: Wesleyan University Press, 1997.

cloud-net. New York: Art in General, 1999.

El Templo. New York: Situations, 2001.

Instan. Berkeley: Kelsey Street Press, 2002.

i tu. Buenos AiresL Tsé-Tsé, 2004.

Palabrarmas. Santiago, Chile: RIL Editores, 2005.

Sabor a Mí. Santiago, Chile: Ediciones Universidad Diego Portales, 2007.

V. Lima, Peru: tRope, 2009.

Soy Yos: Antología, 1966–2006. Santiago, Chile: Lom Ediciones, 2011.

Saborami. Philadelphia: ChainLinks, 2011.

Chanccani Quipu. New York: Granary Books, 2012.

Spit Temple. Brooklyn: Ugly Duckling Press, 2012.

El Zen Surado. Santiago, Chile: Editorial Catalonia, 2013.

About to Happen. Catskill, NY: Siglio, 2017.

New and Selected Poems of Cecilia Vicuña. Ed. Rosa Alcalá. Berkeley: Kelsey Street Press, 2018.

EDITED VOLUMES

Artists for Democracy: El Archivo de Cecilia Vicuña. With Lucy R. Lippard and Paulina Varas Alarcón. Santiago, Chile: Museo Nacional de Bellas Artes, 2014.

Adan, Martin. *The Cardboard House*. Minneapolis: Graywolf Press (The Palabra Sur Series of Latin American Literature), 1988.

Casares, Adolfo Bioy. *A Plan for Escape*. Minneapolis: Graywolf Press (The Palabra Sur Series of Latin American Literature), 1988.

Castellanos, Rosario. *The Selected Poems of Rosario Castellanos*. Minneapolis: Graywolf Press, 1988.

Huidobro, Vicente. *Altazor*. Minneapolis: Graywolf Press (The Palabra Sur Series of Latin American Literature), 1988.

The Oxford Book of Latin American Poetry. New York: Oxford University Press, 2009.

Ül: Four Mapuche Poets. Pittsburgh: Latin American Review Press, 1998.

SELECTED INTERVIEWS

Horsfield, Craigie. "What Art May Be." *Chain* 9 (2002): 112–24.

Isbell, Billie Jean, and Regina Harrison. "Metaphor Spun: A Conversation with Cecilia Vicuña." In *The Precarious: The Art and Poetry of Cecilia Vicuña*, ed. M. Catherine de Zegher (Middletown, CT: Wesleyan University Press, 1997), 47–58.

Levi Strauss, David. "The Memory of the Fingers." In *cloud-net* (New York: Art in General, 1999), 18–21.

Lippard, Lucy. "The Vicuña and the Leopard: Chilean Artist Cecilia Vicuña Talks to Lucy Lippard." *Red Bass / Women's International Arts Issue* 10 (1986): 16–18.

Selected Criticism and Reviews

Alvergue, José Felipe. "The Material Etymologies of Cecilia Vicuña: Art, Sculpture, and Poetic Communities." *Minnesota Review: A Journal of Committed Writing* 82 (2014): 59–96.

———. "Twentieth-Century Experiments in Form: A Critical Re-reading of Cecilia Vicuña's Indigenism as Episteme." *Comparative Literature* 68.3 (2014): 1, 10.

Amich, Candice. "From Precarity to Planetarity: Cecilia Vicuña's Kon Kon." *The Global South* 7.2 (2014): 134–52.

Barnitz, Jacqueline. *Twentieth-Century Art of Latin America*. Austin: University of Texas Press, 2001.

Bianchi, Soledad. "Pasaron desde aquel ayer ya tantos años, o acerca de Cecilia Vicuña y la Tribu No." *Hispamérica: Revista de Literatura* 17 (1988): 87–94.

Brown, Julie Phillips. "'touch in transit': Manifestation/Manifestación in Cecilia Vicuña's *cloud-net*." *Contemporary Women's Writing* 5.3 (2011): 208–231.

Clark, Meredith Gardner. "Navegando el Espacio Háptico Cuerda por Cuerda: La Abstracción y la Lógica del Khipu en la Obra Visual de Cecilia Vicuña." In *Vicuñiana: El Arte y la Poesía de Cecilia Vicuña: Un Diálogo Sur/Norte*, ed. Meredith Gardner Clark (Santiago, Chile: Cuarto Proprio, 2016), 193–214.

———. "Warping the Word: The Technology of Weaving in the Poetry of Jorge Eduardo Eielson and Cecilia Vicuña." *Textile: The Journal of Cloth and Culture* 10.3 2012): 312–27.

Kuhnheim, Jill. *Spanish American Poetry at the End of the Twentieth Century*. Austin: University of Texas Press, 2004.

Lippard, Lucy. "Spinning the Common Thread." In *The Precarious: The Art and Poetry of Cecilia Vicuña*, ed. M. Catherine de Zegher (Middletown, CT: Wesleyan University Press, 1997), 7–15.

Lynd, Juliet. "Precarious Resistance: Weaving Opposition in the Poetry of Cecilia Vicuña." *PMLA* 120.5 (2005): 1588–1607.

Méndez-Ramírez, Hugo. "Cryptic Weaving." In *The Precarious: The Art and Poetry of Cecilia Vicuña*, edited by M. Catherine de Zegher (Middletown, CT: Wesleyan University Press, 1997), 59–71.

Nómez, N. "La poesía chilena: Representaciones de Terror y Fragmentación del Sujeto en los Primeros Años de Dictadura." *Acta Literaria* 36 (2008): 87–101.

Osman, Jena. "Is Poetry the News?: The Poethics of the Found Text." *Jacket* 32 (2007); jacketmagazine.com/32/p-osman.shtml.

Sepúlveda, Magda. "Cecilia Vicuña: La Subjetividad Poética como una Operación Contracanónica." *Revista Chilena de Literatura* 57 (2000): 111–26.

Sherwood, Kenneth. "Elaborate Versionings: Characteristics of Emergent Performance in Three Print/Oral/Aural Poets." *Oral Tradition* 21 (2006): 119–47.

———. "Sound Written and Sound Breathing: Versions of Palpable Poetics." In *The Precarious: The Art and Poetry of Cecilia Vicuña*, edited by M. Catherine de Zegher (Middletown, CT: Wesleyan University Press, 1997), 79–93.

Toledo, Eugenia. "Tejer y Destejer en Cecilia Vicuña." *ALPHA: Revista de Artes, Letras y Filosofia* 11 (1995): 51–62.

Ugalde, Sharon Keefe. "Hilos y Palabras: Diseños de una Ginotradición (Rosario Castellanos, Pat Mora y Cecilia Vicuña)." *Salina: Revista de Lletres* 16 (2002): 219–26.

Weinberger, Eliot. "Basuritas / Little Litter." *Poliester* 3 (1992): 28–32.

Witzling, Mara R. "Cecilia Vicuña." In *Voicing Today's Visions: Writings by Contemporary Women Artists* (New York: Universe Publishing, 1994), 310–32.

de Zegher, M. Catherine. "Ouvrage: Knot a Not, Notes as Knots." In *The Precarious: The Art and Poetry of Cecilia Vicuña*, edited by M. Catherine de Zegher (Middletown, CT: Wesleyan University Press, 1997), 17–46.

ROSMARIE WALDROP

POEMS

FROM *Blindsight*

Evening Sun

for Sophie Hawkes

1

On a balcony onto the Seekonk stands. And full of thoughts of winter. My friend. And drunk with red wine I. Think of the power. Of a single word. Like for example "fact." When I know what matters. Is between.

But how with gnarled hands hold the many and how? The sun and shadow of Rhode Island? Let alone the earth?

Down swoops the hawk. From the sky over Providence. The sky over my head. Down to the leaves inward curled on the ground. But not like buds. Yellow. A cat is buried here and the leaves. Swirl up in the wind.

In the hour of the hawk. What is meant by: I think? Or even: I sit under clouds in which. Rain gathers weight. I sit in my mother's shawl which is. Threadbare. In my head I sit. By the river Euphrates. Strange like water the skies of the dead.

And high from the branches of the maple. Like a prelude to snow. White feathers.

2

But music. Quickens the house down into its shadows. So trembles air in the sun and the shape of the tree blurs as if through a flame seen. Swarms of monarch butterflies stir and brush your cheeks. In celebration. In memory.

Almost visible the words of the song. Leave the singer's mouth and rise up into the sun. Which goes crazy instead of down.

Floods, storms, fires. But a tank won't be stopped by a word. Not even if you shout it from the middle of the road, with hands thrown forward and fingers spread out.

Nor by music. Though its power is great. Like the heat of noon it slants between body and soul. Difficult, then. Unaccustomed as we are to beauty. To know which is effect and which cause.

Not merely as a sailor is present in a ship am I. In my body. Intermingled.

3

My father thought he had the gift to read the stars. To know if the light in a person's eyes. Had gone out. To hypnotize. I stayed awake. Weak in the knees am I. Not a spiritual woman. And pulled toward the earth.

He said, you have to look from afar: what children we are, so gravely at play. In worn out light, in afterglow. Yet fire present is in words.

Which is why we try to read. The stone, the wood and grass, the cloud and lightning and air. And the ancients and poets. And the frogs croak in the swamps.

And to stand. Sky around your shoulders high on a mountain. Or balcony. And know you must cast. Like so many shadows. Your words onto the distance. Or paper. But will they span?

And the next morning you go to the bakery and ask for a loaf of rye. This too is work and without it the dream crumbles inside its glass case. And we must travel the ocean just to see it.

4

With great force our bodies are pulled out of our mothers. And ever since, we walk like almost orphans. With a scar on the brain.

And remember childhood among strings and puppets. Crutches. Knees under the chin tucked. And toy warriors with lance and shield and red badge to ensure courage.

Which we need to live in three dimensions. Of dry air. Or wet. Among gauges for measurement made of wire and string. That my father had looked at before.

And tapped with his finger to make sure. They were steady, not broken. And hitched his pants against gravity and tried to discern. The tether between particle and wave.

Tea has dribbled on his book. The letters under the drops enlarge till a wavy gray absorbs the excess. If however too deep you plunge, he thinks. Into thought. You can't rest till you get to the bottom.

5

Let us take our time, Sophie, fitting bones to the earth. Though they are turning visible inside the flesh, and our blood. No longer overflows and spills.

Much work still to be done. And the smell of ripe peaches. And Long-Jing tea. And lungs full of words. And being an opaque body that intercepts the rays of the sun.

Initial Conditions

IF THOUGHT IS, from the beginning, divorced from itself, a picnic may fade before the first bottle is pulled from the basket. If you ask: Do I know what I am holding? I will offer it to you.

If a father touches the neck of his son's girlfriend, he'll fall into a Freudian sleep. If he intends to, has his palm already felt her gasp?

If you think: A young girl's a vacuum, you mean to rush and fill it. If you ask: Why? one whole chapter of life may close.

Perhaps we can't ask these questions. The traffic moves too fast. We can only throw up our arms. As in a wind tunnel?

The question: Why? is most nostalgic. In twenty years of marriage one might be in love with one another. Or with another?

Can we utter sounds and mean: young girl's neck? With one foot slightly in front of the other? Say: Come have a sandwich, and mean: best to slow down?

Could we say that listening to familiar words is quite different from a girl seen both full-face and from the side at once? Like Cleopatra? If we agree that "Have a sandwich" means: "best to slow down," can we separate marriage to her brother at eleven from being carried in to Caesar in a carpet?

Either we don't move or much follows. The history of the universe predicated on ten seconds of initial turbulence?

If you ask: Where did it all begin? do I answer with a cry of distress, the tip of a triangle, a plan to picnic, a sudden toothache?

If in doubt I will offer it to you.

Intentionalities

MY HAND MOVES along your thigh. When we describe intentions, is the ventriloquist taken over by the dummy? Or pretending to be a ghost?

Instead of "I meant you" I could say, "we walked through wet streets, toward a dark well." But could I speak of you this way? And why does it sound wrong to say "I meant you by pulling away?" Like lovers caught in headlights?

If I talk of you it connects me to you. By an infinite of betweens, not by touching you in the dark. Touch is the sense I place outside myself for you to ride.

When I mean you I may show it—if we stand close—by putting my head on your shoulder. You can show you understand by describing the well under the trap door. What will you say? Don't be frightened?

The feeling I have when I mean you draws an arc of strength between my hips and the small of my back. It doesn't follow that "meaning you" is being exhilarated by terror. Of course not, you say: We need a red thread to run through, but it's entangled with space, form, future. Is this true?

It would be wrong to say that meaning you stands for a forgotten part of myself, a treatise on labyrinths, a path leading nowhere. Am I living in a shell where the sea comes in along with its sound? And drowns us?

I was speaking of you because I wanted to think about you. "I wanted" does not describe a general before battle. Nor, on the other hand, a ship heading for shipwreck. There is no way to decide whether this is an autobiography or a manifesto.

Feverish Propositions

You told me, if something is not used it is meaningless, and took my temperature, which I had thought to save for a more difficult day. In the mirror, every night, the same face, a bit more thread-bare, a dress worn too long. The moon was out in the cold, along with the restless, dissatisfied wind that seemed to change the location of the sycamores. I expected reproaches because I had mentioned the word love, but you only accused me of stealing your pencil, and sadness disappeared with sense. You made a ceremony out of holding your head in your hands because, you said, it could not be contained in itself.

•

If we could just go on walking through these woods and let the pine branches brush our faces, living would still make beads of sweat on your forehead, but you wouldn't have to worry about what you call my exhibitionism. All you liked about trees was the way the light came through the leaves in sheets of precise, parallel rays, like slant rain. This may be an incomplete explanation of our relation, but we've always feared the dark inside the body. You agree there could be no seduction if the structures of propositions did not stand in a physical relation, so that we could get from one to the other. Even so, not every moment of happiness is to hang one's clothes on.

•

I might have known you wouldn't talk to me. But to claim you just didn't want to disguise your thoughts! We've walked along this road before, I said, though perhaps in heavier coats not designed to reveal the form of the body. Later, the moon came out and threw the shadows of branches across the street where they remained, broken. Feverishly you examined the tacit conventions on which conversation depends. I sighed as one does at night, looking down into the river. I wondered if by throwing myself in I could penetrate to the essence of its character, or should I wait for you to stab me as you had practiced in your dream? You said this question, like most philosophical problems, arose from failing to understand the tale of the two youths, two horses, and two lilies. You could prove to me that the deepest rivers are, in fact, no rivers at all.

•

From this observation we turned to consider passion. Looking at the glints of light on the water, you tried to make me tell you not to risk the excitement—to recommend cold baths. The lack of certainty, of direction, of duration, was its own argument, unlike going into a bar to get drunk and getting drunk. Your face was alternately hot and cold, as if translating one language into another—gusts from the storm in your heart, the pink ribbon in your pocket. Its actual color turned out to be unimportant, but its presence disclosed something essential about membranes. You said there was still time, you could still break it off, go abroad, make a movie. I said (politely, I thought) this wouldn't help you. You'd have to kill yourself.

•

Tearing your shirt open, you drew my attention to three dogs in a knot. This served to show how something general can be recorded in unpedigreed notation. I pointed to a bench by a willow, from which we could see the gas tanks across the river, because I thought a bench was a simple possibility: one could sit on it. The black hulks of the tanks began to sharpen in the cold dawn light, though when you leaned against the railing I could smell your hair, which ended in a clean round line on your neck, as was the fashion that year. I had always resented how nimble your neck became whenever you met a woman, regardless of rain falling outside or other calamities. Now, at least, you hunched your shoulders against the shadow of doubt.

•

This time of day, hesitation can mean tottering on the edge, just before the water breaks into the steep rush and spray of the fall. What could I do but turn with the current and get choked by my inner speed? You tried to breathe against the acceleration, waiting for the air to consent. All the while, we behaved as if this search for a pace were useful, like reaching for a plank or wearing raincoats. I was afraid we would die before we could make a statement, but you said that language presupposed meaning, which would be swallowed by the roar of the waterfall.

•

Toward morning, walking along the river, you tossed simple objects into the air which was indifferent around us, though it moved off a little, and again as you put your hand back in your pocket to test the degree of hardness. Everything else remained the same. This is why, you said, there was no fiction.

Time Ravel

1

With the mind's eye. We see against the light. The way we see the dead. My father reading at his desk. Read, road, door. Remains unclear how my brain chose to store this image rather than another. Or how it veers toward the surface. Ulysses fights his way back to an Ithaca with four-lane highways. Where serfdom has been replaced by alienation, anomie, anxiety. Returns, reverts, replies. A borrowed book, the sword to its scabbard, in recompense, response.

2

The assumption is that the sirens have drowned in the alphabet. And been replaced by warnings, war, warp. My father's stopped reading to watch a magpie rising black and white against the sky. Memories are many. Glitter in the brain, ready to be pilfered. Does this fit my image of the real? Where the norms of social interaction have multiplied, and spontaneous acts come back as mistake? Or combustion? Natural feeling, temperament, disposition, impulse, energy all lashed fast to the mast. The rubrics of the dictionary meaning business.

3

Columbus' crew were afraid they would not come back, unable to close the loop time won't permit, but sometimes a ghost or shifting winds. Or the memory of a big slab of ice that a man with leather mittens splits across the middle. To reveal the time hidden within where I might not find my body for the cold. And though my mother wraps the slab in a rag before putting it in the icebox, it would not warm me enough to have a self. Same, identical. Interest, confidence, esteem, reliance, respect. Skin, though it takes pains to remember caresses, is marked by the roads that pain takes.

4

Color of fables, the Indies, scarves, curves. Every island Columbus found was a vow kept toward a map with no elsewhere. High spirits and cloud theory reflect in the sea and stitch coordinates toward a flight of gulls, of stairs. America becomes a continent while numbers pass through the air, soar out of bounds. Or run from danger, flicker of fear. How can I remember my parents if I need to run my hands over my body to make sure it is there. Or lean forward to brace against *our element*, deflect its head-on force into a more general time. Where God for love of us wears clothes.

5

I can't hear my father's voice, moored as if among antipodes, articulation hindered by head hanging down and a spill of oceans. Spell, sperm, spatter, splash. If the mechanisms of subjectivity are disturbed it requires total restructuring of the world. As when I first learned that the earth turns on its axis, that spleen, n., is a highly vascular ductless gland which serves to produce certain changes in the blood. Merriment (obs.), caprice, spite, anger, malice, moroseness, melancholy. Most marked in complex civilizations where the pace of events and cordless voices exceeds all the running one can do just to stay in one place. Though silver, on clear days, is the light.

6

In haste we now blast ourselves beyond the clouds, and get lost
in skies behind the sky. It's hard to rescue time from such a sight.
And though they cast a shadow, perspective has no power over
clouds. "Bodies without surface," they vanish the moment before
the move into abstraction. The way my mother's large body evap-
orates before I can ask her to show me the breast I did not take.
Columbus, though, Magellan, Vasco, in the name of Christ and
King took firm hold of new markets. A mirror for a parrot, scis-
sors for cinnamon, a playing card for a girl naked to the waist, a
kingdom for a horse. And dust in everyone's eyes for private pur-
chase and sale. What does it mean to recall the past if I have little
sense of the present?

7

Names multiplied in the wake of caravels, clippers, communicat-
ing vessels. The spelling capricious (see spleen) as the winds. Track
itineraries, track vanished and erased, track how many pages be-
tween Circe's island and Charybdis. It is not that our sensations
need to match images in the brain, but that the brain needs a body
for frame of reference. No matter if it be square or cant, short,
squat, parts fitted together to enclose a window, door, picture or
disposition of the mind. Just as emotion shows if we're ready for
the future hovering at the edge of our eye.

8

Great beginnings too can end up a small world. Whorl, old. Set sail on the power of imagination for hearsay geographies and real dangers. With greed as secret motor. It drove them back home to cities crazy for spices and gold. In between, waves and more waves. When I think of my mother I am heavy in the pelvis with the children she wanted, and begin to sing. A complex song of if and though I never had a voice. To introduce an exclamation, condition, stipulation, untenable argument, or wish. On condition, in the event that, allowing that these long-term memories are abstractions, a different mode of thought from short-term ones. And that their differences shape my sense of time. A violet's blue as a sign of distance.

From "A Little Useless Geometry & Other Matters"

Point

Beginning or end? Visible to the eye? the microscope? the myopic? So much for definition applied in public. Coiled up and withdrawn within itself, nevertheless a stronghold of vectors. I'd say a point's not meant to start a sentence, but no one's immune to anger, greed or, on the other hand, missiles solid in the sky. If a point of pain is reflected off a field of objects the painting constructs a surface of implacable geometry. Sometimes, however, reaching to the bones. It doesn't have to be lift-off, wing-tear, and steep fall. Every step lands us in ambiguities, how much more a hike across the city, beyond fatigue or tightening in the chest. It's then I think therefore I am beside the point.

Line

I dreamed of stroking a line, caressing its ambition as long as time itself. It flew off without a tangent. To protest the direction from left to right? Because the sun was suddenly blocked? My ruler not long enough? We're supposed to know our way, as if going somewhere, but not talk to ourselves. This brings us to the difficulties of existence and accepted theories. Not to mention childbirth. What if, fluent in frustration, I want to fall silent or out of season with the leaves, without leaving a track in the cloud-chamber? Was the line an illusion of my finger or despair dashing straight at me, en route from Washington to Baghdad?

Figure to Proposition

If the eye of god is a triangle that allows him to see beyond lines (of soldiers?), then is atheism denying geometry? When you've stipulated that a cross is more than an obstructed vertical much remains to be said. (About hairs?) Words come tumbling out before I can pose them for the camera or polish the lens. Is it too late to explore local customs, the way these costumes don't cling close? Or why the view is widespread that the soul's immortal? Anxiety, I must tell you, is the main artery from heart to head that no square can bypass. The equality of its sides ought to reassure, but actually upholds the social divisions: top, bottom, right, left. When it squares your circumstance can you hold on to the gun in hand or to the hand?

POETICS STATEMENT

Composition With With

FROM "Thinking of Follows"

In the beginning there is Stein: "Everything is the same except composition and as the composition is different and always going to be different everything is not the same."

Framework

Every speech act consists of selection and combination (Saussure, Jakobson), of a double reference: to the code and to the context. The code gives us a vertical axis where the elements are linked by similarity. We choose from it whether to say young man, guy, fellow, whether to say walk, run, hurry, etc. Then we combine the selected words on a horizontal axis to say: "the guy was running down the street." We put them in a relation by syntax, by contiguity.

Literary language tends to divide according to an emphasis on one axis or the other. Some are more concerned with *le mot juste*, with *the* perfect metaphor, others, with what "happens between" the words (Olson).

For the long stretch from Romanticism through Modernism (and on?), poetry has been more or less identified with the axis of selection, relation by similarity, metaphor. This implies that the "world" is given, that the poem is an epiphany which is then "expressed"; that content is primary and determines its ("organic") form.

The alternative is emphasis on composition and process.

Here, nothing is given. Everything remains to be constructed. The poem is not "expression," but a cognitive process. I do not know beforehand where the poem will take me. As I begin working I have only a vague nucleus of energy, a few words. As soon as I start *listening* to the words, they reveal their own vectors and affinities, pull the poem—often away from the initial semantic charge.

Valéry: "When the poets enter the forest of language it is with the express purpose of getting lost."

But it is not true that "nothing is given." The blank page is not blank. We always write on top of a palimpsest. This is not a question of "influence," but of writing as dialog with a web of previous and concurrent texts, with tradition, with the culture and language we breathe and move in.

Many of us have foregrounded this awareness as technique, transforming, "translating," collaging parts of other works.

The fact that I am a woman clearly shapes my writing: thematically, in attitude, in awareness of social conditioning, marginality—but does not determine it exclusively. I don't really see "female language," "female style or technique." Because the writer, male or female, is only one partner in the process of writing. Language, in its full range, is the other. And it belongs as much to the mothers as to the fathers.

In crossing the Atlantic my phonemes settled somewhere between German and English. I speak either language with an accent. This has saved me the illusion of being the master of language. I enter it at a skewed angle, through the fissures, the slight difference.

I do not "use" the language. I interact with it. I do not communicate *via* language, but *with* it. Language is not a tool for me, but a medium infinitely larger than my intentions.

What will find resonance is out of my hands. If the poem works (and gets the chance to be read) it will set off vibrations in the reader, an experience with language—with the way it defines us as human beings.

I like the image in *Don Quixote* that compares translation to working on a tapestry: you sit behind the canvas, with a mess of threads and a pattern for each color. You follow out patterns, but have no idea what image will appear on the other side. This holds just as much for writing. We work on technical aspects, on the craft. We make a pattern that coheres. Our obsessions and preoccupations find their way into it no matter what we do.

What will appear "on the other side," what the text will "mean," is another matter. I can only hope that it gives a glimpse of that unreachable goal (which, paradoxically, is also its matrix), the concentration, the stillness of those moments when it seems we are taken out of ourselves and out of time.

Practice

> I don't even have thoughts, I have methods that make language think, take over and me by the hand. Into sense or offense, syntax stretched across rules, relations of force, fluid the dip of the plumb line, the pull of eyes . . . (*A Form / Of Taking / It All*)

I. EXPLORING THE SENTENCE

Both in "As If We Didn't Have to Talk" (in *The Aggressive Ways of the Casual Stranger*) and in *The Road Is Everywhere or Stop This Body*, I worked on making the object of one phrase flip over into being the subject of the next phrase without being repeated:

> weightless inside a density
> about to burn
> the air
> won't take the imprint we
> talk
> doubles the frequencies
> brought up short

I was interested in having the flow of a quasi-unending sentence play against the short lines that determine the rhythm. So, on one level, I was simply exacerbating the tension between sentence and line that is there in all verse. And since the thematic field is circulation systems (walking, car traffic, blood, breath, sex, economics, language) I liked the effect of hurtling down main clause highway at breakneck speed.

It was only gradually that I realized this challenge to a fixed subject-object relation has feminist implications. In many cultures, woman has been treated as object par excellence. These poems propose a grammar in which subject and object functions are reversible roles, where there is no hierarchy, but fluid and constant alternation.

After a while, though, I began to long for subordinate clauses, complex sentences. So I turned to writing prose poems. I became fascinated by Wittgenstein and the extreme closure of propositions. I tried to subvert the closure and logic from the inside, by constantly sliding between frames of reference.

> You took my temperature which I had meant to save for
> a more difficult day (*The Reproduction of Profiles*)

> I also set into play the old gender archetypes (logic and mind being "male," whereas "female" designates the illogical: emotion, body, matter), hoping to challenge these categories.

2. FRAGMENTS

Edmond Jabès, like the German Romantics, holds that the fragment is our only access to the infinite. I tend to think it is our way of apprehending anything. Our inclusive pictures are mosaics.

Juxtaposing, rather than isolating, minimal units of meaning. Hoping for the glint of light on the cut.

3. COLLAGE OR THE SPLICE OF LIFE

I turned to collage early, to get away from writing poems about my overwhelming mother. I felt I needed to do something "objective" that would get me out of myself. But when I looked at the collage poems a while later: they were still about my mother.

This made me realize that subject matter is nothing to worry about. Our concerns will surface in any case. Hence we are free to work on form. For the rest, all we can do is try to keep our mind alive and open.

Even more important was the second revelation: that *any* constraint stretches the imagination, pulls us beyond what we started with. For though the poems were still about my mother, something else was happening.

Collage, like fragmentation, allows us to frustrate the expectation of continuity, of step-by-step linearity. And if the fields we juxtapose are different enough there is hope for sparks from the edges. Here is a paragraph from *A Key into the Language of America* that tries to get at the clash of Indian and European cultures by juxtaposing phrases from Roger William's 1743 treatise with contemporary elements from anywhere in my Western heritage.

> OF MARRIAGE
> Flesh, considered as cognitive region, as opposed to undifferentiated warmth, is called woman or wife. **The number not stinted, yet the Narragansett (generally) have but one.** While diminutives are coined with reckless freedom, the deep structure of the marriage bed is universally esteemed even in translation. **If the woman be false** to bedlock, **the offended husband will be solemnly avenged,** arid and eroded. He may remove her clothes at any angle between horizontal planes.

4. "TRANSLATION"

By this I mean taking one aspect of an existing work and translating it into something else. For instance, *Differences for Four Hands* began with following the sentence structure of Lyn Hejinian's prose poem *Gesualdo* and "translating" it into an invocation of Clara and Robert Schumann. In the finished version this is not always easy to trace. Hejinian's sentence structure is much quirkier than what I ended up with, because I needed to be closer to the tension of fluidity and stillness in Schumann's music. Also, a sentence about the increasing number of children ("Run. Three children through the house.") became a refrain or ostinato that changed the structural feel. But here is a passage that has remained quite close:

> Lyn Hejinian, *Gesualdo*:
> Two are extremes. You place on noble souls. The most important was an extraordinary degree. What has been chosen from this, but a regular process of communication, shortly implored for long life and forgiveness. You are a target of my persuasion. I am overlooking the city. At times I am most devout and at others most serene, and both pleasure and displeasure haunt me. My heart is not above the rooftops.

Differences for Four Hands:
Any two are opposite. You walk on sound. The coldest wind blows
from the edges of fear. Which has been written down. Passion's not
natural. But body and soul are bruised by melancholy, fruit of dry,
twisted riverbeds. Loss discolors the skin. At times you devour apples,
at others bite into your hand.

5. RHYTHM

Rhythm is the elusive quality without which there is no poem. "Upper limit
music, lower limit speech," said Zukofsky. Rhythm, I mean, not meter. It is
difficult to talk about, impossible to pin down. It is the truly physical es-
sence of the poem, determined by the rhythms of my body, my breath, my
pulse. But it is also the alternation of sense and absence, sound and silence.
It articulates the between, the difference in repetition.

6. REVISIONS

I think on paper, revise endlessly. I am envious of Robert Duncan's con-
fidence that anything that came to him was right. "Speaking in the God-
Voice," I heard him call it. But I feel closer to what John Ashbery said in
conversation with Kenneth Koch, that he feels any line could have been
written some other way, that it does not necessarily have to sound as
it does.

I am slow and need to think about things for a long time, need to hold
on to the trace on paper. Thinking is adventure. Does adventure need to
be speedy? Perhaps revising is a way of refusing closure? Not wanting to
come to rest?

NOTE

Adapted from Rosmarie Waldrop, "Thinking of Follows," available at the Elec-
tronic Poetry Center, writing.upenn.edu/epc/authors/waldropr/thinking.html.

ROSMARIE WALDROP

Attending to Absence

Richard Greenfield

Rosmarie Waldrop—poet, translator, publisher—began publishing poetry in the late 1960s, experimenting with lineated poetry in a highly elliptical and minimalist lyric style. By the early 1980s, she had mostly abandoned lineated poetry for prose writing, shifting from an interest in the poetic to a focus on the sentence. In the conventional definition, the prose poem frames a diminishment of the effect (in meaning and music) of line breaks while emphasizing a more organic whole. Consequently, the energy of the prose poem courses through the sentence rather than the line. Additionally, the organizing effect of the stanza break is managed instead in the paragraph unit. Waldrop builds on these traditional prose poem foundations while also departing from them. In "Why Do I Write Prose Poems," she explains that once she lost interest in the traditional lyric line, she began to experiment with "complex sentences, for the possibility of digression, for space,"[1] sketching a kind of abstract manifesto of what's important about the composition of sentences. Evelyn Reilly has said Waldrop's writing might best be described as "investigations in paragraph-based forms,"[2] eschewing familiar formal patterns of prose for justified and quantitatively similar blocks of text composed of free-floating sentences, fragments, and phrasal units. Waldrop's decades-long motivations for pursuing a uniquely rigorous and experimental kind of prose poetry has been mostly uninformed by the French-American lineage of the prose poem traditionally viewed as starting with Charles Baudelaire. In contrast, her touchstones are philosophical writers with a poetic bent: the language games of Ludwig Wittgenstein, the collage writings of Walter Benjamin, the opaque cultural criticism of Theodor Adorno, the literary-mathematical writing of Alfred North Whitehead, Samuel Beckett's poetics of negation, and the spiritual investigations of Edmond Jabès. All of these writers and thinkers share an interest in "the gap"—be it understood as an absence, as presence or matter—and their resistance to, and investment in, understanding the oppression of dialectical thinking; they unflinchingly gaze into the divide between language and meaning.

Similarly, Waldrop has no interest in concealing these gaps through the measured use of transitions, normative grammar, and consistent reinforcement of a set of subjects and objects that is characteristic of much conventional, traditional poetry that aligns itself with late capitalist reality, reinforcing stability, homogeneity, solidity, infrastructure, historical progression, and social and economic hierarchies: hegemony. Her work intersects with the resistant, oppositional writing associated directly and indirectly with Language poetry, and indeed, reached this widening community through its inclusion ("the opening of the field") in the late 1980s in Language-associated journals. Her work engages with many of the same values: Marxist concerns about the value of poetry within society as condoning open reading practices, poststructuralist inquiry into the fallacies of referential language, and an agenda for poetry to decenter or critique the hegemonic modes of language attached to class, ideology, gender, and race. Extraordinarily intimate and sensual in its relationship to these late century openings in reality, her work has a hardened skepticism toward the illusions of seamless late capital continuity. Like many avant-garde writers, Waldrop seeks to critique this alliance with heterogeneous reality. Indeed, the most relevant reading of these gaps in contemporary American avant-garde practice is influenced by a desire—perhaps even faith—that such slippage shall challenge, subvert, and negate hegemonies.

Waldrop herself tends to use the terminology of negation or absence to describe her work: she says it is "lacking coordinates," that it inhabits "unstructured space," and that it explores "uncharted territory."[3] Though her work is primarily poetic prose, it retains the relationship between presence (line) and absence (the white space) suggested by lineated poetry. That relationship remains, for Waldrop, forever dialectical or binary: the poem as material language pushing against absence, which is the space of the page. Prose, however, transfers the open-ended ambiguities of line breaks, or the boundaries against the absence within the blank page space, away from the inherently traditional organizing principles of the lineated lyric poem to new possibilities of unconventional gaps between clauses and phrases. It is true that unconventionally lineated poems can and do achieve a similar effect, but in prose poems, such clefts are less highlighted than they would be as line breaks. These fissures are more insidiously invisible within prose sentences.

Moreover, early in her career, Waldrop came to believe that line management tended to obscure, obviate, or even self-correct the pressures she was attempting to place on normative syntax, which is characterized by causality and logic. Lineated poems, in Waldrop's perspective, limited her early experiments in "gapping" subject-object and main and subordinate clauses perhaps most overtly in the way lineated poems tend to over-emphasize that such gaps occur primarily in the lyric-openings, ambiguities, and *entendres* of the line breaks themselves. Line breaks tend to shift possibility away from the interior gaps she wanted equally emphasized. She came to see more potential in deforming normative syntax, working against subordinated structure, and decentering familiar rhetorics within the long, muscular, seemingly "complete" sentence unit. In a sense, for Waldrop, poetic space shifted from the page as a vacancy against which the line enjambs and refracts to the sentence as a site within which can be planted new, generative gaps. Waldrop became more focused on the use of subordinate clauses in her writing, extending her sentences into more complex sentences after having already opened the boundaries of sentences by sliding sentences together or by fragmentation. Waldrop says she "accepted the complete sentence (most of the time) and tried to subvert its closure and logic from the inside, by constantly sliding between frames of reference" while at the same time found herself attracted to "the possibility of digression, for space. The space of a different, less linear movement: a dance of syntax. The prose paragraph seemed the right kind of space where form could prove 'a center around which, not a box within reach.'"[4]

Waldrop's sense of the decentered potential of poetic prose—of its unique relationship with language, space, and meaning—evolved into a two-decade project of a trilogy of books: *The Reproduction of Profiles*, *Lawn of Excluded Middle*, and *Reluctant Gravities*, collected in *Curves of the Apple*. The striking trilogy defined Waldrop's voice for a generation of readers and for many of her contemporaries offered a more intimate and embodied challenge to questions of subjectivity that were haunting the Language poets in the 1980s and '90s. The trilogy considers the long-standing Western divisions of body and mind and heart and mind. Waldrop's aesthetic practice of investigation is effected through sentences that nimbly play on a scale between the semantic and autobiographical, the everyday material and metaphysical immaterial. Frequently intermeshing biblical historiography and quantum physics, Waldrop positions Eve's apple both with and against Newton's apple in two paradigms of cosmic law, two "falls," two deterministic attractions, both engendered and not engendered, divided by a void.

In works written outside of this project during this period, Waldrop eerily refrains, reframes, and self-ventriloquizes this voice. Arising organically out of the resistance in her early work to the normative subject-object bind of user and used, Waldrop's work of this era actively blurred pronoun relationship to anterior subjects and objects, creating inviting and dizzying equivocal "spaces" of thought or feeling. These spaces—perhaps voices or characters—were barely distinct from each other, even when readers might be tempted to engender as positions or subjectivities spaces she intended to be read as androgyne. Working against the binaries of gender, reflected in a patriarchal grammar of subordination between masculine subject and feminine object, she developed a poetry that worked against a synthesis or union between binaries, what Michel Delville has argued is an "ambiguous and polysemous entity contesting the rigid binarism of masculine rationality . . . an 'excluded middle' enshrined in the process of logi-cal thought."⁵ Waldrop has insisted that she did not seek in this work to represent the presence of subjects so much as create synaptic spaces shaped by both flashes of intimate exchange and veerings of monological "train of thought."⁶ Indeed, bold juxtaposition and fusion of diverse subject mat-ter, without transitions, continues into the millennium to be prominent in Waldrop's prose.

The Ruins of Metaphysics

Driven to Abstraction (2010) suggests a new direction to Waldrop's in-terest in an affect of "present absence" or "distracted presence." Marked by phrases or fragments enacting a kind of temporal slowing, in which a claim is expanded upon or negated by its following phrase, Waldrop's work is no less material in its engagement with the sources, and no less intimate. But it is ineffably slower in its unfolding sentences (more often fragmented than in the earlier work) and emphasizes more brevity; poems are shorter on the page, with white space functioning as the meditative si-lence between poems within shorter sequences. For example, the poem "A Feeling of Absence" meditates on the Platonic divide between the world as it is and the world as we perceive it in the familiar allegory of the cave. The poem unfolds in discrete units to produce an effect of assertion followed by the deconstruction or subversion of the assertion. Waldrop begins with a challenge to Plato: "If shadow be the cause of substance, thought pro-voking matter, then it's illusory to think objects come first,"⁷ while at the same time she desires for Plato to have been right on this count: "And I thought one day to learn about reality." As the poem develops, living within the divide between the object and its sign is enacted through paral-lelism. First, "The world of things, says Plato, is insubstantial. Is the reflec-tion of another world that contains only forms." Then the slippage into infinite reflections or *mise-en-abyme* begins with another theory: "Some say the world of forms in turn is but reflection of another world." Waldrop then offers the following sequence of fragments: "That contains nothing at all. And are disturbed." To contain nothing at all suggests that there would be nothing to reflect upon, and thus there would be no source at all for the world of forms, negating the theory in the first place. The last of these fragments suggests "some" are disturbed by this phenomenon of absence; this is not so much a tracing of shifting Platonic meditations on subjects in relation to objects and ideas as much as a meditation on how such vacil-lations are rooted in the anxiety that nothing at all may be the source of the shadows. In other poems in *Driven to Abstraction*, phrases break away from the clauses they support in so disjunctive a manner as to suggest there is no relative connection.

Waldrop's interest in the fragment (which she humorously calls "the splice of life") variously stems from her interest in how it functions as interruption to produce dissonance and to estrange coherence. A distinction might be made, however, in the manner in which Waldrop thinks about the fragment. First, she thinks of the fragment in a grammatical context—as a unit missing a key piece, such as a subject, a predicate, or an object. Secondly, Waldrop's relationship to the fragment works, in opposition to the Modernist desire to elegize the end of the system ("the system remaining a challenge in the background"[8]) that can be found in the obsessive fragmented epics of Eliot, Pound, and Zukofsky, as a symbolic liberation from totalizing systems.[9] While such fragments may point toward an inherent incompleteness and insufficiency, the rhythms of these fragments (and the way the reader attempts to contextualize these fragments) create a playful sense of suspension and polyphony, where things are separate and yet newly unified: "How the words are. Suspended around you."[10] In an anecdotal introduction to "The Ground Is the Only Figure: Notebook Spring 1996," Waldrop confesses her early tendencies to compartmentalize her writing into separate categories such as lines for poems, reading notes, theater programs, and diaries. She sought through prose to arrange her various jottings from diverse categories of notebooks with the abandon a visual collagist might use, engaging with the possibilities of new networks of discursive play between seemingly distinct forms of writing. Just as in Walter Benjamin's observation that "Interruption is one of the fundamental devices of all structuring," Waldrop found that fragments "cut out" explanations.[11] While fragmentation results in a methodical unfolding of thinking in Waldrop's poems, these phrases are also released subversively from their normative sentence grammar of clausal and phrasal relation through delineation by periods. There is a halting but measured breathing to Waldrop's sentences. In an interview with Christine Hume, she notes that she uses periods in the same way that some poets use line breaks, delineating measures, "as rhythmic markers rather than, or in addition to, using them as grammatical markers."[12] Waldrop makes a similar claim in an interview with Matthew Cooperman: "Recently I have created silence inside the sentence by using periods rhythmically where they don't belong grammatically."[13] Her use of periods (a punctuation strategy that replicates the sonic gap of the line break) affects reading, where the text before the period retains meaning in isolation and simultaneously receives new context from the next consecutive fragment.

In her use of tesserae, however, Waldrop is not so much invested in creating an effect of fragmentation as to suggest the natural congruence of diverse parts: "Displacement matters less to me than the glint of light on the cut, the edges radiating energy. The fragmentary, 'torn' nature of the elements."[14] Waldrop has also described this radiating quality as "blindsight," a term developed by the neuroscientist Antonio Damasio addressing the human ability to see a whole from the fragments of which we are only actually unconsciously cognizant. In *Blindsight* (2003), Waldrop further develops the "figure, foreground, and ground" pattern fragmentation that distinguishes *Driven to Abstraction* from *Curves of the Apple*. Waldrop has said that "blindsight" encompasses her joining her "fragments to other people's fragments in a dialogue, a net that might catch a bit more of the 'world.'"[15] Take for example the poem "Lens," from *Blindsight*. The first paragraph demonstrates a sense of disjunction and a feeling for organic association within sentences and between sentences simultaneously:

> Our capacity for learning is closely concerned with memories of milking cows. Nothing repeats itself except history. The palace, in winter. Now that long sentences are in disuse, blood is not diverted into causes. Nor does the gesture of shivering produce the sensation of labor pains. The first picture of a person wearing spectacles is in a fresco of 1352.[16]

The idea of "our capacity for learning" is linked to the physical knowledge learned through repetitive physical activity that requires little knowledge. On its surface, the leap from learning to milking cows is disorienting, and this disjointedness is compounded when the next sentence jumps to the idea of history repeating. The associative relation is the idea of repetition itself. The dissonant gap between this sentence and the fragment "The palace, in winter" is vertigo-inducing at its surface. There is the hint of a relation when the terms of the fragment link to history, perhaps in the most famous of winter palaces of the last czars of Russia, within the cycles of revolution. Waldrop, following the process she has referred to as "gap gardening," does not explain the relationships of these terms: their radiating proximity to each other suggests the possibility of open-ended transformation. Indeed, Steve Evans observes, "The absence of a gap is tantamount to the absence of transformative possibility."[17]

Nevertheless, Waldrop's rigorous adherence to her compositional processes signals much more than the development of an authorial or authoritative coherence typified in the lyric. Her poetic voice arises organically from her speaking voice. As a German immigrant to the United States, her "phonemes settled somewhere between German and English," so that she now has accents in both languages. As a result, she sees herself entering language from "a skewed angle, through the fissures, the slight difference."[18] Consequently, the stylistic or formal fissures in her work originate in procedural investment and are reinforced by the natural rhythms of her voice: "The enormous migration from Europe to America, wave after wave of explorers, immigrants. Being part of this has marked me. . . . It surfaces again and again in my writing."[19] Steve Evans similarly observes,

"The biographical experience of linguistic dislocation not only informs Waldrop's theoretical and practical orientation toward language, it also represents a historical link to preceding generations of avant-garde writers."[20] Waldrop finds a similar and perhaps influential mode in the writing of Edmond Jabès (for whom she is the primary English translator. Here, she makes evident her keen sense of what's at stake in projecting the illusion of self with certitude:

> Everything in his work—the shifting voices and perspectives, the breaks of mode, tautologies, alogical sequences and contradicting metaphors, the stress on uncertainty (the constant subjunctive)—all combine to subvert the authority we expect in a book. Authority of statement, of closure and linearity, the confidence in a narrative thread, continuity of temporal and causal sequence. And most of all the authority of the author.[21]

In our slowing down of our left-to-right reading of Waldrop's prose, as readers we might come to notice the gaps; with her frequent emphasis on absence itself, it becomes more apparent that the purpose of this prose is to enact that absence—not within the words in the sense of aporia, but between them. Gaps may be detected between words. These fissures are space with dimension and connective energy, too—between-ness—energy bridging *abîmes* between words. The concept of *khora* takes on relevance here. Meaning space, receptacle, or site in Greek, its first usage involved understanding the relationship between elusive phenomenon and materiality, such as the reflection in a mirror. Heidegger suggests a utility of *khora* as a clarification of sight to achieve an unconcealing of being itself—which Heidegger also links to Truth (*Aletheia*) in terms of space in Plato's allegory of the cave. We (perhaps even blindly) shift perspectives from the shadows to the outside of the cave in an attempt to "unconceal" the truth of the phenomenon.

Similarly, and in contrast, Derrida emphasizes the blind nature of the *khora* as a non-utilitarian phenomenon of truth—but as a blind truth, one which may not be seen but may be perceived nonetheless. In her interview with Hume, Waldrop invokes Ernest Fenollosa's criticism of grammar which focuses too much on the distinct and separate parts of speech: "A true noun, an isolated thing, does not exist in nature. Things are only the terminal points, or rather the meeting points, of actions, cross-sections cut through actions, snapshots. Neither can a pure verb, an abstract motion, be possible in nature. . . . Thing and action cannot be separated."[22] Waldrop's alliance with Fenollosa is evident in the blurring of the distinct functions of parts of speech into bridges across what would be considered in standardized grammar to be gaps. Reading every syntactical charge and possibility in what we read, and reading toward looking for and at the space between sentences, too, and when perceiving these gaps, we may see past the illusion of coherence. The text is a polyphony of subjectivities brought into some semblance of a whole merely through the positioning of sentences next to each other. Of course, there are analogs here in Mikhail Bakhtin's notion of the inherent heteroglossia of texts, but Bakhtin argues that much rhetorical effort is made by a writer to conceal these gaps—to make the polyphony so seamless, a larger heterogeneous coherence or surface becomes the purpose of the text. Rosmarie Waldrop works to unconceal these gaps.

Such gaps are also indirectly connected to subjectivity. The effort to conceal such gaps to create coherence mirrors a fragile attempt to build a coherent world or self. Waldrop is interested in the otherness found within the *khora* or the slippage or the inhalation between utterances, words, phrases, and sentences, and how such slippages enact concealments, erasures, and deathly and horrific absences of time. Waldrop's project, like those of Susan Howe and Myung Mi Kim, emphasizes looking at the languaged subjectivity that creates material fissures between the text and the world. This deconstructionist-like inquiry frequently enacts how that subjectivity, often engendered and always semiotic in nature, is revealed momentarily within such gaps. Citing Charles Olson's "Projective Verse," Waldrop is particularly tuned toward his assertion that "what is, is no longer THINGS but what happens BETWEEN things, these are the terms of the reality contemporary to us—and the terms of what we are."[23] Waldrop has approached writing, within and at the same time past the terms of grammar, of these elusive gaps in subjectivity through the lenses (sometimes appropriated from various disciplines) of "gap gardening," "blindsight," "lavish absence," and "law of excluded middle," to name a few. In most cases, Waldrop has intrinsically defined these absences in terms that eschew metaphysics for forms of physicality or for the materiality of space itself. Again, while Waldrop is aware of how absence points toward presence and the fragmentation of the whole, these seemingly metaphysical questions arise first from the grammar of their propositions and how the prose physically pushes out white space to and from the margins, which Waldrop considers to be "the greatest challenge" of the prose poem:

> I've worked with absences, esp. in *Lawn of Excluded Middle*: absence of center, empty center, the womb, the resonating space of a musical instrument, the space between words that makes them words, words carrying absence as a sea shell carries the roar of the sea: "words shelling the echo of absence onto the dry land," or "the empty space I place at the center of each poems to allow penetration." But as for the "metaphysical presence" I have no experience of it.[24]

Waldrop seems particularly suspicious of a metaphysics most recognizable in Cartesian dualism as the "mind-body" problem, where the object may not physically exist beyond its cognition by the subject. Problematically, the subject assumes an entitled use of, or mastery over, the object—a conclusion that centralizes the subject in relation to others, refuses to see the inherent materiality of all beings, and discounts the material contingencies that shape subjectivity. As a dominant paradigm of Western thought that has its origins in Platonism, this definition of metaphysics has been concurrently disseminated through lyric poetry. Thus, what Waldrop suggests here in having "no experience" of "metaphysical presence" is a compressed expression of her very resistance to metaphysical claims in her poetic writing. One of the closing poems of *Driven to Abstraction*, "Nothing and Its Shadow," resonates with this resistance. Waldrop begins:

> To be webbed with the world I turn my back on my husband's body.
> I see photo-ops on a ground of oil and bourbon. And see tortured
> bodies. And in my head, words. Act, fact, pact, tract, intact, abstract.
> Hacked, racked, cracked, sacked, stacked, nackt.[25]

First, there is the estranging feel of being "webbed." In a sense, this means joined to the world, presumably through the Internet. A choice must be made between intimacy with the husband and connection to the world—the divide between inwardness and outwardness. To be "webbed," then, is also to be focused virtually away from the physical world but to be then faced with access to the simulacra of the world—the news feeds filled with images of destruction and war. These, in turn, trigger a string of floating signifiers that may have referents within the world—or at least the virtual representation of the world.

Perhaps it is this slippage between the way the world is framed as a "photo-op" and trying to understand the assignation of these terms, like keywords, even while one's physicality has been sacrificed for this ambiguous engagement with the World Wide Web. These literally "floating" signifiers may arise from the context of war and violence (act, pact) or from the context of bodies (the notion of *body, bodies, embodied* showing up multiple times), as in "intact," "hacked," and "stacked." A word like "hacked" or "cracked" points in the direction of the body and the Internet at the same time as a form of fragmented syllepsis. Bodies placed in body bags might be thought of as "sacked," and "sacked" is a synonym for "terminated"—yet again a slippage into violence through syllepsis. Similarly, "fact" means "a thing done." "Nackt" is a German cognate for naked—again suggesting a link to the body. Indeed, what might appear to be floating signifiers here can turn out to be ascribed to signified objects—signs. Bodies lead to words. In what becomes a provocative inversion of William Carlos Williams' poetic insistence of "No ideas but in things," Waldrop tentatively offers, "No thing without words, no fact before signs, no specie, no prior body?" Later in the poem, Waldrop observes, "Signs are irreparably dislocated from what is supposed to be their signified." To not know for certain what it is we see from the vantage of a computer screen—what Waldrop calls "Not a painting with perspective fixed on the infinite"—is a reality we experience as we passively receive information about our world from a distance, obscured, manipulated, propagandized. Such information forms a virtual pastoral framed within limits of the computer screen, one that is "peaceful because nothing can matter from such a distance."

Finally, thinking of "key words," there is an architectural aspect to this kind of sonic "slippage" in Waldrop's poems, as well. In the sequence "All Electrons Are (Not) Alike," there is usually one instance of aleatory spillage derived from the terminal word of a sentence. For example, contrast in the first segment, "Profusion of languages out of the *blue. Bluster*, blur, blubber" (emphasis added here and below), with the following sentences in the second segment: "Actual observations served to confirm what he already *knew. True*, clue, loop and thimbles, line up to the mast."[26] The last term of a sentence seems to echo across the gap into the next sentence and sometimes to become the genesis of that sentence if not dissonantly fusing into/onto it. While Waldrop takes "Sound must seem an echo to the sense" to its most organic state, the recurrence of this method once per poem creates an architectural repetend to the larger sequence of poems. It also enacts a limited viewpoint, showing that exploration is "like the foot of a snail, held on to the planks of their vessels, not communicating." We move sequentially (as in language) from one phenomenon to the next, not seeing past the vanishing point from our momentary vantage. Waldrop's prose—though crafted from the collaging of textures and discourses and driven by an engine of disjunctive fragmentation never only anchored on the "I"—is located in how she brings all of this together to dwell within the fissures between language and the world.

Against Citation: Historiography as Collage

Driven to Abstraction draws on a dizzying array of materials: Brian Rotman, Pol Bury, John Cage, Stephen Greenblatt, Yoel Hoffmann (a source in *Blindsight*, as well), John Keegan, Gérard Macé, Antonio Pigafetta, Eliot Weinberger, Elizabeth Willis, and Ludwig Wittgenstein. This diverse range of sources typifies Waldrop's ongoing exploration of disjunctive movement between discourses. Such disjunction was true of *The Reproduction of Profiles* (1987), where her sources included phrases from Wittgenstein and A. S. Eddington, of *Blindsight*, which worked with sources as diverse as Hölderlin, Angela Carter, Dore Ashton, and Hans Reichenbach, and of *A Key into the Language of America* (1994), which worked with Roger Williams. Waldrop's prose often interweaves dialogically with that of other materials. Despite the radical juxtaposition of materials on the page,

Waldrop's framing of that material is often quite cohesive and even lyrical in its agenda to bring totality to different strains. Waldrop's interest in collage and procedural writing beginning in the 1980s links her to avant-garde writers and artists with a specific interest in the materiality of language, such as Dada and Surrealism.[27] Waldrop, however, resists the notion of collage as a form of "citation," pushing for more than intertextuality and attempting to create "suspended" material texture within the poem:

> I mostly collage unidentified fragments and use them for texture the way Picasso or Schwitters tore a piece of newspaper and glued it in, the way Rauschenberg will work in a piece of a reproduction of a painting. . . . This is more what I am after: elements formally suspended to form a new composition.[28]

Walter Benjamin likewise observes that citation, at least for the historian, results in tearing the historical object from its context. The suspension of elements, enhanced through the transitory unfolding of fragments and phrases into larger sections of prose, does enact a feeling of suspension of time and of distinct thoughts coming into clarity (and Waldrop herself has referred to gap gardening as the suspension of time).[29] One movement in the sequence, "By the Waters of Babylon," for example, extends Waldrop's ongoing argument about how the world is dangerously manifested through language in pronouncements of power over reality, where "Language plays a great part in our life."[30] The poem proceeds with a description of the void before the world or life on it existed: "There are chaos and void. No man or beast. Not a fly or stalk of ragweed. We think 'primal soup,' and already there is a world. And fed." Language might be used to describe the origins of that world, but the world exists before language. Any etiological concepts such as "primal soup" are formulated as narratives long after the event, a paradox of meaning-making. The seemingly disjunctive movement between free-floating philosophical observations about the nature of the world in relation to language subsumes into gnomically isolated prose paragraphs:

> Then somebody thinks "Operation Ivy Cyclone." "Operation Plymouth Rock." "Operation Iron Hammer."
> In 2005, in Baghdad, 92% of the people did not have electricity, 39% did not have safe drinking water, 25% of children under the age of five were suffering from malnutrition.

Much of the material here is from Eliot Weinberger's description of Baghdad in 2005, from a piece titled "What I Heard About Iraq," and it is either reshaped or used verbatim by Waldrop. Waldrop's "Then somebody thinks 'Operation Ivy Cyclone.' 'Operation Plymouth Rock.' 'Operation Iron Hammer'" is shaped from Weinberger's "I heard about Operation Ivy Cyclone. I heard about Operation Vigilant Resolve. I heard about Operation Plymouth Rock. I heard about Operation Iron Hammer, its name taken from Eisenhammer, the Nazi plan to destroy Soviet generating plants."[31] What becomes clear here is that Waldrop thinks of collage as deep listening, and how suspension for a moment, tearing material from its context, reveals greater epistemological complexities in isolation. As Kenneth Burke states, "Even if any terminology is a reflection of reality, by its very nature as a terminology it must be a selection of reality, and to this extent, it must also function as a deflection of reality."[32] To whom, for example, does "somebody" refer? Who is "thinking" here? Is it the reader, having just encountered and apprehended the unfolding language of the phrase upon the page? Is it the speaker of the poem, or Waldrop, having read Weinberger's essay? At the level of source material of the essay, is it Weinberger, having thought it as he composed it? Is it the rhetoricians on staff at the Pentagon, "deploying" the rhetoric of operations to euphemize and conceal the violent outcomes of war? Collage here evokes a provocative anatomy of how narrative is transmitted piecemeal and becomes constructive of reality, as enacted in Gertrude Stein's dictum, "The world as we see it looks like this. They used to think that the world was there as we see it but this is not so the world is there as it is human nature is there as it is and the human mind."[33] This sequence of poems was composed from 2004 to 2008, in response to the Iraq War, at a time of a major redefining of "reality" following the September 11th terrorist attacks on the World Trade Center. Conversations about the nature of American political and military "reality" took a surreal turn when *New York Times* journalist Ron Suskind published a disquieting revelation of the Bush administration's view on history itself. A senior Bush aide (later identified as Karl Rove) characterized those who "believe that solutions emerge from [a] judicious study of discernible reality" as "the reality-based community."[34] Rove criticizes the assumptions underlying the paradigms of this community:

> That's not the way the world really works anymore. We're an empire now, and when we act, we create our own reality. And while you study that reality—judiciously, as you will—we'll act again, creating other new realities, which you can study too, and that's how things will sort out. We're history's actors . . . and you, all of you, will be left to just study what we do.[35]

Waldrop is aware of the connection between power and language, of this terrifying project of "new realities" resulting from "white-gloved White House memos," but she also wants to engage with the unconscious acts of violence shaping our perception of the world through "The word's power to kill . . . it's violence against what it names, what it can name only by taking its materiality, destroying its presence."[36] Waldrop's collage technique results in the isolation and suspension of these rhetorical pieces, refusing to remold them into an all too palatable humanistic form of witness that is exemplified in the political realism of protest poetry or romantic "poetry of witness" popularized in the 1980s. Waldrop's political investment, already seemingly decentered through sidestepping her own subjectivity through the use of collage materials ("Collage as a way of getting outside myself") also enacts the writer's direct disconnection from these events as second-hand retellings or framed CNN narratives. Weinberger's repeating phrasing of "I hear" focuses similarly on a witness of apprehension without valorizing that witness as the sufferer or victim of the hearing, positioning the consequences of war where they actually lie: outside, out of reach, like floating pieces of a whole. The precession of the moments —each a set piece of an invasion—can only result in a construct of the whole. Collage is no different than the biased work of the historian, however. On the one hand, an open-ended heuristic, in what may be deemed a valid definition of collage as "literary montage," is best characterized by Walter Benjamin as presenting the materials to speak for themselves:

> I needn't *say* anything. Merely show. I shall purloin no valuables, appropriate no ingenious formulations. But the rags, the refuse—these I will not inventory but allow, in the only way possible, to come into their own: by making use of them.[37]

On the other hand, Charles Olson's maxim, "The poem is an act of poetry + history made as one, a redisposition of the force we have known as 'poetry' and a retaking altogether almost, of what 'history' has been since history,"[38] seeks to reground poetry as an activity of historiography. But such "regrounding" is also lodged in a problematic sense of historical witness. Contemporary witness poetry falls into the same trap as it participates in an unwitting transmission of the controlling conceits and propaganda that power would have us disseminate, confirming how fraught the relationship between poetry and historiography remains. Any discourse, indeed, the very conceits of that discourse's metaphors, when they are faithfully subsumed, consumed, or mimicked, become the unwitting carriers of authoritative discourse. As Mikhail Bakhtin proposes, authoritative discourse "demands our allegiance" and cannot be represented—"only transmitted":

> It enters our verbal consciousness as a compact and indivisible mass; one must totally affirm it, or totally reject it. It is indissolubly fused with its authority—with political power, an institution, a person—and it stands or falls together with that authority. . . . It is, so to speak, the word of the fathers. Its authority was already acknowledged in the past.[39]

Wallace Stevens similarly feared that war could only be "a set of events, not only beyond our power to tranquilize them in the mind, beyond our power to reduce them and metamorphose them."[40] Waldrop argues that metaphor thus functions as "hotline to transcendence, to divine meaning, which casts the poet in the role of a special being, a priest or prophet."[41] Evelyn Reilly argues that Waldrop's relation to organic form as it has been inherited by poets since Romanticism is not merely one of resistance but also reformation, paralleling the quantitative formalism of Language poetry and participating in a "renaissance" of constructivist writing.[42] Though Waldrop's use of collage underscores the context of her sources by taking them out of context, the sources are drained of their original propagandistic and didactic purposes, providing a fragmentary snapshot within "its own space" in the same sense with which Maurice Blanchot describes the creative and destructive properties inherent in writing:

> Write in order not simply to destroy, in order to conserve, in order to not transmit; write in the thrall of the impossible real, that share of disaster wherein every reality, safe and sound, sinks. . . . Trust in language is the opposite—distrust of the language—situated within language. Confidence in language is language itself distrusting—defying—language: finding in its own space the unshakeable principles of a critique.[43]

This is the manner in which Waldrop's concept of "gap gardening" relates directly to collage. Deborah Meadows has noted that "gap gardening" reveals or overly underscores how, "at the syntax level, the sentence is an axiomatic structure that both: 1. annihilates what it uses as a vehicle of expression, of evidence; and 2. restores and preserves its vehicle as an inseparable structure of meaning, of evidence." Thus, "Waldrop shows us the gap between language as a self-referential system and experience."[44]

In the context of collage, juxtaposition, which creates these gaps, enacts how language functions in its own space and is always in a state of turning against itself—self-annihilating, self-restoring, self-preserving. Waldrop often collapses historiographical reports from wildly different historical periods, or places private autobiographical notation next to that of historical personages, underscoring parallels between sweeping historical viewpoints and those at an individualistic scale. In *Driven to Abstraction*, this is potently explored in the juxtaposition between Waldrop's father's concerns about the connections between language and phenomenon ("my father was disturbed by Being and Time"[45]) and Christopher Columbus's ambitions to explore and conquer the New World. The sequence links Columbus to imperialistic dialogues with the world, such as Columbus's "legal" proclamations claiming lands on behalf of Spain, or Cabeza de Vaca's "pass[ing] through many dissimilar tongues."[46] A layer of European removal is evoked in Karl May's romantic idealization of the American West after it arrives in the twisted form of manifest destiny. Christian narratology provides even further removal in Adam's naming of the animals with their "true names" (engaging with the mythic but ultimately empirical quest for eidetic language. Waldrop's implication of patriarchal ("explorer") uses of language aligns with materialist characterizations of its use to control the world: "the explorer's attention, like the foot of a snail, held on to the planks of their vessels, not communicating. Too intent on the physical fact, waves, whales, or poison arrows."[47]

Waldrop's overt emphasis on exploring the psychological dimensions of semiotics and its connection to power is unique in expressing it as an absence of communication. Indeed, Waldrop iterates how the distrust of language, in the absence of language used for genuine inquiry, justifies that distrust: "Yet when an object has never been seen back home what good is a word? You have to bring the thing itself and empty your bag to make conversation." In tragic belatedness, Waldrop alludes to André Breton's metaphorical use of "communicating vessels," a notion that the unconscious dictates our choices and chance meetings so that these choices and chance meetings become the belated fulfillment of the unconscious. "Their vessels, not communicating" suggests the very absence of communication between interior and exterior—the self-deluding narratives told to themselves as agents of the Western imperialistic imagination. The taxonomic layering of the material world as envisioned by this deadly invention starts with the material space (the waves), envisions the animals or resources within it (whales), and then envisions the 'hostile natives' lastly within that encompassing gaze (poison arrows). Nothing interrupts this delusional arrangement of the world, as "observations served to confirm what he already knew." Waldrop follows this taxonomy of dominance with the sentence: "Later, though, poured forth stories never dreamed of by the natives." The "later" here is ominous and insidious, understating the genocidal success of these campaigns in the subdual and subjugation of people, which were concealed by romantic fantasies of encounter.

Narrative, Text, and World

Rosmarie Waldrop has spoken of how her sequences, instead of being argumentative, are suggestive of narrative and are often narrative in structure, but that narrative closure rarely happens. Evocative aspects of narrative might include the character-like figures that reappear in a sequence, such as that of Waldrop's father in "All Are (Not) Alike" and "By the Waters of Babylon," both from *Driven by Abstraction*. The reoccurrence of her father in these elliptical references to autobiography also suggests a baseline of a story of which we only see glimpses. These two prose poem sequences respectively open and close a series titled "Sway-Backed Powerlines (2004–2008)," a kind of "book-ending" and circling back to the beginning, a narrative structure used to create an arc across the sequence. In "Music Is An Oversimplification of the Situation We Are In," interrogative sentences probe how to re-start from innocence or naivety. Provocative questions circle from a disembodied perspective and form the semblance of an ongoing internal conflict. This interest in narrative form is not a recent development in Waldrop's writing. Over the years, while she has ventured into occasional novelistic projects such as *The Hanky of Pippin's Daughter* (a book she still considers a given "reality"), her poems have formed analogues to narrative writing or narrative form, such as the organizing chapters in *A Key into the Language of America* used as titles, which in turn approximate Roger Williams' *A Key into the Language of America*, written in 1643. In *Reluctant Gravities*, song and narrative structures organize sequences of conversations, beginning with a prologue that introduces or "stages" two voices. After each series of four conversations (each conversation is always divided on the page into two paragraphs as an analog to two voices in dialogue), an interlude composed of a song and meditation bridges the next four conversations, and so on, until it concludes in "Conversation 24." Additionally, the rhetoric of narrative surfaces in her sentences. Take for example the opening from the first book of the trilogy, *The Reproduction of Profiles*:

> As the streets were empty in the early morning, I had made the spaces between words broad enough for a smile which could reflect off the enamel tower clock. Being late is one of my essential properties. Unthinkable that I should not possess it, and not even on vacation do I deprive myself of its advantages.[48]

The excerpt demonstrates how Waldrop's writing engages the idea of the world as a text and as a representation of one's perception of it, both in a state of reflection (past tense) and in the moment of its construction from language (present tense). Sometimes it is presented as an unfolding apperception of the world in language as it has just been constructed in language (present tense following past tense). There are no illusions that the text can create the world as it is, and in this sense, there is an overall unity and coherence of narrative structure. Ideas move associatively here. The emptiness of the street gives way to the notion of empty spaces between words "broad enough" to be filled. The image of a clock associatively links to the concurrent idea of time and lateness as a property. Though Waldrop plays with the idea of where or when the world unfolds as a text, to a reader blind to these semiotic concerns and perceiving the world of the book as a kind of verisimilitude, the effect is the same as of a narrative. The narrator reflects in a "real" present on a "real" past, which is not to say that this narrator would not enter into such a contract, too. Setting, as one of the more potent illusions of verisimilitude in narrative, plays a role in this contract. On the one hand, this is merely setting—a morning scene of empty streets with broadly sketched lines on a canvas to be interpretively filled. On the other hand, Waldrop is interesting in expressing how this exteriority is constructed, and follows the scaffolding of setting with a brilliant poetic turn against mere verisimilitude, refusing a reality "correspond[ing] to any one color or tableau vivant."[49] Actively filling in the scene with the apprehension of its viewer, Waldrop highlights the writerly theatrical staging of a scene as a *living picture*—a contradiction that captures the duality of the mutable world and the world in stasis. The tone of Waldrop's resistance to this game of realism is both elegiac and liberating: "But what if I had made the spaces too wide to reach the next word and the silence."[50] The narrator as semiotician is caught in a binary: having no less desire for the real ("the next word") than the contracted reader, this narrator at the same time relishes the abysmal gap ("the silence") that proves the world (the empty street, the sky, the rain) is a construction of language. The precise placement of natural elements in this excerpt emphasizes much more associative movement and interconnection by conjunctive relations between sentences to open "as many glimpses from as many different perspectives as possible, rather than trying to develop a linear argument where one follows from another."[51] Note the effect of the first introductory clause in the poem above in creating a semblance of a narrative. Note the effect of the conjunctive adverb of "nevertheless" to suggest the larger relation or the relational pull of the final sentence beginning with a conjunction ("but") that suggests tension against the earlier optimism of the width of her spaces, "broad enough for a smile." Such tension epitomizes Waldrop's lifework of testing the possibilities and limits of these spaces—these gaps. Between instances of political resistance to the seamless illusions of a reified reality and philosophical play, and a burning questioning of what is at stake in the act of writing and the insistence of inquiry over authoritative assertion, there exists the solace and pleasure her utterances take in incompletion—in leaving questions open and unanswered without distress—with a sensual attendance to absence.

NOTES

1. Rosmarie Waldrop, *Dissonance (if you are interested)* (Tuscaloosa: University of Alabama Press, 2005), 262.

2. Evelyn Reilly, "Dislocation Orchestration in the Work of Rosmarie Waldrop," *ON: Contemporary Practice* 2 (2009): 115.

3. Rosmarie Waldrop, "Artist's Statement," www.foundationforcontemporary arts.org/recipients/rosmarie-waldrop.

4. Waldrop, *Dissonance*, 262.

5. Michel Delville, *American Prose Poem: Poetic Form and the Boundaries of Genre* (Gainesville: University Press of Florida, 1998), 215.

6. Waldrop, *Dissonance*, 263.

7. Rosmarie Waldrop, *Driven to Abstraction* (New York: New Directions, 2010), 111.

8. Waldrop, *Dissonance*, 229.

9. For example, see Ezra Pound's *The Cantos* (1915–1969), T. S. Eliot's "The Waste Land" (1922), and Louis Zukofsky's *"A"* (1927–1978).

10. Rosmarie Waldrop, *Blindsight* (New York: New Directions, 2004), 5.

11. Ibid., 226.

12. Christine Hume, "A Conversation with Rosmarie Waldrop," in *12 x 12: Conversations in 21st Century Poetry and Poetics*, ed. Christina Mengert and Joshua Marie Wilkinson (Iowa City: University of Iowa Press, 2009), 78.

13. Matthew Cooperman, "Between Tongues: An Interview with Rosmarie Waldrop," *Conjunctions Online*, December 17, 2005; www.conjunctions.com/online /article/matthew-cooperman-12-17-2005.

14. Waldrop, *Dissonance*, 263.

15. Waldrop, author's back cover note for *Blindsight*.

16. Waldrop, *Blindsight*, 89.

17. Steve Evans, "Rosmarie Waldrop," *Dictionary of Literary Biography 169: American Poets Since World War II* (Detroit: Gale Research, 1996), 286.

18. Waldrop, *Dissonance*, 208.

19. Joan Retallack, "A Conversation with Rosmarie Waldrop," *Contemporary Literature* 40.3 (Autumn 1999): 372.

20. Evans, "Rosmarie Waldrop," 286.

21. Rosmarie Waldrop, *Lavish Absence: Recalling and Rereading Edmond Jabes* (Middletown: Wesleyan University Press, 2002), 142–43.

22. Hume, "A Conversation with Rosmarie Waldrop," 78.

23. Charles Olson, "The Escaped Cock," in *Collected Prose* (Berkeley: University of California Press), 138.

24. Cooperman, "Between Tongues."

25. Waldrop, *Driven to Abstraction*, 131.

26. Ibid., 6.

27. This interest in the materiality of language is further informed by her involvement in publishing hand-set books on the press that she and her husband Keith Waldrop founded in 1961, Burning Deck. In her dual biographical with Keith Waldrop, *Ceci n'est pas Keith / Ceci n'est pas Rosmarie* (Providence, RI: Burning Deck, 2002), she describes the slow process of hand-setting type as being instructive in "close reading" and the awareness she developed from this process for seeing excess "fat" in writing (77).

28. Cooperman, "Between Tongues."

29. Rosmarie Waldrop, *Curves to the Apple* (New York: New Directions, 2006), 103. "Gap gardening which, moved inward from the right margin, suspends time."

30. Waldrop, *Driven to Abstraction*, 67.

31. Eliot Weinberger, *What I Heard about Iraq* (London: Verso, 2005), 35.

32. Kenneth Burke, *Language as Symbolic Action* (Berkeley: University of California Press, 1966), 45.

33. Gertrude Stein, "Geographical History of America," in *Stein Writings 1932–1946* (New York: Library of America), 385.

34. Ron Suskind, "Faith, Certainty and the Presidency of George W. Bush," *The New York Times*, October 17, 2004 (retrieved October 24, 2015); www.nytimes.com/2004/10/17/magazine/faith-certainty-and-the-presidency-of-george-w-bush.html.

35. Ibid.

36. Waldrop, *Driven to Abstraction*, 125.

37. Walter Benjamin, *The Arcades Project* (Cambridge, MA: Harvard University Press, 1999), 460.

38. Charles Olson, Letter to Alan Pryce-Jones, 30 May 1961.

39. M. M. Bakhtin, "Discourse in the Novel," in *The Dialogic Imagination: Four Essays by M. M. Bakhtin*, ed. Michael Holquist, trans. Caryl Emerson and Michael Holquist (Austin: University of Texas Press, 1981), 343.

40. Wallace Stevens, *The Necessary Angel: Essays on Reality and the Imagination* (New York: Alfred A. Knopf, 1951), 22.

41. Waldrop, *Dissonance*, 199.

42. Reilly, "Dislocation Orchestration in the Work of Rosmarie Waldrop," 115.

43. Maurice Blanchot, *The Writing of the Disaster* (Lincoln: University of Nebraska Press, 1986), 38.

44. Deborah Meadows, "Rosmarie Waldrop and the Poetics of Embodied Philosophy," *How2*, 1.8 (2002); www.asu.edu/pipercwcenter/how2journal/archive/online_archive/v1_8_2002/current/readings/meadows.htm (retrieved October 25, 2015).

45. Waldrop, *Driven to Abstraction*, 9.

46. Ibid., 7. This line is quoted from de Vaca's account and used in the poem.

47. Ibid., 5.

48. Waldrop, *Curves to the Apple*, 19.

49. Ibid.

50. Ibid.

51. Retallack, "A Conversation with Rosmarie Waldrop," 372.

BIBLIOGRAPHY

Works by Rosmarie Waldrop

POETRY

The Aggressive Ways of the Casual Stranger. New York: Random House, 1972.
The Road Is Everywhere or Stop This Body. Columbia, MO: Open Places, 1978.
Differences for Four Hands. Philadelphia: Singing Horse, 1984.
The Hanky of Pippin's Daughter. Barrytown, NY: Station Hill, 1986.
Streets Enough to Welcome Snow. Barrytown, NY: Station Hill, 1986.
The Reproduction of Profiles. New York: New Directions, 1987.
A Form / of Taking / It All. Barrytown, NY: Station Hill, 1990.
Peculiar Motions. Berkeley: Kelsey St. Press, 1990.
Lawn of the Excluded Middle. New York: Tender Buttons, 1993.
A Key into the Language of America. New York: New Directions, 1994.
Another Language: Selected Poems. Jersey City: Talisman House, 1997.

Split Infinites. Philadelphia: Singing Horse Press, 1998.
Reluctant Gravities. New York: New Directions, 1999.
Ceci n'est pas Keith / Ceci n'ext pas Rosmarie. Providence: Burning Deck, 2002.
Love, Like Pronouns. Richmond, CA: Omnidawn Publishing, 2003.
Blindsight. New York: New Directions, 2004.
Splitting Image. La Laguna, Tenerife: Zasterle Books, 2005.
Curves to the Apple: The Reproduction of Profiles, Lawn of Excluded Middle, Reluctant Gravities. New York: New Directions, 2006.
Driven to Abstraction. New York: New Directions, 2010.
Gap Gardening: Selected Poems. New York: New Directions, 2016.

CHAPBOOKS AND LIMITED RELEASES
A Dark Octave. Durham, CT: Burning Deck, 1967.
Change of Address. With Keith Waldrop. Providence: Burning Deck, 1968.
Camp Printing. Providence: Burning Deck, 1970.
The Relaxed Abalone; or, What-You-May-Find. Providence: Burning Deck, 1970.
Letters from Rosmarie and Keith Waldrop. With Keith Waldrop. Providence: Burning Deck, 1970.
Spring Is a Season and Nothing Else. Mount Horeb, WI: Perishable Press, 1970.
Body Image. With Nelson Howe. New York: G. Wittenborn, 1970.
Alice ffoster-Fallis: (an outline). With Keith Waldrop. Providence: Burning Deck, 1972.
Until Volume One. With Keith Waldrop. Providence: Burning Deck, 1973.
Words Worth Less. With Keith Waldrop. Providence: Burning Deck, 1973.
Kind Regards. Providence: Diana's Bimonthly Press, 1975.
Since Volume One. With Keith Waldrop. Providence: Burning Deck, 1975.
Acquired Pores. Paris: Orange Export, 1976.
The Ambition of Ghosts. New York: Seven Woods, 1979.
When They Have Senses. Providence: Burning Deck, 1980.
Psyche & Eros. Peterborough, UK: Spectacular Diseases, 1980.
Nothing Has Changed. Windsor, VT: Awede Press, 1981.
Morning's Intelligence. Grenada, MS: Salt-Works Press, 1986.
Shorter American Memory. Providence: Paradigm, 1988.
Peculiar Motions. Berkeley: Kelsey St. Press, 1990.
Light Travels. With Keith Waldrop. Providence: Burning Deck, 1992.
Fan Poem for Deshika. Tucson: Chax, 1993.
Cornered Stone, Split Infinites. Elmwood, CT: Potes & Poets Press, 1994.
Blindsight. Saratoga, CA: Instress, 1998.
In a Flash. Saratoga, CA: Instress, 1998.
Blackwards. Bray, Ireland: Wild Honey Press, 1999.
Cornell Boxes. Los Angeles: Seeing Eye Books, 2001.
Trace Histories. New York: Belladonna Chapbooks #29, 2001.
Second Language. Orono, ME: Backwoods Broadsides Chaplet Series #92, 2005.
Time Ravel. Marly, France: Ink 6, 2010.
Velocity but No Location. San Francisco: Sardines Press, 2011.
Otherwise Smooth. Ottawa: Above/Ground Press, 2013.
In Pieces. Philadelphia & Providence: O'Clock Press, 2015.

Mandarin Primer. San Francisco: Hook Press, 2015.
Third Person Singular. San Francisco: Anomalous Press, 2015.

SELECTED CRITICAL PROSE

*Against Language? 'dissatisfaction with language' as theme and as impulse
   towards experiments in twentieth century poetry.* The Hague: Mouton, 1971.
Lavish Absence: Recalling and Rereading Edmond Jabès. Middletown: Wesleyan
   University Press, 2002.
Dissonance (if you are interested). Tuscaloosa: University of Alabama Press, 2005.
"Translating the Sound in Poetry: Six Propositions." In *The Sound of Poetry / The
   Poetry of Sound*, ed. Marjorie Perloff and Craig Dworkin (Chicago: University
   of Chicago Press, 2009), 60–65.

TRANSLATIONS

"Berlin (plus) Portfolio." *Exact Change Yearbook* 1 (1995): 61–90.
Celan, Paul. *Collected Prose.* Manchester, UK: Carcanet, 1986; Riverdale-on-
   Hudson, NY: Sheep Meadow Press, 1990.
Czurda, Elfriede. *Almost 1 Book / Almost 1 Life.* Providence, Burning Deck,
   2012.
Daive, Jean. *Under the Dome: Walks with Paul Celan.* Providence, Burning Deck,
   2009.
Dichten = No. 10: 16 New (to American Readers) German Poets. Translated with
   A. Duncan, T. Frazer, N. Grindell, and C. Hawkey. Providence, Burning Deck,
   2008.
Erb, Elke. *Mountains in Berlin.* Providence: Burning Deck, 1995.
Hocquard, Emmanuel. *Late Additions.* Peterborough, UK: Spectacular Diseases,
   1988.
———. *A Test of Solitude.* Providence: Burning Deck, 2000.
Guglielmi, Joseph. *Dawn.* Peterborough, UK: Spectacular Diseases, 1991.
Jabès, Edmond. *Elya.* Bolinas, CA: Tree Books, 1973.
———. *The Book of Questions* [four volumes]. Middletown: Wesleyan University
   Press, 1976–1984.
———. *The Death of God.* Peterborough, UK: Spectacular Diseases, 1979.
———. *The Book of Dialogue.* Middletown: Wesleyan University Press, 1987.
———. *The Book of Shares.* Chicago: University of Chicago Press, 1989.
———. *The Book of Resemblances.* Middletown: Wesleyan University Press,
   1990.
———. *Intimations the Desert.* Middletown: Wesleyan University Press, 1991.
———. *From the Book to the Book: An Edmond Jabès Reader.* Middletown:
   Wesleyan University Press, 1991.
———. *The Ineffaceable The Unperceived.* Middletown: Wesleyan University
   Press, 1992.
———. *The Book of Margins.* Chicago: University of Chicago Press, 1993.
———. *A Foreigner Carrying in the Crook of His Arm a Tiny Book.* Middle-
   town: Wesleyan University Press, 1993.
———. *The Little Book of Unsuspected Subversion.* Palo Alto: Stanford Univer-
   sity Press, 1996.

———. *Desire for a Beginning / Dread of One Single End*. New York: Granary Books, 2001.

Mayröcker, Friederike. *Heiligenanstalt*. Edinburgh, Scotland: Morning Star, 1992; Providence: Burning Deck, 1994.

———. *With Each Clouded Peak*. Translated with Harriet Watts (Los Angeles: Sun & Moon Press, 1998).

Pastior, Oskar. *Many Glove Compartments: Selected Poems*. Translated with Harry Mathews and Christopher Middleton. Providence: Burning Deck, 2001.

Roubaud, Jacques. *Some Thing Black*. Elmwood Park, IL: Dalkey Archive Press, 1990.

———. *The Plurality of Worlds of Lewis*. Normal, IL: Dalkey Archive Press, 1995.

———. *The Form of a City Changes Faster, Alas, Than the Human Heart*. Translated with Keith Waldrop. Normal, IL: Dalkey Archive Press, 2006.

Rühm, Gerhard. *I My Feet: Poems & Constellations*. Providence: Burning Deck, 2004.

Schowghi, Farhad. *End of the City Map*. Providence, Burning Deck, 2014.

Stolterfoht, Ulf. *Lingos I–IX*. Providence: Burning Deck, 2007.

Veinstein, Alain. *Archaeology of the Mother*. With Tod Kabza. Peterborough, UK: Spectacular Diseases, 1986.

The Vienna Group: Six Major Austrian Poets. With Harriet Watts. Barrytown, NY: Station Hill, 1985.

Waterhouse, Peter. *Where Are We Now*. Sausalito, CA: Duration Press, 1999.

———. *Language Death Night Outside*. Providence, Burning Deck, 2009.

Weiss, Peter. *Bodies and Shadows*. New York: Delacorte, 1969.

SELECTED INTERVIEWS

Burch, Wendy J. "Interview with Rosmarie Waldrop." *Poetry Flash* 243 (1993): 1–13.

Cooperman, Matthew. "Between Tongues: An Interview." *Conjunctions*, December 17, 2005; www.conjunctions.com/online/article/matthew-cooperman-12-17-2005.

———. "Love, Like Sentences: An Interview with Rosmarie Waldrop." *Denver Quarterly* 40.3 (2006): 35–50.

Foster, Edward. "An Interview with Rosmarie Waldrop." *Talisman* 6 (Spring 1991): 27–39.

Hansen, Jefferson. "Interview with Rosmarie Waldrop." *Poetics Briefs* (1993).

Retallack, Joan. "A Conversation with Rosmarie Waldrop." *Contemporary Literature* 40.3 (Fall 1999): 329–77.

Weinberger, Christine. "A Conversation with Rosmarie Waldrop." *Chicago Review* 53.4–54.2 (Spring 2008): 252–61.

Selected Criticism

Broqua, Vincent. "Le Creux ou la ville en procès chez Rosmarie Waldrop [The Hollow or the City in Process in Rosmarie Waldrop]." *Anglophonia* 25 (2009): 203–13.

Duffy, Nikolai. *Relative Strangeness—Reading Rosmarie Waldrop*. Bristol, UK: Shearsman Books, 2013.

Freitag, Kornelia. *Cultural Criticism in Women's Experimental Writing: The Poetry of Rosmarie Waldrop, Lyn Hejinian, and Susan Howe*. Heidelberg: Universitätsverlag, 2006.

Keller, Lynn. "'Fields of Pattern-Bounded Unpredictability': Recent Palimptexts by Rosmarie Waldrop and Joan Retallack." *Contemporary Literature* 42.2 (2001): 376–412.

———. "'Just one of / the girls:— / normal in the extreme': Experimentalists-To-Be Starting Out in the 1960s," *differences* 12.2 (2001): 47–69.

———. "'Nothing, for a Woman, is Worth Trying': Key into the Rules of Rosmarie Waldrop's Experimentalism." In *We Who Love to Be Astonished: Experimental Women's Writing and Performance Poetics*, ed. Laura Hinton and Cynthia Hogue (Tuscaloosa: University of Alabama Press, 2002), 103–115.

Monroe, Jonathan. "Untranslatable Communities, Productive Translation, and Public Transport: Rosmarie Waldrop's *A Key into the Language of America* and Joy Harjo's *The Woman Who Fell from the Sky*." In *We Who Love to Be Astonished*, ed. Laura Hinton and Cynthia Hogue (Tuscaloosa: University of Alabama Press, 2002), 90–102.

Perloff, Marjorie. "'A Small Periplus along the Edge': Rosmarie Waldrop's Auto-Graphs." *How2* 8 (2002); www.asu.edu/pipercwcenter/how2journal//archive/online_archive/v1_8_2002/current/readings/perloff.htm.

Reed, Brian. "'Splice of Life': Rosmarie Waldrop Renews Collage." *How2* 8 (2002); www.asu.edu/pipercwcenter/how2journal//archive/online_archive/v1_8_2002/current/readings/reed.htm.

CONTRIBUTORS

KAZIM ALI's books of poetry include *Inquisition* (Wesleyan 2018); *Sky Ward* (Wesleyan 2013); *The Far Mosque* (Alice James 2005); *The Fortieth Day* (BOA Editions 2008); *All One's Blue: New and Selected Poems* (HarperCollins India 2015); the cross-genre text *Bright Felon: Autobiography and Cities* (Wesleyan 2009) and *The Voice of Sheila Chandra* (Alice James 2020). His fiction includes *The Secret Room: A String Quartet* (Kaya 2017); the novels *The Disappearance of Seth* (Etruscan Press 2009) and *Quinn's Passage* (blazeVox books 2004); a volume of short fiction, *Uncle Sharif's Life in Music* (Sibling Rivalry 2016); and *Wind Instrument* (Spork Editions 2014). Among his books of essays are *Silver Road: Essays, Maps & Calligraphies* (Tupelo 2018), *Fasting for Ramadan: Notes from a Spiritual Practice* (Tupelo 2011), *Orange Alert: Essays on Poetry, Art, and the Architecture of Silence* (University of Michigan Press 2010), *Resident Alien: On Border-crossing and the Undocumented Divine* (University of Michigan Press 2015), *Anaïs Nin: An Unprofessional Study* (Agape Editions 2017), and *Northern Light: Hydroelectric Power and the Pimicikamak of Manitoba* (Milkweed Editions 2020). He is the editor of *Agha Shahid Ali: Mad Heart Be Brave* (University of Michigan Press 2016) and *This-World Company: On the Poetry of Jean Valentine* (University of Michigan 2011), as well as a special issue of *Poetry* focusing on global Indian Anglophone writing, and the anthology *New Moons: Contemporary Writing by American Muslims*. He is the translator of two novels by Marguerite Duras, *L'Amour* (Open Letter 2013) and *Abahn Sabana David* (Open Letter 2016), and two volumes of poetry by Sohrab Sepehri, *Water's Footfall* (Omnidawn 2011) and *The Oasis of Now: Selected Poems* (BOA Editions 2013). He is a professor of Literature at the University of California, San Diego.

JULIE PHILLIPS BROWN is a poet, painter, critic, and book artist. After earning an MFA and a PhD at Cornell University, she served as the NEH Post-Doctoral Fellow in Poetics at Emory University's Bill and Carol Fox Center for Humanistic Inquiry. She is currently completing a scholarly monograph, *Tactual Poïesis: Material Translation in Contemporary Women's Poetry*, an examination of tactile, material, and spatial textuality in twentieth- and twenty-first-century experimental women's poetry. Her poems and essays have appeared or are forthcoming in *Columbia Poetry Review*, *Contemporary Women's Writing*, *Crab Orchard Review*, *Denver Quarterly*, *The Fight & The Fiddle*, *interim*, *Jacket2*, *The Oakland Review*, *Plume*, *Posit*, *Rappahannock Review*, *Tahoma Literary Review*, *Talisman*, *Tulsa Studies in Women's Literature*, *Vinyl*, *Yemassee*, and elsewhere. She lives in Lexington, Virginia, where she is associate professor of English at Virginia Military Institute.

MARILYN CHIN was born in Hong Kong and raised in Portland, Oregon. She received a BA from the University of Massachusetts and an MFA from the University of Iowa's Writers' Workshop. She is the author of five collections of poetry, including most recently *A Portrait of the Self as Nation: New and Selected Poems* (W. W. Norton 2018) and *Hard Love Province* (W.W. Norton 2014), which won the 2015 Anisfield-Wolf Book Award. In addition to writing poetry, she has translated poems by the modern Chinese poet Ai Qing and co-translated poems by the Japanese poet Gozo Yoshimasu. She is also the author of a novel, *Revenge of the Mooncake Vixen* (W.W. Norton 2009). She has won numerous awards for her poetry, including a 2019 Literature Award from the American Academy of Arts and Letters, the Radcliffe Institute Fellowship at Harvard, the Rockefeller Foundation Fellowship at Bellagio, two National Endowment for the Arts fellowships, the Stegner Fellowship, the PEN/Josephine Miles Award, five Pushcart Prizes, a Fulbright Fellowship to Taiwan, the Sea Change fellowship from the Gaea Foundation, and the United Artist Foundation Fellowship, as well as residencies at Yaddo, the Mac-Dowell Colony, the Lannan Foundation, and the Djerassi Foundation. Her work has been featured in a variety of anthologies, including *The Norton Anthology of Modern and Contemporary Poetry*, *The Norton Introduction to Poetry*, *The Oxford Anthology of Modern American Poetry*, *Unsettling America*, *The Open Boat*, and *The Best American Poetry of 1996*. She was featured in Bill Moyers' PBS series *The Language of Life*. Chin has taught at the Iowa Writers' Workshop and served as guest poet at universities in Singapore, Hong Kong, Manchester, Sydney, and Berlin. In 2018, she was elected a chancellor of the Academy of American Poets. She is currently professor emerita at San Diego State University.

MICHAEL CROSS is the author of *In Felt Treeling: A Libretto* (Chax Press 2008), *Haecceities* (Cuneiform Press 2010), and *The Katechon: Book One* (Compline 2018). He edited the volumes *Involuntary Vision: After Akira Kurosawa's Dreams* (Avenue B 2003) and *The George Oppen Memorial Lectures* (National Poetry Foundation, forthcoming). He co-edits *ON: Contemporary Practice* with Thom Donovan and runs a fiercely independent poetry press called Compline in Oakland. He teaches at Skyline College.

CATHERINE CUCINELLA taught in the Literature and Writing Studies Department at California State University San Marcos, where she also directed the General Education Writing Program. She is the author of *Poetics of the Body: Edna St. Vincent Millay, Elizabeth Bishop, Marilyn Chin, and Marilyn Hacker* (Palgrave 2010), "The Avant-Garde and Marilyn Chin" (The Gale Researcher 2017), as well as journal articles, essays, and reference entries on Elizabeth Bishop and other women poets. Cucinella also edited *Contemporary American Women Poets: An A–Z Guide* (Greenwood 2002) and two textbooks, single-subject readers for first-year composition, *Border Crossings* (Bedford/St. Martin's 2015) and *Funny* (Fountainhead Press 2014). In her retirement, she looks forward to sipping tea, savoring the words of the poets, and rediscovering the magic of sitting within the poetic.

RICHARD GREENFIELD is the author of *Subterranean* (Omnidawn 2018), *Tracer* (Omnidawn 2009), and *A Carnage in the Lovetrees* (University of California Press 2003), which was named a Book Sense Top University Press pick. His work has been anthologized in *Joyful Noise: An Anthology of American Spiritual Poetry*, *The Arcadia Project: North American Postmodern Pastoral*, and most recently in *Privacy Policy: The Anthology of Surveillance Poetics*. He is one of the founding editors of Apostrophe Books and is currently editor-in-chief of *Puerto del Sol*. He teaches at New Mexico State University in Las Cruces.

FANNY HOWE was born in Buffalo, New York. She is the author of more than twenty books of poetry and prose. Her recent collections of poetry include *Second Childhood* (Graywolf 2014), *Come and See* (Graywolf 2011), and *The Lyrics* (Graywolf 2007). Howe is also the author of several novels and prose collections, including *The Winter Sun: Notes on a Vocation* (Graywolf 2009), *The Lives of a Spirit/Glasstown: Where Something Got Broken* (Nightboat Books 2005), and *Nod* (Sun & Moon Press 1998). She has written short stories and novels for young adults, and a collection of literary essays *The Wedding Dress: Meditations on Word and Life* (University of California Press 2003). Howe was the recipient of the 2009 Ruth Lilly Poetry Prize. She also received the 2001 Lenore Marshall Poetry Prize for *Selected Poems* (University of California Press 2000) and has won awards from the National Endowment for the Arts, the National Poetry Foundation, the California Council for the Arts, and the *Village Voice*. She has received fellowships from the Bunting Institute and the MacDowell Colony. She was shortlisted for the Griffin Poetry Prize in 2001 and 2005. She has lectured in creative writing at Tufts University, Emerson College, Columbia University, Yale University, and Massachusetts Institute of Technology. She is professor of Literature and Writing at the University of California, San Diego.

LYNN KELLER is the Martha Meier Renk Bascom Professor of Poetry in the English Department at the University of Wisconsin-Madison and the Bradshaw Knight Professor of the Environmental Humanities, an honor awarded her as the current director of the Center for Culture, History and Environment (CHE) in the University of Wisconsin's Nelson Institute for Environmental Studies. Her most recent book, *Recomposing Ecopoetics: North American Poetry of the Self-Conscious Anthropocene* (University of Virginia Press 2017) examines twenty-first-century poetry that addresses some of the urgent environmental challenges we face today. She also is the author of *Re-Making It New: Contemporary American Poetry and the Modernist Tradition* (University of Michigan Press 2004), *Forms of Expansion: Recent Long Poems by Women* (University of Chicago Press 1997), and *Thinking Poetry: Readings in Contemporary Women's Exploratory Poetics* (University of Iowa Press 2009), as well as numerous articles and a co-edited collection, *Feminist Measures: Soundings in Poetry and Theory* (University of Michigan Press 1994). She co-edits the Contemporary North American Poetry Series of scholarly books from the University of Iowa Press. Her current project concerns recent ecopoetic explorations of plant life and its significance in the Anthropocene.

KAMRAN JAVADIZADEH is associate professor of English at Villanova University, where he works on the long history of poetry and poetics, with a particular emphasis on the twentieth- and twenty-first centuries. He is the author of *Institutionalized Lyric: American Poetry at Midcentury* (Oxford University Press, forthcoming). His essays have appeared or are forthcoming in *PMLA*, *Modernism/modernity*, *Arizona Quarterly*, and *The Yale Review*, as well as in several edited anthologies. With Robert Volpicelli, he is coeditor of *Poetry Networks*, a forthcoming special issue of *College Literature*.

ELLINE LIPKIN is a poet, academic, and nonfiction writer. Her first book, *The Errant Thread* (Kore Books 2005) was chosen by Eavan Boland for the Kore Press First Book Award. Her second book, *Girls' Studies* (Seal Press 2009) explores contemporary girlhood in America. Her poems have been published in various contemporary journals and she has been a resident at Yaddo, the Virginia Center for the Creative Arts, and the Dorland Mountain Arts Colony. From 2016 to 2018, Lipkin served as poet laureate of Altadena, California, and co-edited the *Altadena Poetry Review*. Currently a research scholar with UCLA's Center for the Study of Women, she also teaches poetry for Writing Workshops Los Angeles.

ALICE NOTLEY was born in Bisbee, Arizona, in 1945 and grew up in Needles, California, in the Mojave Desert. She was educated in the Needles public schools, Barnard College, and the University of Iowa's Writers' Workshop. She has lived most extensively in Needles, New York and, since 1992, in Paris, France. She is the author of numerous books of poetry and essays and talks on poetry, and has edited and co-edited books with Ted Berrigan and Douglas Oliver. She edited the magazine *Chicago* in the 1970s and co-edited with Oliver the magazines *Scarlet* and *Gare du Nord* in the 1990s. She is the recipient of various prizes and awards, including the Los Angeles Times Book Award for *Mysteries of Small Houses* (Penguin 1998), the Griffin Prize for *Disobedience* (Penguin 2001), the Academy of American Poets' Lenore Marshall Prize for *Grave of Light: New and Selected Poems 1970–2005* (Wesleyan University Press 2008), and the Poetry Foundation's Ruth Lilly Prize, a lifetime achievement award. Recent books include *Certain Magical Acts* (Penguin 2016), *Benediction* (Letter Machine Editions 2015), *Manhattan Luck* (Hearts Desire Press 2014), *Negativity's Kiss* (Presses Universitaires de Rouen 2014), and *Songs and Stories of the Ghouls* (Wesleyan University Press 2011). Notley is also a collagist and cover artist. Above all she is a full-time poet, at this point an internationalist and haunter of Paris, remaining an American, an ex-New Yorker, and a desert denizen.

KHADIJAH QUEEN is the author of five books, most recently *I'm So Fine: A List of Famous Men & What I Had On* (YesYes Books 2017). Her verse play, *Non-*

Sequitur (Litmus Press 2015) won the Leslie Scalapino Award for Innovative Women's Performance Writing, which included a full staged production in New York City at Theaterlab in December 2015. Individual poems and prose appear in *Poetry*, *Fence*, *Tin House*, *American Poetry Review*, *The Poetry Review* (UK), and widely elsewhere. She is assistant professor of creative writing at University of Colorado, Boulder.

CLAUDIA RANKINE is the author of five collections of poetry, including *Plot* (Grove Press 2001), *Don't Let Me Be Lonely* (Graywolf 2004), and *Citizen: An American Lyric* (Graywolf 2014); and two plays, including *The White Card* (Graywolf 2019), which premiered in February 2018 (ArtsEmerson/American Repertory Theater). She has participated in numerous video collaborations and is the editor of several anthologies, including *The Racial Imaginary: Writers on Race in the Life of the Mind* (Fence Books 2015). Among her many awards and honors, Rankine is the recipient of the Bobbitt National Prize for Poetry, the Poets & Writers' Jackson Poetry Prize, and fellowships from the Guggenheim Foundation, United States Artists, the MacArthur Foundation, and the National Endowment for the Arts. Rankine teaches at Yale University as the Frederick Iseman Professor of Poetry. In 2016, she co-founded The Racial Imaginary Institute (TRII). She lives in New Haven, Connecticut.

MARTHA RONK is the author of eleven books of poetry, most recently *Silences* (Omnidawn 2019); *Optical Proof* (Omnidawn 2016), on the deceptive nature of photographs; *Partially Kept* (Nightboat Books 2012); *Transfer of Qualities* (Omnidawn 2012), long-listed for the National Book Award; and *Vertigo* (Coffee House Press 2007), a National Poetry Series selection. Her earlier *In a landscape of having to repeat* (Omnidawn 2004) won the PEN Center USA Award for Poetry. Her work has been included in the anthologies, *American Hybrid* and *Lyric Postmodernisms*. She is the recipient of an NEA fellowship and several residencies at the MacDowell Colony and the Djerassi Foundation. She worked with visual artists Tom Wudl and Don Suggs on chapbooks and has been interested in the relationship between the visual and verbal in both her academic and poetic work. After receiving her PhD from Yale, she taught for thirty-five years at Occidental College in Los Angeles, teaching sixteenth- and seventeenth-century British literature, publishing essays on Shakespeare, and also organizing a college-wide creative writing program; recently she has been team-teaching with a book designer in the art department.

LESLIE SCALAPINO was raised in Berkeley, California, and received a BA from Reed College and an MA in English from the University of California, Berkeley. She is the author of over thirty collections of poetry including *Flow-Winged Crocodile and A Pair/Actions Are Erased/Appear* (Chax Press 2010); *It's go in horizontal: Selected Poems 1974–2006* (University of California Press 2008); *Zither & Autobiography* (Wesleyan University Press, 2003); *Sight* (Edge Books 1999), a collaboration with Lyn Hejinian; *way* (North Point Press 1988), which received the Poetry Center Award, the Lawrence Lipton Prize, and the American Book Award from the Before Columbus Foundation; *that they were at the beach* (North Point Press 1985); *Considering how exaggerated music is* (North Point Press 1982); and *O and Other Poems* (Sand Dollar Press 1976). In 1986, Scalapino founded O Books, which published emerging and prominent innovative writers, including Ted Berrigan, Robert Grenier, Fanny Howe, Tom Raworth, Norma Cole, Will Alexander, Alice Notley, Norman Fischer, Laura Moriarty, Michael McClure, Judith Goldman, and many others. She received a fellowship from the National Endowment for the Arts in 1976. She taught at the Naropa Institute, Bard College, Mills College, and the University of California, San Diego, where her papers are held in the Mandeville Special Collections Library.

LISA SEWELL is the author of several books of poetry, most recently *Impossible Object* (Word Works 2015), winner of the Tenth Gate Prize. She is also co-editor, with Claudia Rankine, of *American Poets in the 21st Century: The New Poetics* (Wesleyan University Press 2007) and *Eleven More American Women Poets in the 21st Century: Poetics Across North America* (Wesleyan University Press 2012). She has received grants and awards from the Leeway Foundation, the National Endowment for the Arts, the Pennsylvania Council on the Arts, and the Fine Arts Work Center at Provincetown, and fellowships from the Oak Springs Garden Foundation, Yaddo, the Virginia Center for the Creative Arts, the MacDowell Colony, The Tyrone Guthrie Center, and the Sitka Center for Art and Ecology. Recent work has appeared in *Louisville Review*, *Prairie Schooner*, *Ploughshares*, and *Crab Orchard Review*. She lives in Philadelphia and is professor and Luckow Family Chair in English at Villanova University.

LISA RUSS SPAAR is the author/editor of over ten books of poetry and criticism, including *Monticello in Mind: 50 Contemporary Poems on Jefferson* (University of Virginia Press 2016), *Orexia: Poems* (Persea 2018), and *"More Truly and More Strange": Contemporary American Self-Portrait Poems* (Persea 2019). Her honors include a Rona Jaffe Award, a Guggenheim Fellowship, the Carole Weinstein Poetry Prize, and the Library of Virginia Award for Poetry. Spaar's poems have appeared or are forthcoming in the *Best American Poetry* and *Pushcart Prize Anthology* series, as well as *Poetry, Boston Review, Denver Quarterly, The New Yorker, The Kenyon Review*, and elsewhere. She was a 2014 short-list finalist for the National Book Circle Critics Award for Excellence in Reviewing and one of three national finalists for the 2016 Cherry Award for Excellence in Teaching. Her commentaries, reviews, and columns about poetry have appeared regularly or are forthcoming in *The Chronicle of Higher Education*, the *Washington Post*, the *New York Times*, the *Los Angeles Review of Books*, *On the Seawall*, and elsewhere. She is a professor and director of the Creative Writing Program of the Department of English at the University of Virginia.

COLE SWENSEN is the author of seventeen collections of poetry, most recently *On Walking On* (Nightboat Books 2017), *Gave* (Omnidawn 2017), and *Landscapes on a Train* (Nightboat Books 2015). She is also the author of a volume of critical essays, *Noise that Stays Noise* (Michigan University Press 2012). Her poetic collections turn around specific research projects, including ones on public parks, visual art, illuminated manuscripts, and ghosts. Her work has won the National Poetry Series, the Iowa Poetry Prize, the San Francisco State Poetry Center Book Award, and the PEN USA Award in Literary Translation. A former Guggenheim Fellow, she is the co-editor of the anthology *American Hybrid* (W. W. Norton 2010) and founding editor of La Presse Poetry (www.lapressepoetry.com). She teaches at Brown University.

BRIAN TEARE is the recipient of poetry fellowships from the Pew Foundation, the National Endowment for the Arts, the MacDowell Colony, the American Antiquarian Society, the Fund for Poetry, and the Headlands Center for the Arts. He is the author of *The Room Where I Was Born* (University of Wisconsin Press 2003), *Sight Map* (University of California Press 2009), *Pleasure* (Ashata Press 2010), *Companion Grasses* (Omnidawn 2013), *The Empty Form Goes All the Way to Heaven* (Ashata Press 2015), and *Doomstead Days* (Nightboat Books 2019). A recipient of the Brittingham Prize, the Thom Gunn Award, and the Lambda Literary Award, his work has also been a finalist for the Kingsley Tufts Award. Teare is also the author of eight chapbooks, most recently *Headlands Quadrats*, *SORE EROS*, and *Paradise Was Typeset*. As a critic, he has published essays, interviews, and reviews in *Boston Review*, *Jacket2*, and the *Los Angeles Review of Books*, as well as in *At the Barriers: The Poetry of Thom Gunn*, *Jean Valentine: This-World Company*, and *From Our Hearts to Yours: New Narrative as Contemporary Practice*. After over a decade of teaching and writing in the San Francisco Bay Area, he is now an associate professor at Temple University and lives in South Philadelphia, where he makes books by hand for his micropress, Albion Books.

NATASHA TRETHEWEY served two terms as the nineteenth Poet Laureate of the United States (2012–2014). She is the author of five collections of poetry, *Domestic Work* (Graywolf 2000), *Bellocq's Ophelia* (Graywolf 2002), *Native Guard* (Mariner Books 2007)—for which she was awarded the 2007 Pulitzer Prize—*Thrall* (Mariner Books 2012) and, most recently, *Monument: Poems New and Selected* (Houghton Mifflin Harcourt 2018). In 2010 she published a book of nonfiction, *Beyond Katrina: A Meditation on the Mississippi Gulf Coast* (University of Georgia Press 2015). A member of both the American Academy of Arts and Letters and the American Academy of Arts and Sciences, she is the recipient of fellowships from the Academy of American Poets, the National Endowment for the Arts, the Guggenheim Foundation, the Rockefeller Foundation, the Beinecke Library at Yale, and the Radcliffe Institute for Advanced Study at Harvard. In 2017 she received the Heinz Award for Arts and Humanities, and in 2019 she was elected to the Board of

Chancellors of the Academy of American Poets. She is Board of Trustees Professor of English at Northwestern University.

MEG TYLER was the 2016 Fulbright Professor of Anglophone Irish Writing at Queen's University in Belfast. She teaches humanities at Boston University where she also directs a poetry series and chairs the Institute for the Study of Irish Culture. She is the author of a chapbook of poems, *Poor Earth* (Finishing Line Press 2014), and *A Singing Contest: Conventions of Sound in the Poetry of Seamus Heaney* (Routledge 2005). Her poems and prose have appeared in *Agni, Literary Imagination, Kenyon Review, Harvard Review, Irish Review*, and other journals. A chapter on Heaney's last two volumes appears in *"The Soul Exceeds Its Circumstances": The Later Poetry of Seamus Heaney*, edited by Eugene O'Brien (Notre Dame University Press 2016). She won the 2018 Peyton Richter Award for Outstanding Interdisciplinary Teaching at Boston University.

JEAN VALENTINE was born in Chicago, earned her BA from Radcliffe College, and has lived most of her life in New York City. She won the Yale Younger Poets Award for her first book, *Dream Barker*, in 1965 and has since published thirteen books of poetry, most recently *Shirt In Heaven* (Copper Canyon 2015). *Door in the Mountain: New and Collected Poems, 1965–2003* (Wesleyan University Press 2004) was winner of the 2004 National Book Award for Poetry. She was the State Poet of New York from 2008 to 2010. She has received many awards and honors including the Wallace Stevens Award from the Academy of American Poets, the Maurice English Prize, the Teasdale Poetry Prize, and Poetry Society of America's Shelley Memorial Prize. She has also received fellowships from the Guggenheim Foundation, the National Endowment for the Arts, the Bunting Institute, the Rockefeller Foundation, the New York Council for the Arts, and the New York Foundation for the Arts. In 2014 she was given an award for exceptional accomplishment in literature from the American Academy of Arts and Letters. She has taught at Sarah Lawrence College, the Graduate Writing Program of New York University, Columbia University, and the 92nd Street Y in Manhattan.

CECILIA VICUÑA is a Chilean poet, artist, and filmmaker whose work addresses ecological destruction, human rights, and cultural homogenization. She has lived in exile since the overthrow of the Allende government in the early 1970s. Vicuña's poems in space and ephemeral site-specific performances/installations, set in nature, streets, and museums, combine ritual and assemblage. She calls this practice "lo precario" (the precarious): transformative acts that bridge the gap between art and life, between the ancestral and the avant-garde. Her early paintings of revolutionary heroes and poets, depicted in the style of colonial saints, are considered pioneering examples of indigenous-led cultural decolonization. In Chile she founded the legendary *Tribu No* in 1967. In 1974, exiled in London, she co-founded Artists for Democracy to oppose dictatorships in the Third World. She co-founded www.oysi.org in 2011, an educational site dedicated to indigenous oral culture. Her work has been widely exhibited, including at documenta 14, Athens and Kassel; the Hammer Museum; Museu de Arte Moderna; Institute of Contemporary Art, Boston; Museo Nacional de Bellas Artes; Whitechapel Art Gallery; Institute of Contemporary Art, London; Whitney Museum of American Art; and the Museum of Modern Art. Her survey exhibition *Cecilia Vicuña: About to Happen*, organized by the Center of Contemporary Arts of New Orleans, toured museums in the United States from 2018 to 2019. Vicuña has published twenty-five art and poetry books, including *New and Selected Poems of Cecilia Vicuña* (Kelsey Street Press 2018), *AMAzone Palabrarmas* (University of Chicago Press 2018), *About to Happen* (Siglio Press 2017), and *Read Thread, The Story of the Red Thread* (Sternberg Press 2017). She co-edited *The Oxford Book of Latin American Poetry* (Oxford University Press 2009), and edited *Ul, Four Mapuche Poets* (LARP l997). She was appointed Messenger Lecturer at Cornell University in 2015, an honor bestowed on authors who contribute to the "Evolution of Civilization."

ROSMARIE WALDROP's most recent books are *The Hanky of Pippin's Daughter* (Dorothy 2019), *Gap Gardening: Selected Poems* (New Directions 2016), *Driven to Abstraction* (New Directions 2010), and *Curves to the Apple* (New Directions 2006). Her collected essay, *Dissonance (if you are interested)*, was published by University of Alabama Press in 2005. She has translated from the French fourteen volumes of Edmond Jabès's work (see her memoir, *Lavish Absence: Recalling and Rereading Edmond Jabès*, published by Wesleyan University Press in 2002), as well as volumes by Emmanuel Hocquard and Jacques Roubaud, and, from the German, Friederike Mayröcker, Elke Erb, Gerhard Rühm, Ulf Stolterfoht, and Peter Waterhouse. She was born in Germany in 1935. At age ten she spent half a year acting with a traveling theater, but was happy when schools reopened and she could settle for the quieter pleasures of reading and writing, which she has pursued in and out of universities, in several countries, but mostly in Providence, Rhode Island, where she lives with Keith Waldrop (with whom she co-edited Burning Deck Press). The linguistic displacement from German to English has not only made her into a translator but given her a sense of writing as exploration of *what happens between*. Between words, sentences, people, cultures.

INDEX

gesture: in Ronk, 193; in Scalapino, 230–31; in Swensen, 273–74, 280; in Tretheway, 317
Glück, Louise, 142
The Grand Permission: New Writings on Poetics and Motherhood, 109–13, 115–16
Greek lyric poetry in Ronk, 186–88
Greenfield, Richard, "Rosmarie Waldrop: Attending to Absence," 18, 434–50
grief. *See* erotics of grief
Griffin, Susan, 111
Grosz, Elizabeth, 40
Grosz, Elizabeth, *In the Nick of Time*, 50
Grubin, Eve, 358
Guattari, Felix, 236
Guest, Barbara, 179–80

Haggerty, George, 44–49
haiku in Howe, 84–85
Hardwick, Elizabeth, 142, 146–47
Hardy, Thomas, "The Voice," 74
Hartman, Saidiya, 145
heaven in Valentine, 362
hegemonies in Waldrop, 435
Heidegger, Martin, 235–36, 440
Hejinian, Lyn, 240
Hejinian, Lyn, *Gesualdo*, 432–33
Henniger, Katherine, 314–15
history: Chin on, 36–37; in Rankine, 142–45, 157–58; Rankine on, 140; in Ronk, 188–90; in Scalapino, 15; in Swensen, 272–78; in Tretheway, 15–16, 311–24, 327–29; Tretheway on, 307–10; in Vicuña, 390, 392–96, 399–409; in Waldrop, 439–40, 443–48
A History of Inventions, Discoveries, and Origins, 279–80
Howe, Fanny: alliteration in, 84; blank space in, 74; closure in, 86; collective/communal poetics, 10, 82–83; disjunction in, 9; ego in, 82–83; ellipses in, 84–85; form in, 78–80, 83, 89; fragmentation

in, 9–10, 77–78, 83–85; haiku in, 84–85; on identity, 72; language and, 9–10, 74, 81–82, 87–88; light in, 75–76; lyric in, 9–10, 77, 80–81; metaphor in, 75–76, 83; overview of work, 9–10; permanence in, 89; poetics statement, 72–73; on prose, 72; questions in, 76, 83; on responsibilities of poetry, 4–5; silences in, 74, 76, 80–83, 85–86, 89; simile in, 79; Sontag and, 74, 81; sound-lines in, 74–75; sound patterning in, 77–79, 85–86; spirituality and, 79–81; Tyler's analysis, 73–89
Howe, Fanny, works of: *Come and See*, 62–68; "Evening," 70; "For the Book," 68, 77–78; "Forty Days," 60–61; "The Garden," 69; *Gone*, 82–83, 85–87; *On the Ground*, 88; "A Hymn," 9, 62–68; *Introduction to the World*, 78–79; "Joy Had I Known," 80–81; *The Lyrics*, 60–61; "The Ninth Hour," 71; "The Nursery," 79; *O'Clock*, 79–80, 84–85; "Parkside," 69–70; "Person, Place and Time," 82; "The Sea-Garden," 89; *Second Childhood*, 68–71, 77–78; *Selected Poems*, 81; "The Source," 75, 78; "2002," 88; *The Vineyard*, 75–76, 79; *The Winter Sun: Notes on a Vocation*, 82–89; "The World Bank," 88–89
Howe, Susan, 268, 271
Hume, Angela, 156
Hume, Christine, 438, 440
humor in Swensen, 291n21
Hunter, Walt, 323
hybridity, 2
hybrid poetics in Swensen, 267–72

illusion in Scalapino, 228–29
inclusiveness. *See* poetics of inclusion
indigenous identity in Vicuña, 390, 399
indigenous models of time in Vicuña, 395–96
informal interviews in Swensen, 283–84

installations in Vicuña, 404
Internet in Waldrop, 442–43
interrogative sequences in Waldrop, 449
irony in Chin, 41–42

Jabès, Edmond, 431, 440
Jackson, Virginia, 143, 200; *Dickinson's Misery: A Theory of Lyric Reading*, 182–83
Jakobson, Roman, 154–55
James, Henry, *The Spoils of Poynton*, 180
Jameson, Frederic, *Postmodernism, or the Cultural Logic of Late Capitalism*, 190–91
Jara, Víctor, 392
Javadizadeh, Kamran, "The Atlantic Ocean Breaking on our Heads: Claudia Rankine and the Whiteness of the Lyric Subject," 11–12, 141–58
Jones, Meta DuEwa, 312
joy in Vicuña, 390, 404

Kane, Daniel, 74, 78
Keller, Lynn, "Truths Surpassing Fact: Cole Swensen's Research-Based Poetics," 14–15, 267–89
khora in Waldrop, 440–41
Kuhnheim, Jill, 404

lacework aesthetic in Swensen, 274
language, 5–6; in Howe, 9–10, 74, 81–82, 87–88; in Notley, 10, 116; Notley on, 5; in Rankine, 11–12, 142–44, 154–55, 156–57; Rankine on, 6–7; in Ronk, 12–13, 183–86, 189–201; Ronk on, 5–6, 179–80; in Scalapino, 13, 237–38; Scalapino on, 5, 223–25; in Swensen, 14, 268–86, 289; Swensen on, 6, 191, 264–67; Tretheway on, 5; in Valentine, 364–65; Valentine on, 346; in Vicuña, 17–18; Vicuña on, 389–90; in Waldrop, 18, 434–36, 439–40, 443–50, 451n27; Waldrop on, 6–7, 429–31

Language poetry, 3; and Howe, 10, 84; Rankine on, 142; and Ronk, 182–83, 187, 190–91, 200–201; and Swensen, 268; and Waldrop, 435–36, 447
Lauterbach, Ann, "As (It) Is: Toward a Poetics of the Whole Fragment," 189
leaf motif in Vicuña, 404–5
Leighton, Angela, 39
Lejeune, Philippe, *On Autobiography*, 194
Licad, Abigail, 41
light in Howe, 75–76
liminality: in Swensen, 281; in Valentine, 17, 358–59, 366–67
liminally controlled world in Chin, 40, 51–52, 54
Lindsay, Vachel, "The Congo: A Study of the Negro Race," 147
lineated poetics in Waldrop, 434–36
linguistic fragility in Ronk, 185
Lipkin, Elline, "Resist, Reframe, Insist: Alice Notley's Poetics of Inclusion," 10–11, 108–23
Lippard, Lucy, 396
literary traditions in Tretheway, 312–13, 328–29
Loffreda, Beth, 143–44, 148
Logan, William, *The New Criterion*, 321–22
Lonewolf, Don, 47–50, 57n54
loss in Chin, 39, 42–49, 54
Love, Heather, 151
"Love and Loss: An Elegy" (Haggerty), 44
love in Chin, 38–55
Lowell, Robert, 142–58, 159nn6–7, 352
Lowell, Robert, works of: "Holy Matrimony," 146–47; *Life Studies*, 142, 144–47, 149, 152, 157–58; "Man and Wife," 142, 145–46, 148; "Skunk Hour," 155
Lynd, Juliet, 403
lyric, 2, 4; Chin on, 36–37; in Howe, 9–10, 77, 80–81; in Notley, 10–11;

questions in Howe, 76, 83
quiet. *See* silences
quotation mark manipulation, in
 Notley, 118–21

race in Tretheway, 308, 311–27
race/racism in Rankine, 141–58
Rahv, Philip, "Paleface and Redskin,"
 146–47
Rankine, Claudia: aesthetics, 142–43;
 autobiography in, 142, 144, 148;
 collective/communal poetics, 11,
 140, 151; collective memory, 157;
 confessional poetics and, 142–45,
 150–52; erasure in, 143, 153, 155;
 experimental poetics and, 142–43;
 familial structures in, 152–55,
 162n45; first-person mode in,
 149–52; on genre, 140–41; on
 history, 140; history in, 142–45,
 157–58; Javadizadeh's analysis,
 141–58; on language, 6–7; language
 in, 11–12, 142–44, 154–55,
 156–57; and Lowell, 142–58; lyric
 in, 3, 11–12, 141–45, 148–52,
 154–58; lyricization and, 143–44;
 lyric subjectivity and, 11–12, 141,
 144–45, 148–52, 154, 156, 162n52;
 mimetic writing, 11; overview of
 work, 11–12; poetics statement,
 140–41; race/racism in, 141–58
Rankine, Claudia, works of: *Citizen:
 An American Lyric*, 129–36,
 141–42, 144–45, 149–58, 161n40;
 Don't Let Me Be Lonely, 150; "July
 29-August 18, 2014/Making Room:
 Script for Public Fiction at Hammer
 Museum*," 137–39; *Nothing in
 Nature is Private*, 144; *The Racial
 Imaginary*, 143–44, 148; "Skunk
 Hour," 161–62n43
Ransom, John Crowe, 148
recognizability in Scalapino, 241–42
redemption in Vicuña, 394–96, 409
reduplications in Chin, 53–54
Reed, Anthony, "post-lyric," 150
Reed, Brian, 286–89

Reilly, Evelyn, 434, 447
re-inscription in Tretheway, 314–17,
 320, 327
remembrance in Chin, 39
repetition: in Howe, 84; in Notley,
 120; in Swensen, 270; in Waldrop,
 433, 438–39
representation in Ronk, 183–85
research-based poetics in Swensen,
 269–79, 282–89
responsibilities of poetry, 4–6, 107–8,
 310–11
reterritorialization in Scalapino,
 231–32
return in Vicuña, 394–97, 399, 408–9
revisions in Waldrop, 433
revolutionary poetics in Vicuña, 404
rhythm: in Notley, 110–11; in
 Scalapino, 229–33; in Waldrop, 18,
 438–39; Waldrop on, 431, 433
Rich, Adrienne, 116, 351; *Of Woman
 Born: Motherhood as Experience
 and Institution*, 351–52
Riding, Laura, 87–88
Ronk, Martha: aesthetics, 183,
 189–90, 199–201; apostrophic in,
 195–96; artifice in, 192, 195–97;
 collage, 189–90, 193; collective/
 communal poetics, 180; disjunction
 in, 183, 188–89, 191, 193; doubt in,
 191–93; estrangement and, 197–98;
 fragmentation in, 187–90, 193;
 gesture in, 193; history in, 188–90;
 on language, 5–6, 179–80; language
 in, 12–13, 183–86, 189–201; lyric
 "I," 13; lyric in, 12–13, 182–201;
 mimetic writing, 183–84; natural
 voice and, 195–98; overview of
 work, 12–13; poetics of failure
 and, 185–86, 190–92, 198–99; on
 poetics of memory, 180–81; poetics
 statement, 179–82; representation
 in, 183–85; on responsibilities of
 poetry, 6; Teare's analysis, 182–201;
 uncertainty and unknowing in, 191,
 199–201
Ronk, Martha, works of: "As I

understand my job, it is, while suggesting order, to make things appear as much as possible to be the way they are in normal vision," 177; "Below the moon, above the sun," 188–89; "A blurry photograph," 176; "the book," 175–76; "Closer to My Natural Voice," 195–99; "Collage," 193; "corroded metal," 174; *Desire in L.A.*, 192; "Elegy (and a photograph by Robert Adams)," 178; *Eyetrouble*, 193; "a glass bowl," 173; *Glass Grapes*, 197–98; "Her Subject/His Subject," 197–98; "I cannot remember anything about this journey other than this," 169; "In a landscape of having to repeat," 167; "It is only a question of discovering how we can get ourselves attached to it again," 170; *In a Landscape of Having to Repeat*, 167, 184–85, 195–99; "No sky (after Robert Adams's *California: Views*)," 177; "Odi et amo 4," 186–88, 193; *Oracular Proof*, 176–78, 182; "Paraphrase," 192; *Partially Kept*, 171–72, 180, 185, 200; "A Photograph of a Plate Glass Window," 168; "Photography Loves Banal Objects," 192–93; "Poetics of Failure," 189, 192, 198–99; "Poetry and Photography and the Transitory," 183; "Remembrance," 172, 200; "Rhetoric No. 3," 192; "The shadows of clouds scudded across the steep slopes and through the ravines," 170; *State of Mind*, 192; "The," 171; *Transfer of Qualities*, 173, 180; "Trying," 168, 184–85; *Vertigo*, 169–70, 180, 188–89; *Why/Why Not*, 179, 186–88; "the window," 174

Rosenbaum, Susan, 120
Roussel, Raymond, 88
Rove, Karl, 445
Rukeyser, Muriel, "The Book of the Dead," 141

Scalapino, Leslie: anarchic text, 226–27, 237; animality in, 231–37; antilandscape in, 237–42; autobiography in, 240; awakening in, 237–43; body in, 224–27, 232–39; collective/communal poetics, 226–27; Cross's analysis, 226–43; defamiliarization in, 230–35; dialectical image in, 237–42; disjunction in, 227–29; eroticism in, 233–35; fragmentation in, 13; gesture in, 230–31; history in, 15; illusion in, 228–29; language in, 13, 237–38; lyric in, 15; mimetic writing, 230, 242; mind-body split, 224; mind formation in, 14, 226–27, 234; misrecognition in, 242–43; movie posters in, 242; overview of work, 13–14; poetics statement, 223–26; recognizability in, 241–42; on responsibilities of poetry, 5; reterritorialization in, 231–32; simile in, 228–30, 243n8; subjectivities in, 233–34, 236, 241–42; testing-space in, 14, 226–30, 232, 235–38, 241–43

Scalapino, Leslie, works of: "Autobiography," 227; *Day Ocean State of Stars' Night*, 217–20; "Dead Souls," 221–22; *Defoe*, 214–17, 223–24, 238–40; "DeLay Rose," 217–20; "Dog," 230–32; "Floating Series 1," 208–13; *The Front Matter, Dead Souls*, 221–22, 240; *hmmmm*, 227–31, 239; "In Sequence," 233–34; "Notes to Waking Life," 214–17; *The Return of Painting*, 234–35; *R-hu*, 238; *Sight*, 240; *That they were at the beach*, 233–34; *way*, 208–13; *Zither and Autobiography*, 240

Schumann, Clara and Robert, 432–33
scientific language in Swensen, 280
second person of lyric address in Rankine, 150–53, 155–56
self-love in Chin, 45

Form," 252; *American Hybrid: A Norton Anthology of New Poetry*, 267–68, 289n2; *Art in Time: Soutine*, 261–62; "Birds," 251; *The Book of a Hundred Hands*, 251; "Debord," 264; "December 25, 1456: Je Françoys Villon escollier," 250; "The First Movies", 251; "The Flight into Egypt," 273–74; "The Fold," 268–69; "A Garden is a Start," 254–56; "George Sand: Promenades autour d'un village," 263–64; "A Ghost," 257; *The Glass Age*, 252–53, 280–82; *Goest*, 279; *Gravesend*, 257–59, 283; "Gravesend," 258; *Greensward*, 283–89; "A History of the Incandescent," 279–80; "Introduction," 276–77; "The Invention of Equal Hours," 277; "June 1: Reaping," 278–79; "June 15, 1416: The Death of Jean, Duc de Berry," 277–78; "Kent," 257–58; *Landscapes on a Train*, 259–60; "May 21, 1420: The Signing of the Treaty of Troyes," 249; "News that Stays News," 270–71; *Noise that Stays Noise*, 268; *Noon*, 270; "One No," 258; *Ours*, 253–56; Paysage à Céret, 1921, 262; "Paysage à Céret, 1920," 261; *Pierce-Arrow*, 271; "Prologue," 272–73, 275–76; "Shadow Puppets," 251–52; *Such Rich Hour*, 249, 275, 278; "There," 274–75; "Triptych," 274; *Try*, 272–75; *On Walking On*, 262–64; "Who Walked," 259; "Wordsworth," 262

syntactic gestures in Swensen, 273–74, 280

Tate, Allen, 148
Teare, Brian, "Martha Ronk's Distressed Lyrics," 12–13, 182–201
technology of lyric in Ronk, 184–85, 188, 191
temporality in Vicuña, 394–97

Terada, Rei, "After the Critique of the Lyric," 183
tesserae use in Waldrop, 438–39
testing-space in Scalapino, 14, 226–30, 232, 235–38, 241–43
[three]3AM Magazine, 112
time in Chin, 38–41, 50–55
time in Vicuña, 394–96, 399, 404
translation, Waldrop on, 430
translation in Waldrop, 432–33
Treacle, Geoffrey, 9
Très Riches Heures du Duc de Berry, 276–77
Tretheway, Natasha: anti-pastoral in, 314–15; autobiography in, 312, 321; biographical details, 307–9; body in, 317–22; collective/communal poetics, 309; ekphrasis in, 312–14, 316–23, 329; gesture in, 317; on history, 307–10; history in, 15–16, 311–24, 327–29; on language, 5; literary traditions and, 312–13, 328–29; national narratives and, 313, 327–29; objects in, 314–17; and Orwell, 325; Orwell and, 307; overview of work, 15–16; palindromic rhyme schemes in, 328–29; on personal experience, 310; persona poems and, 316–17; photography in, 312–17, 323–25; poetics statement, 307–11; Queen's analysis, 311–29; race in, 308, 311–27; re-inscription in, 314–17, 320, 327; on responsibilities of poetry, 5, 310–11; and Smith, 325; on social justice, 308–9; subjectivities in, 15; visual arts in, 312–13, 317–22
Tretheway, Natasha, works of: "The Americans," 322; "Before Katrina," 299–300; "Bellocq," 294, 316; *Bellocq's Ophelia*, 294, 313, 316, 323–24; *Beyond Katrina*, 299–300, 313–14, 324–26, 329; "Calling," 304–5, 314, 320; "Congregation," 325–26; *"De Español y Negra; Mulata,"* 321; *Domestic Work*, 313,